Digital Storytelling

Digital Storytelling

A creator's guide
to interactive entertainment

Third Edition
Carolyn Handler Miller

Focal Press
Taylor & Francis Group

NEW YORK AND LONDON

First published 2004 by Focal Press

This edition published 2014
by Focal Press
70 Blanchard Road, Suite 402, Burlington, MA 01803

and by Focal Press
2 Park Square, Milton Park, Abingdon, Oxon OX14 4RN

Focal Press is an imprint of the Taylor & Francis Group, an informa business

Notices
Knowledge and best practice in this field are constantly changing. As new research and experience broaden our understanding, changes in research methods, professional practices, or medical treatment may become necessary.

Practitioners and researchers must always rely on their own experience and knowledge in evaluating and using any information, methods, compounds, or experiments described herein. In using such information or methods they should be mindful of their own safety and the safety of others, including parties for whom they have a professional responsibility.

Product or corporate names may be trademarks or registered trademarks, and are used only for identification and explanation without intent to infringe.

Library of Congress Cataloging in Publication Data
Miller, Carolyn Handler.
Digital storytelling : a creator's guide to interactive entertainment / by Carolyn Handler Miller.—Third edition.
    pages cm
Includes bibliographical references and index.
1. Interactive multimedia. 2. Storytelling—Data processing. 3. Digital storytelling. I. Title.
QA76.76.I59M55 2014
372.67'70285—dc23
                                                    2013046539

ISBN: 978-0-415-83694-4 (pbk)
ISBN: 978-0-203-42592-3 (ebk)

Typeset in Times New Roman PSMT
By diacriTech

Printed in Canada

Bound to Create

You are a creator.

Whatever your form of expression — photography, filmmaking, animation, games, audio, media communication, web design, or theatre — you simply want to create without limitation. Bound by nothing except your own creativity and determination.

Focal Press can help.

For over 75 years Focal has published books that support your creative goals. Our founder, Andor Kraszna-Krausz, established Focal in 1938 so you could have access to leading-edge expert knowledge, techniques, and tools that allow you to create without constraint. We strive to create exceptional, engaging, and practical content that helps you master your passion.

Focal Press and you.

Bound to create.

> We'd love to hear how we've helped
> you create. Share your experience:
> **www.focalpress.com/boundtocreate**

This edition of <u>Digital Storytelling</u> is dedicated to my husband, for his unwavering and cheerful support . . .

And in memory of my mother, who always enjoyed a good story, no matter how told.

Table of Contents

Foreword

Digital storytelling. In its true essence, it is so much more than simply "writing for the Web." The secret to any degree of long-term "success" lies with storytelling and attracting and then engaging a captive audience in a digital space where banner ads, clicks, pokes, cat videos, and a host of other distractions are rife is no mean feat.

Crafted in a way that only a great storyteller might, *Digital Storytelling* is delivered in a cohesive arc of five parts as Carolyn Handler Miller takes you by the hand and walks and talks you through new technologies and the creative opportunities that they bring for writers and creators, pausing to consider convergence, interactivity (and most importantly its effects), and digital storytelling tools. Vital topics are finely balanced, not focusing too intently on the digital and choosing instead to bring core fundamentals of storytelling to your toolbox. Characters, dialogue and emotion, story structure, and a laser focus on your audience and their behaviors are woven throughout this third edition of *Digital Storytelling: A Creator's Guide to Interactive Entertainment*. Carolyn expertly takes a close look at dovetailing digital techniques with storytelling principles and how they apply to video games, online, mobile and apps, ARG, TV, toys, and immersive environments, concluding with the much puzzled upon question of career considerations and finding *paid* work as a digital storyteller.

Which is perhaps where I come in …

In 2006 I was a bestselling novelist, having penned three "rom coms," and had begun to flex my playwriting muscles too. My first three novels were written with a "promise" that I'd made to myself. In an era where Bridget Jones was klutzing through life, documenting her calorie and nicotine intake and where romantic comedy and chick lit were being constantly dumbed down, I made a deal with myself.

Each of my books would organically weave three things:

1. a foreign destination;

2. an art form; and

3. a genre of music.

And so *Class Act*, *Look Before You Leap*, and *Three of a Kind* were set in dual locations and took readers from Paris to Valencia, Dublin to Lisbon, set against a backdrop of classical, jazz, and blues with a splash of additional color courtesy of Edgar Degas and his ballerinas. I was frustrated as I yearned for these stories to live and breathe beyond their book jackets. I imagined readers *listening* to *Canon in D* whilst reading the slower paced scenes. I wanted a postcard print of Degas ballerinas, with their pastel blue tutus, inside my front cover. But this was 2004 and the only way this would happen would be with a clunky CD in a sleeve inside the back cover. A "multimedia" add-on.

Disillusioned with the confines of restricting my characters and their stories within the jacket of a book I also realized that I was one in a stable of similar writers. Our books were simultaneously hitting the shelves, I had a series of uncomfortable photo shoots in shop windows (once holding a book in one hand and a yogurt in the other—don't ask), and was gracing the sofas of breakfast and afternoon shows for interviews, not so much about the books, but more about the female-centric (and sometimes comedic) themes within them.

My publisher wanted me to keep doing the same thing.

I didn't.

I focused on playwriting and showcasing my plays was my first experience of audience reactions to my storytelling, in real time. It was pivotal, shocking, and hugely exciting. That dialogue and those scenes I'd expected them to bust their sides laughing at? They merely tittered … The poignant relationship-split scene that I'd cried over as I wrote? They barely sniffed. And a couple of people blew their nose, loudly. But nobody bawled. At least not like I did. I had a lot to learn—about writing for performance and connecting with my audience. Disillusioned with the limited scope for my writing, the range for reaching out to, interacting with, and engaging an audience was stifling and so I turned to the Internet, specifically to Google …

Ironically, although probably not surprisingly, I first met Carolyn digitally, six months later. The disillusionment had led me to enroll as a full-time student on a Master's Program teaching Creative Writing & New Media. As a guest lecturer, Carolyn immediately captivated us with her knowledge, processes, awareness of fluidity and yet focus when writing to entertain an audience that were so blinkered to "traditional" or "old" media. Within an hour of "meeting" and asking her a barrage of questions I'd clicked to buy the first edition of *Digital Storytelling: A Creator's Guide to Interactive Entertainment.*

And yet it was only the beginning. At the very least, of a friendship between Carolyn and I.

A further year later, under the direction of my mentor Christy Dena, Ph.D. and with a (now embarrassing) amount of emails to both Christy and Carolyn, my fourth novel had fragmented and was living and breathing online through a series of blogs, YouTube videos, *Second Life* meet-ups, email interactions, fictitious magazine articles, spoof magazine covers, postcards sent to readers around the world, and forums. Within days agents, newspapers, magazines, production companies, and networks were pinging my inbox and calling my phone. It was clear I was on to something. Tim O'Reilly's "Tools of Change in Publishing Conference" whisked me to New York to present my project and publishers, broadcasters, and filmmakers around the world invited me to talk to their storytellers.

It was the ultimate baptism of fire and whilst it sometimes burned, I mostly glowed with excitement and opportunity.

Digital storytelling has been the cause of excitement, debate, and discussion for a while, bandied around under broader terminology such as pervasive storytelling, transmedia storytelling, and storytelling 2.0, brings forth animated discussions of narrative design, experience design, engagement, and interaction, and is the topic of conversation for many conferences that focus on entertainment and all things "new."

I now work with storytellers and producers across a global entertainment industry, with a close-knit community of great people with awesome job titles, and on my travels, my time as Producer and Chair of StoryWorld Conference, teaching at film and media schools, and conversations with renowned Hollywood storytellers and consultants, there remains one statement that rings loud and clear: "there just aren't enough writers who know how to *really* do this."

There are plenty of strategists, architects, and theorists—but never enough writers who *really* understand the complexities of digital storytelling—the interactions, pacing, calls to action, storylines. Somewhere amongst the bells and whistles, human behaviors tend to be forgotten and many are the novice storytellers who believed they can *make* their audiences behave differently.

If this book serves only to make you do one thing—let it be to write.

To experiment, to understand your audience, to prototype, to strategize, but to write and "get it out there."

In balance to there being "not enough writers who know how to *really* do this" there is also a huge opportunity for experimentation—which brings experience, failure, and then growth.

If there's one thing I learned from my Master's story project, it's that I learned more from what went wrong than what went right. That's where the learning is—in the experimentation. Storytelling is intrinsic to our DNA and at many a conference I've heard an "expert" preach about the days of cave painting and campfire oratory tales. We know this. What we're still trying to catch up with is how to turn our storytelling ship and navigate digital whilst keeping tight with our audience, weaving entry points, jump-off points, and opportunities for interactivity—all whilst retaining exemplary fundamentals of storytelling.

I am absolutely honored and delighted to be writing this foreword for Carolyn's third edition of *Digital Storytelling: A Creator's Guide to Interactive Entertainment*.

So, at the risk of repeating myself …

Digital storytelling. In its true essence, it is so much more than simply "writing for the Web." The secret to any degree of long-term "success" lies with storytelling and attracting and then engaging a captive audience in a digital space where banner ads, clicks, pokes, cat videos, and a host of other distractions are rife is no mean feat.

Because without "story" it's all just noise and here's where Carolyn truly excels.

Alison Norrington
CEO
storycentral

Preface

THE EVOLVING WORLD OF DIGITAL STORYTELLING

Since the second edition of this book came out, back in 2008, a staggering number of new developments and innovations have taken place in this field. I cannot think of one area of digital media where tremendous change has not occurred. Furthermore, whole new areas of content have been created where virtually nothing existed in 2008. These include storytelling on smart phones and tablets; new forms of interactive TV, like second-screen and social TV; the huge wave of popularity of social media, which is turning into a viable platform to tell stories; and the growth of transmedia storytelling. New digital platforms and technologies have also been introduced, such as Google Glass and the Kinect. In this new edition, I have done my best to include all major new developments in this arena as clearly and completely as possible.

As in the two earlier editions, the focus here is on storytelling, not on the technology. I have discussed the technology only to the degree that such a discussion can be used to clarify how a particular technology can be used for storytelling purposes. I leave it to others to delve deeply into the technological aspects of this field. While I fully acknowledge that the technology is extremely important, it is not only beyond the scope of this book, but it is also, to be honest, beyond my expertise. I have instead focused on the areas where I do have a certain expertise, which is in storytelling and in creating interactive digital media projects. Thus, I have covered storytelling essentials: character development, plot, emotion, and structure. And I have also focused on the impact of interactivity on narrative, and the way it can change everything about classic storytelling.

One interesting observation I made in preparing this new edition is the fact that many recent projects defy neat categorization. For example, a single project may be a work of transmedia storytelling, and simultaneously be a work of social media, an interactive experience for the Web, and a new form of gaming. It is becoming increasingly challenging to slot projects into specific chapters. Perhaps we are looking towards a world where all forms of digital media will be multi-platform. If multi-platform stories become the norm, labeling them by the platform they live on will no longer make sense. The one thing we can count on is that significant changes will continue to take place in this field. While some may be predictable, many will not be.

THE VARIOUS DEFINITIONS OF DIGITAL STORYTELLING

It should be noted that people use a variety of definitions for "digital storytelling." The way we use it in this book is this: digital storytelling is the use of digital media platforms and interactivity for narrative purposes, either for fictional or for non-fiction stories. Under this definition, we include everything from video games to smart toys to virtual reality, and a number of other story forms as well.

Quite often the projects highlighted in his book have been produced by a professional team, and with the expectation that the work would be seen by a large audience and in the hopes that there would be some financial compensation for producing it. While a great many of these works are made for entertainment purposes, others are made to train, to promote, to educate, and to inform. But even when employed for pragmatic purposes, these works always contain elements of storytelling.

In the educational arena, however, "digital storytelling" is used to mean the employment of still images and a recorded script, and possibly some video or animation, to tell personal stories or stories relating to an element in the curriculum. Often children are given the opportunity to create these stories to teach them narrative skills and to excite them about learning. In the anthropological field, "digital storytelling" is used as a way to preserve stories of a culture or historic period that might otherwise be forgotten.

In journalism, the term is used to indicate a true story that is told via multiple media, such as audio, text, video, and still images. In the last several years, we have seen a significant growth in interactive documentaries, and some of these have been made for prestigious institutions like the *New York Times* and the John F. Kennedy Presidential Library and Museum.

Although these definitions and intentions differ, they all do have some critical elements in common: they are narratives, they employ digital media, and they are meant to be engaging.

THE ORGANIZATION OF THIS EDITION

This edition is organized much like the second edition, although some new chapters have been added, and several chapters have been merged. Nevertheless, the five large divisions used in the second edition have been retained here. They include:

- PART 1: NEW TECHNOLOGIES, NEW CREATIVE OPPORTUNITIES

  This section covers the history and development of digital storytelling, and also examines what is meant by convergence and how it relates to digital storytelling.

- PART 2: CREATING STORY-RICH PROJECTS

  This section examines the fundamentals of storytelling (such as plots, character development, emotional content, and structure) and how they are impacted by interactivity. It also investigates important developmental considerations like one's audience; the use of social media and transmedia; and the steps that one can take to make the production process as smooth as possible.

- PART 3: HARNESSING DIGITAL STORYTELLING FOR PRAGMATIC GOALS

This section discusses how digital storytelling can be used in education and training, in promotion, and for informational purposes.

- PART 4: MEDIA AND MODELS: UNDER THE HOOD

The chapters in this section delve into specific forms of digital storytelling, including video games, immersive environments, projects for the Web, smart toys, and many other areas. These chapters offer a cross-section of examples and case studies of successful projects in each area. Several projects that did not flourish are also examined, along with the reasons for their lack of success. This is done in the belief that one can learn as much from failures as from successes.

- PART 5: CAREER CONSIDERATIONS

This section is devoted to questions that must be answered if one wishes to work in the digital storytelling field or wishes to sustain a successful career in this arena. Should one create a showcase? What are the different ways of working in this field and what are the advantages and disadvantages of each? What legal matters should you be aware of?

Each chapter in this book opens with a series of thought-provoking questions relating to the contents of the chapter. Most chapters close with several "idea-generating exercises." These exercises give you, the reader, the opportunity to try out the concepts discussed in the chapter and to stretch your imagination. The chapters in Part 5 contain practical suggestions and tips instead of exercises, a better fit for this section.

SOURCES AND PERSPECTIVE

The material in this edition, as with the first two editions of the book, is based in part on interviews conducted with practitioners and experts in the field of digital storytelling. Twenty-two new interviews were done for this edition. The book also retains many of the highlights of interviews done for the older editions, so, in a sense, it is a compendium of wisdom from the field. Much of the information offered in this edition is supported by facts or opinions found in blogs, magazines, surveys, and publications dedicated to various aspects of digital media. The sources of this information are given in the text, after the relevant content, rather than in footnotes, which many readers find distracting.

In addition to information from experts and from printed sources, some of the content here is based on my own professional experience in the field. My personal perspective is that of a writer and a storyteller, a person on the creative side of this field, and that perspective also forms the thrust of this book. In addition, much of the content is based on many hours of playing games and exploring various works of digital storytelling, which is the great pleasure of writing a book like this.

The majority of information contained in this edition relates to projects or developments that had not yet seen the light of day when the second edition was published. In addition, some solid examples of digital storytelling from the first two editions have been retained, because these projects broke new ground and are still highly useful as models.

ADDITIONAL RESOURCES

The field of digital storytelling moves so quickly that it is inevitable that even a brand new edition of this subject will not be able to contain everything that is new and worth noting. Whenever possible, I have offered up specific sources of information that will enable the reader to stay current, including online publications and the websites of important trade groups and organizations. I have worked hard to bring this edition up-to-date and even project into the future, but ultimately you, the reader, must take on the responsibility to carry on where I have had to leave off, and make your own discoveries.

When possible, I will post new information on the book's companion website and on my own website, www.CarolynMiller.com. I also welcome your questions and comments. These may be sent to me at Carolyn@CarolynMiller.com. The companion website can be found at www.focalpress.com/cw/miller.

Acknowledgments

In writing the third edition of *Digital Storytelling*, I received invaluable help from a number of individuals. First and foremost, these include the 22 experts in a variety of fields who allowed me to interview them and pick their brains. They were extremely generous with their time and their ideas, and this book would not be what it is without their contributions. Unfortunately, space does not allow me to list them all by name, but they are acknowledged in the sections of the book where they are quoted. I would like to give one special thank you, however, to Nick DeMartino, who kindly straightened me out on a number of matters and pointed me to some excellent projects that I've described in this book. His help was invaluable.

In addition, I would like to thank my editor, David Bevans, who has been extremely supportive and patient with me. I hope very much that this book justifies his kindness, which is greatly appreciated. Thanks also to my production editor, Emma Elder, who made the final steps so pain free for me.

My technical advisor, Douglas Lee Miller, was extremely helpful in making sure that the technical information I offered was accurate, and he also offered up some interesting information of a non-technical nature. I've included as many of these curious tidbits as possible.

I would also like to acknowledge my literary agent, Susan Crawford, who has been wonderfully level-headed and an enormous help in getting this edition nailed down properly. As always, she has been a pleasure to work with.

In addition, I would like to thank the students I have taught at the University of New Mexico and the Santa Fe Community College for their thought-provoking questions and comments. In a similar fashion, I would like to thank the people who have come to my talks and workshops in recent years. As always, I feel I learn more from my students than they learn from me!

And one last thank you goes to my two donkeys, Minnie and Pearl, who cheered me up when the going got rough and refreshed my mind when it was bogged down with a heavy load of material for this book. There's nothing like feeding fresh hay or apples to two hungry donkeys to give you a fresh perspective!

PART 1

New Technologies, New Creative Opportunities

CHAPTER 1

Storytelling, Old and New

In what ways is digital storytelling like traditional forms of storytelling and in what ways is it quite unique?

What ancient human activities can be thought of as the precursors of digital storytelling, and what can we learn from them?

What are the similarities between athletic games and digital storytelling, and why are they important?

What ideas can we find in classic literature, movies, and theatrical works that may have influenced digital storytelling?

STORYTELLING: AN ANCIENT HUMAN ACTIVITY

Storytelling is a magical and powerful craft. Not only can it transport the audience on a thrilling journey into an imaginary world, but it can also reveal the dark secrets of human behavior or inspire the audience with the desire to do noble deeds. Storytelling can also be pressed into service for other human goals: to teach and train young people, for example, or to convey important information. Although digital storytelling is humankind's newest way to enjoy narrative entertainment, it is part of this same great tradition.

Digital storytelling is narrative entertainment that reaches its audience via digital technology and media. One of its unique hallmarks is *interactivity*—back-and-forth communications between the audience and the narrative material. Digital storytelling is a vast field. It includes video games, content designed for the Internet, mobile apps, and even intelligent toy systems and electronic kiosks—at least 11 major and very different areas in all.

On the vast timetable of human achievements, this type of storytelling is a mere infant, only coming into being in the mid-twentieth century with the development of computer technology. As to be expected with something so young, it is still growing and evolving. Each new development in digital media—broadband, wireless signals, mobile apps, virtual reality—sees a corresponding development in digital storytelling.

The biggest difference between traditional types of narratives and digital storytelling is that the content of traditional narratives is in an *analog* form, whereas the content in digital storytelling comes to us in a *digitalized* form. Digital data is made up of distinct, separate bits: the zeroes and ones that feed our computers. Analog information, on the other hand, is continuous and unbroken—a continual stream of information. The oldest stories were conveyed by the human voice and actors; later, narratives were printed on paper; more recently, they were recorded on audiotape, film, or video. All these older forms are analog.

To distinguish between these older forms of content and the computerized forms, people coined the term "new media." New media content includes the words and images we see on our computer screens; material that comes to us on DVDs and other discs; via streaming audio and video; and on our video game consoles, mobile phones, and tablets. All of these forms are digital. The difference between analog and digital can easily be seen by comparing an analog clock to a digital clock. An analog clock displays time in a smooth sweep around the dial, while a digital clock displays time in specific numerical increments of hours, minutes, and seconds.

Digital information can be stored easily, accessed quickly, and transferred among a great variety of devices. It can also be readily reassembled in an almost infinite number of ways, and thus becomes a viable form of content for interactivity. The digitizing of content is what makes digital storytelling possible.

Yet, as new as digital storytelling is, it is part of a human tradition that stretches back to preliterate times. Furthermore, it has much in common with other forms of narrative—theatrical performances, novels, movies, and so on. (A narrative is simply an account of events which are interesting or exciting in some way; the word is often used interchangeably with "story.") In essence, all stories have the same basic components. They portray characters caught up in a dramatic situation, depicting events from the inception of the drama to its conclusion. "Story," of course, does not necessarily mean a work of fiction, something that is make-believe. Descriptions of things that happen in real life can be stories, too, as long as they are narrated in a dramatic manner and contain characters. Newspapers and TV news shows are major vehicles for non-fiction stories. And documentaries, which are long-form explorations of true events, are also stories.

Scientists believe that storytelling can be traced back to sometime in the Pleistocene Age (1.8 million to about 11,000 years ago) and was developed as a critical survival tool. Manuel Molles, Professor Emeritus of Biology at the University of New Mexico, theorizes that storytelling was used to communicate important information about the environment, behavior of wildlife, and availability of food (from his paper "An Ecological Synthesis: Something Old, Something New," delivered at a 2005 ecology conference in Barcelona).

Dr. Dan Schwarz, a professor of English at Cornell University, also believes that storytelling shapes a basic human need. He stated in a recent interview that it was his bedrock belief "that humans are defined in part by an urge for narratives that give shape and form to their experience" (*English at Cornell*, Vol. 13).

Storytelling is such a powerful craft that telling the wrong story can even get you killed. Jeff Gomez, CEO of Starlight Runner Entertainment, a transmedia production company, commented to me in an email interview: "When you think about it, many have been killed throughout history for articulating narratives out of sync with popular notions. Shamans, spiritualists and others have historically been accused of witchcraft and sorcery, targeting them for death." To back up his point, Gomez sent me a link to an article published in the *Peruvian Times* (October 5, 2011), reporting that as recently as 2011, 14 shamans had been murdered in Peru over a 20-month period.

EXPERT OBSERVATIONS: HUMANS HARD-WIRED TO TELL STORIES?

Dr. Daniel Povinelli, a psychologist from the University of Louisiana, has made some interesting observations about the origins of storytelling. Dr. Povinelli, who studies the differences between the intellect of humans and apes, feels our species has an inborn impulse to connect the past, present, and future, and in doing so, to construct narratives. As reported in the *Los Angeles Times* (June 2, 2002), Dr. Povinelli feels this ability gives us humans a unique advantage. For example, it enables us to foresee future events based on what has happened in the past; it gives us the ability to strategize; and helps us understand our fellow human beings and behave in a way that is advantageous to us.

INTERACTIVITY AND STORYTELLING

One of the things that distinguishes digital storytelling from classical storytelling is that members of the audience can become active players in the narrative and even have a direct impact on it. Surprising as it may seem, however, interactive narrative experiences like this existed long before the invention of computers.

Some professionals in interactive media hypothesize that the earliest forms of interactive storytelling took place around the campfires of prehistoric peoples. I can remember this theory being enthusiastically touted back in the early 1990s, when the creative community in Hollywood was first becoming excited about the potential of interactive media. At almost every conference I attended at the time, at least one speaker would allude to these long ago campfire scenes. The prehistoric storyteller, according to this theory, would have a general idea of the tale he planned to tell, but not a fixed plot. Instead, he would shape and mold the story according to the reactions of those gathered around him.

This model evokes an inviting image of a warm, crackling fire and comfortable conviviality. It was no doubt a reassuring scenario to attendees of these first interactive media conferences, many of whom were intimidated by computers and the concept of interactive media. But to me, this model never sounded particularly convincing. For one thing, how could anyone really know what took place around those smoky old campfires? And even if it were true that ancient storytellers constructed their tales to fit the interests of their listeners, how much actual control or participation in the story could these campfire audiences have had? At best, it would have been an extremely weak form of interactivity.

But no matter what one thinks of this campfire model, it is unquestionably true that a form of interactive storytelling—a far more profound and participatory form—dates back to extremely ancient times. According to the renowned scholar Joseph Campbell (1904–1987), one of the earliest forms of story was the myth, and storytellers did not merely recite these old tales. Instead, the entire community would reenact them, in the form of religious rituals.

PARTICIPATORY DRAMAS

These ancient reenactments of myths described by Campbell were a form of participatory drama. He and other scholars in the field have observed that the myths acted out by a community generally contained deep psychological underpinnings, and that one of their most common themes was death and rebirth. Campbell noted that participants who took part in myth-based rituals often found the experience so intense that they would undergo a catharsis, a profound sense of emotional relief. (The word catharsis comes from the Greek, *katharsis*, and means purgation, or purification.)

In agrarian communities, these rituals would often commemorate the death of the earth (winter) and its joyous rebirth (spring). One such ritual, well known to scholars of Greek drama, was called the Festival of Dionysus. Celebrated twice annually throughout ancient Greece, these festivals were a ritual retelling of the myth of Dionysus, the Greek god of wine and fertility (see Figure 1.1). They not only depicted important events in the deity's life, but were also closely connected to the cycle of seasons, particularly the death and rebirth of the grapevine, a plant closely associated with Dionysus.

Figure 1.1 The Greek god, Dionysus, pictured on this ancient vase (ca 500 BC) was honored in intense ritual ceremonies that were an early form of interactive storytelling. Note the grapevine and clusters of grapes in the decoration. Dionysus was closely associated with the cultivation of grapes. Photograph by Maria Daniels, courtesy of University Museums, University of Mississippi.

While some details of the Dionysian rituals have been lost over time, a fair amount is still known about them. They involved singing and dancing and the playing of musical instruments. The male participants would dress as satyrs, drunken creatures who were half man and half goat (the goat being one of the animal forms associated with the god), while the women would play the part of maenads, the god's frenzied female attendants. In some Greek communities, the festival included a particularly bloodthirsty element—the participants would take a live bull (symbolizing another animal form of the god) and tear it apart with their teeth.

Ultimately, these festivals evolved into a more sedate ceremony, the performance of songs called *dithyrambs* that were dedicated to Dionysus. These choral performances in turn evolved into classic Greek drama, both tragedy and comedy, which continued to retain the influence of the early rites. The word "tragedy," in fact, comes from the Greek word *tragoidia*, which means "goat song."

MYTHOLOGICAL SYMBOLISM AND DIGITAL STORYTELLING

The Greeks were by no means the only ancient community to reenact its myths in dramatic performances. The ancient Egyptians also held religious rituals based on their mythology. Over time, they evolved into staged performances, with actors playing the role of various gods. These early forms of drama actually pre-dated Greek theater. Campbell asserts that the reenactment of myths was a common element of all preliterate societies. Even today, in regions where old traditions have not been erased by modern influences, isolated societies continue to perform ceremonies rich in mythological symbolism.

One such group is the Dogon people of Mali, West Africa, who live in clay dwellings tucked into the steep cliffs of the Bandiagara Escarpment, not far from the Sahara desert. Because this region is so remote and relatively inaccessible, the Dogon have managed to preserve their ancient traditions and spiritual practices to this day. Many of the Dogon's beliefs are reenacted in elaborate dance ceremonies, during which participants don masks and full body costumes. Unlike dancers in Western culture, where troupes are made up of a select few talented individuals who perform for an audience of nonparticipants, in Dogon society, every member of the community takes part in the dances put on by their clan.

One of the most dramatic of these ceremonies is the Sigui dance, which takes place just once every 60 years. It contains many of the elements Joseph Campbell noted as being customary in important ritualistic ceremonies, such as a representation of death and a rebirth. In this case, the Sigui dance symbolizes the passing of the older generation and the rebirth of the Dogon people.

Although the actual ceremony is performed at such great intervals, every so often a version of it will be presented to visitors who make the difficult trek to the Dogon's cliff dwellings. Some years ago, I had the great privilege of witnessing the Sigui dance. It was an extraordinary sight to see the costumed dancers appear, as if from nowhere, and make their way into the center of the village where we waited. A number of them danced on stilts, making them as tall as giants, and all the more impressive.

Each dancer plays a highly symbolic and specific role. Their masks and costumes represent important animals, ancestors, and spirit figures in their belief system (see Figure 1.2). In the eyes of the community, the dancers are more than mere human beings; each is an *avatar* for a mythological being or spirit—the embodiment or incarnation of an entity who is not actually present.

Figure 1.2 The Dogan dancer on stilts represents a female *tingetange*, or water bird. Dogan dancers don masks and costumes to portray mythological beings or spiritual figures much in the same way as game players control avatars in digital dramas and games. Photograph courtesy of Stephenie Hollyman.

A student of mine who lived on the Navajo Nation recalls another example of a participatory drama that was reenacted every fall by the Apaches. He told me: "I'd always be afraid of the 'Apache dancers.' They danced around with sticks and have their faces covered with black cloths with their bodies all painted in black. They looked like a nightmare coming into reality and once I'd hear those bells on their ankles jiggling I'd be the first running behind my parent to hide. Trust me, there is a reason. The dancers would stop in front of a crowd and go out and grab people to dance with them or have them participate in the story they were performing."

Odd though it may seem, the rituals performed by the Apaches, the Dogons, and the ancient Greeks have a great deal in common with modern-day digital storytelling. After all, they involve the use of avatars; they are a form of role-play; participants interact with each other and work toward accomplishing a particular goal; and they play out scenes that can be highly dramatic and even have life and death significance. To me, these ritual reenactments are a far more intriguing model of interactivity than that of the old campfire stories.

FAMILIAR RITUALS AND DIGITAL STORYTELLING

Closer to home, and to our own lives, we can examine our own holidays and traditional religious practices and discover other surprising similarities to digital storytelling. These celebrations are often forms of participatory drama and contain items of important symbolic or mystical value, just as works of digital storytelling do. And in some cases, they are also *multi-sensory*. In other words, they involve the senses in a variety of ways.

The Jewish holiday of Passover is a particularly good example of this. Passover commemorates the exodus of Jews from Egypt and their liberation from the slavery imposed on them by the Pharaoh. The traditional way to observe Passover is at a ceremonial meal called the Seder, where the dramatic story of exodus is recounted, and is recreated by the symbolic foods that are part of the ritual.

For example, one eats a flat unleavened bread called *matzo*, which recalls the bread hurriedly made during the exodus, when the escaping Jews had no time to let their bread rise. Another special Seder food is a bitter herb called *maror* (customarily horseradish), which symbolizes the bitterness of slavery. It is eaten together with *charoset*, a sweet chopped mixture of apples, nuts, and spices, which represents the mortar the Jews used to build the pyramids and also hints at the sweetness of freedom to come. These are among the many symbolic foods eaten during the ritual. And in addition to the foods consumed, a traditional Seder includes another sensory element: the participants recline on pillows instead of sitting upright in chairs. This is a reminder of another aspect of the exodus story (through body position and the softness of the cushions): once the Jews were liberated, they were free to eat like noble families, in a reclining position.

Many forms of digital storytelling are multi-sensory in this way, involving tactile feedback, aromas, motion, and other stimuli. The addition of multi-sensory components adds to the immersiveness and emotional power of works of digital storytelling.

STRANGE BUT TRUE: HALLOWEEN AND DIGITAL STORYTELLING

Our yearly celebration of Halloween is just one of many Western holidays that bear some surprising similarities to digital storytelling. This holiday originated as a Celtic celebration called *Samhain*, and it marked the end of summer and the beginning of the dark half of the year. It was considered a time when the spirits of the dead might return and interact with those who were still living. Again, we have the recurring theme of death and rebirth found in so many other rituals. And though we might not be aware of what the holiday symbolized to ancient Celts, Halloween still retains reminders of death (skulls, skeletons, gravestones) and of the supernatural (ghosts, witches on broomsticks, zombies).

One of the most alluring aspects of Halloween is, of course, the opportunity to wear a costume. Just as in works of digital storytelling, we can take on a new role and "be" something we are not in real life. Halloween also gives us a chance to transition into a world that is quite different from our ordinary reality, a world filled with magic and the supernatural and spooky reminders of the afterlife. This ability to get a taste of another reality is something else we can do, thanks to digital storytelling.

RITES OF PASSAGE AND DIGITAL STORYTELLING

Joseph Campbell, the scholar who did the groundbreaking work on mythology, also noted that traditional myth-based rituals frequently reflected major life passages, such as a coming of age for young boys and girls. According to Campbell, the ceremonies held for boys typically required them to undergo a terrifying ordeal, during which they would "die" as a child and be reborn as an adult. Girls also went through coming-of-age ceremonies, he found, though they tended to be less traumatic.

Campbell discovered that cultures all over the world and across all cultures told myths about this universal coming-of-age experience, a type of mythology he analyzed in 1949 in his seminal work, *The Hero with a Thousand Faces*. This genre of myth is often referred to as the *hero's journey*. As we will see in Chapter 5, its core elements and recurring characters have been incorporated into many popular movies and, most importantly for us, the hero's journey has also served as a model for innumerable works of digital storytelling, particularly video games.

GAMES AND DIGITAL STORYTELLING

We can look back at a very different type of human activity and find another important precursor to digital storytelling: the playing of games. As we will see later in this book, many works of digital storytelling are either full-fledged games or include game-like elements. And like rituals, games date back to ancient times and once served important functions.

The earliest games were developed not for idle amusement but for serious purposes: often to prepare young men for the hunt and for warfare. By taking part in games, the youths would strengthen their bodies and develop athletic skills like running and throwing. By playing with teammates, they would also learn how to coordinate maneuvers and how to strategize. Over time, these athletic games evolved into formal competitions. Undoubtedly, the best known of these ancient sporting events are the Greek Olympic Games. We can trace the Olympic Games back to 776 BC, and we know they continued to be held for more than 1,000 years.

Athletic competitions were also held in ancient Rome, India, and Egypt. In many old societies, these competitions served a religious function as well as being a form of popular entertainment. In Greece, for example, the games were dedicated to the god Zeus, and the athletic part of the program was preceded by sacred religious rites.

Religion and sporting games were even more intricately mixed in the part of the world that is now Mexico and Central America. The Olmecs, Mayans, and other peoples throughout Mesoamerica played a ball game somewhat like basketball. We now know this game had great spiritual and symbolic significance to them, and was a central ritual in their culture. The game served as a conduit to the gods they believed dwelt beneath the earth and was a way of communicating with divine powers.

The game was played by two competing teams in an outdoor court marked by a set of high parallel walls. The players had to keep the ball in the air, and could use any part of their body to do this except for their hands. As in a modern ball game, the two teams vied to lob the ball into a specific target to make a goal; in this case the target was a high stone ring. However, unlike modern ball games, once a goal was scored, the game ended, and so did the life of at least one of the players. Scholars still are debating whether this fate fell to the captain of the winning team or the losing team. They do agree, however, that the leader of one of the teams was ritually executed by decapitation, and that this action was meant as a religious sacrifice, to please their gods. Visitors to the excavated ball court at Chichén Itzá, in Mexico's Yucatan Peninsula, can still see a stone relief depicting the decapitation ceremony (see Figure 1.3).

Figure 1.3 This carving at Chichén Itzá of a postgame decapitation ceremony illustrates that games can play a deadly serious role in the spiritual life of a culture. The circle in the carving represents the ball, and the figure inside the ball is the skull of the decapitated player. Photograph courtesy of E. Michael Whittington, Mint Museum of Art, Charlotte, North Carolina.

Over 1,500 years ago, all the way across the ocean, in Asia, players faced each other in another athletic competition with deep spiritual significance. In this case, the country was Japan and the game was sumo. Sumo is closely tied to Japan's Shinto religion, and it symbolizes a legendary bout between two gods, a contest upon which the fate of the Japanese people rested. The Japanese emperor himself is believed to be a descendant of the victor. As different as sumo and the Mesoamerican ball games are, they both illustrate that games can have intensely meaningful significance. The same can be true for the games found in works of digital storytelling, where game and narrative can be closely interconnected, and where the players can be enormously invested in achieving a positive outcome.

ANCIENT GAMES AND DIGITAL STORYTELLING

The sporting competitions that have come down to us from ancient times were inherently dramatic. Two opponents or two teams were pitted against each other, each attempting to achieve a victorious outcome for their side and to defeat their opponents. These old games contained many of the key elements that continue to be hallmarks of today's athletic games. Furthermore, they are also the distinguishing characteristics of the gameplay found in many works of digital storytelling. Sporting competitions as well as many works of digital storytelling are:

- dramatic and exciting;
- full of action;
- intensely competitive;
- demanding of one's skills, either physical or mental;
- regulated by specific rules;
- clearly structured, with an established way of beginning and ending;
- and played to achieve a clear-cut goal; in other words, to succeed at winning, and to avoid losing.

BOARD GAMES AND DIGITAL STORYTELLING

Athletic competitions are not the only type of game that has come to us from ancient times and that have strong similarities to many works of digital storytelling.

Board games dating back to 2700 BC have been found in the temples of the Egyptian pharaohs. They were also highly popular in ancient China, Japan, and Korea; and the people of India played chess and card games thousands of years ago. According to mythologist Pamela Jaye Smith of MYTHWORKS, some board games were used in ancient and premodern times to train players in strategy and diplomatic skills. She cites chess as a prime example of this, saying they called for "the need to analyze the other player's move, to think three, four or more moves down the line, to recognize feint, and to know when and how to make sacrifices." The ancient Chinese ancient board game of go is another game that demands strategic skills.

Another type of game, distantly related to board games, are tabletop war games. The earliest forms of such games were war game simulations developed in the eighteenth and nineteenth centuries. These games were used to train officers in strategy, and were typically played on tabletops with miniature soldiers made of metal (see Figure 1.4). In the latter part of the twentieth century, games like these, married to elements of improvisational theater, morphed into computerized role-playing games.

Figure 1.4 War game simulations played with miniature soldiers like these were the precursors of today's massively multiplayer online games (MMOGs). Photograph courtesy of Lloyd Pentacost.

Many board games involve a mixture of skill and luck, and the element of chance is one of the things that makes them particularly enjoyable. The draw of a wild card or the throw of the dice can dramatically change one's fortunes. Also, many people are attracted to board games primarily because of the social interactions that are a major part of the experience. And although board games can be competitive, they offer a safer, less stressful playing environment than athletic games. And these are all features that attract players to works of digital storytelling, as well.

CHILDREN'S GAMES AND THE "FUN FACTOR"

In addition to the structured games played by adults, children in every era and every culture have played games of all sorts. Many of them are more free-flowing and less formalized than adult games. Children's pastimes range from "quest" games like hide-and-seek, to games that are more social in nature, like jump rope, to games of skill, like jacks. Children also enjoy make-believe activities like fantasy role-play. Two old favorites, for example, are cowboys and Indians and cops and robbers.

FANTASY ROLE-PLAY FOR ADULTS

Even adults engage in fantasy role-playing activities, as evidenced by the popular Renaissance Faires, which are elaborate reconstructions of Elizabethan England, complete with jousting, a royal court, and someone playing the part of Queen Elizabeth I. Many attendees come to these faires dressed in period costumes and attempt to speak in Elizabethan English.

In the Spanish-speaking world, *Moros y Cristianos* (Moors and Christians) is another immensely popular variation of adult role-play. In these spectacular recreations of long-ago martial conflicts, participants garb themselves in medieval dress and take on the part of either Moors or Christians. Over several days, they parade through the streets and fight non-lethal battles. In some of these recreations, the Christians are riding horses and the Moors are atop camels or elephants.

For the most part, fantasy role-play activities are not strictly games, because they are not competitive in nature. They also don't follow a fixed set of rules or have a clear-cut end goal. But though they differ from more formalized games, the two pursuits have an important element in common: both activities are experienced as "play." In other words, people engage in these activities for pleasure, and they perceive them as fun.

Yet fantasy role-play is also an important part of the *Dungeons and Dragons* series of games, one of the most popular and best-selling role-playing games of all time. David Arneson, the co-creator of *Dungeons and Dragons* (along with Gary Gygax), originated many of the key concepts of role-playing games, such as the hero gaining power through his adventures. After his untimely passing in 2009, his daughter issued a statement saying: "The biggest thing about my dad's world is he wanted people to have fun in life" (*Minneapolis Star Tribune*, April 10, 2009).

The expectation of having fun is one of the primary reasons that both adults and children have traditionally engaged in games and other play activities. This continues to be true in contemporary society, even when the playing is done on game consoles or computers instead of on a ball field or in a schoolyard. The importance of this fun factor was underscored in a survey conducted a few years back by the Entertainment Software Association, a professional organization for publishers of interactive games. In the survey, game players were asked to name their top reason for playing games. Over 85 percent said they played games because they were fun.

NONLINEAR FICTION BEFORE THE COMPUTER

Traditional entertainment, especially material that is story based, is almost always *linear*. In other words, one event follows another in a logical, fixed, and progressive sequence. The structural path is a single straight line. Interactive works, on the other hand, are always *nonlinear*. Plot points do not necessarily follow each other in fixed sequence, and even when interactive works do include a central storyline, players or users can weave a varied path through the material, interacting with it in a highly fluid manner.

Nevertheless, a few innovative individuals working in long-established media—printed fiction, the theater, and more recently in motion pictures—have attempted to break free of the restrictions of linearity and have experimented with other ways of presenting story-based material.

One of the first was Laurence Sterne, author of the novel *The Life and Opinions of Tristram Shandy, Gentleman*. The nine-volume work was published between 1759 and 1766, not long after the first English novels were introduced to the public. In *Tristram Shandy*, Sterne employs a variety of unconventional ways of presenting the narrative flow, starting down one story path only to suddenly switch over to an entirely different one, and then a short while later turning down still another path. He also played with the sequence of chapters, taking chapters that had allegedly been misplaced and inserting them seemingly at random into the text. Sterne asserted that such unexpected narrative digressions were the "sunshine" of a novel and gave a book life.

Several mid-twentieth-century authors also experimented with nonlinear narrative. William Burroughs caused something of a sensation when he introduced his "cut up" works, in which he took text that he had cut into fragments and reassembled it in a different order. He believed that these rearrangements enabled new meanings to emerge. His technique was akin to the making of collages in the art world—works composed of bits of assorted materials.

As for the brilliant modern author James Joyce, many now consider his novels to be a precursor of *digital hypertext*, where words are linked to other related "assets," such as photographs, sounds, video, or other text. The user who takes advantage of these links is rewarded by a deeper experience than would have been possible by following a simple linear thread. Joyce, particularly in his sweeping novels *Ulysses* and *Finnegan's Wake*, used a similar technique of associations, allusions, word pictures, and auditory simulations, though all on paper and within the covers of his novels. Entire websites are now devoted to the topic of the hypertext aspects of Joyce's work.

Joyce died in 1941, long before the development of modern computers, but contemporary writers are now using digital technology to compose short stories and novels utilizing hypertext. Their works are available online, and electronic books are published by several companies. Most prominent among them is Eastgate, an evangelist for serious works of hypertext.

But dropping back for a moment to books that are printed the old-fashioned way, on paper, another example of interactive narrative should be mentioned: a series of books introduced in 1979. Going under the general heading of *Choose Your Own Adventure*, and primarily written for the children's market, these unusual books actually presented a form of interactive fiction. At various points in the novel, the narrative would pause and the reader would be offered a number of different ways to advance the story, along with the page number where each option could be found. Many of these books offered dozens of alternate endings. Do these novels sound a little like works of digital storytelling with branching storylines? Well, not surprisingly, this type of structure has been used in many interactive narratives, as we will see.

NONLINEAR DRAMA IN THEATER AND MOTION PICTURES

Writers and directors of plays and motion pictures have also experimented with nonlinear methods of telling stories. The Italian playwright Luigi Pirandello (1867–1936) wrote a number of plays that probed the line between reality and fiction. His plays deliberately broke the *fourth wall*, the invisible boundary that separates the audience from the characters on stage, and divides reality (the audience side) from fiction (the characters' side). In his play

Six Characters in Search of an Author, Pirandello breached the wall by having actors in an uncompleted play talk and refer to themselves as if they were real people. They fretted about the need to find a playwright to "complete" their plot lines, or lives. Pirandello won the Nobel Prize in literature in 1934 for his groundbreaking work, and his dramas influenced a number of other playwrights, including Samuel Beckett and Edward Albee.

Pirandello's boldness at smashing the fourth wall is also echoed in Woody Allen's film, *The Purple Rose of Cairo*. In this picture, Mia Farrow plays the part of a woebegone filmgoer with a passionate crush on a character in a movie (played by Jeff Daniels). Much to her astonishment and delight, her film hero speaks to her as she sits in the audience watching the movie, and even steps out of the screen and into her life.

This breaking of the fourth wall, while relatively unusual in the theater and in movies, is a common occurrence in interactive media. Video game characters address us directly and invite us into their cyber worlds; fictional characters in Web-based stories and games send us emails and faxes and even engage in instant messaging with us; smart toys joke with us and remember our birthdays. This tunneling through of the fourth wall intimately connects us with a fictional universe in a way that is far more personal than was ever possible in older media.

Another revolutionary technique that first appeared in theater and films, and was later employed more fully in interactive entertainment, is the use of multiple pathways or points of view. The play *Tamara*, written by John Krizanc, utilized a multiple pathway structure, and it created quite a stir in Los Angeles in the 1990s. Instead of being performed in a theater, *Tamara* was staged in a large mansion, and multiple scenes were performed simultaneously in various rooms. Members of the audience had to choose which scenes to watch (which they did by following characters from room to room); it was impossible to view everything that was going on during a single performance.

Tamara had a direct influence on the producers of the CD-i mystery game *Voyeur*. Like the play, the game also made use of multiple pathways. It, too, was set in a mansion with many rooms, and simultaneous action occurred throughout the mansion. But as a player, you could look through only one window of the mansion at a time (much like a member of the *Tamara* audience, who could only observe the action in a single room at a time). To successfully play the game, you had to select a sequence of windows to peer through that would give you sufficient clues to solve the mystery.

A more recent nonlinear theatrical work, *Sleep No More*, like *Tamara*, was also meant to be experienced by moving from room to room and floor by floor. The work, loosely based on Shakespeare's *Macbeth*, was created by Punchdrunk, a British theatre company. It was set in the fictitious abandoned McKittrick Hotel (actually three adjoining warehouses in Manhattan, dressed to look like a luxurious 1930s hotel), and performed primarily without dialogue. As with *Tamara*, much of the action occurred simultaneously in various rooms, so it was impossible to experience every scene. Members of the audience were instructed not to talk to each other, and everyone was required to wear a mask. No two people experienced *Sleep No More* in exactly the same way, and it was thus up to each member of the audience to piece together his or her own version of the narrative. *Sleep No More* ran in New York during 2011–2012, with earlier productions in London and in Brookline, Massachusetts.

Writers and directors of feature films have also experimented with narrative perspective. One notable example is the Japanese film *Rashomon*, made in 1950 by the renowned director-screenwriter Akira Kurosawa. *Rashomon* is the story of a woman's rape and a man's murder, but what made the film so striking was not its core story but Kurosawa's use of multiple points of view. The story is told in flashback by four different characters, each of whom was a witness to the crimes, but each giving a different version of what really happened. In the end, we are not told which the "correct" version is; we are left to puzzle out which person's perspective is the most plausible. Kurosawa's concept of offering multiple points of view has been borrowed by a number of works of interactive cinema, as we will see later in this book.

The American film director Robert Altman often uses another narrative approach, that of multiple overlapping and interconnecting storylines. *Nashville* and *Gosford Park* are two of his films that do this. A viewer watching them has the impression of multiple events occurring simultaneously, and sometimes wishes for the freedom offered by interactive media to jump from one storyline to another.

THE SPECIAL CHARACTERISTICS OF DIGITAL STORYTELLING

As we can see from the various examples we've examined here, ranging from ancient rituals to twentieth-century films, many of the techniques that are characteristic of today's digital storytelling can actually be found in far earlier forms of storytelling and other human activities. Yet, thanks to computer technology, we can incorporate these techniques into interactive stories in a much more fluid and dynamic fashion to give us quite a new way to experience narrative.

Let's now take a look at the special characteristics of digital storytelling to see what makes it unique as a form of narrative. Some of these characteristics have already been mentioned, and some will be discussed later in the book.

Works of digital storytelling are always:

- types of narratives: they involve a series of connected dramatic events that serve to tell a story;
- works that contain characters, including types of characters found only in digital media: characters controlled by the user or by the computer, and synthetic characters with the appearance of *artificial intelligence* (AI);
- interactive: the user controls, or impacts, aspects of the story;
- nonlinear: events or scenes do not occur in a fixed order; characters are not encountered at fixed points;
- deeply immersive: they pull the user into the story;
- participatory: the user participates in the story;
- navigable: users can make their own path through the story or through a virtual environment.

Works of digital storytelling often:

- break the fourth wall: the user can communicate with the characters; the fictional characters behave as if they were real people;

- blur fiction and reality;

- include a system of rewards and penalties;

- use an enormous narrative canvas, tying together multiple media to tell a single story;

- may be *multi-sensory*;

- attempt to incorporate some form of *artificial intelligence* (AI);

- allow users to create and control avatars;

- offer a shared community experience;

- manipulate time and space (contracting or expanding time; allowing users to travel enormous virtual distances);

- put users through a series of challenges and tests (modeled on rites of passage and *The Hero's Journey*);

- offer opportunities to change points of view, either seeing the story from the vantage point of different characters or by changing the visual point of view;

- include overt and non-overt gaming elements, such as:
  o clear-cut objectives: to score points; to win;
  o high stakes;
  o governed by clear set of rules;
  o demanding of high skill level;
  o played within a defined space;
  o making users engage in risk-taking behaviors;
  o set within a specific time frame;
  o requiring the use of strategy;
  o calling for team play;
  o requiring the overcoming of obstacles and dealing with opponents;
  o requiring players or avatars to wear elaborate uniforms that alter their appearance;

- include elements of play:
  o experienced as pleasurable, as fun, rather than as work;
  o very loosely structured; no formalized set of rules;
  o involve a degree of chance or the unexpected;
  o offer opportunities for interactions with other people; social experiences;
  o may be set in a fantasy environment or call for fantasy role-play.

WORTH NOTING: CLASSIC STORYTELLING AND DIGITAL STORYTELLING: IMPORTANT DIFFERENCES

While digital storytelling shares many characteristics with other forms of narratives, such as plays, novels, movies, and news stories, there are important differences, as well.

TRADITIONAL STORIES:	WORKS OF DIGITAL STORYTELLING:
• are preconstructed; story elements cannot be changed;	• are malleable; not fixed in advance;
• have a linear plot; usually told in linear fashion;	• are nonlinear, nonchronological;
• author/writer is sole creator;	• the user co-creates the story;
• are experienced passively;	• are experienced actively;
• have one unchangeable ending.	• different outcomes are possible.

CONCLUSION

As we have seen, two extremely old forms of social interaction—rituals and games—were two of the major precursors to digital storytelling. Despite the obvious differences between the activities that have come down to us from ancient times and today's computerized narratives, rituals and games help to define some of the critical components of this new form of storytelling.

Namely, they are interactive; they are participatory; they facilitate role-play; they are dramatic; and they are deeply immersive. In addition, the type of myth known as the *hero's journey* has served as a direct model for works of digital storytelling. However, one significant aspect of rituals and games has not yet become part of most works of digital storytelling: these ancient human activities aroused intense emotions in those who participated in them. Ancient rituals were capable of producing a powerful feeling of catharsis, or emotional release, in the participants, and communities that played ancient games felt a profound sense of being connected to the divine. In fact, this ability to elicit strong emotions is a characteristic of all classic narratives. The emotional potential of digital storytelling, however, is still largely untapped, waiting for a Shakespeare or a Sophocles of this new form of narrative to take it to a higher level.

IDEA-GENERATING EXERCISES

1. What traditional ritual have you participated in, or are aware of, that reminds you in some way of an interactive narrative? What is it about this ritual that you think is like a work of digital storytelling?

2. Think of a time when you wore a costume or engaged in some form of role-play that did not make use of electronic technology. Describe the experience and how it made you feel. How do you think it was similar to or different from the role-playing that occurs in works of digital storytelling?

3. Take a fictional character from a movie, TV show, or novel and list some ways that hypertext could be used to give a fuller picture of this individual.

4. Can you think of any work of traditional entertainment (poem, short story, novel, play, movie, TV show, etc.) that breaks the "fourth wall"? Describe how the fourth wall is broken in this work. Could the fourth wall be broken in a similar way in an interactive work? Why or why not?

CHAPTER 2

Backwater to Mainstream: The Growth of Digital Entertainment

How did international conflicts spur the development of modern computers and the Internet?

What challenges do people face when creating content for a new medium?

Who was a more likely candidate to invent the first computer game, a physicist working with an oscilloscope or a teenage kid fooling around on a PC?

What effect is digital media having on traditional forms of entertainment like movies and TV?

AN EXTREMELY RECENT BEGINNING

The development of the modern computer gave birth to a brand new form of narrative: digital storytelling. Sometimes it is difficult to keep in mind that even the oldest types of digital storytelling are quite recent innovations, especially when compared to traditional entertainment media, like the theater, movies, or even television. For instance, the first rudimentary video game wasn't even created until the late 1950s, and two more decades passed before the first form of interactive storytelling for the Internet was developed. Most other types of digital storytelling are much more recent innovations. Thus, we are talking about a major new form of narrative that is little more than half a century old.

While today's children have never known a world without computers or digital entertainment, the same is not true for older adults. Individuals who were born before the 1960s grew up, went to college, and got their first jobs before computers ever became widely available. As for today's senior citizens, a great number of them have never even used a computer and frankly aren't eager to try. Almost certainly, though, they have taken advantage of computerized technology embedded in familiar devices, from microwaves to ATM machines to home security systems.

A BRIEF HISTORY OF THE COMPUTER

While computers are newcomers to our world, only having been introduced in the middle of the twentieth century, the conceptual roots of computer technology date back to antiquity. Historians of information technology often point to the use of the abacus, the world's oldest calculating tool, as being the computer's original starting place. They believe that the Chinese, the Babylonians, and the Egyptians used various forms of the abacus as long ago as 3000 BC. It was the first implement in human history to be employed for mathematical computations.

Thousands of years later, in the late nineteenth century, humans moved one step closer to modern computer technology. In 1890, Herman Hollerith and James Powers invented a machine that could perform computations using punch-card technology. Their machine was designed to speed up computations for the US Census Bureau.

STRANGE BUT TRUE: THE WORLD'S FIRST COMPUTER PROGRAMMER

Ada Lovelace, Countess of Lovelace (1815–1852) was the daughter of the great Victorian poet, Lord Byron, and is regarded as the world's first computer programmer. She worked closely with the brilliant Charles Babbage, who created the "analytical engine," an early version of a punch-card computer. Though this device was not completely built at the time of Babbage's death, Lovelace created a working algorithm for it in the early 1840s, which means Babbage's computer was conceived far earlier than the punch-card computer built by Hollerith and Powers. Lovelace was highly gifted in mathematics—so much so that Babbage termed her "The Enchantress of Numbers."

Punch-card machines like theirs became the computing workhorses of the business and scientific world for half a century. The outbreak of World War II, however, hastened the development of the modern computer, when machines were urgently needed that could swiftly perform complex calculations. Several competing versions were developed. While there is some debate over which machine was the world's first all-electronic computer, the majority of historians believe the honor should go to the ENIAC (Electronic Numeric Integrator and Computer). This electronic wonder was completed in 1946 at the University of Pennsylvania. It could perform calculations about 1,000 times faster than the previous generation of computers (see Figure 2.1).

Despite the ENIAC's great speed, however, it did have some drawbacks. It was a cumbersome and bulky machine, weighing 30 tons, taking up 1,800 square feet of floor space, and drawing upon 18,000 vacuum tubs to operate. Furthermore, though efficient at performing the tasks it had been designed to do, it could not be easily reprogrammed.

Figure 2.1 The ENIAC, built in 1946, is regarded as the world's first high-speed computer, but it was a hulking piece of equipment by today's standards. Photography courtesy of IBM corporate archives.

During the three decades following the building of the ENIAC, computer technology progressed in a series of rapid steps, resulting in computers that were smaller and faster, had more memory, and were capable of performing more functions. Concepts such as computer-controlled robots and Artificial Intelligence (AI) were also being articulated and refined. By the 1970s, computer technology developed to the point where the essential elements could be shrunk down in size to a tiny microchip, meaning that a great number of devices could be computer enhanced. As computer hardware became smaller and less expensive, personal computers (PCs) became widely available to the general public, and the

WORTH NOTING: MOORE'S LAW

In 1965, Gordon Moore, the co-founder of Intel, made an observation that has become known as Moore's Law. He predicted that the processing power of microprocessors would double every 18 months—an incredibly fast speed. Moore's prediction was pretty much on target, though the pace has slowed somewhat.

use of computers accelerated rapidly through the 1970s and 1980s. It wasn't long before computer technology permeated everything from children's toys to supermarket scanners to household telephones.

THE BIRTH OF THE INTERNET

As important as the invention of the computer is, another technological achievement also played a critical role in the development of digital storytelling: the birth of the Internet. The basic concept that underlies the Internet—that of connecting computers together to allow them to send information back and forth even though geographically distant from one another—was first sketched out by researchers in the 1960s. This was the time of the Cold War, and such a system, it was believed, would help facilitate the work of military personnel and scientists working on defense projects at widely scattered institutions. The idea took concrete shape in 1969 when the United States Department of Defense commissioned and launched the Advanced Research Project Association Net, generally known as ARPANET.

Although originally designed to transmit scientific and military data, people with access to ARPANET quickly discovered they could also use it as a communications medium, and thus electronic mail (email) was born. And in 1978, there was an even more important discovery from the point of view of digital storytelling: some students in England determined that ARPANET could be harnessed as a medium of entertainment, inventing the world's first text-based role-playing adventure game for it. The game was a *MUD* (Multi-User Dungeon or Multi-User Domain or Multi-User Dimension), the forerunner of today's enormously popular Massively Multiplayer Online Games (MMOGs).

In 1982, Vint Cerf and Bob Kahn designed a new protocol for ARPANET. A protocol is a format for transmitting data between two devices, and theirs was called TCP/IP, or Transmission Control Protocol/Internet Protocol. Without it, the Internet could not have grown into the immense international mass-communication system it has become. The creation of TCP/IP is so significant that it can be regarded as the birth of the Internet.

In 1990, the Department of Defense decommissioned ARPANET, leaving the Internet in its place. And by now, the word "cyberspace" was frequently being sprinkled into sophisticated conversations. William Gibson first coined the word in 1984 in his sci-fi novel, *Neuromancer*, using it to refer to the nonphysical world created by computer communications. The rapid acceptance of the word "cyberspace" into popular vocabulary was just one indication of how thoroughly electronic communications had managed to permeate everyday life.

Just one year after ARPANET was decommissioned, the World Wide Web was born, created by Englishman Tim Berners-Lee. Berners-Lee recognized the need for a simple and universal way of disseminating information over the Internet, and in his efforts to design such a system, he developed the critical ingredients of the Web, including URLs, HTML, and HTTP. This paved the way for new forms of storytelling and games on the Internet. The Internet's popularity has continued to zoom upward all over the globe, reaching a total of almost 2.5 billion users worldwide by mid-2012.

THE FIRST VIDEO GAMES

Just as the first online game was devised long before the Internet was an established medium, the first video games were created years before personal computers became commonplace. They emerged during the era when computer technology was still very much the domain of research scientists, professors, and a handful of graduate students.

STRANGE BUT TRUE: THE WORLD'S FIRST VIDEO GAME

Credit for devising the first video game usually goes to a distinguished physicist named William Alfred Higinbothem, who created his game in 1958 while working at the Brookhaven National Laboratory in Upton, New York. His creation, *Tennis for Two*, was, as its name suggests, an interactive ball game, and two opponents would square off to play it. In an account written over 20 years later and posted on a Department of Energy website, Higinbothem modestly explained he had invented the game to have something interesting to put on display for his lab's annual visitors' day event. The game was controlled by knobs and buttons and ran on an analog computer. The graphics were displayed on a primitive-looking oscilloscope, a device normally used for producing visual displays of electrical signals. It was hardly the sort of machine one would associate with computer games. Nonetheless, the game was a great success. Higinbothem's achievement is a vivid illustration of human ingenuity when it comes to using the tools at hand.

A game called *Spacewar*, although not the first video game ever created, was the most direct antecedent of today's commercial video games. *Spacewar* was created in the early 1960s by an MIT student named Steve Russell. Russell, working with a team of fellow students, designed the game on a mainframe computer. The two-player game featured a duel between two primitive-looking spaceships, one shaped like a needle and the other like a wedge. It quickly caught the attention of students at other universities and was destined to be the inspiration of the world's first arcade game, though that was still some 10 years off.

In the meantime, work was going forward on the world's first home console games. The idea for making a home console game belongs to Ralph Baer, who came up with the revolutionary idea of playing interactive games on a TV screen way back in 1951. At the time, he was employed by a television company called Loral, and nobody would take his idea seriously. It took him almost 20 years before he found a company that would license his concept for a console, but finally, in 1970, Magnavox stepped up to the plate. The console, called the Magnavox Odyssey, was released in 1972, along with 12 games. The console demonstrated the feasibility of home video games, and paved the way for further developments in this area.

At just about the same time as the console's release, things were moving forward in the development of arcade games. Nolan Bushnell and Ted Dabney, the future founders of Atari, created an arcade version of *Spacewar*, the game that had been made at MIT, and released it in 1971. Their game, *Computer Space*, was the first arcade game ever, but it was a failure, reportedly because people found it too hard to play. Dabney lost faith in the computer game business and he and Bushnell parted company. Bushnell, however, was undaunted. He went on to produce an arcade game called *Pong*, an interactive version of ping-pong, complete with a ponging sound when the ball hit the paddle. Released in 1972, the game became a huge success. In 1975, Atari released a home console version of the game, and it too was a hit.

Pong helped generate an enormous wave of excitement about video games. A flurry of arcade games followed on its heels, and video arcade parlors seemed to spring up on every corner. By 1981, less than 10 years after *Pong* was released, over 1.5 million coin-operated arcade games were in operation in the United States, generating millions of dollars.

During the ensuing decades, home console games similarly took off. Competing brands of consoles, with ever more advanced features, waged war on each other. Games designed to take advantage of the new features came on the market in steady numbers. Of course, console games and arcade games were not the only form of interactive gaming in town. Video games for desktop computers, both for the PC and Mac, were also being produced. These games were snapped up by gamers eager for exciting new products.

THE DEVELOPMENT OF OTHER IMPORTANT INTERACTIVE PLATFORMS

Not counting the great variety of video game consoles, four other significant platforms were introduced during the 20 years between the late 1970s and the late 1990s. All of these technologies—laser discs, CD-ROMs, CD-is, and DVDs—were used as vehicles for interactive narratives, some more successfully than others.

LASER DISCS

Laser discs, also called video discs, were invented by Philips Electronics and made available to the public in the late 1970s. The format offered outstandingly clear audio and video and was easy to use. Consumers primarily used laser discs for watching movies, while its interactive capabilities were more thoroughly utilized in educational and corporate settings.

The laser disc's potential as a vehicle for pure interactive fun came into full bloom in the arcade game *Dragon's Lair*, released in 1983. The game not only fully exploited the capabilities of laser disc technology but also broke important new ground for video games. Unlike the primitive graphics of other games up until then, *Dragon's Lair* contained 22 minutes of vivid animation. It also had a far more developed storyline than the typical "point and shoot" arcade offerings. As a player, you had the heady experience of "becoming" the hero of the story, the knight Dirk the Daring, and as Dirk, you had a dangerous mission to fulfill: to rescue Princess

Daphne from a castle full of monsters. The game was an entertainment phenomenon unlike anything seen to date. So many people wanted to play it that arcade machines actually broke down from overuse.

CD-ROMS

CD-ROMs (for Compact Disc-Read Only Memory) were introduced to the public in 1985, a joint effort of Philips and Sony, with prototypes dating back to 1983. These little discs could store a massive amount of digital data—text, audio, video, and animation—which could then be read by a personal computer. Prior to this, storage media for computer games—floppy discs and hard discs—were far more restrictive in terms of capacity and allowed for extremely limited use of moving graphics and audio.

In the early 1990s, the software industry began to perceive the value of the CD-ROM format for games and *edutainment* (a blend of education and entertainment). Suddenly, these discs became the hot platform of the day, a boom period that lasted about five years. *Myst* and *The Seventh Guest* were two extremely popular games that were introduced on CD-ROMs, both debuting in the early 1990s. It also proved to be an enormously successful format for children's educational games, including hits like the *Carmen Sandiego* and the *Putt-Putt* series, *Freddie Fish, MathBlaster, The Oregon Trail*, and the *JumpStart* line.

The success of the CD-ROM as a platform for games was largely due to its ability to combine story elements with audio and moving visuals (both video and animation). Even professionals in Hollywood started to pay attention, intrigued with its possibilities, and hoping, as one entrepreneur put it back then, "to strike gold in cyberspace."

Unfortunately, CD-ROMs went through a major downturn in the second half of the 1990s, caused in part by the newest competitor on the block, the Internet. Financial shake-ups, mergers, and downsizing within the software industry put the squeeze on the production of new titles, and many promising companies went out of business. Despite this painful shake-up, however, CD-ROMs have remained a major platform for delivering games, education, and even corporate training, along with DVDs and the Internet.

CD-Is

The CD-is (Compact Disc-interactive) system was developed jointly by Philips and Sony and introduced by Philips in 1991. Termed a "multimedia" system, it was intended to handle all types of interactive genres, and was the first interactive technology geared for a mass audience. The CD-i discs were played on special devices designed for the purpose, and connected to a TV set or color monitor. The system offered high-quality audio and video and was extremely easy to use.

Although CD-ROMs were already out on the market at the time CD-is came along, the new platform helped spur significant creative advances in interactive entertainment, in part because Philips was committed to developing attractive titles to play on its new system. Among them was *Voyeur*, a widely heralded interactive movie–game hybrid.

DVDS

DVD technology was introduced to the public in 1997, developed by a consortium of 10 corporations. This group, made up of major electronics firms, computer companies, and entertainment studios, opted to pool their resources and work collaboratively, rather than to come out with competing products, a practice that had led to the demise of prior consumer electronics products. In a few short years, the DVD became the most swiftly adopted consumer electronics platform of all time.

The initials DVD once stood for "Digital Video Disc," but because the format could do so much more than store video, the name was changed to Digital Versatile Disc. The second name never caught on, however, and now the initials themselves are the name of the technology.

DVD technology is extremely robust and versatile. The quality of the audio and video is excellent, and it has a far greater storage capacity than either CD-ROMs or laser discs. While primarily used to play movies or compilations of television shows, it is also used as a platform for original material, including interactive dramas and documentaries.

LESS FAMILIAR FORMS OF INTERACTIVE ENTERTAINMENT

As we will see in future chapters of this book, a number of other important technologies and devices are employed for digital storytelling, and new ones are introduced on a frequent basis. Some platforms for interactive narrative are extremely familiar to the general public and highly popular—such as video game consoles, the Internet, mobile apps, and social media—while others, such as interactive television and interactive cinema, have been slower to catch on. We will be exploring both the highly popular forms and the less familiar forms throughout this book.

THE EVOLUTION OF CONTENT FOR A NEW MEDIUM

As we have seen, digital storytelling is an extremely new form of narrative, and has only had a very brief period of time to develop. The first years of any new medium are apt to be a rocky time, marked by much trial and error. The initial experiments in a new field don't always succeed, and significant achievements are sometimes ignored or even ridiculed when first introduced.

THE EARLY DAYS OF A NEW MEDIUM

The very first works produced for a new medium are sometimes referred to as *incunabula*, a term which comes from the Latin word for cradle or swaddling clothes, and thus means something still in its infancy. The term was first applied to the earliest printed books, those made before 1501. But now the term is used more broadly to apply to the early forms of any new medium, including works made for various types of digital technology.

When creating a work for a brand new medium, it is extremely difficult to see its potential. People in this position must go through a steep learning curve to discover its unique properties and determine how they can be used for narrative purposes. To make things even more challenging, a new technology often has certain limitations and these must be understood and ways must be found to cope with them. Creating works for a new medium is thus a process of discovery, and a great test of the imagination.

Typically, projects created for a new medium go through evolution, with three major steps:

1. The first step is almost always *repurposing*, which is the porting over of materials or models from older media or models, often with almost no change. For instance, many early movies were just filmed stage plays, while in digital media, the first DVDs just contained movies and compilations of TV shows, and many of the first CD-ROMs were digital versions of already existing encyclopedias.

2. The middle step is often the adaptation approach, or a spin-off. In other words, an established property, like a novel, is modified somewhat for a new medium, like a movie. Producers of TV series have been taking this approach with the Internet by creating *webisodes* (serialized stories for the Web) and *mobisodes* (serialized stories for the mobile devices) based on successful TV shows.

3. The final and most sophisticated step is the creation of totally original content that makes good use of what the new medium has to offer and does not imitate older forms. For example, the three-camera situation comedy is a unique TV genre that takes full advantage of the medium of television. The same can be said of the MMOG, which takes full advantage of the opportunities offered by the Internet.

Developing works for digital media has presented challenges almost never before faced by the creative community. For example, how could you tell a story using interactivity and a nonlinear structure? And how would the user be made aware of the interactivity, and know how to use it?

THE PROFOUND IMPACT OF DIGITAL MEDIA

Since the days when it was first called ARPANET, the Internet has matured as a major medium of distribution. A critical mass of users now has broadband connectivity, making it possible to receive and send large quantities of audio and video. Users can download and stream audio and video on their computer in real time and even watch entire feature-length movies, not to mention the wealth of shorter pieces of video and animation that are so abundant on the Internet. Broadband has also helped to turn the Internet into a robust vehicle for original content of all types, including new genres of games, new forms of drama, and new types of journalism. Broadband has also made it possible to create whole new types of social communities, such as virtual worlds, social media sites, and video file sharing sites.

The maturing of the Internet is just one reason for this digital revolution. Another important factor is the creation of new digital devices and systems that make it possible to watch and listen to programming no matter where you are. Apple has been an important innovator in this area. It built the iTunes website, which allowed users to download music for a small fee, and also created the iPod, a conveniently portable and stylish piece of playback equipment for listening to your downloaded music and other kinds of audio programming. Then, in 2005, Apple introduced the video iPod, a portable media player that enabled users to download video as well as audio content from the Internet.

When Apple released the video iPod, it also announced that it would make episodes of hit television shows available on its iTunes website for a small fee. Within the first year, it sold 45 million TV shows. In addition, the iPod can be used to watch full-length movies and play simple video games. It can also be used to watch or listen to *podcasts* (Internet audio and video broadcasts that can be watched online or downloaded to mobile devices). Sophisticated cell phones and other types of mobile devices can also be used to enjoy all kinds of audio and video content, as can many types of video game consoles.

In 2010, Apple released another revolutionary device: the iPad. This small one-piece touchscreen tablet computer allowed users to take photos, read books, shoot video, play music and games, and browse the Internet. Since the 2010 release, new versions of the iPad have been released in a steady stream. Other companies have also jumped into the craze for tablet computers, including Microsoft, Samsung, Sony, Dell, and Toshiba. While tablet computers have become enormously popular, the sales of PCs have been declining. Some analysts believe it will not be long before the sales of tablets overtake the sales of PCs (*Digital Trends*, May 9, 2013). Much of the content that is accessed via these tablet computers (as well as via smart phones) is available in the form of *apps*, which can be downloaded from app stores. "App" is the abbreviation of the term *application*. Essentially, an app is a small downloadable program designed for a particular purpose. Apps include ebooks and games as well as programs designed for pragmatic purposes (for more on tablets, smart phones, and apps, please see Chapter 17).

Another device that has played a role in the digital revolution is the personal video recorder (PVR), also known as the digital video recorder (DVR). This type of device allows TV viewers to select and record TV programs and play them back whenever they wish. Viewers also have the option of fast-forwarding through the commercials, a feature that many appreciate. And viewers who own a piece of equipment called the Slingbox can even send recorded programming to their computers, no matter where their computers happen to be. Let's say, for example, your TiVo is in your apartment in Manhattan but you are on a business trip to Paris. With a Slingbox, you could "forward" your TV favorite show to your laptop in your Paris hotel room.

TiVos, PVRs, iPods, and other digital devices have freed television viewers from the tyranny of the television schedule. As one media analyst put it, "Appointment-based television is dead." Perhaps this is an overstatement, but there's no question that developments in recent years—including the development of the Internet as a major new medium, new forms of digital distribution, and the enormous popularity of video games and other kinds of digital entertainment—are having a profound impact on the Hollywood entertainment establishment. This digital revolution is also having a number of other ramifications. For example, it is impacting on how and where advertising dollars are spent, and is profoundly changing the world of journalism. It is also bringing about innovations in the way students are taught and how employees are trained. And, most relevant to this book, it is sparking the creation of exciting new forms of storytelling.

Digital media is also impacting our lives in myriads of unexpected ways. For example, fewer people are now sending out paper greeting cards and holiday cards, finding it much faster and less expensive to send their good wishes electronically. And authors increasingly want to publish their creations as ebooks. With ebooks, they have more control over the process and make a higher percentage of royalties than they would by going with a traditional publisher that still prints exclusively on paper.

People are even experiencing nature differently. A study by the National Park Service reveals that people expect to travel through the parks with portable, mobile information that travels with them. Furthermore, they expect this information to be interactive, personalized, age-appropriate, and culture-appropriate.

Finally, the use of digital media, specifically mobile phones, is even creating a new language, according to Columbia linguistics professor John McWhorter. He calls this new language *textspeak* and says of it: "Texting is fingered speech. Now we can write the way we talk" (*All Things D*, February 28, 2013). Furthermore, a new field of academic study has opened up called cyborg anthropology. Led by Amber Case, it is the study of how humans and nonhumans, such as computers, interact with each other.

CHANGES IN THE CONSUMPTION OF ENTERTAINMENT

From the debut of the world's first commercial video game, *Pong*, in 1972, to the present-day explosion of digital content, the popularity of digital entertainment has grown at a steady and impressive rate. Not only are more people consuming digital entertainment, but they are also spending more hours enjoying it. As a result, the audiences for traditional forms of entertainment have shrunk. We are now at the point where digital content can no longer be considered a maverick outsider because it has become an accepted part of the mainstream entertainment world.

Young people, in particular, are enormous fans of digital entertainment and everything digital. They text message each other on their cell phones, instant message (IM) each other and watch streaming video on the Internet, listen to music on their iPods, and play games on their game consoles and their parents' tablet computers (see Figure 2.2). As far back as 2007, a study released by Jupiter Research reported that people between the ages of 18 and 24 spend twice as much time online as they do watching television.

Older people and women are also spending more time on pursuits typically considered the domain of teenage boys. According to statistics released in 2013 by the Entertainment Software Association (ESA), the average age of gamers is now 30, and these gamers have been playing for an average of 13 years. A total of 51 percent of US households own at least one game console. Furthermore, women over the age of 18 now make up 45 percent of the gamer population, a much larger proportion of the gamer population (31 percent) than boys 17 and younger (19 percent).

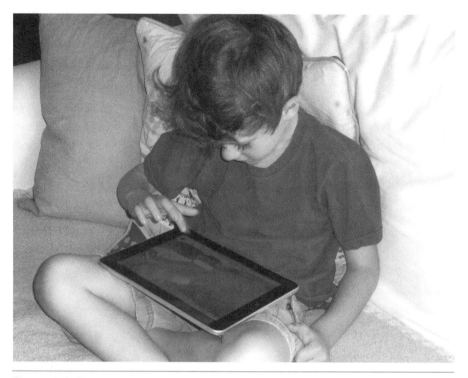

Figure 2.2 Children love doing things on digital devices, and particularly love the interactive apps offered on the iPad.

Digital media is having a major impact on broadcast television, which is slowly being overshadowed by the penetration of broadband Internet access. According to the *Hollywood Reporter*, for example, more homes in the United States have broadband access than subscribe to HBO.

While once there were only two entertainment screens that mattered—TV screens and movie screens—there is now a powerful "third screen" to contend with. This so-called third screen is really composed of multiple types of screens, a mixture of game consoles, computer screens, cell phones, and tablets.

THE IMPACT ON HOLLYWOOD

Television networks and movie studios are by no means unaware of the digital revolution, and the most forward looking of them are taking steps to minimize the negative impact and even to take advantage of it as much as possible. They clearly want to avoid being blindsided the way the music industry was in the late 1990s with illegal file sharing. Until the courts put an end to it, people were able to download songs for free, using Napster's file sharing services. This online piracy caused the recording industry to suffer tremendous financial losses, and now that video can easily be downloaded from the Internet, Hollywood is taking steps to avoid a similar debacle.

Thus, following Apple's lead, a number of film studios and TV networks have been making their movies and TV shows readily available for legal downloads for a small fee. Some are also adapting an innovative *multi-platforming* strategy. With multi-platforming, not only do they create entertainment content for their two traditional screens—movie theaters and TV sets—but also create auxiliary content for the third screen. When the same narrative storyline is developed across several forms of media, one of which is an interactive medium, it is known as *transmedia entertainment*.

Content created for a multiple media approach may take the form of dramatic material such as *webisodes* (also known as Web series) and fictional blogs. They may also use digital media to involve viewers in a mystery that's part of the plot of a TV show, giving them clues on websites and other venues so they can help solve the mystery. Or sometimes, especially with television shows, the producers will find ways to involve the viewers while the show is being broadcast. For example, viewers may use their cell phones or laptops to participate in contests or polls, vote a contestant off a reality show, or voice an opinion. This is referred to as *second-screen TV*.

The multi-platforming and transmedia approach to content is being used across the spectrum of television programming, including sitcoms, reality shows, dramas, news shows, and documentaries. These strategies serve multiple purposes. They:

- make the shows more attractive to younger viewers—the demographic that is particularly fond of interactive entertainment;
- keep viewers interested in a show and involved with it even when it is not on the air—in the days between its regular weekly broadcast, and during the summer hiatus;
- attract new viewers to a show; and
- take advantage of new revenue streams offered by video on demand (VOD), the Internet, and mobile devices.

These techniques are equally important in the feature film arena, although here very often digital platforms are primarily used for promotional purposes. We will be exploring the multi-platforming and transmedia approach to storytelling, and the kinds of interactive content that grow out of it, throughout this book, with Chapters 10 and 18 specifically devoted to this topic.

Despite various efforts to embrace the digital revolution, it is clear that traditional Hollywood entertainment is taking a hit from the third screen. Not only is television viewing down, but also movie attendance is being impacted. The big event movies remain popular, as do the specialized low-budget genre pictures, but the films that are middle of the road, with mid-level budgets, are doing poorly. It indicates that while people may be willing to spend money to go to films they really want to see, they'd sooner stay home and watch a DVD or play a video game than go to movies that don't sound particularly appealing.

Beginning in 2002, the sale of tickets for feature films began to decline, particularly with the prime demographic: young people between the ages of 12 and 24. Sales did experience a bounce in 2012 and for the first half of 2012, but many observers feel the feature film arena will never fully recover, much as broadcast television has not seen the return of young male viewers.

When an innovation in media creates a new market that disrupts an existing market, it is called *disruptive media*. It is fair to say that the popularity of various forms of new media has caused them to become disruptive media.

THE IMPACT ON HOLLYWOOD'S TALENT POOL

The popularity of digital media is also rocking the boat with Hollywood professionals. Writers, actors, and directors are demanding that they be paid fairly when their work is downloaded from the Internet or when they contribute to a new form of content like a webisode. The long-established compensation system for top talent was created well before the digital revolution and doesn't cover these situations. Not surprisingly, payment issues have grown contentious. As of this writing they have already led to one major strike, by the Writers Guild of America, the union that represents Hollywood writers. Digital technology is raising some unexpected concerns, as well. For example, actors worry that their voices and images may be digitalized and used in productions without their consent, meaning that they could lose jobs to a virtual version of themselves.

HOW ADVERTISERS ARE RESPONDING

People inside the world of the Hollywood entertainment business are not the only ones grappling with the sea changes created by the explosion of digital media. These changes are also creating upheavals for the advertising industry. In the past, television commercials were a favored way of promoting products, and advertisers spent a staggering amount of money on them—approximately $350 billion globally in 2012 alone (Nielsen, April 18, 2013). But advertisers are becoming far less willing to make such an investment under the present circumstances. Not only is television viewing down, but people are also downloading commercial-free shows from the Internet, fast-forwarding through commercials on their PVRs, and viewing commercial-free television programming on DVDs. Another major medium for advertising—the daily newspaper—is also becoming less attractive to advertisers. Circulation numbers are plummeting almost everywhere, and readership is especially low with young people, who prefer to get their news online or through their mobile devices.

Thus, advertisers are shifting their ad dollars to other areas. An ever-larger portion is going to the Internet. In 2012, one in five advertising dollars went to the Internet, and online advertising topped $100 billion, while it was virtually nothing 20 years previously (Forbes, January 1, 2013). Advertisers are also investing in product placement in video games. In a car racing game, for example, the track might be plastered with billboards promoting a particular product, or in a sports game, the athletes may be wearing shirts emblazoned with the name of clothing line, or in *The Sims*, a character might be driving around in a Prius.

In addition, advertisers are devising new forms of digital narratives and games to promote products, which is of particular interest to those of us involved in digital storytelling. For example, they are putting money into *advergaming*—a form of casual gaming that integrates a product into the game, and is often set in a narrative frame. They are also producing webisodes and elaborate multi-platform games that subtly or not so subtly make a particular product shine. Advertisers are also employing social media to get their messages out. We will be exploring these new types of content throughout this book.

THE IMPACT OF DIGITAL MEDIA ON THE ECONOMY

Along with shifts in the way advertising dollars are being spent, the digital revolution is impacting other areas of the economy, often in quite positive ways. Several years ago, the Entertainment Software Association released a report focusing on the economic impact of video games, *Video Games: Serious Business for America's Economy*. According to the report, games were responsible for creating 144,000 full-time jobs. Many of these jobs are high paying; recent college graduates employed by game companies earn significantly more money than the average college graduate. In addition, the report noted that software developed for games is being applied to other endeavors. For example, gaming software had been adapted by the real estate market and the travel industry, which uses it for virtual online tours. Video game techniques (*gamification*) have been successfully incorporated into educational and training games used by schools, as well as by projects funded by corporations and the military.

THE IMPACT ON JOURNALISM AND HOW WE RECEIVE INFORMATION

The digital revolution has both hurt and helped the field of journalism, and has profoundly impacted the way information is disseminated. While newspaper circulation is down, as is the viewership of television newscasts, we have a whole universe of new sources of information and journalism, thanks to digital media, and they can deliver the news in real time—no more waiting to get the news in the morning paper. On the Internet, we can receive up-to-the-minute news stories, complete with audio and video, and we also get information from blogs, informational websites, online news magazines, and podcasts. And via our mobile devices, we can receive news bulletins, check stock prices, get weather reports, and keep tabs on sports events.

Digital media has forced some newspapers to go out of business or to be sold for low prices. In August 2013, the sale of the *Washington Post* to Jeff Bezos, founder and CEO of Amazon. com, sent shockwaves through the journalistic community, especially because Bezos bought the paper for what was considered the seriously undervalued sum of $250 million.

This sale indicates the vulnerability of print newspapers. According to conventional wisdom, the Internet is to blame for the decline in newspapers. However, a study conducted by Harvard's John F. Kennedy's School of Government and released in 2013 revealed that long-time journalists had a different opinion: they actually believed the Internet sustained journalism. But they also believed the Internet destroyed the long-standing business model that supported newspapers. According to Martin Nisenholtz, former digital chief of the *New York Times*, "The oxygen got taken out of the financial model."

THE INTERNET AS A JOURNALISTIC MEDIUM

The *Red Bull Stratos* mission is an excellent example of how important the Internet has become to journalism. Before dawn on Sunday morning, October 14, 2012, millions of people around the world were anxiously watching YouTube as Austrian pilot and skydiver Felix Baumgartner was preparing to do something no one else on Earth had done before. Baumgartner was going to ascend 24 miles above the planet, carried aloft by a hot air balloon in a tiny space capsule, and then … jump! (see Figure 2.3). If he succeeded, it would be breaking a multitude of records: the greatest height anyone had ever jumped from; the longest free-fall ever achieved; and breaking the speed of sound. If he failed … it would become a fatal accident witnessed by millions. But fortunately, Baumgartner succeeded on all counts. His altitude at the point of his jump was 128,097 feet (over 24 miles above the Earth); he was in free-fall for 4:19 minutes; he broke the

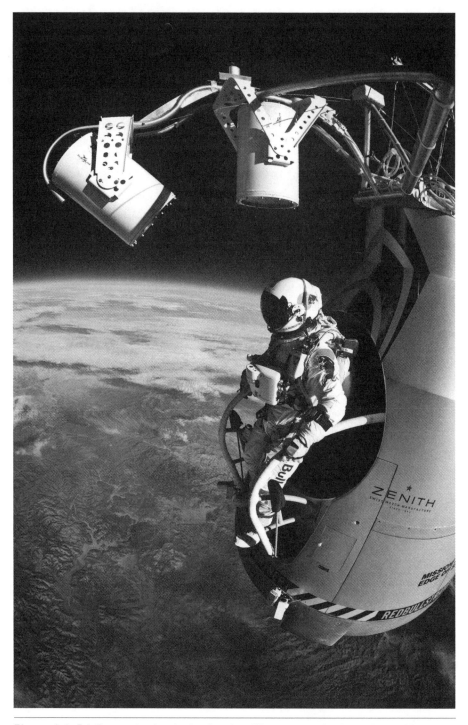

Figure 2.3 Felix Baumgartner is poised on the edge of his space capsule, about to jump—this moment being watched by millions on YouTube. Image courtesy of Balazs Gardi.com, Red Bull content pool.

sound barrier; and he landed safely in a remote corner of New Mexico. Moreover, he set a new record for the largest ever simultaneous viewing audience on YouTube: eight million people. The previous record of 500,000 viewers had been set by that summer's Olympics. Clearly, the Internet proved that day that it could attract a massive live audience.

WHAT THE DIGITAL REVOLUTION MEANS FOR CONTENT

As we have seen, digital technology has had a colossal impact on content, giving us many new forms of entertainment and new ways to receive information. Furthermore, digital technology is providing individuals with new ways to express themselves.

TYPES OF USER-GENERATED CONTENT

Unlike other types of digital entertainment, the material found on sites that support user-generated content is largely created by the users themselves. These online destinations can roughly be divided into four general genres: virtual worlds; social media sites; video sharing sites; and sites featuring fan fiction. In some cases, private citizens have become "Citizen Journalists," reporting about ongoing events like Occupy Wall Street from their mobile phones. In addition, there is another type of user-generated digital content, *Machinima*, though it is not primarily an online form.

Virtual Worlds

Virtual worlds are online environments where users control their own avatars and interact with each other. These worlds may have richly detailed landscapes to explore, buildings that can be entered, and vehicles that can be operated, much like a massively multiplayer online game (MMOG). However, these virtual worlds are not really games, even though they may have some game-like attributes. Instead, they serve as virtual community centers, where people can get together and socialize, and, if they wish, conduct business.

Second Life is the most successful of these virtual worlds. It is a complex environment, offering different types of experiences to different residents, much like real life. It is a thriving center of commerce, for instance, where residents can buy and sell real estate, crafts, and other goods. People who like to party can fill their social calendar with all kinds of lively events. But *Second Life* can also be a place of higher learning. Real universities, including Harvard, Oxford, and Cornell, have a presence there, and many universities conduct classes in *Second Life*. In addition, real corporations hold shareholder meetings there and politicians set up campaign headquarters there. It can also be a romantic destination. Residents have met in *Second Life*, fallen in love, and gotten married in real life.

Social Media Sites

Social media sites are designed to allow users to share details of their personal or professional lives and to connect with others. The most popular of these sites is Facebook, which has an estimated 750,000,000 unique monthly visitors. Along with personal profiles, users can post

STRANGE BUT TRUE: PINT-SIZED VIRTUAL WORLDS

While *Second Life* is intended for grown-ups, children need not feel left out of the chance to enjoy virtual worlds. Software developers have created a host of virtual worlds just for them. For example, capitalizing on the popular craze for penguins, New Horizon Interactive created a virtual world called *Club Penguin* in 2005 for children aged 6 to 14. Kids get to control their own penguin avatars and play in a wintery-white virtual world. Another site called *WeeWorld* lets small children control avatars called WeeMees, play games, and send messages to each other. And at *Sqwishland*, which is based on a line of toys, kids enter the game after acquiring a real life toy, which comes with a code. The code serves as a free entry into the game and their toys come to life in *Sqwishland*. Players can earn in-game currency (Squash) with which they can buy clothes for their avatars and other items. *Sqwishland* is designed and managed by a team in Manila, Philippines.

updates about their lives to Facebook, as well as photos and videos. Different social media sites specialize in different types of content. On Twitter, for example, the focus is on extremely brief comments, limited to 140 characters, while Pinterest is primarily designed for posting photos and arranging them by categories onto boards. For storytelling and gaming on social media sites, please see Chapter 9.

Video Sharing Sites

Some websites primarily serve as online spaces where users can share their own creative works, primarily videos and animation. YouTube is the best known and most successful of these. Created in 2005, it has become an enormously popular place for people to upload their own videos and view videos made by others. While much of the content is made by non-professionals, it also hosts slickly made commercial material. For example, politicians sometimes use YouTube to try to woo prospective voters.

Fan Fiction

Fan fiction, also known as fanfic, is a type of narrative that is based on a printed or produced story or drama, but is written by fans instead of by the original author. Works of fan fiction may continue the plot that was established in the original story, may focus on a particular character, or may use the general setting as a springboard for a new work of fiction. This genre of writing began long before the advent of digital media. Some experts believe it dates back to the seventeenth century, beginning with sequels of the novel *Don Quixote* that were not written by Cervantes himself but by his admirers. Since then, other popular novels have been used as launching pads for fan fiction. In the twentieth century, until the birth of the Internet, this type of writing primarily revolved around the science fiction TV series, *Star Trek*. With the Internet, however, fan fiction has found a welcoming home and a wider audience. Sites for this type of user-generated content abound, with fans creating stories for everything from Japanese anime to Harry Potter novels, as with *Potter Puppet Pals*.

Machinima

Machinima, a term which combines the words "machine" and "cinema," is a form of filmmaking that borrows technology, scenery, and characters from video games but creates original stories with them. Though it is a form of user-generated content, it is not, as noted above, an Internet-based form, though works of machinima can be found on the Web.

One well known machinima production is *Red vs Blue*, a multi-episode tongue-in-cheek science fiction story about futuristic soldiers who have strange encounters in a place called "Blood Gulch." Works of machinima are often humorous, possibly because the characters, borrowed as they are from video games, are not capable of deep expression.

Film connoisseurs have begun to regard machinima as a genuine and innovative form of filmmaking. A group of these films were shown at Lincoln Center in New York City, where they were described as "absurdist sketch comedy." Machinima has even found a foothold in the documentary film community, where it has been used to recreate historic battle scenes.

Thus, as demonstrated by these very different types of user-generated content, digital tools can give "regular people" the opportunity to do things that may be difficult to do outside of cyberspace—the opportunity to socialize, express themselves, be creative, and share their creations.

DIGITAL TECHNOLOGY AND THE ARTS

It should be stressed that amateurs are not the only ones to use digital tools. Professionals in the fine arts are also using them. Although for the most part outside of the scope of this book, innovative works using computer technology are being made in the fields of visual arts, music, performing arts, poetry, fiction, and creative non-fiction. For lack of a better term, these works are often labeled as "new media art."

In some cases, these works can be found in mainstream environments. Just as one example, in 2007 the London Philharmonic performed a virtual reality version of Igor Stravinsky's ballet, *Le Sacre du Printemps*, at the newly refurbished Royal Festival Hall in London. Using Stravinsky's music as a springboard, media-artist and composer Klaus Obermaier designed a piece in which dancer Julia Mach interacted with the music and the three-dimensional images projected onto the stage. Members of the audience watched the performance wearing 3D glasses. Musicians are also experimenting with the Vocaloid and Utau programs, which are singing voice synthesizers.

In the area of visual arts, several major museums, such as the Metropolitan Museum and Whitney Museum in New York City, contain new media artworks in their collections, and in some cases museums have held exhibits that heavily feature such works. For instance, the Museum of

Contemporary Art in Los Angeles held an exhibition in 2005 called *Visual Art*, which contained a number of new media art pieces. The exhibit explored the relationship between color, sound, and abstraction.

For the most part, however, artists who work in new media are still struggling to find an audience, and most of them support themselves by teaching at universities. This is also the case of writers who work in digital literature. This type of writing is sometimes called *hyperliterature*, a catch-all phrase that includes hypertext, digital poetry, nonlinear literature, electronic literature, and cyberliterature. Several websites specialize in this kind of writing, including the Hyperliterature Exchange, and Eastgate, a company which publishes hypertext. In addition, the Electronic Literature Organization promotes the creation of electronic literature and *The New River* is a journal devoted to digital writing and art. A particularly lovely example of this kind of work is the hyperliterature version of the Wallace Stevens poem, *Thirteen Ways of Looking at a Blackbird*, recreated as short Flash animation pieces by British artist/writer Edward Picot (http://edwardpicot.com/thirteenways/blackbirdsinterface.html).

Unfortunately, there is not sufficient room in this book to delve deeply into the realm of fine arts. However, we will be covering a number of works that fall into this category, particularly in the fields of interactive cinema and immersive environments.

A GLOBAL PERSPECTIVE

Although many of the developments mentioned in this chapter, as well as many of the statistics cited, refer specifically to the United States, it is important to keep in mind that digital entertainment is popular throughout the world, and that software production centers are also scattered worldwide. The United States does not have the same stranglehold on digital media as it does on the television and motion picture industry, and even lags behind other developed countries in some forms of digital technology, such as high-speed Internet access. Countries from India to South Africa to Australia are creating innovative content for digital media and devices, with especially strong production centers in Japan, South Korea, Germany, Great Britain, and Canada.

Furthermore, some forms of digital technology and entertainment are better established outside of the United States than within its borders. Cell phones and content for them are tremendously successful in Japan, and Scandinavian countries lead the way in innovative transmedia storytelling.

In addition, China has its own microblogging site, Sina Weibo (http://us.weibo.com/gb), which is enormously popular. Like Twitter, Weibo has a 140-character limit. It has over 500 million users—one-third of all Chinese Internet users. India has a growing video games development community, led by Dhruva Interactive, the oldest gaming company on the subcontinent. Singapore is leading Asia when it comes to transmedia development, but transmedia production is also taking place in South Korea, Japan, and Malaysia. China is the home of the new, government sanctioned online combat game *Glorious Mission*, a first-person shooter which extols the values of the People's Liberation Army. A variety of digital storytelling projects, at least one of which involves augmented reality, are being funded in Australia by Screen Australia. And according to Marco Sparmberg, Festival Director of the Hong Kong Webfest, Web series are being produced in Hong Kong and video game development is in high gear all over South East Asia.

CONCLUSION

Clearly, digital storytelling is no longer the niche activity it was several decades ago. While once barely known outside of a few research labs and academic institutions, it can now boast a worldwide presence and a consumer base numbering in the millions. It can be enjoyed in homes, schools, offices, and, via wireless devices, virtually anywhere. Furthermore, it is also no longer just the domain of teenage boys. Its appeal has broadened to include a much wider spectrum of the population, in terms of nationality, age, gender, and interest groups. It is powerful and universal enough to become a serious contender for the public's leisure-time dollars and leisure-time hours, and muscular enough to cause consternation in Hollywood.

A striking number of the breakthroughs that have paved the way for digital storytelling have come from unlikely places, such as military organizations and the laboratories of scientists. Thus, we should not be surprised if future advances also come from outside the ranks of the usual suppliers of entertainment content.

Various studies have documented the enthusiasm young people have for interactive media. This demographic group has been pushing interactive entertainment forward much like makers of snowmen roll a ball of snow, causing it to expand in size. Almost inevitably, as members of this segment of the population grow older, they will continue to expect their entertainment to be interactive. But will the same kinds of interactive programming continue to appeal to them as they move through the various stages of life? And how can emerging technologies best be utilized to build new and engaging forms of interactive entertainment that will appeal to large groups of users? These are just two of the questions that creators in this field will need to address in coming years.

IDEA-GENERATING EXERCISES

1. Try to imagine yourself going through a normal day, but as if the calendar had been set back 50 years, before computers became commonplace. What familiar devices would no longer be available to you? What everyday tasks would you no longer be able to perform, or would have to be performed in a quite different way?

2. Imagine for a moment that you had just been given the assignment of creating a work of entertainment for a brand new interactive platform, one that had never been used for an entertainment purpose before. What kinds of questions would you want to get answers to before you would begin? What steps do you think would be helpful to take as you embarked on such a project?

3. Most children and teenagers in developed countries are major consumers of interactive entertainment, but what kinds of interactive projects do you think could be developed for them as they move into adulthood, middle age, and beyond? What factors would need to be considered when developing content for this group as they mature?

4. Analyze a website that facilitates social networking or the sharing of user-generated material (if possible, not one described in this chapter). What demographic group is this site primarily geared for? What about the site should make it attractive to its target demographic? What are its primary features? Is there anything about this site that you think could be improved upon?

CHAPTER 3

Moving Towards Convergence

Over the years, there has been a great deal of talk—some say hype—about convergence. But what do people actually mean by the term?

Where are we today in terms of convergence? Have there been any success stories so far?

Why should people who create interactive entertainment be aware of developments in convergence? How is convergence related to digital storytelling at all?

CONVERGENCE: AN ONGOING DEBATE

The topic of convergence has sparked many a debate within the world of interactive technology. For years, people in media have been awaiting the coming of convergence as eagerly as the people in ancient days awaited the Messiah. Nevertheless, industry professionals argued back and forth about what "convergence" really meant and when we might see it and if we would recognize it if it ever did arrive. And as time went on, some doubters even began to suggest that convergence was an unrealistic expectation, an empty buzzword that had lost all useful meaning. More recently, though, hope has been renewed, and some now contend that convergence is actually here, right in our midst, an overlooked but significant reality, and assert that ever more exciting forms of convergence are on the way.

But why all this disagreement about a word that in essence means a coming together of two or more different elements, a blending of these entities into one seamless whole? And why has its arrival or non-arrival been the subject of so much dispute? After all, in the non-technical world, convergence has seemingly always been with us. For example, a mule is a convergent animal, the offspring of a horse and a donkey. And the building of Europe's great cathedrals, as a student pointed out to me, was a convergence of multiple talents, including masons, sculptors, weavers, artists, glaziers, and carpenters. So what does it matter whether convergence within interactive technologies ever takes place?

CONVERGENCE AND DIGITAL MEDIA

First of all, let's try to pinpoint what convergence means in the context of interactive technology. Unfortunately, this is no easy task—even experts in media have trouble pinning down a fixed definition of the concept.

If anyone should have a clear grasp of what convergence means, it should be Gary Arlen. Arlen is president of the media research and consulting firm, Arlen Communications, and an acknowledged expert in the convergence of interactive media and telecommunications. Yet during the two telephone interviews I had with him, he struggled to come up with a precise and universal description, saying there is no one "right" way to define the term. The reason for this, he explained, is that we are in the early stages of a business that is still defining itself as it goes, and furthermore, the term has been used in multiple technologies, where it is given different meanings.

"I've given up trying to define it," he admitted. "I think it's kind of like Scotch tape. It will define itself by the way it is used." Nevertheless, Arlen was able to lay out a lucid description of what the term means within the hardware and software worlds, the arenas most central to the interests of interactive entertainment. "The hardware and software people see convergence as the technology of voice, video and data delivery coming together through a single package," he said.

For many within these industries, the idea of convergence is built in large part on the wide-spread availability and consumer adaptation of broadband—high-speed access to images and other data via various delivery systems. Broadband is considered a critical element because it makes feasible such things as:

- interactive TV;
- VOD (video on demand—a system that lets viewers select video content to watch from the Internet or from digital cable or satellite systems);
- streaming audio and video (listening and watching audio and video in real time, without delay, as it is being downloaded);
- and the receiving of moving images over wireless devices.

It is easy to see why the melding together of voice, video, and data in a single device or network is so desirable. It makes possible an exciting array of new electronic products and services and offers potentially lucrative commercial opportunities to those in the business of making and selling hardware and software for consumer use. And, to creators of entertainment, it offers new types of entertainment experiences that mean both greatly expanded storytelling opportunities and a greatly expanded marketplace for interactive programming.

However, convergence also has a potential negative side. When different technologies are bundled together, the devices that are built to utilize them can be clumsy and complicated to use, and they can be highly susceptible to malfunctions or design flaws. They may not work as smoothly and efficiently as devices built for single purpose, and consumers may either be reluctant to try them or become quickly disenchanted with them.

> **WORTH NOTING: THE ART WORLD AND CONVERGENCE**
>
> It is interesting to note that in the art world convergence is more easily described using the German word *gesampkunstverk*, which means a synthesis of various art forms, like an opera, which can incorporate music, dancing, painting, and performance.

THE DIGITIZING OF CONTENT

In order for convergence to be possible, the content must be available in digital form. This is a significant requirement. Until fairly recently, critical visual and audio elements have been available only in analog form. But the digitizing of content is so important to the merging of technology and media that some people even refer to convergence as "digital media integration."

The digitizing of content is particularly critical when it comes to video. Once video is digitized, its audio and visual elements can be compressed into tiny units of data—making it feasible to send and receive, and usable by digital devices. It also can be easily accessed and readily reassembled in an almost infinite number of ways.

Book publishing is an arena which has seen a significant degree of experimentation with the digitizing of content. For example, the digital book publisher Vook, founded in 2009, specializes in books that combine text, video, audio, links to the Internet, and social media sites. Its series of digital field guides for birds, *iBird*, contains a wealth of easily accessible information about hundreds of birds, including recordings of their songs. Readers can even record their own bird songs and match the sounds up to a bird in its database, thus easily identifying it. And Theodore Gray's *The Elements: A Visual Exploration*, produced for the iPad by Touch Press, is a dazzling book about chemistry. It visually investigates the 118 elements in the periodic table, allowing readers to explore each in vivid detail. The book transforms what is often a dull subject into a fascinating feast for the eyes.

When it comes to fiction, there have been numerous experiments with digital books. For instance, in 2008, Penguin UK commissioned six authors to recreate six classic books using six different forms of digital media in a project called *We Tell Stories*. The authors made use of such disparate digital services as Google Maps, blogging and Twitter, and used various forms of structure, such as branching storylines. *Cathy's Book* and others in the same series are interactive teen novels done in the form of sketch pads for the iPhone and iPod written by Sean Stewart and Jordan Weisman. It is full of videos, links to websites, and even phone numbers you can call. And for adults, Anthony Zuiker has written a series of what he calls *digi-novels* about an especially creepy serial killer. When read on a mobile device, the books are embedded with video clips, which are called cyberbridges.

As noted in Chapter 2, content goes through a three-step process when it is being created for digital media:

1. *Repurposing*, or the porting over of the content from one medium to another, essentially without changing it. Many ebooks, for example, are just text-based works that are made available on portable devices.

2. *Adaptation*, in which a work is modified for the new medium. Using the example of an ebook, the concept of a "book" is adapted into a new kind of work that now contains not only print but interactive assets, like animations or games, as in the ebooks mentioned above.

3. *The creation of a totally a new genre*, specifically designed for the new medium. For example, a brand new genre is a mobile app that uses social media to tell you a story.

WORTH NOTING: THE FOUR COMPONENTS OF CONVERGENCE

Convergence might be regarded as a four-part formula, a compound that requires four elements, or types of "ingredients," to work. They are:

1. A communications delivery system (via satellite, cellular, dial-up, cable, Wi-Fi, Bluetooth, or some other means).

2. Hardware (such as a TV set, a game console, a wireless device, or a computer).

3. Digitized content (data such as text, audio, graphics, video, or animation).

4. Computerized technology (to access, manipulate, and interact with the content).

CONVERGENCE ON THE CORPORATE LEVEL

The dazzling promise of convergence has tempted a number of companies to impetuously plunge into the convergence waters, anticipating that this coming together of interactive media and technologies would result in significant strategic gains and profits. Unfortunately for some of these companies, their headfirst dive proved to be premature at best, and resulted in heavy losses, giving convergence a bad name.

One of the most infamous of these corporate ventures was the merger of AOL and Time Warner in 2000. Things went sour in just two years. The stock of the newly merged enterprise plummeted and shareholders lost an estimated $200 billion. Entertainment mogul David Geffen might have had this unfortunate union in mind when he quipped that convergence "is the most expensive word in history," a quote captured by Gary Arlen in an article he wrote for *Multichannel News* (August 12, 2002). Time Warner finally spun AOL off in 2009. But over the years, AOL itself has made a number of newsworthy acquisitions, including the *Huffington Post*, *MapQuest*, *Moviefone*, and numerous others.

Other corporate mergers seem more promising, and could lead to a true corporate convergence. For example, Disney acquired Lucasfilm in 2012, a deal that included all the *Star Wars* intellectual property and a treasure trove of other Lucasfilm endeavors. Disney was not merely interested in possible new *Star Wars* films but also in using *Star Wars* as the basis of mobile and social media games, according to Disney's CEO, Robert Iger (as reported in Digital Media Wire, October 20, 2012). By the time this deal took place, Disney had already acquired Marvel Entertainment and Pixar Animation, so Disney was on a roll.

When it comes to a digital media company to digital media company merger, that has taken place as well. In 2006, Google acquired YouTube, much to the distress of many YouTube fans. But the merger seems to have gone smoothly. And, in 2012, Google acquired Motorola Mobility, which, in 2013, resulted in the birth of a new smart phone, the Moto X, which uses Google's Android software. In 2013, Yahoo acquired the blogging company Tumblr, though as of this writing, it is too soon to know how that deal has worked out. A more intriguing type of corporate convergence was suggested by April Arrlington in her blog post (thearrglingtonjump. com) of April 24, 2012: a convergence of Hollywood, Silicon Valley, and Madison Avenue. She believes this type of convergence is accelerating because "the creative community is interested in content, the technology community just wants to facilitate channels of distribution, and marketers are focused on selling you beautifully branded products and services."

CONVERGENCE IN DEVICES

Corporate wheelings and dealings aside, convergence has been quite successful when it comes to multiple-media, multiple-use devices. There are three major categories of such devices: games consoles, mobile phones, and tablet computers. The latest generation of game consoles can connect to the Internet, play CDs and DVDs, and support multi-player gameplay as well. As for many of today's mobile phones, they cannot only be used to make calls and send text messages, but they can also connect to the Internet and can be used to take photos and videos—images that can be posted online immediately. They usually also come with built-in games, and can access additional games and other entertainment content from the Internet. As for tablet computers, most of them can do everything a mobile phone can do, and more, except for the most part they do not operate as phones.

One of the first convergent devices was the Nokia N-Gage. It was both a cell phone and a handheld game console, thus converging media and capabilities that had never been available before on a single device (see Figure 3.1). In addition to its main duties as a phone and game console, this little piece of hardware also connected to the Internet and functioned as a digital music player and an FM radio. Nokia introduced the N-Gage in 2003 to great fanfare, but unfortunately, it had some serious design flaws. As noted earlier, creating convergent devices can be a risky proposition, and in the case of the N-Gage, consumers found it looked somewhat ridiculous when held up to the ear as a phone, dubbing it "taco phone" and "elephant ear." It had other drawbacks as well, including problems with the keypad and difficulties with swapping games in and out. To Nokia's credit, the company paid attention to the complaints and redesigned the N-Gage, improving its sales, but the device is now mostly sold in China and India, and no new games for it have been made since 2006.

Figure 3.1 A first generation Nokia N-Gage, an early convergent device. Image courtesy of Nokia.

In 2007, another innovative convergent device made a big splash—Apple's iPhone. Among its main features, it functioned as a cell phone, a music player, and a video player; it also connected to the Web and had email service. In addition, it worked as a camera, a calendar, and a calculator. And this is just a partial list of what it could do. The iPhone caused a sensation when it was introduced, and people lined up for days for a chance to buy one. "This is cyberspace in your pocket!" exclaimed one enthusiastic Silicon Valley consultant, Paul Saffo (as quoted in the *Los Angles Times*, January 10, 2007).

Other convergent devices have included the iPod, the iPad, and a variety of other smart phones and tablet computers, along with sophisticated game consoles like the PSP (PlayStation Portable) and the Xbox One. The iPod is a portable media player, primarily used to play music and games. It has many of the features of the iPhone, though it cannot be used as a telephone. The iPad, introduced by Steve Jobs early in 2010, resembles a much larger iPhone, and via this touchscreen device, users can check email, play videos, surf the Web, play games, read ebooks, and run most of the thousands of apps on Apple's App Store. These devices are living, breathing proof that convergence is not only possible but has actually arrived. Quite possibly, we will see even smarter convergent devices in the future. One thing we can be sure of, though: the creative community will put these new devices to work and come up with revolutionary new kinds of stories.

CONVERGENCE AND TELEVISION

Interactive television (iTV) and video on demand (VOD) have been two of the most widely anticipated manifestations of convergence, and to a limited degree, they are already available to us. VOD can be accessed through various digital cable and satellite TV services and downloaded from the Internet, and we can watch video on a variety of handheld devices.

Streaming video is also common online, although not everyone would agree that streaming video is actually VOD. In any case, as broadband access spreads to more homes, we will almost certainly find an increased amount of VOD available to us there.

As for iTV, it is already fairly well established in the UK and in several other countries. In the United States, single-screen iTV, the kind they have in the UK, is only available on a limited basis. With single-screen iTV, the programming is broadcast right to your television set, and is controlled by a remote control device. In the United States, single-screen interactivity is just offered by a few satellite and cable services, and an upgraded set-top box is needed to access it.

However, second-screen TV is available to anyone who has online access and a TV set. It is the most common form of iTV in the US. With second-screen TV, viewers can interact with the television content by posting comments, voting, interacting with characters, and even helping to solve mysteries (for more on second-screen TV, see Chapter 19).

CONVERGENCE AND DIGITAL STORYTELLING

There is a close connection between advancements in digital convergence on one hand and advancements in digital storytelling on the other. Creators of new media are quick to take note of significant advances in technology and experiment with ways to incorporate them into entertainment experiences. For example, when Global Positioning Systems (GPS) were embedded in sophisticated cell phones in Europe, a Swedish company devised a way to use this new technology for urban adventure role-playing games. And a very old form of entertainment, the comic book, is being re-invented for the digital age by Marvel Entertainment. In an initiative called ReEvolution, introduced in March, 2012, Marvel outlined its plans for digital comic books that would be read on digital devices. These new comics would still be presented in a panel format, but would be more cinematic, using such movie conventions as zooms and close-ups. Some would incorporate Augmented Reality, which would unlock special features like 3D, audio clips, and video clips.

STRANGE BUT TRUE: DOLLS AS CONVERGENT DEVICES

Surprising though it might be, smart dolls (life-like dolls embedded with microprocessing chips) are some of the most advanced forms of convergent devices on the market. Toy inventors are always on the lookout for new technologies they can use to make their dolls seem more alive, more interactive, and more able to take a central role in an interactive story experience. Smart dolls incorporate nano technology and voice recognition systems; have built-in clocks and calendars; they can connect to the Internet; and they have sensors that let the doll know what outfit she's wearing and that can detect motion, touch, and light conditions.

Sometimes it is users themselves who discover new or enhanced storytelling potential in a convergent device. For example, the Microsoft Xbox game console has an accessory device called the Xbox Communicator, which is an aural communications system. It is meant to enable players to speak to each other in real time so they can strategize as they play and issue commands and so on. But the device also has a feature called a "voice mask" that lets players disguise their voices, much like wearing a Halloween mask disguises a person's face. Players have had great fun using the voice mask system to enhance the experience of "becoming" a fictional character. Thanks to the device, a young teen could sound like a tough Mafioso or a creepy space alien instead of the squeaky-voiced 13-year-old kid he really happened to be.

It is a mistake, however, to think that advancements in digital storytelling are entirely dependent on breakthroughs in convergence, or on technology in general. A number of innovations in digital storytelling occur because storytellers are looking for new ways to involve users, or are searching for a new way to construct an interactive narrative. As we will see, we can also find a number of instances of "soft" forms of convergence that impact on digital storytelling but are independent of any specific technology.

TRANSMEDIA STORYTELLING AS A FORM OF CONVERGENCE

Transmedia storytelling, which also goes by the name of multi-platforming, integrated media, and cross-media productions, is a relatively new approach to narrative. In this approach, which we briefly discussed in Chapter 2, a single entertainment property is merged over multiple forms of media, at least one of which is interactive. It is a special way of combining media to tell a single story. Although primarily employed for story-based projects and games, a few productions of this type have also been produced for information-based projects. It has also been employed by non-profit organizations to make the public more aware of their missions and to raise funds (for more about transmedia storytelling, see Chapters 10 and 18).

ADAPTATION AS A FORM OF CONVERGENCE

A far older approach to story-based material, which sounds similar to transmedia storytelling but is actually quite different, is the process of adaptation. Properties have been adapted from one medium and used in another ever since the days when we had at least one other medium to borrow (or steal) from. The ancient Greeks freely took stories from their myths and oral traditions and turned them into works for the theater, just as many of today's movies are based on earlier source material, such as novels, plays, and comic books. Unlike the cross-media approach, however, an adaptation is not something that is developed simultaneously for several media. Instead, it is just a retelling of the same story—a way to get more mileage out of good material.

In terms of interactive media, adaptation has primarily involved turning video games into movies and vice versa. In 1993, *Super Mario Brothers* became the first game to become a movie. Unfortunately, the adaptation was not the box office sensation that was hoped for, and other such adaptations in the years that followed did not do well, either. Two other game-to-movie failures include *Doom* and *Max Payne*. However, the huge success of *Lara Croft: Tomb*

Raider proved that it was indeed possible to turn a popular game into a popular movie. *Lara Croft: Tomb Raider* spurred a great increase in such adaptations.

Undaunted by previous game to movie failures, the French video game company Ubisoft is producing a movie based on its own game: *Assassin's Creed*. It remains to be seen if a game company can have greater success at adapting a game than Hollywood has had. It has also become increasingly common to develop a video game and a movie simultaneously, as Peter Jackson did with *King Kong*. But whether done simultaneously or many years apart, the process of adaptation is filled with challenges. This was as true for Greek playwrights who ventured to turn a myth into a dramatic stage play as it is for today's writers, when they try to turn a linear comic book into an interactive game.

All types of adaptations have their own inherent problems. In adapting a novel into a movie, for instance, you must figure out how to translate passive descriptive material and internal monologues into a visual narrative told through dramatic action. You also have to pare down or eliminate an abundance of plot and characters. In adapting a game into a movie, you need to figure out how to convey the sense of interactivity and choice that is so much part of a video game, but without making this seem repetitive. You also need to take what are typically one-dimensional characters in games and fill them out with more richly shaded personalities and backstories. Characters in movies usually need to be given a "character arc" so that they change and grow in the course of the story. This is something that movie audiences expect to see, but is far less common in games. You almost inevitably need to condense what is often a huge game environment with many worlds and locations into a more contained film-like environment. These are a few of the issues that today's screenwriters are grappling with when they turn a game into a movie.

In the reverse sort of situation, turning a movie into a game, you are faced with an opposite set of problems. Most importantly, you need to work out how to convert a linear storyline with a single through-line into a multidimensional interactive experience. How will the user participate in the storyworld; what kinds of things will he or she do; and what will the overall goal or mission be? Characters usually need to be simplified, and their most important traits highlighted. More plot lines or layers of action will need to be provided than are usually found in a movie, and the storyworld will generally need to be built out. Game developers have as many challenges in adapting a movie as film producers have in adapting a game, if not more.

In addition to video games, film producers have been eyeing other interactive media for prospective works to turn into movies. The first Internet-based material to make it to the big screen was Urban Entertainment's webisode *Undercover Brother*, in 2002. The trend has gone the other way, too, with movies sometimes becoming material for the Web. For example, *Star Wars* has been turned into a MMOG. Sometimes TV shows become video games, too, as with the *X-Files, Law and Order, Buffy the Vampire Slayer*, *Sabrina the Teenage Witch*, and *24*. And in at least one case, a social media game is being adapted into a TV series. The game in question is Zynga's immensely popular *Farmville*. Early in 2013, Director Brett Ratner announced he would produce a half-hour animated television series based on the game. This migration of a property from one medium to another is hardly a new phenomenon. What is relatively new, though, is that interactive media have joined the great pool of work that is regarded as attractive source material.

INTERMEDIA INFLUENCES AS A FORM OF CONVERGENCE

In addition to adaptations and transmedia narratives, we can find another, though quite subtle, form of convergence involving digital storytelling—the way traditional forms of narrative and new media narratives are influencing each other in terms of structure, visual presentation, style, and a general approach to storytelling.

This is most clearly apparent in the way video games are influencing motion pictures. Just as one example, consider the German film *Run, Lola, Run*. The film is about a young woman who goes on a life-and-death mission to save her boyfriend. With its eclectic mix of animation and high-speed live action, it has a distinctly game-like look, feel, and pace. The movie is structured in three "rounds," each giving Lola 20 minutes to successfully achieve her goal. The first two rounds end badly, so the game (or story) is "reset" and Lola gets another chance. In each round she has to deal with many of the same obstacles, but it is not until round three that she manages to figure out how to deal with all of them, and is able to "win."

The Hunger Games, a film released in 2012, is, as screenwriting expert John Truby has pointed out, another feature film that has been influenced by video games. The story is about a contest where children in a fictional world must fight to the death, with only one winner possible. Thus, as Truby points out, the story is firmly set within a game, and not only a game, but, like many video games, a game in which there can only be one winner. To add to its video game-like quality, throughout the movie we see an ever-updated score, so we know at every moment how the various competitors are doing. Though we cannot "play" the movie, we as viewers closely identify with Katniss, who is, in a sense, the avatar character.

To a lesser extent, we can also find examples of the impact of the Internet on linear entertainment, particularly on television. Certainly the influence can be seen in the way material is presented visually on a TV screen. Instead of one single image, the frame is now often filled with multiple images like a Web page. Often the frame is divided into separate boxes, and we even find text scrolling at the bottom of the screen. The visually dense style we have become familiar with from Web surfing has become common in news programs, documentaries, and sports shows. In another borrowing from the Internet, we can now see commercials that look strikingly like the amateur videos posted on YouTube, complete with cute-only-to-their-parents children and irritating pets.

On TV, we can also find cases where video game-like influences have crept into dramatic series. The hit Fox series, *24*, for example, was quite game-like in terms of its story content, structure, and main character. The main character, Jack Bauer, played by Kiefer Sutherland, worked for a government counter-terrorist agency and each season was faced with preventing a new and horrifying catastrophe from happening. In the series, Jack resolves one set of challenges only to be forced to deal with another set, much like advancing level by level in a game. In each of these "levels," he encounters a new group of bad guys and must overcome new obstacles or solve new puzzles, many of them quite game-like in nature. And as with a video game hero, we become extremely knowledgeable about Jack's physical and intellectual skills, but learn little about his thoughts or feelings. Not surprisingly, the series was turned into a video game.

Just as TV and films contain elements influenced or directly borrowed from interactive media, the converse is also true. Interactive media borrow from established media, too. The cut scenes in video games are highly cinematic in content and style. Genres developed for radio and television, like quiz shows and reality TV, regularly turn up on the Web. Techniques of character development and structure first devised for the theater and for film are now employed in video games and interactive cinema. Thus, in the cross-pollination among media, we have a form of narrative convergence.

CONCLUSION

Though industry leaders may not always agree on a definition of convergence and some even doubt that convergence can ever be fully realized, we can nonetheless find concrete examples of digital convergence in today's world. We can also look at transmedia storytelling and adaptation as two "soft" forms of convergence.

Many content creators have found innovative ways to incorporate new forms of digital convergence into their narratives. It behooves us as digital storytellers to be aware of developments in convergence and so we too can utilize them in our stories.

IDEA-GENERATING EXERCISES

1. Describe a convergent device that you have used and are quite familiar with. What can this device do? What do you most like about it? What design flaws, if any, does it have?

2. On a sheet of paper, make a list of 10 simple electronic devices. Then randomly select two of them and try to determine how they could be converged into a single device. Can you think of any way your new invention could be used as part of a work of interactive entertainment?

3. What movie or TV show have you seen recently that seemed to be influenced by video games? In what way was this influence apparent?

4. What computer game have you played that might make a good movie? What about it would lend itself well to a cinematic adaptation? What about it would need to be changed in order to make it work as a movie?

5. What movie have you seen lately, or what novel or other material have you read, that might make a good video game or online game? What about it would lend itself well to such an adaptation? What about it would need to be changed in order to make it work as a game?

PART 2

Creating Story-Rich Projects

CHAPTER 4

Interactivity and its Effects

How does the use of interactivity radically change the way an audience experiences a narrative?

How does the use of interactivity radically change the narrative material itself?

What are the pros and cons of giving the audience some control over story?

What techniques can be used to help create cohesion in works of digital storytelling?

WHAT IS INTERACTIVITY?

Without interactivity, digital entertainment would simply be a duplicate of traditional entertainment, except that the medium in which it is presented, such as video or audio, would be in a digital format rather than an analog format. To the audience member or listener, however, the difference would be minimal except perhaps in the quality of the picture or sound. Essentially, the experience of "consuming" the entertainment would be exactly the same.

It is interactivity that makes digital media such a completely different animal from traditional storytelling forms, like movies, television, and novels. All stories, no matter how they are told—whether recited by a shaman, projected onto a movie screen, or played out on a game console—have certain universal qualities: they portray characters caught up in a dramatic situation, depicting events from the inception of the drama to its conclusion. Interactivity, however, profoundly changes the core material, and profoundly changes the experience of those who are the receivers of it.

We've all probably heard and used the word "interactivity" hundreds, even thousands, of times. Because of overuse, the word has lost its fresh edge, somewhat like a kitchen knife that has grown dull because it's been used so often. Let's take a moment to consider what interactivity means and what it does.

Interactivity is a two-part word. The first part, *inter*, a prefix, means "between," implying a two-way exchange, a dialogue. The second part, *active*, means doing something, being involved or engaged. Thus the word as a whole indicates an active relationship between two entities. When used in the context of narrative content, it indicates a relationship where both entities—the audience and the material—are responsive to each other. You, the audience member, have the ability to manipulate, explore, or influence the content in one of a variety of ways, and the content can respond. Or the content demands something from you, and you respond.

Essentially, interactivity is one of only two possible ways of relating to narrative content; the other way is to relate to it passively. If you are passively enjoying a form of entertainment, you are doing nothing more than watching, listening, or reading, though you might also be making connections in your mind, or questioning something about the story. But with interactive content, you actually become a participant, and in robust works, your input can have an impact on how the story unfolds or ends. This is radically different from the way narratives have traditionally been experienced.

INTERACTIVITY AS A CONVERSATION

Interactivity can be thought of as a conversation between the user and the content, a concept articulated to me by Greg Roach during a conversation about the subject. Roach is CEO of HyperBole Studios, the company that made such award-winning games as *The X-Files Game* and *Quantum Gate*, and as a digital media pioneer, he has given a great deal of thought to the subject of interactivity.

Roach compared the act of designing interactivity to the act of writing a sentence in a language like English, which uses the grammatical structure of a subject, object, and verb. As an example, he used a simple interactive scene in which you give your character a gun. The interactive "sentence" would be: he (the subject) can shoot (the verb) another character (the object). Carrying Roach's grammatical analogy a step further, the sentences you construct in interactive media use the active voice, and are not weighed down by descriptive phrases. ("He watered his horse" rather than "he was seen leading his dusty old horse down to the rocky creek, where he encouraged it to drink.") These interactive sentences are short and to the point, far more like Hemingway than Faulkner.

Roach is not alone in using grammatical terms to talk about interactivity. Many game designers use the phrase *verb set* in referring to the actions that can be performed in an interactive work. The verb set of a game consists of all the things players can make their characters do. The most common verbs are walk, run, turn, jump, pick up, and shoot.

WORTH NOTING: LEANING BACK VERSUS LEANING FORWARD

Passive entertainment and interactive entertainment are often differentiated as "lean back" and "lean forward" experiences, respectively. With a passive form of entertainment like a movie or stage play, you are reclining in your seat, letting the drama come to you. But with an interactive work—a video game, for instance—you are leaning forward toward the screen, manipulating the action with your controller or keyboard or even your body movements.

WHAT HAPPENS TO THE AUDIENCE?

The way one experiences interactive entertainment is so different from the way passive entertainment is experienced that we rarely even use the word "audience" when we are talking about interactive works. More often than not, we talk about such people in the singular rather than in the plural. This is probably because each individual journeys through the interactive environment as a solo traveler, and each route through the material is unique to that person.

Because each user is in control of his or her own path through the material, interactivity can never truly be a mass audience experience. This is the case even when thousands of people are simultaneously participating in an interactive work, as they may be doing with a MMOG. Think how different this is from how an audience partakes of a movie or TV show, watching the same unvarying story unfold simultaneously with hundreds—or even millions—of other viewers. Of course, each member of the audience is running the story through his or her own personal filter and is probably having a somewhat different emotional response to the material. Yet no matter how intensely people might be reacting, there is nothing any member of the audience can do to alter a single beat of the tale.

It is an entirely different case when we are talking about interactive entertainment, and we may call upon one of several terms to describe the person who is in the process of experiencing it. If we're referring to someone playing a video game, we will use the term "player" or "gamer," while if a person is surfing the Web, we may use the term "visitor," and for simulations and immersive environments, we often call the person a "participant." One term that fits all types of interactive experiences is the word "user," which is the standard term we are employing in this book.

THE USER, THE AUTHOR, AND INTERACTIVITY

The people who participate in interactive entertainments are given two gifts that are never offered to audiences of passive entertainments: choice and control. They get to choose what to see and do within an interactive work, and the decisions they make have an impact on the story. Less than 50 years ago, such freedom to manipulate a work of entertainment would have been unimaginable.

The user's ability to control aspects of the narrative is called *agency*. Essentially, agency gives the user the ability to make choices and to see and enjoy the results of those choices. Agency is one of the unique pleasures of digital storytelling. It is not limited to the kinds of verb sets we discussed earlier (run, jump, shoot, and so on) but also allows the user to navigate through the storyworld, create an avatar, change points of view, and enjoy many other kinds of interactive experiences that we will discuss later in this chapter.

Agency is something that is built into an interactive work right from the start, as an integral part of the concept, and in fact helps define what kind of work it will be. It is up to the creative team to decide what kind of agency the user will have and how it will be integrated into the work. Experienced interactive designers and producers know that great care must be given to crafting the way the user can interact with the work. Interactivity must be meaningful to be satisfying. In other words, the choices offered must make sense, must have consequences that make sense, and what the user does must have a true impact on the story. Users will quickly become dissatisfied with pointless, empty interactivity.

STRANGE BUT TRUE: HOW AGENCY CAN BACKFIRE

Experienced designers also know that it can be a risky proposition to give users agency without thinking ahead to the various ways they might use or misuse it. A 2007 interactive advertising campaign for the Chevy Tahoe SUV underscores how agency can be used in unintended ways and can backfire on the producers. This online ad campaign gave users the chance to make their own commercial for the car, offering them a generous selection of videos of the interior and exterior of the vehicle, exotic settings in which to place the car, and background music, plus the ability to write their own text. To encourage participation, Chevy presented this as a contest, a version of Donald Trump's TV show, *The Apprentice*.

But the campaign went terribly wrong for Chevy. People who detested the Tahoe and hulking SUVs in general gleefully used the tools to make scathingly satirical commercials about the vehicle's role in creating pollution, waste, environmental destruction, and global warming. To its credit, Chevy actually ran some of these commercials on the contest website, but it was an embarrassing situation for the company and the commercials were pulled after a short time.

Many kinds of interactive works, most particularly virtual worlds and MMOGs, have been plagued with run amuck agency, with a handful of players threatening to spoil the fun the designers had intended to offer. These ill-spirited players have had their avatars bully other players, engage in lewd acts, and even rob, steal, and murder.

As the Chevy Tahoe campaign illustrates, agency is a gift to the user but can cause serious trouble for the creative team. Designers invest a significant amount of time in devising ways of preventing the agency they offer from getting out of hand, while not unduly restricting the sense of freedom they want to give to the users. Agency can also thrust writers of interactive works into an unfamiliar and uncomfortable position, particularly if they come from the worlds of more traditional forms of writing, like screenplays, novels, or TV shows. In those fields, the writer has God-like powers over the narrative. The writer gets to choose who the characters are, what they do, and what they say. And the writer controls what happens to them. But in an interactive work, this kind of God-like control over the material must be shared with those individuals who in an earlier era would have been powerless and in your thrall—the members of the audience.

Producer Nuno Bernardo, in an article he posted to MIPBlog (January 24, 2012), wrote how the creators of *Sofia's Diary* controlled the possibility of runaway agency in that story. *Sofia's Diary* was a teen drama created for social networking site, Bebo. It was a bit like *LonelyGirl15*, in that it was about a young girl with many personal problems, and actually pre-dated *LonelyGirl15* by a few years. The creators encouraged users to become friends with the fictional characters and to offer their help when she was in difficulty. But, he noted, "if you give your audience power over the story they will get rid of your antagonist, solve all the major problems and erase all the drama."

Thus, the creative team realized that the writers had to have complete control over the A plot line of the story, the main plot line. However, "What they [the users] *could* alter was the 'B plot', which contained all the minor episodic dilemmas that were contained in Sofia's life … We allowed the audience to make minor changes in the show – so they felt that this was their show and was responding to their suggestions – but avoiding dramatic changes that could ruin all the drama of the story we wanted to tell."

Although agency gives users exciting new powers, not all the benefits go to them, and the creators of interactive narratives benefit, too. While it's true that those of us who are writers must give up a certain amount of control, we now have the opportunity to work on a far vaster canvas than in previous media, and with story tools never before available. We also have the exhilarating chance to create brand new kinds of narratives. And despite the amount of agency given to the user, we still do retain ultimate authorial control. We, along with our fellow design team members, create the project's storyworld and its possibilities, the kinds of characters who will live there and the kinds of challenges they will face.

IMMERSIVENESS

One of the hallmarks of a successful interactive production is that it envelops the user in a rich, fully involving environment. The user interacts with the virtual world and the characters and objects within it in many ways and on many levels, and the experience might even be *multi-sensory*, meaning that it may stimulate multiple senses. In other words, an interactive production is immersive. It catches you up and involves you in ways that passive forms of entertainment can rarely do.

The power of immersiveness was brought home to me by an experience I had during the Christmas season one year in Santa Fe, New Mexico. It was my first year of living there, and I'd heard a great deal about the city's traditional holiday procession called *Las Posadas*, so I decided to see it for myself.

Las Posadas originated in medieval Spain as a nativity passion play and was brought to New Mexico about 400 years ago by the Spanish missionaries. They felt *Las Posadas* would be a simple and dramatic way to ignite the religious spirit of the local Pueblo Indians, and hopefully turn them into good Catholics.

Las Posadas, which is Spanish for "the inns," recreates the Biblical story of Mary and Joseph's search for a night-time shelter and place where Mary can give birth. It is performed with different variations in towns all over the Southwest and Mexico, but the basic elements remain the same. In Santa Fe, the procession takes place around the historic town plaza. Mary and Joseph, accompanied by a group of musicians and carolers, go from building to building asking for admittance, but each time they make their appeal, the devil emerges and denies them entrance, until at last they find a place that will receive them.

On the evening of Santa Fe's *Las Posadas*, my husband and I waited in the crowd with the other spectators, all of us clutching candles and shivering in the icy night air, waiting for the event to begin. Finally the first members of the procession appeared, holding torches to light the way. Mary and Joseph followed, with a group of carolers around them. The group paused in front of a building not far from us and all proceeded to sing the traditional song, which pleads for lodging. The devil popped up from a hiding place on the roof and scornfully sang his song of refusal. It was very colorful, very different from anything I'd seen before back in California, and I was glad we had come (see Figure 4.1).

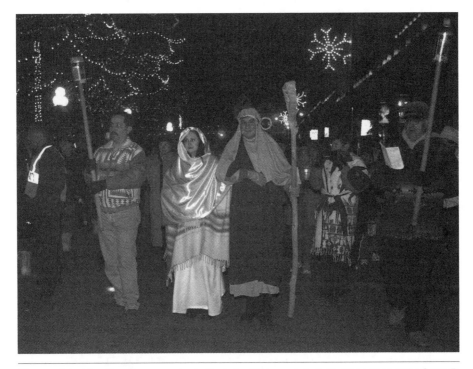

Figure 4.1 A *Las Posadas* procession in Santa Fe. Photograph by Kathy De La Torre of the *Santa Fe New Mexican*, courtesy of the *Santa Fe New Mexican*.

But then I noticed that a number of people were breaking away from the throng of bystanders and joining in the procession. Spontaneously, I pulled my startled husband into the street after them. In a flash, we went from being observers to being participants, and began to experience

Las Posadas in an entirely different way. Marching with the procession, we became part of the drama, too, and fully immersed in it.

For the hour or so that it lasted, I became someone else. No longer was I a twenty-first century Jewish writer. I became a pious Catholic pilgrim transported back to a wintry medieval Spanish village. Some of this I experienced on a personal and physical level: I had to watch my step, taking care not to slip on a patch of ice or trip on a curb or get ahead of the Holy Family. I was aware of the scent of burning candles all around me, and the press of the crowd. Much of the experience was emotional and communal: my husband and I would do our best to sing along with the carolers and Holy Family when it came time to ask for a room at the inn. Whenever the devil would appear on a rooftop or balcony, we would join in the hearty boos and derisive shouts of the processioners.

The best moment came when Mary and Joseph stopped in front of the heavy gates of the historic Palace of the Governors, the former seat of New Mexico's colonial government. Once again we all sang the imploring song, but this time the gates swung open! A joyous cheer went up from the processioners, our voice among them, and we all surged into the courtyard. Welcoming bonfires and cups of hot cocoa awaited us.

Becoming part of *Las Posadas* instead of merely observing it transformed the experience for me. It was like the difference between watching a movie and suddenly becoming a character in it. To me, it vividly demonstrated the power of immersiveness—one of the most compelling and magical aspects of interactive media.

Immersiveness can involve all the senses. I have even had a student experiment with the sense of taste. The student, Keredy Scott, developed a story in which you, the user, were instructed to eat chocolate at certain points in a story she had created.

TYPES OF INTERACTIVITY

Users can interact with digital content in a variety of ways, and different types of interactive media lend themselves to different types of interactivity. For instance, the Internet is particularly good at providing opportunities to communicate with fictional characters and other users; smart toys excel at offering one-on-one play experiences; video games gives us great control over objects. Each of the interactive media has its limitations, as well. In an immersive environment, a participant's ability to control objects may be limited. Game consoles, unless connected to the Internet, are restricted to just a few players at a time. When it comes to the types of interactivity offered by the various digital media, no one size fits all.

That said, however, six basic types of interactivity can be found in almost every form of digital storytelling. They are like the basic foodstuffs a good cook always keeps in the pantry, and can be used to make a wide variety of dishes. The basic types of interactivity are as follows:

1. *Stimulus and response.* The stimulus might be something as simple as a highlighted image that the user clicks on and is rewarded by a little animated sequence or hearing a funny sound, or it might involve having to solve a puzzle, after which the user is

rewarded by the occurrence of some sought-after event: the door to the safe swings open, or a character reveals a secret. Generally speaking, the stimulus comes from the program and the response from the user, although there are exceptions. For instance, smart toys recognize and respond to actions taken by their child owners, such as squeezing the toy's hand. The stimulus–response exchange is a universal component of all interactive programming.

2. *Navigation*. Users can move through the program in a free-form manner; in other words, they can simply choose what to do. Navigation may offer a vast, 3D world to explore, as in a video game or MMOG. Or it may be more limited, restricted to choosing options from a menu offered on a DVD or icons on a website. Navigation, like the stimulus-response exchange, is a universal component of every form of interactive programming.

3. *Control over objects*. The user can control virtual objects. This includes such things as shooting guns, opening drawers, and moving items from one place to another. While a fairly common form of interactivity, this one is not entirely universal.

4. *Communication*. The user can communicate with other characters, including those controlled by the computer and other human players. Communication can be done via text that the user types in, or via choosing from a dialogue menu, by voice, or by physical actions (such as waving a hand in front of a Wii). Generally, communication goes both ways—characters or other players can communicate with the user, too. As with #3, it is a common, but not universal, form of interactivity.

5. *Exchange of information*. This can include anything from sending in comments to online forums to sending in videos to a fictional character on YouTube. This form of interactivity is generally found in devices that have a connection to the Internet.

6. *Acquisition*. The nature of the material can range from virtual to concrete, and the methods of acquiring it can range greatly as well. Users can collect information (such as news bulletins or medical facts) or purchase physical objects (books or clothing). They can also collect virtual objects or assets in a game (a magic sword; the ability to fly) or receive an upgrade in status. This type of interactivity is common in any medium that involves the Internet, as well as almost all video games.

Using these six basic "ingredients," digital creators can "cook up" a great diversity of experiences for people to participate in. They include:

1. Playing games. There is an almost infinite variety of games users can play: trivia games; adventure games; shooters; mysteries; ball games; role-playing games; and so on.

2. Participating in a fictional narrative.

3. Exploring a virtual environment.

4. Controlling a simulated vehicle or device: a fighter jet, a submarine, a space ship, or a machine gun.

5. Creating an avatar, including its physical appearance, personality traits, and skills.

6. Manipulating virtual objects: changing the color, shape, or size of an object; changing the notes on a piece of music; changing the physical appearance of a room.

7. Constructing virtual objects such as houses, clothing, tools, towns, machines, and vehicles.

8. Taking part in polls, surveys, voting, tests, and contests.

9. Interacting with smart physical objects: dolls, robotic pets, wireless devices, animatronic characters.

10. Learning about something. Interactive learning experiences include edutainment games for children, training programs for employees, and online courses for students.

11. Taking part in a simulation, either for educational purposes or for entertainment.

12. Setting a virtual clock or calendar to change, compress, or expand time.

13. Socializing with others and participating in a virtual community.

14. Searching for various types of information or for clues in a game.

15. Sending or receiving items, for free or for money, including physical objects, virtual objects, as well as information.

This is by no means an exhaustive list, though it does illustrate the great variety of experiences that interactivity can offer, and the uses to which it can be put.

HOW INTERACTIVITY IMPACTS CONTENT

These various forms of interacting inevitably affect one's content. Users expect to be offered a selection of choices, but by offering them, you give up your ability to tell a strictly determined linear story or to provide information in a fixed order.

To see how this works, let's compare a linear and interactive version of a familiar story, the Garden of Eden episode from the Bible. The Garden of Eden episode is one of the best-known creation stories in the Western world, and thus seems an appropriate choice to illustrate the creative possibilities of changing a linear story into an interactive one.

As it is handed down in Genesis, the story involves three characters: Adam, Eve, and the serpent (see Figure 4.2). Each of them behaves in exactly the same way no matter how often one reads about them in the Old Testament. And the alluring tree that is the centerpiece of the story is always the Tree of the Knowledge of Good and Evil. God has warned Adam and Eve not to eat its fruit, though they are free to enjoy anything else in the garden. The serpent, however, convinces Eve to sample the forbidden fruit, which she does. She gets Adam to try it, too, at which point they lose their innocence and are expelled from the Garden. It is an extremely simple but dramatic story.

Now let's construct an interactive version of the same story. We'll use the same three characters and the same tree, but offer the player an array of choices. Let's say the tree now offers five kinds of fruit, each with the potential for a different outcome. If Eve picks the pomegranate, for instance, she might immediately become pregnant; if she eats too many cherries, she

TAV. XV   STANZA DELLA SEGNATURA Vaticano [n. 85 C]
           Particoiare della volta: *Adamo ed Eva* (cm. 170).

Figure 4.2 Raphael's Garden of Eden, showing Adam, Eve, the serpent, and the tree. An interactive version of this simple Bible tale can quickly spin out of control.

might get fat; only if she eats the forbidden fruit would the narrative progress toward the results depicted in the Bible.

As for the serpent, let's allow the user to decide what this character should be: malevolent or kindly, wise or silly. And we'll let the user decide how Eve responds to him, too. She might ignore him, or tell him to get lost, or try to turn him into a docile house pet … or, she might actually listen to him, as she does in the Bible. We'll give the user a chance to determine the nature of Adam and Eve's exchange, too. Adam might reject Eve's suggestion to try the fruit, or might come up with several suggestions of his own (open up a fruit stand, or make jam out of the tree's cherries). Or they may hotly disagree with each other, resulting in the Bible's first marital spat. Suddenly we have a vast multitude of permutations springing out of a simple story.

Note that all of this complexity comes from merely allowing the player one of several options at various nodes in the story. But what if you gave the players other types of interactive tools? You might allow them the opportunity to explore the entire Garden of Eden and interact with anything in it. They could investigate its rocky grottos, follow paths through the dense foliage, or even snoop around Adam and Eve's private glade. Or what if you turned this into a design challenge, and let users create their own Garden of Eden? Or how would it be if you turned this into a role-playing game, and let the user play as Adam, as Eve, or even as the serpent? Or what if you designed this as a community experience, and gave users the chance to vote on whether Eve should be blamed for committing the original sin?

Our simple story is now fragmenting into dozens of pieces. What once progressed in an orderly manner, with a straightforward beginning, middle, and end, and had a clear and simple plot, has now fallen into total anarchy. If adding interactivity to a simple story like the Garden of Eden can create such chaos, what does it do to a more complex work?

USING GAMING TECHNIQUES TO SUPPLY THE MISSING COHESION

Because interactivity can break up the cohesiveness of a narrative, it becomes necessary to look for other ways to tie the various elements together and to supply the momentum that, in traditional storytelling, would be supplied by the plot. Many professionals in digital media believe that the best solution is to use a gaming model as the core of an interactive work, and build narrative elements around it. Games provide an attractive solution because they involve competition, contain obstacles and a goal; and offer a clear-cut goal. While stories in traditional media use these same elements, they are less obvious, and great attention is placed on other things, such as character development, motivation, the relationship between characters, and so on.

Designer Greg Roach, introduced earlier in this chapter, is one of those professionals who is inclined to turn to games to help knit the various pieces of an interactive work together. "When you discard all aspects of gaming, how do you motivate people to move through the narrative?" he asks rhetorically. "The fundamental mechanisms of games are valuable because they provide the basic tool sets."

Roach sees stories and games as two very different types of artifacts—artifacts being objects created by human beings. Roach says, "A story is an artifact you experience as dynamic process while a game is a process you enter into that creates an artifact when it ends." Roach feels that interactive works have, as he puts it, "immense granularity." Granularity is a term Roach and others in interactive media use to mean the quality of being composed of many extremely small pieces.

Roach describes films and other types of linear narratives as "monoliths, likes of block of salt," and for interactivity to be possible, he says the monoliths must be broken up into fine pieces. "These granules of information can be character, atmosphere, or action. But if a work is too granular, if the user is inputting constantly, there are no opportunities for story." Roach stresses that in order to have an interactive story, "you must find a balance between granularity and solidity. You need to find the 'sweet spot'—the best path through the narrative, the one with the optimum number of variables."

Despite the differences between stories and games, Roach believes a middle ground can be found, a place to facilitate story and character development in an interactive environment.

One of the challenges Roach sees in constructing a nongaming interactive story is the task of providing the player with motivation, an incentive to spend time working through the narrative. But he suggests an answer as well. Roach believes that people like to solve problems, the tougher the better, and feels that a major distinction between games and stories is the types of problems they present, plus the tools that can be used to solve them. In a game, he suggests, the problem might be getting past the monster on the bridge. In a story, the problem might be getting your son off drugs and into rehabilitation.

GAMES AS ABSTRACT STORIES

Janet H. Murray, a professor at the Georgia Institute of Technology and the author of one of the best-known books on interactive narrative, *Hamlet on the Holodeck*, takes things a step further than Roach. In her book, she asserts that games and drama are actually quite closely aligned, and that games are really a form of "abstract storytelling."

To underscore the close connection between stories and games, Murray points out that one of our oldest, most pervasive, and popular types of games—the battle between opposing contestants or forces—is also one of the first and most basic forms of drama. The Greeks called this opposition *agon*, for conflict or contest. Murray reminds us that opposition, or the struggle between opposites, is one of the fundamental concepts that we use to interpret the world around us (big/little; boy/girl; good/evil).

Although Murray does not say so explicitly, every writer of screenplays is keenly aware of the importance of opposition, and realizes that unless the hero of the drama is faced with an imposing challenge or opponent, a script will lack energy and interest. For an interactive narrative to work, it too must pit opposing forces against each other. Thus, games and dramas utilize the same key dynamic: opposition. As we will see in Chapter 6, which focuses on character, this concept of opposition is so key to drama that it defines how we think of our heroes and villains.

Opposition is not the only way that games and drama are alike, Murray believes. She suggests, in fact, that games "can be experienced as symbolic drama." She holds that games reflect events that we have lived through or have had to deal with, though in a compressed form. When we play a game, she says, we become the protagonist of a symbolic action. Some of the life-based plot lines she feels can be found in games include:

- being faced with an emergency and surviving it;
- taking a risk and being rewarded for acting courageously;

- finding a world that has fallen into ruin and managing to restore it; and, of course,

- being confronted with an imposing antagonist or difficult test of skill and achieving a successful outcome.

DRAMA IN AN ABSTRACT GAME

Janet Murray is even able to find a life-like symbolic drama in abstract games like *Tetris*. In *Tetris*, players have to maneuver falling puzzle pieces so they fit together and form a straight row. Each completed row floats off the bottom of the game board, leaving room for still more falling puzzle pieces. To Murray, the game resembles our struggles to deal with our over-busy lives, and is like "the constant bombardment of tasks that demand our attention and that we must somehow fit into our overcrowded schedules and clear off our desks in order to make room for the next onslaught" (*Hamlet on the Holodeck*, p. 144).

Games, Murray asserts, give us an opportunity to act out the important conflicts and challenges in our lives, and to create order and harmony where there was messiness and conflict.

In many ways, Murray's view of games is much like Joseph Campbell's view of ritual ceremonies—activities that provide us with a way to give meaning to important life experiences and to provide us with emotional release. In its most powerful form, this emotional release is experienced as a catharsis.

STORIES THAT ARE NOT GAMES

In examining the relationship between stories and games, let us not forget what designer Greg Roach asserted: that it is possible to create interactive stories that are not based on game models. We can find examples of game-free narratives in many genres of digital storytelling. One small enclave of such narratives is called, fittingly enough, Interactive Fiction (IF). Works of IF can be found on the Internet and they are also available on CD-ROMs. Though the creators and fans of IF are a fairly small group, often found within academic circles, they are dedicated to advancing this particular form of storytelling.

Traditional works of IF are often text-based (although the term is sometimes used for adventure games and other works that are animated or are done on video). To see/read/play a work of IF, you need to be sitting in front of a computer, inputting your commands with a keyboard. The story advances and reveals itself as the user types in commands ("open the door" or "look under the bed" or "ask about the diamond"). Unlike hypertext, you must do more than click on a link; you must devise phrases that will give you the most meaningful and useful way to advance the story.

IF stories can be about almost any topic, and can be written in just about any fictional genre, although they work best when the plots call for you to be active, to explore, and to make things happen. They need not be plot driven, however. *Galatea*, written by Emily Short, is an intriguing character sketch that is constructed as a dialogue between the user and a Nonplayer Character (NPC)—a character controlled by the computer. The story is based on the Greek myth of Pygmalion, a sculptor who carves a beautiful statue, Galatea. The statue comes to life after he falls in love with her. It is the same myth that inspired the Broadway musical, *My Fair Lady*.

In this interactive version of the myth, you visit the art gallery where *Galatea* is displayed and discover that you are able to talk with her. As you converse with her, you gain insights into her history and troubled emotional state. Her responses to your questions vary, as does her attitude toward you, depending on how you treat her (see Figure 4.3).

```
>ask about eyes
"What was it like, having your eyes carved?" you ask.

"He drilled at the corners," she says.  "And that was
agony -- waiting to see whether he would go too deep.  He
never did, but there was always doubt."

>ask about seeing
"When did you first begin to see?" you ask.  "Was it when
your eyes were finished, or could you somehow see before
that?"

"Before that," she says.  "Certainly before he began to
drill in the corners.  It was a gradual thing: everything
was dim and shadowed, and it grew brighter and sharper
the closer he came to the surface of my eyes, until I
could recognize colors, and know his face."

>ask about face
She just shrugs.
```

Figure 4.3 A segment of the IF work *Galatea* by Emily Short. Image courtesy of Emily Short.

IF stories resemble text-based adventure games as well as online MUDs and MOOs. Unlike MUDs and MOOs, however, they are played by a single individual rather than with a group. Furthermore, they do not have the win/lose outcomes that are so much a part of adventure games, though they do often include puzzles that must be solved in order to progress. These narratives cannot be as tightly plotted as linear fiction, but they do generally have overarching storylines.

Throughout this book, we will be examining other works of digital storytelling that contain no overt elements of gaming, particularly works of iCinema (interactive cinema). These stories demonstrate that even though games are extremely useful vehicles for holding interactive narratives together, works of digital storytelling do not need to be dependent on game models in order to succeed.

CONCLUSION

Interactivity, as we have seen, profoundly changes the way we experience a work of entertainment. We go from being a passive member of the audience to becoming a participant with an active and meaningful role, wielding a new power called agency.

Interactivity, however, changes the role of the storyteller. Instead of being the sole creator of the story, this role must now be shared with the user. And interactivity makes the telling of a fixed, sequential, linear story impossible. To knit the story together and make it compelling, storytellers must find new models to use. Many rely on game techniques to achieve narrative cohesion, although some digital storytellers are finding other ways to construct satisfying interactive narratives.

While interactivity creates new challenges for storytellers, it also gives them new powers. Thanks to interactivity, it is possible to tell stories that are deeply immersive and intensely absorbing; that take place on a much vaster canvas; and that can be experienced from more than one point of view. The challenge for storytellers is to find ways to use interactivity effectively, so that users can enjoy both agency and a meaningful narrative experience.

IDEA-GENERATING EXERCISES

1. Describe an event or occasion where you went from being a passive observer to an active participant. How did this shift affect the way you experienced the event? Your example could be something as simple as going from being a passenger in a car to actually driving the vehicle, or it could involve a more complex situation, like the *Las Posadas* procession described in this chapter.

2. If you are working on a project for a specific interactive medium or platform, make a list of the types of interactivity the medium or platform lends itself to most strongly, and the types of interactivity it does not support well or at all. Is your project making good use of the platform's strengths and avoiding its weaknesses?

3. Take a very simple, familiar story and work out different ways it would be changed by injecting interactivity into it, as with the Garden of Eden example. Your examples might be a story from the Bible, a child's nursery rhyme, or a recent news item.

4. Using a simple story like one chosen for the exercise above, redesign it as two different interactive experiences: one that is very story-like, and the other that is very game-like.

CHAPTER 5

Old Tools/ New Tools

What can an ancient Greek like Aristotle teach us that we can apply to modern interactive entertainment?

What aspects of traditional storytelling can be successfully ported over to digital storytelling?

When writers of traditional stories at first move into digital storytelling, what do they find most challenging?

What 10 entirely new tools must creators learn to use when they construct interactive narratives?

AN ASSORTMENT OF STORYTELLING TOOLS

Embarking on a new work of digital storytelling is usually a daunting proposition, even for veterans in the field. Each new project seems to chart new ground. Some call for a unique creative approach; others utilize new technology; still others combine media in new ways. And those who work in the newer areas of interactive entertainment—mobile apps, transmedia productions, and innovative types of immersive environments—are faced with having to be a pioneer almost every time out. Furthermore, the complexities posed by interactivity, plus the sheer volume of material contained in most works of digital storytelling, can be overwhelming. No wonder starting work on a new project can feel like plunging into the abyss.

Nevertheless, even though we may feel we are starting from scratch, we actually have a wonderfully serviceable set of tools and techniques at our disposal, some of which we glimpsed in Chapter 1. Aristotle first articulated a number of these tools over 2,000 years ago. Other tools go back still further, to preliterate storytellers. And we can also borrow an array of tools from more recent storytellers—from novelists, playwrights, and screenwriters. Furthermore, we can raid the supply of tools originally developed for pre-electronic games of all types, from athletic competitions to board games.

As is to be expected, of course, the majority of these borrowed tools and techniques need to be reshaped to some degree for digital media. And at some point, we finally empty out our old toolbox and reach the point where we need to pick up and master some entirely new implements. Ultimately, it is a combination of the old and the new, seamlessly integrated together, that enables us to create engaging works of digital storytelling.

LEARNING FROM GAMES

Some of the most effective tools of storytelling, tools that can inject an intense jolt of energy into any type of narrative, were not even developed by storytellers. They originated in games. Games are an ancient form of human social interaction, and storytellers in both linear and nonlinear media have borrowed heavily from them, as we saw in Chapters 1 and 4. Games can be used as a form of glue to hold an interactive work together.

Above all else, games teach us the critical importance of having a clear-cut goal, and also show us the importance of putting obstacles in the way of that goal. In games, the ultimate goal is to win the competition, and the players on the other side—the opponents—provide the biggest impediment to achieving that goal. This player versus player opposition is what provides much of the excitement and drama in an athletic competition, in much the same way it does in storytelling. In addition, participants in sporting competitions must contend with physical obstacles and challenges, such as the hurdles on a track field, the net on the tennis court, or the steep roads in a cycling race.

WORTH NOTING: GOALS IN GAMES AND STORIES

In a good game, as well as in a good story, the best goals are:

- Specific;
- Simple to understand;
- Highly desirable; and
- Difficult to achieve.

Try to imagine a game or story without a goal. What would the players or characters be trying to do? What would keep the audience interested in watching something that has no clear objective? What would give the experience meaning? Virtually every story and every game has a goal, although some would argue that sandbox games like *Minecraft* have no goal. Nevertheless, players of sandbox games construct their own goals, whether it be to survive in a hostile world or to create a magnificent structure.

The essential mechanics of stories are remarkably similar to games, especially when it comes to goals and obstacles. In a story, the protagonist wants to achieve a goal, just as an athlete does, even though the type of goal being sought after is of a different order. The objective may be to find the buried treasure; win the love of the adored one; track down the killer; or find a cure for a desperately sick child. A goal provides motivation for the main character, a sharp focus for the action, and a through-line for the plot, just as a goal provides motivation and focus for a game. And in a story, as with a game, obstacles provide the drama, and the most daunting obstacles are human ones—the antagonists the hero has to contend with.

Of course, some novels and works of short fiction present narratives in which the protagonist has no apparent goal, and so do some art house films. But even though such "slice of life" stories may be interesting character studies or be admirable for some other artistic reason, the narrative will usually feel flat because nothing is at stake. That is why it is difficult for such works to attract a wide audience.

The conflict between achieving a goal and the obstacles that hinder this victory is what creates conflict, and conflict is the heart of drama. The clearer the goal, and the more monumental the obstacles that stand in the way of achieving it, the greater the drama. The very first storytellers—those who recited the ancient myths and heroic epics of their culture—understood this, and made sure to emphasize all the difficulties their heroes had to overcome. Later storytellers, working in succeeding waves of media from classic theater to television and everything in between, recognized the value of goals and obstacles just as clearly. Not surprisingly, these fundamental story ingredients are just as useful in the creation of digital entertainment.

Games have provided storytellers with other valuable tools as well. From games, we learn that the most thrilling competitions are those that demand the most from a player—the most skill, the most courage, the most strategizing. Similarly, a good story demands that the protagonist give his or her all to the struggle. In an interactive work, the same demand is made on the user or the player. The greater the personal investment and the tougher the challenge, the sweeter the ultimate victory.

In addition, games are governed by specific sets of regulations. These not only add to the challenges but also help to keep the game fair. For example, players are only allowed to use approved types of equipment, or employ certain maneuvers and not others, or score a goal by doing X and not Y. Without such rules, victory would be too easy and the game would lack interest. Games not only have rules but also follow a set structure or format, though the specifics vary greatly among types of games. For example, a football game begins with a kickoff; a baseball game has nine innings; a basketball game is divided into quarters. No doubt, the first players of ancient sports soon found that without structure or rules, their games would quickly disintegrate into anarchy, and one side would use tactics that seemed completely unexpected and unfair to the other side. Rules and structure provide an equally fair, consistent playing environment to all players.

For the same reason, stories in every medium have a structure and format for how they begin, how they develop, and how they end. Furthermore, although stories don't follow set rules, they are guided by internal conventions. This ensures that behaviors and events within the fictional universe are consistent and logical and make sense within the story. Even a fantasy universe like the one portrayed in the Harry Potter novels, films, and games must remain faithful to its own internal set of rules. For instance, if it is established that characters cannot pass through physical structures unless they recite a secret spell, Harry or one of his classmates should not suddenly be able to blithely walk through a wall without using the spell. That would violate the rules of magic already established in the story. Internal conventions provide a narrative equivalent of a fair playing field.

LEARNING FROM MYTHS

Contemporary storytellers, whether working in linear or interactive media, are also indebted to the great mythmakers of ancient days. These master tellers of tales built their stories upon themes with deep emotional and psychological underpinnings. As noted in Chapter 1, many of these old stories feature young heroes and heroines who must triumph over a series of harrowing obstacles before finally reaching their goal, and in the course of their adventures undergo a form of death and rebirth.

Joseph Campbell, introduced in Chapter 1, analyzed the core elements of the hero's journey and found that such myths contained characters that were remarkably similar from story to story, and that the myths contained extremely similar plot points. He held that the hero's journey tapped into the universal experiences shared by humans everywhere, reflecting their hopes and fears, and thus resonated deeply with the audience.

More recently, Christopher Vogler interpreted Campbell's work for contemporary readers and writers in a book called *The Writer's Journey*. The book profiles the archetypal figures who commonly populate the hero's journey—characters with specific functions and roles to play—and he describes each of the 12 stages of the journey that the hero must pass through before being able to return home, victorious.

The hero's mythic journey has had a deep influence on storytellers throughout the world. Countless works of linear fiction—novels, plays, comic books, and movies—have been built on the model provided by the hero's journey. Among them are the films made by the great filmmaker George Lucas, who has often spoken of his debt to Joseph Campbell and the hero's journey. Even the magnificent film *Spirited Away*, a work of Japanese anime about a little girl trapped in a mysterious resort for ghosts, closely follows the 12 stages of this ancient myth.

This enduring model works equally well for interactive narratives. For example, the immensely involving game, *Final Fantasy VII*, contains many of the elements of the hero's journey. And a number of MMOGs incorporate it as well. After all, as a player, you set off for a journey into the unknown, meet up with various helpful, dangerous, or trickster characters along the way, find yourself tested in all sorts of ways, and do battle against powerful opponents.

Do writers, producers, and designers of these interactive versions of the hero's journey deliberately use this genre as a model? In some cases, yes, this modeling is conscious and intentional.

For example, Katie Fisher, a producer/designer for the game company Quicksilver Software, Inc., is quick to acknowledge that she based the game *Invictus* on the hero's journey, and used Christopher Vogler's book as a guide. In other cases, though, the hero's journey is probably an unconscious influence. After all, it is a story that is familiar to us from childhood—even many of our favorite fairy tales are simplified hero's journeys. And many a designer's most beloved movies are also closely based on this model, too, including such films as the *Wizard of Oz* and *Star Wars*. Obviously, elements in the hero's journey strike a deep chord within audiences both past and present. There is no reason why creators of interactive entertainment should not be able to find inspiration, as Katie Fisher has, in this compelling model.

LEARNING FROM ARISTOTLE

Mythological themes have provided fodder not only for our first narrative tales, but also for our earliest theatrical works. As noted in Chapter 1, rituals based on the myths of Dionysus led to the development of classic Greek theater. Aristotle, one of the greatest thinkers of the ancient world, closely studied Greek theater, particularly the serious dramas, which were then always called tragedies. Based on his observations, he developed an insightful series of principles and recorded them in a slender, densely written volume, *The Poetics*. Though drafted in the fourth century BC, his ideas have held up astoundingly well right up to the present day. The principles discussed in *The Poetics* have been applied not only to stage plays, but also to movies, TV shows, and, most recently, are finding their way into interactive narratives.

Aristotle articulated such concepts as dramatic structure, unity of action, plot reversals, and the tragic flaw. He also made perceptive comments about character development, dialogue, plot, and techniques of eliciting a strong emotional response from the audience. Furthermore, he warned against using cheap devices that would undermine the drama. One such device he felt was unworthy of serious theater was the *deus ex machina*, Latin for "God from a machine." This device was called into play when a writer was desperate for a way to get a character out of a predicament, and would solve the problem by having a god suddenly descend to the stage from an overhead apparatus and save the day. Aristotle decried such techniques and believed that plot developments should be logical and grow naturally out of the action.

One of Aristotle's greatest contributions to dramatic theory was his realization that effective dramas were based on a three-act structure. He noted that such dramas imitated a complete action, and always had a beginning, middle, and an end (acts I, II, and III). He explained in *The Poetics* (Chapter VII, Section 3) that "A beginning is that which does not itself follow anything by causal necessity, but after which something naturally is or comes to be. An end, on the contrary, is that which itself naturally follows some other thing, either by necessity, or as a rule, but has nothing following it. A middle is that which follows something as some other thing follows it. A well-constructed plot, therefore, must neither begin or end at haphazard, but conform to these principles."

Entire books have been written on the three-act structure, derived from this short passage, applying it to contemporary works of entertainment, particularly to films. One of the most widely used in the motion picture industry is Syd Field's *Screenplay: The Foundations of Screenwriting*. The book breaks down Aristotle's points and expands on them in a way that modern writers can readily understand. The three-act structure is so widely accepted in Hollywood that even nonwriters, professionals like studio development executives and producers, feel completely comfortable talking about such things as "the first act inciting incident," "the second act turning point," and the "third act climax."

The idea of the three-act structure has also found a place in interactive media, most noticeably in games. But it is used in other types of interactive entertainment as well, including virtual reality simulations, location-based entertainment, interactive movies, and Web series. Of course, inserting interactivity into a narrative project impacts enormously on its structure, so additional models must also be called into play. Often they are used in conjunction with the classic three acts first spelled out by Aristotle. (For a more detailed examination of structure in interactive works, please see Chapter 7.)

Aristotle also had valuable things to say about character motivation. He noted that motivation is the fuel which leads to action, and that action is one of the most important elements of drama. Just as the players' striving toward a goal is the driving force in a game, a character striving toward an objective is the driving force of a drama. Aristotle believed that there are two types of human motivation. One, he felt, is driven by passion and based on emotion. The other, he said, is based on reason or conscious will. In other words, one comes from the heart, the other from the head.

In interactive media, motivation is also of tremendous importance. It is what pulls the user through a vast universe of competing choices. By understanding motivation, we can create more compelling works of interactive entertainment.

Aristotle also believed that drama could have a profound effect on the audience, eliciting such emotions as pity and fear. The most effective dramas, he felt, could create a feeling of catharsis, or emotional purging and relief—the same sort of catharsis Joseph Campbell said occurred when people took part in a reenactment of a powerful myth. Creators of interactive works have not, as a rule, put much effort into trying to produce projects with an emotional punch. Today, however, more attention is being paid to this subject, and it will be discussed in more detail in Chapter 6.

LEARNING FROM CONTEMPORARY STORYTELLERS

When it comes to interactive entertainment, we can also learn a great deal from the creators of linear narrative, particularly from film and TV. These forms of entertainment already have great similarities to interactive media because they are stories told in moving images and sound, which is also how most interactive narrative is conveyed.

Two of the most important skills that can be ported over from film and television are character development and story construction. These are the fundamental building blocks of any type of narrative. Of course, they cannot be adapted without some adjustments, for interactivity has a profound impact on all aspects of the creative process.

Because I have made the transition from television and film into the interactive field myself, I am well aware of how closely the techniques of character and story development used in filmed narratives work in digital storytelling. For example, one of my first jobs in interactive media was as a freelance writer doing some work on Broderbund's pioneering *Carmen Sandiego* series, a game that had kids playing the part of a detective and trying to track down the thieving Carmen or one of her henchmen. My assignment called for me to create four new characters for the game and to write dialogue for two of its already-established characters, the Chief of Detectives and Wanda, his assistant. These tasks were almost identical to work I might have done for a TV show, except that I had to write numerous variations of every line of dialogue. Thus, I found myself coming up with about a dozen different ways to say "you bungled the case."

Another early assignment had me working out an interactive adventure story for children based on an idea proposed by actress-producer Shelly Duvall. Called *Shelly Duvall Presents Digby's Adventures* and developed by Sanctuary Woods, the CD-ROM was a story about a little dog who goes exploring, gets lost, and tries to find his way home. It was the kind of tale that could have easily been a kid's TV show, except for one thing: this was a branching, interactive story, so the little dog gets lost in three completely different ways. Each version offers the player numerous opportunities to become involved in the dog's adventures and help him find his way home.

OTHER USEFUL OLD TOOLS

Aside from character development and story construction, what else can be borrowed from traditional storytelling? One excellent tool is tension. Although tension is something we try to avoid in our daily lives, it serves an important function in both linear and interactive narratives. It keeps the audience riveted to the story, experiencing a mixture of apprehension and hope, wondering how things will turn out. Tension is particularly important in interactive narratives because they don't have the benefit of linear plots—the carefully constructed sequence of events that advances the action and builds up the excitement in traditional stories. Creators of interactive stories have to work extra hard to keep users involved with their narratives, and ramping up the tension is a good way to keep them hooked.

One reliable method of inserting tension in a nonlinear story is to put your main character (who is often the player, via the avatar he or she is controlling) into great jeopardy … risking death in a snake-infested jungle, caught behind enemy lines in a war, or pursued by brain-sucking aliens in a sci-fi story. But the jeopardy need not be something that could cause bodily harm … the risk of losing anything of great value to the protagonist can also produce dramatic tension. Thus, the jeopardy can involve the threat of relinquishing everything your hero has worked so hard to achieve in the story, whether it is a vast sum of money, solving a baffling mystery, or becoming a mafia godfather.

Introducing an element of uncertainty can also increase dramatic tension. Which of the characters that you encounter can you trust? Which ones are actually enemies in disguise? Which route through the forest will get you to your destination quickly and safely, and which one might be a long and dangerous detour? Uncertainty is a close cousin to suspense, which is the burning desire to know what will happen next. It is the feeling of suspense that keeps us turning the pages of a novel until long past our bedtime, and keeps us glued to a TV movie when we know we really should be paying bills or doing something similarly responsible.

To pump up the adrenaline and keep the audience glued to the story, many works of both linear and nonlinear narrative use a device called a *ticking clock*. With a ticking clock, the protagonist is given a specific and limited period of time to accomplish his goal. Otherwise there will be serious and perhaps even deadly consequences. A ticking clock is an excellent way to keep the momentum of a story going. The ticking clock can even be found in children's fairy tales. Cinderella, for example, has to rush out of the ballroom before the clock strikes 12, or else she will be caught in public in her humiliating rags. Movies and TV shows are full of ticking clocks, and an entire TV series, *24*, is build around a literal ticking clock counting off the minutes and hours the main character has left to save the day. The awareness of time running out is as effective in digital storytelling as it is in films and television.

THE STORYLINE IN LINEAR AND INTERACTIVE NARRATIVES

As we have seen, many techniques first developed for linear narratives also work extremely well in interactive media. Yet when it comes to the role of the *storyline*—the way the narrative unfolds and is told, beat-by-beat—we are faced with a major difference. In traditional linear narratives, the storyline is all-important, and it needs to be strong and clear. It is "the bones" of a story. But narrative works in digital media are nonlinear, which means events cannot unfold in a tight sequential order the way a carefully plotted linear story does. Digital storytelling also needs to support interactivity, which, as we've seen, can be extremely disruptive to narrative. And, in the case of games, the actual gaming elements of the work become paramount. In order to offer players a pleasurable and dynamic experience, gameplay is usually given prominence over a developed storyline.

Works of digital storytelling vary enormously when it comes to how developed a storyline they can carry. Some genres, especially *casual games* (short, lightweight entertainments), often contain little or no storyline to speak of. They may not even have characters or a plot; they may be totally abstract, like an electronic version of tic tac toe. Simulations might have just enough of a storyline to give users a framework for what they'll be doing. But at the other extreme, we have projects with richly plotted through lines, dramatic turns and twists, and even subplots, as is true with certain video games and works of interactive cinema. Given the fact that there is such a vast spectrum of interactive entertainment media, and a great variety of genres within each of the media, it is not possible to formulate a set of rules to govern the "right" amount of story that is appropriate for a given project. The best guide is the project itself. You need to consider its genre, its target audience, its goal, and the nature of the interactivity.

NOTES FROM THE FIELD: WHAT IS "JUST ENOUGH" OF A STORYLINE?

The *JumpStart* line of edutainment games for children seems to have found just the right balance between storyline and other demands of educational titles. The *JumpStart* products are developed by Knowledge Adventure, part of the Universal Vivendi portfolio of game companies, and they are great fun for kids. Their actual purpose, however, is to drill the young users in specific skills they need to master at school, like multiplication or spelling. The drills are incorporated into games that are so entertaining that they feel more like play than like learning. So where do storylines fit in here?

According to Diana Pray, a senior producer on the *JumpStart* titles, the storyline is important to give the game a context; it drives the game toward a particular desired outcome. The *JumpStart* titles feature a cast of highly appealing animated characters, and, in a typical storyline, one or more of the characters has a problem, and the child's help is needed to solve it. "The story encourages kids to reach the end goal," she explained. "We give them enough story so they feel they are in the game. The storyline gives them the incentive to play the games and get the rewards. Incentives are embedded in the story. But kids want to play; they don't want a lot of interruptions. So we don't do very deep stories. We don't want to risk boring the child. We have to be efficient in the storyline."

A HOLLYWOOD WRITER'S VIEW OF INTERACTIVE MEDIA

Writers moving from the linear world of Hollywood screenwriting into the field of interactive media are often as struck, as I was, by the similarities in crafting scripts in these two seemingly antithetical arenas. A number of people interviewed for this book remarked on this. Among them was Anne Collins-Ludwick. Collins-Ludwick comes from the field of mainstream night-time television and had worked on such successful television series as *Vegas*, *Fantasy Island*, and the mystery series *Matlock*. In 2002, she made a major career switch and became a scriptwriter and producer for Her Interactive, which makes the *Nancy Drew* mystery-adventure games. It was her first professional exposure to interactive media and she plunged in headfirst. In just a little over a year, she helped develop four new titles, including *The Haunted Carousel* (see Figure 5.1).

Figure 5.1 Box art for one of the Nancy Drew games, which utilize many of the tools drawn from linear storytelling. Image courtesy of Her Interactive.

"The parallels between what I do here and working on a weekly TV show are phenomenal," she told me. "Lots of the elements are just the same." Chief among them, she noted, was the process of developing the story and characters and the designing of the environments (though they are called "interiors" and "exteriors" in Hollywood scripts). "I found I knew everything I needed to know," she added. "It was just a different application."

For Collins-Ludwick, accustomed to the taut linear scripts of Hollywood, the one major difference was the way interactivity impacted on the story. "Giving the player choices was the hardest part for me," she recalled. "We want to give the players as much freedom to explore as possible, but we also want to relate a story. We need to move them from A to B to C." The challenge was to find a way to reveal the mystery while also offering the players a significant amount of choice, and to balance the need to tell a story against the need to give players the opportunity to explore.

The other big challenge for her, and what she considered to be her steepest learning curve, was mastering an interactive script format. She had to learn how to flag material so that once the player had performed a certain task, something could happen that could not have happened previously. For instance, if a player found a hidden letter, she could now ask a character an important question, or could enter an area that had previously been off-limits.

"It was a lot to keep straight in my head; there was a lot of logic to get used to, and a lot of details. It's a matter of training your brain to think in a certain pattern," she said. But she was taken in hand and helped by a staffer with a great deal of technical savvy, and she also found that the company's thorough documentation process helped her keep track of things. "It's easy now," she reports, "but in the beginning it was very intimidating."

Of course, works of digital storytelling may contain segments that are not interactive but are, instead, like a linear scene from a movie. In video games, these linear passages are called *cut scenes*. They are usually found at the beginning of a game, serving as an introduction to the world where the game is set. They also give enough information to make it clear what you as a player need to do in this virtual world, and why. Cut scenes are also sprinkled through most games, often triggered when a player has accomplished a particular task. At such points they function as an opportunity to advance the narrative aspects of the game. They may also give important pieces of the *backstory* (elements of the narrative that took place before the game opens and are important to the understanding of the game's story). These scenes are really no different from scenes you'd find in a movie or a television show except that in today's games they are almost always animated rather than live action. Thus, any of the cinematic or dramatic techniques employed in these older media can be used just as successfully in the linear sequences of interactive works, though cut scenes should be kept as short and used as sparingly as possible.

TEN NEW TOOLS

We have seen how many well-seasoned tools of traditional storytelling can, with certain modifications, still be used in digital storytelling. Working in this arena, however, also requires utilizing some entirely new tools. And it also calls for something else: an attitude adjustment. In order to create these new kinds of stories, we must release our mental grip on sequential narrative and be open to the possibilities offered to us by interactivity.

This is not only true for those who are accustomed to working in traditional screen-based media, like Anne Collins-Ludwick. It also applies to anyone who has grown up watching TV and movies and has developed the expectation that stories should have tightly constructed linear plots. It is usually less of an issue for those people who, from childhood on, have played video games. Yet even members of this generation can have trouble functioning in a nonsequential story world.

But no matter which category you fall into—the group who embraces nonlinearity or the group who is uneasy with it—you still need to learn how to use a new set of tools if you want to work in digital storytelling. They will be explored in detail in future chapters, but we will offer a brief rundown of 10 of the most essential tools here.

1. INTERFACE AND NAVIGATION

The users of an interactive work need a way to connect with the material, perform actions, and move around. This is where interface design and navigational tools come in. They provide a way for users to make their wishes known and control what they see and do and where they go. The many visual devices used in interface design and navigation include menus, navigation bars, icons, buttons, cursors, rollovers, maps, and directional symbols. Even sound effects have a role to play in user interface. Hardware devices include video game controllers, touch screens, and VR wands. With the Wii and the Kinect, even your body can be used to control the content, and the interface must take this into consideration (see Chapters 7, 15, 17, and 22).

2. SYSTEMS FOR DETERMINING EVENTS AND ASSIGNING VARIABLES

In order for the events within an interactive project to occur at an appropriate time, and not have the narrative self-destruct into chaos, there needs to be an orderly system of logic that will guide the programming. Most members of the creative team are not expected to do any programming themselves, but they still must understand the basic principles governing *what* happens *when*.

Also, interactive projects typically involve a great number of variables. For example, characters may be constructed from variables including body types, physical attributes, and special skills. To organize such variables, the design team will often construct a *matrix* to help assign and track them. As a member of the design team or as a writer, it is necessary to understand how to work with the variables and the system of logic in your project (see Chapters 6, 7, and 11).

3. ASSIGNING A ROLE AND POINT OF VIEW TO THE USER

Users have many possible roles they can play in an interactive narrative, and they can also view the virtual world from more than one possible point of view. One thing the creative team decides early on is who the user will "be" in the story and how the user will view the virtual world portrayed in the narrative (see Chapter 6).

4. WORKING WITH NEW TYPES OF CHARACTERS AND ARTIFICIAL INTELLIGENCE

Thanks to interactive media, a strange new cast of character types has sprung into being. Among them are avatars, chatterbots, and nonplayer characters (characters controlled by the computer, usually called NPCs). In some cases, digital characters have artificial intelligence (AI). They seem to understand what the player is doing or saying, and act appropriately in response. The way characters are developed and given personality and AI calls for considerations never encountered in linear media (see Chapter 6). Furthermore, the computer program itself may possess AI. It may recognize the user's patterns and offer scenario A to one group of users and scenario B to a different group of users.

STRANGE BUT TRUE: AI'S IQ

A group of researchers at the University of Illinois at Chicago conducted a study recently to see just how bright an advanced system of AI developed at MIT really was. Their discovery? That it was just about as smart as the average four-year-old. Though it was good at vocabulary and did well at recognizing similarities, it fell quite short when it came to basic common sense. Evidently, common sense calls for the ability to recognize both hard facts and implicit facts. Though computer programs can grapple with hard facts, they lack the life experience to deal with implicit facts—things like a pan can be extremely hot if it has stayed in the oven for a long time. Implicit facts tend to be obvious to humans but not to computers (University of Illinois at Chicago News Center, July 15, 2013).

However, some computers *are* extremely intelligent. IBM's Watson computer, for example, was capable of understanding questions presented to it in text. Watson was a contestant on Jeopardy, winning $1 million dollars! Watson has most recently been employed at the Sloan-Kettering Cancer Center, answering nurses' questions about lung cancer.

5. NEW WAYS OF CONNECTING STORY ELEMENTS

In linear entertainment, the various media elements—audio, graphics, moving images, and text—come "glued" together and cannot be pried apart, as do the various scenes that constitute the story. But in interactive media, media assets, scenes, and major pieces of story can be presented or accessed as separate entities, and connected in various ways. These various ways of connecting story pieces exist on both micro and macro levels.

As we saw in Chapters 1 and 2, *hypertext* and *hot spots* are two ways of connecting assets. They require an active decision on the part of the user to make the connection. But story elements can also be connected indirectly. In Chapter 7, on structure, we will see how pieces of a story such as a cut scene or the appearance of a new character or the discovery of a clue can be triggered indirectly, once the user has performed a specific set of actions or solved a puzzle.

On the macro level, works of digital storytelling can be constructed to exist across a number of media platforms such as mobile devices, broadcast television, and the Internet, with parts of each story available on different media platforms and with the whole story interconnected. As noted earlier, this is *transmedia storytelling*, and it includes a new type of narrative/game hybrid, the *alternate reality game* (see Chapters 10 and 18).

6. GAMEPLAY

As we have discussed, many works of digital storytelling are built around games, and in such works, the creative team must give a serious amount of attention to developing satisfactory *gameplay* for the project. Gameplay is the overall experience of playing a game and what makes it fun and pleasurable; it is what the player can do in the game. It includes the game's challenges; how they can be overcome; the game's rules; and what it takes to win (or lose).

Even works that are not primarily games may require users to solve puzzles, answer trivia questions, or play a series of mini-games. Thus, it is important to understand games and have a basic grasp of what constitutes good gameplay (see Chapters 15 and 18).

7. REWARDS AND PENALTIES

Rewards are an effective way to keep users motivated, while penalties keep them on their toes and add an agreeable amount of tension. They are usually found in games, but may be used in other types of digital storytelling, as well. Rewards may be in the form of points, play money, or a valuable object for one's inventory. Players may also be rewarded by rising to a higher level, getting a virtual career promotion, or receiving extra powers for their avatars. Penalties, on the other hand, can be the deduction of anything that can be earned as a reward. The ultimate penalty is a virtual death or losing the game. It is important to know what kinds of rewards and penalties work well for your genre and are appropriate for your audience (see Chapters 8, 12, and 15).

8. NEW KINDS OF STRUCTURES

Most forms of linear narrative use the same basic building block or unit of organization: the scene. Scenes move the overall story along, but are also complete little dramas in themselves. Interactive media, however, uses very different units of organization. Each of these units offers a specific set of possibilities—things the user can do or discover within them. As part of the creative team, you need to have an understanding of the basic building blocks of whatever genre you are working in (see Chapter 7).

9. THE USE OF TIME AND SPACE

Time and space are far more dynamic factors of interactive narration than they are of linear media. For example, games may present a persistent universe, where time moves on and events occur even when the game or story is turned off. Thus, if users fail to log onto a MMOG they've subscribed to, they may forego the opportunity to take part in an exciting adventure, or if a user has adopted a virtual pet, it may die if not fed regularly.

In a different use of time, the interactive medium may keep track of things like holidays and important anniversaries in your personal life. For instance, a smart doll may wish its child companion a happy birthday or a Merry Christmas on the appropriate dates.

In many fictional interactive worlds, time is cycled on a regular basis, so that during a single session of play, the user might experience dawn, the midday sun, and sunset. The virtual world may also cycle through different seasons of the year, and sometimes the changing of a season will trigger a dramatic event in the story. In some games, you can slow down time or speed it up. And in some works of interactive cinema, you may be able to select which time period of a story you want to visit.

In addition, geographical space is experienced on a different scale and in a different way in interactive media than in linear media. Some games contain multiple parallel universes, where events are going on simultaneously in more than one place and you can hop back and forth between these worlds. In other games, the geographical scope of a game can be vast, and it can take hours or even days for the player to travel from one point to another.

As part of a creative team, you need to have a basic knowledge of the various possibilities of space and time, and you should have some idea of how they might be utilized in the type of project you are working on (see Chapters 15 and 21).

10. SENSORS AND SPECIAL HARDWARE

Certain forms of interactive entertainment require sensors or other devices in order to simulate reality or control or trigger events. These include gyroscopes, accelerometers, and GPSs. In addition, a smart doll might have a built-in sensor that can detect light and darkness, and be sleepy when it grows dark and wide-awake in the morning. In immersive environments, users need to wear special equipment to see virtual images, and such environments may use a variety of other devices to simulate reality. As a member of the creative team of a project that uses sensors or other special hardware, you will need to know enough about what the devices can do so that you can use them effectively (see Chapters 20 and 22).

THE COLLABORATIVE PROCESS

Working with an unfamiliar and complex set of tools—even a single new tool—can be an anxiety-producing experience. For someone who has never worked in interactive media, the first exposure can be something of a culture shock. Fortunately, professionals in interactive media seldom work in a vacuum. It is not a field populated by hermit-like artists slaving away in lonely garrets. On the contrary, it is a field that almost evangelically promotes the team process. Colleagues are encouraged to share ideas in freewheeling brainstorming sessions. Even staffers low on the totem pole are encouraged to contribute ideas. Since almost every company has its own idiosyncratic methods of operating, newcomers are taken in hand by veterans and shown the ropes.

NOTES FROM THE FIELD: ONE NEWCOMER'S EXPERIENCE OF COLLABORATION

Anne Collins-Ludwick, who came from the highly competitive, dog-eat-dog world of prime-time television, is one person who has found the working conditions of interactive media to be extremely supportive. She said she was immediately struck by that when she began working on her first *Nancy Drew* title for Her Interactive. "It was one of the most collaborative works of fiction I'd ever been involved with," she reported enthusiastically. "It was collaborative from Day One, when I was first brought into the game."

At virtually all software companies, projects are developed by an entire team rather than by a single individual. The team typically includes specialists from several key areas, such as game design, project management, art direction, and programming. Thus, no one person has the burden of having to be an expert in every facet of the project.

CONCLUSION

Interactive entertainment utilizes an array of tools, some drawn from extremely ancient sources, others from contemporary linear storytellers, and still others that are unique to new media. Although ancient and more contemporary storytelling tools are highly useful, we must move beyond them and master 10 new tools.

Often, the greatest challenge for people new to digital storytelling is overcoming the discomfort of working with unfamiliar concepts. Depending on our mindset, the chance to pick up and use the new tools employed in this field can be either exhilarating or intimidating.

For those willing to jump in and try them out, a great deal of help is available. As Collins-Ludwick and others have been pleased to discover, digital entertainment is an enormously collaborative field, and even when the learning curve is steep, newcomers can count on getting the support they need from their teammates.

IDEA-GENERATING EXERCISES

1. Analyze a computer game you are familiar with and compare it to a specific type of athletic game. In each case, what is the goal, what are the obstacles, and how do you win or lose? In what major ways are they alike or different?

2. Pick a movie, TV show, or novel that you think used tension effectively. What kept you riveted to this story? Is this something that you think could be used effectively in digital storytelling?

3. Select an interactive project that you are familiar with, and describe what was built into this material that would make users want to invest their time in it. What would keep them interested and involved?

4. Which of the 10 tools unique to interactive storytelling do you feel is the most challenging or intimidating for you? Why do you feel this is so?

5. Which of the 10 new tools do you feel is the most creatively exciting? Can you describe something you'd like to try to do with this tool?

CHAPTER 6

Characters, Dialogue, and Emotions

How do characters in interactive stories differ from characters found in linear media?

Why is it worthwhile to give time and attention to creating your villains?

How does interactivity affect the way characters communicate with us?

What can you do to increase the user's emotional response to an interactive work?

CHARACTERS IN AN INTERACTIVE ENVIRONMENT

Characters are an essential element of all forms of storytelling, from our ancestors' oral recitations of myths and epics to today's high-tech computer-assisted narratives. Characters pull us into the story and give it life. We empathize with our heroes and identify with their struggles; we fear the villains and long to see them defeated. Thanks to characters, both noble and malevolent, we connect with the story on a deep emotional level.

THE ROLE OF CHARACTERS IN DIGITAL STORYTELLING

If anything, characters are even more important to digital storytelling than they are to linear narratives. In addition to adding life to these narratives and an emotional context, they also serve some specialized roles. They can:

- give users entry into an unfamiliar or intimidating world and allow them to explore it in a way that feels inviting and safe;

- increase a project's perception of being entertaining, even if the underlying purpose of the project is educational or instructional;

- add refreshing touches of humor;

- keep people hooked, willing to spend hours immersed in the character's life and environment;

- offer assistance to users when they are confused, and answer their questions; and

- add excitement, obstacles, and challenges, in the form of antagonists.

In addition to all these contributions, strong, unique characters can make a work stand out from others in the market and become a hit. After all, why is it that so many people love the *Tomb Raider* games? The primary reason people love these games is because of the appeal of Lara Croft. She not only leads an exciting life, but she's rich, beautiful, brave, and a phenomenal athlete. Lara is a great aspirational figure for girls, and, as a plus for the guys, well, she's got a great body (see Figure 6.1).

Figure 6.1 Lara Croft in a screen capture from *Lara Croft tomb raider: The angel of darkness*. Image courtesy of Eidos interactive.

Lara Croft and other vivid characters from computer games—characters like Mario, Sonic the Hedgehog, Carmen Sandiego, and Angry Birds—have begun to take their place alongside other icons of popular culture like Dick Tracy and Mickey Mouse. In the short time that interactive entertainment has existed, it has proven that it is capable of producing enduring characters, characters who have what it takes to become household names and to sell everything from plastic action figures to lunch boxes.

THE DIFFERENCES BETWEEN CHARACTERS IN LINEAR AND INTERACTIVE STORYTELLING

The characters we find in traditional media and the ones we find in digital storytelling are different both in what gives them life and in what they can do. Characters in linear media are created exclusively by writers and can never change. The Hamlet created by Shakespeare, for example, will always be plagued by the same doubts and will always speak the same soliloquies, even 400 years after the Bard wrote a play about him. As much as members of the audience might want to make Hamlet act differently, there is nothing they can do.

In interactive narratives, however, users can share the job of character creation with the writer, and they can step right into a story. Furthermore, characters in interactive narratives can, as discussed in Chapter 1, break the fourth wall and talk directly with the user. They can also possess artificial intelligence and respond in believable ways to things that the users do. Just imagine, then, what a digital storytelling version of *Hamlet* would be like if it could have a cast of interactive characters, and these characters could play a meaningful part in the enfolding of events facing the troubled prince in long ago Denmark!

In digital storytelling, we have two major categories of characters. The terminology to describe them comes from video games. One large group consists of the *player characters*. These are the characters over which the users have direct control. The second large group consists of *nonplayer characters*, or *NPCs*. These are the characters that, as the term indicates, are controlled by the computer and not the user.

Interactivity makes it more difficult to construct complex characters and portray how they transform emotionally over time, a change known in linear media as a *character arc*. Without a fixed sequence of events, how do you reveal a character's flaws, needs, and special gifts? How do you show the character growing as a human being? How can you even produce a vivid portrait of your protagonist when that character might never even be seen, because your user has stepped into that character's shoes and has "become" the character? Yet techniques do exist that deal with these challenges, as we will see later in the chapter.

WHERE DID ALL THE CHARACTERS GO?

If good characters add so much appeal to a work of interactive entertainment, how can it be that some immensely popular interactive games don't have any characters at all? After all, the world's first successful computer game, *Pong*, consisted of only a ball and paddle, and *Tetris*, an ever-popular puzzle game, lacks characters, too. And so does the simple but addictive mobile game, *Snake*. In *Snake*, you try to lengthen a skinny snake-like shape by "eating" dots. It's a stretch to call the snake a character, though, as it has no personality whatsoever.

True, a number of interactive works have no characters. But they do have something that traditional stories lack: the user. Users actually share many of the qualities possessed by protagonists in linear works, and to a great degree fill in for a missing main character. They are active; they strive for a goal; they are challenged by obstacles. Furthermore, users are personally invested in the outcome of the story. Their actions, not those of a fictional character, will determine how things turn out. It is the user who brings an interactive construct to life.

CLASSIC CHARACTERS FROM LINEAR MEDIA

Let's now turn to the basic character types of traditional storytelling, and see how these models might serve us in interactive media. The two classic archetypes, the must-haves of every work of linear storytelling, originated in the Greek theater. The first is the protagonist, the central figure of the drama, whose mission, goal, or objective provides the story with its forward momentum. The second archetype is the antagonist, the adversary who stands in the way of the protagonist, and whose opposition gives heat to the drama and provides the story with exciting conflict.

For anyone who might still have a lingering doubt about the critical role competitive games have played in the origin of drama and storytelling, consider this: the words "antagonist" and "protagonist" are both formed around the same Greek root, agon. As mentioned in Chapter 4, the word *agon* means a contest for a prize at a public game. The protagonist is literally one who goes after the prize and the antagonist is the one who tries to prevent this; their struggle is the core of the story.

In works of linear storytelling, the protagonist is the character the audience is rooting for. Audience members invest their emotions in the protagonist's struggle and want to see this character succeed. In an interactive work, the emotional investment is often even greater, for in most cases, the protagonist and player are one and the same. The protagonist is a player character, controlled by the user. A protagonist in an interactive work can give the user an opportunity to live out a fantasy by virtually walking in that character's shoes. Antagonists, on the other hand, stand in the way of the outcome the user most wants. Almost inevitably, antagonists in digital storytelling are NPCs.

The same basic struggle between archetypal characters can be found in many ancient myths. For example, two continually warring goddesses can be found in Irish mythology. Cailleach, which means "the old veiled one," ruled during the dark season of the year, and represented death and rebirth. However, she was replaced by Bridget in the spring. Bridget represented healing, the eternal flame, and creative inspiration, as described in a post on April 22, 2012, by Elyn Aviva on Your Life is a Trip.com.

THE USER AS PROTAGONIST

As we have learned from traditional media, a protagonist need not be a saint. After all, Walter White in the TV series, *Breaking Bad*, was hardly a man of virtue. He cooked meth and killed people and lied to his family. Yet White was unquestionably the protagonist of the series. It is easy to find tarnished protagonists in interactive media as well; we need look no further than the enormously successful video game *Grand Theft Auto* series. Our protagonists here are all violent criminals.

Many authorities in drama, beginning with Aristotle, have contended that the most interesting characters are not perfect. In classic Greek theater, as with Shakespeare's plays, the main characters are afflicted by what is often termed "a tragic flaw." Though noble in many ways, these characters also possess some weakness—jealousy, self-doubt, ambition—a trait that leads to their undoing. In lighter stories, protagonists usually have flaws, too, though of a less serious nature. These flaws in their personality will not lead to tragic consequences, but will often cause them trouble, and can also be the source of comic moments.

Not every protagonist in interactive media has a flaw or a quirk, but such weaknesses are not uncommon. That's even true of the little mouse, Mia, who is the star of a hit series of children's titles. Mia has a perky, adventurous, can-do personality, but she has some flaws as well. She can be stubborn and recklessly curious and doesn't always think ahead, and all of these traits can land her in a world of trouble (see Figure 6.2).

Figure 6.2 Mia, the perky little mouse who stars in a hit series of children's titles. Image courtesy of Kutoka interactive.

According to Richard Vincent, president of Kutoka, the Canadian company that makes the *Mia* edutainment titles, good character design is critical. "Games really end up being about character," he told me. "If people don't identify with the character, they won't play it. I admit in the beginning I wasn't thinking like that; I wasn't thinking characters were that important." But the success of Mia convinced him of the pivotal role characters play, and the company has changed its preproduction process accordingly, devoting time to preparing a complete bible of all the characters, their personalities, and their worlds.

What we need in a protagonist are qualities that make them likeable, believable, and attractive enough for us to want to spend time in their company. We need to understand why they have chosen to go after the particular goal they are seeking—their passion to do this must make sense to us. In other words, we must be able to identify with them—be able to imagine ourselves in their position and feel what they are feeling. This becomes even more important in interactive media, where in so many cases we actually take on the role of the protagonist. If the main character is distasteful to us, or if the character's motivation baffles us, we are not going to want to invest our time in this particular work of digital entertainment.

THE USER'S AVATAR

Player characters often appear on the screen in the form of an *avatar*—a graphic representation of the player-controlled character. The word *avatar* comes from the Hindu religion, where it means an incarnation or physical representation of a deity. In some interactive works, avatars are predefined and unchangeable, but in other cases, players can construct avatars out of a selection of heads, body parts, and clothing and gear, and also choose such things as special skills and powers for them. The make-it-yourself avatars are extremely common in MMOGs and in many video games. As yet another possibility, users can sometimes pick their avatar from several predefined character choices.

It is important to note that in some forms of digital storytelling, we have no physical representation of the user on the screen at all. This is true in works where the user sees things from the first-person point of view, as we will be discussing. It is also true when the user plays a God-like role and is able to see and do things, but is not actually a character in the story. Furthermore, in some kinds of non-screen-based forms of digital storytelling, the user is actually physically present and is interacting directly with the narrative or game. This is the case when the user is participating in an immersive environment or playing with a smart toy or playing a game on the Wii or other motion-sensitive console.

THE USER'S POINT OF VIEW

One of the most unique aspects of digital storytelling is its use of point of view (POV). The user has two, or possibly three, very different ways of seeing things in a virtual world: via the first-person and third-person POV. Some would argue that there is a second-person POV as well.

With a first-person POV, we see the action as if we were actually right there and viewing it through our own eyes. We see the world around us, but we don't see ourselves, except for perhaps a hand or a foot or a weapon we are holding. It is the "I" experience … I am doing this, I am doing that. The first-person POV is much like the way we experience things in real life. For instance, I don't see myself as I type on my computer, though I can see my hands on the keyboard. This is the same way first-person perspective works in interactive media. With this POV, it is quite easy to put ourselves completely into the role of the character we are playing and invest in the illusion that we really are the hero of the story. There is nothing visual on the screen to remind us we are not really that character (see Figure 6.3).

In some cases with the first-person POV, the cursor on the screen may indicate where we are in the virtual world, and may even change into an iconic symbol in certain situations. For example, if we are playing a detective, the cursor may change into a magnifying glass when we are physically close to a clue.

Figure 6.3 With the first-person POV, we do not see the character we are playing, except perhaps for a hand, a foot, or a weapon, as demonstrated in this screenshot from *Thief*. Image courtesy of Eidos interactive.

With the third-person POV, on the other hand, we are watching our character from a distance, much like we watch the protagonist in a movie. We can see the character's body in motion and can see his or her facial expressions, too. With the third-person POV, our protagonist can be extremely well-developed visually (see Figure 6.4). Cut scenes show characters from the third-person POV, as well.

Figure 6.4 In a third-person POV, as in this screen capture from *Lara Croft tomb raider: Angel of darkness*, we can see the character we are playing, much like watching a movie. Image courtesy of Eidos interactive.

Some professionals in the field also contend that a number of interactive works also offer a second-person POV, a view that combines the intimacy of first person with the objectivity of third person. In a second-person POV, they hold, we largely see things as if we were really in the scene, but we also see a little of our avatar—the back of the head, perhaps, or a shoulder. It's almost like being right on top of your character, but not "inside" the character. Others would argue that the so-called second-person POV does not actually exist, but is actually a variation on the third-person POV.

The first- and third-person POVs each have their advantages and disadvantages. The first-person perspective gives us great immediacy and immersiveness. However, we never get to see what our characters look like and cannot watch their reactions. It's also difficult to portray certain kinds of actions with the first-person POV. How can you show the character drinking a glass of whiskey, for instance, or hugging another character? On the other hand, the third-person POV allows us to see the character's movements and facial expressions, but since the character is so well-defined visually, it is more difficult for us to put ourselves into the role. It can create a sense of disconnect between the user and the material.

In video games, the decision whether to use the first- or third-person POV depends to a large degree on the kind of gameplay being offered. In games that emphasize shooting action, the first-person POV is the most often used, since that gives the player the sense of actually controlling the gun. In fact, such games are usually referred to as *first-person shooters*. On the other hand, when games have the main character doing a great deal of running, jumping, and climbing, like the *Tomb Raider* series, it is advantageous to use the third-person POV. That way, you can see your character's body and have better control over what the character is doing.

Many interactive works try to get around the perspective problem by offering different POVs in different situations. They give the user the first-person POV for the most adrenaline-intense action scenes, and use the third-person POV for exploratory situations. However, the jump between the different perspectives can be jarring and break the user's sense of immersion.

Determining which point of view to use for your project is an important decision, and one that must be made early on, because so many other factors will be impacted by it, from character design to graphics issues to types of interactivity.

THE USER'S MANY POSSIBLE ROLES

Another critical matter to determine is what role the user plays in the narrative. So far, we have been focusing on the user as the hero of the story—as the protagonist. Often this character truly is heroic. He or she saves the princess, saves the city, saves the planet. But this hero role is not necessarily as clear-cut as you might imagine. Author David Straker, on the website Changing Minds, has identified no less than 18 types of hero characters. These include the accidental hero, the martyr, the anti-hero, the noble savage, and the savior. Thus, as you develop your protagonist, give careful thought to what motivates this character, what the users might feel about this character, and also what the expectations are of the individuals this character is saving.

In some digital storytelling works, you play the assistant or helper of the "star" of the story and help this character reach a particular goal. Who are you in a case like that? You might be thought of as a sidekick or pal, but you could also claim to be the protagonist, since your actions will determine how things end.

In some interactive narratives, you are assigned to a particular role at the very beginning, such as a rookie detective or a junior Mafioso, and from there try to work your way up to the top of your virtual profession. In other interactive narratives, you play a voyeur and spy on people, but you are also a character in the story and can get caught spying, with possible fatal consequences. In yet other works, you become a deity-like figure, controlling the destiny of a virtual world, or a particular piece of that world—a military unit or a sports team. As still another possibility, and quite a common one, you just play yourself, though you interact with fictional characters. And sometimes, you are not a character at all, and do not take a direct part in the story. Instead your choices determine what part of the story you will see.

As a member of the creative team for a digital storytelling project, among the first decisions you will need to make is who the user is in the story and what the user will be able to do.

COMPUTER-CONTROLLED CHARACTERS: ANTAGONISTS AND OTHERS

While it is impossible to conceive of a story-based interactive work without a protagonist, or at the very least, without a player/participant, can the same be said for the necessity of an antagonist? Is it essential to include an oppositional character or series of them in every work of digital entertainment?

In order to answer this question, you must first consider the nature of your project. Where does it fit within the overall entertainment spectrum, with free-form experiences on one end, and works with strong storylines and goals on the other? If it leans more toward the free-form end, you probably won't need an antagonist. Such projects tend to be more like unstructured play (activities involving smart toys or a Sims game, for example) or offer the user the opportunity to construct items with digital tools (artwork, simulated neighborhoods, or theme park rides). Activities like these can be quite engrossing without inserting an antagonist; in a sense, the challenges they offer serve the same function. For the most part, antagonists can be an unwelcome and disruptive presence in free-form projects, unless they are created by the users themselves.

On the other hand, interactive experiences that have clear-cut goals and the other hallmarks of games and stories will definitely require oppositional forces. Most frequently, these forces will be characters. However, opposition can also come from natural forces, such as violent storms, or from physical challenges, such as negotiating a boot camp obstacle course. Opposition may also come from nonhuman but living characters, such as dangerous animals, or from human but non-living characters, like zombies.

In general, opposing forces in the form of sentient characters will make the conflicts more dramatic and more "personal." Being pitted against an intelligent adversary will ratchet up the user's feeling of danger and jeopardy. An opponent who is capable of reason and strategy is far more formidable and far scarier than any inanimate obstacle can be.

NOTES FROM THE FIELD: FAMILY FRIENDLY AND COMIC ANTAGONISTS

Even games made for young children usually include villains of one kind or another. The opponents in projects for young children tend to be humorous bad guys, rather than the truly menacing opponents that are found in works for older users. For instance, one of the antagonists in the *JumpStart* line is a snail named

Dr. O. Senior producer Diana Pray described him to me as "spineless, armless, slimy and silly, sort of a family-friendly villain." She told me that research had shown that kids really like to have bad guys in their games, and that parents didn't mind as long as the characters weren't evil. As with *JumpStart*, the bad guys in the Kutoka's children's titles are done with a light touch. In the *Didi and Ditto* games, for example, the antagonist is a wolf, but not a vicious, carnivorous one. This wolf happens to be a vegetarian, and he's a little embarrassed about his unusual food preferences.

Even humorous opponents fill an important function:

- They help sharpen the conflict.
- They supply obstacles.
- They pit the protagonist against a force that is easy to comprehend.

CREATING WORTHY OPPONENTS

Just as the time spent developing your protagonist pays off in a more engaging product, so does the time invested in creating your antagonists. Well-drawn antagonists, especially ones that are not stereotypes, can give your work depth and richness. In interactive media, opponents are almost always violent and evil characters who cannot be overcome except by the use of physical violence. But is it inevitable that they must follow this model? Certainly not if we follow the examples set in traditional storytelling.

For instance, in romantic comedies, the antagonist can be an otherwise nice individual who just happens to cause the protagonist a great deal of trouble. The antagonist in this case is often the love interest of the protagonist. In domestic dramas, too, the protagonist is usually pitted against a mostly decent, likeable person, often a spouse or family member. Such adversarial relationships are the staple of novels, independent films, and TV sitcoms and soap operas. They demonstrate that opponents do not have to be villainous or pose a physical threat in order to be compelling.

Here are a few other factors to keep in mind when you are creating an opponent for your protagonist:

- For maximum sizzle, make your antagonist and protagonist evenly matched. If your opponent is too menacing or overpowering, the protagonist's struggle will seem hopeless, and the users will be tempted to give up. On the other hand, if the antagonist is too weak, users will lose interest, perceiving the struggle as unchallenging.

- Provide your antagonist with an understandable motive to explain why he or she is blocking the hero's way. The more intensely motivated the antagonist, the more dramatic the story. And the motive must seem logical and justified, at least to the opponent.

- The more the hero knows about the opponent, and the more the opponent knows about the hero, the more interesting and personal the battle will be.

A MULTIPLE NUMBER OR SUCCESSION OF ANTAGONISTS

In some interactive works, the protagonist might be pitted against multiple opponents, one after another. The fiercest and scariest of these opponents will usually make an appearance right toward the end of a level or other segment of the work, and must be defeated in order for the player to make further progress in the story. In games, this formidable type of antagonist is known as a *boss monster*, and the fight between the boss monster and the player is known as the *boss battle*.

In works with a succession of antagonists, creative teams sometimes cut corners and make all of these bad guys practically indistinguishable from one another (nearly identical enemy soldiers or werewolves, for example). However, projects are far more interesting when each opponent is unique and intriguing.

OTHER TYPES OF NPCS

Antagonists are by no means the only type of NPCs to be found in digital storytelling. They can also be allies of the protagonist (friends, family members, fellow warriors) and neutral characters (shopkeepers, customers, drinkers in a bar). NPCs often serve the same purpose as the minor characters in a movie or TV show, though they may also have specialized functions in digital works that do not exist in traditional narratives, such as helper characters you can call on when you are stuck or have a question.

NPCs serve many functions. They populate a virtual world, provide clues, serve as gatekeepers, add color, and supply comic relief. They can also act as employers, providing users with a way to earn money and an incentive to perform particular actions.

Even minor characters, if well developed, can help inject richness and originality into a project. Just as with a succession of opponents, it is a wasted opportunity to have a group of minor characters—be they hairy monsters, little bears, or school kids—all resemble each other. To help illustrate this point, there's a wonderful story about the making of the Disney classic, *Snow White and the Seven Dwarfs*. Evidently, Walt Disney was originally planning to make all the dwarfs alike; they'd all just be little old men. But then he decided to give them each a name that reflected something about them and he dubbed them Sleepy, Dopey, Sneezy, Bashful, Happy, Doc, and Grumpy. Suddenly these little guys sprang to life and each became a vivid individual in his own right. Many adults can still remember and name these beloved characters long after having seen the movie in childhood.

INTELLIGENT CHARACTERS

Within the vast population of nonplayer characters, just as within the human population, you can find a great range of mental capabilities. On the low end, NPCs can be extremely dumb; on the high end, they can be impressively bright. The dumbest of the computer-controlled characters do not have the ability to communicate and do not have variable behavior. In the middle range, users and characters can "converse" with each other, though the ability of the NPCs to understand and react is limited. But on the smartest end of the scale, we have characters who seem to understand human language and who respond in a life-like way to what the users are saying to them. Characters who behave in a life-like way are said to possess *artificial intelligence*.

The very first of these seemingly human characters was a "virtual psychiatrist" named *ELIZA*. She was created in the mid-1960s by Joseph Weizenbaum, who at the time was a professor of computer science at MIT. He programmed ELIZA to meet the rigorous standards of AI set in 1950 by Alan Turing. In what is now known as the "Turing Test," both a human and a computer are asked a series of questions. If the computer's answers cannot be distinguished from the human's, the computer is regarded as having AI.

ELIZA, the intelligent character that Professor Weizenbaum created, would ask the user probing questions much like a real psychiatrist, and she would comment on the user's responses in a surprisingly thoughtful and life-like way, often with questions of her own. ELIZA did not actually appear on the screen but manifested herself only through the typed questions and comments she would send to the user. Nevertheless, she was evidently so convincing that the people who interacted with her, including the professor's own secretary, were convinced that ELIZA truly understood them.

STRANGE BUT TRUE: BEATING THE TURING TEST

Although the Turing Test was first proposed by Alan Turing in 1950, humans have rarely beaten the computer. However, Charles Platt managed to beat it in 1994 by displaying such unpleasant human characteristics as being obnoxious, moody, and irritable. And Brian Christian managed to beat it and be named "the Most Human Human" in 2009 by employing very human-like conversational techniques: finishing someone else's sentence and answering a question before the judge has completed asking it. Thus, at least for now, humans who compete against the computer need not worry about their mastery of facts or their mathematic abilities. They just need to figure out how to display uniquely human attributes, as unpleasant as they might be.

CHATTERBOTS

ELIZA gave birth to a new kind of digital character, the *chatterbot*—in other words, a bot (artificial character, short for robot) with whom you can chat. Dozens of chatterbots "live" on the Internet and are available to converse around the clock. You chat with them by typing in your part of the conversation, and they respond either by typing back or by speaking. And unlike ELIZA, who was invisible, many of these contemporary chatterbots have an animated presence on the screen.

Among those that I have conversed with is *A.L.I.C.E.*, who lives on the website of the Artificial Intelligence Foundation. During a recent rather mundane chitchat about the weather,

I mentioned that we were having a hot day where I was. She surprised me by asking if we were experiencing global warming. Pretty smart! Another is Cybelle, who lives in AgentLand, which she describes as being high in the skies of cyberspace. She apologized for misunderstanding one of my questions, explaining that her botmaster was still working on her brain (unfortunately, according to a chatbots website, Cybelle is no longer available). The most surreal chatterbot of all is God, with whom you can converse by visiting a website called *iGod*. God tells me he is a chatterbot "created by Myself" and goes on to say that he is a "flawless entity."

There are also animated bots who "live" on Twitter and who are activated by words triggered by other Tweets. Most of these Twitter bots deliver spam, but sometimes people create these bots for humorous or philosophical purposes.

SYNTHETIC CHARACTERS

When a character can "understand" the words the user freely types or says, and is able to respond appropriately, it is called *natural language interface*. Sometimes characters with this capacity are fully animated and highly life-like, unlike the more cartoony chatterbots on the Internet. These realistic intelligent beings are called synthetic characters.

Some of these synthetic characters have been put to work in military training simulations made for the US Army. Unlike ELIZA and her kin, these synthetic characters are capable of a wide range of behaviors, and their backgrounds, personalities, and motivations are developed in depth in much the same way as major characters are developed for feature films and television scripts.

The goal is to make these synthetic characters as life-like as possible, and to make the exchanges between them and the user feel emotionally authentic. These synthetic characters have individual attitudes and agendas, and their behavior toward the trainee is influenced by the conversations between them. If the trainee handles the conversation in one way, the attitude of the synthetic character might possibly change from cordial to hostile, but if it goes a different way, the character becomes extremely cooperative.

The holy grail of natural language interface is *voice recognition*. Voice recognition allows the user to talk in a normal way instead of typing, and the character responds orally, thus duplicating a human conversation. Though voice recognition exists, it is still far from perfect. To have a truly realistic conversation with a synthetic character, four goals must be accomplished:

1. The synthetic character (actually, the computer) has to be able to understand what a user is saying.

2. The synthetic character (the computer) has to be able to formulate and express a verbal response.

3. The synthetic character must look convincing while speaking, with the lip movements in sync with the words and with appropriate facial expressions.

4. The synthetic character must sound convincing, with natural inflections and speech rhythms.

Despite the challenges of voice recognition, Apple has managed to develop a fairly successful voice recognition "personal assistant" named *Siri* who lives on their mobile devices.

Siri performs tasks much like a concierge, making dinner reservations for you and buying you the movie tickets you've requested. Although at this time Siri does not have an animated presence, she can not only understand your requests or questions but will also helpfully answer you.

STRANGE BUT TRUE: TAKING "LIFE-LIKE" TO THE OUTER EDGE

While most digital characters are total fabrications of the imagination, the technology now exists to recreate the images, voices, and personalities of real people, including those who have passed away. In 2007, Orville Redenbacher, the popcorn guru, became the first digital character to rise from the dead. He was reconstructed 12 years after his demise by the well-known special effects house, Digital Domain, enabling him to pitch his beloved popcorn in TV commercials once again.

CREATING CHARACTERS FOR AN INTERACTIVE ENVIRONMENT

Creating complex and dimensional characters is more challenging in digital storytelling than it is for works of linear media, since we don't have a number of the same techniques available to us. For example, in films and TV shows, we can cut away to scenes the protagonist is not part of, and during these scenes we can learn important things about our main character by listening to what other characters are saying about him. But cutaways are not usually possible in interactive narratives since the protagonist and the user are often the same. In addition, the scenes and dialogue exchanges in interactive media tend to be short, leaving little room to reveal subtle character traits.

Furthermore, because events in interactive narratives do not occur in a fixed sequence, it is extremely difficult to portray a *character arc*, a process during the course of the story in which the protagonist grows and changes. In linear stories, for example, the heroine may go from being self-centered and egotistical to becoming a loving and caring individual, or the hero may go from cowardly to brave. Such change is a staple element of linear drama, but the protagonists in interactive narratives tend to remain essentially unchanged from the beginning to end.

Despite these challenges, however, it is possible to create dimensional, original, and evolving characters for works of digital storytelling, and, as we will see, it is also possible to portray dramatic character arcs.

TECHNIQUES FOR DEVELOPING MEMORABLE CHARACTERS

As we have noted, works of digital storytelling benefit when they are populated by dynamic, unique, and memorable characters. Here are seven pointers that can help you create them:

1. *Develop character biographies.* Invest time in working out the backstories and psychological profiles of each of your main characters. What are their personal and

professional histories? What are their hopes and fears? What kind of world do they live in, and how do they (or do they not) fit into this world? Though you may never use most of this information, it will help you develop rich and interesting characters.

2. *Motivate your characters.* Your protagonist, antagonist, and other important characters should have clear goals. This will energize them and make them understandable. What are they striving for and why is it so important to them?

3. *Make them vivid.* Interactive media does not leave any room for subtlety. Your characters' most important traits should shine through clearly. For models, study comic strips, graphic novels, and animated movies, all of which use shorthand techniques to convey character.

4. *Avoid stereotypes, or alternatively, play against them.* Stereotypes can make your work seem predictable and bland. Either avoid them completely or take a familiar stereotype and give it a twist it. For example, make your mad scientist a little old lady, or have your tough enemy solider be an expert on French champagne.

5. *Give characters a distinct look.* The appearance of your characters can telegraph a great deal about them. Consider their body language, how they hold themselves, and how they move (arms clenched to their bodies, stooped over a walker, a cocky swagger). Their clothing can also provide clues, as can the objects they typically have with them.

6. *Make them fun.* Not all characters can be humorous, but people do love characters that are amusing. A droll appearance, an eccentric quirk, or an amusing way of speaking will help characters stand out. Be aware, however, that "fun" and "cute" are not necessarily the same thing. Cute characters may feel too young to teenagers, though they tend to be popular with all age groups in Asia.

7. *Give them a standout name.* Some designers are fervent in their belief that a catchy name is critical. While not all popular characters have arresting names, we can find some distinctive ones from the world of video games, including Duke Nukem, Max Payne, Earthworm Jim, and Sonic the Hedgehog. Certainly a memorable name can't hurt.

ADAPTING CHARACTERS FROM ANOTHER MEDIUM

Frequently, a character who is "born" in one medium—a novel, a movie, a TV show, a comic book, or even a board game—will be ported over to a work of interactive entertainment. Such an adaptation calls for careful handling, especially if it involves a well-known figure. The primary consideration is to be as faithful as possible to the original. Otherwise, you risk disappointing the character's fans.

One company that is familiar with this adaptation process is Her Interactive, which develops the *Nancy Drew* mystery titles. Each title is based on one of the beloved novels in the Nancy Drew novels, books that have been popular with young girls since 1930. By transporting Nancy Drew from a 1930s-era print series to a contemporary interactive game, Her Interactive has managed to retain Nancy Drew's core personality and values while updating her devices. Yes, Nancy now has a laptop and a cell phone, but she still has the same spunky personality and the same enthusiasm for sleuthing she had decades ago.

CONSTRUCTING A CHARACTER ARC

Even though the protagonists in most works of digital entertainment do not grow or change, such static characters are not inevitable. Several techniques can be employed to show your hero or heroine learning, evolving, and changing—in other words, undergoing the emotional transformation that is characteristic of a character arc.

One technique is to employ the structure of your work to your advantage. This works particularly well if your narrative is broken into levels or other progressive units and your protagonist must overcome specific challenges in each level in order to progress to the next structural level. This type of structure is typical of video games and you can use it to show your protagonist changing in small increments level by level as he or she advances through the story.

For example, in a video game I worked on recently, the player starts out as a mercenary only interested in his own welfare and getting his job done, no questions asked. But in each level the player learns a little more about his corrupt bosses and their sinister objectives, and by the end of the game, if he survives, he is transformed into a true hero, willing to sacrifice his own life in order to defy the immoral organization he works for. He undergoes a character arc worthy of a first class film, evolving from a cynic to a highly altruistic individual.

A second way to build in a character arc is to allow your user-protagonist to attain new strengths or attributes by earning them through succeeding at certain challenges, by trading with other players for them, or by buying them. This is a common device in video games and MMOGs. Although it is primarily used in settings which feature physical challenges, quests, and combats, there's no reason why it couldn't be used in other types of digital storytelling. For example, consider an interactive drama about a young man who is poor and uncouth but extremely ambitious. You could give him a series of challenges, which, if he succeeds at them, would enable him to acquire a smoother set of social skills, a higher degree of business savvy, and a more ruthless way of dealing with people, along with a better wardrobe and a country club membership. Ultimately, by the time he has attained the success he has dreamed of—becoming a rich and powerful CEO and marrying a beautiful socialite—he would have undergone a significant character transformation.

A third technique is one that is employed in interactive training projects, particularly ones focusing on interpersonal skills. For example, after working through a module on dealing with disgruntled customers, the trainee takes part in a simulation calling for encounters with a series of rude, demanding customers. By handling these situations well, the trainee demonstrates the mastery of the new skills. The protagonist in such cases is a real person, not a fictional character; but even so, this technique could be used in story-based environments to test out new skills and demonstrate change.

EMERGENT BEHAVIOR

In certain extremely sophisticated works of digital storytelling, computer-controlled characters may act in ways that go beyond the things they have been specifically programmed to do. At moments like these, they almost seem to have an inner life and be capable of human thought. Janet Murray, in *Hamlet on the Holodeck*, describes this as *emergent behavior*.

As she explains it (pp. 239–242), a character is capable of emergent behavior when we give it a repertoire of actions, motivations, and behaviors. Programmed with a large cluster of these attributes, each one simple in itself, an NPC is capable of performing in complex and unexpected ways. Sometimes these behaviors may seem very reasonable and understandable and sometimes they may seem ludicrous.

According to Murray, the more abilities we program into our characters, the more unpredictable they can become, and the more apt to surprise us. A character programmed to do only one thing—toss snowballs, for example—can be counted on to only toss snowballs. But if we program a character to whistle at women, steal food when feeling hunger, fear men in uniform, and to run fast, we have a character capable of acting in some extremely interesting ways.

Procedural animation is, along with motion-capture and a few other techniques, a way to endow characters with life-like behavior and a wider range of actions. In procedural animation, characters are generated on the fly, in real time, based on the principles of physics, rather than being rigidly pre-rendered. To make such a character, the animator provides a set of rules and initial conditions—in other words, a procedure.

At this point in time, works containing these life-like kinds of characters are found primarily in academic computer labs at places like MIT and New York University. However, it is tantalizing to think of being able to employ them in works of digital storytelling.

DIALOGUE AND OTHER FORMS OF VERBAL COMMUNICATION

Characters in movies, plays, and TV shows communicate their thoughts and feelings most directly through dialogue—the verbal exchanges they have with other characters. Dialogue is used to advance the story and to supply critical information necessary for understanding it. It's also a way to gain insight into the characters, their relationships, and their feelings about each other.

In documentaries and educational programs, dialogue spoken "voice over" by a narrator can be used to impart, inform, and act as an unseen tutor.

Dialogue in interactive media entertainment fills exactly the same role, and serves other functions as well. It can be used to:

- welcome users to a program;
- explain the program's interface;
- provide help functions; and
- coach and correct the user in an educational or training program.

In interactive media, not only do verbal communications serve more functions than in linear media, but we also have a more varied communications palette to work with. For one thing, characters can speak directly to the user, which makes for a far more personalized experience. And for another thing, the user can have an active part in dialogue exchanges.

But in addition to dialogue, we have many other forms of verbal communications we can use, written as well as oral. In terms of oral communications, not only do we have dialogue exchanges but player characters can also "turn on" a TV or radio and hear a news broadcast that contains key information. Characters also communicate through telephone calls—and often users themselves, as the protagonist, can place the calls and get phone messages from NPCs.

In terms of written communications, player characters can find and read old newspaper clippings, diaries, letters, and documents of every kind, all of which can provide important information about characters and events. They may also be able to read a character's emails and computer files, even "deleted" ones. In addition, fictional characters may have their own Web pages and blogs and social media pages and posts, which can offer excellent insights into their personalities and motivations. They can also send users emails, faxes, and text messages to their cell phones. By using contemporary methods of communications as part of a story, we have an abundance of new ways that characters can tell us about themselves.

CLASSIC DIALOGUE

Despite all these new ways of communicating, classic dialogue—a verbal exchange between two or more characters—is still a supremely important tool in most forms of digital storytelling. It is a tool that has been refined and shaped though centuries of use. Even Aristotle, in his typically pithy way, offered some good pointers on writing effective dialogue. In the *Poetics* (Chapter XI, Section 16), he explained that dialogue is "the faculty of saying what is possible and pertinent in a given circumstance." In other words, the character's lines should be believable and reveal only what is possible for him or her to know. And the speech should not ramble; it should be focused on the matter at hand.

In addition to Aristotle, we can learn about dialogue from modern-day screenwriters. One of the most valuable things they can teach us is to use dialogue sparingly, only when there is no other means of conveying the information. "Show," they always advise, "don't tell." But when screenwriters do use dialogue, they make sure the exchanges are brisk and easy to understand. They use simple, clear words, knowing this is not the place to show off one's vocabulary. And they break the exchanges between characters into short, bite-sized pieces, because long speeches make an audience restless. These are all practical principles we can port over to digital media.

DIALOGUE IN DIGITAL STORYTELLING

Writers and producers in interactive media have discovered that dialogue needs to be even leaner than it is in traditional media. Users become impatient with long stretches of speech; they want to move on to the action or gameplay. Furthermore, interactive dialogue doesn't lend itself very well to subtlety. In traditional media, when actors say a line of dialogue, we look at their faces for an indication of their emotional state. But the computer-generated animation in most digital programs is usually not up to the task of conveying shades of emotion. Thus, we are better off using more direct language than we would in a play or film.

In interactive media, exposition can be a particular challenge. Exposition is information that is essential for the understanding of the story. It includes the relationships of your characters to each other, salient facts about their backstory, and their goals. Many writers are tempted to dump a huge amount of exposition in one speech, very near the beginning of a work, and are relieved at having disposed of it. But beware! When characters reel off a big lump of exposition, the speech sounds unnatural. Furthermore, it brings everything to a halt while it is being delivered. The trick is to work it in naturally, in small doses. And if you can find ways other than dialogue to slip in some of this exposition, all the better.

When dialogue is written as text rather than spoken, we have additional limitations. We don't have the cues available to us that an actor's voice would give us, so it is difficult to suggest nuances such as irony or sarcasm. Written dialogue also rules out some common devices available in oral speech. How do you have a character angrily interrupt another? How do you show a character speaking with hesitation? How can you have two characters excitedly talking at the same time?

Though dialogue in interactive media, whether written or spoken, has certain limitations, it also offers us a tremendous opportunity: the user/player character can actually participate in it. Interactive dialogue can be done in one of several ways.

Some works of digital storytelling support natural language interface, which, as we saw earlier in this chapter, gives the user the opportunity to type a line of dialogue, or speak it, and an NPC will respond in a believable and appropriate way.

Other works of digital storytelling utilize a technique called a *dialogue tree*, in which the player character or user is presented with several lines of dialogue to choose from. Each line will trigger a different response from the NPC being addressed and in some cases may even lead the user or player character down different narrative paths. For example, let's say the player character is walking along the street of a virtual city and encounters a scruffy beggar. The beggar says to the player: "Say, friend, can you spare some change?" The player can now pick one of the following replies:

Choice A: "Well, sure, here's a few bucks. Go get yourself something to eat." (In which case, the beggar makes a sweeping bow and thanks the player profusely.)

Choice B: "No. Can't. I'm in a rush." (In which case, the beggar says sarcastically, "Yeah, you have a nice day, too.")

Choice C: "Are you kidding?! You panhandlers make me sick! Go get a job like the rest of us!" (In which case, the beggar whips out a knife and threatens to stab the player, saying, "Yeah? Well, how do you like this for a job?")

Choice A, furthermore, might result in the beggar giving the player an important piece of information, while Choice B might have no consequences, and Choice C might have disastrous consequences, or, on the other hand, might trigger a surprise twist.

For another example of a dialogue tree, see Chapter 11.

In some dialogue trees, the line chosen by the user may be spoken aloud by his avatar and the character who is being addressed will reply out loud as well. But in some cases, the whole exchange is done in text. Sometimes we don't hear the avatar speak the line, though we do hear the NPC's response.

As a third possibility, the user can select from a choice of attitudes and intentions rather than lines of dialogue, a technique that we will call, for lack of a commonly used term, an *attitude selection*. The player's choices in the beggar scenario, for example, might be "kind and obliging," "brusque," or "hostile." We will then hear our avatar speak a line matching the attitude we selected and the NPC react accordingly. Usually the types of choices given for attitudes or intents are provocative, and are designed to elicit a strong response from the NPC.

In terms of the user's part of the exchange, the important question is how this dialogue will impact the narrative. Will it have consequences, and if so, how profound might they be? This varies greatly from project to project. In some cases, the impact is minimal to none. Though there's an illusion of interactivity, the dialogue choices don't have any effect on the story. This is a weak use of interactivity and a meaningless form of agency. But in other cases, the choices have a significant impact on the narrative. Though this sort of interactive storytelling is more challenging to create, it results in a far more robust project than one with inconsequential dialogue.

GUIDELINES FOR VERBAL COMMUNICATIONS

In addition to the points already mentioned, a few other basic guidelines can be helpful for writing effective dialogue and other forms of oral communications:

1. The lines a character speaks should be "in character." In other words, what the character says should reflect his personality, his age, his mood, his educational level, his profession, his goals, and his point of view.

2. If writing lines to be delivered by an unseen narrator, particularly an authority figure, you will want to use a somewhat formal style. But it is still important to use easy to understand words and to avoid complex sentence construction.

3. If writing for a telephone conversation, study how people talk on the phone. Such exchanges tend to be breezy and brief.

4. If writing a fictional news broadcast, study the format, pacing, and style of a professional news show. Also, listen to how the announcer "teases" an upcoming story.

5. Read what you have written out loud, listening for inadvertent tongue twisters, awkward phrases, unnatural speech, and overly long lines. Then cut and polish.

And here are a few guidelines for written communications:

1. If producing a document that one of the fictional characters supposedly wrote, the writing should be "in character," as with #1 above.

2. To make the document look authentic, include some typos or misspellings—but only if your character is likely to make such mistakes.

3. Keep the document short. People don't want to spend much time reading.

4. If writing an email, model the telegraphic style of real emails, and even include an *emoticon* or two. (An emoticon is a symbol used in text messages to express an emotion.)

5. In the same way, model any other specialized type of written communication—including Web pages, blogs, and newspaper articles—on real life examples. Strive to make the piece of writing as authentic looking as possible. From a user's point of view, part of the fun of stumbling across a fictional document is the sense that it could be "real."

THE ROLE OF EMOTION

In character-centric media like novels and movies, not only do the characters in the stories experience strong feelings, but so do the readers and viewers of these stories. Even comic animated films like the *Shrek* series portray characters with easily identifiable emotions, such as loneliness, fear of rejection, fright, and budding love. The audience easily identifies with their feelings and is moved by them. For some reason, however, most people do not associate interactive projects with deep emotion except, perhaps, for the feelings of tension and excitement and the thrill of combat aroused by the more violent types of video games.

Yet emotions can and do play a role in digital storytelling, and the contribution of emotions can be extremely significant. They can make the work seem less computerized and more real. They also add richness and dimension to the narrative. Above all, they make the experience more immersive and compelling, intensifying the connection between the user and the material.

Video games, the oldest form of digital storytelling, clearly have the power to arouse a wider repertoire of emotions than they are generally given credit for. In a groundbreaking study conducted by Hugh Bowen in 2005, *Can Video Games Make you Cry?*, 535 gamers were surveyed about the importance of emotions in games. The gamers described feeling a great many non-typical emotions while playing games. They reported strong empathy with many characters and being brought to tears when a favorite one died. They also admitted to becoming moved to tears by certain love stories, by the self-sacrifice of a brave heroine, and by the plight of a broken-hearted parent whose child has disappeared. Most surprisingly, two-thirds of them believed that video games presently excelled, or could excel in the future, in the emotional richness found in other major forms of art and entertainment.

The potential of digital storytelling to stir the emotions has sparked the interest of a number of people in the interactive media industry. Many of the people interviewed for this book were consciously developing ways to inject emotion into their work, and a number of the projects I investigated contained strong emotional elements.

Some experts interviewed for this book even asserted that when an interactive work is emotionally potent, it will make a greater impression on the user than an emotionally barren work, and that building emotion into an educational project can help people remember the instructional content for an extended period of time.

Some experimental training projects are specifically designed to rouse strong emotions in order to make a deep impression on trainees. One such project, *DarkCon*, is a virtual reality simulation designed to train US soldiers on how to conduct a surveillance mission. This mission is extremely dangerous, but to make the simulation even more frightening and life-like, it is enhanced by some cutting-edge technology. These include a *rumble floor* (a floor that vibrates at appropriate times, such as when there is an explosion) and a *scent necklace* (a device that emits certain smells, like gunpowder).

Jacquelyn Ford Morie, who is producing this project, explained to me that making the simulation emotionally powerful was a deliberate and stated goal. "Studies show you remember emotionally charged events better than neutral ones," she said. So important is putting an emotional bang into *DarkCon* that Morie has actually designed what she calls an "emotional score," a document not unlike a musical score. It maps out the high and low points the participant can experience during the simulation—including feelings of anxiety as well as feelings of relief. The emotions are paced for maximum impact (see Figure 6.5).

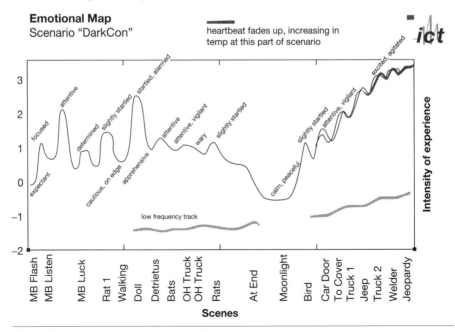

Figure 6.5 The emotional score of *DarkCon*, a VR simulation, maps out the feelings a participant should experience at each point in the story. Image courtesy of Jacquelyn Ford Morie.

Though the *DarkCon* scenario is designed to induce feelings of tension and fear, Morie believes many other types of emotions could be incorporated into a simulation and could also have a powerful impact. She has also worked on another VR project, *Memory Stairs*, that centers on an entirely different set of emotions, such as nostalgia and tenderness (for more on this work, please see Chapter 22).

CONCLUSION

As we have seen, characters in interactive dramas can be every bit as vivid and interesting as those in traditional media. However, when we develop fictional beings for our projects, we have to ask ourselves questions we'd never need to ask in creating a traditional story, and such questions are never simple to answer. They are among the most demanding issues that we have to deal with in creating a work of digital entertainment. But when they are addressed thoughtfully, and the necessary time is invested in working them out, they can help us produce outstanding characters who in turn can make the narratives they are in truly memorable.

There's every reason to think that interactive narratives, containing characters and storylines as they do, should be able to be as emotionally rich as traditional narratives. Perhaps it is even possible for an interactive work to induce the ultimate emotional experience that Aristotle described in his analysis of drama: the feeling of catharsis, the profound sense of release. After all, the creators of interactive stories have a powerful tool that wasn't available to Greek dramatists: immersiveness. Our "audience"—our users—can actually step inside the story world and experience it in a highly personal way. With immersiveness and the other tools at our disposal, we have the potential to produce highly charged works of entertainment, should we choose to do so.

IDEA-GENERATING EXERCISES

1. Create two characters for an interactive work, a protagonist and antagonist, coming up with brief descriptions of each. What is it that your protagonist most wants, and why is the antagonist standing in the way? Try, however, to avoid using the familiar good versus evil model or the need for either one to resort to violence. Instead, strive to invent an antagonist who has some positive qualities, though has some reason to create trouble for the protagonist.

2. Using the same antagonist, come up with three characters who might act as his or her assistants. Do a brief character description of each, striving to make each unique and different from each other, as Disney did with *Snow White and the Seven Dwarfs*.

3. Take your protagonist from Exercise #1 and describe how this character might change from the start of the work to the end. In other words, what kind of character arc might this character experience? Discuss how you could show this transformation in an

interactive narrative, using one of the techniques described in this chapter for portraying a character arc.

4. What emotions is your protagonist likely to experience in this conflict with the antagonist? What could add even more emotional richness to this clash between the two characters?

5. Write an interactive dialogue exchange between your protagonist and antagonist, using a dialogue tree. For reference, see the Dick and Jane script in Chapter 11.

CHAPTER 7

Structure in Digital Storytelling

How is it possible to organize an experience that is all about free choice … how can you order something that is supposed to be nonlinear?

What kinds of structural "building blocks" exist in interactive media, and how can you use them to help build a work of digital storytelling?

What do you need to know or decide before you begin to structure a new project?

STYROFOAM PEANUTS

Structure: it is the unseen but all-important method of organizing a work of digital storytelling. It functions much like the bones in our bodies. Without our internal skeleton, we would have no shape, and our flesh would have nothing to support it. In a work of digital storytelling, the structure not only supports the narrative and gaming elements but also helps determine the nature of the interactivity.

Structure should not be confused with plot. Plot consists of the basic beats of a story, the "what happens next." Structure is the framework of the story. It connects the basic pieces of the narrative and ensures that the work flows in a satisfying way.

Without question, structure is one of the most daunting aspects of creating a work of interactive entertainment. Yes, character design and the issues that go with it create a host of challenges, as we saw in the previous chapter, but the questions springing up around structure can make one's head spin. How do you organize and shape an experience that is supposed to be free-flowing? How do you create a pathway through a nonlinear environment, and when is trying to do that even a good idea? Where do you find usable structural models, when a great many people in the field can't even articulate the models that they are currently using? When you're dealing with interactive structure, it can be extremely hard to find anything solid enough to grasp hold of—it can feel somewhat akin to trying to construct a house out of Styrofoam peanuts.

The job of designing the structure falls to specialists—the game designers in the game world, the information architects of the Internet and information-based projects, and the engineers and computer programmers and designers and inventors and producers in other fields of interactive media. But even if you are not tasked with designing the structure yourself, that doesn't mean you can ignore the topic. That's because every member of the creative team needs to have a basic understanding of the framework that's being used in order to do his or her job. Furthermore, each member of the creative team has valuable input to give, since each is viewing the structure from a unique professional vantage point.

Curiously enough, considering that structure is such an essential aspect of creating an interactive project, the language we have to describe it is still largely unfixed. Even basic words like "node" or "level" may be used one way at company A and in quite a different way at company B. As for company C, it is very possible they have no language at all to cover structural terms. Yes, they will probably be able to describe the structure in a loose sort of way, but if you really want a clear understanding of it, you'll have to work your way through several of their projects to learn how they are put together.

Fortunately, we do have some basic structural concepts and models that we can use as a starting place to discuss structure. Furthermore, the fundamental questions of structure are essentially the same across the board, for all types of interactive media. And, as always, we can look to traditional linear narratives for some initial guidance.

THE BASIC BUILDING BLOCKS OF TRADITIONAL DRAMA

Structure plays an important role in every type of narrative, whether the work is linear or interactive, and it is built in the same fundamental way across all kinds of stories as well. Small units of material are assembled into a greater, interconnected whole. The units are the basic building blocks of the work, and they may be combined together to form still larger building blocks and these, in turn, are assembled and become the final product.

In a linear work of drama, such as a movie or play, the smallest building blocks would be the story beats. They'd then be organized into scenes, and from there into acts. If we look at classic drama, as we did in Chapter 5, we see that Aristotle believed that every effective theatrical work contained three acts, with Act I being the beginning, Act II being the middle, and Act III being the end.

Although Aristotle was talking about classic Greek drama when he described the three-act structure, the same basic structure can be applied to video games and other forms of interactive media as well, as long as the work has at least a thread of a story. In other words, interactivity

NOTES FROM THE FIELD: THE THREE-ACT STRUCTURE IN MOTION PICTURES

Dr. Linda Seger, an internationally known script consultant and author of many books on screenwriting, describes the three-act structure this way: "In the first act, a catalyst begins the action—an event that gets the story going and orients the audience to genre, context, and story. The middle act (which is usually twice as long as Acts One and Three) develops and explores conflict, relationships, and theme, using action and events (whether large or small) to move the story forward. The final act is the consequence of the work of Act One and Act Two, paying off all the development, strategizing, and struggle that went on throughout Acts One and Two."

and the three-act structure are not mutually exclusive; on the contrary, this structure still plays an important role even in the most cutting-edge kinds of storytelling. Sometimes the three acts can be hard to spot and they may not be connected in a sequential order, but if you study the work closely, the three acts will shine through.

At some companies, the creative teams are highly aware of the three-act structure and use it consciously. In other organizations, however, it may be employed in a less conscious fashion, although it still shapes their products. After all, we are inundated almost since birth in story-based material organized around the three acts. How could this degree of exposure not affect our interactive storytelling?

Her Interactive, the company that makes the *Nancy Drew* mystery-adventure games, finds the three-act structure a highly useful organizational tool. Max Holechek, who at one time was the company's Creative Director, told me that they definitely think in terms of a beginning, middle, and end. "We have to make sure there's a good story that keeps evolving," he said. "And the characters have to evolve in one way or another." He echoed many of the things Dr. Seger said about the function of the second act. "In the middle act we do things like up the dangers, or put in some plot twists, or add some intrigue," he said. "These things help keep the game fresh."

Quicksilver Software is another software developer that consciously employs the classic three-act structure. This company has developed dozens of strategy, simulation and action/role-playing games, including *Master of Orion 3*, *Invictus*, *Castles*, *Star Trek: Starfleet Command*, and *Shanghai: Second Dynasty*. Katie Fisher, a producer-designer for the company, told me without equivocation: "The three-act structure is the backbone of everything we do here." But she also noted that the nonlinear nature of games added a special wrinkle: "How you get to the plot points—that's where interactivity comes in." That, of course, is the critical question. How and where does the interactivity come in, and how do you structure it into your storyworld? How do you combine story and interactivity—and gaming elements, as well, if you are making a game—into one organic, seamless whole?

THE BASIC BUILDING BLOCKS OF INTERACTIVE NARRATIVES

In any type of narrative, in order to form a structure, you must work with both your smallest and largest building blocks. In interactive narratives, your smallest building blocks are your decision or action points—the places where the user can make a choice or perform an action. They are the equivalent of story beats in a linear narrative. Decision and action points are also known as *nodes*, although to make things especially confusing, node is also a term used for some types of macro units. In order to create your structure, you need to determine the kinds of things the users can do at each node. Can they pick things up? Shoot weapons? Converse with characters? Rearrange objects?

In some cases, users are given several specific options to choose from, in the form of a menu. For example, let's say we have a story in which the player character is a young woman, and let's say she's being followed down the street by an odd-looking man. A menu will pop up and present the user with three choices: A: the young woman can run, B: she can turn and confront the stranger, or C: she can ask a policeman for help. Each choice will result in a different outcome. Decision points are rarely so obvious, though. In most cases, the player is not given a menu of possibilities to select from. For instance, let's say our same player character, the young woman, has successfully dealt with the odd-looking man and is continuing down the street toward her destination. As she is walking along, a piece of paper flutters out of a window above her. She must decide whether to pick it up or to continue walking, and this is a decision point.

On the macro level, you'll need to work out the nature of your biggest units or divisions. In video games, where there is a relatively standardized approach to structure, the most common type of large division is the *level*. Each level takes place in a different setting and has a different group of NPCs and a different set of challenges. The player usually (but not always) works through the levels in sequential order. The challenges become more difficult as he or she ascends through the levels, with the ultimate challenges awaiting the player in the final level. Each level is much like a chapter in a book, and like a chapter, it needs to fulfill a meaningful role in the coverall game. In fact, each level can be regarded as a miniature game, with its own goals and challenges.

For a level to offer satisfying gameplay, make sense in terms of the narrative, and serve the overall game in a satisfactory way, certain things must be determined:

- What is its overall function in the game? (For example, to introduce a character, provide a new type of challenge, or introduce a plot point?)
- What is the setting of this level? (What does it look like; what features does it contain?)
- What NPCs will the player encounter here?
- What are the major challenges the player will face here, and where in this setting will they take place?

- What is the player's main objective in this level?
- What narrative elements will be revealed in this level?

Instead of levels, some games are instead organized by missions, where users are given assignments they must complete one at a time. But it is important to note that there are games that use an *open world* structure (discussed in detail in Chapter 15), where players are invited to move around freely. These games may have an overall goal, but they lack a linear structure. Players do not have to follow any set sequence to achieve the goal. So what kind of structure do such games use? Some of these games use a *world structure*, where the play space is divided into different geographical spaces, such as the different parts of a city or different locations in outer space, each with its own set of characters and challenges.

Still another type of organizational unit is the "module," which is often used in educational and training projects. Each module customarily focuses on one element in the curriculum or one learning objective. Yet other types of interactive projects may be divided into episodes, as in a Web series, or into chapters, as DVDs often are. Or, if this work is being made for the Internet, your macro units may be Web pages.

Once you know the type of large building blocks you'll be using, you can begin to determine the core content of each unit, what the user does in each one, and how many units you will have in all. You'll also be able to begin populating them with characters. Thinking in terms of large building blocks can help bring order to the organizational process.

THE IF/THEN CONSTRUCT

As we noted a little earlier, the decision or action points are the smallest building blocks of interactive narratives. These choices or actions will trigger specific events to happen during the narrative—sometimes immediately, sometimes further down the road. The logic system that determines the triggering of events is implemented using a piece of computer code called an *algorithm*. An algorithm determines such things as what the player needs to do before gaining access to "X" or what steps must be taken in order to trigger "Y." Algorithms are a little like recipes, but instead of the ingredients being foods, they are events or actions. For instance, an algorithm for opening a safe may require the player to find the secret combination for the lock, get past the growling guard dog, and dismantle the alarm system. Only then can the safe be opened.

Logic in digital storytelling is often expressed in *if/then* terms. If the player does "A," then "B" will happen. Another way of expressing the steps needed to trigger an event is through *Boolean logic*. Boolean logic is based on only two variables, such as 0 and 1, or true and false. It allows for only two possible outcomes for every choice (live/die; open/close; explode/not explode). A string of such variables can determine a fairly complex sequence of events. Boolean logic can be regarded as a series of conditions that determine when a "gate" is opened—when something previously unavailable becomes available, or when something previously undoable becomes doable.

Having only two possible options for each decision or action is also called *binary choice*. However, there's also a more subtle type of choice mechanism available, the *state engine* approach, which allows for a greater range of stimuli and responses instead of a simple if/then. Game producer Greg Roach, introduced in Chapter 4, described to me how a state engine works in a video game. In his sample scenario, the player wants to smash open a wooden crate with an axe, the one tool available to him. With binary choice, the crate could only exist in one of two possible conditions: broken or unbroken. It would remain unbroken until the user succeeded in smashing it. At that point, Roach said, its status would switch to broken.

"But a state engine approach works differently," Roach explained. "It tracks cumulative force and damage, allowing for a richer set of player choices. Each player can make a different set of choices and the state engine construct will respond appropriately. So a player who chips away at the crate with a pen-knife will take ten times longer to get it opened than a player who runs it over with a vehicle and breaks it open with a single move."

Thus, the state engine approach offers users a broader range of actions and responses than simple binary choice.

BRANCHING STRUCTURES

Many, if not most, interactive narratives still rely to a greater or lesser degree on the if/then construct, and this construct is the foundation of one of the most common structural models of digital storytelling: the *branching structure*. A branching structure is made up of a great many interconnected if/then constructs. It works a little like a pathway over which the user travels. Every so often, the user will come to a fork in the path—a decision or action point—which may offer several different choices. Upon selecting one, the user will then travel a bit further until reaching another fork, with several more choices, and so on. Thus, this structure is extremely similar to the old *Choose Your Own Adventure* books, described in Chapter 1. (To see a script using a branching structure, see Figure 11.2, *Dick and Jane*, in Chapter 11.)

The problem with a branching structure is that in a very short time it escalates out of control. After just two forks in the path, with three choices at each, you'd have racked up 13 possible choices, and by the third opportunity for choice, you'd have a total of 39 possible outcomes. Although the user would only experience three of them, your company will still have to produce the other 36, in case the user made a different selection. A branching structure like this squanders valuable resources (see Figure 7.1).

A Duck Has an Adventure (http://e-merl.com/stuff/duckadv.html) is a simple interactive story that employs a branching structure. It is a good example of how the different branches can take the story in wildly different directions. The story has 16 possible endings.

Designers employ a number of techniques to rein in runaway branching, some of which, like the *faux choice*, offer little or no meaningful agency. In a faux choice construct, the user is presented with several options, but no matter which is picked, the end result will be the same. Runaway branching can also be contained by *cul-de-sacs*, *loop backs*, and *barriers*. Cul-de-sacs are areas off the main story path that the user is free to explore, but these areas are walled in, and ultimately force the user back to the main story path. In a loop-back construct, the user must return to a previously visited area in order to fulfill a task or acquire some necessary information. In a barrier construct, the user can only activate a choice or move forward by first succeeding at a "gateway" task, such as solving a puzzle.

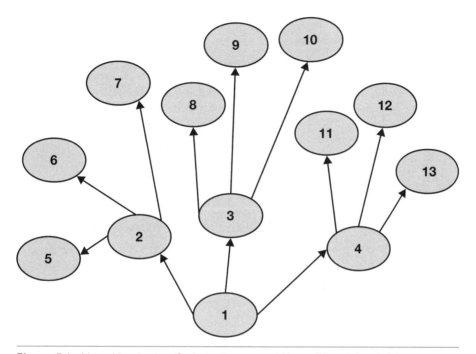

Figure 7.1 A branching structure. Such structures can quickly escalate out of control. Image courtesy of Terry Borst.

Some designers rein in runaway branching trees by constructing more modest branching "shrubs," each with a specific subgoal. The branching shrubs all link to the major story path, but the branching is more contained. For instance, the ultimate goal might be to save the princess in the tower. Subgoal number one requires that you poison the dragon (shrub #1); subgoal number two requires that you pass over the bridge guarded by ogres (shrub #2); and subgoal number three requires that you outwit the princess's evil stepsisters who are keeping her locked up (shrub #3).

Other designers strive for an illusive structural form called "bushiness," which offers a maximum amount of choice but which prevents unlimited branching by having many of the links share communal outcomes.

The branching structure is often used within large structural building blocks, such as levels, missions, and worlds.

THE CRITICAL STORY PATH

In works of digital storytelling, the underlying structure has a great impact on the overall user experience. Structures can range from quite restrictive in terms of choice to being extremely free-ranging. The structure for a particular project is typically determined by the type of interactive experience the designers want to provide.

If the goal is to allow users to be able to explore freely, interact with other users, and make up their own adventures, the structure will be designed for maximum openness and the least amount of restraint. But if the project is essentially a story-based one, such as an adventure game, a mystery, or a drama, it will need a fairly restrictive structure that invisibly nudges the user down a linear narrative passageway.

Many professionals within the new media industry refer to this linear passageway as the *critical story path*. This path contains everything the user must do or must discover in order to achieve the full story experience and reach a meaningful ending point.

The critical story path makes it possible to reveal key pieces of information in an incremental way and at an optimal time. It also facilitates dramatic intensity. With the critical story path, you can ratchet up the spookiness of a scary story by controlling when the player will see the shadowy figure outside the window, or hear the scurry of footsteps on the roof, or find the dead dog in the refrigerator. The critical story path can also be used to dramatize the protagonist's character arc. It is useful whenever you want certain things to happen in some rough order.

Devising the critical story path is a four-step process. To create one, you:

1. Make a list of all the *critical beats*—the things the users must experience or the information they must discover in order for the narrative to make sense and to build in an appropriate way.

2. Determine what needs to be conveyed through cut scenes.

3. Determine the essential actions the user must perform in order to trigger the critical beats.

4. Determine the optional interactive possibilities between the essential actions—things that might enrich the narrative or heighten the gameplay, but are not strictly necessary to make the story progress.

Her Interactive, which develops the *Nancy Drew* mystery-adventure games, is one of the software companies that utilizes a critical story path. Players can travel down this path in many different ways and can collect items and clues at their own pace, but they must perform certain actions in order to solve the mystery.

"We want to give players as much freedom to explore as possible," writer-producer Anne Collins-Ludwick told me. "But we also want to relate a story, so we have to move them from A to B to C." She said sometimes the methods to get the players to move down this path will be obvious, but sometimes they go on behind the scenes. "For instance," she said, "you might not be able to get inside a certain environment until you've done something else."

However, the company also wants to pace each adventure so players don't race down the critical story path too quickly, or else the experience won't feel like a game. Thus, they devise puzzles, activities, and various kinds of obstacles to heighten the gameplay and make the mystery more challenging to solve.

While the creative team of the *Nancy Drew* titles uses the term "critical story path," over at Quicksilver Software they use a different way to talk about the through-line for their games. Producer-designer Katie Fisher calls it a *malleable linear path*. She said: "Even though we use a three-act structure, we give the players lots of ways to get to the end. We want to avoid the need to hang things on one specific event to move the story forward. We don't know what order things will happen in, but we can say that five different things will happen before X happens."

STRUCTURAL MODELS THAT SUPPORT THE CRITICAL STORY PATH

An often-used structural model for the linear story path is *a string of pearls*. Each of the "pearls" is a world, and players are able to move freely inside each of them. But in order to progress in the story, the player must first successfully perform certain tasks. Sometimes they cannot enter a new pearl until every task in the prior one is completed; sometimes they can enter other pearls, but access to certain areas within them will be blocked (see Figure 7.2).

Figure 7.2 The string of pearls structure. With this type of structure, the player progresses through a series of worlds. Image courtesy of Terry Borst.

NOTES FROM THE FIELD: A ROPE WITH NODES

Game designer Greg Roach calls structures like the string of pearls *a rope with nodes*. He explains that the nodes offer a rich degree of interactivity, but they are strung together in a linear fashion. According to Roach's model, players can do three different things in each node:

- They must "eat their meat and potatoes"—a term he uses for tasks that must be performed in order for the story to proceed properly, make sense, and become emotionally satisfying. The "meat and potatoes" can be such things as acquiring objects or information, encounters with characters, or experiencing events.

- They can choose to have as much or as little "candy" as they like—by which he means they can do enjoyable things that enrich the story and add depth to the experience but which are not critical to the overall narrative success.

- They can activate triggers—they can do or encounter things that bring about a change in the mood, narrative structure, character attitudes, environment, or experience.

In this model, players cannot move to the next node until they have eaten all the meat and potatoes in the node they are currently in.

THE PASSENGER TRAIN MODEL

A number of other structures also channel users down a linear path, some more restrictive than others. Most are applicable both to story-based material and to non-fiction material. One that offers the least amount of freedom is *sequential linearity*, a structure that I prefer to call the *passenger train*. It was the model used in the first children's interactive storybooks. It is still used for this purpose, and is also commonly employed in interactive training applications. It is similar to the string of pearls structure.

In the passenger train model, users begin at the engine end of the train and work their way down car by car until they reach the caboose end. They can explore the interior of each car at will, but usually cannot leave until the program releases them—sometimes they must first listen to some narration, or watch some animation, or work through some exercises. They must also move in sequence; they cannot jump, say, from car number two to car number six. Once users reach the caboose, they are usually able to explore more freely. Many projects built on this model offer a menu to allow users to revisit a particular car or to go directly back to a specific game, activity, or exercise.

OTHER STRUCTURAL MODELS

If you look closely at interactive models, you might see that they fall into two broad groups, rounded and angular. Angular structures tend to channel users along a particular path and have a more linear core. On the other hand, rounded structures do not support much of a story thread, but do promote a great deal of freedom and exploration. Some structural models combine rounded and angular elements, and thus can combine narrative with a certain amount of freedom.

SPACES TO EXPLORE

Some people refer to an unrestricted, free-range environment as an *exploratorium*. I prefer to think of this structure as an *aquarium*, because it is so much like a three-dimensional fish bowl. Users can navigate through it in any direction, and though it may be dotted with "islands" of story elements, it is better suited for experiential interactive journeys or "scavenger hunt" types of experiences than for dramatic narratives.

The aquarium model is frequently found in MMOGs, which typically offer a number of free-ranging worlds through which players can journey. A MMOG universe can be vast in scale. Robert Pfister, senior producer of *EverQuest*, told me that his game contains about 220 adventure zones. It would take months for a player to visit them all. And Ben Bell, producer of the PlayStation2 version of *EverQuest*, said of MMOGs in general that: "Most are loosely structured in terms of plot and level design." He feels that in such games, setting is more important than the story, because "supporting thousands of players in a single game world is prohibitive to supporting a single story line." He said designers of these games generally convey a linear plot through suggestions in a handful of subplots. "Quests, items, and the movement of NPC populations are all tools that we use for plot exposition."

Some designers call the most free-form structures a *sandbox* or an *open world*, described above. They provide users with objects to manipulate and things to do, and they have spatial boundaries; sometimes they also have a specific end goal. Players are creating their own stories as they play. *The Sims* is a sandbox experience, as is *Minecraft*; virtual worlds like *Second Life* have many of the characteristics of the sandbox; and *Saints Row* and *Grand Theft Auto* are open world games.

Another structural model is *indexical storytelling*, as reported in *Gamasutra* by Leigh Alexander on September 25, 2012. The concept was developed by Clara Fernandez Vara and her team during the Singapore-MIT Gambit Game Lab. In such a work, users are tasked with the job of finding hidden objects, each of which represents a piece of a narrative, and then they must thread these objects together to form a story. Vara's team created a game in which players try to work out a mystery about a deceased composer, *The Last Symphony*, to demonstrate this concept. According to Vara, the play *Sleep No More*, described in Chapter 1, was an important influence on the development of the game.

Marie-Laure Ryan, in her book *Narrative as Virtual Reality*, describes an extremely free-form structure she calls *the complete graph*. In these works, each node can be connected to every other node, and all paths are bi-directional. In this type of structure, the user can move in any direction. It is hard, however, to imagine how it could be capable of sustaining any kind of narrative thread.

STRUCTURES THAT ARE MORE ANGULAR

Several basic structural models have been devised for works that have a narrative through line, though they also offer a certain amount of navigational freedom. These structures include the funnel, the pyramid, the coal mine, parallel worlds, and the hero's journey.

The hero's journey, described in Chapter 5, is one of the best known of these quasi-linear models. This type of work is structured around the classic myth about the youth who must survive and triumph over a number of terrible ordeals and is transformed by the experience. The classic journey contains 12 stages, so an interactive model using the hero's journey would incorporate a critical story path and could logically be broken into 12 levels or missions or "pearls on a string," although there could be less or more structural units.

Another model is the *funnel*, which is sometimes called a *pyramid* (a pyramid is essentially just an upside-down funnel). It is often used in games. In this structure, players start at the "fattest" end, where there is a great deal of freedom of movement. But as they work their way through the game and are nearing the conclusion, their choices become more constrained, and they also may be more challenging.

In interactive environments that call for users to "drill down"—a term frequently used in regard to the Internet—we can find several different types of structures. In general, however, they can be clustered together as *coal mine* models. The coal mine is most common on the Web, but it can be employed for any project that encourages a burrowing process for fictional or informational material. In a coal mine model, you gather new material via a series of links, and move through lateral as well as vertical passageways.

The parallel world, also known as *parallel streaming* or even *harmonic paths*, is another quasi-linear structure. It contains several layers of story, each set in its own virtual world, and the user can jump between them. Often each world is a persistent universe, meaning that events continue to unfurl there even when the user is not present. Since it is not possible to be in more than one world at a time, the player must carefully decide which to visit, because being in one of these places inevitably means missing out on events taking place in the others.

THE MODULAR STRUCTURE

As noted earlier, the modular structure is often used in education and training. These kinds of projects often open with a noninteractive introduction, and then the users are presented with a choice of modules, which they visit in any order. Modules within a single work may vary greatly in style, much like a variety show with different acts. Once all the modules have been visited and the required tasks in each have been completed, the program may end with a linear wrap-up or the user might be offered a "reward" activity.

At *JumpStart*, they refer to this structure as a *hub-and-spoke* model. The player starts from a central location (the hub), and all the modules radiate out from there (the spokes). This structure is extremely clear and simple to navigate, making it especially suitable for children's projects (see Figure 7.3).

Figure 7.3 The hub-and-spoke model is used here, in *JumpStart Advanced First Grade*. The modules, represented by the various structures, are accessed from the main screen, illustrated here. A reward activity is offered in the Race Arena, in the upper left corner. Image courtesy of Knowledge Adventure and used under license.

SOPHISTICATED STORY MODELS

Designers of interactive content have come up with a number of structural models that work particularly well in supporting complex interactive narratives.

One such structure is what I refer to as the *Rashomon* model. This model contains several versions of the same story, each version seen from the POV of one of the characters. The model resembles the Japanese movie *Rashomon*, described in Chapter 1, about a crime viewed by four people, each of whom saw it differently. In interactive narratives that use this model, the user can move between storylines to get a full picture of the incidents at the core of the story. Though it is primarily used for works of fiction, it has also been used in interactive documentaries, such as *What Killed Kevin?*, discussed in Chapter 14.

The model I call the *archeological dig* uses quite a different approach. The narrative in these works takes place over a long stretch of time, and the user digs down through these different time periods to reconstruct the story. In Chapter 21, we will be looking at works that utilize both the archeological dig model and the Rashomon model.

In *Hamlet on the Holodeck*, Janet Murray deconstructs a number of narrative models, some of which resemble ones already discussed here, though they go by different names.

Two, however, are quite different. The *rhizome* model takes its name from the field of botany, where it is used to describe an interconnecting root system. Murray applies this term to stories where each piece can be connected to every other piece, and where there is no end point and no way out. Thus, it is much like a maze. This model, she feels, is particularly good for journey stories and can offer many surprises, though navigating the rhizome can be challenging to the player.

The maze itself is an ancient concept and a key element in the Greek myth about the Minotaur: a ferocious creature who is part man and part bull. The Minotaur is kept confined in a labyrinth (a maze-like structure) on the island of Crete by King Minos. The labyrinth or maze is often a feature of cathedrals, such as Chartres in France, where people walk its paths as an act of meditation and prayer. In modern times, the maze has become a popular structural feature for video games and other digital works. In an article about mazes by Gabriella Marks (*Local Flavor* magazine, October 2012), she writes that it is clear "that the human psyche is drawn to these adventures and endless possibilities presented for playing hide-and-seek, for getting lost, for finding our way."

Another model Murray describes is the *electronic construction kit*. In this model, users are given a number of story components, like characters and settings, and they can use them to assemble their own narratives. It is an open-ended construct, with the user in control of how the story will unfold. *The Sims* would be a good example of this type of structure.

In *Narrative as Virtual Reality*, Marie-Laure Ryan describes two particularly interesting narrative models. One, which she calls *the hidden story*, contains two layers of narrative. The top layer contains clues to a story that took place in the past. The user explores this top layer to uncover the second layer, the hidden story, and to assemble the pieces of the hidden story into a coherent and linear whole. Although not specifically noted by Ms. Ryan, this type of structure is often used in alternate reality games (ARGs). In these games, players uncover clues to a deeper mystery and reassemble them to form a cohesive narrative, often working on the clues at the same time as the fictional characters in the game (for more on ARGs, please see Chapter 18).

Another model she offers is the *fractal structure*. "Fractal" is a mathematic term for a pattern that repeats itself endlessly in smaller and larger forms. Ryan uses this term in an interactive narrative context to describe a story that does not advance but instead expands. In the example she gives, a miniaturized version of the core story is presented right at the start. It grows in scope as the player interacts with it, but the essence of the story never changes.

Video game scholar Joris Dormans sees great potential in this model, which he discusses in an article called "Lost in a Forest," posted on the Game Research website. He feels that fractal stories contain many of the pluses found in other structures, but avoids some of the problems that are also characteristic of them. Like interactive stories with a fairly linear plot and clearly defined goal, the fractal story also has an ultimate destination, but it does not narrowly push the user toward it. And like structures that emphasize exploration, it offers a great deal of freedom, but without sacrificing the narrative elements. Thus it is a middle ground between the two ends of the spectrum: strict linearity on one hand, and unrestricted freedom on the other. It also supports replayability, because with each play, users can experience the story differently.

CREATING YOUR OWN STRUCTURAL MODEL

Sometimes no ready-made model exists for the type of interactive narrative you have in mind, and in cases like this, you need to invent your own structural model. I faced a situation like this when I was pitching a series of interactive stories for a children's website. I wanted a structure that contained a linear entrance and exit but that was interactive in the center. I thus came up with a model that I named the *python that swallowed a pig*. In this model, the head portion, or entrance to the story, is narrow, and the tail portion, which is the exit, is also narrow. But the middle is fat, and here is where the interactive events occur. Though you can experience these interior events in any order, you must be careful about your choices, or else you will not succeed in accomplishing your goal and will be forced to exit from the snake prematurely. Thus, the beginning and the end are essentially linear, while the middle is interactive, a model that combines the rounded and angular forms. This structure lends itself well to a goal-oriented narrative experience. Multiple pythons can be connected together in various ways to produce a more dimensional experience, somewhat like a lumpy string of pearls.

Another model I took the liberty of naming is one of my favorites: *the balloon man*. Like the python, it combines angular and rounded elements, but it is far more complex. The balloon man can be an effective vehicle for exploring psychological themes and revealing hidden facets of a character. It resembles a hand holding a cluster of strings, and every string is attached to a balloon—each a world in the balloon man's universe. Your mission begins in the hand, and from there you choose which string—or pathway—to move along. When you reach a balloon, you experience events much as you would in the interior of the snake, except that you are free to leave at any time. To visit another balloon, you must first travel back to the balloon man's hand and select another string. Each journey along the same string produces new experiences or yields new insights. Once you have neared your overall goal, the ultimate revelation or triumph often awaits you back in the balloon man's hand.

DETERMINING A STRUCTURE

It is one thing to talk about structure in an abstract way, and to examine a variety of models; it is an entirely different thing to decide which structure to use for a particular project or line of titles. Often, the decision is guided by practical considerations or by the type of experience the creative team wants to provide for the user.

Different factors come to the forefront at different software companies. For instance, at Training Systems Design, which makes interactive training programs, they regularly use a modular structure with an open architecture because it can accommodate a variety of ways of presenting material and multiple learning styles. Dr. Robert Steinmetz, the company's president and senior designer, told me they like to promote "discovery learning" rather than a tutorial approach. A modular structure with an open architecture lends itself well to this type of learning.

EXPERT OBSERVATIONS: WHY ONE STRUCTURE AND NOT ANOTHER?

The *JumpStart* edutainment games typically employ a hub-and-spoke structure, as noted earlier. When I asked Senior Producer Diana Pray why they use it, I was surprised to learn that the needs and desires of the ultimate purchasers—the parents—heavily factored into this choice. Of course, the needs and desires of the end-users—the kids—have also been given consideration. Of the hub-and-spoke structure Pray said: "It's an easy kind of navigation. We have tried more complex ways, but parents had trouble with them. They don't want to spend time showing the kids how to do the game. They want to cook dinner, do the laundry. They don't want to hear: 'Mom, I'm stuck!'"

And, she went on to say: "Kids don't like the computer to tell them what to do; they like to choose. They like a game that gives them the power to go where they want. If the kids don't like the style of gameplay in a particular module, they can go into another module. We don't force them along one story path."

Obviously, there is no "one size fits all" when it comes to structure. And in some cases, as we've seen, you might find that no off-the-shelf model will work for what you want to do, and it may be necessary to customize a unique structure for your project. Your decisions about structure will be determined, to a large extent, by the project itself. Here are some questions you can ask that will help guide you:

1. What platform or device is this project being made for, and what structures are most suitable for it?

2. What projects like it already exist, and what structural models do they use? What can you learn from them, in terms of where they work well and where they are weak?

3. What types of structures are your target audience likely to be comfortable with?

4. How important is it that the users move down a predetermined story, informational, or training path?

5. How important is it that users can navigate freely?

6. What kinds of choices will be offered?

7. What kinds of large building blocks will be most useful in organizing this project?

CONCLUSION

We have described a variety of structural models here, some widely recognized in the field, others not. Often professionals use different names to describe the same models. Perhaps, because of the evolving nature of digital media, we will never reach the point of having one standard set of models, each with a specific name and architectural form. And in some cases, it is left to the creative team to shape their own structures.

Fortunately, it is not necessary to completely start from scratch. We can study the models that are most frequently used, and we can deconstruct already-made projects to see how they work. And, as we begin to shape one of our own projects, we can be guided by its specific purpose and requirements. Once we do that, we will find that it is not as impossible as it might seem to give order to an experience that should, to the user, feel free of constraint. In actuality, we do have far more to work with than Styrofoam peanuts.

IDEA-GENERATING EXERCISES

1. Select a work of interactive entertainment—one that you are very familiar with, or have access to—and analyze its structure. What are its major structural units and how does the user move from one to another? Is it possible to travel anywhere in this interactive environment right from the start, or do certain activities need to be performed before wider access is allowed? Why (or why not) do you think this structure works well for this particular project?

2. Come up with an example of an if/then choice and reaction. Express the same situation using a state engine approach.

3. If you are familiar with any structural models that have not been identified in this chapter, how would you describe them, and what name would you give them?

4. Pick a myth, story, movie, or TV show that you are familiar with. Imagine that you have been tasked with turning it into an interactive narrative. Take one section of this story and devise a critical story path for it.

CHAPTER 8

Your Audience

In developing products for niche audiences, how useful are professional experts, focus groups, and testing?

In what ways, if any, does designing a project for a largely female audience differ from designing a project for males?

What special considerations must we be aware of in designing a work of digital storytelling for children?

Are seniors at all interested in digital content, and if so, what should you keep in mind when developing a project for them?

WHO IS YOUR AUDIENCE?

It is common fallacy for inexperienced developers to assume that the digital storytelling project they are working on will have broad appeal, and that it will be something that "everyone" will love. These inexperienced developers have no concept of how varied the tastes, needs, and interests are for different segments of the population. Yes, it would be wonderful if all projects could be hits across a great swath of the population, but the truth is that such projects are extremely uncommon. When trying to specify exceptions, *Angry Birds* is one of the few digital media projects that comes to mind. This game manages media to appeal to children and adults alike, as well as males and females, and Americans, Europeans, and people in far-flung corners of the world. I even saw the familiar *Angry Birds* motif emblazoned on batik cloth in a fabric store in Malaysia.

In truth, however, it is rare for any work to have such broad appeal. Audiences differ greatly, depending on age group, education, gender, geographic location, income level, ethnic group, and special interests. It is almost impossible to make a work that will appeal to "everyone," and it is best not even to try, for all too often such works end up appealing to no one. It is far better to clearly define who your audience is, and then design a work that will meet its needs and interests. In this chapter, we will explore a number of specific audiences and define how they differ from each other.

CHILDREN: A SIGNIFICANT PIECE OF THE DIGITAL PIE

Some people are fairly dismissive of projects made for young audiences and do not take this sector of new media seriously, but this is a sadly shortsighted attitude. Content made for children and teens is not only every bit as demanding as content made for adults, but it is also a tremendously important arena in terms of the volume of products produced for it. Furthermore, children and teens are among the most enthusiastic fans of digital media, and often lead the way when it comes to the adaptation of new forms of interactive entertainment. Thus they often help push the entire field forward.

In the decade between 2000 and 2010, children between the ages of 8 and 18 tripled the time they spent on computers, and much of that time was spent online, according to a study conducted by the Kaiser Family Foundation. In the 2010 report, *Kids and Games: What Boys and Girls are Playing Today*, research showed that over 90 percent of kids between 8 and 11 play games online. A report by the Pew Research Center in 2012 found that 75 percent of teens regularly send text messages, and one-third of them send as many as 100 messages a day.

It is interesting to note that young people typically *multitask* while online, simultaneously listening to music or texting. By 2010, according to the Kaiser report, they were spending 7.5 hours on various forms of digital media every day, a two-hour increase of use in just five years. When multitasking was accounted for, the total time spent on digital media added up to 10 hours and 45 minutes, more hours than a full-time job! This proclivity to multitask is not lost on producers of children's media, who build multitasking components into many entertainment products made for this group.

STRANGE BUT TRUE: WHAT LITTLE KIDS ARE GOOD AT

The skill sets of very young children seem to have radically changed in recent years. Children from two to five are more likely to be able to navigate with a mouse, use a smart phone, or play a simple computer game than they are likely to be able to tie their own shoes, ride a bike, or swim. These startling findings were reported in 2010, based on a series of studies conducted by AVG, an Internet security company. The reports, called the *AVG Digital Diaries*, also found that by the time most babies are six months old, they already have a digital footprint. Backing this up is a widely seen video of a baby girl repeatedly poking at the pages of a magazine, confusing it with an iPad, and claiming in baby talk that the magazine was broken!

Young people have enthusiastically taken to mobile phones, portable consoles, and tablets. When it comes to mobile phones, they actually spend more time playing games and texting on them than actually using them to talk. Many transmedia entertainments now usually contain a mobile phone component, recognizing that this feature particularly appeals to young people.

Theme parks, which are also primarily geared for children and teens, include many interactive attractions, which often go under the heading of "immersive environments." Cultural institutions, too, recognize the innate appeal interactivity has for children, and they build interactivity into their exhibits whenever their budgets permit.

Entire segments of the interactive market are devoted primarily to young people. They include smart toys, edutainment games, and *lapwear*, software products made for little tots between nine months and two years of age. And an arena that was once the exclusive domain of older teens and young adults, the MMOG, has offerings for younger children, as well. Most prominent among these worlds is *Club Penguin*, owned and operated by Disney.

Thus, interactive entertainment for children spans a vast spectrum of media and products.

UNDERSTANDING THE YOUNG USER

Although creating content for young users is full of special pleasures, it is also replete with daunting challenges. Even though the individuals who make up this particular demographic are young, relatively unsophisticated, and hungry for amusement, it is a dangerous mistake to believe they are an easy group to please. Making successful products for children and teens requires an awareness of many special factors, including:

- the developmental stages of childhood;
- gender considerations;
- the desires and fears of parents;
- the desires and aspirations of children;
- an understanding of what sort of content is most appealing to young people and the type of content that can repel them.

Children and teenagers have their own culture, language, and values. In order to be able to make content that will appeal to them, we have to understand them. But right here is where many content developers make a serious error: this audience cannot be lumped into an all-inclusive "them." Children at different ages are vastly different from each other in terms of what they enjoy doing, are capable of doing, and are able to understand. Furthermore, boys and girls do not necessarily like the same kind of content.

NOTES FROM THE FIELD: A CASE OF MASSIVE MISJUDGMENT

Chinese Hero Registry, an online game sponsored by the government of China and targeted at Chinese youth, is a perfect example of misjudging one's target audience. According to the *Los Angeles Times* (November 4, 2005), the game was built to lure kids away from violent online games and to entice them to play something more "wholesome." And from the perspective of a Chinese adult and dedicated Communist, this game probably sounded like wonderful fun. Players are given virtuous role models from Chinese history to emulate, and are rewarded for performing good works that reflect good old-fashioned Communist values. They score high by mending socks, helping old ladies home during a rainstorm, and stopping people from cursing and spitting on the sidewalks. Not surprisingly, when real kids in China got a chance to test it out, they found it to be incredibly dull and abandoned it after just a few minutes of play.

Fortunately, we do not have to rely on guesswork when creating content for young users. We have several forms of guidance available to us: developmental psychologists, educational specialists, and children themselves. In addition, we can study the market and analyze the most successful products made for the group we wish to reach. By doing this, we can glean useful clues about what works in terms of subject matter, tone, humor, characters, and style of graphics.

HOW CHILDREN DEVELOP

One excellent place to turn for help is the field of developmental psychology. The specialists in this area make it their business to study the different stages of childhood, and understand how a child progresses mentally, physically, and emotionally from the diaper stage to the drivers' ed stage. One of the foremost experts in this field is Jean Piaget, the great twentieth-century Swiss psychologist. Piaget systematically and scientifically explored the mental growth of children and documented his findings in 1948 in his seminal work, *The Origins of Intelligence in Children*. Almost everyone who develops products for children and who is concerned with age-appropriateness uses Piaget's work as a guide.

Piaget divided childhood into four stages. Within each of these stages, he asserted, children have a particular preoccupation and favored type of play. For those of us who create interactive entertainments for children, Piaget's theories regarding play are particularly relevant. He felt that play was serious business for children, a critical activity necessary in order to achieve a healthy adulthood. He held that play was a form of mental gymnastics which helped train and exercise the developing mind and prepared the individual for the challenges of life.

WORTH NOTING: AGE GROUPS AND PLAY PATTERNS

Like Piaget, the children's software industry breaks children into four distinct groups, but it uses a slightly different division of ages than Piaget did. This list combines the widely used age categories of the software industry with the developmental stages that Piaget described:

1. *Toddlers, preschool, and kindergarten*: young children love to experiment with objects and enjoy activities involving practice. They particularly love to repeat a task over and over until mastery is accomplished.

2. *Children 5 to 8 (early elementary)*: children at this age are fascinated with symbols, such as letters and numbers. They are also absorbed with fantasy pastimes, such as games which give them a chance to try out different roles and to feel powerful and unafraid.

3. *Children from 8 to 12 (late elementary; also known as "tweens")*: at this age, children like to try out their reasoning skills and prefer play activities that emphasize rules, order, and predictability.

4. *Teenagers*: teens are most concerned with trying to understand abstract concepts and testing out hypotheses. They enjoy activities that involve constructing things and making models.

Although Piaget linked each form of play to a specific stage of childhood, he also recognized that these preferences were not etched in stone. For example, a seven-year-old might experiment with forms of play that were characteristic of older children, such as making simple models, while teenagers might well still enjoy activities associated with earlier developmental stages, like fantasy role-play, and incorporate those earlier play patterns into their current games.

The principles laid down by Piaget and other developmental psychologists can help us build age-appropriate interactive entertainments, and can also guide us in making products that will appeal to a broad spectrum of young people.

SOLICITING HELP FROM EXPERTS, LARGE AND SMALL

While obtaining the assistance of a developmental psychologist or child psychologist might not always be feasible, it certainly makes sense to become familiar with the literature of Piaget and others in the field. Also, it is usually possible to seek help from educational specialists, a group that includes professors of education, consultants to schools and cultural institutions, and classroom teachers. These professionals deal with children and how they learn, and are almost certain to be familiar with the tenets of developmental psychology. Most software companies that make edutainment products regularly consult with such specialists.

A final and excellent source of help can be obtained from children themselves. You can seek this type of help by forming focus groups; by visiting classrooms (with permission from the school, of course); or by talking with individual children. A word of warning here, though. For an objective opinion, it is best to try your ideas out on young strangers. Your own children or children who know you will try to please you by telling you what they think you want to hear.

AGE-APPROPRIATENESS

When undertaking any work for a young audience, one essential question that must be asked and answered is whether the project is *age-appropriate* for its target audience. Do the characters, story, or content feel too young or too old or just right for the intended users?

Children like to feel they are more grown up than they really are and as a rule prefer to have their characters be a bit older than they are, too. To borrow a term from the child psychologists, kids have *aspirational* desires. In other words, they aspire to accomplish certain things or behave in certain ways that seem grown-up to them, and they look to their favorite characters to serve as models. Even a character like Barbie is seen as an aspirational figure: she is older, more glamorous, more sophisticated, and more accomplished than are the children who play with her.

Aspirations are engines that help push children toward maturity and hence serve a useful purpose in development. It is understandable that when a product seems too babyish, a child will be insulted and will not want to have anything to do with it. Designing something "just right" in terms of age-appropriateness can be quite challenging, and children can be devastatingly sensitive when they feel a project is not targeted correctly. According to the report *Children (Ages 3-12) on the Web*, a six-year-old tester scathingly rejected a test website, saying "This website is for babies, maybe 4 or 5 years old. You can tell because of the cartoons and trains."

Along with age-appropriateness, one must also determine whether a product will appeal across both genders or be more attractive either to boys or to girls. Entertainment products made for very young children, as well as for older teenagers, may well be acceptable to both genders, but this is far less true of products made for children in between these age extremes. Thus, many children's products are marketed either to girls or to boys.

THE PARENTS' POINT OF VIEW

In designing products for children, you cannot afford to concern yourself only with what the young users might like or not like. You must consider their parents' attitudes as well. After all, in most cases, it is the parents who will be purchasing the product or allowing access to the content.

So what are parents looking for in interactive entertainment for their kids, and what do they NOT want it to contain? On the positive side, they are hoping for a product that offers high-quality entertainment and content that is wholesome and that supports family values. Furthermore, parents see it as a big plus if the work is educationally enriching. In addition, parents of young children are greatly pleased when the material is enjoyable for them as well as for their kids, since they will probably by playing it with them. For models of family-friendly entertainment that appeals to both adults and children, study hit animated films like *Shrek* and *Toy Story*.

On the negative side, almost without exception and no matter what the interactive medium, parents do not want their children exposed to graphic violence, and they are equally against products that contain sexual content. When it comes to the Internet, parents have more specialized concerns. The things they most fear revolve around the three Big Ps: Predators,

Pornography, and Privacy (children being manipulated into giving personal or financial information to strangers). To a degree these fears were realized in 2012, when people were shocked to learn that the popular teen online virtual world, *Habbo Hotel*, was riddled with cybersex and pornographic chat. The Finnish company that runs the site swiftly responded by shutting down the chat feature. As a result of this scandal, the site lost its CEO, as well as many of its investors, staff, and users. Now renamed simply *Habbo*, it remains active, but it is unclear how popular it currently is.

A number of recent reports have significantly downplayed the dangers of young online users coming into contact with predators, but in the meantime, the spotlight has been thrown on another, more prevalent danger for child users: *cyber bullying*. Cyber bullying is harassing another person online, sometimes with immense cruelty, and it can lead to deadly consequences. In 2006, a 13-year-old girl hanged herself because a boy she'd met online and liked, and believed was interested in her, suddenly turned on her. Unbeknownst to the girl, the boy never even existed. He was a fiction invented by the mother of one of her friends, supposedly in retaliation for something the victim had done to her daughter (see http://abcnews.go.com/GMA/story?id=3882520). Cyber bullying is surprisingly common, though fortunately, it rarely inflicts as much pain as in this case. A study conducted in 2011 by Pew Internet and American Life Survey reported that 33 percent of teens have been victims of this form of harassment.

In order to protect young users, many sites for this demographic build in safety features that restrict communications that can occur between users. Many also restrict which sites the young users can link to, making sure whatever sites they can visit are safe. Although this makes for a less expressive, freewheeling experience for the child, it provides some measure of reassurance to the parent.

On the positive side of the safety issue, more than one study has reported that young people actually benefit from being online and from using other forms of digital media. These studies assert that not only does digital media give young users the opportunity to learn technical skills and explore interests, but that it is also a venue for participating in peer socialization, especially in their use of social media. An extensive study by the John D. and Catherine T. MacArthur Foundation found that not only does digital media offer positive benefits to young people, but it is the youngsters who are not active on social media sites who are at risk of being maladjusted.

Software developers who make edutainment products for children invest a great deal of time in the development of the characters in their titles. Character development is influenced by the overall needs and goals of the project. At Knowledge Adventure, which makes the *JumpStart* line of edutainment games, the cast of regular characters for *JumpStart* was revamped to make them more efficient within the educational context of the titles. Thus, for *JumpStart Advanced First Grade*, each character was given a special skill as a way to help the young learner. For example, Eleanor, the pink elephant, is gifted in linguistic skills and hosts the reading modules, while Kisha, the artist of the bunch, supports the players by providing helpful pictures. The revamped cast is now collectively called the Learning Buddies (see Figure 8.1).

Figure 8.1 The Learning Buddies from the *JumpStart* educational games. Image courtesy of Knowledge Adventure, Inc., and used under license.

But even at *JumpStart*, where educational objectives are taken very seriously, they recognized that perfection can be a little boring and thus gave the cast some little flaws. "We built in more conflict," senior producer Diane Pray reported. "We aren't the 'village of the happy people' anymore."

THE USE OF HUMOR

Kids love to laugh, and an interactive work that is full of humor will make it extra attractive to them. But comedy is a slippery beast, especially when you are working in children's media. Despite the willingness of young people to be amused, it is not necessarily easy to make something funny for them. What tickles children is sometimes quite different from what we adults consider amusing.

For one thing, kids' taste in humor is often what many adults regard as bad taste. They are drawn to content that causes nice grown-ups to squirm. They giggle at bathroom humor, at foul language, at odd-looking people, and at characters who break the rules of polite society. Kids also have a great sense of the absurd. They see what a silly place the world is, and they appreciate anything that celebrates its ridiculousness. Humor that pokes fun at adults, or that has a rebellious tinge, is therefore greatly relished. They love humor that is wacky, unexpected, and off the wall.

In general, visual humor works better than verbal humor; puns and word play will mostly go right over the heads of younger children. The young ones, on the other hand, love to click or roll over an object and have something silly or unexpected happen—an amusing piece of animation or a funny sound. But if you want to expand the age range of your product, it is a smart strategy to include humor that appeals to children in different age groups. And, if you think their parents might be playing along with them, throw in some funny things for them, too, as they did at *Toontown Online*. The adults will appreciate it, and the kids won't even realize that they've missed a joke or two.

Overall, the best kind of humor in children's interactive works is not very different from the best kind of humor in children's linear works: it is built into the character or into the situation, and is integrated into the work from the concept stage on. It isn't just pasted on as an afterthought. So, if you want your projects to be truly funny, begin factoring in the humor from the earliest development stages. One final thought about humor: to be on the safe side, test your comic elements on kids, to make sure they find it as amusing as you do.

OFFER SATISFYING CHALLENGES AND REWARDS

Rewards are a powerful motivator. A key strategy for grabbing the attention of children is to break the content into a series of small, exciting challenges, and to offer rewards each time a challenge is met. Challenges should increase in difficulty as the child's mastery increases, thus keeping the work interesting.

Rewards provide positive reinforcement, and also serve as a measuring stick for how well the child is doing. The trick is to emphasize success and to downplay failure. If the player makes a mistake, soften the sting with a little humor, and with words of encouragement from one of the nonplayer characters. You want to keep them involved and eager to do more, rather than become discouraged and quit. Rewards can be in the form of a burst of audio, words of congratulation from another character, or a cute little animation. Rewards can also be objects that the child collects during the game—such as pieces that work as currency, or upgrades in clothing or possessions.

A FINAL TIP: BE RESPECTFUL

In developing quality works for young audiences, one critical strategy is to be respectful. Being respectful, first of all, means not talking down to the young users or patronizing them. Being respectful also means creating a product for them that is age-appropriate and truly engaging. Finally, being respectful shows you care enough about your young audience to make something that challenges them, but not beyond their abilities, and that is entertaining, but isn't "dumbed down." Overall, it means offering them plenty to do and lots of fun, but meaningful, content, too.

HELPFUL RESOURCES

- To stay up-to-date on children's software, websites, and smart toys, you might consider subscribing to *Children's Technology Review* (www .childrenssoftware.com). This excellent monthly publication is available both as a print publication and in electronic form. A subscription also gives you access to its online archives, which include a stash of thousands of product reviews.
- To read the Pew report on teens and texting, go to http://www.pewinternet .org/Reports/2012/Teens-and-smartphones.aspx.
- To read the Kaiser Family Foundation report on kids and media, go to http://www.kff.org/entmedia/upload/8010.pdf.

- To seek out information on children, media and technology, go to Common Sense Media (http://www.commonsensemedia.org/).
- To learn more about designing websites for children, you can purchase the study *Children (Ages 3-12) on the Web* at http://www.nngroup.com/reports/children-on-the-web/.

CREATING PROJECTS FOR GIRLS AND WOMEN

The idea that girls inherently like one kind of thing and boys inherently like another is not a popular one in today's world. A fierce dispute has been raging for years about the origins of gender preferences—it is a major issue in the famous nature versus nurture debate. Proponents on the nature side assert that gender preferences are inherited, and are among the traits one is born with; those on the nurture side, on the other hand, contend that such preferences are determined by one's social environment and by how one is raised. In the end, however, our opinions about gender do not matter. Gender preferences are a reality in today's world, and one must be aware of them.

In broad strokes, experts in child development have noted the following differences between boys and girls:

- When playing with others, girls prefer collaborative activities while boys like activities that are competitive.
- Boys are drawn to activities that involve objects while girls are drawn to activities that involve other people or animals and particularly like activities with a social component.
- Girls are good at activities that employ fine motor skills; boys prefer activities that call for gross motor skills.
- Boys look for opportunities to be aggressive, while girls are more comfortable in nonviolent, socially peaceful play situations.
- Girls enjoy activities that call for organizing and arranging; boys like activities that require building, digging, and constructing.

Gender differences between boys and girls can even involve such minute matters as color preferences. Girls are notoriously fond of two colors, purple and pink, and software companies that want to attract girls tend to bow to this color preference.

The 2010 Kaiser Family Foundation Study on Children and Media reported a number of differences in the amounts of time boys and girls spend on different activities. For example, boys spend an average of 19 minutes a day on social media sites, while girls spend 25 minutes, but girls only spend an average of 14 minutes playing games on video game consoles, while boys play for 56 minutes.

Jesyca Durchin, who owns Nena Media, a consulting company that specializes in media content for girls, has made a number of interesting observations about the preferences of young females. She says that girls generally prefer play that involves fashion, glamour, and nurture, though also enjoy play that involves adventure, action, collecting things, and communication. Unlike boys, girls do not enjoy meaningless or repetitive violence, though if the violence makes sense in terms of the story, they are not opposed to it.

According to Durchin, girls do not necessarily want everything to be sweet and happy; they do enjoy mystery and suspense, and even like works that are spooky. But they are not pleased if spookiness crosses over into scariness—a firm distinction Durchin makes. Something that is spooky, she points out, means you might be startled or frightened (for example, at a carnival at night). But something scary is much more intense and can put you in real danger, like being out alone when there's a murderer on the loose.

Durchin also notes that girls like attractive environments, and these environments should be realistic or make sense in terms of the story. She also asserts that girls especially like sensual interfaces—ones that are colorful and that contain sound and that change shape when activated. They don't like a row of grey buttons that are all the same shape.

It should be noted, however, that preferences differ from culture to culture, which is an important consideration if a product is to be marketed internationally. For example, boys in North America over the age of eight or nine find cute animal characters "too young," but such characters are highly popular in Asia across all age groups and both genders.

Thus far, girls have largely been left out of the market for video games and most other forms of digital media, which is generally targeted to male audiences. But that doesn't mean that they do not hunger for works that more closely fit their interests. This hunger was dramatically demonstrated in 2012 when Lego, a company well-known for its toys for boys, introduced a new line of construction sets for girls. Called Lego Friends and launched after Lego conducted extensive research, the construction sets more closely match the tastes of girls. The sets are all environments of a fictional place called Heartland City. They include miniature plastic figures, each of which has a personality and a backstory. Players can build a cruise ship and play with dolphins, construct a high school that can be anywhere from one to three stories high and even put together and play with an equine-centered summer camp. Lego introduced several new colors for this line, including azure and lavender. The sets were instant hits. In the first six months, sales were double the projected figures. Lego Friends has been one of the biggest successes in Lego's history and illustrates what can happen when the female audience is taken into consideration. There is no reason the same could not be true in interactive digital media, but thus far, few companies have ventured into this arena.

CREATING PROJECTS FOR WOMEN

Girls, of course, grow up to be women, and though their interests and tastes mature, their inclinations do not change dramatically. For example, women, like girls, still lean more toward projects that offer them opportunities to socialize rather than to engage in meaningless violence. And they enjoy opportunities for self-expression, such as customizing their avatars. A study sponsored by PopCap found that women are particularly fond of social games, with 55 percent of all social gamers in the United States being female and 60 percent in the UK. Games on Facebook are a particular favorite with these players. And although girls and women do enthusiastically play social media games and casual games, they are also a substantial segment of the video game audience. According to the Entertainment Software Association (ESA), women over 18 constitute a far larger slice of the gaming population (31 percent) than do boys 17 and younger (19 percent).

When it comes to the use of digital media for informational and educational purposes, women often have a significant role. For example, in the Arab world, women played a major part in employing digital media to disseminate news about the Arab Spring to a global audience. And many educational software companies are headed by women, and largely staffed by them, too.

SENIORS AND DIGITAL MEDIA

Contrary to the stereotype of older people being incapable of acquiring new skills, and being skittish of new technology, a significant segment of the senior population uses various forms of digital media on a regular basis. They use email, social media sites, do research, and play games online. They also use mobile phones and play games on various kinds of game consoles, with the Wii being a particular favorite (see Figure 8.2). These digital devices offer them an opportunity to stay connected with friends and family members and also offer them a way to engage in physical activities, despite any health issues they might be dealing with.

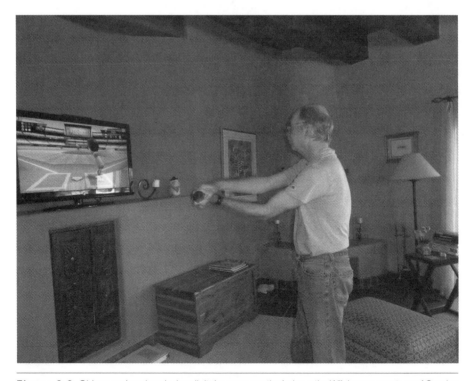

Figure 8.2 Older people enjoy playing digital games, particularly on the Wii. Image courtesy of Carolyn Handler Miller.

Since 2009, the mega technology trade show, Consumer Electronics Show (CES), has been holding a day-long event called Silvers Summits, focusing specifically on technology that relates to older people. It recognizes that people aged 50 and over make up almost 45 percent of the US population and control 70 percent of its wealth—obviously not a demographic to be overlooked. The event held in 2013 revealed some interesting data. For example, people 55 and older represent the fastest growing segment of the population to engage in online dating, and seven million older Americans without children at home own video game systems.

Other statistical studies underscore how popular digital media has become with the older generation. Between 2005 and 2009 alone, broadband usage in this group tripled, and by June of 2011, one-half of all Americans 65 and older were online. One-third of these individuals were on Facebook, 86 percent used email, and 69 percent had a mobile phone. Even many seniors are actively enjoying video games. A study published in July 2013 in *Computers in Human Behavior* revealed that elderly adults, age 77 and beyond, recruited from senior centers, retirement homes, and religious centers, played video games at least once a week, and 17 percent played every day. The games they played tended to be less high action than *World of Warcraft* or *Halo*, and more along the lines of puzzle games, but the study showed they benefited greatly by playing these games, with better functioning for everyday activities and less depression than non-gamers.

Wii bowling in particular has caught on with seniors. A retirement community called Greenspring has 30 teams with 200 members that compete in Wii bowling, some of them while sitting in wheelchairs. A number are in their eighties and one woman is in her mid-nineties. The game offers not only physical activity (without the requirement to lift a heavy bowling ball) but an opportunity for socialization, ending the isolation that often goes along with advanced years. In Illinois, there is even a state-wide Wii bowling competition between teams from assisted living facilities.

STRANGE BUT TRUE: A THERAPEUTIC ROBOTIC SEAL

Paro, a robotic stuffed animal who resembles a baby harp seal, has become a beloved companion animal at nursing homes all over the world. It was developed in Japan as a digital aid to the rapidly growing number of aging seniors there. The furry white creature with big black eyes moves and makes sounds much like the real animal it is modeled on, and responds in a believable way when petted, though in fact it is an animatronic robot. While living companion animals like dogs and cats are often barred from nursing homes, Paro has been welcomed with enthusiasm. Seniors who are agitated or are generally non-responsive, many with dementia, find Paro a comforting presence, and some will actually sing to the cuddly creature (http://www.parorobots.com/, http://www.gizmag.com/paro-robot-baby-seal-companion/13753/).

Seniors typically enjoy the kinds of activities online that are popular across the board: email, sharing photos, visiting social media sites, and checking the news and weather. But they also visit sites that are of special interest to individuals in their demographic: those on health, finances, and travel. Several sites also offer what has become known as *brain games*, entertaining games that are designed to keep the brains of elders active and fit. One interesting new trend is the development of sites designed to offer play opportunities for seniors and their grandchildren. One such site is Wizard 101 (www.wizard101.com). The site contains a suite of family-friendly games that are fun, easy to play, and safe.

THE MEDICALLY ILL AND DISABLED

Digital technology has been a boon to many individuals who are dealing with health problems or who are physically disabled. Special games and other forms of digital works have been designed to help them cope with their illnesses and help the outside world understand what they are going through. For example, *Re-Mission* is a video game and Web destination for young cancer patients that helps them combat their disease. NAMI (National Alliance on Mental Illness) is an organization and a specialized website to help people deal with mental illness. Dozens of other websites serve as support groups for individuals with specific illnesses, while other websites offer general medical information. And for combat veterans who are suffering from Post-Traumatic Stress Disorder, virtual reality treatment is now available. These virtual reality simulations re-create battlefield conditions, thrusting the user into situations that feel very real, but done at a pace that the user can handle, gradually becoming more intense. This kind of treatment is called *exposure therapy*, and the user is guided by a trained therapist. The experience is made exceedingly real with sound effects and even disturbing smells, but it enables users to confront their traumas and overcome them. VR is also being used to treat debilitating phobias suffered by non-military personnel, such as the fear of flying or the fear of crowds.

Even works designed for the general public can be a boon to those with handicaps, as exemplified by the massive ComicCon Convention, a gathering celebrating all forms of popular culture, held annually in San Diego. Many of the ComicCon attendees travel through the vast convention hall on wheelchairs, and many of these attendees are dedicated gamers and participants in virtual worlds like *Second Life*. These digital works give them opportunities that they are usually denied. For example, one woman who uses a wheelchair is a great fan of *World of Warcraft*. She told a *Los Angeles Times* reporter (July 25, 2009) that in the game "you can be someone you are not in real life." And, she added: "You can feel like you can be one of them – you have legs! – and you can become a warrior."

OTHER PARTS OF THE WORLD AND OTHER ETHNIC GROUPS

When it comes to one's audience, we must remember to look beyond our own national borders and our own ethnic group. What if we are asked to develop a project for housewives in Japan or English-speaking middle-class Africans or for tween girls in the Middle East? These projects do come about, and before we can delve into them, we must ask and answer a variety of questions that will help us better understand an audience that might be unfamiliar to us.

In my own case, I was asked by a producer based in Saudi Arabia to help develop a virtual world and series of interactive stories for pre-teenage girls in the Middle East, a demographic that is seriously underserved. It was a dream assignment, but I needed to know a great deal before I could actually begin to create this fictional world. For example, what kinds of relationships, if any, do girls in this part of the world have with boys who are not members of their own families? At what age do girls typically get engaged? What kinds of customs are traditional throughout the Arab world, and which are specific to Saudi Arabia? Are there international schools in the Middle East, and do Muslim girls ever go to school with girls from other backgrounds? What kinds of pets might a family have? What do girls typically enjoy doing during their leisure time and during vacations? How closely supervised are they? I had dozens of such questions, but fortunately, my producer was able to answer them or point me to the answers. Such questions would be totally different if one were to develop a project for Japanese housewives or middle-class Africans, but in order to understand your audience you must learn as much about this target population as possible.

Digital works are often designed for highly specialized audiences. For instance, a website called *Live/Hope/Love* is directed specifically at Jamaicans who are living and struggling with HIV/Aids (www.livehopelove.com), though of course this beautiful website can be viewed and enjoyed by anyone. The site utilizes videos, poetry, photos, and music to tell the story of these Jamaicans and to humanize their illness. Another highly specialized website, *JewishGen* (www .jewishgen.org), has been created to help those who are Jewish construct their genealogy and trace their familial roots. One particularly fascinating feature of JewishGen is the collection of pages devoted to shtetls (villages where Jewish communities once thrived) scattered across Europe, North Africa, and the Middle East. Though many of them thrived before World War II, they were largely destroyed during the war and events that followed. These moving pages about the past, indexed under http://kehilalinks.jewishgen.org/, include family stories, still photos, maps, paintings, and sometimes even videos. It was an exciting day for me when a colorful page was launched to commemorate Ostropol, the shtetl that my father's side of the family originated from (http://kehilalinks.jewishgen.org/ostropol/). Another site with an international audience is *WiseMuslimWomen* (http://www.wisemuslimwomen.org/), which in part serves to counter gender-based inequality experienced by Muslim women across the globe.

Ultra-Orthodox Jews even have their very own Internet provider, eNativ (http://www.enativ .com/about_en.aspx), which recognizes how necessary the Internet has become for work and for one's personal life. However, it blocks out material that is inappropriate for ultra-Orthodox Jews to view. Its goal is to make it possible to surf the Web without encountering material that is not kosher.

Devout Christians, not to be left out of the digital media world, have developed a number of Christian-themed video games. Among them are games based on the *Left Behind* books, about those who are called to Heaven (the Rapture) and those who are left behind to deal with the apocalypse. *Left Behind, Eternal Forces* and its sequels are games that feature real-time strategy and even violent combat (though only when necessary), with the goal of saving people from the Antichrist. The *Left Behind* games are primarily geared for teen boys—the same ones who might be tempted to play *Grand Theft Auto*. For a much younger Christian audience, a number of games have been produced based on the *VeggieTales* series of videos.

When it comes to entertainment for ethnic minorities, YouTube has a vast number of them. Many YouTube stars, such as Japanese-American comedian Ryan Higa, are Asian-Americans. As of January 2014, Higa's YouTube channel, Nigahiga, has over 11 million subscribers. Other YouTube stars are African American or Latino. Although Hollywood might not have put out the welcome mat for these entertainers, they have found success on the Internet. And they can do their shows without having to modify them according to the dictates of network or studio execs.

SPECIALIZED WORKS FOR DOMESTIC POPULATIONS

Obviously, many works of digital media are not intended for an international audience, but for audiences much narrower in scope. Two projects with a sharply local focus are *It Takes a Thousand Voices* (http://www.nrcprograms.org/site/PageServer?pagename=Thousand Voices_home) and *Cerrillos, New Mexico* (http://www.cerrillosnewmexico.com/). The first site is intended for Native Americans, and they are encouraged to use the site to videotape their own personal stories. The second site focuses on the northern New Mexico village of Cerrillos, which used to be a booming center of mining but now is almost a ghost town. The site records the history of the village and contains a number of true stories about life there under a forum called the Spit & Whittle Club. It also serves as a source of information about current businesses and events going on in Cerrillos. Thus the site works as an historic record, a virtual community center, and a promotional vehicle to attract tourists. A far more global endeavor is *Ushahidi* (http://www.ushahidi.com/), a platform developed to support citizen journalism around the world. Ushahidi means "testimony" in Swahili.

CONCLUSION

A major reason digital works do not succeed is because the designer did not create them for a specific audience. Before undertaking any digital storytelling project, you need to understand in as much detail as possible who the audience is and what will attract the audience to the site.

Major considerations in terms of defining your audience include: age range, gender, educational level, economic status, ethnicity, geographic region, what their interests are and what they enjoy doing, what they dislike, and what is inappropriate for them.

Three major considerations in terms of the project are:

1. The subject matter: is it appropriate for the audience you have in mind and is it something that would strongly appeal to them?

2. The platform: do members of your intended audience own the platform you intend to release your project on, and are they comfortable with it?

3. The difficulty level: is it targeted correctly for your audience, or is it too easy, too demanding, or too intimidating?

Also, it can be unsafe to develop a project without outside guidance. It is often helpful to bring in subject matter experts (SMEs) that can help you determine what will most interest your audience, the accuracy of your material, and what is and is not appropriate for them.

As we have seen here, audiences vary enormously in terms of age range, gender, and a variety of other factors. Thus, it is no surprise that the "one size fits all" approach is a dangerous one to adopt. It is far better to have a clear idea of what group you are targeting and build a project with their needs and interests lucidly in mind.

IDEA-GENERATING EXERCISES

1. Take a familiar myth or children's fairy tale (like *King Midas* or *Cinderella*) and analyze what the core story is; in other words, what its "bones" are. Then discuss how this story could be used as a framework for an interactive work project that would appeal to each of the four major age groups of young audiences. How would it need to be changed to be appropriate to each group? Do you think your ideas could appeal equally to boys and girls in each of these age groups, or would a different approach be needed for each?

2. Imagine that you were tasked with developing an interactive piece of digital storytelling for Japanese housewives or English-speaking middle-class Africans. Develop a series of questions that you'd want to have answered before you could begin the creative work on the project.

3. How do you think developing a project for young children differs from developing a project for senior citizens? What are the primary factors to keep in mind if you are going to create a project for either of these groups?

4. Work your own way through an existing interactive game or other project designed for a specific audience, and analyze its strengths and weaknesses. What about it do you think would hook this audience and keep them involved? What needs, if any, does it satisfy?

CHAPTER 9

Social Media and Storytelling

Is it really possible to construct a story using only social media?

What kinds of characters can "live" on social media?

How can social media be used to tell non-fiction stories?

What role does humor play in social media?

INSERTING THE SOCIAL INTO THE MEDIA

Social media—online communities that exist to let people share news, opinions, personal information, photos, and videos—are a relatively new phenomena. Yet new as social media sites are, they have had an enormous impact on our online lives and also on the way we tell interactive stories.

Some observers point to early BBS systems, newsgroups, and usenets as the start of social media. Others feel that GeoCities in 1994 represents a more accurate starting point. Users of GeoCities would post their Web pages in virtual geographic locations appropriate to their content. For instance, if you were interested in the movie business, you'd put your page in Hollywood; if you were a jazz musician, you would likely put your page on BourbonStreet. GeoCities was extremely popular for several years and had 38 million users by 2009. Today, however, it is only available in Japan.

The launching of other sites more familiar to contemporary users is even more recent. They include the start of Friendster in 2002; MySpace and LinkedIn in 2003; Facebook in 2004; YouTube and Bebo in 2005; and Twitter in 2006. The enormously popular Pinterest didn't even launch until 2010. But new as these social media sites are, by 2013 Americans were already spending an average of 16 minutes on them out of every hour they were online (from Experian). The average time in other Western countries was only slightly less. And by the beginning of 2013, Facebook alone had 800 million active users, while Twitter had 100 million and LinkedIn had 64 million.

It should be noted that the popularity of particular social media sites can wax and wane, and new forms of social media are introduced quite frequently. While Facebook remains the most popular form of social media, it is losing some of its appeal to teenagers, its prime demographic. Some teens are suffering from "Facebook fatigue," according to a 2013 Pew Research Report. Twitter is fast growing in popularity with teens, and Reddit is also quite popular. Other popular sites with teens include Tumblr, Vine, and Snapchat, while a new Pew Research Center study showed that adults favor Pinterest and Instagram.

Users are drawn to social media sites for a number of reasons. For some, the appeal is fluff content, such as watching videos of cute pets or cute children doing cute things. For

STRANGE BUT TRUE: WHERE PEOPLE CONNECT

Many users are so tied to social media that they connect to it from places that might give others pause. For example, 32 percent of people aged 18 to 24 use social media in the bathroom. And 51 percent of people aged 25 to 34 connect to social media sites while at work, in their offices. Even some astronauts have been heavy users of social media and regularly tweeted to global audiences from the International Space Station (from http://www.uncp.edu/home/acurtis/NewMedia/SocialMedia/SocialMediaHistory.html).

others, the appeal is more serious. It may be the chance to promote a political cause or to witness a natural disaster as it unfolds. Increasingly, social media is employed as a way to disseminate news. Reportedly, the first time a social media site broke a hard news story was in 2009, when a person tweeted that a plane was down in the Hudson River. Furthermore, and in line with the focus of this book, social media is being used to tell fictional and non-fiction stories.

THE POWER OF SOCIAL MEDIA

The upstart social media sites have surprisingly powerful muscle power. One small example of this power was an incident that took place in the spring of 2013 when the Walt Disney Company announced plans to trademark the term *Dia de los Muertos*. The term is Spanish for Day of the Dead and is an important holiday in Mexico. The holiday traces its roots back to the Aztecs and it is an occasion when the observant honor the souls of their departed ones. As soon as Disney announced its plans, a huge protest occurred on social media sites. Disney quickly withdrew its trademark plans and most observers believe it was because of the outcry on social media. Graham Harvey, owner of Matthew Media LLC, had this to say about incident: "Any company or organization that wants to protect its brand needs to understand the powerful, viral nature of social media. A backlash can occur in the blink of an eye" (as reported in the *Los Angeles Times*, May 9, 2013).

Social media have been playing an important role in politics and social unrest, too. They helped fuel the Arab Spring protests that began in 2010 (as noted in Chapter 14). Later in the book, in Chapter 21, we cover the YouTube film, *Kony2012*, which raised awareness of the Ugandan tyrant Joseph Kony. Comedians are now even telling jokes about social media, which means they have definitely penetrated the public consciousness. One, by an unknown jokester, goes like this: "A guy walks into his doctor's office and says, 'I think I'm addicted to Twitter.' The doctor responds 'Sorry, I don't follow you.'"

Of course, like all forms of power, the power of social media can be used for evil as well as for good. Unfortunately, one negative effect of social media is the increase in cyber bullying—the online belittlement of an individual, usually by a group of his or her peers. Several vulnerable young people who have been victims of this kind of harassment on Facebook and other sites have even taken their own lives.

CHARACTERS ON SOCIAL MEDIA

Characters—some fictional, some real, and some real but given fictional personas—can thrive on social media. They can tweet, have Facebook pages, post photos to Pinterest and post videos to YouTube. Social media sites can be an excellent way to amplify a character's personality or show shades of that person that might not be revealed by other forms of media. One of the special "gifts" of social media is that it gives characters a first-person voice.

Prominent individuals and celebrities from all over the world have taken to tweeting. In fact, it would be difficult to find an actor or musician who doesn't tweet. These famous tweeters include entertainers like Britney Spears, Justin Bieber, and Lady Gaga; TV personalities like Oprah Winfrey and Conan O'Brian; and political and religious leaders like Queen Elizabeth, Barack Obama, the Dalai Lama, and Pope Francis. The Mayor of Chicago, Rahm Emanuel, also has a Twitter account, but unfortunately for him, it is a fake account and quite sarcastic. The Pope, the real one, has even granted rewards to the faithful in the form of indulgences—less time spent in purgatory—for those who followed his posts on social media during Catholic World Youth Day. (This was not a free pass, however. In order to receive an indulgence, the person must have already confessed and be truly penitent.)

Fictional personalities are also creating Facebook pages and tweeting on Twitter. One such Twitter posterer is Betty Draper (@BettyDraper), the ex-wife of Don Draper, the central character of the TV series, *Mad Men*. She writes about her new life as a single mom, her clothes, and the trials and tribulations she suffers that are caused by her daughter Sally. Of course, since Betty Draper is not a real person, she is not actually writing these tweets, even though they perfectly capture the persona of an upper-middle-class woman living in the 1960s. Interesting, the tweets are not written by anyone on the *Mad Men* staff, either. Instead, they are created by Helen Klein Ross, a former ad agency creative director who is now out on her own. Ross calls what she does "Twittertainment" and brand fiction, describing this as "original narrative and mythology built around a brand's unique premise." Apparently, the *Mad Men* staff have no problem with members of the larger public tweeting in voices of the characters on the TV show, because 90 Twitter accounts have been opened in the name of *Mad Men* characters or characters from that era who converse with them.

In some cases, real living people (and, quite often, animals) are given the opportunity to participate on social media. For example, Grumpy Cat (real name: Tardar Sauce) became an overnight celebrity when a video featuring her, and her dour expression, appeared on YouTube. Not only has she received over two million views on YouTube, but she also puts up grouchy posts on Twitter (#grumpycat).

STRANGE BUT TRUE: DOGS CAN TWEET

If cats can tweet, dogs, of course, will want to be part of the action, too. Luckily for them, the toy company, Mattel, came up with a way to enable them to do that. The company is now marketing a device called "Puppy Tweets" that can be attached to a dog's collar. It is motion and sound sensitive. The dog's owner has to help out, though, by putting an associated USB receiver in a computer and setting up a Twitter account for the pup. They will then be able to receive regular updates from their pet (from a sound bank of 500 pre-recorded tweets). For example, if the dog is having a lazy day, he might send out a Tweet saying "Somedays it feels like my paw is permanently on the snooze button."

One of the most followed animals on Twitter is Wolf_OR-7. He's a real grey wolf who was given a GPS collar in Oregon when he was a pup and has been wandering between Oregon and northern California since then, traveling over 1,000 miles in a year and a half (OR7 is his tracking number—OR is for Oregon, where he was born). He captured the public's attention when he crossed into California in December, 2011, the first living wolf in the state since 1924.

He adamantly tweets "Don't call me Journey," a name given to him by some school children and that he detests. He also says his hobbies include wandering and ungulates (hooved mammals). Biologists think he left home to find a mate and some territory of his own, and followers anxiously hope he doesn't suffer from the same fate as his brother, shot illegally by a hunter in Idaho. He also has his own Facebook page, where he is shown cavorting with a group of coyotes. It's a rare glimpse of his odyssey, illustrating that his solo travels have not been entirely lonely. But he doesn't seem to have yet found the love of his life and he's now back in Oregon. Wolf_OR7 could be a compelling figure in a work of fiction, although in most fictional works featuring wolves, they are the villains, not the heroes. But the portrayal of this wolf on Twitter and Facebook demonstrates that with social media tools alone, you can construct a highly engaging character.

WORKS OF FICTION USING SOCIAL MEDIA

As to be expected, since social media sites are relatively new on the scene, so are fictional works that employ them, particularly works that employ them as a primary means to tell a story. *My Darklyng*, co-written in 2010 by Lauren Merchling and Laura Moser, was one of the first works of social media fiction to do this. The authors say they wrote the story because they were disappointed in the ebooks at the time, which they felt was almost entirely text-based and did not use media creatively. Both writers had previously written young adult fiction, so they decided to create a young adult novel that would intensively use digital media. Their "book," although it does not exist as a physical book, is the story of 16-year-old Natalie Pollock who gets sucked into a world that might (or might not) be populated by vampires. They told their story using a number of different Facebook pages, tweets by various characters, and YouTube videos. In addition, a large part of the story was serialized online on Slate. They took special pains to capture the way teens write on Facebook—with lots of caps, excessive enthusiasm, and intense emotion about almost everything, and they received praise from the *New York Times* for their efforts.

STRANGE BUT TRUE: EVEN HAMLET HAS A FACEBOOK PAGE!

One early work of social media fiction was the retelling of Shakespeare's *Hamlet*, written entirely in Facebook posts. This comic version of *Hamlet* was written in 2009 by Sarah Schmelling (http://www.angelfire.com/art2/antwerplettuce/hamlet.html). As with the posts by the fictional characters of *My Darklyng*, the writer has made good use of Facebook conventions. For example, one post reads "Hamlet and the queen are no longer friends" and another reads "Ophelia joined the group Maidens Who Don't Float." In 2010, Juliet Capulet of *Romeo and Juliet* started tweeting, thanks to the Royal Shakespeare Company. Will Macbeth be next to join the social media fray?

In Chapter 21 on iCinema, we discuss a film, *Inside*, which relied heavily on social media to reach its resolution. Two other recent works of fiction that heavily employ social media are *The Social S#ctor* and *The Lizzie Bennet Diaries*.

The S#cial Sector (also spelled as The Social Sector, http://socialsector.usanetwork.com/) was an ancillary online show for the USA Network series, *Psych*. The eight-week series was an interactive online comedy/murder mystery featuring the same two characters who star in the TV show, Shawn and Gus. It was, in part, built on the success of another *Psych* ancillary series, *Hashtag Killer*. *The S#cial Sector* revolved around a fictional online reality show. Just as in non-fiction reality shows, one contestant is eliminated each week, but in this case, the elimination is literal. The unlucky contestant is murdered. Gus and Shawn ask for your help in finding the secret location of the reality show house and in catching the murderer.

The experience, which unfolded early in 2013 in real time and largely took place on a dedicated website, involved a great deal of interactive dialogue, crowd-sourced challenges, mini-games and YouTube videos. Adding to the social nature of the experience, players could also make videos of themselves discussing theories about the case and post them on the "Fan Theory Board," which was powered by the Theatrics collaborative storytelling platform. The experience spilled over onto Facebook and Twitter. The ultimate goal as a player was to become Top Digital Assistant.

I learned about *S#cial Sector* from a colleague and decided to try it out. But before getting into the action, I first had to register. Some years ago, when registering for a two-screen TV game, *Boys Toys* (see Chapter 19), I hastily picked my own first name, Carolyn, as a user name. The first time the leader board popped up, I was number 6! But I was mortified to find myself up against a bunch of macho guys with names like GunDoc and Scuba Steve. I vowed never to pick such an uncool girlie name again. So with *The S#cial Sector*, I was determined to use something much tougher and decided to call myself TwoFist. I was glad I did, because the two TV characters immediately made me, TwoFist, their digital assistant, and engaged me in a great deal of amusing dialogue. Much of this involved simple questions such as what their favorite fruit was (pineapple—which was easy because it was noted in every write-up of the show). Though it was a little disconcerting, though flattering, to be addressed as TwoFist, I did manage to hold up my end without tripping. A victory for my gender! Unfortunately, by the time I got involved with *S#cial Sector*, the eight episodes were coming to a close, so I was unable to participate in the full experience. I did succeed, though, at getting a taste of the social nature of the project, its videos, its interactive dialogue, and quiz questions. Even though my time with it was brief, I could easily understand why it was so popular, especially with fans of *Psych*.

The enormously popular *Lizzie Bennet Diaries*, which won an Emmy in 2013 for Best Interactive Program, relied even more heavily on social media, and was in fact told entirely through social media. These included YouTube, Facebook, Tumblr, Twitter, Google Plus, OK Cupid, Pinterest, and LOOKBOOK. It should be noted that the *Lizzie Bennet Diaries* is also considered a work of transmedia storytelling, since it uses a multitude of different forms of media to tell the story. The series was a modern retelling of Jane Austen's *Pride and Prejudice*, as if Elizabeth Bennet (the Lizzie in the title) lived in a world with the Internet, smart phones, video cameras, and social media. The story is told as a video diary, but augmented with social media. The videos are highly entertaining, in part because Lizzie and her best friend Charlotte, who is shooting them, role-play various characters in the story, like Lizzie's mother and father, and dress in appropriate costumes. While this might have been a budgetary decision to reduce the number of actors needed, it works well in the somewhat off-the-wall way Lizzie tells her story.

In general, the adaptation follows the classic Austen story of a mother eager to find husbands for her five daughters, and of the daughter's encounters with various suitable and unsuitable bachelors. In the modern version, the household has been reduced to just three daughters. They are Lizzie herself, who is the middle child and a grad student in mass communications, destined to be the love interest for the seemingly cold Darcy; her older sister, the fashionable, perfect Jane; and her baby sister, the flirtatious, frenetic Lydia. In addition, Charlotte, Lizzie's best friend, functions almost as a fourth sister. The slimming down of the Bennet household helped make the complex story more manageable and made it possible to focus more intensively on several characters.

I was extremely fortunate to snag an interview with Bernie Su, the head writer and show runner for the series. In addition, the modest Su was also its co-creator and directed most of the episodes. In terms of work that inspired the *Lizzie Bennet Diaries*, he told me that *LonelyGirl15* was definitely an influence. I was curious about the social media sites that were used, and Su told me they were used in different ways. Some were used more to portray the characters, while others, including LOOKBOOK, Tumblr, and Twitter, were used more for narrative purposes. LOOKBOOK, a fashion social network, was one of the most unique social media sites used in the story. Lizzie's sister Jane, who loved fashion, was very active on LOOKBOOK. Su told me her posts there were highly popular: "I think the fans who were very immersed really appreciated LOOKBOOK because that was a thing they hadn't seen before." The photos used on LOOKBOOK, he said, were story-enhancing because they showed what Jane had worn to different events in the story.

He said Facebook was used mostly to reinforce what Lizzie had talked about in her video blog, while the perspectives of other characters primarily came from Twitter and other YouTube channels, serving almost as parallel storylines. He said they worked as "four almost complete timelines in real-time, some more in-depth than others." Although the different perspectives were not as sharply differentiated as *Rashomon*, he pointed out, they offered a much more enriched version of the story. As to the importance of the social media sites, Su told me they were contributed hugely to the popularity of the show. He said they "enriched the fandom to such a high level that it propelled the series into the success it has."

I asked Su what the biggest change was in adapting the Austen novel. He said: "telling the story and having it be all about marriage, or meeting the right guy, or getting the guy, felt very anachronistic. It didn't feel very genuine to us. And even though some of the purists wondered 'how could you tell *Pride and Prejudice* and not have it be about marriage?!' You go like 'well, it's not 1800.' It was about marriage, but I think it was also about *independence*."

Aside from shifting the focus away from the importance of marriage, what was most true from the Austen novel was the way the characters came through. The only significant one to be changed was Darcy's sister, he told me; the others were essentially modern versions of Austen's creations.

The audience could participate in the story by asking Lizzie questions, which she would answer in character. Su told me: "Toward the end we were getting thousands of questions, and in the beginning we were getting hundreds, so it was certainly a very, very cool thing."

Sometimes Lizzie would directly invite fan participation. For example, she would ask people how they spent their holidays, and fans would respond by sending her videos about their celebrations. And, of course, fans could and did comment on any of the posts the fictional characters made. The fans even created their own completely independent website to discuss the series, *Darceny.com*. Charlotte and the three sisters each had a dedicated fan base. Charlotte's fans, for example, could make comments about her on Twitter at #thatssocharlotte. He told me that Charlotte "has become an icon of our series as the counterpoint to Lizzy's point of view, which is not always correct."

The *Lizzie Bennet Diaries* ran for 100 episodes, just short of an entire year, an achievement attained by very few Web series. In the beginning, though the team did not know exactly how many episodes there would be, they realized it would be an extended run. Su told me: " I approached it very much like a television show. I said 'this is a long game … I'm building it to be evergreen, to last a long time, to be a long series'." And, he said, the success of the *Lizzie Bennet Diaries* did not come easily. Though he believes it is possible to create a successful Web series, "You have to go fight for it, and work hard," he stressed. "It's a journey. It's difficult … I know I put in a lot of hours, for sure. And I do enjoy it. I'm not complaining." But, he said emphatically, "you've got to work for it, or else you're not going to get it."

AUSTEN LIVES ON

Fortunately, the *Lizzie Bennet Diaries* has not been the end of the line for social media Web series based on Jane Austen's writings nor the end of the characters that Lizzie introduced. A new series, *Welcome to Sanditon* (http://www.welcometosanditon.com/), premiered in May 2013 and ran over the summer of 2013. It was based on Austen's unfinished novel, *Sanditon*, which she abandoned after only 11 chapters, but the new online series greatly expanded and modernized the story.

As with the *Lizzie Bennet Diaries*, which are conveyed to a large extent by Lizzie in the form of vlogs (video blogs), *Welcome to Sanditon* is told in a series of vlogs narrated by Gigi, Darcy's sister. The story revolves around the seaside community of Sanditon in California (see Figure 9.1), which is striving to modernize and to attract more visitors.

Gigi has been enlisted to help her brother's company introduce a new video platform called Domino to help with this endeavor. Thus, the fictional residents of Sanditon will be beta testing Domino, and their employment of it is featured in Gigi's vlogs. (Most of these videos are fan-made and are powered by the Theatrics collaborative storytelling platform.) In addition to the vlogs, the story is told by an array of social media sites, including Twitter, Reddit, Facebook, Tumblr, and This is My Jam (a social media site focused on music), using them as the fictional characters in the story would. Since Austen never finished this novel, the creative team has had the liberty to conclude the series in the way they feel serves it best.

Figure 9.1 The logo for the Web series, *Welcome to Sanditon*, based on the unfinished novel by Jane Austen. Image courtesy of Adam Levermore.

WORKS OF NON-FICTION USING SOCIAL MEDIA

Social media has quickly become a workhorse form of communications for all kinds of organizations, both for-profit and nonprofit, and for all kinds of endeavors. Charities use social media to raise funds; artists use them to draw attention to their art work; universities use them to enroll new students. My old journalism school, the Medill School at Northwestern University, has integrated the teaching of social media into the curriculum, believing that these new platforms have become another significant method of connecting with audiences. In addition to these functional applications of social media, they are also being used to create new kinds of non-fiction entertainment experiences and to tell fairly complex stories as they happen in real time.

One quite unusual non-fiction project was launched by YouTube in 2008. It was a collaborative symphony project, *The YouTube Symphony Orchestra* (http://www.youtube.com/user/symphony). The project had a global reach because musicians from all over the world were invited to send in audition videos. An original piece of music, *The Internet Symphony No 1*, written by Chinese composer Tan Dun, was commissioned for this project. A decidedly modern piece, it called for such unusual instruments as disc brakes and rims from automobiles. Prospective orchestra members had to submit a tape showing them playing this music, as well as another audition piece. The YouTube community itself voted on the selection of the musicians.

The winners participated in a live performances directed by Michael Tilson Thomas at the Carnegie Hall in 2009 and a second YouTube Symphony Orchestra competition was announced in 2010. The musicians for the second concert assembled and performed at the Sydney Opera House in 2011. Again directed by Thomas, it involved 101 musicians from 33 different countries and another original piece of music. The exterior of the iconic opera house was illuminated by stunning projections made by Obscura Digital. The event became the largest live stream ever made by YouTube: over 30 million watched the concert on computers and almost three million on mobile devices. Even though this project involved classical music, not normally a type of music favored by a great many people, this project illustrates that there is an enormous potential audience for unique events that involve social media, competition, and glamour, as well as new kinds of experiences that can be created using digital media.

Another unusual social media project—*@Summer Break*—played out over the summer of 2013. It was an eight-week reality show that exclusively used social media rather than TV. Playing out in real time, it followed nine newly graduated high school seniors as they enjoyed their last summer before college, and presumably, before growing up. It utilized Twitter, YouTube, Tumblr, and Instagram. Obviously, *@Summer Break* is a fairly juvenile story, and unlike the YouTube Symphony Orchestra it does not involve high art, but it illustrates another way new ground can be broken by using social media.

The Grapes of Wrath Journey (http://www.grapesofwrath75.org/), organized by the National Steinbeck Center in California, also used social media exclusively, but it was a far more serious enterprise than *@Summer Break*. The 10-day road trip, much of it along old Route 66, was made in honor of the 75th anniversary of John Steinbeck's renowned book, *The Grapes of Wrath*. It retraced the route of the fictional Joad family across Oklahoma, Texas, New Mexico, Arizona, and into California, where the Joads were hoping for a better life after nearly being wiped out during the Dust Bowl. The modern group of travelers was made up of a team of three artists and their crew, among them a visual artist, a playwright, and a filmmaker.

Although members of the public could not travel with them, they could vicariously participate in the journey through the project's website, blog, Facebook page, tweets, and Instagram posts. Along the route, the artists did over 16 programs at partner organizations, including performances, workshops, and the recording of oral histories, and some of these programs were streamed live. In part, the team was trying to answer the same question the Joad family had been grappling with: how do you survive as a family in hard times? Storytelling was a major part of this project, because not only did it honor the story that Steinbeck told, but also told the story of the modern travelers and the stories of the people they met along the way. This project is a solid example of how social media can be used to document an unfolding story in real time, and how it can involve members of the audience.

SOCIAL MEDIA GAMES

Social media games, also called social games, are games that you play on social media sites with your community of friends. Thus, they are multiplayer games, unlike many video games that you play alone against NPCs. What is new about social media games is, first of all, they are generally asynchronous, meaning that players are not playing with each other at the same time, though there are a few exceptions to this. Furthermore, unlike most other kinds of games, these have no victory or loss conditions, because they are ongoing experiences, though they do generally have missions that the user must complete before advancing in the game. For the most part, these games are free to play but their business model is based on microtransactions, which means that players must make small purchases with real money in order to be successful in the game. These games have varying degree of story content, from almost none to quite a large amount, and new approaches to this genre are being developed on a continuing basis.

Farmville, published by Zynga in 2009 and played on Facebook, was the first social media game to become a massive hit. Its premise was quite simple: you have a plot of undeveloped farmland and it is your job to plant crops, raise livestock, build barns, and create the most thriving farm possible. Another early game, *Scrabulous*, was also quite popular on Facebook. The game dates back to 2005, but due to its close similarity to Scrabble, its developers were sued and the game was removed. In contrast another game, *The Godfather, Five Families*, which was made by Kabam and came out in 2011, contains far more narrative and includes video, and is a fairly dark story. The game is set in the 1930s during Prohibition, and the story revolves around five mafia families warring against each other to gain control of New York. If your game strategy is clever enough, you might become Don of the city.

Zynga Elite Slots, launched late in 2012, combines typical slot machine play with fantasy-adventure game elements, and thus is quite different from other social media games. Players choose a pet avatar to represent them in the game and, as they advance, they venture through a succession of themes, such as the Enchanted Forest and the House of Fangs. The players' pets progress in experience points and gems as the player spins, and eventually players can engage in a big boss fight. In terms of story, the richest elements are the characters and the fantasy environments.

In contrast to the other social media games discussed here, *Pearl's Peril* offers quite a rich narrative. The episodic game, made by the German company Wooga, is set in the 1930s. You play the game as Pearl, a young woman trying to solve the mystery of her father's death. The gameplay involves hidden object scenes and puzzle-solving adventure sequences, all of which help you solve the mystery. You are also asked to construct and decorate buildings that will help you gain insight into the life of Pearl's father (and possibly his death). Although the story elements here are quite deep, the social elements are more limited. The game contains leaderboards and friends can send energy to each other, so it is almost like a game meant for solo play. It will be interesting to see if developers find a way to combine the social part of gaming with rich narratives so that social media games can offer the deeply immersive experiences of video games.

DOES HUMOR HAVE ANY ROLE TO PLAY IN SOCIAL MEDIA?

Humor, if appropriate, can be a very effective component of social media. When people are amused by something, they are apt to pass it along to their friends, and thus humor can promote viral marketing. And when people get a good laugh from something, they tend to remember it longer than something that was serious. Thus, yes, humor can be your ally, but there is a large BUT here. If the humor used is insensitive when it comes to race, gender, culture, or other forms of personal identity, it can backfire and instead of being an ally, it will become an enemy of your content. Furthermore, the humor you use should always be in keeping with the overall story. Not every project can or should support humor, and it is clearly inappropriate if your content relates to such topics as the Holocaust, deadly diseases, assassinations, and the like. But when applied judiciously, and to the right project, humor can definitely be an asset.

CONCLUSION

Although using social media to tell stories is still a relatively new development, these narratives have already demonstrated that they can be used to portray characters and be the "bones" of both fictional and non-fiction stories. And it seems that with every passing year, developers are finding new ways to employ them for storytelling.

Here are a few things to keep in mind for using social media as a storytelling device:

- If you are developing a work of fiction, select the forms of social media that your characters would be likely to use, rather than the form that is currently most popular (though a highly popular one might also be right for your piece).

- When writing social media posts for your fictional characters, use the conventions of that particular form and model these posts on the way living people write.

- Remember that sometimes a social media site that is less well known can be perfect for your piece, so don't be afraid to use it, since you can point your users to it from the more popular sites you are employing.

- When writing a work of non-fiction, select the forms of media best suited to convey different facets of your piece, including photos, text, and video.

- Make sure your piece leaves space for users to participate and welcomes their contributions. This can include the opportunity to make comments, post images and videos, or even contribute new characters. Remember that in social media, it is the *social* that makes this form of communication as popular as it is.

- Use humor when appropriate, but do not use it in an insensitive fashion.

IDEA-GENERATING EXERCISES

1. Select a character from a TV show, movie, or game that you are very familiar with and write at least five tweets in this person's voice.

2. Develop a Facebook page for this character. What information would you put in the "about" section. What kinds of photos do you think this character would include? Write a few posts, and responses to those posts, for this Facebook page.

3. Take a novel or motion picture or TV show that you are highly familiar with, and consider how that same story could be told using only social media. What social media would you employ? Try creating the opening of the story using these social media.

4. Sketch out a work of social media non-fiction for an ongoing endeavor that you are familiar with. What forms of social media would you use? How could users add their own contributions? This endeavor could be about archeology, exploration, a conservation effort, or many other things, but ideally it should be ongoing and the outcome should be uncertain.

5. Select a social media game that you have played and analyze how the game worked. Describe the narrative content and the gameplay. What made this a social game? What do you think worked best in this game and what could have been improved?

Transmedia Storytelling

What makes the transmedia approach so different from other forms of storytelling?

What are *cheese holes* and *rabbit holes* and what do they have to do with transmedia storytelling?

Why is the transmedia approach so attractive from a creative person's point of view?

How is the transmedia approach being used for non-fiction endeavors like retail and education?

A DIFFERENT APPROACH TO STORYTELLING

With rare exceptions, narratives have been created for a single and specific medium—to be acted on the stage, for instance, or to be printed in a book or filmed for a movie. Sometimes a work might later be adapted into another medium, but such adaptations are rarely planned in advance; essentially, adaptations are just another way to tell the same story. Recently, however, content creators have begun to take a very different approach to storytelling. They have started to devise narratives that are designed from the ground up to "live" on several forms of media simultaneously. Each relates a different aspect of the story, or relates it in a different manner. In this new approach, at least some of the story is offered on an interactive medium, so that people can participate in it. This new type of storytelling, which we briefly discussed in Chapters 2 and 3, uses a *transmedia* approach to narrative.

Although transmedia storytelling might seem like a brand-new concept, we can actually find a strong example of it thousands of years ago, going back to the ancient Egypt of the pharaohs. The Egyptians' monumental temple complexes and tombs often employed architecture, painting, sculpture, symbols, and hieroglyphics to tell a single united story (see Figure 10.1). The story could be about a god, a great pharaoh, or a victorious battle. Each medium would contribute a piece to the overall story, just as the various elements have a part to play in modern transmedia storytelling. Another older example is the German concept of *gesampkunstverk*, introduced in Chapter 3, which is an artist work that spans several forms of art, such as an opera.

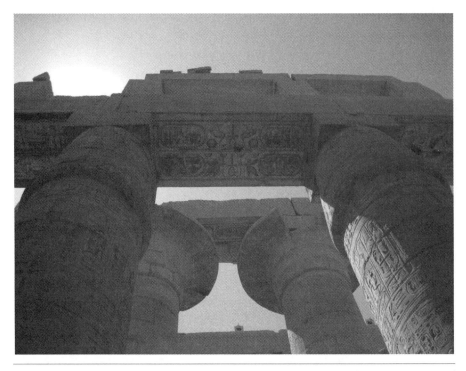

Figure 10.1   The ancient Egyptians employed a form of transmedia storytelling. Image courtesy of Carolyn Handler Miller.

In modern times, the first transmedia production to catch the attention of the public was *The Blair Witch Project*, which was made in 1999. It consisted of just two components—a movie and website. The movie told the story of three young filmmakers who venture into the woods to make a documentary about a legendary witch, and then vanish under terrifying circumstances, leaving behind their videotapes. The movie is constructed solely of the footage that is allegedly discovered after their disappearance, and it is presented as a factual documentary.

The website focused on the same central story that was told in the film. At the time of the movie's release in 1999, plenty of other websites had already been tied into movies. But what made *The Blair Witch Project* so remarkable, and what created such a sensation, was the way the website enhanced and magnified the "documentary" content of the film. It bore no resemblance to the typical promotional site for a movie, with the usual bios of the actors and director, or behind-the-scenes photos taken on the set. In fact, it contained nothing to indicate that *The Blair Witch Project* was a horror movie, or that it was even a movie at all.

Instead, the material on the website treated the account of the filmmakers' trip into the woods as if it were absolute fact. It offered additional information about the events depicted in the movie, including things that happened before and after the three filmmakers ventured into the woods. Visitors to the site could view video interviews with the filmmakers' relatives, townspeople, and law enforcement officers, or examine an abundance of "archival" material. Thus, they could construct their own version of the mystery surrounding the missing filmmakers.

The content of the website was so realistic that many fans were convinced that everything depicted in *The Blair Witch Project* actually took place.

Of course, the website was, in fact, just an extremely clever and inexpensive way to promote the low-budget movie. It accomplished this goal supremely well, and created such intense interest and curiosity that *The Blair Witch Project* became an instant hit. Though simple by today's transmedia productions, made up of just a movie and a website, it dramatically illustrated the synergistic power of using multiple platforms to expand a story. The website (www .blairwitch.com) has become an Internet classic, and remains popular even now, though not all of its features are still functioning.

DEFINING THE TRANSMEDIA APPROACH

Partially because transmedia storytelling is still so new, it goes by several different names. Some call it "multi-platforming" or "cross-media producing." It is known to others as "networked entertainment" or "integrated media." When used for a project with a strong story component, it may be called a "distributed narrative." Gaming projects that use the transmedia approach may be called "pervasive gaming" or sometimes "trans-media gaming." When this kind of gaming blurs reality and fiction, it is often called "alternate reality gaming" or an "ARG." The terms "transmedia entertainment" and "transmedia storytelling" seem to be gaining the most favor, however, and these are the terms we are using here.

In any case, no matter what terminology is employed, these works adhere to the same basic principles:

- The project in question exists over more than a single medium, usually three or more.
- It is at least partially interactive.
- The different components are used to expand the core narrative.
- The components are closely integrated.
- The story contains at least one public point of entry (the *rabbit hole*).
- The story contains spaces which are designed to encourage members of the audience to contribute content (*cheese holes*).
- Transmedia stories, while not necessarily games, often contain some gaming elements and a playful sensibility.

In addition, several other terms are often used in conjunction with transmedia storytelling. One universally important term is s*toryworld*, which is the universe of the story. A storyworld can be either fiction or non-fiction, but in any case it contains everything the story revolves around. This includes the plot, the characters, and the setting. Storyworlds are deep and, ideally, contain a past and a future as well as a present. There should be something about the storyworld that makes people want to participate in it. Furthermore, the storyworld must be consistent across all platforms. In academic circles, the term *diagesis* is sometimes used to mean storyworld.

Developers will often refer to the *canon* of the story, which is the official version of the narrative, consistent on all the different media on which the story is carried. Professionals within the transmedia world will also talk about navigating *silos*, which are media organizations like TV production companies, ad agencies, and newspaper publishers— organizations that are used to operating independently and being non-collaborative. In building a transmedia story, however, these organizations must learn to work with each other and to breach the rigid silo-like walls that once enclosed them.

Finally, and all importantly, transmedia storytellers, like all good storytellers, aspire to captivate their audiences and induce them to experience a *willing suspension of disbelief*. In other words, they want their audiences to buy into the story, become totally absorbed in it, and at least temporarily believe it to be true and not question its validity. Yes, this is a form of lying, because the story is not true, but at some level the audiences realize that the story is a fiction. This is quite different from a hoax, which is a fiction the storyteller intends for the audience to take at face value, believe as factual, and act accordingly. A hoax can cause panic, as Orson Wells' *War of the Worlds* did. Some listeners to this radio broadcast believed aliens were actually invading Earth, and in the following days a great deal of outrage was expressed about the show. In transmedia storytelling, because so many media are employed and because the stories comprise a *persistent universe*, they have even greater potential to seem real. This was the case of an alternate reality game (ARG), *The Truth about Marika*, a story produced for Swedish television about a young woman who had disappeared. Many people believed she was a real person and helped search for her. Understandably, they were not at all happy when it was revealed the story was a complete fiction, as is noted below. Thus, to avoid an angry backlash, transmedia storytellers must take care not to be creating a hoax.

Transmedia productions typically include both traditional media and digital media platforms. The traditional components may be a movie, a TV show, a newspaper ad, a novel, or even a billboard. The digital media elements may be a Web series, a video game, an app, or a social media feed. In addition, these projects may also utilize everyday communications tools like faxes and voicemail. A number of these projects also include the staging of live events, with actors portraying the fictional characters in the story. The choice of platforms is totally up to the development team; no fixed set of components exists for these projects.

INSIGHTS FROM THE EXPERTS

In order to gain a better understanding about where transmedia is today, and where it might be going, I interviewed four experts in the field. They included Jeff Gomez, CEO of Starlight Runner Entertainment, a transmedia production company. As one of the leading authorities in the field, Gomez and his company have transformed many Hollywood blockbusters, such as Disney's *Pirates of the Caribbean*, into vibrant transmedia experiences. The group also included Alison Norrington, based in London and LA. She is an accomplished writer and transmedia producer, and also the CCO/Founder at storycentralDIGITAL and the newly launched storycentralLABS. In addition, Norrington was Conference Chair of the first two StoryWorld Conferences, which focused sharply on transmedia storytelling. My third expert was Sean Stewart, whom I had interviewed previously and whose further contributions can be found in Chapter 18 on alternate reality games (ARGs). Stewart is a transmedia storyteller and one of the brilliant creators of *The Beast*. He continues to break new ground in transmedia while simultaneously teaching at the University of Southern California (USC). My fourth expert, Robert Pratten, also appears extensively in Chapter 18. Based in London, Pratten is CEO of Transmedia Storyteller Ltd. His company has developed a software program, *Conducttr*, which coordinates and manages all the assets of transmedia stories, including social media, and releases pieces of the story at appropriate times.

One of the topics I quizzed them about was the willing suspension of disbelief, and how important they believed it was to the transmedia experience. In the opinion of Jeff Gomez (see Figure 10.2), "That's just good storytelling, no matter what the medium. Every so often it's fun to think that what we are experiencing is 'for real,' and every generation has a cool hoax story, from Orson Welles' depiction of *War of the Worlds*, to *The Blair Witch Project*." But, he added, "I think it's a practice over which the audience tires very quickly." He cited *The Truth About Marika*, the Swedish production about a young woman who has allegedly been kidnapped and whom the audience believed to be in great danger. When the audience learned it was a totally fictional story, Gomez said, it "left a bad taste in the mouths of many."

Sean Stewart also agreed that there can be a downside to trying to induce the suspension of disbelief. He and his teams have an approach guided by the philosophy of "we will make a world for you. We will make this a good time. But we will never make you feel dumb for having done this." He told me that it has always been fundamental to his practice to be extraordinarily respectful of the players. In part, he said, being respectful was just common courtesy, but also because "the suspension of disbelief is as gossamer as a soap bubble and requires great effort on a player's part to maintain." He added that "anything you do that makes them feel dorky for having done it for you is a terrible mistake." He went on to tell me: "People are really worried that someone, somewhere is trying to screw them over or make them look stupid. And you really have to avoid doing that. If you lose an audience's trust, then you're in a world of trouble, and you should be."

Stewart went on to describe a metaphor he and a co-worker often use about the relationship between the developers and the audience: that it's like asking someone to dance. "The gentleman asks the lady to dance," Stewart explained. "He [the development team] will propose a step, and if the lady [the audience] accepts and chooses to follow the step, there will be a dance. But it's respectfully done, and you have to know that the lady does not have to accept that suggestion."

All four of my experts offered their ideas about choosing the best platforms to use. Gomez feels that the platforms with the greatest untapped potential are the ones that are capable of generating the greatest level of intimacy. He includes mobile devices and tablets in this category and says: "Transmedia narratives have the potential to become highly personalized through these devices, and that in turn can generate powerful responses on the part of the audience participant."

Alison Norrington believes that there's no single template for choosing platforms because of diverse audience types, genres, and stories. She feels the selection of platforms can only

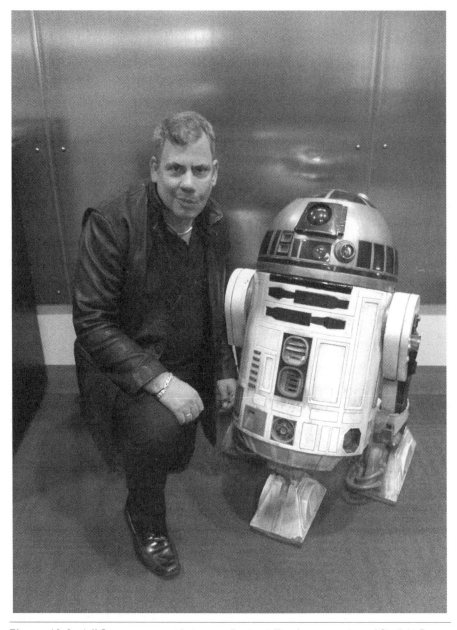

Figure 10.2 Jeff Gomez, an expert in transmedia storytelling. Image courtesy of Starlight Runner Entertainment.

sensibly be made toward the end of the R&D process: "Only when the developmental work that looks at core message, theme, story world build, genre, audience demographics and behaviors, experience design and budgetary restrictions is completed can writers begin to really consider platforms." Not surprisingly, she asserts that the most effective platforms depend on the specific project and that "it's about the conversation with the audience, tone of voice, exploring where they already 'hang out' and echoing their behaviors."

Robert Pratten concurs with Norrington that research work must be done before selecting specific platforms for a transmedia work. He told me: "I'd say that the platforms are often initially being driven by what we think would make a cool experience for the story or the need to 'spread the word' or the need to generate revenue but then quickly sanity-checked against the audience. Are they likely to have access? Are they familiar and comfortable with this platform?" Pratten shared with me a diagram he created that indicates the four elements that must be considered before an intelligent selection of platforms can occur (see Figure 10.3).

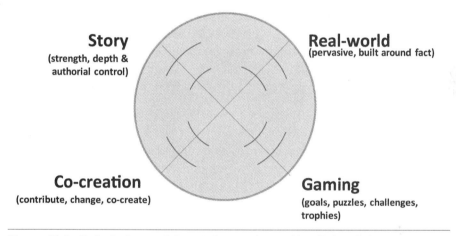

Story
(strength, depth & authorial control)

Real-world
(pervasive, built around fact)

Co-creation
(contribute, change, co-create)

Gaming
(goals, puzzles, challenges, trophies)

Figure 10.3 Pratten's diagram of elements that must be considered before platforms are selected. Image courtesy of Transmedia Storyteller Ltd.

Sean Stewart had a much simpler perspective on the selection of platforms. He feels that the focus should be audience centric, rather than platform centric, and boiling it all down, he said that as to the choice of platform "we're just going to take whatever is the best and most interesting way to bring you your story or your entertainment."

As for cheese holes, Jeff Gomez confessed to me that it was he who had come up with using the concept in transmedia storytelling. He said: "The 'Swiss cheese' model of story-telling first occurred to me in the 1980s while I was designing stories for my players to run through in early games of Dungeons & Dragons … I needed to 'drill holes in the cheese' that were mysterious and alluring enough for them to want to climb into and fill. My story world became a block of Swiss cheese, and my players loved it! So there were questions to be answered, riddles to solve, gaps in history that required speculation, and we were off and running."

Alison Norrington told me that for her, "Cheese hole design is about recognizing the opportunities within the story … Cheese holes are the places where you would like or will actively steer an audience to create content, perhaps in the form of back story, additional characters, ancillary storylines, Rashomon-style alternative perspectives or around artifacts from the storyworld. It doesn't necessarily mean disruption to impact the storyline." Surprisingly, Norrington told me that she isn't convinced that cheese holes are absolutely necessary in transmedia stories, since the interaction and conversation between storyteller and co-creators can take place by alternative methods means beyond filling gaps in the story. However, she feels that cheese holes can be "a fun place for co-creation with fans and audience."

Both Norrington and Gomez feel that story creation for transmedia requires a somewhat different mindset than story creation for a single medium story. Gomez said: "like any rising art form, good transmedia storytelling will require a combination of established talents and techniques, but it also will need something new. A native talent and skill set that I believe is coming up just over the horizon." And Norrington stressed "a story created with a specific transmedia approach in mind requires a wider lens than a single-platform, contained story in order to expand it to a storyworld." She advises writers interested in working in this form to "take a step back and consider whether they have a concept of a story that's big enough to be built out to a world."

Norrington has observed a number of common mistakes that are made in the creation of transmedia stories:

- a rush to platforms because they are free;
- the storytellers' unbridled excitement and passion to launch their story, which causes them to hurry the development process and results in a confusing base line of mythology;
- a disregard for audience demographics and behaviors;
- a weak core theme and message; and finally
- the use of heavy marketing language in the calls-to-action.

Gomez added two mistakes that he has observed:

- Building the narrative without a forum or apparatus to house and process user feedback. Why, he wonders, "wouldn't you be interested in hearing what your audience has to say about it?"
- And second, he says, "too many transmedia narratives feature characters we don't care about." He asserts: "Creators and producers have to remember that the technology and unique nature of the implementation is not nearly enough to hold an audience to a transmedia narrative. Good story, accessible and compelling characters, and ease of use will do that."

As to the future of transmedia storytelling, Sean Stewart believes we are still in the "horseless carriage days"—the early days of discovering what we can do with this new type of narrative. He is confident people will stick with it but believes in the future these stories will have "a pleasant degree of agency. I tend to think that many of the most successful ones will have very strong interactivity that does not change the outcome of the story, but that's just my bet."

AN INTERNATIONAL PHENOMENON

As an indication of the widespread popularity of transmedia storytelling, it is worth noting that transmedia projects have been developed throughout the world.

For example, Singapore has hosted a number of multi-platform projects, one of them being the popular children's show, *Mat Yoyo*. Kuwait was the home of *Find Fahad*, a transmedia mystery story. South Korea, a hub of high-tech enterprises, has been a fertile location for transmedia, while in Malaysia, the TV and radio broadcaster Astro, as well as the integrated media company MediaPrima, are both producing transmedia elements in conjunction with their established programs. Transmedia is a comfortable fit in Japan, with its long tradition of integrating manga comics, TV, merchandising, and live events. And Java is the home of *Wakfu*, a transmedia MMOPG that also integrates comics and a card game.

In Europe, producers in France are creating a transmedia Web series, *3X3*, while Denmark hosted the transmedia music video show *Boogie*. Finland and Sweden were the home of a cluster of clever transmedia games centered on mobile devices and in South Africa, the reality show *Big Brother, Africa* has been designed from the ground up to encompass a transmedia storytelling approach. We cover a collection of American transmedia works in this chapter and in Chapter 18, on alternate reality games (ARGs). In addition, transmedia storytelling is being studied in academic institutions around the world, from MIT's august program of Comparative Media Studies in North America to the University of Sydney in Australia.

GOING PRIME-TIME WITH TRANSMEDIA STORYTELLING

In the fall of 2002, a bold new kind of transmedia venture was introduced to the public and was the first prime-time TV series to employ transmedia storytelling. Entitled *Push, Nevada*, it combined both a story and a game; blurred fiction and reality; and used multiple media. The project was produced by LivePlanet, a company founded, in part, by Ben Affleck and Matt Damon, and the project had some of Hollywood's most sophisticated talent behind it. With a first-class production team, network television backing, and over a million dollars in prize money, *Push, Nevada* was Hollywood's first major step into transmedia waters.

The components that made up the *Push, Nevada* galaxy revolved around a quirky mystery that was devised to unfold in 13 60-minute television episodes on ABC. The unlikely hero of the story is an IRS investigator, Jim Prufrock, a clean-cut and earnest young man. One day, Prufrock receives a fax alerting him to an irregularity, possibly an embezzlement, in the finances of a casino in a town called Push, Nevada. He sets off to Push to investigate, and becomes entangled in the strange goings on of this extremely peculiar town. The mostly unfriendly residents clearly have something—perhaps many things—to hide. An uneasy aura of corruption hangs over the town, and the tone of the television show is intriguingly off-center, reminiscent of the TV series *Twin Peaks*. With its complex plot, allusions to T.S. Eliot, and unresolved episode endings, the series was not the kind of TV fare that most viewers were used to.

The TV show, although obviously a critical element, was just one of several components employed to tell the story and support the game. Other elements included a number of faux websites, mobile apps, a book, and text messaging. During the preproduction process, great attention was paid to the development of both the story and the game, and to make sure all the elements worked together, LivePlanet created a document called an Integrated Media Bible and an Integrated Media Timeline, which showed the relationship between the various media as the story and game played out over a number of weeks (see Figure 10.4).

Figure 10.4   A portion of the Integrated Media Timeline developed for *Push, Nevada*. Image courtesy of LivePlanet.

EXPERT OBSERVATIONS: WADING, SWIMMING, AND DIVING

Just before the airing of the first episode of *Push, Nevada*, LivePlanet's CEO, Larry Tanz, addressed a group of industry professionals at the American Film Institute. In his talk, he described the project "a treasure hunt for waders, swimmers, and divers." In other words, members of the audience could determine the degree of involvement they wished to have. Some might only want to "wade" into its fictional world, which they could do just by watching the TV show. Others might choose to "swim," and sample parts of the story on other media. And still others might want to "dive in" and actively follow the clues and try to win the prize money, in which case they would be able to make full use of the other platforms that were part of *Push, Nevada*. Ideally, as Tanz suggested, transmedia narratives should accommodate the full spectrum of audience members, from those who are primarily interested in passive entertainment to those who relish an extremely active experience.

LivePlanet referred to *Push, Nevada* as an "integrated media" approach to storytelling. As Larry Tanz described it to me, it means developing a property and having it operate over three platforms: traditional media (TV, film, and radio), which is the "driver" of each project; interactive media (the Internet, apps, and so on), which allows the audience to participate; and the physical world, which brings the story into people's lives. The goal is to have these three platforms overlap in such a way that they are integrated at the core (see Figure 10.5).

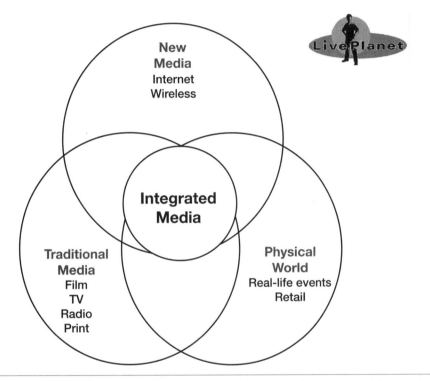

Figure 10.5 LivePlanet's integrated media approach to transmedia. Image adaptation courtesy of LivePlanet.

Despite the high hopes for the project, and despite the fact that the interactive components proved to be extremely popular, the TV component of *Push, Nevada* failed to catch on, and after only seven episodes, ABC discontinued the show.

By many other measurements, though, it was clear that many people were closely following the *Push, Nevada* story/game. About 200,000 people visited the *Push, Nevada* websites, which at the time made it one of the largest online games in history, according to ABC's calculations. Over 100,000 viewers followed the clues closely enough to figure out the phone numbers of fictitious people on the show, call the numbers, and hear the characters give them recorded messages. In addition, about 60,000 people downloaded the "Deep Throat" conspiracy book written for the project. All told, ABC estimates that 600,000 people actively participated in the experience.

TRANSMEDIA STORYTELLING AND FEATURE FILMS

Less than a year after *Push, Nevada* debuted, another high profile transmedia narrative was released, and like *Push, Nevada*, it, too, had roots in glamorous Hollywood media. This venture was the sequel to the enormously popular feature film, *The Matrix*. Unlike a regular movie sequel, however, it was not just another feature film. Instead, the producers, the visionary Wachowski siblings, created a transmedia sequel of breathtaking scope. It was composed of two feature films, *The Matrix Reloaded* and *The Matrix Revolutions*, and it also included a video game, *Enter the Matrix*; a DVD, *The Animatrix*; and a website, ThisistheMatrix.com.

This high-tech, new media crossover was particularly apt, given that the *Matrix* story depicts a society in which the digital and physical worlds collide, and in which virtual reality runs amok.

Each component of the *Matrix* collection of properties tells a somewhat different piece of the *Matrix* story, but the story is consistent across all media. The two movie sequels and the video game were actually developed as one single project. The Wachowskis, Andy and Lana, reputed to be avid gamers, were at the helm of all three projects. All were shot at the same time. Not only did the Wachowskis write and direct the two movies but they also wrote a 244-page dialogue script for the game and shot a full hour of extra footage for it—the equivalent of half a movie. In terms of the filming, the movies and game shared the same 25 characters, the same sets, the same crews, the same costume designers, and the same choreographers.

Although it is not necessary to see the movies in order to play the game, or vice versa, the game and movies, when experienced as a totality, are designed to deepen *The Matrix* experience and give the viewer-player a more complete understanding of the story. As one small example, in *The Matrix Reloaded*, the audience sees a character exit from a scene and return sometime later carrying a package. But only by playing *Enter the Matrix* will people understand how the character obtained that package.

At the time, it was one of the most expensive video games in history to make, costing $30 million, and took two-and-a-half years to complete. Nevertheless, despite the cost and a certain amount of criticism of the game and films, the game and the movies were a great success and benefited from the transmedia storytelling approach. Both the game and the first of the sequels, *The Matrix Reloaded*, debuted on the same day in May 2003 (a first in media history). By the end of the first week, the game had already sold one million units, selling a total of five million copies in all. As for *The Matrix Reloaded*, it earned a record-breaking $42.5 million on its opening day and a stunning $742 million worldwide (the second sequel, *The Matrix Revolutions*, fared somewhat less well, but still earned a respectable $427 million worldwide).

HOLLYWOOD'S KEEN INTEREST IN TRANSMEDIA STORYTELLING

Both the *Push, Nevada* story/game and *The Matrix* transmedia sequels were pioneering projects and ahead of their time, but more recently, as noted in Chapter 2, mainstream Hollywood studios and producers have woken up to the fact that a transmedia approach to content can be an effective antidote to shrinking audiences, and can also give them new revenue streams to tap.

In many cases, the transmedia material created for TV series has been in the form of Web series, sometimes called *webisodes*, which are serialized stories told in short episodes. These mini-dramas have spun out the TV series in a number of different ways. For example, a 10-part Web series was produced for the hit comedy, *The Office*. Called *The Office: The Accountants*, it was a story about a large sum of missing money. The story involved some of the background characters in the series, rather than the stars, giving the audience a chance to know them better. Sometimes a Web series will fill in pieces of the backstory of a TV series or will fill in story gaps between TV seasons, as with the 10-part webisode of the sci-fi show, *Battlestar Galactica*.

Sometimes, instead of creating a Web series, the TV series will create fictional blogs for their main characters, and fictional bios and posts for social media sites like Facebook, Pinterest, and Twitter. But in some cases, a TV series will pull out all the stops, as has been the case with the hit Showtime series, *Dexter*, who is a serial killer with a strong moral code. As of this writing, *Dexter* is in its eighth and final season. The producers have created a wealth of transmedia material for this show, including several Web series, an ARG, a Flash game, Facebook and mobile games, and a wiki. In addition, and most uniquely, they created a pseudo magazine campaign with magazine covers of Dexter displayed in magazine racks across the country. The covers closely imitated the covers of real magazines but had Dexter posing as the cover model. In another transmedia element, they set up working fountains in 13 US cities, all spewing a red liquid, hinting at Dexter's fascination with blood.

Nigelblog.com was another extremely clever transmedia venture tied to a TV series. Nigel was a character on *Crossing Jordan*, a crime drama set in a city coroner's office in Boston. Nigel shared his observations with viewers on a blog written in his character's voice. Occasionally, he even posted videos he made with a webcam, sometimes secretly taping interchanges with other fictional characters. Though this example of transmedia storytelling only uses two media (TV and the Internet) it is highly interactive, and also completely immerses viewers in the fictional world of the television drama. For example, during the first season of the blog, Nigel solicited viewers' help in solving several "cold case" murders, posting a number of clues on his blog. The blog created for the second season had a more personal twist to it, with Nigel asking viewers to help him handle a messy office love triangle. Throughout the season, Nigel encouraged viewers to offer their advice on how to handle this complicated romance and frequently quoted their comments on his blog. Thus, real living people—the viewers—got to enter this fictional story and to feel as if they were playing a meaningful part in it.

Sometimes TV series producers will focus on mobile devices, with spin-offs in the form of *mobisodes* (serialized stories produced for mobile devices) being one such approach. For example, the six-part mobisode made for *Smallville*, a TV series about Superman's boyhood, told the backstory of an important character featured in the TV show, the Green Arrow. In a somewhat different approach, the mobisode *24: The Conspiracy* (a spin-off of the TV suspense drama, *24*), used the same type of storyline and same setting as the TV show, but offered a completely different cast of characters.

The Lost Experience, however, is possibly one of the most ambitious of transmedia storytelling applied to an American TV series. *The Lost Experience* is an alternate reality game created around the TV drama, *Lost*, about a group of survivors of an airline crash marooned on a mysterious tropical island. The game was created by three TV companies, ABC in the United States, Channel 7 in Australia, and Channel 4 in the UK. The clues and narrative content were embedded in faux TV commercials and websites, in phone messages, in emails from characters, and in roadside billboards. In one eerie beat of this unfolding ARG, a "spokesperson" (actually an actor) from the Hanso Foundation even appeared on an actual late night TV show to defend his organization, which has played an ongoing and possibly nefarious role in the mystery.

It is worth noting that the *Lost* ARG did not reveal any essential parts of the narrative. Thus TV viewers who didn't participate in the ARG would not miss any essential parts of the story, while viewers who played the ARG would enjoy a fuller experience of the *Lost* drama.

As ambitious as *The Lost Experience* was, it was by no means the series' sole venture in transmedia storytelling. *Lost* was always a leading innovator in the use of multiple platforms. For example, it created a mobisode called the *Lost Video Diaries* that featured the stories of other characters who were in the fictional airline crash, but were not part of the TV drama. And in another bit of transmedia storytelling, viewers of the TV show would see a character find a suitcase from the wrecked plane that has washed up on the beach. Upon opening the suitcase, he discovers it contains a manuscript for a novel. Careful viewers who go to the trouble of looking up the title and author on Amazon.com will actually find the book listed, along with some information about the author being one of the passengers of an airline lost in mid-flight. Viewers could actually order the full-length book and read it, should they wish, or buy the audio version, and possibly pick up more clues about the *Lost* saga.

The Lost Experience and other transmedia narratives based on TV series have been extremely popular with viewers, giving them new ways to enjoy their favorite TV shows. From the networks' point of view, they have been successful in achieving their twin goals of keeping audiences involved between episodes and seasons and sometimes providing new revenue streams. And, for TV writers and producers, these new ventures have offered fresh ways to expand the fictional worlds they have created.

FULLY DIGITAL WORKS OF TRANSMEDIA STORYTELLING

It is important to note that many works of transmedia are not built around TV series or films but stand entirely on their own. For example, *Dirty Work*, created by Fourth Wall Studios, was an original Web series augmented by a multi-platform approach. The episodes aired on Fourth Wall's proprietary website, Rides.TV. The show was an interactive comedy about a trio of twenty-somethings who worked for a company called Bio-Tidy and whose gory job it was to clean up crime scenes. *Dirty Work*'s goal was to imitate the way people interact with their digital devices while watching TV. If viewers wished, they could simply watch the episodes on the Web, but they could also choose to sign up for the full experience. This included receiving text messages and phone calls from the characters, getting additional content on Twitter and Facebook, and watching bonus videos. *Dirty Work* received an Emmy in 2012 for Outstanding Creative Achievement in Interactive Media.

TRANSMEDIA TV IN EUROPE

When it comes to outstanding transmedia productions, Europe is by no means being left in the dust by the United States. For example, *The Truth About Marika*, mentioned previously, was a riveting transmedia drama about the disappearance of a young woman, Marika, and the search instigated by her close friend. It aired in Sweden during the fall of 2007, and its transmedia elements—centered around the search and theories about her disappearance— took place on TV, on the streets, over the Internet, and on mobile phones.

Several years later, citizens of the Netherlands were alarmed to find people in frightening Zombie makeup and costumes wandering around their cities. These performers turned out to be an element of *Saligia-7*, a transmedia sci-fi thriller. The project was not only covered by Dutch TV news but also included print media, online videos, blogs, mobile devices, and social media.

In 2012, company P, the same production company that created *The Truth About Marika*, aired an even more ambitious project, *The Spiral*. The five-episode TV series aired not only in Sweden, but also in Denmark, Belgium, Finland, Norway, and the Netherlands. The story focuses on a group of young artists who hope to make their mark by stealing six price-less paintings, including a work by Picasso and another by Rubens. The museums which housed these paintings actually took them off their walls during the run of the series. The audience is invited to help try to find the invaluable artworks and an international chase ensues. *The Spiral* was an international sensation and was nominated for an International Emmy Award in 2013.

UNUSUAL VARIATIONS ON TRANSMEDIA PRODUCTIONS

Three of the most unusual works of transmedia storytelling are *Prison Dancer*, *The Seed*, and *The Due Return*.

Prison Dancer began as a YouTube video shot in Cebu Prison in the Philippines. The video records actual convicts, 1,500 of them, rehearsing a dance to Michael Jackson's *Thriller*. The dramatic video quickly went viral. From there, Canadian producers created a fictional version of this phenomenon called *Prison Dancer*. It featured six prisoners, one of whom was the transgender choreographer, Lolo, plus a cast of hundreds. At the end of each episode, viewers can decide which, if any, of the actors they want to hear tell their story. From the Web, and this is the most surprising point, the series became the springboard of an off-Broadway musical based on the same fictional story. The stage musical mixed live actors (including several from the Web series), film, and audience participation.

To date, *Prison Dancer* is one of the only transmedia musicals ever produced. However, if we look across the Atlantic, we can find another theatrical work, *The Seed*, which lived in a larger transmedia universe. *The Seed* was both an online game played out in the real world and a series of four plays written and produced for London's 2012 Cultural Olympiad. The work was inspired by the biographies of real Victorian botanists with a great sense of derring-do. These gentlemen would brave practically anything, Indian Jones style, to find rare plants that would flourish in British gardens. Players of *The Seed* were tasked with finding an especially precious specimen, the Chinese Gold, and clues could be found practically anywhere. One clue was actually written in moss. The four plays were staged in the gardens of the real-life botanists who inspired this story.

As for *The Due Return*, it was a full scale intergalactic sailing ship that was the centerpiece of a highly unusual art installation (see Figure 10.6). The project was created by Meow Wolf, a Santa Fe, New Mexico, artists' collective. Although Meow Wolf itself did not call the installation a work of transmedia but instead termed it a work of "immersive multimedia" or an "interdisciplinary work," it had all the hallmarks of a transmedia storytelling. These included

Figure 10.6   The exterior of *The Due Return*. Image courtesy of Ken Wilson.

a multi-platform narrative, interactive elements, digital media, and live performances as well as hundreds of artist-created artifacts, even including handmade barnacles.

According to the ship's archives (http://loci.theduereturn.com/), *The Due Return* had been traveling through space and time for decades. During the late spring and summer of 2011, it had docked in Santa Fe, New Mexico, at the Center for Contemporary Arts. Not only was it a full-sized ship, measuring 75 feet in length, 25 feet in width, and 14 feet from the ground up to the main deck, but it also contained hundreds of mysterious artifacts and pieces of sculpture. In addition, it was the setting for various live performances. Surrounding the ship was an extraterrestrial landscape of caves and glowing lights. Visitors to the vessel could explore the crew's bunks, the captain's chambers, a scientific lab, a lounge, and a greenhouse full of living plants that crew harvested for food. They could also spend time out on the captain's deck, an interactive control room. There they could not only spin the steering wheel but also try out its many electronic devices (see Figure 10.7).

Figure 10.7   The interactive captain's deck of the *Due Return*. Image courtesy of Ken Wilson.

In addition, a rich narrative was woven around the *The Due Return*'s history, covering the 161 years that the ship had been traveling. The history was not only written as text but also contained audio and video and could be accessed online. The archives included artists' books and sculpture, photos, YouTube videos, and various artifacts that visitors on the ship could study and even handle.

STRANGE BUT TRUE: NORWEGIAN ROT

One particularly unusual element of *The Due Return*'s transmedia story was a powerful drink called Norwegian Rot. This cocktail, a blue liquid with white orbs floating in it, evidently controlled the ship's navigation. When enough of the crew had consumed Norwegian Rot and had become intoxicated by it, the ship would move. On certain occasions, visitors to the ship could purchase Norwegian Rot and sample it themselves.

The creation of *The Due Return*'s history and archive was under the helm of Nicholas Chiarella, a poet with a background in museum work. Chiarella told me that it took a year of planning and building to construct *The Due Return* and its artifacts, and that up to 125 people had contributed to it. It was clear to me that *The Due Return* was a collaborative project but I wondered if anybody who wished could work on it. I asked Chiarella: "If Joe Smith from down the block wanted to contribute something, would he be able to?" "We're all Joe Smith," Chiarella replied.

Clearly, Meow Wolf is as inclusive as possible. Chiarella, giving a beautiful definition of transmedia storytelling, told me: "We didn't want to tread on either the artist's intention in trying to shape peoples' experience, or always control everything an audience member was feeling or thinking. We wanted their imaginations to become as much a part of our story as our art was."

Thanks in part to this interdisciplinary, collaborative spirit, *The Due Return* is a powerful creation and one of the most unusual transmedia works built so far. It illustrates that transmedia storytelling can move far beyond traditional television and film and venture into realms that we are just beginning to explore.

USING THE TRANSMEDIA APPROACH FOR A VARIETY OF ENDEAVORS

Most of the works of transmedia produced thus far have been made for entertainment purposes. However, a number of very clever and successful works have also been produced for marketing, information, education, training, and other uses.

For example, *Traces of Hope* was a transmedia game produced by the British Red Cross to promote awareness of its work in war-torn countries and to raise funds. The game is a story about Joseph, a 16-year-old Ugandan teenager who is searching for his mother. Their village has been ransacked by civil war violence and Joseph knows his sister and father have been killed in the bloodshed, but he doesn't know what happened to his mother. It's your job as the player to help reunite Joseph with his Mom. The game has its own website (http://tracesofhope .com/) and is played out over blogs, Linkedin, Flickr, and mobile apps. Launched in 2008, it was the first major transmedia work to be undertaken by a large charity.

However, for-profit organizations have been heavy users of transmedia for many years. One of my personal favorites was *Meow Mix House*, a promotional venture produced by Del Monte Foods back in 2006. *Meow Mix House* closely imitated TV's popular survivor shows and was aired in three-minute segments on Animal Planet. The contestants were cats who had been rescued from animal shelters in three major cities and were living in a specially built house which was displayed on a Manhattan boulevard. The winning feline would become an executive vice president of *Meow Mix House*. In order to win, the cats had to beat the other contestants in stunts like Best Post Climber. Webcams were trained on them around the clock, and viewers could watch them online, share their opinions, and vote for their favorite contestant. After the show ended, every participant was adopted into a good home. Thus, *Meow Mix House* not only promoted a brand of cat food, but also promoted the idea of pet adoption.

Catch the Kid was another clever promotional project. The game, built in 2011, was designed to promote tourism in my home state of New Mexico and was built around a famous, long dead New Mexican outlaw, Billy the Kid. According to the game's conceit, Billy is still alive and you are a lawman trying to find his hideout and catch him. If you're successful, you'll win $10,000, and along the way you can also win a variety of tourist-themed prizes, like free meals. An entire family could register as a "sheriff's posse" on the game's website, and by following the clues on the website, you'd arrive at various real destinations around the state. Posters were made for each location in the game, and you and your posse were to snap photos of the posters to prove you were there, and send them back to the game headquarters. The game worked well in part because it featured a strong charismatic character, a clear-cut goal, and gave players a meaningful role to play.

STRANGE BUT TRUE: THE *LOVE PLUS+* TRANSMEDIA GAME

Japan was the home of another transmedia promotional game, this one with a highly unusual twist: to promote geek (*otaku*) tourism. *Love Plus+* was a virtual romance game created for lonely-hearted bachelors, primarily computer geeks who not only lacked social skills but who also lacked real-life girlfriends. The game itself gave these young men an opportunity to court virtual girlfriends and develop a life-like relationship with them. If they earned enough points, they could take their girlfriend on a romantic getaway to a real Japanese resort town, Atami, which is a bit like going on a honeymoon to Niagara Falls. The hospitality industry in Atami happily played along with the game, and didn't ask any questions when a young man would register for a double room but had no visible companion with him. Evidently, over 1,500 players have turned up in Atami clutching their hand-held devices but not the hand of a young woman.

At least one toy company, Mattel, has also found a comfortable home in transmedia. It has successfully created an entire transmedia world based on its line of Monster High dolls—dolls who are the offspring of famous monsters. A dynamic and ever-growing website, Monster High (http://www.monsterhigh.com/en-us/index.html), has been created to support these dolls. Users can register as students in Monster High, decorate their lockers, send a scream to their best friend, check out the year book ("fear book"), and play games, of course. The Monster High universe also includes a set of fashion dolls, Facebook posts, and monster clothing for real-life young girls.

Although in most cases, the transmedia approach to storytelling has been used for works of fiction, this technique can also be successfully employed in non-fiction projects. For example, public television station KCET in Los Angeles used multiple media to tell the story of Woodrow Wilson, the president of the United States from 1913 to 1921, a project we will discuss in more detail in Chapter 14.

Another, more recent and groundbreaking work of non-fiction transmedia is *Snow Fall: The Avalanche at Tunnel Creek* (http://www.nytimes.com/projects/2012/snow-fall/#/?part=tunnel-creek), by John Branch. It is a stunning piece of new-style reporting published in print and digital form by the *New York Times* in 2012. This Pulitzer Prize winning article is about a group of skiers caught in a devastating avalanche. It was stitched together as an interactive piece consisting of text, video, still photos, and audio interviews. Readers make their own path through the harrowing story.

In previous or future chapters, we will discuss how transmedia is used in education, in training, and we will also examine how the publishing industry is utilizing transmedia.

GUIDELINES FOR CREATING TRANSMEDIA NARRATIVES

In this chapter, we have described a number of transmedia narratives, and these projects used a great diversity of techniques and media to tell a story across multiple platforms. As different as they are from each other, however, we can learn some important general lessons from them that can be applied to other transmedia projects:

- As always, you need to understand your audience, and provide it with an experience they will perceive as enjoyable, not as too difficult nor too simple, not too confusing nor overwhelming.
- Give members of the audience some way to enter the story and participate in it in a meaningful way (rabbit holes and cheese holes). They want to contribute to the story, too.
- When at all possible, develop all components of a project simultaneously, from the ground up, and work out how these components will be integrated.
- Each platform should contribute something to the overall story. Don't just paste new components onto an already existing property without considering how they will enhance the narrative.

THE CREATIVE POTENTIAL OF TRANSMEDIA PRODUCTIONS

One reason that the transmedia approach is such a powerful storytelling technique is because it enables the user to become involved in the material in an extremely deep way, and sometimes in a manner that can eerily simulate a real-life experience. By spanning a number of media, a project can become far richer, more detailed and multifaceted. It also offers the story creators an exceptional opportunity to develop extremely deep stories. Unlike TV shows or a feature film, there is no time constraint on how long they can be. Some of these works utilize hundreds of fictional websites to spin out their narratives, including many that contain audio, animation, and video clips. It is not unusual for a full-length book to be commissioned as one of the media elements. And because these narratives can utilize virtually any communications medium in existence, they offer a tantalizing variety of ways to play out the story, limited only by the creators' imaginations and by the budget.

Commercial considerations are not necessarily the primary attraction for those who work on them. Many creative teams are drawn to this approach because of its untapped creative potential. They find the experience exhilarating despite the many complexities they inevitably engender.

ADDITIONAL RESOURCES

To broaden your understanding of transmedia storytelling, the following resources may be helpful:

- TedX talks on transmedia: http://www.YouTube.com/playlist?list=PLsRNo Ux8w3rNPAwznV550YjismvZN5zGl&goback=%2E gde_3178836_member_206963172.

- Transmedia lab's case studies: http://www.dailymotion.com/playlist/ x2278b_Transmedialab_transmedia-case-studies/1#video=xrebh.

- Case studies and news about the field: http://storycode.org/.

- An excellent timeline of *Dexter's* transmedia elements: http://www .transmedialab.org/en/the-blog-en/case-study-en/dexter-in-transmedia/.

- You also may consider joining Linkedin's transmedia storyteller's group: http://www.linkedin.com/groups?gid=2129889&trk=vsrp_groups_cluster_ name&trkInfo=VSRPsearchId%3A19745713742121136523%2CVSRPtarg etId%3A2129889%2CVSRPcmpt%3Agroups_cluster.

- Or joining Linkedin's Transmedia Producers' group: http://www.linkedin .com/groups?gid=2944923&trk=vsrp_groups_cluster_name&trkInfo=VS RPsearchId%3A19745713742122245139%2CVSRPtargetId%3A2944923 %2CVSRPcmpt%3Agroups_cluster.

CONCLUSION

As we have seen from the projects discussed in this chapter, the transmedia approach can offer the user a new and extremely involving way to enjoy narratives and to interact with content. Forward-thinking broadcasters are looking at this approach as a way to potentially strengthen the connection between their viewers and their programming, an especially important goal as television audiences steadily decline.

Unfortunately, however, not all projects utilizing the transmedia approach have been successful, not even when supported by high budgets and produced by highly talented individuals. Yet it should always be kept in mind that creative ventures inevitably carry the possibility of failure, even in well-established areas like motion pictures and television.

The risk is even greater when undertaken in a relatively uncharted area such as transmedia storytelling.

Clearly, the transmedia approach is an area that invites further exploration. Almost certainly, more experience with this approach will help content creators to find successful new ways of combining media platforms. We can also expect to see combinations of media not tried before. More work in this area should result in the creation of exciting new storytelling experiences.

IDEA-GENERATING EXERCISES

1. A variety of different media and communications tools have been employed in transmedia productions. Can you think of any medium or tool that, to your knowledge, has not yet been employed? If so, can you suggest how such media or tools could be employed in an entertainment experience?

2. Discuss some possible transmedia approaches that could make a documentary or reality-based project extremely involving for the audience.

3. Try sketching out a story that would lend itself to a transmedia approach. What media would you use, and what would be the function of each in telling this story?

CHAPTER 11

Guidelines: Creating a New Project

What is the very first step that needs to be taken in developing a new project, and why is it so important?

What are the five most common mistakes people make when developing an interactive project?

Why is so much time and attention spent on creating certain types of documents during the development process, and are these documents even necessary?

What are the 10 most important questions that must be addressed before production begins?

THE DEVELOPMENT PERIOD AND WHY IT IS CRITICAL

Before a work of interactive entertainment is ever built—before the interactivity is programmed or the artwork is produced, or the sound is recorded—a tremendous amount of planning must first take place. This phase of the work is known as the development process or the preproduction period. It is a time of tremendous creative ferment. In its own way, it is not unlike the period described in ancient creation myths when all was nothingness and then, after a series of miraculous events, the Earth was formed and its myriad beings were given life.

The creation of a work of interactive entertainment is a totally human endeavor, of course, but it, too, begins with nothingness, and to successfully bring such a complex endeavor to fruition can almost seem miraculous. To achieve the end goal, a tiny sliver of an idea must be nurtured and shaped, amplified and refined. And, instead of miracles, it requires a tremendous amount of hard work. Bringing a project up to the point where it is ready for production requires a team of individuals with diverse skills who perform an array of different tasks.

Surprising though it may be, the work that goes on during preproduction is much the same for every type of interactive project, whether the end product is a video game, content for the Web, a VR simulation, or a mobile app. The specific documents that are called for may vary, and the specific technical issues may be different, but the core process varies little, no matter what the interactive medium may be.

WORTH NOTING: THE ADVANTAGES OF GOOD DOCUMENTATION

A well-utilized preproduction period can save not only time and money during production, but can also help avert the risk of a product that fails. Furthermore, the documents generated during development can go a long way toward keeping the entire team on track while the project is actually being built. Good documentation can mean that everyone is working with the same vision of the end product in mind. It helps avoid confusion, prevents mistakes, and reduces the likelihood of work having to be redone. It also avoids the dangers of the dreaded *project creep*: a situation in which a project expands beyond its original concept and sucks up staff time, often without additional financial compensation. And if a new member is added to the team midway through, the documentation can quickly bring that individual up to speed.

The tasks that take place during the development period include the conceptualizing of the project; addressing marketing issues; producing design documents, artwork, and other materials; building a prototype; and doing testing. Not every task done during this period deals specifically with creative issues, although invariably everything does impact the content, including the drawing up of budgets and schedules and the preparing of marketing plans.

The development process typically lasts an average of six months. However, it can be as brief as a few days or take as long as a year or more, depending on the complexity of the project, the experience of the creative team, and whether or not it involves a new type of technology or content. At the end of the development process, the company should be ready to swing into full-scale production.

FIVE ALL-TOO-COMMON ERRORS

Unfortunately, certain serious mistakes tend to be made during the development process. Some of these errors are caused by inexperience. Others may be fueled by the team's admirable intention of making something remarkable, yet being unable to rein in their ideas and set reasonable limits. And quite often, problems arise because the creative team is eager to plunge into preproduction and is too impatient to invest sufficient time in planning. Based on my own experience and on interviews with experts, here are five of the most common and serious errors that occur during the creative process:

1. *Throwing too much into the project.* In cases like this, the creative team may have become intoxicated with a promising new technology or with exciting new ways to expand the content. But this sort of enthusiasm can lead to many problems. It can cause the project to go over budget or require it to carry too expensive a price tag for the market. The project may take far longer to produce than the time originally slotted for it, causing it to miss an important market date. Or the finished product may be too complex for the end-user to enjoy.

2. *Not considering your audience.* This error can be fatal to a project. If you do not have a good understanding of your audience, how can you be sure you are making something it will want, or will have the ability to use? Misjudging your audience can lead to:

   o creating subject matter they are not interested in, or find distasteful;

   o developing content for a platform, device, or technical ability they do not possess;

   o developing an educational or training program that omits key points they need to know, or that goes over their heads;

   o developing content for children that is not age-appropriate.

3. *Making the product too hard or complicated.* This error can stem in part from Error #2, not knowing your audience. You need to understand what the end-users are capable of doing, and not make unrealistic demands on their abilities. Sometimes this error is caused by poor design, and is allowed to slip by because of inadequate testing. Whatever the cause, an overly difficult product will lead to unhappy end-users. As game designer Katie Fisher of Quicksilver Software said: "When a game becomes work, it's not fun for the player." Her comment is true not just of games but for any type of interactive content, be it a smart toy, an immersive movie, or an iTV show. If it is too hard to figure out, people are not going to want to invest their time in it.

4. *Making the product too simple.* This is the other side of the coin for Error #3. We are not talking here, however, about the product being too simple to use—simplicity in functionality is a good thing. We are referring to overly simple content. The content of an interactive work needs to be challenging in some way; otherwise, users will lose interest. It should also contain enough material to explore, and things to do, to keep the users absorbed for a significant amount of time. If it is too thin, they will feel they have not gotten their money's worth. To gauge the appropriate amount of playing time for your product, it is advisable to become familiar with similar products on the market. Focus group testing is also helpful in this matter.

5. *Not making the product truly interactive.* In such cases, users are not given sufficient agency to keep them involved. When this happens, the flaw can usually be traced back all the way to the initial concept. In all likelihood, the premise that the product was

built upon was weak in terms of its interactive potential, even if it might have been an interesting one for a noninteractive type of entertainment. In a successful interactive product, the interactivity must be organic from the outset and not just an afterthought.

THE FIRST STEP: CREATING THE CORE CONCEPT

The development phase begins with deciding what, in essence, the new project will be—the core concept. The initial idea may come about in one of several ways, and how it is initiated varies from medium to medium, company to company, project to project. Sometimes the concept is proposed by the CEO or president of the company; sometimes a staff member comes up with the idea; and sometimes it emerges during a staff brainstorming session. In a long-established software company, the concept may be a sequel to an already existing title. In a start-up company, it may be the dream project of a single individual or a small group of colleagues.

Ideas for new projects can come about in many ways. Sometimes they are inspired by a myth or true event from history or from an incident in someone's personal life. Sometimes the starting place begins with someone dreaming up an intriguing fantasy setting or exciting world to explore. Many times ideas take shape just by letting the imagination run free or by a group brainstorming session. In other cases, an idea is sparked by a new technology, when someone envisions how it could be used as a medium for an interactive narrative.

In many instances, of course, a company is given an assignment by an outside client, and needs to find a creative way to fulfill it: to come up with an entertaining way to teach high school physics, for example, or to use digital storytelling techniques to promote a movie or sell a line of automobiles.

In many companies, the raw idea is set before the entire creative team and subjected to some rigorous brainstorming. During brainstorming, even the wildest ideas are encouraged, in order to explore the full potential of the project.

Once a consensus of the core idea is reached, a description of it needs to be articulated in a way that adequately reflects what the group has worked out. Ideally, one person on the team will boil the concept down to a clear and vivid *premise*. The premise, which is usually just one sentence long, describes the concept in a way that indicates where its energy will come from, what the challenges might be, and what will hook the users. Ideally, the premise should also indicate who the major characters are and the world that is the setting for the story. The premise is often written in the second person, "you," to put the listener or reader right into the action.

For example, a description of the premise of a new game might sound something like this: "In *Runway*, you are thrust into the glamorous but cut-throat world of the fashion industry, where you play the head of a small fashion house competing against powerful rivals and try to come up with the winning line for the new season." Or a description for a smart toy might be described this way: "Perry the Talking Parrot can be trained to speak and repeat phrases, but you can never predict what Perry might say, because he has a mind of his own!"

In the film business, they call this one sentence description a "log line." The term got its name from the concise descriptions of movies given in television logs and other entertainment guides. However, the idea of boiling down a premise to a few words is equally useful for interactive entertainment. By nailing it down this way, the team will have a clear grasp of what it is setting out to do. They will also be able to communicate this vision to everyone who will be working on it, or whose support will be needed to bring the project to fruition. And ultimately, this log line will be a valuable marketing tool.

OTHER EARLY DECISIONS

Early on during the development period, the creative team needs to make certain fundamental decisions about the project, assuming they are not already incorporated into the basic concept. First of all, what specific medium and platform is the project being made for, and what genre does it belong to? Once these basic "What is it?" questions have been addressed, it is time to consider important marketing issues. Who will the target audience be? What competing products are already available? And, if this a retail product, what will the intended price tag be? All these matters can have a significant impact on the design.

To help answer these questions, many companies either use a marketing person on staff or hire an outside consultant. This marketing expert might determine, for example, that the idea you have in mind sounds too expensive for your target audience, and if you don't want to overprice your product, you will need to rethink the design and leave out some of the cutting-edge features you were hoping to build in. Or your marketing expert might tell you your product would have a better chance with a different demographic than you had in mind. This information would require a different kind of adjustment. For instance, if you found out it would have more appeal to teens rather than to preteens, you may need to make the product more sophisticated and edgier than you'd intended at first.

Somewhere early on during the development period, the project manager will also be working out a preproduction and production schedule which will include specific milestones—dates when specific elements must be completed and delivered. A budget for the project will also be drawn up. Now, armed with a clearer idea of your project and its parameters, the team can brainstorm on refining the concept and begin to develop its specific features. Unlike the very first brainstorming sessions, where the sky was the limit, these later brainstorming sessions are tempered by reality.

EXPERT OBSERVATION: FIVE POUNDS OF STUFF

Designer Greg Roach, introduced in Chapter 4, points out that you only have limited resources for any project you undertake, and you have to decide how best to use them. "It's like being given five pounds of stuff," he said. "You can't do everything you want." Thus, you have to make trade-offs—if you really want Feature X, then you may have to scratch Feature Y or Feature Z. In other worlds you can't build a 10-pound project with only five pounds of stuff.

HOW PROJECTS EVOLVE DURING DEVELOPMENT

As a project moves through the development process, it evolves from a raw idea to a polished state where it is capable of being produced.

During this preproduction phase, many projects require the input of *subject matter experts*, known as *SMEs*. Projects designed for educational, informational, or training purposes will inevitably require help from experts on the content and often on the target learners. But even when the sole goal of the project is to entertain, it might be necessary to seek expert help, or to assign someone to do research. For instance, if you are actually doing a game about the fashion industry, you will want to find out everything you can about the world of high fashion, from how a new line of clothes is designed to how a fashion show is staged. Based on this knowledge, you can build specific challenges and puzzles into the game, and make the project far richer and more realistic than it would be if you had attempted to rely on your imagination alone.

As the project develops, the team will be setting the ideas down in various types of documents. They will also be producing flowcharts, character sketches, and other visuals to further refine the interactivity, characterization, and look of the project. The various documents and artwork will be described in more detail a little later in this chapter, in the section entitled "Documents and Artwork" (see pp. 191–203).

At various points during the development process, ideas and visuals may be tested on *focus groups*—representative members of the target audience. If a client company is involved in this project, it will also need to be briefed on ideas and shown visuals. Based on the feedback that is received, further refinements may be made. The final step in preproduction is often the building of a prototype, a working model of a small part of the overall project. This is especially typical in cases where the project incorporates novel features or new technology, or is the first of an intended line of similar products.

The prototype will demonstrate how the project actually operates, how the user interacts with the content, and what the look and feel of it will be like. For many interactive projects, the prototype is the make-or-break point. If it lives up to expectations, and funding for the product and other considerations are in place, the project will receive the green light to proceed to development. But if the prototype reveals serious flaws in the concept or in its functionality, it may mean going back to the drawing board or even the end of the line for that particular concept.

EXPERT OBSERVATIONS: THE PROTOTYPE

The *Harvard Business Review* has created an interesting short video on prototyping. It can be seen at http://www.youtube.com/watch?v= N-BX0jzmS1w&feature=player_profilepage

A 10-STEP DEVELOPMENT CHECKLIST

As we've already seen, the process of creating an interactive project involves the asking and answering of some fundamental questions. Based on my own experience and on the interviews done for this book, I have put together a list of 10 critical questions that must be addressed early in the development process, each with its own set of subquestions. These questions and subquestions apply to virtually any type of work of interactive entertainment. The answers will help you shape your concept, define your characters and structure, and work out the project's interactivity. The 10 questions are:

1. *Premise and purpose:*

   o What is the premise of the project … the core idea in a nutshell? What about it will make it engaging? Try to capture its essential qualities in a single sentence.

   o What is its fundamental purpose? To entertain? To teach or inform? To make people laugh? To market a product?

2. *Audience and market:*

   o Who is the intended user?

   o What type of entertainment do people in this group enjoy? How technically sophisticated are they?

   o Why should your project appeal to them?

   o What other projects like yours already exist, and how well are they doing?

3. *Medium, platform, and genre:*

   o What interactive medium or media is this work being made for (such as the Internet, smart phones, video game console, or several media together); what are the special strengths and limitations of this medium and how will the project take advantage of these strengths and minimize these limitations?

   o What type of platform (hardware) will it use? (For example, a PC, a game console, a mobile phone, etc.)

   o What genre (category of programming, such as simulation, Web series, or action game) does it fall into, and in what ways does your work contain the key characteristics of this genre?

4. *Narrative/gaming elements:*

   o Does your work contain narrative elements (such as a plot or characters)? If so, has the storyline been fully worked out? What are the major events or challenges that the user will need to deal with during the narrative?

   o What is the tone of your narrative? Is it comic, dark, scary, or a light-hearted romp?

   o Does this work utilize gaming elements? If so, is the gameplay thoroughly worked out? What constitutes winning or losing?

5. *User's role and POV:*
   o What character or role will the user play in this interactive environment?
   o What is the nature of the user's agency? How will the user impact the narrative or the outcome?
   o Through what POV will the user view this world: first person, third person, or a mix of both?

6. *Characters:*
   o Who are the nonplayer characters in this project?
   o What role or function do they serve (allies, adversaries, helper figures)?
   o If your project contains a number of characters, have you developed a character bible to describe them?

7. *Structure and interface:*
   o What is the starting place in terms of the user's experience and what are the possible end points?
   o How will the project be structured? What are the major units of organization (such as modules or levels), and how many of them will there be? What structural model are you using?
   o How will the user control the material and navigate through it? How will the user be able to tell how well he or she is doing? Will your project be making use of navigation bars, menus, icons, inventories, maps, or other interface devices?

8. *Storyworld and sub-settings:*
   o What is the central fictional world where your project is set?
   o How is it divided, geographically? What are its major settings, what do they look like, and how are they different from each other?
   o What challenges, dangers, or special pleasures are inherent to each of these settings?
   o In what time period is your story set? Does it take place in the past (if so, when?) or the future, or is it a contemporary story?

9. *User engagement:*
   o What about your project will keep the user engaged, and want to spend time with it?
   o What important goal is the user trying to accomplish by the end of this work, and why would this be something of significant importance to the user?
   o What will add tension to the experience? Will there be a ticking clock?
   o Are you building in a system of rewards and penalties?
   o What kind of meaningful interactivity are you offering the user, and will this interactivity have a significant impact on the material?

10. *Overall look and sound:*

   ○ What kinds of visuals will you be using (animation, video, graphics, text on the screen, a mix)?

   ○ Is the overall look realistic or a fantasy environment?

   ○ How do you plan to use audio in your work? Will characters speak? Do you have plans for ambient sound? (Rain, wind, traffic noises; background office sounds?) Will there be sound effects? Music? Dialogue?

Once you have answered these 10 questions as completely as possible, you should have a pretty good grasp of the major elements of the project, or know what needs to be developed more fully. If your project is one that blends entertainment with other goals, such as education or promotion, it will be helpful to also review the checklist given in Chapter 12, in the section entitled "Guidelines for Projects that Blend Storytelling with Teaching and Training."

DOCUMENTS AND ARTWORK

While each company may have its own unique method of doing documentation and pre-production artwork, certain types of written materials and visuals are universal throughout the interactive entertainment universe, even though their names may vary from company to company. The most frequently used forms of documentation and visual presentations are:

1. THE CONCEPT DOCUMENT

The concept document is a brief description of the project and is usually the first piece of written material to be generated. It includes such essential information as the premise, the intended medium and platform, and the genre. It also notes the intended audience for the project and the nature of the interactivity, and gives a succinct overview of the characters and the main features of the story. Concept documents may be used as in-house tools to give everyone on the team a quick picture of what the project will be, and they can also be used as sales tools to secure support or funding for a project. If intended to be used in the second capacity, the concept document should be written in a vivid, engaging style that will convince readers of the project's viability. Concept documents tend to be quite short, generally under 10 pages in length.

2. THE BIBLE

A bible is an expanded version of a concept document, and it is strictly an in-house working document. Bibles are most frequently used for complex, story-rich projects; they may not be written at all for certain types of interactive projects, such as puzzle games. A bible fully describes significant elements of the work. It includes all the settings or worlds and what happens in them and all the major characters, and may also give the backstories of these characters (their personal histories up to the point where the story or game begins). Some bibles, called character bibles, only describe the characters. Other bibles are used to describe all the weapons in the work. Bibles vary quite a bit in length, depending on the breadth of the project and their intended purpose within the company. In some companies, the bible is a collection of all the preproduction documents written for the project.

3. THE DESIGN DOCUMENT

The design document serves as a written blueprint of the entire interactive work. It vastly expands the information given in either a concept document or bible, and contains specific technical information about the interactivity and functionality. It is the primary working document of any new media project. At some companies, the design document evolves from the concept document or bible; at other companies, it is written from scratch.

The design document is a living construct, begun during preproduction but never truly completed until the project itself is finished. As new features are added to the project, they are added to the design document, or if a feature is changed, the design document is revised accordingly. Because a design document is such an enormous and ever-changing work, and because so many different people contribute to it, it is vital that one person takes charge of overseeing it. This person coordinates and integrates the updates and makes sure that only one official version exists and that no outdated versions are still floating around.

Generally speaking, because design documents change so frequently, it is impractical to try to keep paper copies of your design document. It is far more efficient to make an electronic version that can easily be amended or added to. It is also useful to keep the design document on the company intranet. That way, everyone on the team can have immediate access to it.

Design documents are organized in various ways. Some are organized by structure, with a section for each module, world, environment, or level. Others are organized by topic. For instance, the design document for the strategy game *Age of Empires* contained a section just on buildings and how they worked.

To get an idea of the type of information that can be included in a design document, let's take a look at a few pages of one prepared for *JumpStart Advanced First Grade* (see Figure 11.1). The document is organized module by module; this module is for Hopsalot's Bridge, a sorting game. It is hosted by a character named Hopsalot, who is a rabbit.

At the top of the first page is a picture of Hopsalot's Bridge, from the POV of the player. Beneath it is a list of the curriculum points the game will teach, followed by brief summaries of the introduction speeches, one for first-time visitors and one for repeat visitors. This is followed by a detailed description of the game play, levels, and functionality. The full documentation of this module would also note what objects on the screen are clickable and what happens when the player clicks on them—what the pop-ups will be and what the audio will be, as well as a description of all the buttons on the screen and on the tool bar, and what each of them does. It would also indicate every line of dialogue that Hopsalot would speak, and would include special notes for the programmer and graphic artist.

Hopsalot's Bridge Module
(Hb)

Access

Click Hopsalot's House, on the Main Menu Screen to get here.

Page Description

The curriculum for this module is the <u>Sorting</u> of:
- <u>Parts of speech</u>
- <u>Words</u>
- <u>Geometry</u>: shapes
- <u>Science</u>: Health/Nutrition, Animals, Weather

On Your First Visit:
Hopsalot gives long intro. Hopsalot's turbo carrot juice is one of the most prized power-ups for the scooters. Or at least he thinks it is, so he has gone to extremes to protect his supply.

Return Visit:
Gives short intro.

Gameplay

Hopsalot has made an island to hide his high-octane carrot juice on and he has to build a bridge to get to it. He has columns in the water that divide the bridge into 3 sections. He has also created little remote controlled balloon blimps to drop into place and create the bridge.

Each balloon has a word or picture on it (depending on the content selected for the session). For example: each word would be a Noun, Verb or Adjective. You must sort the balloons so that each column of the bridge has the same type of word. Use the left and right arrow keys to steer the balloons and use the down arrow key to make them drop faster.

If you send a balloon into the wrong column it will bounce back up into the air so that you can try again. Hopsalot will also hold a pin that will pop the balloons that you don't need (distractor blimps in L2 and L3).

(Continued)

When the bridge is complete, Hops will run over to grab a carrot power-up and bring it back. Now for the fun part! He can't leave the bridge up or Jimmy Bumples might sneak across, so you'll need to repeat the activity, but this time matching object will pop the balloon underneath.

Reward:
After you've destroyed the bridge, Hops will reward you with the power-up.

Content Leveling

Note: the levels are related to each topic.

1.   Parts of speech
Level 1: Verbs, Adjectives and nouns
Level 2: Verbs, Adjectives and nouns
Level 3: Verbs, Adjectives and nouns
Add words that do not fit into the category such as an adverb or preposition.

2.   Syllables
Level 1: 1 to 3 syllables; pronounced
Level 2: 2 to 4 syllables; pronounced
Level 3: 2 to 4 syllables; regular pronunciation

3.   Health-Nutrition (food groups)
Level 1: 3 categories: Grains, Meats, Dairy
Level 2: 4 categories: Grains, Meats, Dairy, Fruits
Level 3: 5 categories: Grains, Meats, Dairy, Fruits, Vegetables

4.   Animals
Level 1: Habitat: water, land, air
Level 2: Attributes: scales, fur, feathers
Level 3: Zoological type: mammals, reptiles, insects; amphibians as distracters

5.   Science - Weather
Level 1: 3 categories: sunny, rainy, snowy; outdoors activities
Level 2: 3 categories: sunny, rainy, snowy; outdoors activities + clothes
Level 3: seasons: winter, spring, summer; fall as distracter

6.   Geometry – Shapes and Forms
Level 1: 2D shapes: squares, triangles, circles, rectangles
Level 2: 3D shapes: cubes, cones, cylinders, spheres
Level 3: everyday objects by their 3D shape: cubes, cones, cylinders, spheres

Game Play Leveling

Level 1: Slow falling pieces.
Level 2: Medium speed falling pieces.
Level 3: Fast falling pieces.

Functionality

I.   On entering the Module:

A.   Play Background: BkgG1HbBackground
B.   Play Background Music: G1HbAmbient.wav

(Continued)

II.   Introduction Functionality

    A.   Long Introduction (played the first time a player visits this module)
       Follow standards for interruptability
          a)   Play Hopsalot waiving at Player
               ■   Hopsalot's Body: AniG1HbHopsalot, FX Wave
          b)   Play Hopsalot giving his Long Intro
            (Note: during Intro, Hopsalot will be Pointing at item as he speaks about them; items
            will highlight, and Hopsalot will have corresponding "Point" FX going on)
            i)   Long Intro:
               ■   Hopsalot's Body: AniG1HbHopsalot, FX Point01
               ■   Hopsalot's Talk: AniG1HbHopsalotTalk, FX LongIntro01
               ■   Hopsalot's VO: DgG1HbHopsalotTalkLongIntro01.wav
          c)   Go to Gameplay

    B.   Short Intro (played on any return visits)
       Follow standards for interruptability
          a)   Play Hopsalot giving one of the 3 Short Intros: (Random without repetition)
               ■   Hopsalot's Body: AniG1HbHopsalot, FX Point{01-03}
               ■   Hopsalot's Talk: AniG1HbHopsalotTalk, FX ShortIntro{01-03}
               ■   Hopsalot's VO: DgG1HbHopsalotTalkShortIntro{01-03}.wav
          b)   Go to Gameplay

III.   Gameplay Interaction

    A.   Display
       1.   <u>Hopsalot</u>
          a)   Hopsalot's Body: AniG1HbHopsalot, FX Still
          b)   Hopsalot's Talk: AniG1HbHopsalotTalk, FX Still

       2.   <u>Device to throw Balloons</u>
          a)   Device: AniG1HbDevice, FX Still

       3.   <u>Falling Balloons</u>
         (note: will appear on screen one after the other, according to order set for current level;
         those will be the same sprite, replicated at {x} instances; use datadict for coordinates)
          a)   Play first Balloon ready on the Device: AniG1HbBalloon, FX Still

       4.   <u>Carrot Case</u>
         (note: at the right side of screen = case containing the power-up)
          a)   Case standing there: AniG1HbCarrotCase, FX Still

       5.   <u>Labels</u>
         (Note: located at the bottom of each section of the bridge, they will display the name of
         each category; they will appear one by one when Hopsalot gives instruction: see below)
          a)   Labels sprites are not visible when entering the module

Figure 11.1   A few pages from the design document of *JumpStart Advanced First Grade*. Document courtesy of Knowledge Adventure, Inc., and used under license.

Because design documents incorporate such a vast amount of detail, they sometimes reach 1,000 pages or more in length. Some companies also produce a "lite" version for a quicker read.

To see the table of contents for an extensive design document, visit: http://www.runaway-studios.com/articles/ctaylordesigntemplate.doc. Although this sample design document was produced some years ago, its main features are still completely valid.

Not only does the design document help keep things on track during development and production, but it is also the point of origin for many other important documents. For example, the programming department will use the design document for creating its own technical design document and the test team will use it to prepare a list of all the systems to be tested. The design document also helps the marketing group put together promotional materials and prepare for the product launch. If an instructor's guide or novelization is to be written for the project, the design document will come into play for those endeavors as well.

4. THE DIALOGUE SCRIPT

In some companies, as we've seen, the dialogue script is incorporated into the design document, but quite often these scripts are stand-alone documents. The dialogue script sets down all the lines that the characters will speak during the interactive program. These scripts often describe the visuals and the actions that accompany the dialogue, as well. Dialogue may either be spoken by characters on the screen (animated figures or actual actors shot in video), or spoken voice-over by characters who are not visible. Their voices may be heard via a telephone, a radio, or some other device, or the dialogue may be delivered by an off-screen character who is offering help and support. In cases when only voice-over actors will be used, and no live characters appear on screen, a separate voice-over dialogue script will be prepared that contains nothing but lines of dialogue.

Formats for interactive scripts vary widely, and no single industry standard exists at this time. Companies will use a format that works best for the types of projects they develop, and many customize their own formats.

One fairly common script style resembles the format for feature film screenplays, except that it incorporates instructions for the interactive elements. This format works particularly well in story-rich projects and games in which the level of interactivity is not too complex. In such scripts, the dialogue is centered in the middle of the page, with the descriptive material extending out further to the left and right margins. When using such a format, it is important to clearly indicate all the dialogue choices being offered to the user, and the responses the other character gives to each one of them. For an example, see Figure 11.2, *Dick and Jane*, a sample script I wrote for instructional purposes. The script incorporates an if/then branching structure.

Some companies prefer to use a multi-column format. This formatting style roughly resembles the traditional audio/video two-column format used in the making of documentaries and other types of linear programs, where one column is used for visuals (the video) and the other is for voice and sound (the audio). Interactive scripts, however, may use several more columns. At Training Systems Design, the company uses anywhere from three to five columns. The number of columns varies from script to script and even from module to module. The

DICK AND JANE
(Sample script using if/then technique)

JANE, the player character, leaves her house to go for a walk. She is a pretty young woman in her early 20s.

She can 1.) go straight; 2.) turn to the left or 3.) turn to the right.

1.) Straight path:
If she goes straight, **then** she must cross a busy street and dodge heavy traffic.

[The script would continue to follow her actions from this point on]

2.) Left path:
If she turns to the left, **then** she will pass a pretty flower garden.

If she stops to pick a flower in the flower garden, **then** a bee will sting her.

[The script would continue to follow her actions from this point on]

3.) Right path:
If she turns to the right, **then** she will come to the house of her handsome neighbor, DICK. Dick is trimming a hedge. Jane can either ignore him or wave at him.

If Jane ignores him and walks on, **then** Dick will continue to trim the hedge.

[The script would continue to follow her actions from this point on]

If Jane waves at Dick, **then** he will speak to her.

> DICK
> (awkwardly, very shy)
> Oh, hi, Jane. Nice to see you.
> (beat)
> … Uh, any chance you'd be interested in going on a long walk with me on the beach tonight? It's a full moon, and…

User can pick one of three responses for Jane to give:

Response A:

> JANE
> (clearly not interested)
> Oh, sorry, I can't. There's this great sale at the mall tonight… half off designer pumps. Fabulous! Thanks, though.

If A is selected, then go to A1.

Response B:

> JANE
> (with genuine enthusiasm)
> Gee, Dick, I'd love to!

If B is selected, then go to B1.

(Continued)

Response C:

> JANE
> No way! For heaven's sake, Dick, has
> anyone ever told you you sound like
> a total cliché?

If C, then go to C1.

A1:

> DICK
> (sagging with humiliation)
> Uh, OK. Guess I can take the hint.

B1:

> DICK
> Great! How 'bout I swing by your
> place about 7:30?

C1:

> DICK
> Well, Jane, has anyone ever told you
> you sound like a total [bleep]?!

Figure 11.2 *Dick and Jane*, a sample dialogue script, uses a modified screenplay format. This script was written for instructional purposes, and thus each if/then has been emphasized. Script courtesy of Carolyn Handler Miller.

number of columns used depends on the needs of the programming and graphics groups. Their scripts also contain artwork indicating what will appear on the learner's screen. The company calls this type of formatting "scripts and screens."

One example of a five-column scripts and screens format is the company's script for the *Save Your Co-Worker* game, part of the *Code Alert* training program discussed in Chapter 12 (see Figure 11.3). The script for the game was written by Dr. Robert Steinmetz. The artwork depicts the setting for this portion of the game, an office cubicle, and also shows the bar that keeps track of the learner's score, as well as an icon the learner can click on to receive help (upper left). Column one, labeled Spot, indicates the hot spots on the screen—objects the learner can click on to get some sort of response from the program. Column two, Programming Instructions, gives notes to the programmers, explaining what needs to happen when the user clicks on a specific hot spot. Column 3, Value, shows how the learner's choice will affect his or her score. Column 4, Audio Label, gives the code for the audio that will be heard in Column 5. Column 5, Sound Effect/Voice-Over, describes the audio effects that will be heard and the voice-over dialogue that the narrator will speak.

The multi-column style of formatting is extremely precise and works particularly well for educational, informational, and training programs. However, it is cumbersome to use for projects that involve a number of dialogue exchanges.

Yet another scripting option is to use a spreadsheet. Spreadsheets are most popular when characters have numerous lines to say, and when there are multiple variations of the same speech, such as five different ways for a character to say "Yes! You're right!"

Scene 2: Toni & Joseph Cubicle
5.1.2-1

Spot	Programming Instructions	Value (if selected)	Audio label	Sound effect / voice over
1 Printer	If selected, add value to score bar, play good beep and play audio VO 5.1.2-1A	1	5.1.2-1 A	(Good Beep) it all depends on frequency of use. But, based on where she has her mouse, we can assume this person is right handed, therefore it might be better to swap the phone position and the printer. However, sometimes it is good to move things around to avoid repetitive motion syndrome.
2: Phone	If selected, add value to score bar, play good beep and play audio VO 5.1.2-1A	1		
3: Monitor	If selected, add value to score bar, play good beep and play audio VO 5.1.2-1B	3	5.1.2-1B	(Good Beep) Right! She really should orient herself so that her eyes are level with the monitor and her neck is in a neutral position.

Spot	Programming Instructions	Value (if selected)	Audio label	Sound effect / voice over
4: Head position	If selected, add value to score bar, play good beep and play audio VO 5.1.2-1B	3		
5: Keyboard	If selected, add value to score bar, play bad beep and play audio VO 5.1.2-1C	1	5.1.2-1C	(no beep)The problem isn't really with keyboard… though you could consider it part of a larger overall work habit problem.
6: Mouse	If selected, add value to score bar, play bad beep and play audio VO 5.1.0-3	0		
7 Lifting position	If selected, add value to score bar, play bad beep and play audio VO 5.1.2-1D	0	5.1.2-1D	(Bad Beep) Nope, he is lifting with his legs, and he is tucking the load in toward his torso.

Figure 11.3   A five-column script for the *Save Your Co-Worker* game, written by Dr. Robert Steinmetz for the *Code Alert* training program. Document courtesy of Training Systems Design.

In some cases, a company will create its own in-house software program for script formatting, as Training Systems Design has done.

5. FLOWCHARTS

Flowcharts are a visual expression of the narrative line of the program, and illustrate decision points, branches, and other interactive possibilities. Flowcharting often begins early in the development process as a way to sketch out how portions of the program will work. As the project evolves, flowcharts serve as a valuable communications device for various members of the team, for everyone from writers to programmers. They are also useful for explaining the project to people not directly on the team, such as marketing specialists or clients. As a visual method of illustrating how the program works, they can be much easier to grasp than a densely detailed design document.

Flowcharts vary a great deal in style and appearance. The least adorned ones, such as the one designed by Terry Borst to illustrate the interactivity for a short script called *Pop Quiz*, are composed of lines and geometric shapes like a simple diagram (see Figure 11.4). More detailed, higher-level flowcharts may also be made for programming, with each element coded to reflect specific functions or types of content.

More elaborate flowcharts may include detailed visuals of the screens and short explanations of functionality, such as the flowcharts produced for *Code Alert*

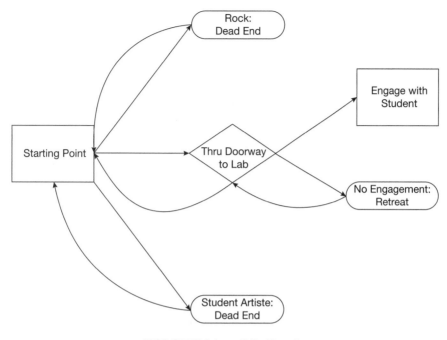

"POP QUIZ" Interactivity Flowchart

Figure 11.4   An unadorned flowchart designed by Terry Borst to illustrate the interactivity of *Pop Quiz*. Image courtesy of Terry Borst.

(see Figure 11.5). Flowcharts like these are particularly useful for explaining the program to the client or to potential investors.

According to Dr. Steinmetz, the company uses two levels of flowcharts. A macro level flowchart, like the one pictured here, gives an overview of the training program and is the type of flowchart that would most likely be used in a company proposal. Such flowcharts are made once the major instructional objectives have been identified. A more detailed flowchart, made later in the development period, would indicate all the branching. It would be produced once the specific teaching points had been identified, and would be cross-referenced to the document that laid out the teaching points.

Several off-the-shelf software programs are available to make flowcharts. Two that are popular with people in the software industry are Inspiration and Microsoft Visio. A blog by Prof. Howard Rheingold offers some addition tools for concept mapping: http://ltlatnd .wordpress.com/2011/05/10/best-tools-and-practices-for-concept-mapping/.

6. CONCEPT ART

Concept art, also called concept drawings or concept sketches, is a visual rendering of some aspect of the program. Such artwork is often used to depict characters and locations. The

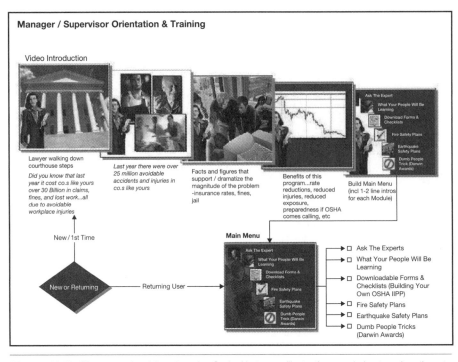

Figure 11.5   The macro level flowchart for *Code Alert* uses illustrations and short explanations to describe how the program works. Document courtesy of Training Systems Design.

images may be used as trial balloons and shown to team members or focus groups to test possible character designs or settings. They will then be refined until a consensus is reached, and the team agrees on a final version.

When members of the art department are working on a character design, they might make a series of poses for each character. For example, at Her Interactive, for the *Nancy Drew* games, each character is given a set of eight different poses that reflect the character's personality and emotional state. The clothing the character is wearing can serve as a useful way to reveal character, too. For instance, a depressed young woman may be wrapped in layers of dark clothing, while a cocky politician may have his thumbs stuck in his suspenders.

7. STORYBOARDS

Storyboards are graphical illustrations of the flow of action and other elements of the content, and are displayed sequentially. They are somewhat similar to illustrated flowcharts. In the feature film world, movie directors storyboard every scene before filming begins. Storyboarding is often used in interactive media in much the same way. At some companies, it is used primarily for linear sequences, though other companies use them to work out interactive elements as well.

Storyboards resemble comic book art in that each frame advances the story. Each frame will indicate the location of the objects within the scene, the placement of the character or characters, the position of the camera, and the direction of the movement within the scene. Because storyboards are so visual, they are simple to comprehend. They are a useful preproduction tool for many kinds of interactive projects, including VR simulations, immersive environments, and interactive movies—in short, for any interactive endeavor that contains rich visual sequences.

8. PROTOTYPE

As noted earlier in this chapter, a prototype is a working model of a small portion of the program. It is the ultimate way of testing a concept. Many people within the interactive community consider it a more useful method of trying out the concept's viability than flowcharting or storyboarding because it gives a more accurate indication of the look, feel, and functionality of the program. It's a chance to find out how the navigation works and to actually interact with the material. Prototyping is not necessarily done only at the end of the preproduction process. Small prototypes might also be built along the way to test out specific features. Also, it should be noted that prototyping is not necessarily done for every interactive project. For example, if the company has already made many similar products and if this is just another product in an already-established line, prototyping may not be called for.

SPECIALIZED DOCUMENTS AND ARTWORK

Many other types of documents can be generated during the development process as well, although they do not specifically focus on the creative aspects of the project. These would include a technical document containing the technical specifications; a budget; a schedule; a marketing plan; and a test plan. In addition to the fairly ubiquitous types of documents, visuals, and models already described, many companies work with customized tools that are particularly helpful for the type of project they are creating.

For example, at Her Interactive, they use several kinds of special documents when they make the *Nancy Drew* mystery-adventure games. One is the "critical path document," which lists the events that must occur, the discoveries that the player must make, and the obstacles that must be overcome in order to successfully reach the end point in the game. This critical path document is extremely succinct, about a page and a half of bullet points. Another document they produce is the "environmental synergy document," which is organized around specific environments (locations) in the game. For instance, for an interior of a room, it would note how the furniture is arranged, how the room is decorated, what "plot critical" objects it contains, what other less essential clues can be found here, and information about any characters who will be found in this room. It also notes what puzzles need to be solved within this environment. In addition to these two documents, the company also creates a highly detailed puzzle document, which lists all the game's puzzles and specifies how they work. All these documents are cross-referenced and collected together as a project bible, so that if a team member needs more information on any aspect of the game, it will be easy to find.

When a project contains a great many variables in terms of characters or types of actions, some companies create matrixes to keep track of them. A *matrix* looks much like a table, with horizontal rows and vertical columns. For instance, when I worked on the *Carmen Sandiego* series and was writing dialogue clues to help identify various suspects, I was given a matrix to use. It organized the variable characteristics of the suspects by categories, such as hair color, eye color, favorite hobbies, favorite sport, and favorite foods, and then listed all the possibilities for each category. I was to write four lines of dialogue clues for each variable.

Within the world of smart toys, inventors and designers create something they call a skeleton logic chart or logic flow document. This tool illustrates how the toy and the child will interact with each other, and shows the direction of the narrative line. And for projects that are designed to train or teach, a document is often prepared that lists the main teaching points or training goals.

CONCLUSION

As we have seen here, during a well-utilized preproduction period, a concept for an interactive work moves from an extremely rudimentary premise to a well-thought-out project that is detailed enough in every regard to be moved into production. This outcome is only obtainable, however, when teams go through the steps described here, or through similar ones that might be more appropriate to their particular project.

Unfortunately, teams are sometimes tempted to jump into production before they've worked out important details, thinking they can do the detail work as they move along. But moving into production prematurely can be a costly mistake.

The development process, when undertaken with care, generates a number of highly useful documents, but it also involves an even more important task: conceptualizing. The creative team needs to work out exactly what the project is, whom it is for, and how people will interact with it. Above all, what about the project will make people eager to spend their time engaged with it? Finding satisfactory answers to questions like these can go a long way toward helping you create a viable project with genuine appeal.

IDEA-GENERATING EXERCISES

1. Pick a work of digital storytelling that you have just begun to work on or that you are interested in doing. The work can be in any medium or for any type of platform. Take this project through the 10-Step Development Process to determine if any aspect of the project needs more thought or needs to be strengthened before moving more deeply into development.

2. Using the same project from #1 as your model, determine what types of specialized tasks would need to be done during the preproduction process.

3. Again, using the same project as above for your model, determine what kinds of documents you would need to generate in order to effectively take this project through the preproduction stage. What would each type of document contain?

4. Using the same project as your model, consider your marketing specialist. What information do you think this person could give you and the rest of the team that would be helpful? And what documents do you think your team could give to the marketing specialist that would be useful in terms of launching the product?

PART 3

Harnessing Digital Storytelling for Pragmatic Goals

CHAPTER 12

Using Digital Storytelling to Teach and Train

In what ways can projects designed to teach or train benefit by an interactive storytelling approach?

Why are organizations as different from each other as the United Nations, a chain of ice cream shops, the United States Department of Defense, and a group of Christian fundamentalists all turning to digital storytelling to help them fulfill their objectives?

What is a "serious game," and isn't this a contradiction in terms?

In what important ways should projects designed to teach or train be approached differently from projects whose only goal is to entertain?

"A SPOONFUL OF SUGAR"

Many tasks in life are important, but not necessarily appealing. Of such activities, Mary Poppins had some excellent advice, declaring that "a spoonful of sugar helps the medicine go down." What's true of swallowing medicine is also true of other tasks in life that are usually regarded as uninviting—such as doing schoolwork or undergoing on-the-job training. When digital media are used to teach and train, that spoonful of sugar is an infusion of entertainment content and interactivity. This sweet combination helps to make learning far more appealing than it ordinarily would be, and works equally well for teaching students in the classroom as it does for teaching employees in a workplace setting, although, as we will see, the techniques used in these situations are somewhat different.

The idea of integrating entertainment and education is not new. Our grandparents, and probably our great-grandparents, too, learned to read from schoolbooks that looked just like attractive children's storybooks. They played with educational toys like building blocks and magnets, and took part in costume dramas where they reenacted important moments in history. It's also not a new concept to use the latest technology to teach. Both film and video, for example, were quickly put to use in the classroom and for training purposes as soon as it became possible to do so.

What is entirely new, however, is the use of digital technology as a vehicle to teach and train, and the packaging of educational content in a format that is both entertaining and interactive. This new approach often uses digital storytelling techniques, and is effective for young learners and older ones alike.

The "sugar" in this approach, as we've noted, is made up of both entertainment and interactivity. By incorporating entertainment into a work designed to teach or train, we create something that engages and engrosses the learner. The experience of learning the material is perceived as pleasurable, and learners are more willing to spend time working their way through it instead of trying to dodge it.

Furthermore, an entertaining environment is not perceived as intimidating. Let's face it: classroom learning can be extremely uncomfortable for many people. In this public environment, surrounded by your peers, you are expected to perform and seem knowledgeable. No one relishes making a mistake in such a setting. But interactive education, especially when it is entertaining, is not only private but is also perceived as nonthreatening and nonjudgmental. Thus, learners don't feel the need to put up their defenses. They are more receptive to the educational objectives.

In many cases, projects that blend entertainment with teaching or training employ a game-like format, though they may employ other digital storytelling techniques as well. Some rely on compelling storylines and dramatic narrative. Others use appealing characters to put a human face on the material. Still other projects employ humor as their primary form of appeal. And some projects use a Chinese-menu approach, employing a variety of storytelling techniques.

Interactivity is the other powerful component in the "spoonful of sugar." Interactive content engages multiple senses and offers multiple ways of acquiring information and new skills. Instead of just obtaining information from a textbook or a classroom lecture, for example, learners may take part in interactive simulations where they are called upon to observe their surroundings, converse with characters, manipulate objects, search for clues, and analyze data. This type of educational experience requires them to be fully alert and active, and the wealth and variety of stimuli make for a deeply engaged learner.

Moreover, interactive learning is highly flexible: the same program can usually accommodate different levels of learners and different learning styles. Many interactive titles offer several levels of difficulty and various kinds of learning activities, making it more likely that users will be challenged—but not beyond their ability—and will find material that matches their preferred personal style of acquiring new knowledge. Unlike traditional classroom learning, the students can proceed at their own pace. They are not held captive by the teacher's need to get through certain curriculum points by a certain time. They are also not held back by other students who may be slower at catching on than they are. Nor are they in danger of finding themselves lost if the rest of the students are ready to move on while they are still struggling to understand a key point in the lesson. They can repeat a section of the program, drop down a level, or access a help function or tutorial for extra guidance. However, there is one potential pitfall with many online courses, especially the ones with a massive group of students: there is no teacher available to answer questions or offer feedback.

Thus, these programs accommodate struggling learners as well as ones who learn more readily. And they can be enormously empowering to students of all abilities. As learners work their way through an interactive program, they gain a satisfying feeling of mastery and accomplishment.

DIGITAL MEDIA AND YOUNG LEARNERS

Interactive educational software for young learners often goes by the term *edutainment*, a word that combines both education and entertainment. Although the term may be jarring to the ear, it effectively expresses its intent: to blend educational content with entertainment in a way that makes the material appealing to the intended learners. This technique, it should be noted, is not exclusive to interactive media. Television series like *Sesame Street* also use an edutainment approach to content.

Educational software titles are made both for home use and for the classroom. Edutainment titles were among the biggest success stories of the early 1990s, during the CD-ROM boom. Among the biggest hits during this period were the *Carmen Sandiego* series (used to teach geography, history, and astronomy) and the various *Math Blaster* and *Reader Rabbit* titles.

Children's edutainment software continues to be highly popular today. Some of these titles are curriculum-specific, geared for a particular school grade, and cover several core skills that need to be mastered for that grade, such as *JumpStart Advanced First Grade*. Other titles target just one subject, such as *Mia: Romaine's New Hat*, a science title developed by the Canadian company, Kutoka. Some of these single-subject titles are tied to the curriculum of a specific school grade while others are appropriate for several grades. Still other edutainment titles have a softer focus. They may center on such subjects such as wildlife or geography, or they may be designed to develop a child's reasoning skills or appreciation of art. Such titles are not curriculum-specific, and are meant to be inclusive of a broader age group.

Educational mobile apps are extremely popular both with parents and with their children. They include the apps made by Brainpop (http://www.brainpop.com/) and Agnitus (http://www.agnitus.com/).

STRANGE BUT TRUE: NOT FOR BABIES!

Babies are well known for being gifted at learning languages, but it turns out that their success greatly depends on how they are being taught. In an experiment done by Patricia Kuhl of the Institute for Brain and Learning Science at the University of Washington, babies were taught Mandarin sounds in one of three ways: by humans, by audio, or by video. It turns out that the babies who were taught by humans learned to reproduce the sounds quite successfully, but the babies who were taught via audio or via video actually became worse over time. The lesson here? It may be that while older children often thrive on screen-based learning, including video games, these tools are not appropriate for the youngest learners.

GAMES IN THE CLASSROOM

A surprisingly large number of elementary school teachers regularly use video games in the classroom. A study conducted in 2012 by the Joan Ganz Center at Sesame Workshop found that video games were "a regular and beneficial part of today's classroom." Fifty percent of the K-8 teachers in the study used video games in their classes at least two days a week, and 18 percent used them daily. The games used included simulations and games played on computers, tablets, game consoles, and mobile devices. The teachers reported that games helped them motivate and engage their students. The most difficult challenge one teacher reported having was convincing the parents that games were an important component of her curriculum, and yes, playing games really was part of their children's homework.

AN ADDITIONAL RESOURCE

To see a selection of video case studies demonstrating the use of video games in the classroom, go to http://www.youtube.com/playlist?list=PLA3C69D48D4FFE87E

To a certain extent, edutainment titles build on the inborn desire of all children to acquire new skills and information. Producer Diana Pray of Knowledge Adventure, the developers of the *JumpStart* titles, noted this when she said to me: "Younger kids love learning, even when it means lots of repetition. When they accomplish something, you can see the pride and pleasure in their faces. They think it's fun."

THE "DRILL AND KILL" GAME

Edutainment titles like the *JumpStart* line offer a great deal of repetitive practice, and this genre of game often goes by the name of "drill and kill." Though not an especially flattering term, it reflects that a certain amount of repetition is necessary in order to master basic skills.

Although children obviously learn from these drill and kill games, the companies that make them do not necessarily feel that they "teach," in the true sense of the word. Diana Pray of Knowledge Adventure believes their value lies in offering an interactive supplement to what the children are learning in school. "The products are meant to help kids practice their skills, never to replace the teacher. They are not a substitute to what goes on in the classroom," she said. And the students enjoy these games far more than the more traditional way of practicing skills, which used to call for hours spent with flash cards.

DIGITAL MEDIA AND OLDER LEARNERS

While countless edutainment software titles have been developed for schoolchildren since the early 1990s, it is only recently that serious attention has been paid to using the same approach for older students. Complex subjects like Newtonian physics and microbiology were considered too difficult to teach using digital media and entertainment techniques. However, this reluctance to develop such software for advanced subjects has changed radically in recent years, thanks in large part to work that was initiated at MIT under a program called the *Games-to-Teach Project*.

The two-year program, a collaboration between MIT and Microsoft, was launched in 2001 with the goal of developing conceptual prototypes for a new generation of games based on sound educational principles. It brought together an eclectic mix of specialists from various fields—game designers, teachers, media experts, research scientists, and educational technologists. The 15 game concepts developed under this program tackled difficult subject matter in science, math, engineering, and humanities, and were geared for advanced placement high school students or lower level college students. By taking advantage of the latest technology and design principles, these games were meant to excite the curiosity and imagination of the students while giving them the opportunity to explore complex systems and concepts.

Many of these projects offered networked gaming environments, and these multiplayer games were designed to deeply engage learners by competing, collaborating, and interacting with their peers, and overcoming challenges in a communal environment. Research suggests that the kind of trial-and-error experimentation and problem solving that takes place in such environments can promote the retention of newly gained knowledge.

Professor Henry Jenkins, who at the time was director of MIT's Department of Comparative Media Studies, served as principal director of *Games-to-Teach*. Discussing the philosophy behind the project in an article published on the TechTv website, Professor Jenkins made an interesting comment about what games can do. "Games push learners forward, forcing them to stretch in order to respond to problems just on the outer limits of their current mastery," he said.

Like Diana Pray of *JumpStart*, Jenkins believes that the role of educational games is not to replace teachers, but to enhance what they do. Games help make the subject matter come alive for students, he noted in the article; they motivate them to learn. He said he felt educational games could be of particular value in the areas of science and engineering because they offer "rich and compelling problems" and model the scientific process.

The 15 game concepts developed under the MIT program focused on many different educational subjects and used a variety of digital storytelling techniques. For example, in a game called *Hephaestus*, designed to teach mechanical engineering and physics, players find themselves on a formidable volcanic planet. Here they must work together to build and operate a workforce of specialized robots in order to survive. Another game, *La Jungla de Optica*, was a role-playing adventure game set in the Amazon jungle and designed to teach optical physics. It involved two primary characters, an archeologist and his niece, who must contend with a bunch of criminal minded marauders … something like a *Tomb Raider* for the physics set.

The *Games-to-Teach* project helped spur the *serious games movement*—a movement which promotes the development of games designed to teach difficult subjects, and which we will be discussing later in this chapter.

GAMIFICATION IN EDUCATION

Recently, a technique called *gamification* has gained a great deal of traction in higher education circles. Gamification is the application of gaming techniques to projects that are not games and not designed for entertainment. In academic circles, this translates into creating an awards system for taking quizzes and handing out badges for completed assignments. Badges are a particularly popular incentive, because they can be displayed on websites, social networking sites, and job sites. However, not everyone is enthusiastic about gamification in education. Henry Jenkins, for one, feels that it greatly waters down the concept of employing video games to motivate students to learn challenging material, as they were doing at MIT under the *Games-to-Teach* project. We will be taking another look at gamification in Chapter 13, where we will investigate how it is used for promotional activities.

GAMES FOR ORGANIZATIONS

In should be noted that games are not only being used to teach students but are also being used by organizations like the US Navy to study complex problems. For example, the Navy developed an online game featuring the operations pirates in Somali, opening the game to the public in 2011 and seeking potential solutions from players. Unlike commercial

STRANGE BUT TRUE: YOUR DIGITAL DOPPELGANGER

In a massive project called Sentient World Simulation (SWS), the stated goal is to create "a synthetic mirror of the real world" (as quoted in the project's concept page and noted in an article in *The Register* written by Mark Board on June 23, 2007). This is a war game on an enormous scale, and it is updated with new data on a regular basis. It is purportedly being used to see how individuals and groups will respond to stressors like a military coup or earthquake or urban warfare. Evidently, corporations are also using it to test new products.

> In this game, there are nodes not only for buildings like hospitals and mosques, but also for human beings. In 2007, the game contained five million nodes, with some parts of the game having one node for every 100 human beings. The stated goal, however, has been to include a node for every human being on Earth. Your personal node or digital doppelganger would resemble you in terms of age, occupation, and other details, but would not include your name. Thus far, SWS includes 62 nations, with the Iraq and Afghanistan models being the most highly developed. The project, which is also called SEAS (for Synthetic Environment for Analysis and Simulations), has been under development for many years at Purdue University. The simulation was fairly widely covered by the press in 2006–2007, but in recent years, almost nothing new has been reported about it, so it has not been possible to determine whether or not we are now all represented by our digital doppelganger.

video games, however, this game did not possess highly cinematic visuals, but was instead *message based*. In other words, players could send brief messages, somewhat like tweets, suggesting how to handle specific situations. The pirate game was the first in a series of online games focusing on complex problems. Overall, the series is called MMOWGLI, which stands for massively multiplayer online war game leveraging the Internet. Other themes have included climate change in the South Pacific and the potential impact of the first ice-free Arctic summer.

ONLINE COURSES

One of the newest developments in recent years is the growth of Massive Open Online Courses (MOOCs). These are free courses that are available to thousands of students at a time and are often taught by professors at elite universities. The first MOOC was offered in 2008 by the University of Manitoba. Called Connectivism and Connective Knowledge, its students included 25 from the Canadian university and 2,300 from the general public. In 2011, when Stanford University offered a MOOC on artificial intelligence and enrolled 160,000 students, this type of teaching suddenly became an overnight sensation. A tidal wave of other MOOCs were soon made available. Coursera and Udacity, two companies that offer MOOCs to the public, were launched in 2012. By early 2013, Coursera alone had 2.4 million students with offerings from 33 universities. Some of these courses are offered for college credit. edX, launched in 2012, also offers courses from top universities, including Harvard, MIT, and the University of California at Berkeley.

MOOCs offer wonderful opportunities to students without the financial resources to attend college, but thus far, most students who enroll in a course do not complete it. Cheating on quizzes and exams can also be an issue, so students are sometimes monitored by webcams and their typing patterns. Despite low retention and cheating issues, however, the number of courses offered continues to swell.

Although MOOCs are generally university level courses, it should be noted that in my home state of New Mexico, and quite possibly elsewhere, online courses are also being offered at the middle and high school level. In New Mexico, the New Mexico Virtual Academy is a statewide school that offers classes entirely online. It is the first virtual school in the state, and already has 500 students. The pupils enrolled there enjoy the flexibility it offers in terms of when they can "attend" class and the freedom to work as quickly or slowly as they choose.

USEFUL TECHNIQUES FOR COMBINING TEACHING WITH DIGITAL STORYTELLING

Educational video games and gamification are among a number of approaches utilized in order to create a project in which teaching goals and entertainment goals are both successfully met. Let's examine some additional techniques that can be employed to help accomplish this.

DETERMINING WHERE THE EDUCATIONAL CONTENT FITS IN

The key to a successful edutainment title seems to be in finding the right mix of educational material and entertainment and to blend them seamlessly together. But what guidelines can be used to work out the ratio of fun to education? In other words, how do you integrate the "edu" and the "tainment," and balance the two?

Experts in the field unanimously advocate starting with the educational goals, and building the entertainment around them. For example, at Knowledge Adventure, they always begin by setting the educational objectives of a new *JumpStart* game. The creative team starts the process off by soliciting the input of outside experts. Typically, these experts are classroom teachers who teach the grade or subject matter of the title. In some cases, they also use subject matter experts (SMEs)—specialists in a particular field—particularly when a title focuses on a specific topic. For instance, during the development of *JumpStart Artist*, which dealt with the visual arts and was a game I worked on, they used art experts from the Los Angeles County Museum of Art.

Organizations that make educational software for older learners, including companies that make training software and the US Army, start the development process in the same way—by first defining the pedagogical goals.

SETTING THE CURRICULUM

Once the general educational goals are established, a specific curriculum needs to be established—the specific teaching points that the work will cover. Games designed for grades K-12 face a particular challenge in this regard because curriculum standards can vary widely from state to state. The Common Core State Standards, however, are helping to set national guidelines. When it comes to the international front, curriculum variations can present even more significant obstacles to overcome. For instance, in France they don't teach subtraction until third grade, while in the United States it is taught in first grade.

Educational software designed for older students and for use in the workplace will also need to meet the general standards of the organizations that the project is being designed for. This is usually done by working with subject matter experts and building a consensus on the curriculum.

CREATING A PROGRAM CONDUCIVE TO ACTIVE LEARNING

The great advantage of using digital platforms for teaching is that they are interactive. Interactivity promotes *active learning*, which is also known as *experiential learning*. Both terms mean learning by doing, acting, and experiencing, as opposed to passive forms of learning, such as listening to lectures or reading books. Content designed for digital media should take full advantage of interactivity. Thus, thought must be given to how best to involve the learners. Will your program invite them to role-play? Take part in simulations? Require them to test themselves in quizzes? Have them participate in peer-to-peer learning? Offer them games to play?

SETTING LEVELS OF DIFFICULTY

By setting several levels of difficulty within the educational program, its audience can be extended beyond a specific curriculum or narrow age range or specific skill set. Having levels of difficulty also adds to the program's repeatability. If a learner starts at the easiest level, for example, the game will seem fresh again by progressing to the next more difficult level. A game might be built with three levels of difficulty, with the expectation that the student will fit inside one of these levels. The player or instructor can set the level of difficulty, but many games also include an assessment tool that automatically sets the level for the player, and offers up games that have a natural progression in difficulty. With some educational games, parents and teachers can also receive an assessment report on the child's progress and weaknesses.

Having various levels of difficulty works equally well for children, older learners, and for training programs meant for the workplace.

ESTABLISHING A COMPELLING PREMISE AND END-GOAL

As we have discussed throughout this book, when users are immersed in a nonlinear work, it is extremely helpful to give them a strong incentive so that they will work their way through to the end. This is where effective techniques of digital storytelling come into play. Enticements on the macro level are usually in the form of a dramatic premise and a highly attractive end-goal.

For example, in *Mia: Just in Time*, a game that focuses on math skills, the story begins with a disastrous fire that burns down the quaint Victorian cottage where Mia lives. But, we soon learn, this calamity can be reversed! For this to happen, Mia must assemble and operate an old time machine, but four essential parts are missing. Mia needs the player to help her find these parts, a quest that requires the solving of many math problems (see Figure 12.1). Thus, the entertaining aspects and educational aspects of the game are tightly bound together, and neither dominates.

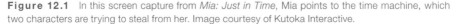

Figure 12.1 In this screen capture from *Mia: Just in Time*, Mia points to the time machine, which two characters are trying to steal from her. Image courtesy of Kutoka Interactive.

Not all edutainment titles have as strong a storyline as *Mia: Just in Time*, but they almost invariably contain a compelling goal to strive for to keep users playing all the way through to the end. Dramatic premises and compelling end-goals are equally effective in works for older learners. Of course, they need to be appropriate for the sophistication level and tastes of the target audience.

CREATING A REWARDS SYSTEM

Rewards are tremendously powerful motivators. They encourage learners through the hard parts and keep them involved for the duration of the program. Adults enjoy winning rewards just as much as children do, though the types of rewards doled out to older people will, of course, be different. There is even a school of thought, advocated by Paul Howard-Jones, a neuroscientist at Bristol University, that the chance of a reward (rather than a guaranteed reward) can increase the production of dopamine and this helps to keep a player engaged in the game.

Rewards come in many different forms, including:

- being praised by a synthetic character;
- receiving a good score;
- winning some kind of prize;
- obtaining a coveted item;
- moving up a level;
- being promoted in rank or power within the fictional world of the project;
- making some type of significant advance within the game or story context; or
- achieving a successful outcome in a simulation.

Rewards can also be in the form of intangible benefits like a boost in self-confidence or the satisfaction that comes with mastering something difficult.

When a learner succeeds at a task, it is common for a graphic (such as a score or a status bar) on the screen to note this and to show the learner's progress in the game. Rewards, however, are not necessarily seen or heard. Often they work as invisible passes, granting the user the ability to advance in the program.

NOTES FROM THE FIELD: BUILDING IN REWARDS

In children's educational games, rewards are especially important in holding the players' attention. "With rewards, the kids want to play longer" Diana Pray of Knowledge Adventure explained to me. Along with major rewards, many titles also offer smaller rewards each time the child successfully completes an exercise within the game. These rewards are the equivalent of a friendly pat on the back. Sometimes it will be in the form of a snatch of triumphant music or a brief piece of reward animation; sometimes a character, usually off-screen, will congratulate the learner with a "bravo; well done!"

Rewards should always be in keeping with the storyline and setting of the work; in effective educational titles, they work hand-in-hand. The incentives are embedded in the story; the story motivates the learners to stay involved and earn the rewards. Rewards can be handed out whenever the learner successfully completes a task, solves a puzzle, or works all the way through a quiz. Programs for young learners tend to be generously sprinkled with rewards, while those made for adults normally use them more sparingly, but they are strategically placed to give them maximum punch.

USING SIMULATIONS

Simulations are a particularly powerful tool for teaching, though they are most often used for older students and adults. Simulations are unfolding dramas that immerse the user in a realistic and engaging scenario. They are experienced from a first-person point of view, and the user's choices determine the outcome. Thus, they promote experiential learning—learning by experiencing and doing, as opposed to passive forms of learning. They can be used for a wide variety of learning situations, from teaching ancient history to training workers in how to serve ice cream cones, and are frequently employed in teaching interpersonal skills.

In a simulation called *Beyond the Front*, US soldiers are immersed in the personal pressures faced by a soldier, driving him to the edge of suicide. Players can help steer him toward recovery or, if they make unsuccessful choices, the fictional soldier will actually shoot himself in the head. The simulation was produced by the army in response to the high suicide rate among soldiers.

A quite different simulation, this one set in a virtual nuclear facility at Los Alamos National Laboratory, has players take on the role of UN nuclear facilities inspectors and inspect every inch of the lab. The project is called *Virtual Simulation Baseline Experience*, and while in the virtual lab, they can even open file drawers and pick up pieces of equipment. The project is extremely realistic from a scientific point of view. For example, gamma rays will behave like gamma rays. The goal of the simulation is to familiarize players with the tasks they will need to perform when they inspect real nuclear facilities.

USING PEER-TO-PEER LEARNING

Peer-to-peer learning is another technique often used in teaching older students. In such a learning environment, students help each other solve problems and work together to carry out tasks. Scholars of educational games have found that such peer-to-peer learning reinforces mastery. The *Hephaestus* game developed at MIT, described earlier, is an excellent example of how peer-to-peer learning can be designed into an educational game.

ADDITIONAL DIGITAL TOOLS FOR EDUCATION AND TRAINING

Thus far, we have concentrated on video games, simulations, and online courses as digital tools that can be employed for education and training. But these are only three of the many tools available for various forms of teaching. Other digital tools include cell phones, mobile apps, virtual reality, full dome immersive experiences, transmedia storytelling, and alternate reality games.

TRANSMEDIA STORYTELLING AND ALTERNATE REALITY GAMES

Cosmic Voyager Enterprises, a transmedia storytelling project for students aged 12 to 17, unfolded over a three-week period and was played by 600 students all over Florida. It employed an ambitious multi-platform approach to teach financial responsibility, economics, and ethics. The story revolved around a rocket headed for the International Space Station that instead crashes into the small town of Millisville, Florida. The center of the town is largely destroyed and at least one business, a local restaurant, is pulverized. Dangerous toxins might have been released during the crash, as well. Students play executives in the fictional company that sent the rocket into space, and must come up with a fair and ethical way of dealing with an extremely complex situation. How best can the town and its victims be recompensed for the disaster without bankrupting the company? Pieces of the story are told by extremely realistic looking faux news broadcasts (see Figure 12.2), websites, Twitter and Facebook posts, YouTube videos, blogs, and emails. Students become active participants

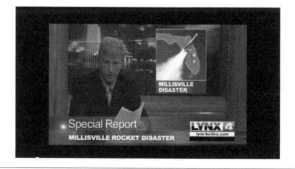

Figure 12.2 Screen capture of a faux news broadcast for *Cosmic Voyager Enterprises*. Image courtesy of Doubletake Studios, Inc.

in the story, making the project an experiential learning tool. At least one student initially believed the rocket disaster had actually occurred. Robert Pratten's company, Transmedia Storyteller Ltd., discussed in Chapters 10 and 18, played a key role in facilitating and coordinating the various components of the project, and it was produced by Doubletake Studios, Inc., in Tampa, Florida.

Another work of transmedia storytelling, this one designed as an alternate reality game (ARG), was used in the UK to teach genetics and educate students about the human genome. The eight-week project was called *Routes* and its components included a murder mystery, documentary segments, Flash games, mobile elements, and live theatrical events. Players could amass points by engaging in the ARG and playing the games, and high scorers could win valuable prizes.

MOBILE PHONES, TABLET COMPUTERS, AND APPS

Mobile phones, tablet computers, and apps are increasingly being used in the classroom, or at home to complete assignments. According to a survey by the Pew Research Center in early 2013, 73 percent of middle and secondary teachers in the study said they used mobile phones in their teaching, while 45 percent used e-readers (like Kindle) and 43 percent used tablets. And almost half of the teachers surveyed (42 percent) admitted that their students were more versed in using digital tools than they were.

It's interesting to note that English teachers used these digital tools more than math teachers did, finding them especially helpful in teaching language arts. Also, not too surprisingly, 39 percent of teachers employed by schools with a mostly low income student body felt their schools were "behind the curve" in digital education, while only 15 percent of teachers with high income students felt that way. The report can be found at http://www.pewinternet.org/Reports/2013/Teachers-and-technology.aspx.

When it comes to choosing educational apps for their students or children, teachers and parents are faced with what can seem to be far too many candidates. By early 2012, there were already 200,000 educational apps on the market, with approximately 100 or more being issued every day. Not all apps offer the same degree of educational content, of course. For more on educational apps, see Chapter 17.

IMMERSIVE EXPERIENCES

Various forms of immersive experiences (experiences that put the user virtually inside the story) are been used for education and training. The US armed forces, for example, is using full dome structures (bowl-shaped structures that project images on all sides) for training exercises. Some of these domes are even inflatable, and can be set up in two hours by two people and a screwdriver. To see a video of one such dome, go to http://www.cubic.com/News/Technology-Innovation-Media-Center-Articles/ID/678/Cubic-Immersive-Training-Dome--Air-Force-Association-Convention-2012.

In a project called *Virtual Army Experience* or *VAE*, the US Army is now using virtual reality to give civilians a taste of combat. Participants are seated in a Humvee and are given facsimiles of machine guns and other weapons (but no live ammunition) and are thrust into a realistic combat scenario. After the mission is complete, an after-action review is given, in which scenes from their mission are critiqued. The goal of *VAE* is to interest civilians in joining the military, much like *America's Army*, the game that it was spun off from. For more on *America's Army*, see Chapter 13 on promotion and for a video on *VAE*, see http://www.youtube.com/watch?v=8rAEtv7UtX0.

OTHER DIGITAL STORYTELLING TECHNIQUES

A number of other digital storytelling techniques are used effectively in interactive educational titles. For example, most titles for young children contain generous amounts of humor because they enjoy it so much. Attractive settings are also an important draw for this group—favorite places like the beach, a zoo, or an amusement park, or fantasy settings like outer space or an underground "alternate" universe. Fantasy settings can also be attractive to older audiences, though titles designed for training are usually set in realistic contemporary workplaces.

Well-developed characters are an important element in all works meant to be both educational and entertaining, no matter what the target age group is. And, as always, a solidly designed structure, appropriate for the project's pedagogical goals, is an important asset.

THE GROWTH OF THE SERIOUS GAMES MOVEMENT

As noted earlier in this chapter, serious games are games designed to teach difficult subjects, either to advanced students or to learners outside of academic settings. Because serious games are meant to be entertaining as well as vehicles for teaching, they make intensive use of digital storytelling techniques. We will be examining a variety of serious games during the rest of this chapter and throughout the book.

The *serious games movement* is a loosely organized group of designers, developers, and scholars who promote the development of such games. The movement got its start around 1996, when the US Army began to work with Hollywood professionals and the games community to develop games and simulations for military training. Serious games went mainstream in 2004, when the first Serious Games Summit was held at the Game Developers Conference.

Serious games cover a great variety of topics and are built for many different kinds of users. In fact, there is no one generally agreed upon definition of what constitutes a serious game. Most people involved in the field, however, would agree that serious games include:

- high level academic games;
- corporate training games;
- simulations used to train military personnel;
- training for emergency workers and "first responders," such as police officers, medical personnel, and firefighters;
- social impact games (games designed to have a social impact and raise public consciousness of important issues, such as famine and international conflicts);

- news games (games designed to shed light on topics currently in the headlines); and

- games meant to help individuals deal with physical, emotional, and spiritual health.

Some people in the field would also include games designed to advertise and to promote products in the broad category of serious games, an area we will be covering in Chapter 13. In addition, some also include games designed to inform, a topic covered in Chapter 14.

Many games already mentioned in this chapter would be considered serious games, such as *Beyond the Front*, *Sentient World Simulation*, *Cosmic Voyage Enterprises*, and *Virtual Army Experience*. But as we will see, serious games include a number of other endeavors as well.

A CROSS-SECTION OF SERIOUS GAMES

Serious games, as we've noted, cover a vast spectrum of projects. Let's take a brief look at several of them, to get an idea of the diverse subjects they tackle and the range of approaches they use.

- Stone Cold Creamery (http://www.icmrindia.org/Short%20Case%20Studies/Human%20 Resource%20Management/CLHR015.htm), a chain of ice cream shops, created a fast-paced online training game for its employees. A simulation, the game is set in a virtual ice cream store, and players strive to dish up ice cream, and in the correct amounts, before time runs out.

- *Glorious Mission* (http://www.digitaltrends.com/gaming/chinese-video-game-glorious-mission-chooses-us-army-for-its-enemy/) is an online military first-person shooter developed in China to counteract the influence of Western video games and also possibly to make a more popular game than the failed *Chinese Hero Registry*, described in Chapter 8. The game, which uses high quality graphics to promote patriotism and the core values of the People's Liberation Army, is thought to be modeled on *America's Army*. Unfortunately, though, the enemies the player is fighting are US soldiers.

- *iCivics* (http://www.icivics.org/) is a series of games to teach middle schoolers about civics and how the US government works. No less a luminary than former Chief Justice Sandra Day O'Connor has been involved with its development. The game is being used throughout the United States, in approximately 55,000 classrooms.

- Persuasive Games (http://www.persuasivegames.com/) is the website of Ian Bogost's company, which specializes in serious games. The website contains a portfolio of serious games dealing with such topics as airport security, pandemic flus, and the politics of nutrition.

- *Earthquake in Zipland* (http://www.ziplandinteractive.com/) is a children's adventure game that helps youngsters cope with the emotional trauma of their parents' divorce or separation. Designed for ages 7 to 13, it is set in a colorful fantasy environment. The lead character, Moose, lives on an idyllic island, but an earthquake (symbolizing a divorce) tears apart this once happy place. The player must help Moose try to put things to right again.

- *Re-mission* (http://www.re-mission.net/), mentioned in Chapter 8, is a third-person shooting game for young cancer patients. The original game is now joined by five new games, all with the same goal: to give the patients a sense of control over their cancer, help them adhere to treatment programs, and improve the quality of their lives. All five games are set inside the human body and use real-world techniques to blast away at malignant cells. The games are distributed at no charge through the game's website.

- *Endgame: Syria* (http://www.desura.com/games/endgamesyria) is a news game about the civil war in Syria. Users play as a rebel against the regime of Bashar al-Assad, and must make hard choices about the best way to handle various situations. They then see the consequences, often negative, of their choices.

- *Aftershock* (http://www.impactlab.net/2008/11/15/aftershock-reality-game-simulates-next-big-one-for-los-angeles/) was a three-week alternate reality game dealing with the aftermath of a major earthquake in Southern California. Players are sent on real world missions and tested on their earthquake preparedness skills. The game was run by the Institute for the Future and Art Center College of Design.

- *SnowWorld* (http://www.slate.com/blogs/future_tense/2012/01/31/snowworld_a_ experimental_virtual_reality_game_to_distract_burn_victims_from_pain_.html) is a virtual reality game to help burn victims deal with their pain while undergoing extremely painful treatment for their wounds. Set in a beautiful icy world, they are diverted from the grim reality of their hospital room by engaging in snowball fights with snowmen and penguins.

DEVELOPING SERIOUS GAMES FOR THE MILITARY

As we have already noted, the US Army was one of the first organizations to recognize the value of using gaming techniques and digital technology for training purposes. The Army and other military organizations continue to be leaders in the development of serious games. Not only does the military have an ongoing need for training, but games are also safer and less expensive than live exercises. Furthermore, games are highly portable and deployable. In addition, using gaming techniques for training builds on the recognized popularity of video games, especially with the young people who comprise such a large percentage of the armed forces.

Dr. Elaine M. Raybourn, one of the leading experts in this field, talked with me recently about creating games for military training. She said she has found that serious games are well-suited for experiential learning and can help the trainees master critical skills in decision-making and communication. Dr. Raybourn designs, writes, and produces games for the Sandia National Laboratories in New Mexico, a multi-program laboratory under the US Department of Energy that develops technologies to support national security. The games Dr. Raybourn develops focus on interpersonal skills rather than on procedural training (such as how to load a gun or toss a grenade). They are used to train individuals in leadership, cultural awareness, problem solving, flexible thinking, and making difficult decisions under stress.

Dr. Raybourn calls the approach she uses in her games *adaptive training systems*. By this she means the games are designed to facilitate feedback and communication during and after play, as well as the sharing of strategies and solutions. The end-goal is to help the players understand their personal strengths and weaknesses in terms of leadership and to acquire skills they need to carry out to the real world. Such an approach fosters what she terms an *emergent culture*, an experience that begins during the game but continues long after gameplay, as trainees continue to think and talk about what they learned.

Most of the projects she works on are multiplayer role-playing games. Trainees are divided into two teams of 8 to 10 players who do the role-playing, while the rest of the players serve as observers and offer feedback. Trainees switch positions at least three times during the game, giving everyone a varied perspective. While role-playing, the trainees communicate with each other by speech, talking through microphones that mask their voices to preserve anonymity. Dr. Raybourn explained to me that she is not fond of dialogue trees because "the answers have always been pre-scripted."

Though the projects she designs are for training, she believes that they are also very game-like, noting that they are full of action; that players have the goal of winning; and that they contain rewards and consequences. "That's what makes them fun," she said. The rewards in these games, she pointed out, go beyond the game itself. They increase the players' self-confidence and self-understanding.

One of the most important aspects of her preproduction process is creating a profile of a single target user, an approach to character design termed the *persona method*. It involves developing the characteristics of one fictitious but realistic individual who will represent the target player. She establishes this individual's stressors; values and belief system; strengths and weaknesses; and what this person has been through. She uses this representative individual as a guide for developing the game's narrative, its rewards system, and the creation of character arcs.

Once the persona has been created and the training objectives determined, she will then design the narrative flow of the game: where it starts and what situations the players will encounter in it. As with most games, however, there is no one set finishing point; the participants themselves create the resolution as well as many of the narrative elements. She strives to create scenarios that will pump up the players' adrenalin levels and that are emotionally engaging, though leaving room for improvisation.

The narratives she develops are extremely realistic, with every detail appropriate to the part of the world where the game is set. The visuals, the audio, and even the vegetation are as accurate as possible. For example, a game she created for the US Army Special Forces on cross-cultural engagements is set in Afghanistan. It includes a mission where players try to remove a vehicle that is blocking the road to a village. This vehicle in this particular mission is a colorfully decorated *jingle truck*, an important mode of transportation in Afghanistan (see Figure 12.3).

In the simulations she designs, she strives to create what she calls a *crucible experience*, an in-game experience that will be emotionally powerful and believable enough for the player to undergo a meaningful changing in thinking, understanding, and perception—that will cause the

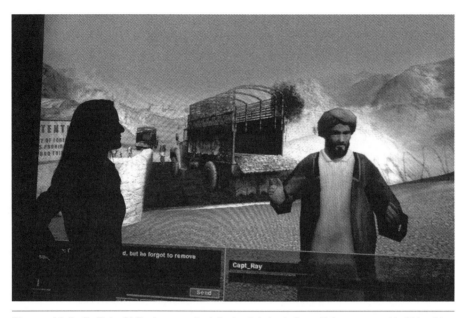

Figure 12.3   Dr. Elaine M. Raybourn, on the left, stands in front of a multiplayer game set in Afghanistan that she developed for the US Army Special Forces. The vehicle in the center is a jingle truck. Image courtesy of Randy Montoya and Sandia National Laboratories.

ADDITIONAL RESOURCES

The following websites provide a great deal of information on serious games topics and relevant conferences:

- The serious games page on Gamasutra: http://www.gamasutra.com/topic/serious/sgs/index.php;

- Games for Health Conference website: http://gamesforhealth.org/;

- Games for Change: http://www.gamesforchange.org/;

- Social Impact Games, a catalogue in progress of serious games: http://www.socialimpactgames.com/.

player to have, as she puts it, "an aha moment." This epiphany, she explained, is somewhat similar to the experience of the hero's journey, which can transform the person who undertakes it. The hero's journey, as you might recall, was first articulated by Joseph Campbell, and is described in Chapters 1 and 5.

Dr. Raybourn's simulations are often designed with built-in tools so that the instructor can modify elements during gameplay—increasing or decreasing the stress level, for example, or inserting twists in the scenario, or even building scenarios of their own. These simulations also contain in-game and after-game assessment tools. Players can analyze actions and share their observations while the game is in progress, and the instructor can bookmark segments of the game and play them back later in the session, even from different angles, so players can analyze them and discuss alternate strategies. Dr. Raybourn emphasizes that post-game discussions are an extremely important part of the learning experience.

COMBINING DIGITAL STORYTELLING AND TRAINING

Training is an activity that is essential to business. Sooner or later, almost everyone who holds a job will be asked to participate in a training session, whether the employee is a new hire whose job it is to stock shelves or a seasoned manager who oversees a large staff. Training sessions can cover anything from a basic company orientation to leadership skills, and from customer service to complex legal or scientific topics. At one time, such sessions were usually led by a facilitator and conducted much like a school or college class. Increasingly, however, training is done via computer technology, including the Internet, CD-ROMs, DVDs, and various blends of media.

The use of digital media to train employees has all the advantages of interactive software designed for education, including the facilitation of active learning. The chief difference between them is that interactive training courses focus on practical or interpersonal skills, while educational software focuses on academic learning. But as with educational software, the learners find training software more stimulating and engaging than traditional classroom experiences and appreciate the opportunity to learn at their own pace.

In addition, digital training has another advantage that appeals to businesses: it is cost-effective. Employees can do the coursework while sitting at their workstations or from home, eliminating the need to travel to a training seminar.

Given the fact that corporate training is usually a mandatory part of one's employment, and that these courses focus on the skills that employees must master in order to succeed at their jobs, it is reasonable to wonder if it is necessary, or even possible, to make such courses entertaining. Nevertheless, the companies that create training software, as well as the companies that purchase it, recognize the value of making training engaging, and understand that entertainment elements can help hold the users' attention. And they are also mindful of the fact that interactive training is competing to some extent with other forms of interactive programming, particularly games. This is especially true when the training material is directed at younger learners.

For example, Dr. Robert Steinmetz, who heads the software firm Training Systems Design, noted that he was very aware of the developments in interactive gaming and of the expectations of the younger generations for interactivity and for visual richness. Dr. Steinmetz, who holds a Ph.D. in Instructional Technology and Educational Psychology and has had over 20 years' experience in training, has a good grasp of what these courses need to be like in order to make them effective with the designated learners. He said it was necessary not only to take the expectations of the younger learners into consideration but also to consider the older learner, the person who says "just give it to me in spoon-sized bites. Don't overwhelm me."

Although story scenarios can be effective teaching tools, training specialists recommend that they be set in a realistic workplace environment in order to make them meaningful to the user. The more similar a story scenario is to real life, the easier it is for learners to transfer the training to their jobs. Care must also be taken to make sure the gaming elements reinforce the training message and don't divert attention away from it. Like story scenarios, they should be as closely related to the users' jobs as possible. Games, simulations, and story-based scenarios can all be part of the courses' mix, offering users a variety of ways to learn.

A SAMPLE INTERACTIVE TRAINING COURSE

At Training Systems Design, the company employs an open architecture that can accommodate many types of learners. Typically in their courses, the subject matter is divided into modules, and each module is given an engaging and appropriate theme. A single interactive course may contain a great variety of interactive approaches, including game-like activities, simulations, and modules that offer a user-directed path through informational material.

For example, the company's course on office safety, *Code Alert*, makes good use of simulations as a training technique. One especially tense simulation features a disgruntled employee who is armed and potentially dangerous. You, the user, have to calm him down and get him to leave the office without the encounter erupting into violence. Another simulation has you dealing with a suspicious package that has just been delivered to your office and that could contain an explosive device. If you don't handle the situation correctly, the device will go off. Without question, such simulations give users the sense that a great deal rides on whether they make the right decisions. Immersive dramas like these are likely to keep them highly involved in the training program.

Using a different approach, the module called *Save Your Co-Worker* is a game in which the user must navigate around the office and spot things that could be unsafe (see Figure 12.4). Potential "hot spots" include a man with a necktie bending over a shredder; a man perched high on a ladder; and a top-heavy file cabinet. If you leave the office without spotting all the potential hazards, the consequences can be disastrous to your fellow workers. For instance, if you have

Figure 12.4 A screen capture from the *Save Your Co-Worker* segment of *Code Alert*. The objective is to spot potential hazards and to prevent accidents from happening. Image courtesy of Training Systems Design.

failed to note the man on the ladder, he will topple over backwards. For those learners who respond better to more traditional learning, a mentor can be accessed from the upper right corner of the screen and is available to give a tutorial on the subject.

Still another module is called *How Safe Are You?*, which is a Cosmo-style quiz about the user's own office safety practices. Thus, *Code Alert* offers a diverse array of activities, some game-like, some with touches of humor, some highly dramatic. "We took a topic which most people would say 'ho hum' to," Dr. Steinmetz said of *Code Alert*, "and tried to make it engaging and attention sustaining." As *Code Alert* illustrates, storytelling and entertainment techniques can play an important role in enhancing the effectiveness of interactive training.

USING VIRTUAL WORLDS FOR TEACHING AND TRAINING

One relatively new digital venue for learning is the online virtual world. Over 100 academic institutions have conducted classes in *Second Life* alone. They have included such top-notch American universities as Harvard, Stanford, Cornell, and Columbia, as well as academic institutions in the UK, Australia, New Zealand, Austria, Singapore, and Germany.

Instructors who have taught courses in this virtual world have had positive things to say about the experience, reporting that unlike other online educational education, virtual worlds promote a real sense of community among the students and instructors, and people are far more likely to interact with each other. The virtual world environment is conducive to the building of collaborative projects, and thus promotes active learning and peer-to-peer education. And, unlike on-the-ground classes, shy students are more willing to participate (perhaps because they can act through their avatars, or because they can type in their comments), while students who tend to be domineering lose the ability to control the classroom. On the downside, however, some people new to virtual worlds complain of the steep learning curve, and others have mentioned strange distractions, such as people teleporting overhead.

NOTES FROM THE FIELD: VIRTUAL WORLD TEACHING PROJECTS

As an example of a virtual world educational project, a physics professor at the University of Denver planned to build a nuclear reactor in *Second Life* to explore issues relating to nuclear waste … which, of course, would be far safer than experimenting with nuclear waste in the real world. And at Whyville, a virtual world for 8- to 15-year-olds, sixth-graders took part in an experiment involving the spread of disease, learning about epidemics, infection, and contagion. During the experiment, their avatars broke out in red spots and started sneezing involuntarily.

The Internet, CD-ROMs, and DVDs are not the only digital options for teaching. As we've already mentioned, military organizations use virtual reality and other types of immersive environments to prepare officers and troops for active duty.

It should be stressed that digital instruction does not necessarily replace live teachers. Often these programs are played in a classroom setting, and the teacher uses them to stimulate discussion and reinforce important points. And sometimes students log into an online course in a classroom with a live instructor acting as facilitator, a combination sometimes called a *webinar*.

GUIDELINES FOR PROJECTS THAT BLEND STORYTELLING WITH TEACHING AND TRAINING

Obviously, big differences exist between making an edutainment game for young students, making a training simulation for the workplace, and making an interactive educational title for advanced students. However, as we have seen, digital storytelling techniques can successfully be applied to a wide spectrum of projects designed to teach or train. All such projects begin with the same basic considerations and questions. Here are some of the things that need to be thought out at an early stage:

- What is the need for this particular project? What is the ultimate goal of the organization that is sponsoring it?
- What are the specific teaching or training objectives of this project?
- Who is the intended audience, and how comfortable is this group with interactive media?
- What digital platform is this project best suited to?
- Will you be using subject matter experts? If so, what kinds of expertise do you want them to furnish?
- What interactive educational techniques will you use to make this an effective teaching tool?
- What will make the content engaging? What digital storytelling approach might work well to teach this particular subject?
- How will you integrate the educational content with the entertainment content?

The answers to these questions, along with the 10-step development guide offered in Chapter 10, will help you shape almost any project that blends digital storytelling with teaching and training.

CONCLUSION

Projects with workhorse missions like teaching and training might at first seem to be unlikely venues for entertainment. Yet, as we have seen in this chapter, such projects can successfully be blended with traditional techniques of storytelling and contemporary techniques of gaming.

Unfortunately, because these types of projects are not works of "pure" entertainment, they may be perceived as lacking the glamour of areas like video games. Nonetheless, we have seen many examples here of titles that are extraordinarily creative and cutting-edge, just as much so as projects that have no other mission but to entertain.

Furthermore, endeavors like these perform a genuine service in the world. In addition, they offer a great many employment opportunities. As the use of interactive media continues to spread, it is highly likely that the use of digital media for teaching and training will expand as well. If this prediction is correct, we can expect to see a steady demand for people with the creative ability to stir sugar and medicine together and turn it into a palatable, tasty brew.

IDEA-GENERATING EXERCISES

1. Select a topic that is taught in elementary school and sketch out a general concept for an edutainment game that would teach this subject.

2. Select a subject for older learners that could be taught as a serious game. This game could be for training purposes, for an advanced educational topic, or to educate people about a health, social, or public policy issue. What is the "spoonful of sugar" in this game?

3. Devise an over-arching goal for the player in each of these games.

4. Devise a rewards system that would be appropriate for each of these games. How would the rewards for the younger learners differ from those developed for the older group?

5. What types of teaching techniques would you use for each of these games? Why do you feel one approach is better suited for schoolchildren and the other for adults?

Note: if these exercises are being done in a group setting, divide the group in half. One half should work on the game for the schoolchildren and the other half on the game for adults. Once all the exercises have been completed, the two groups can compare and discuss their approaches.

CHAPTER 13

Using Digital Storytelling for Promotion and Advertising

How can digital storytelling techniques be applied to serious business endeavors like promotion and advertising?

In terms of digital storytelling and promotion, what could the US Army and a story about a pig possibly have in common?

Why are alternate reality games catching on as promotional vehicles?

What role does gaming play in promotional digital storytelling?

OLD ENDEAVORS/NEW TECHNIQUES

On the face of it, it may be difficult to see any similarities between a music video featuring a group of preppy rappers, an alternate reality game about a mysterious crop circle, a gritty video game about military combat, and a reality show where all the contestants are house cats. Yet all four of these projects do have key characteristics in common: they use interactive media and storytelling for advertising and promotional purposes.

The need to advertise and promote probably goes all the way back to the time when humans were still living in caves. Perhaps the first manifestation of this type of activity began when an enterprising caveman set up shop under a tree and tried to trade his surplus chunks of woolly mammoth meat for some sharp pieces of flint. But when he attracted more flies than customers, he realized he would never do any business unless he could make his fellow cavemen aware that he had mammoth meat to trade, and excellent meat at that. Thus the first attempt to promote and advertise might have been born.

While no one can say for sure if such a scenario ever took place, we can be quite confident that the need to promote and advertise has existed as long as people have had products, services, or ideas that they wanted other people to purchase or willingly accept.

The methods have changed with the technology, of course. Our enterprising caveman would only have had his own voice and his gestures to make people aware of his excellent woolly mammoth meat. In time, however, merchants would be able to tout their wares on strips of papyrus, and then in printed newspapers and magazines, and ultimately, in radio and television commercials. Today we have yet another technology at our disposal, and an incredibly powerful one: interactive digital media.

Unlike earlier forms of promotion and advertising, which used passive forms of media, interactive digital media encourages an active involvement with the message. Because this form of promotion and advertising can be so entertaining, people willingly become involved with it. Furthermore, they enjoy it so much that they even tell their friends about it—a phenomenon known as *viral marketing*, which is the voluntary spread of information by means of digital media. And, unlike earlier forms of advertising and promotion, the exposure to the message is not a fleeting experience. In some cases, the involvement can last for days or weeks, and can even lead to a life-long connection to the product or idea. Think how different this is from fast-forwarding through a commercial or barely skimming the ads in a magazine or newspaper!

With interactive digital media, we have an enormous variety of techniques we can use to promote and advertise. The ones we will focus on in this chapter are not "hard sell" forms of advertising like the online pop-up and banner ads that most people find intrusive and annoying. Instead, they use various aspects of digital storytelling such as plot, characters, suspense, immersive storyworlds, conflict, competition, humor, and heart—the warm and touching emotional core of a story.

As we will see, many of these projects are remarkably ingenious. The techniques we will be examining can be used to promote products (automobiles, shoes, candy, cat food); entertainment properties (movies, TV shows, video games, theme parks); ideas and causes (health issues, international crises, social issues); and organizations or groups (political parties, religious faiths, professions).

THE DIFFERENCE BETWEEN PROMOTION AND ADVERTISING

With promotion and advertising, we are, of course, talking about two somewhat different endeavors. Although both have the goal of attracting people to certain goods, services, organizations, or ideas, they are somewhat unalike in terms of their end-goals. Promotional activities are designed to attract favorable attention to a product, organization, or idea, while advertising goes one step further and tries to encourage a purchase or a commitment. The line between promotion and advertising can get quite blurry in digital media, although most projects that use a digital storytelling approach fall along the promotional end of the spectrum.

One of the most desired outcomes of both advertising and promotion is something called *branding*, a concept briefly introduced in Chapter 8. Branding is a way of establishing a distinctive identity for a product or service, an image that makes it stand out from the crowd. By successful branding, the product is differentiated from its competitors and is made to seem alluring in a unique way. As has been pointed out to me, companies can be fiercely protective of their brands, creating bibles and style guides to make sure the brand is presented in a consistent fashion.

VIRAL MARKETING

Many promotional works that use digital storytelling techniques are spread by viral marketing, as mentioned above. The beautiful thing about viral marketing is that it costs virtually nothing outside of the production costs to the company or organization that has created the piece. Instead, its fans willingly spread it to their friends and colleagues, who in turn spread it to others.

The Danish website Baekdal.com (for media professionals) published an insightful article several years ago offering a number of common-sense pointers on creating projects that are likely to be spread virally (http://www.baekdal.com/media/viral-marketing-tricks). Among the points stressed was the importance of developing a good story that creates strong emotions and does something unexpected. Baekdal advises that the star of the piece be the story and not the product or organization being promoted, which should take a back seat—a point I totally agree with. Baekdal also advises that you should make your piece easy to share, using a format that is commonly used, and not creating impediments, like forcing people to register or become members in order to see it. In addition, Baekdal feels it is important to allow people to make comments, and to not be afraid of negative ones. After all, if you have created something that engenders strong emotions, you are bound to step on a few toes.

We must be aware, however, that digital media has the immense capability of spreading pieces that are negative to a product or company's image, as happened several years ago with the Domino's Pizza fiasco. A couple of disgruntled employees created a video, posted to YouTube, showing them doing some highly unsanitary and disgusting things with the company's pizzas. This was not a situation that Domino's had done anything to encourage, unlike the Chevy Tahoe do-it-yourself commercial described in Chapter 4, and Domino's responded promptly and intelligently to the bad publicity. But the overall lesson here is, first, to pay attention to what people on social media are posting about your organization, and second, do not give users tools with which they can make mischief.

DIGITAL MEDIA VENUES FOR PROMOTION AND ADVERTISING

As we saw in Chapter 12, many different forms of digital media can be used to teach and train. The same is true of promotion and advertising, which can also use a wide variety of digital media and storytelling techniques to accomplish their goals. Before discussing the specific techniques of narrative-based promotion and advertising, let's first take a look at the major digital venues and see how they are being used. They include:

- *The Internet*: the Internet is quite possibly the most heavily used digital medium for promotion and advertising. Among the many online narrative-based genres used for these purposes are real and faux websites, fictional blogs, webisodes, virtual worlds, MMOGs, and short, fast-paced games known as *advergames*. Advergaming will be discussed in more detail later in this chapter.

- *Mobile devices*: in the last several years, mobile devices have become an important venue for promotion and advertising. They are often used for advergaming and as part of an overall transmedia promotional campaign. In addition, mobisodes (episodic dramas for mobile devices) are sometimes used to promote entertainment properties, and may also be used to promote consumer products like automobiles.

- *iTV*: although iTV (interactive television) is not flourishing in most parts of the world, some companies do use interactive commercials for advertising. Some companies also sponsor entire entertainment programs, incorporating promotional messages into the content itself. Second-screen TV is a fairly new venue for promotion and advertising, but advertisers are starting to wade into these waters as well.

- *Video games*: video games are being used to promote and advertise both on the macro and micro levels. On the macro level, entire games are devoted to a single promotional goal. On the micro level, various products or companies are promoted through *product placement*—the integration of products into a game or other form of screen-based entertainment. Product placement will be discussed in more detail later in this chapter.

- *Virtual reality*: full-scale VR installations are sometimes used for promotional purposes, and portable VR kits have been developed to advertise various products.

- *Smart toys and theme park rides*: toys and rides are primarily used to reinforce consumers' awareness of branded entertainment properties.

- *Additional venues*: in addition, organizations use short films, mobile apps, virtual worlds, and transmedia storytelling for promotional and advertising purposes.

APPLYING DIGITAL STORYTELLING TECHNIQUES AND GENRES TO PROMOTION AND ADVERTISING

In the short time that digital media has been used to promote and advertise, content creators have developed an extremely varied palette of techniques to engage their target audiences and get their messages out to the public. Let's take a look at some of the most widely used of these techniques.

PRODUCT PLACEMENT

As we noted in Chapter 2, product placement is the integration of products into a game or other form of screen-based entertainment. Product placement can be found in video games, where you might see NPCs wearing ball caps embellished with clothing logos or skimming the waves on surfboards decorated with soft drink logos. One might think that players would find product placement intrusive, but a focus group conducted by a New York ad agency showed that to the contrary, 70 percent of those in the group felt that seeing familiar products in a game "added realism."

Product placement is also finding its way into virtual worlds and MMOGs. For example, players of the *Sims Online* can set up McDonald's restaurants or equip their offices with PCs from Intel. Furthermore, major corporations have set up outposts in *Second Life*.

For the most part, product placement is a static form of advertising and not directly related to digital storytelling. However, product placement can become a more active promotional technique and at times does contain elements of narrative, in the form of characters and little storylines.

For example, the famed science fiction novelist, William Gibson, via his avatar, visited *Second Life* to promote his new novel, *Spook Country*, and did a reading of his book there. And during the holiday season a few years ago, NBC held a tree-lighting ceremony in *Second Life*. The ceremony took place at a virtual version of Rockefeller Center, which even had a virtual skating ring. Avatars of characters from the cast of an MTV show visited MTV's virtual world, *Virtual Hills*, and interacted with the avatars of fans, and avatars of famous movie stars and musicians are becoming increasingly common.

If this phenomenon of active product placement continues, we can expect content creators to become involved by creating little scenarios or even larger dramas to integrate the products into some kind of engaging narrative.

BRANDED CONTENT

Branded content is programming that is funded by an advertiser and integrates promotional elements with the entertainment content. Unlike traditional advertising sponsorship, where the advertising is done through commercials, the entire program can be thought of as a "soft" commercial. To be effective, the promotional elements need to be woven into the narrative content, and the narrative content must be highly attractive to the audience.

Many examples of branded content can be found on the Internet and, to some degree, on mobile devices, as well. Advergaming is a form of branded content, and so are a number of amusing videos found on sites like YouTube. Sometimes entire websites are forms of branded content. For example, the Official Harry Potter Website, described in Chapter 8, invites users to explore and play in Harry Potter's world. It is highly entertaining and interactive, but its true goal is to promote the Harry Potter films.

The Way Beyond Trail, an online interactive adventure story created to promote the Jeep Patriot, is another example of branded content, and a good illustration of how digital storytelling techniques can be applied to promotion. It follows the same model as the old *Choose Your Adventure* books mentioned in Chapter 1 where the user (the reader, in the old days) is asked to make a choice at crucial points in the story and the choices affect the way the game will end. It thus uses the classic branching structure described in Chapter 7. But even though the structure is hardly innovative, the story is clever and fresh, and you as the user feel quite engaged.

The Way Beyond Trail, shot on video, is a tale about three hip young adults traveling around the backcountry—in what else but a shiny new Jeep Patriot. When you first log onto the story, you are asked to fill out a passport with your name and gender. Thus, you become the fourth member of the party and are even addressed by name at a few points. The camping trip soon turns into a search for buried treasure and things soon become a little wacky—just how wacky depends on the choices you make. But you will almost certainly make several wrong turns before you find the treasure, and encounter some bizarre individuals along the way, a little like characters from the classic TV series, *Twin Peaks*.

The Way Beyond Trail works well as a branded content story because the user is actively involved and pulled into the adventure. Furthermore, the promotional material does not intrude in the story. Of course, as you and your new friends drive around the woods and search for the treasure, you get a good look at the Jeep's interior and exterior, and get to see how well it maneuvers on rough terrain. Also, it has a subtle subtext: by owning one of these Jeeps, the story implies, you, too, can go on cool adventures with cool friends and have a great time.

In quite a different application of branded content, Meow Mix cat food created a reality show in 2006 that followed all the conventions of the genre, except that the contestants in this case were all house cats. The show, *Meow Mix House*, was a transmedia entertainment, using television (broadcast on the Animal Planet network), the Internet, and a real-world venue, a custom built home for the cats in a storefront on New York's Madison Avenue. Visitors to the website could view the 10 competitors, all cats rescued from shelters, through webcams. They could read their bios, see recaps of the episodes, and vote for their favorite feline. Just as with a human reality show, the cats were given challenges, but these were more in line with their natural talents. They were judged on such things as purring, climbing, and catching toy mice. The website was an enormous success, receiving over two million unique visitors, and a success for the cats, too, because after the show they were all adopted into good homes.

SOCIAL MARKETING

Social marketing is a specialized form of promotion that is designed to change the way people behave—to motivate them to break harmful habits like smoking or overeating, and to encourage them to take up positive behaviors, like wearing seat belts or exercising. Though digital platforms have only recently been used in social marketing campaigns, the concept itself has been around since the 1970s, when social marketing campaigns were mostly conducted through televised public service announcements.

Today's digital social marketing campaigns are far more sophisticated. They avoid lectures and scare tactics and instead are positive, upbeat, and involving. *America on the Move*, for example, is a healthy lifestyle campaign to get people to become more physically active. One technique the site used to offer was "virtual hikes," like China's Silk Road or the Appalachian Trail. You, the user, picked a trail, tracked how many steps you took each day (measured on a pedometer), and entered them on your virtual trail. Your steps were converted into miles along the trail and your progress was charted on an online map. You could even enjoy some sightseeing as you "hiked."

PUBLIC ADVOCACY CAMPAIGNS

Like social marketing, public advocacy campaigns are meant to sell ideas, not products. Such campaigns are intended to raise public consciousness about serious issues and to inspire people to take action. One way of doing this with digital media has been to combine Flash animated cartoons with calls to action. Unlike objective informational pieces, social advocacy cartoons take a strong position on whatever issue they are tackling, though the stand they take should be supported by facts.

One highly successful public advocacy campaign was a series of clever little Flash animated cartoons called *The Meatrix*. The cartoons, which are still available on YouTube (http://www .youtube.com/watch?v=rEkc70ztOrc), are a parody of the popular film, *The Matrix*, and are a call to action against factory farming. The first *Meatrix* debuted online in 2003, with sequels *Meatrix II* and *Meatrix II½* coming out in succeeding years.

Produced by the design firm, Free Range Graphics, *The Meatrix* tells the story of a naïve young pig, Leo, who is living contentedly on a bucolic family farm until he meets a cow named Moopheus, an underground resistance fighter. When Leo takes the red pill Moopheus offers him, he is introduced to a ghastly alternate reality and learns the shocking truth: family farms are mostly a fantasy, having been stomped out by agribusiness and replaced by cruel, filthy, and diseconomic factory farms (see Figure 13.1). Leo joins Moopheus as a resistance fighter, and the sequels continue his adventures and include more shocking revelations about the meat industry.

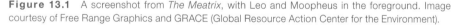

Figure 13.1 A screenshot from *The Meatrix*, with Leo and Moopheus in the foreground. Image courtesy of Free Range Graphics and GRACE (Global Resource Action Center for the Environment).

More recently, another animated story about factory farming, *A Pig's Tail*, has created a great deal of buzz. This sweet, earnest story of a little pig who happily discovers a real family farm was produced by the Humane Society of the US and Aardman Animations.

Still another public advocacy campaign, this one designed to call attention to pollution caused by plastic bags, used a short live action film to get its message across. The project, *The Majestic Plastic Bag* (http://www.youtube.com/watch?v=GLgh9h2ePYw), is a mockumentary narrated by Jeremy Irons and sponsored by Heal the Bay. Though not interactive in itself, it does contain a call to action.

WEB SERIES

Web series, which are sometimes called webisodes, are serialized dramas typically broadcast in short installments. They are often used as promotional vehicles for TV series, as we saw in Chapter 9, where we discussed several examples. Mobisodes, which are like Web series except made for mobile devices, can be employed in this way, too. In addition, however, Web series are being used to promote such products as automobiles and beauty products, and can be viewed as a form of branded content.

In 2006, Dove, which makes beauty products for women, created a somewhat loony webisode, *Nighttime Classics*, that highlighted its Calming Night line of products. In the series, Felicity Huffman, star of the TV series *Desperate Housewives*, dreams she is visiting the fictional homes of vintage TV shows like *Leave It to Beaver* and *The Brady Bunch* and interacting with the characters who live in each household. With veteran director Penny Marshall at the helm, new footage was shot and skillfully interwoven into excerpts from the classic TV shows, so it looks as if Huffman is actually conversing with the characters in the old series. The escapist dreams that Huffman enjoys tie in nicely with Dove's night-time beauty products, and the campaign included a call to action: women who viewed *Nighttime Classics* were invited to request free samples of the products.

Promotional Web series can be non-fictional stories, too. For example, Nissan produced a series about its cutting-edge racing car, the DeltaWing. The major storytelling device here? Suspense. How would the brand new car do in the Le Mans 24, the Grand Prix of endurance races?

GAMING

A number of different forms of gaming are used as vehicles for advertising and promotion. They include advergaming (mentioned above), casual games, video games, alternate reality games (ARGs), and massively multiplayer online games (MMOOs). Gamification, discussed in Chapter 12, also has a role to play in promotion and advertising.

Advergaming and Casual Games

Advergaming, introduced briefly above, is, as the name suggests, a combination of gaming and advertising. Advergaming, also known as *promotional gaming*, began on the Web, but now these games are also appearing on mobile devices, where they work equally well.

Advergames are meant to be short pieces of entertainment, lasting just a few minutes, essentially making them a sub-genre of casual games. Like casual games (which are discussed more thoroughly in Chapter 15), they are designed to be highly addictive and fun. Usually they start off as very easy to play but quickly become more difficult. Thus, people become hooked on them and play again and again, trying to do better with each go-round. Furthermore, they are not demanding in terms of the skill level needed to play them, so they are as enjoyable for inexperienced players as they are for people who play games regularly. Thus, they are a robust form of promotion and advertising.

Advergames are popular with advertisers because they:

- are so engaging that consumers will willingly play them;
- increase brand awareness;
- can be spread to an ever-expanding group of players through viral marketing; and
- are an effective way to highlight a brand's special features.

Often these games contain a little backstory to set up the gameplay and put it in context, though the backstory needs to be established quickly, because users want to get into a game as soon as possible. Advergames often contain an indirect message reinforcing positive aspects of the product.

For example *The Race to School Game* was developed around a particular type of athletic shoe, Reebok's Traxtar. It features a character named Sammy Smartshoe. In the backstory, we learn Sammy has missed his school bus and has to get to school in time for an important math test. So Sammy decides to beat the bus to school. As the player, you help Sammy race against the bus, making him leap over a variety of obstacles and avoid hazards like slippery mud puddles. Sammy's jumps in the game have a springy, bouncy quality that sends him effortlessly over obstacles—a subtext indicating what the user can look forward to if he purchases this particular brand of shoe.

Advergames are most likely to catch on when they are a good fit with the tastes and sensibilities of the target audience, which is one of the reasons cited for a game called *King Kong Jump* becoming an international hit a few years ago. This zany game promotes two different products: the movie, *King Kong*, and Pringles potato chips. Though tying potato chips and an adventure movie together in the same advergame might seem like quite a stretch, the company that made it recognized that both products were perceived as fun and both appealed to the same demographic. You, as the player, are the would-be hero of the game, and you must save a helpless young woman from King Kong's jungle. For some reason, this is accomplished by dodging and jumping over cans of Pringles potato chips, which are rapidly rolling down a hill directly at you. If you fail to get out of the way in time, you get squished flat. But if you achieve enough points, the gorilla beats his chest and roars approvingly, and you move on to the next level.

Chipotle's Mexican Grill, a restaurant chain committed to humanely raised meat and locally grown produce, commissioned a game called *The Scarecrow* which charmingly depicts its mission. The Scarecrow's enemy in the game is a crow, who represents Crow Foods, a fictional company that mass produces food. The game is available as a free app, and high-scoring players can even win coupons for food. Chipotle's also produced a companion film for the game: http://www.scarecrowgame.com/.

Video Games

As briefly noted earlier, entire video games are sometimes devoted to a single promotional objective. *America's Army*, launched in 2002, is one highly successful example of a dedicated promotional game. It was made by the US Army with the goal of recruiting young people to join the armed forces. The game and its sequels realistically but excitingly portray army life and combat, taking players from boot camp training right through to dangerous combat missions. The weaponry and tactics are all authentic. The developers took great pains to be accurate, while focusing, of course, on the most thrilling and glamorous parts of military life; KP (Kitchen Patrol) and push-ups are not featured in the game.

The game exceeded all expectations, in part because of is content and in part because it was perfectly aimed at its target demographic, the young men and women who love to play video games. It has become one of the most successful video games ever. The producers offer regular updates, and versions have been made for comic books, mobile phones, the latest game consoles, and, as we saw in Chapter 12, even for a virtual reality experience.

Alternate Reality Games

Alternate reality games (ARGs) are often used to promote entertainment properties, and we noted one example in Chapter 10, *The Lost Experience*. But in addition, ARGs are being used to promote restaurant chains, automobiles, and other products. They are particularly effective as promotional vehicles because players become deeply invested in them and in the brand being promoted, often for weeks at a time. Furthermore, these games are especially enjoyed by people between the ages of 18 and 34, a prime demographic for advertisers.

For example, *Who is Benjamin Stove?*, sponsored by General Motors, promoted the awareness of ethanol fuel and, in an extremely low-key way, promoted their Flex Ford line of vehicles. The mystery story involves an enigmatic character named Benjamin Stove as well as crop circles, sacred geometry, and mystical archeological sites. According to the late Dave Szulborksi, the game's puzzle designer and a story consultant on the project, the game was unusual in that it kept the identity of the sponsor, General Motors, a secret until very near the end. General Motors actually stepped into the game as a character, addressing the fictional Benjamin Stove in an ad that appeared in the *USA Today* newspaper and website (see Figure 13.2). *Who is Benjamin Stove?* is discussed in more detail in Chapter 18, as well as some other promotional ARGs.

Massively Multiplayer Online Games (MMOOs) and Virtual Worlds

An entire MMORPG or virtual world can be used as a form of promotion. One newcomer to this arena is Disney Infinity, which as of this writing has just been launched. It is a gaming site that also operates a little like a virtual world, and is a rich venue to promote Disney characters and movies.

MTV, another entertainment giant, has an entire collection of virtual worlds, which operate under the banner of *Virtual MTV*, or *vMTV*. As of this writing, MTV operates six virtual worlds, each based on one of its popular TV shows.

In addition, many companies have been exploring sites like *Second Life*. By mid-2007, at least 85 major brands established outposts there. They were dipping their toes in these virtual waters in various ways: setting up retail stores; offering customer support; testing designs for new products and buildings; collaborating on projects; and holding meetings, events, and

Figure 13.2   General Motors took out this ad on the *USA Today* website as a rabbit hole into the game, without revealing it was the game's sponsor. Image courtesy of Dave Szulborski, GMD Studios, and General Motors' Live Green, Go Yellow campaign.

EXPERT OBSERVATIONS: CREATING A PROMOTIONAL ARG

Dave Szulborksi, who not only served on the creative team of *Who is Benjamin Stove* but on 11 other ARGs as well, was one of the world's most experienced people in the ARG universe. He offered me this perspective on creating a promotional ARG:

In most cases, the very idea to create an ARG for promotional purposes is generated as part of the discussion of a larger marketing campaign, with the ARG representing just a portion of the overall budget and scope of the campaign, so their creative genesis usually is expressly to promote a product, brand, or idea in a way that complements the more traditional marketing they will be doing.

"This doesn't mean, however, that the narratives of promotional ARGs necessarily need to be full of product references or even explicitly mention a company or brand to be successful," he continued. "And that's really the trick of being successful as an ARG designer, isn't it? Finding ways to tell an engaging story that also accomplishes the goals of the sponsors."

international conferences. The results have been mixed, because there is an inherent clash of cultures between the fantasy-role-play typical of virtual worlds and the suit-and-tie mentality of the business world. For example, Nissan retooled its Altima Island in *Second Life* in 2007 to be more in keeping with the spirit of the world, but shortly thereafter, a helicopter smashed into one of its buildings, killing several avatars. It is unknown whether this was an accident or a prank, but in any case, it left a sour impression and, since then, a number of businesses have closed up shops there.

Business ventures in virtual worlds seem to fare best when done in the spirit of these fantasy communities. If you remember William Gibson's book reading described earlier in the chapter, that also had an appropriate virtual world twist. An overflow crowd of avatars squeezed into the hall where the event was to take place and eagerly awaited Gibson's arrival. But Gibson's avatar did not make his entrance from a mundane side door. Instead, he descended from the ceiling in a large object shaped like a tanker container. The doors of the vessel opened and Gibson's avatar stepped out to huge (typed) applause.

Gamification

Gamification, the employment of gaming techniques to works that are not games, has become a highly popular method for businesses and organizations to promote their messages to the public. For example, when I was in London in the spring of 2012, a little before Easter, a massive egg hunt was being carried out. But people weren't searching for typical little painted chicken eggs. These eggs were enormous, at least as waist high as a very tall man, and each was adorned by a leading artist. It was all part of the *Fabergé Big Egg Hunt*, which the jewelry company sponsored in part to celebrate the Queen's Diamond Jubilee and in part to help two charities. And it helped promoted the famous jewelry company's new London boutique as well, by playing off the intricate Easter eggs the company would fashion each year for the Czar's wife or mother prior to the Russian Revolution.

The 200 eggs in the London hunt were hidden all over the city, and the person who found more than anyone else would win a grand prize: a golden Jubilee egg encrusted with jewels (more the size of a chicken egg than the eggs in the campaign!). To help users find these eggs, clues were planted on Twitter and Facebook, and zone maps indicating their location were posted on a special website. Each egg had its own code, and participants who found an egg would photograph it and its code and send the photo to a dedicated phone number, which logged it in as an entry.

In terms of digital storytelling, this campaign incorporated a strong goal (winning the golden egg); challenges (finding the eggs in the campaign); rewards (collecting entries); exploration (of London); and interactivity (using your phone to photograph the egg and send in the code). In addition, the golden Jubilee egg, as well as the 200 hidden eggs, all served as characters in this hunt.

In a very different type of endeavor, the movie *Rio* teamed up with Chiquita, the food company famous for its bananas, to create the *Make Your Way to Rio* campaign. The grand prize was a trip to Rio de Janeiro in Brazil. It was a campaign designed to involve the entire family.

Families that registered to play received a "passport" and played as Blu, a bird character featured in the movie. As Blu, you would interact with activities on the campaign's website—coloring, trying out new recipes, and playing games.

Families accumulated points by completing activities, and could win prizes like badges, DVDs, ringtones, and a year's supply of bananas. The campaign was largely promoted through "Mommy" websites, which are blogs devoted to child-rearing and are a popular genre on the Web. The mommy bloggers were given promotional packets containing tickets to the film, coupons for Chiquita food products, stickers, and recipes, all to encourage them to write about the campaign. In terms of digital storytelling, it contained many of the same elements as the egg hunt in London: a strong goal; challenges (the activities on the website); rewards; and a colorful character, Blu.

MUSIC VIDEOS

In 2006, a music video called *Tea Partay* debuted on YouTube, and may well have been the first music video on the Internet to be used for promotional purposes. The clever tongue-in-cheek video, sponsored by Smirnoff, featured a group of East Coast preppies rapping about a new Smirnoff beverage, Raw Tea. Spread quickly by viral marketing, it was viewed an estimated 5.8 million times on YouTube alone. This was a great coup for Smirnoff, since YouTube viewers are a prime demographic for their new beverage. A year later, in the wake of this success, Smirnoff released a follow-up video, *Green Tea Partay*, featuring a rival group of rappers on the West Coast singing about another Smirnoff beverage.

"CONSTRUCTION KIT" COMMERCIALS

"Construction kit" commercials are online promotions in which users are given all the tools they need to create a commercial for a specific product, competing for prizes and recognition. As we saw in Chapter 4, Chevy used this technique with its Chevy Tahoe campaign, but the venture backfired badly when some users created venomous commercials about the SUV. Nevertheless, the concept itself is a promising one, encouraging interactivity and engagement, though for it to be effective for promotional uses, some restrictions would need to be built in.

FAUX OR FICTIONAL BLOGS

Faux or fictional blogs, like Web series and mobisodes, are often used to promote TV series. We examined one such blog in Chapter 10, *Nigelblog.com*, and there is every reason to think that such blogs can be effectively used to promote other types of things, not just entertainment properties. However, it should be noted that blogs, like construction-kit commercials, have the potential to backfire.

In 2006, NBC attempted to promote a new TV series, *Studio 60*, by a faux blog called *Defaker*, modeled closely on a popular real blog, *Defamer*, which covers entertainment gossip. *Defaker*'s first entry was mostly an uninspired rehash of the first episode of *Studio 60* and almost immediately the negative comments poured in, posted on the blog's own comments section, on other blogs, and even in mainstream news media. Scorn was heaped on *Defaker* for being a poorly written, clumsy, blatant plug for the show. *Defaker* soon became the poster child of a fictional blog gone wrong, making NBC something of a laughing stock. The blog was pulled after just a few days.

The *Defaker* fiasco is a vivid illustration of the importance of using a light hand and a fresh approach when employing digital media for promotion.

SHORT FILMS

Short films for the Internet, both linear ones and interactive ones, are logical vehicles for promotional endeavors. Earlier in this chapter, we examined the interactive film, *The Way Beyond Trail*. The concept of using short online films as branded entertainment dates back to 2001, when BMW began promoting its sleek, high-end vehicles online via a series of sleek, high-end short films. Collectively called *The Hire*, the eight films were united by a recurring character, a mysterious driver-for-hire, who operates the car in all the little movies. Heavy hitters like Guy Ritchie, John Frankenheimer, and Ang Lee directed the films, and one even stars Madonna. No overt advertising was contained in any of them. *The Hire* has received many accolades and brought much favorable attention to BMW. The films have even been screened at Cannes, and they can still be seen online (http://www.bmwblog.com/2009/08/25/video-collection-bmw-films-the-hire/).

Many other organizations have also been utilizing short films as a marketing strategy. For example, the Humane Society of the United States produced a heartwarming work about an endearing little dog named Billy, rescued from a puppy mill. Billy sadly passed away several months after his rescue, but the film and one made to commemorate his life was successfully employed to increase donations for the Humane Society. The Environmental Defense Fund made a series of short films about a fictional family of polar bears struggling to survive during global warming, as the ice was melting. And as we saw earlier in this chapter, the Humane Society of the US created the animated *A Pig's Tale* to raise awareness of the negative aspects of factory farming and to promote the Humane Society.

WEBCAM PEEPSHOWS

Webcam peepshows, where the user can type in commands that the person shown on the webcam video must follow, have to be among the most bizarre methods of promotion ever devised. Evidently, webcam peepshows are fairly common forms of pornography, but it takes a leap of imagination to consider this as a model for a promotional purposes. Yet Burger King did just that with its edgy *Subservient Chicken* (http://www.subservientchicken.com/pre_bk_skinned.swf) campaign in 2004 to promote chicken sandwiches. News of the website spread like wildfire through viral marketing and TV tie-ins.

The show featured a person dressed in a chicken costume (and a garter belt, as well!) who would obey approximately 400 typed-in commands. Though made to look like a live feed, the videos were actually prerecorded responses triggered by key words. The peepshow cleverly reflected Burger King's slogan, "Get chicken your way." The chicken would even turn itself into a chicken sandwich, if requested, by tucking itself in between two cushions.

According to the ad agency that oversaw the website, Crispin Porter + Bogusky, *Subservient Chicken* received a million hits within hours of launching, and over 15 million hits within a few months. *Subservient Chicken*, now many years later, is still going strong.

With a success of the magnitude that *Subservient Chicken* enjoyed, a couple of other promotions have imitated the idea of commanding an animal of some species or other to perform specific behaviors. In one such campaign, this one for Heart Guard (a heart worm medication for dogs), users could type in commands to a cute little dog, who seemed to understand most of them. When he couldn't, he would apologize and explain why. In another, this one for the Tipp-Ex correction roller, you help out a would-be bear hunter who suddenly decides not to shoot a marauding bear. So you can "wipe out" the instructions to shoot the bear, and instead command the bear to do things like kiss, hug, and wave. It should be noted that while both of these campaigns are entertaining and are thematically tied to the product they are promoting, neither one makes use of the peepshow concept.

TRANSMEDIA STORYTELLING

Transmedia storytelling is increasingly being utilized as a promotional tool. In Chapter 10, we discussed several examples of promotional transmedia stories, including *The Beast* (to promote the movie *AI*); the various transmedia extensions to the TV series, *Dexter*; and the *Catch the Kid* campaign to promote New Mexico tourism.

Beginning in the 2008 holiday season, Macy's department store launched a major transmedia campaign, *Believe*, and added additional elements over succeeding years. The campaign was based on a letter written to the New York *Sun* in 1897 by eight-year-old Virginia O'Hanlon. Little Virginia wanted to know if Santa Claus really existed. The reply, known as *Yes, Virginia, There is a Santa Claus*, became one of the most famous editorials ever written, full of hope and positivity. Macy's took Virginia's story and transformed it into an enormously successful campaign, which centered around children writing letters to Santa. "Belief stations" with postal boxes and letter-writing stations and stationary were set up in Macy's stores, and for each letter written, Macy's pledged to give one dollar to the Make a Wish Foundation. The letters resulted in Macy's donating $1 million dollars to the charity.

Other elements included holiday display windows at Macy's animating Virginia's story; balloons in the Macy's holiday parade; shopping bags with the "Believe" logo; various forms of social media; an animated movie about Virginia; a book, a DVD, and holiday ornaments all based on the same story. The campaign also had its own website, http://social.macys.com/believe/?cm_mmc=VanityUrl-_-believe-_-n-_-n#/home, which received 10 million views in just eight weeks. In addition, in 2011, Macy's developed an augmented reality (AR) app placed in the Belief station in which a child could be posed with characters from the animated movie. The photo could then be made into a holiday card and sent to friends on Facebook or by email. The app could also be used at home to see Virginia ice-skating. The Believe campaign is an excellent example of how an "old timey" story can be revived and transformed using both digital media and traditional forms of communication, like handwriting and window displays, into a successful transmedia marketing campaign for today's audiences.

Social Media

Social media is being utilized in a variety of ways to promote products and organizations. Sometimes these stories are conveyed visually. For example, a ski resort in northern California developed a campaign that invited customers and staff members to post photos and videos on social media with the tag "Northstar, Tahoe." Those who do can potentially be rewarded by having their photos or videos posted on the Northstar website or even winning ski resort services. This fairly simple and straightforward endeavor resulted in the ski resort receiving thousands of favorable posts, whereas before there had only been a few hundred entries on the same sites.

Jack in the Box used quite a different approach several years ago after its spokesperson, Jack (the one with the round clown head and dunce cap), was run over by a bus during a Super Bowl commercial and nearly killed. (The commercial can still be seen at http://www.youtube.com/watch?v=kqT_5f08Nxs and was actually the opening event of a relaunch of the company's brand, with a new menu, website, and food choices). The campaign, called *Hang in There, Jack*, invited Jack in the Box fans to send Jack get well messages by social media and the company website. Twenty-seven fans went so far as to create get well videos, which in total received 4.8 million views (*Los Angeles Times*, March 17, 2009). In addition, Jack received thousands of text messages on Facebook and Twitter. Jack's website and social media accounts gave regular updates of his medical condition. Two reliable digital storytelling techniques were used here: having your story revolve around a life-and-death situation and employing a vivid character at the center of the story (in this case, the character was already well known to the public). Though the company took a risk in inviting the public to post anything they wished, the negative messages were minute in comparison to the positive ones. The company did monitor the posts, but only removed ones that were vulgar or included profanity.

MOBILE APPS

Mobile apps are being used in a variety of ways to promote products and organizations. For example, Charmin, a brand of toilet paper, teamed up with *SitorSquat* to produce an app that helps users find the cleanest public toilets wherever they happen to be. Its two cute bear cub mascots are used as visuals for the app. In an extremely different type of app, the World Wildlife Fund (WWF) created *WWF Together*, an educational app that showcases the stories of eight species of animals. In addition, the app contains animal-themed games, a 3D globe that lets you find out where 60 different species of animals live, and teaches you how to fold origami animals.

AUGMENTED REALITY

Augmented reality (AR) is becoming increasingly popular with advertisers and marketers, because it allows users to interact with the brand. Smart phones and other digital devices can be used to "see" 3D images that are invisible to the naked eye. According to ABI Research, advertisers only spent $6 million on AR in 2009, but were expected to spend $350 million by 2014.

As we saw above, Macy's used AR in its *Believe* campaign to allow children to take photos of themselves with animated characters. In a promotion for the *Green Lantern* movie, users could play an AR game to test whether or not they had the stuff to become a Green Lantern. They were tested on strength, focus, agility. Volvo created an app that lets you "drive" a Volvo through whatever room you are in. So, if you are in an office, you need to scoot around chairs and dodge desks, or, if you are in your living room at home, you need to drive around the coffee table and avoid hitting your Siamese cat. And, in a live demo of AR, and perhaps one with the greatest digital storytelling potential, *National Geographic* invited members of the public to play with a group of dinosaurs, pet a cheetah, swim with a dolphin, and interact with an astronaut.

ADDITIONAL RESOURCES

- To keep up-to-date on the use of using interactive digital media for promotion and advertising, visit iMedia Connection or subscribe to its daily newsletter: http://www.imediaconnection.com/index.asp. The publication offers news and features about all forms of interactive marketing; conducts insightful case studies; and does podcasts.

- For news and information about mobile marketing, go to *Mobile Marketer*, http://www.mobilemarketer.com/.

CONCLUSION

As we have seen in this chapter, digital storytelling techniques can be applied to advertising and promotion in a great many ways, and these works can be highly entertaining and engaging. However, we have also seen a couple of instances where projects did not succeed as anticipated and, in fact, some badly backfired. We can learn a great deal both by the successes and failures that we have studied.

First of all, it is important for content creators to give thoughtful consideration to the message they want to send, the culture of the medium they are using, and how best to appeal to their target demographic. Care must be taken to seamlessly integrate the promotional content into the narrative content, without allowing the promotional message to intrude jarringly. Humor is always an asset, and should be used to the maximum degree appropriate, since it is a rare individual who doesn't enjoy a good laugh now and then. As we have seen, material that is fresh, fun, edgy, and original has the best chance of reaching a wide audience.

Finally, it can be risky to give users too much control, because they might be tempted to play havoc with it. This is far less likely to happen, however, when they enjoy and genuinely respect the material. This respect for the material must originate with the creators themselves. If they feel they are "slumming" and don't exert themselves creatively, this attitude will be perceived by the users. The truth is, creating a successful campaign in this arena requires pulling out all creative stops.

It remains to be seen how, in the long run, businesses will adapt to virtual worlds and other new digital genres. It is also too soon to know how, if at all, digital storytelling will fit into this picture. But as these examples illustrate, an element of playfulness and fantasy—close relatives of storytelling—can certainly help bridge the disparate cultures of business and digital media.

When digital storytelling techniques are used imaginatively, and when everything comes together in a well-planned campaign, it can result in a resounding success. Furthermore, the process of developing such a project is hardly drudgery. Instead, the work can be a creative joy.

IDEA-GENERATING EXERCISES

1. Choose a product that you are familiar with, and devise a concept for an advergame or other form of branded content that would highlight its strongest qualities. Try to find an indirect way to give an important message about this product, using subtext rather than a blatant hard sell approach.

2. Select an organization or profession that you know well and that has a specific need. Sketch out a campaign using digital media and digital storytelling that could make the public aware of the organization and its need, as the US Army did with *America's Army*.

3. Think of a social problem that is currently a public concern, and devise a social marketing campaign that could help address this problem.

4. Select an object in the room that you are in and try to create a mobile app or work of AR that would promote this object.

CHAPTER 14

Using Digital Storytelling to Inform

How and why are traditional media outlets like newspapers, news magazines, and television networks turning to interactive media as an adjunct to their news services?

How are digital storytelling techniques being applied to informational content?

In what ways are such disparate forms of digital media like virtual reality, electronic kiosks, and interactive cinema being used to disseminate informational content?

What are some of the criticisms that have been leveled at the way digital media has been used to disseminate information?

THE IMPACT OF DIGITAL MEDIA ON NEWS AND INFORMATION

The proliferation of digital media is rapidly transforming the way we receive news and information. Until recently, most people obtained their news and information from print publications or from radio and television broadcasts. Now, however, digital technology is giving us new options. We can stay informed via websites, blogs, podcasts, and news bulletins delivered by email and in text messages on our mobile devices. We can receive the latest news almost as soon as it happens—and sometimes as it is actually taking place. With digital media, we also have the ability to customize the information we receive. We can choose the categories of content that interest us; we can specify whether we want to receive news bulletins or full stories; and we can determine when and how often we want to receive this content.

In recent years, the popularity of traditional sources of information has been waning steadily and this, in turn, has been impacting the news organizations themselves. For example, the newspaper staffs have been shrinking, with 2,600 fewer editorial jobs (editors, reporters, and photographers) in 2012 than previously, according to a Pew Research Center report. The news departments of television stations are also shrinking and are now about half the size they were in 1980. And while in the past, it was customary for a crew of three or four people to be sent out to cover a story, now it is typical for one individual, a digital, to write, shoot, and edit these stories by themselves. TV stations are also cutting costs by doing more interviews by Skype than on location. As a result of this decrease in robust coverage, many people are abandoning the news sources they once relied upon. The audience for evening network news shows, for example, has been shrinking steadily for many years, losing a startling 55.5 percent of their former viewers by 2011. Furthermore, the average age of these viewers is 53, which is not the ideal demographic for these news shows. Newspapers have been so hard hit that many have been forced to go out of business. Several, including the *Rocky Mountain News* and the *Tucson Citizen*, have gone out of business, and a number of others are on a death watch. Another sign of the instability of the news business occurred in 2013, when the venerable *Washington Post* was sold to Jeffrey Bezos. Jeffrey Bezos, it should be remembered, is the founder and CEO of Amazon.com, but there are no plans to merge the two organizations.

THE GROWING POPULARITY OF DIGITAL MEDIA AS A NEWS SOURCE

By early 2011, only 41 percent of people between the ages of 18 to 29 were still receiving their news from papers, radio, TV, or news magazines, while 65 percent of this group were getting their news from the Internet, according to a report from the Pew Research Center. Furthermore, as another sign of the changing times, newspapers lost $7 on the print side for every $1 they made in digital ad revenue, according to a 2012 report from the Pew Research Center's Project for Excellence in Journalism. By 2012, online ad revenue actually surpassed the revenue earned by newspapers.

Meanwhile, the popularity of digital media as a news source has been soaring. Many people now turn to YouTube for videos of unfolding news, particularly when it comes to natural disasters and political upheavals. YouTube is now the third most popular site on the Internet, after Google and Facebook, with 72 hours of video uploaded every minute. A report published by the Pew Research Center in October 2013 revealed this fact: 30 percent of the population receives its news from Facebook! This seems especially surprising, given that most posts on Facebook are highly personal in nature (my great photo of the sunset!) and not about newsworthy events, but the report noted that these individuals are not going to Facebook in search of the news, but pick up the news while they are there for other reasons.

Many observers believe YouTube, Twitter, and Facebook played a major role in fueling the Arab Spring, which began in Tunisia with the self-immolation of Mohamed Bouazizi in late 2010. In Tunisia and Egypt, videos of protests encouraged other protesters to join in and posts on social media helped define the expectations of democracy and freedom. In the week before

Hosni Mubarak, the president of Egypt, resigned, tweets about the insurgency increased by 10 times, according to a report by Philip Howard, an associate professor in communication at the University of Washington.

One dramatic sign of the popularity of digital media was previously mentioned in Chapter 2: the millions of people watching on the Internet to see the death-defying jump from the edge of space by Felix Baumgartner (see Figure 14.1). The jump broke all previous records of live stream viewing on the Internet: eight million viewers on YouTube. (The previous record of about 500,000 concurrent viewers was set that summer during the Olympics in the UK.) A photo of Baumgartner right after he landed was shared about 30,000 times within 40 minutes and almost immediately gathered 216,000 likes. This event clearly demonstrated that the Internet is capable of attracting a mass audience for a special event.

Figure 14.1   The Red Stratos team preparing the space capsule that Felix Baumgartner will use to ascend into the edge of space, an event watched on the Internet by eight million people. Image courtesy of Jay Nemeth and Red Bull content pool.

The Internet has obviously become the big gorilla in the room when it comes to news and information. But in addition, we can receive information from mobile devices, watch interactive documentaries, and interact with informational works on electronic kiosks and in immersive environments. These information-providing digital platforms can be found almost everywhere, from public spaces like cultural institutions and airports to private spaces like our homes, our schools, and our places of employment. In many cases, we carry them around with us, in our pockets or handbags.

Not only is digital content highly portable and customizable, but it also gives us the opportunity to participate in the content. Newspapers allow for extremely limited forms of participation—readers can write letters to the editor and that's about it. But interactive media allows us to contribute by sharing our stories and videos, voice our opinions in forums and polls, and join in live chats and other types of community experiences.

The radical shift in the way information is sent and received, as we noted in Chapter 2, is having a profound impact on traditional media and on how journalism is practiced. And, of particular interest to those of us involved in digital storytelling, these developments in the sphere of news and information are giving us the opportunity to use powerful new techniques of interactive narrative for informational purposes.

THE DIGITAL REVOLUTION AND TRADITIONAL NEWS MEDIA

As we have seen above and in Chapter 2, the popularity of digital media is putting intense pressure on traditional news outlets. As audiences shrink, so do ad revenues, which puts traditional news outlets in an ever-tighter bind. In business, the customary response to competition is to engage in an all-out battle with the rival, seeking to beat down and eliminate the usurper. But in the case of the competition between traditional and digital news sources, many forward-thinking newspapers and broadcasters are using a more adventurous strategy. They are embracing their rival, digital media, and integrating new types of interactive content into their operations.

For many newspapers, the embracing of digital media involves a shift of self-perception. As an article in the *Santa Fe New Mexican* put it (April 11, 2007), many papers no longer think of themselves as being in the "newspaper business" but simply as being in the "news business." In other words, their primary mission is to deliver the news. The medium of delivery is irrelevant. More recent statistics bear this out. According to the Alliance for Audited Media, during the six months ending on March 31, 2013, the digital editions of newspapers were 19.3 percent of their total circulation mix. In other words, almost one-fifth of readers received their news from digital media. The digital media content was offered via mobile apps and e-reader editions of the papers. Not surprisingly, *The Wall Street Journal* and the *New York Times* were ahead of the pack, having the highest percentages of digital circulation.

Most traditional news organizations that commit to digital media focus on developing a robust website and employ a large website staff. According to recent statistics, the website of the *Washington Post* has a staff of 200—larger than some newspapers. A few news organizations are taking a more proactive stance, teaching their reporters to develop stories for multiple media, using video and audio as well as print. Others are making significant changes in how and where they offer the news. For example, *The Wall Street Journal* puts breaking news and financial data on its website, and uses its print publication for in-depth articles.

The changes in the way news is being covered are even sifting down to journalism schools, and impacting the way news writing is being taught. At my old graduate school, the Medill School of Journalism at Northwestern University, they are now training all students to use digital media to cover stories. Students learn to create blogs and websites; develop content for mobile devices; do podcasts; and write interactive narratives. They also learn to use an array of digital equipment. The professors have had to go back to school themselves to learn how to teach these new courses.

Nationally, about 160 newspapers in the United States offer some type of paid subscription for their websites, according to the Newspaper Association of America. This includes two of the leading papers in the United States, the *New York Times* and *The Wall Street Journal*. The *New York Times* is also taking some innovative approaches with digital media. For instance, it is now publishing video games as part of its op-ed page. These are serious games and, like any op-ed piece, they take a position on an important issue. The first such game, *Food Import Folly*, centers around the problems of imported food and the shortcomings of government food inspectors. Others can be found at http://www.persuasivegames.com/, the website of Ian Bogost's company, which specializes in serious games. The *New York Times* is also producing interactive documentaries, which will be discussed later in the chapter.

STRANGE BUT TRUE: SETTING INFORMATION TO MUSIC

Not only is the *New York Times* beginning to feature games for its editorial page and to produce interactive documentaries, but it has also produced a musical video for its website. Staff writer David Pogue, who covers technology, created the first such project for the paper. Pogue normally writes text-based stories, but when Apple introduced the revolutionary iPhone, he couldn't resist doing something totally different. He went all out and created a humorous musical video about the new device. Though the musical took a tongue-in-cheek, mock-serious tone, the production also contained a thoughtful rundown of the iPhone's assets and shortcomings. Pogue composed his own lyrics (to the tune of "I Did It My Way") and even sang most of the music himself, though a few people waiting in line to buy iPhones were corralled into singing a few lines. The video is still online at http://video.on.nytimes.com/video/2007/07/05/technology/1194817121833/iphone-the-musical.html.

In a quite different approach, the cable TV network MSNBC created an extremely rich and deep community-based website revolving around the Hurricane Katrina disaster in 2005. Called *Rising from Ruin* (http://risingfromruin.msnbc.com/stories.html), the site contains stories written by professional journalists as well as individuals from the affected region. It includes numerous heartbreaking and inspirational first-person accounts of the aftermath of this monumentally destructive storm, told in text, still photos, audio, and video. New stories have been added over the years, and the beautiful site is still maintained.

APPLYING DIGITAL STORYTELLING TECHNIQUES TO NEWS AND INFORMATION

Digital storytelling techniques can make an otherwise dry or difficult subject come alive, and can make the material extremely engaging to users. The combination of information and entertainment gives us another genre of "tainment" programming—*infotainment*—a blending of information and entertainment, much as *edutainment* is a blending of education and entertainment. However, the term infotainment has fallen into disfavor because to some people it connotes a trivialization of factual content. Thus, even though the infotainment approach is perfectly valid when handled responsibly, we will refrain from using the term in this book because it might be distracting.

WORTH NOTING: OBJECTIVE VERSUS SUBJECTIVE

We have many techniques at our disposal for making information engaging. But first of all, a basic decision must be made. Will we be taking a *subjective* or *objective* approach to delivering the content? Traditional journalism is objective. It is told in the third person and the writer avoids voicing his or her personal opinion. The facts in the story are checked out and validated; usually the sources of the facts are cited. A subjective approach, on the other hand, is a more personal one, and the material is often written in the first person. The writer's opinion is clearly expressed, and facts may not be as carefully vetted or noted as with an objective approach. The subjective point of view is often used in blogs and personal websites. It is also fairly common in interactive documentaries and in audio and video podcasts and is even used in some informational games.

A fundamental goal in combining information, entertainment, and interactivity is to offer users an opportunity to relate to the material in an *experiential* manner, as opposed to one in which they are merely passive recipients of the information. The experiential approach to the presentation of information allows users to interact with it, participate with it, and manipulate it. As we will see, a variety of digital storytelling techniques can be used to create experiential forms of informational content.

UTILIZING PERSONAL STORIES

One way to involve users is by creating highly involving and interactive personal narratives. This is the approach used in *Rising from Ruin* about Hurricane Katrina victims, described above. The same approach is being used in a website called the *Hawai'i Nisei Story* (http://nisei.hawaii. edu/page/home), an emotionally rich website featuring the stories of Hawaiians of Japanese decent and their often harrowing experiences during World War II (*Nisei* is a Japanese term for second-generation Japanese Americans). The stories on this website are told in a mixture of video, audio, still photos, archival material, and text. Each person's story is quite detailed, but users have the ability to choose their own path through the narratives and go as deeply as they wish.

This same technique, that of using personal stories as the foundation of a website, is employed in *Jewish Pioneer Women* (http://www.storiesuntold.org/main.html). The stories, which tend to be quite short, are embedded in a quilt design. The quilt serves as an appropriate metaphor, since so many pioneer women stitched quilts. The website, produced by the New Mexico History Museum, focuses on the lives of women who lived in the state from 1850 to 1910. The stories are told by way of text, still images, and audio.

To create an effective narrative, the story or stories should be involving; multiple modes of communication should be employed; and users should have the ability to pick their own path through the material, as these works illustrate.

COMMUNITY-BUILDING ELEMENTS

Users want to be able to personally participate in the story in some way. As we saw earlier in the description of *Rising from Ruin*, one method is to invite users to share their own personal stories. Other community-building techniques include inviting users to participate in polls; share their thoughts on forums, message boards, and listservs; and join in live chat sessions. Some community-building techniques encourage the use of mobile devices: people can use them to vote, send in text messages, or even create videos to share with others.

A website called *Firefly Watch* (https://www.mos.org/fireflywatch/) uses a somewhat different community-building approach, inviting users to participate in a study as citizen scientists. The Museum of Science in Boston, along with researchers at Tufts University and Fitchburg State College, suggests that fireflies (which are actually beetles) may be far less numerous today than in the past, and raises the question: are they disappearing? Users are invited to spend 10 minutes each week during the summer to track the fireflies in their own yards or nearby fields. The website offers simple to understand, but fascinating information about the different types of flashes fireflies send out to help observers track them accurately, much of it through an interactive "virtual habitat." It also contains a discussion board, another key tool in community building. Unfortunately, people living west of the Rocky Mountains aren't able to participate, because, aside from rare exceptions, there are no flashing fireflies that far west.

Community-building websites like these are effective not only because they tell a story but also because they encourage visitors to actively contribute to it, whether it be a story about an environmental crisis or the life-cycle of an insect.

In addition, it is a common practice today for practically any type of website to build in social objects so a community can be formed around it. These community elements are often managed by a Community Manager, a growing job description.

GAMES AND GAME-LIKE ACTIVITIES

Games are a highly effective and popular way to involve users in informational material and to absorb it in an experiential manner. This technique was used by the game developed for the *New York Times* on food inspection, *Food Import Folly*. It was also used in several serious games described in Chapter 12, such as *Endgame: Syria* and the games developed for *iCivics*.

Two other informational games are *Cutthroat Capitalism* (http://www.wired.com/gamelife/2009/07/pirate-game/) and *The Cat and the Coup* (http://www.thecatandthecoup.com/). *Cutthroat Capitalism* is a news game about the pirates off the Somali coast, and was published in 2009 by *Wired* magazine to help explain the economics behind Somali piracy. *The Cat and the Coup* has been described as a "documentary game," and is about the former prime minister of Iran, Dr. Mohammed Mossadegh, the first democratically elected prime minister of that country. In this indie game, which incidentally has wonderfully exotic graphics, you play as the prime minister's cat.

The Internet abounds in informational games for all age groups and on a vast assortment of topics. Just to pick one example to look at more closely, let's focus on a website called *The MesoAmerican Ballgame* (http://www.ballgame.org/). The site was produced in conjunction with a traveling museum show and it does an excellent job of involving the user in games and game-like activities. The focus of this website is the ancient basketball-like sport played in Mexico and Central America, a game that was also a serious religious ritual. As you may recall, this game was described in Chapter 1.

The MesoAmerican BallGame gives users a chance to "play" a version of the ball game itself, though they score points by answering trivia questions about the game instead of tossing the ball through the hoop. In addition, the website contains a number of game-like activities. For example, users can bounce some of the traditional balls, and with each bounce, learn an interesting fact about them. Another game-like activity lets users dress one of the players in his game uniform. In addition to games and game-like activities, visitors can "tour" a virtual ball court and learn more about how the game was played, and also view MesoAmerican artifacts relating to the ball court. The website makes excellent use of animation, sound effects, music, and interactive time charts to make its subject matter vivid and understandable.

USING HUMOR

Humor is a traditional and effective way to make content engaging. We have seen how the *New York Times* used humor in its iPhone musical, a work clearly geared for an adult audience. And, as we discussed in Chapter 8, humor is also an excellent way to involve young people.

Humor can also be used to convey a serious message, as was done by *Dumb Ways to Die* (http://dumbwaystodie.com/). This seemingly light hearted jingle with child-like animation, put out by Metro Trains Melbourne, incorporated a strong message: to observe safe practices around trains. This cute little video received 45 million hits on YouTube. As this work illustrates, there are very few important messages that cannot be conveyed by employing a clever dash or full dose of humor.

OFFERING MULTIPLE POINTS OF VIEW

Because works of digital storytelling are nonlinear and interactive, they can be designed to give users the ability to explore information from more than one point of view. As we will see a little later in this chapter, this technique is sometimes used in interactive documentaries. One such interactive documentary is *What Killed Kevin?* (http://whatkilledkevin.com/), about bullying in the workplace. It is a story about a magazine editor who was allegedly driven to suicide by his boss. Users can view the work from the POV of his sister, his boss, and his co-worker. They can also read emails and other documents, and ultimately decide for themselves whether or not Kevin was the victim of workplace bullying.

Multiple points of view can also be employed in works of virtual reality, as was done in a work called *Conversations*, described in Chapter 22. By allowing users to see a work from more than one point of view, you give them the opportunity to examine the factual evidence in a number of ways and then come to their own conclusions. This is quite different from linear information content, which only provides one predetermined way of viewing the material.

AN ARRAY OF PLATFORMS

Throughout this chapter, we have mentioned many different platforms that are used to deliver informational content. Now let's look at them one by one, and examine how each serves as a vehicle for information.

THE INTERNET

When it comes to informational platforms, the Internet is certainly the grande dame of them all, having been used for this purpose far longer than any other other digital medium. It now rivals traditional media as a delivery platform for information and news, and it is excellent at delivering densely factual material in an easily accessible manner. And, much in the manner of a grande dame, Web content can be beautifully dressed up in a great many ways. It can be enhanced by media elements like animation, video, sound effects, music, and other types of audio, as well as by interactive elements like multiple narrative paths, diagrams with "hot spots," games, timelines, and activities of various kinds.

However, the Internet's content can also be "dressed down," harkening back to the Internet's modest roots as a text-based medium. Many informational websites are still primarily text-based, lacking most or all of the "glittery" elements we have described. In such cases (and even when there is plenty of "glitter"), the content needs to be organized in a way that is logical, easy to find, and "chunked" into small pieces, so users are not forced to read long stretches of text. Also, whenever possible, a narrative thread should be teased out of the source material so the content on the website tells an involving story. As experienced journalists know, engaging stories can be pulled out of virtually any source material and assembled in a compelling way.

WORTH NOTING: TAXONOMY AND THE INTERNET

In scientific circles, *taxonomy* is the discipline of classifying and organizing plants and animals. The underlying concept of taxonomy is extremely useful for organizing informational content on the Internet as well as other digital media.

The word taxonomy comes from the Greek and is composed of two parts: *taxis*, meaning order or arrangement, and *nomia*, meaning method or law. Though the organization of organisms in biology and the organization of text and graphics for a website might seem to be worlds apart, the basic approach is quite similar. In biology, taxonomy is a hierarchical system, starting with the largest category at the top, and then dividing the organisms into smaller and smaller categories, organized logically by commonalities. The same system works well on a website, and the underlying logic makes it easy for users to find the information they are looking for. Note that taxonomy also works well for DVDs and other platforms which offer a large amount of information.

In terms of designing a digital storytelling project for the Internet, we've examined projects that used multiple points of view and ones that used gaming, but another important technique is the strong use of visuals. Whether using just a few stills, or using multiple videos and interactive graphics, visuals can very much make a website come alive. *The Packard Plant. Big. Ugly. Dangerous* (http://www.freep.com/article/20121202/NEWS01/120814070) is one such project that featured the dramatic use of visuals. The website, produced by the Detroit Free Press, focused on the enormous but crumbling plant that used to produce Packard automobiles, but had been shut for years, making it a target of vandals, graffiti artists, and squatters who chopped up the floor for firewood. The site includes a six-minute video about the Packard plant, an aerial interactive map, and a photo gallery with photos both of its years as a fully functioning factory and its years of shocking decline. The Associated Press honored the site by giving it first place for digital storytelling in the Journalism Excellence competition.

Social media has become an essential tool for spreading news on the Internet, especially in parts of the world enveloped by civil war or other forms of unrest. We now have a website, Storyful (http://storyful.com/), that aggregates social media news stories and serves as a newswire for journalists.

MOBILE PHONES AND TABLETS

Mobile devices are increasingly being used as a portable tool to stay informed about breaking news, sports, weather, stocks, and entertainment. They are particularly useful for delivering short pieces of information, though tablets also work well for exploring a topic in depth. One such app for the iPad is *The Elements: A Visual Exploration*. This work has been described as "a love story" to the periodic chart, and it thoroughly examines each element thus far discovered both visually and in text. Even people who are adverse to chemistry have found it mesmerizing.

Owners of mobile devices can subscribe to any number of news services that will send the kinds of information they are interested directly to the cell phones. Some of these news sources, like CNN and Reuters, were originally established for traditional media. Others, like Google Mobile, have their roots in new media. Most mobile devices can play video and can connect directly to the Internet, thus widely expanding their utility. Also, it should be stressed that mobile devices are designed as two-way streets. Not only can owners of them receive information, but they can also capture and send out breaking news—in text, stills, and video.

Thus, mobile phones have become useful tools for collecting data. For example, global health services now conduct surveys about the spread of disease using mobile phones, and with this data are able to put together the story of a particular disease.

AGENT-BASED MODELING

Agent-based modeling is a common technique used to populate and animate scenes in video games and films with virtual characters. In addition, however, agent-based modeling can be used to tell the story of a vanished people, as was done in a fascinating research project called *The Artificial Anasazi*. The modeling was in part to reconstruct the lives of the Anasazi (ancient Native Americans who were the precursors of today's Pueblo Indians) who lived in The Long House Valley in Arizona between 1800 BC to 1300 AD. It was also done to try to solve the mystery of why they suddenly abandoned the place they had called home for centuries. Up until this study, archeologists assumed that the Anasazi throughout the Southwest had deserted their traditional villages because of a disastrous drought that had occurred around 1300. Would the study uphold this theory or not?

The research team populated the valley with "agents" who each represented a household of five individuals, and, based on anthropological information, assigned them life spans, nutritional requirements, and movement capabilities, plus other attributes gleaned from archeological materials excavated in the valley. They were then able to put together a clear picture of how these agents moved around the Valley, how they grouped into clans and villages, and how they responded to changes in the environment and to social conditions. The study clearly demonstrated that, despite the drought, crops could still be raised in the valley, and concluded that the Anasazi's reasons for abandoning this region could still not be determined.

In a slideshow created to explain the project, Dr. George Gumerman, one of the researchers, quoted a line from Pablo Picasso: "Art is a lie that helps us see reality" and paraphrased it thus: "Agent based modeling is also a lie that helps us see reality."

LOCATIVE JOURNALISM

Locative journalism is a term used for audio tours made possible by GPS. Essentially, works that use this technique are essentially the stories of physical places. This form of reporting has also been called *LoJo*, a term coined by a team of graduate students at the Medill School of Journalism at Northwestern University. LoJo has been used to tell the story of the Berlin Wall, using personal narratives and original source material for the content, and can also be a robust way to tell the story of past events. In addition, LoJo can be used to tell the story of future events. For example, the Medill graduate students created a LoJo project to show what Chicago would look like if it won the bid to host the 2016 Olympics.

INTERACTIVE AND SECOND-SCREEN TV

By making television content interactive, viewers can be pulled into the presentation and become actively involved in the program. It offers viewers a much richer connection to the informational content than they would have with a linear TV show. A number of techniques can be used to enhance linear TV programming. They include access to background information (in text, audio, or video); play-along trivia games; participating in polls; and being able to vote in a contest or issue presented on the show and witness the results of the vote. In the UK, the BBC offers a service called BBC Red Button, which is its version of iTV. BBC Red Button was enormously popular during the Olympics held in London in 2012.

Second-screen TV, which is a second device like a smart phone or tablet computer used in conjunction with a broadcast TV show, can be used to access additional information about the TV show and post comments and other material. For instance, if you are watching a baseball game, you can use your second screen to access data about the players, the teams, and the history of this particular competition, and you can also post your thoughts about who will win and why.

VIRTUAL REALITY (VR)

Virtual reality installations are unique in the way they can give participants a chance to connect with information content in a deeply experiential manner. As we will see in Chapter 22, VR can be used to immerse people in a recreated news story and observe it from multiple points of view, as with *Conversations*, the true story of a prison breakout. VR has exciting potential as a platform for experiential treatments of information content, but thus far its potential has barely been explored.

ELECTRONIC KIOSKS

Electronic kiosks are ideal for offering informational content in a public setting, since they are reasonably portable, sturdy, and easy to operate. However, content for kiosk delivery must necessarily be quite concise, since kiosks must serve large numbers of people. They are well suited as informational delivery systems in government buildings, trade shows, and as adjunctions to museum exhibitions. The housing for kiosks can be dressed up in imaginative ways, serving as an enticement for visitors to try them out. Some of the latest kiosks are equipped with facial recognition technology, which can be used to verify a person's identity for such purposes as obtaining a driver's license. Other kiosks, these quite dazzling, project holographic images of "virtual mannequins" who offer various services. Some are positioned in airports and offer security information while others are placed in retail establishments as shoppers' assistants. Non-fiction content for kiosks is more thoroughly explored in Chapter 23.

INTERACTIVE DOCUMENTARIES

Interactive documentaries are made for both large and small screens. Large-screen productions, works that are viewed by audiences in theaters, are primarily found in cultural institutions. They are particularly well suited to content that is emotionally engaging and offers an interactive exploration of a particular theme, such as marine life, human biology, or ancient Egypt. Several examples are discussed in Chapter 21.

The more intimate works of small-screen iCinema, designed for individual use, are an ideal platform for interactive documentaries because they encourage in-depth examinations of a particular subject or event. Such interactive documentaries can offer multiple points of view, allowing users to experience the story from various angles, as was done with *What Killed Kevin*, discussed above. Others, known as *database narratives*, give users the chance to select and assemble small pieces of factual material into a cohesive story.

The *New York Times* has begun to publish interactive documentaries. One, the acclaimed *Snow Fall: The Avalanche at Tunnel Creek* (http://www.nytimes.com/projects/2012/snow-fall/#/?part=tunnel-creek), is the nonlinear story of a group of skiers caught in a devastating avalanche. The work won a Pulitzer Prize. Another, *Jockey* (http://www.nytimes.com/projects/2013/the-jockey/), used stunning photography, audio, and text to explore the world of jockey Russell Bates. Examples of other documentary projects can be found in Chapter 21.

MUSEUM INSTALLATIONS

With digital technology, museum installations have the power to make static displays of artifacts become highly involving and interactive. To do this, museums are making use of animatronic characters, holographic images, and powerful sound and motion effects, as well as immersive environment techniques used in high-tech theme park rides.

For example, Le Domus Romane di Palazzo Valentini is an archeological site in Rome focusing on two long-buried Roman villas that were discovered in 2007 and then excavated. To help visitors understand what these magnificent homes would have looked like at the time they were inhabited, museum curators have virtually reconstructed parts of the villas lost to time, using digital technology to bring them back to life. The exhibit includes a voice-over narration. Other examples of how museums are using digital technology can be found in Chapter 22.

TRANSMEDIA PRODUCTIONS

The transmedia approach to content, explored in depth in Chapter 10, presents an integrated narrative over a number of different platforms, and allows users to experience the content and interact with it in a number of ways. Transmedia productions are not constrained in terms of length or style by a single medium, and provide a deeper and more dimensional understanding of informational material than does content delivered over a single platform. For example, the transmedia project *Half the Sky* (http://www.pbs.org/independentlens/half-the-sky/film/), based on a book, includes a documentary, music, an interactive map, a Facebook game, and a social impact campaign. The project focuses on the plight of women around the globe, particularly in Third World countries, who are dealing with gender-based violence, high rates of maternal mortality, and sex trafficking.

To get a better understanding of how a non-fiction transmedia project works, let's take a closer look at the biography of American President Woodrow Wilson, briefly mentioned in Chapter 10. The project integrated a linear three-hour TV documentary with two interactive productions, a website, and a DVD. Jackie Kain, who at the time was VP of New Media for public station KCET in Los Angeles, was in charge of developing both the website and DVD.

As an initial step, Kain closely studied the core material. She noted that the documentary was "a rich story that was narrative driven" and therefore decided to capitalize as much as possible on its narrative qualities through the interactivity that would be offered. In addition, while the TV biography focused primarily on the international aspects of Wilson's career, she decided to use the website and DVD to portray other parts of his presidency—his domestic policies and personal life. Thus, the interactive elements of the transmedia production would serve to round out this portrait of a president.

The website would be more text based, while the DVD would contain more video, thus coming at the same subject matter in somewhat different but complementary ways. They would be tied by a similar graphic design as well. (It should be noted that this project was undertaken before the widespread ability to stream video, which made the inclusion of the DVD particularly valuable.)

The website included an interactive timeline; commentary by historians; and additional information about the people, issues, and events that were important in Wilson's life. One of the site's most engaging and imaginative features was an activity called "Win the Election of 1912." It challenged users to run their own political campaign to see if they could do better than other contenders in that historic race. Players got to invent the name of their party and then decide their stance on certain critical issues of the time. Based on their selections, they either won or lost the election.

The DVD contained 80 minutes of video expressly produced for it, material not included in the TV show. This additional footage, broken into small, "consumable" chunks, consisted of mini-documentaries and interviews with scholars (see Figure 14.2). Kain described them as "short documentaries that tell you a story." According to Kain, these supplemental documentaries were purposely kept short, about five minutes each, so they would not compete with the film itself. Thus, the DVD and the website enhanced the TV documentary, and did so in a highly engaging manner.

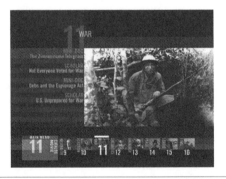

Figure 14.2 The menu of the Woodrow Wilson DVD, showing how the information was broken into small segments using principles of taxonomy. Image courtesy of PBS, WGBH, and KCET.

WIKIS

A wiki is a specialized type of website that allows members of a group, or the general public, to add or edit content. Undoubtedly, the most famous wiki of all is Wikipedia, the huge online encyclopedia. Wikis, however, can be created for almost any topic. One of my students, for example, created a wiki called *The Nanotech Mysteries*, which covered the field of nanotechnology. It included text, audio, visuals, and even a game.

SPECIAL CONSIDERATIONS FOR CREATING INFORMATIONAL PROJECTS

By their very nature, informational projects are based on facts, and factual material needs to be handled more carefully than material that is pure fiction, especially when incorporating the information into an interactive narrative. Care must be taken not to misconstrue or trivialize the facts or "dumb down" a complex issue. But on the other hand, you do want to create an engaging story that is not bogged down with an over-abundance of dry material. The answers to the following questions can help you shape a non-fiction project that marries factual material with digital storytelling and does justice to both:

- Will you be taking a subjective or objective approach to the factual material? If your point of view is a personal one, how will you make this clear to users?

- What digital medium or forms of digital media will you use to tell this story, and why are these forms particularly appropriate for the material and the audience? And what kinds of interactive enhancements can you build in that will contribute to an understanding of the material?

- What narrative thread can you pull out of the source material that will be engaging to users and also give a fair representation of the various sides of the story? If your narrative thread is unbalanced in some way, how can you provide users with the opportunity to explore other sides of the story?

- In dramatizing the non-fiction material, are you providing ways for users to get all the important facts of the story? Will you build in ways for people to access supplementary material that is not part of the main narrative path?

- How will you give users an opportunity to participate in the story, so that it is not just a one-way street? Can they contribute stories of their own, or make comments, or provide additional facts? Can they participate in polls relating to the story, or vote on some aspect of it?

ADDITIONAL RESOURCES

To learn more about using digital media for informational projects, the following resources might be helpful:

- The Pew Research Center's Project for Excellence in Journalism, which offers reports on traditional and digital media, as well as a daily briefing: http://www.journalism.org/.

- iDocs, an organization devoted to interactive documentaries: http://i-docs.org/.

- The Alliance for Audited Media, which compiles facts and figures about newspapers and magazines: www.auditedmedia.com.

- The Idea Lab, a group blog by people who are interested in reinventing media in a digital age: http://www.pbs.org/idealab/about-idea-lab.

CONCLUSION

As we have seen, digital storytelling techniques, if handled carefully, can successfully be applied to virtually any type of informational project. In this chapter alone, we have discussed a diverse array of works, including biographies of unknown private citizens (Japanese Americans in Hawaii) and of a powerful US president (Woodrow Wilson); stories about a natural disaster (Hurricane Katrina) and an interesting creature found in nature (the firefly); interactive narratives about important figures in history (Woodrow Wilson and Dr. Mohammed Mossadegh) and a cutting-edge technology (the iPhone); and others about a contemporary sports ritual (the Olympics) and an ancient cultural ritual (the MesoAmerican ball game).

The "infotainment" approach to informational content has sometimes been criticized for trivializing serious content. Unfortunately, this allegation is quite valid in cases where the subject matter is oversimplified, or when entertainment elements overshadow the informational content, or when important facts are omitted.

However, the judicious use of digital storytelling techniques can actually be a tremendous asset to informational projects. By making the informational content engaging, these works can entice people to learn about a subject they would ordinarily regard as too dull or difficult to be of interest to them. With interactivity, users can connect with the material in an experiential manner, and come to a far deeper understanding of it.

Applying digital storytelling techniques to an informational subject can work surprisingly well even for complex issues. Through interactivity and multiple story paths, these works can offer users more than one way to view the subject. A well-designed project can offer far more than a superficial presentation of a topic, because users can view the material from different angles and dig deeply for additional information.

Thus far, most members of the public have only had limited exposure to interactive informational narratives, and in the great majority of cases, they have encountered these works on the Internet or on mobile devices. However, as other digital platforms become more commonplace, we are likely to see exciting new developments in this area.

IDEA-GENERATING EXERCISES

1. Take a current news story that you have read about in a newspaper or magazine or seen on a TV news show. Imagine that you have been tasked with the job of turning this story into an interactive narrative for a news-oriented website. What digital platform would you use? How would you make it both informative and engaging and how could you involve users in the story?

2. Pick a subject from history and sketch out an idea on how you could develop it as an interactive narrative. What platform would you use? What digital storytelling techniques would you employ?

3. Select a current events topic that is the subject of public concern, such as global warming or terrorism. Sketch out an idea for an informational game on this topic.

4. List several possible informational topics that could be aimed at young audiences. How do you think they might be made enticing by utilizing an interactive informational approach? What techniques would you employ?

PART 4

Media and Models: Under the Hood

CHAPTER 15

Video Games

Can video games be a robust venue for storytelling?

What can we learn from video games that we can apply to other forms of interactive entertainment?

What is *gamification* and how does it relate to video games?

What are *casual games* and how do they differ from other forms of gaming?

What is it about massively *multiplayer online games* (MMOGs) that makes them such a potent form of gaming, to the point that some players become addicted to them?

What common mistakes do inexperienced game developers make in building a new game?

VIDEO GAMES: THE 10,000-POUND GORILLA OF INTERACTIVE ENTERTAINMENT

Video games are the granddaddy of all forms of interactive digital entertainment. *Pong*, the world's first successful video game, debuted in 1972, almost a full two decades before the World Wide Web was even born and long before other types of digital media were introduced. In the intervening years, video games have not only evolved enormously but have also had a profound influence on a great many other forms of interactive digital entertainment. In addition, as we saw in Chapters 12, 13, and 14, games are not just a significant form of entertainment, but are also being used to teach, promote, and inform.

Furthermore, over the years video games have migrated from their original platforms (arcade machines, PCs, and consoles) to a wide variety of venues, including smart phones, social media, and tablets. They have even spilled out into real life locations, such as theme parks, museums, and city streets. Innovative developers regularly roll out new devices to support gameplay and new ways to enhance the experience of playing.

As we will see in future chapters, even forms of interactive entertainment that are not strictly video games, such as interactive cinema, immersive environments, and second-screen TV, often contain gaming elements. Thus, it would be impossible to write a book about digital storytelling without a deep bow of acknowledgment to this pioneering form of entertainment.

VIDEO GAMES AND THEIR PLACE IN THE OVERALL ENTERTAINMENT UNIVERSE

Over the past decade, games have become a dominant form of entertainment, even drawing away audiences from movies and television. It is no longer uncommon for a popular game to generate more revenue than a blockbuster movie. The most successful video game to date, *Grand Theft Auto V*, made $800 million on its first day of release in 2013, while in comparison, the most successful feature film to date, *The Avengers*, only made a little over $207.4 million during its opening weekend in 2012.

Critics of video games sometimes accuse them of being a lesser form of entertainment than novels, stage plays, and movies, and one that does not qualify as art. For example, the late film critic Roger Ebert wrote a famous blog post in his *Chicago Sun-Times* blog entitled "Video Games Can Never Be Art" (April 16, 2010), which enraged the gaming community. However, no less an august body than the US Supreme Court has ruled that video games are every bit much an art form as older forms of narrative. In a decision that came down in 2011, Supreme Court Justice Antonin Scalia declared: "Like the protected books, plays and movies that preceded them, video games communicate ideas—and even social messages—through many familiar literary devices (such as characters, dialogue, plot, and music) and through features distinctive to the medium (such as the player's interaction with the virtual world)." He concluded: "That suffices to confer First Amendment protection." The First Amendment to the Constitution of the United States protects the right of free speech.

It would be nice to think that we don't need the Supreme Court to tell us that video games are an art form, even though not everyone agrees with this. But already in their brief history, games have proven to be a unique and powerful way of involving their audience. Furthermore, as the video game arena matures, games are becoming increasingly sophisticated. Some game reviewers now use the term *cinematic* to describe the quality of today's games, indicating that they are more movie-like, which is regarded as a high compliment. They mean by this that games are now utilizing high-quality visual effects, sophisticated sound effects, and original scores. They are also hiring top Hollywood stars to read the voice-over lines of the characters, and the dialogue these actors are reading is becoming more polished and more extensive.

In addition, today's plots are, for the most part, far more compelling than the plots of earlier games and often sound quite movie-like. One older but often used example of a movie-like plot is the storyline of *Tomb Raider: Angel of Darkness*. In this game, Lara Croft is accused of the murder of her one-time mentor, Von Croy, and becomes a fugitive on the run. With the police in hot pursuit of her, she tries to find out who murdered Von Croy and why (see Figure 15.1). One of the most successful games in the venerable *Tomb Raider* series, the plot contains a strong resemblance to the well-regarded movie thriller, *The Fugitive*.

While it is true, however, that today's games look and sound more like movies, and often have far stronger storylines than in the past, many people within the gaming community are uncomfortable with calling games "cinematic." They stress that the two forms of entertainment are "apples and oranges." In an article for *Wired* magazine (April 2006), game designer Jordan Mechner, who wrote and directed the original *Prince of Persia* game, noted that newer

Figure 15.1   Lara Croft becomes enmeshed in a dark, movie-like plot in *Tomb Raider: Angel of Darkness*. Image courtesy of Eidos Interactive.

media often model themselves on older media until they develop as a unique art form. Mechner went on to say: "As we gamemakers discover new ways to take storytelling out of cut scenes and bring it into gameplay, we're taking the first steps toward a true video game storytelling language — just as our filmmaking forbearers did the first time they cut to a close-up. One day soon, calling a game 'cinematic' will be a backhanded compliment, like calling a movie 'stagy.'"

THE GREAT DEBATE

One ongoing and intense debate that has been raging among game scholars and game developers is the question of whether or not games can even be regarded as a form of storytelling. Two warring groups have squared off on this issue. On one side, we have the *narratology* camp. They say, yes, of course, games are a form of storytelling and they can be studied as narratives (the term "narratology" simply means the theory and study of narrative). Janet Murray, the author of the classic book on interactive narrative, *Hamlet on the Holodeck*, and a professor at the Georgia Institute of Technology, is a leading advocate of the narratology position.

On the other side of the battlefield, we have the *ludology* camp. Espen J. Aarseth, a professor at the University of Bergen, is the most vocal proponent of the ludologist camp. The term ludology comes from the Latin word *ludus*, for game. The ludologists argue that even though games have elements of narrative like characters and plot, this is incidental to the things that make them a distinct creative form, such as gameplay. Thus, they assert, games should be studied as unique constructs. This debate has an emotional undercurrent to it, because the ludologists suggest that the academics who espouse narratology are elitist and fail to recognize games as worthy of study on their own merits. Clearly, if sides must be chosen, this book is most closely in allegiance with the narratologists.

NARRATIVE IN GAMES

While the narratology versus ludology debate may rage on through infinity, no one can flatly deny that games, on the whole, do contain story content. This content includes, among other elements, developed characters, plot, character-based goals, challenges that characters must overcome, and dramatic conflict. The amount of story contained in games varies hugely. Some games contain no story at all while others offer richly nuanced narratives. And in some cases, the story content is formed by the choices the players themselves make, rather than being built into the game. This is particularly true of sandbox games.

It must be acknowledged, however, that the kinds of narratives found in games differ from narratives found in other media. Designer Greg Roach, introduced in Chapter 4, puts it this way: "Novels tell; movies show; games do." In other words, games are all about the things you do, about action. Games are performance experiences. But this focus on action has a downside, as well. Game designer Darlene Waddington notes that "games tend to be all about the 'hows' and not about the 'whys.'" She feels, for instance, that they are good at getting the player into a combat situation, but are less good at probing the psychological or human reasons for getting into combat in the first place.

Waddington's point about the focus being on action while giving scant attention to motivation is a criticism often leveled at games. While games now offer more fully developed characters and storylines, they generally lack the depth of older forms of entertainment. With few exceptions, they do not look deeply into the human psyche or deal with a full spectrum of emotions. How often, for example, do we encounter or play a character who is motivated by shame, love, compassion, guilt, grief, or the dozens of other emotions we humans feel? Yet such emotions are the underpinnings of dramas we can find in movies or the stories we read in novels.

Most game developers will argue that the story is only there to serve a functional purpose rather than being the prime attraction, which is good gameplay. Yet, without a story, the gameplay lacks a context to be meaningful. Story provides the game with objectives and challenges, meaningful victories and defeats, and an overall story world to play in. Thus, even a minimal amount of story content serves a functional role in a game.

Game writer Christy Marx made an interesting observation about storytelling and games many years ago, in an article she wrote for *Written By* magazine (December 2003). She noted that games began as a programmer's medium, and since they were text based, they didn't require a writer or artist. The one essential element these early games did require was code. Marx theorizes that this early game culture, with the dominant role of the programmer and the non-existent role of the storyteller, continues to permeate the game development world. Nevertheless, the game industry is increasingly aware of the importance of good storytelling in games, and top Hollywood screenwriters are often hired to work on games. But even today, many of these screenwriters are only asked to write dialogue, thus bypassing their abilities to make significant contributions to the projects they work on.

Veteran Hollywood writer Randall Jahnson, who successfully made the transition between screen writing and game writing, told the *Hollywood Reporter* (November 23, 2005) that the process of writing for the two media was like apples and oranges. He compared writing for games to writing haiku, because the plot points and dialogue had to be far more compressed than in a screenplay, where you don't have a player itching to jump into the gameplay. On the other hand, he found that games gave him the opportunity to explore subplots and tangents of the story that there would be no time to develop in a screenplay.

NOTES FROM THE FIELD: WRITING A GAME IS LIKE WRITING AN OPERA

An extremely savvy game professional recently compared the job of writing a game to that of writing an opera. Why? Because in both cases, the stories are painted with a broad brush and the plots often lean toward the melodramatic. But, even more importantly, the storytelling in opera needs to leave room for the music and performance, and the storytelling in games needs to leave room for the gameplay. This observation, quoted in the UK version of *Wired* magazine (March 4, 2013), was made by Margaret Robinson, managing director of Hide and Seek, a UK game design company. She said: "the libretto shouldn't have to tell you everything you need to know about the character or the setting or the underlying scene … There's a little bit of that in games, to leave space for the action and the player."

ADAPTING A GAME FROM OTHER SOURCE MATERIAL

When developing a new game, a special type of story development situation arises when the game is being adapted from a property that exists in a different medium. This type of adaptation is full of unique challenges, some of which were mentioned in Chapter 3. Yet stories that were first told in movies, TV series, comics, and novels have been an irresistible source of narrative material for video games. No genre or platform of gaming seems immune from this type of adaptation. Just as one example, the immensely successful *Harry Potter* novels have not only been turned into online games and console games but even a game for the Kinect, which will be discussed a little later in this chapter.

Nonetheless, the process of adapting a game from a different medium is a challenging one, and each adaptation has its own unique set of challenges. For example, a number of years ago I worked on the script and text for Disney and Pixar's adaption of the original *Toy Story* movie. We were turning the movie into *The Toy Story Animated Storybook*, which blended a game with a storybook. As a writer, I had two big challenges. First of all, the hero in the movie is Woody, a toy cowboy, but we couldn't use Tom Hanks (who voiced Woody in the movie) in this adaptation. Instead, we had to tell the entire story from the POV of another character. Fortunately, the substitute narrator who was chosen was a highly engaging, somewhat sardonic toy: Hamm, the piggy bank. So I had to reimagine *Toy Story* from a pig's POV, which was a major change from the source material, though an entertaining writing challenge.

The second difficult task was incorporating meaningful interactivity into the adaptation, and the obvious ways to do it were not necessarily in the best interests of the project. For example, in the film, the toys enjoy playing checkers with each other, and some members of the team believed we should include a game of checkers in the adaptation. The problem here, though, is that a checkers game wouldn't advance the narrative at all and wouldn't involve players in the story. It would just stop everything dead. Instead, I helped create a mini-game where players were challenged to quickly put all the toys in Andy's room back in their proper places before Andy and his birthday party guests could enter the room and make an alarming discovery: that the toys could come to life when humans were not around. This added a sense of urgency to the interactive story and gave the players a meaningful degree of agency.

THE UNIQUE CHARACTERISTICS OF VIDEO GAMES

A well-designed video game has certain characteristics that make it enjoyable to play and that facilitate the experience of playing. These characteristics are also unique to games, as opposed to other forms of media that contain story content. These characteristics relate directly or indirectly to the game's narrative. Let's take a look at three of these characteristics.

GAMEPLAY

In the broadest of strokes, gameplay is two things: it is what makes a game fun, and it is how a person plays the game—the way in which they control it and the way in which it responds. It is what gives a game its energy and makes it exciting. To understand gameplay, you must understand what a game is. Games involve the player in achieving an ultimate goal, but in order to do this, the player must first overcome a series of challenges. If successful, the game is won; if unsuccessful, it is lost. Games also provide a unique kind of instantaneous feedback to the players' input and choices. If this feedback/response mechanism is satisfying, intuitive, and smooth, then the players' experience of the gameplay will probably be a positive one. If the game's response is imbalanced, jerky, slow, or confusing, then the gameplay will probably be perceived negatively.

Gameplay consists of the specific challenges that are presented to the player and the actions the player can take in order to overcome them. Victory and loss conditions are also part of the gameplay, as are the rules of the game. Story enters into this dynamic because it is what puts gameplay in context. The game's overall goal is established through the story, as are the challenges the player encounters and the victory and loss conditions. Story provides motivation for the player to want to keep playing and makes the experience richer.

ARTIFICIAL INTELLIGENCE (AI)

AI in games is the element that can make a game seem eerily life-like, and this is done by giving realistic behaviors to NPCs. AI is primarily the domain of the coders and only exists in digital media. It can make NPCs act like living, intelligent creatures. These AI-enhanced NPCs can interact and converse with player characters and respond to them in an appropriate way, given the context of the situation they are in. Some of these extra-smart NPCs can, through "observation," even learn about a player's weaknesses and strengths. This "knowl-edge" can be used either to the player's disadvantage (to track and kill him) or to the player's advantage, with the NPC acting as a loyal and protective buddy. AI is one of the elements that can distinguish the playing of video games from all other forms of entertainment.

INTERFACE AND NAVIGATION

Interface is what connects the player and the game. It enables the player to receive important information and to take actions within the game. Furthermore, it gives the player a way to evaluate how well he or she is doing. A well-designed interface can help make a game fun, while a poor one can make it frustrating and disappointing.

There are three major forms of interface: manual (hardware such as controllers and keyboards); visual (icons, maps, meters); and auditory (verbal feedback, cues from the environment, music). Interface provides important information about geography, player status, inventory, and whether the player is succeeding or failing. Interface also gives the player the ability to do such things as run, jump, shoot, and use weapons or tools. In addition, a game must have navigational mechanisms so that the player has the ability to move his or her avatars, vehicles, or objects from one point to another in the virtual world.

CATEGORIES AND GENRES OF GAMES

Video games comprise an enormous universe made up of a diverse array of offerings. In order to get a clearer picture of this universe, it is useful to know the different ways video games are played and how games are categorized.

GAME PLATFORMS

Even though members of the general public often lump together all types of games and refer to them generically as video games, gamers themselves and professionals in the field customarily divide them into several large categories, based on the type of platform (hardware and/or software system) that they are designed to run on. Each platform is best suited for a particular type of play experience, and the popularity of the various platforms has shifted over the years.

Among the most popular platforms are console games (devices that are specifically designed to play games); personal computers; smart phones and tablet computers. While the first games were played on arcade machines, and were the only way games could be played, the once bustling arcade parlors have largely vanished, although arcade machines can still be found in sports bars and in the lobbies of movie theaters.

In recent years, a revolutionary new way to play games was introduced: games controlled by one's movements. The first of these motion-based game systems was the Nintendo Wii, launched in 2006. The Wii is operated in part by a hand-held controller, but a camera built into the device "reads" the player's motions, and the player's motions, in turn, determine to a large degree the action one sees on the screen. Special peripherals enhance the experience further. For instance, with Wii Fit, players can control action via a balance board, and can compete in skiing games or whack soccer balls tossed by a rival team. The Wii retractable golf club lets you play golf games on a variety of courses or practice your swing, while the Wii Zapper, a plastic gun-shaped device, enables you to play games where you need to be armed with a weapon. Such games range from war games to horror games to zombie games, and even pit you against dinosaurs.

In 2010, Microsoft launched its own motion-based system, the Kinect for the Xbox 360. Unlike the Wii, it was totally controller free and operated entirely by the player's movements. In addition, the Kinect also offered voice recognition and facial recognition. The Kinect offered entirely new kinds of gaming experiences. For example, in the game *Harry Potter for Kinect*, players can use the facial recognition system to scan their own faces onto that of a witch or wizard in the game, and maneuver that character through Harry Potter's world. In addition, players can use the voice recognition system to cast spells against their opponents by calling out spell names along with the appropriate physical gestures.

Other tweaks on motion-based game consoles have occurred throughout the years. For instance, in 2012, Nintendo introduced Wii U, a successor to the Wii. Its major innovation was a redesign of the controller, renamed the GamePad. It incorporated a touch screen in the center of the device, turning it into something that looked like an iPad surrounded by a traditional controller. Unfortunately for Nintendo, the Wii U was not the success it was hoping for. In 2013, Microsoft unveiled the Xbox One, which incorporates a redesigned Kinect and is meant to serve as an all-in-one entertainment center. It can be used to watch TV, surf the Web, or Skype with friends and family. It retains all the features of the original Kinect, which has been somewhat updated, and can be controlled primarily through voice commands. The gaming system is both cloud-based and can run disc-based games.

In a completely different approach to a controller system, one that involves an app rather than hardware, Microsoft introduced the Xbox SmartGlass in 2012. It is a companion application to the Xbox and, among its many features, SmartGlass works as a second-screen support system, allowing players to use their smart phones or tablets, in part, as game controllers.

STRANGE BUT TRUE: QUIRKY CONTROLLERS

Innovative designers and scientists have invented some surprising new ways to control video games. For example, while Joe Kniss was a Computer Science professor at the University of New Mexico, he devised a way to control a game via riding on a skateboard, and he demonstrated his device by playing a game in which he had to negotiate through space while dodging meteors. A more sophisticated iteration of his concept morphed into what he called the hexdex, a six-sided platform that could be tilted in any direction, this controlling the action on the screen.

And then there's the Virtusphere, a globe-shaped hollow device that resembles a giant hamster ball. The Virtusphere is designed to be used for virtual reality (VR) experiences. The player, wearing a head-mounted display (HMD), climbs into it, and by moving in any direction—walking, running, or even crawling—controls the images he sees.

More extraordinary than either device, however, is a controller that every single player already comes equipped with—the brain. A New Zealand company has developed a 14-sensor headset called the Emotiv EPOC that can harness the power of the mind. A German team has already demonstrated how the headset can be used to operate a real car, to make it speed up, slow down, or turn right or left. If a real car can be controlled in this way, it is not much of a leap to imagine using this technology to control an automobile in a video game. Designers around the world, such as InteraXon, the Canadian team behind a brain-sensing headband called Muse, are currently working on brainwave controllers, experimenting with new ways to use brain power to control video games.

Small is Big

Miniaturization is a relatively new and popular trend in console design. For example, the Ouya, which uses the Android operating system, is a game console that is shaped somewhat like a rounded cube and smaller than a can of soda pop. Often compared in size to a Rubik's Cube, it was a huge hit on Kickstarter in 2013, quickly raising over eight million dollars, even though it had only set a more modest target of under a million dollars. In short order, over 12,000 game developers pledged support to the new console.

Not to be outdone, the GameStick, which also came out in 2013, is even smaller, just the size of a flash drive. Developed by PlayJam, it is designed to plug directly into the TV. Like the Ouya, it uses the Android operating system.

TYPES OF GAMES

Games can be divided and grouped into two very large categories: the way the game is played, and the game's genre. In the discussion of game platforms, above, we reviewed a number of ways games can be played, in terms of the hardware that they are played upon. We will discuss some other, very different, ways games can be played a bit later in this chapter. But first, let's focus on genre.

Game Genres

Just as with films, novels, and other forms of linear narratives, games are often divided into large general categories called genres. Works within a specific genre follow the same conventions, almost like a formula. These commonalities include having similar settings, characters, subject matter, and type of action. Knowledge of game genres gives us a useful shorthand to refer to different games and to understand their prominent characteristics. Furthermore, by studying the various genres, one gets a sense of the scope and variety of experiences possible within interactive media, and one begins to see how some of these elements can be ported over to other forms of interactive entertainment.

As important as it is to have an understanding of game genres, however, the process of assigning a particular game to a particular category can be fairly tricky. No two experts will agree to exactly the same definition of a genre, and no ruling body exists to regulate what game belongs where. To further complicate the situation, the dividing lines separating genres are sometimes blurry, with a particular game having characteristics of more than one genre. Nevertheless, here is a list of what most people would consider to be the most common genres of games:

- *Action games*: these games are fast-paced, full of physical action, and often call for a great deal of hand–eye coordination and strategy. Some, like the popular *Deus Ex* and its sequels, contain a great amount of story (see Figure 15.2). Action games are one of the most popular of all genres.

Figure 15.2 A screenshot from *Deus Ex, Invisible War*. The game tells a complex story involving global conflict and intrigue, and falls into the action genre. Image courtesy of Eidos Interactive.

- *Adventure games*: more than any other type of game, adventure games feature the strongest use of story. Typically, the player is sent on a quest or has a clear-cut mission and must solve a number of riddles or puzzles in order to succeed. Players also explore rich environments and collect items for their inventories as they move about. Generally, these games use a preconstructed protagonist, as opposed to an avatar that the player creates or defines. These games have a very old history, dating back to text-based games such as the *Colossal Cave Adventure*. A subgenre of the adventure game is the mystery-adventure game, which includes the *Nancy Drew* series, discussed in other chapters. While adventure games were highly popular in the 1980s, they have fared less well in recent decades.

- *Action-adventure*: a subgenre of the adventure game and an extremely broad term that can be applied to a wide variety of games. Unlike pure adventure games, which feature very little physical action, these games do involve combat situations and demand quick reflexes.

- *Survival horror*: a subgenre of the action-adventure game. In terms of story and ambience, they are much like a horror film or horror novel. The player is immersed in a terrifying and claustrophobic setting, discovers troubling objects or frightening characters, and must try to use whatever objects or weapons are available in the storyworld to survive and prevail. *Silent Hill* and *Resident Evil* are two popular series of survival horror games.

- *Sports and driving games*: these games focus on various types of team or individual sports, or on car racing. The sports games are highly realistic and call for strategy as well as good control of the action. Gamers may play as an individual team member or may control an entire team. A number of major athletic organizations, such as the National Football League, license their names for sports games, as do star athletes.

- *Role-playing games (RPGs)*: in this genre of game, the player controls one or more avatars, which are defined by a set of attributes, such as species, occupation, skill, and special talents. The genre evolved from the precomputer version of *Dungeons and Dragons*. Contemporary descendants are highly popular as MMORPGS (massively multiplayer online role-playing games) and include *World of Warcraft*.

- *Strategy games*: these games, as the name suggests, emphasize the use of strategy and logic rather than quick reflexes and hand–eye coordination and thus are more cerebral than many other genres. In these games, the players manage resources, military units, or communities. The *Command and Conquer* series are strategy games. Gameplay is generally turn based.

- *Real time strategy games (RTS)*: these games are a subgenre of strategy games, and the gameplay progresses in real time, rather than by the taking of turns.

- *Multiplayer online battle arena (MOBA)*: MOBAs are a subgenre of real time strategy games, and a relatively new form of online gaming. Often two teams of players compete against each other and each player controls a single character. Teams are ideally made up of characters with different and complementary strengths.

- *Massively multiplayer online game (MMOG or MMO)*: an online game in which thousands of players participate at the same time, and typically set in a sprawling fictional landscape. MMOGs are persistent universes, which means that the game action continues even after a player has logged off.

- *Massively multiplayer online role-playing game (MMORPG)*: these are MMOGs in which players control one or more avatars and go on quests with other players. These games typically stress cooperative play. MMORGs are one of the popular subgenres of MMOGs and are discussed in more detail later in this chapter. *Lord of the Rings Online* is an example of an immensely successful MMORPG.

- *Social media games*: games that are designed to be played with one's friends on social media sites like Facebook. They are generally free to play but micropayments are often necessary in order to advance in the game. *Farmville* was one of the first major successes in this genre (see Chapter 9 for more on social media games).

- *Free to Play (F2P)*: these are games that are free to play, or free to download. They can be virtually any genre. As with social media games, players may be invited to make small payments for in-game items or to enhance the gameplay experience. In some cases, an F2P version of a game is designed as a way to promote the pay-to-play version of the game.

- *Otome games*: a genre born in Japan and typically designed for female players, otome games feature a romantic plot and the usual objective is to end up with the desired boyfriend. Their visual style resembles manga (Japanese comic books).

- *Shooters*: Shooters, as the name suggests, involve shooting at things—either at living creatures or at targets. In a shooter, the player is pitted against multiple opponents and can also be a target; in a first-person shooter (FPS), the player is given a first-person point of view of the action. Examples of shooter games include the wildly popular *Halo* series.

- *Puzzle games*: puzzle games are generally abstract and highly graphical and call for the solving of various types of puzzles. Some would also assert that the genre includes games that offer story-based environments that are generously studded with puzzles. *Tetris* is an example of the abstract type of puzzle game, while two classic games, *Myst* and *The 7th Guest*, would be examples of the story-based type of puzzle game.

- *Fighting games*: in these games, players confront opponents in an up-close-and-personal way. The encounter may lead to death, or at least to a clear-cut defeat for one of the opponents. The games typically emphasize hand-to-hand combat instead of guns or other modern weapons. The *Mortal Kombat* games are fighting games.

- *Simulations*: a simulation may offer the player a physical experience such as flying a plane or parachute jumping, or may offer the opportunity to create a simulated living community. Examples of the first type include the *Naval Ops* series. The community-building type of simulation would include *The Sims* series and *Sid Meier's Civilization*, although some would argue that these games belong to the strategy category.

- *Platform game*: these fast-paced games call for making your character jump, run, or climb through a challenging terrain, often while dodging falling objects or avoiding pitfalls. Such games require quick reflexes and manual dexterity. Classics of this genre include *Donkey Kong*, the *Super Mario Brothers*, and *Sonic the Hedgehog*.

- *Casual game*: a game that is easy to learn but difficult to master, and that can be played in a short amount of time. They include a wide variety of genres, such as shooters, puzzle games, and racing games, and they are highly popular on mobile devices. *Angry Birds* is a casual game, as is *Tetris*. Casual games are discussed in more detail later in this chapter.

- *Text-based game*: a game that employs words rather than visual images. Players input word-based commands to control the action. Such games were one of the earliest forms of gaming and though they almost died out once it became possible to use graphics in games, they are enjoying a resurgence, and are a pillar of interactive fiction (IF). Most MUDs are text-based.

- *Serious game*: a game designed to fulfill a pragmatic purpose rather than to be just an entertaining experience. Serious games are made for educational, informational, and promotional purposes and customarily use the same techniques as games made for pure entertainment. Serious games were discussed in more detail in Chapter 12.

- *Cognitive game*: a game designed to sharpen a person's mental capabilities such as memory, math skills, and logic. They are a subgenre of serious games.

- *Open world games*: these games are typically set in vast environments which the player can explore freely, and they offer players a rich variety of activities to enjoy, from shopping to fighting to operating a variety of vehicles and aircraft. Unlike most games, they do not force a player down a set story path via a structure made up of levels. Instead, although they do contain an overall goal and story elements, they are totally nonlinear and they allow the player to choose what to do at any point. The *Saints Row* games are open worlds, and many consider the *Grand Theft Auto* series to also be open worlds. Open world games and *Saints Row* are discussed in more detail later in this chapter.

- *Sandbox games*: these games have much in common with open world games, and in fact, some people use the terms interchangeably and some argue that sandbox games are a subgenre of open world games. Like open world games, they are set in large environments that can be explored freely and they allow players to decide what they want to do throughout the game. However, when distinctions are made between open world and sandbox games, sandbox games are regarded as a "toy box" that contains tools that players can use to modify the game world and gameplay. Instead of containing set story elements like an open world game, players can construct a narrative while playing, creating an *emergent story*.

Ways Games are Played

In addition to the dazzling variety of game genres, games can be played in a variety of ways that go far beyond "traditional" game platforms, like game consoles, which we discussed above. A number of these ways of playing take place outside of one's house, where games are typically played. Location-based games are a good example of this alternative way of playing. These games take place in real life environments, most often in urban settings, and pieces of the game are dispersed or supported through various forms of digital technology, including websites, smart phones, GPS coordinates, and QR readers. Some games also take advantage of augmented reality (AR), which is used to create images or sounds that seemingly exist in the real world but are part of the game. In location-based games, players must venture out into the real world, to specific sites, to uncover clues or pieces of the story. *The Q Game: City of Riddles*, discussed in Chapter 17, is an example of a location-based game.

Alternate reality games (ARGs) are an even more complex form of gaming that is not tied to any single platform. They can be partially played at home (by investigating clues on websites and by collaborating with other players on dedicated websites) and partially in the real world, by following clues in real locations and taking part in live events. These games are forms of transmedia storytelling and often employ multiple digital platforms as well as traditional media. ARGs are discussed in detail in Chapter 18.

A completely different gaming experience that takes place outside of the home is the immersive multiplayer motion-sensing game. To date, this is a fairly rare type of gaming, but it can be found at Disney's Epcot Theme Park in Florida, in a set of games produced for the *Living Landscapes* pre-show for the *Soarin'* ride. In this type of gaming, an entire group of people control the game by their motions (such as waving their hands), much as a single player controls a game made for the Wii or the Kinect (see Figure 15.3). More about this type of gaming, and the kinds of stories they can incorporate, is discussed in Chapter 22.

Figure 15.3 Guests interacting with one of the multiplayer immersive games produced for the *Living Landscapes* pre-show for the *Soarin'* ride at Epcot. Image courtesy of © Disney Enterprises, Inc.

VIOLENCE AND VIDEO GAMES

Physical combat, sometimes gory and extremely graphic, is a feature of many video games. In part because of this, games have been blamed as the cause of violent teenage behavior. This anti-game attitude is something that everyone who works in the game industry encounters. I was personally assaulted at a brunch just this past weekend by a table full of otherwise lovely people, mostly seniors who had probably never played a video game in their lives. They were convinced that games were the cause of great evil, and looked at me strangely for being associated with them.

I reminded them of two things: first, that video games were just the latest form of popular entertainment to be accused of causing teenage violence. Long ago, people accused dime novels and comic books of inciting teenage mayhem, and later movies and television were also vilified. I also pointed out that many video games were violence-free, and games could be highly positive vehicles for education and information. They listened politely but I doubt their minds were changed.

Nevertheless, despite the negative opinions many people hold about video games, psychological studies have been unable to demonstrate a clear relationship between playing violent video games and committing acts of violence in real life. Even the US Supreme Court, in the landmark 2011 case, noted this lack of proof, calling the research work done thus far "unpersuasive." Because of the lack of convincing evidence, the court refused to sanction regulations of the industry. A thoughtful article by Dr. Romeo Vitelli, published in 2013 in *Psychology Today*, reviewed the research done thus far on the connection between playing games and violence. Dr. Vitelli asserted that the studies were inconsistent. He also pointed out that the statistics on youth violence were at a 40-year low, even though video games have gained in popularity during the same period.

In fact, it is possible that it is the teens who do *not* play video games who may be the ones who have social problems. In the book, *Grand Theft Childhood*, Harvard medical school psychiatrists Lawrence Kutner and Cheryl Olson assert that playing games and talking about them has become such a mainstream pastime among teens that those who do not participate in these activities are now "de facto abnormal."

INDEPENDENT ("INDIE") GAMES

Independent games, or indies, were once only a tiny segment of the games world, but in recent years they have become increasingly prominent. Essentially, an indie is a game that has been made without the financial support of a publisher and has usually been produced on an extremely small budget and by a minuscule team or a single individual. However, this independence gives the developers full artistic control of their games, and indie games can be far more experimental and artistic than games that have been made with a publisher's support.

The growth of the indie world is in part because games can be made on far smaller budgets now than in the past. Furthermore, thanks to digital distribution via the Internet, smartphones, and downloadable services on game consoles, it is possible to find an audience for a game without the support of a publisher. In the past, developers had to seek out contracts with publishers for funding, marketing, and distribution, but this is no longer necessary.

Typically, however, indie games are far more modest than blockbuster games with their multimillion-dollar budgets. They usually lack the gorgeous graphics and other features of high-end games, and tend to be much shorter. But they do boldly venture into territory that the risk-adverse publishers have avoided. One of the stars of this world is Jason Rohrer, who has made several indie games. One of them, *Passages*, is a life journey told in just a few minutes of play, with a somber mortality theme. The game brought a leading game executive to tears.

"A realization is dawning that games can be much more than what they are now," Rohrer told a *New York Times* reporter back in 2009. "They even have the potential to be meaningful in deep, fundamental ways." Indie developers are increasingly taking up this challenge and are striving to create games that do have meaning and do contain emotional richness. Indie developers had a dominant presence at the 2013 Game Developers Conference in San Francisco, and for the first time ever, an indie game, *Journey*, won the prestigious game of the year award.

THE CHALLENGE OF STORYTELLING IN NONLINEAR GAMES

One of the most daunting tasks in terms of creating stories for video games is that of constructing a narrative for a totally nonlinear game environment like an open world. This is a very different situation than level-based games, where players are channeled along sequentially level by level. Although there's nonlinearity within a level itself, the level structure makes it relatively easy to construct a plot and a character arc. But in open world games, players can freely choose where to go, what to do, and when to do it, and even fully customize the character they play, the protagonist. How can stories possibly be developed for such freewheeling game worlds?

In order to find answers, I was fortunate enough to do a telephone interview with Steve Jaros, Creative Director and Head Writer for the highly successful *Saints Row* series of open world games. The first two games are set in a gang-infested fictional metropolis. In the first game of the series, you, the protagonist, become a member of the 3rd Street Saints gang, ultimately becoming the gang's leader and helping to bring the entire city under the control of the Saints. In subsequent installments, you continue to exert your gang's dominance over rival gangs and refuse to cave in to a criminal syndicate that demands tribute from you (see Figure 15.4). Meanwhile, you can create a lucrative merchandise empire with your own Saints Row brand of sneakers, energy drinks, and even bobblehead dolls. With its endless opportunities for mayhem and violence and its raucous, over-the-top humor, the series has been described as an open world adult theme park.

Figure 15.4   The *Saints Row* series of games is an open world, known for its intense and often violent action as well as its humor. Image courtesy of Deep Silver Volition.

Jaros, who has a degree in playwriting, unhesitatingly admitted that storytelling in such an environment is difficult. "I think the biggest challenge is having to go and throw out traditional conceptions of what makes good storytelling," he told me. "Good writing and good game writing are different things. There are things that are amazing stories that make for terrible games."

He noted that open world games present special problems. "In a linear game, people are always plowing through the story, with no other choice but for progression. In an open world game, we are competing with ourselves. We have side quests and activities and open world game play and fun things for you to go and do." In other words, there are lots of distractions competing with your story. "So you have to make sure the game is clear and concise and not confusing," he stressed. "Sometimes that means losing the complexity which I normally like to have in my writing. But because of the nature of the beast you sometimes have to make sacrifices."

Unlike the steady progression of challenges and events you'd find in a linear game, Jaros told me: "Often times, the open world is almost more of a lobby, where the player goes and hangs out and does what he wants and waits to get to the next part of the story." In *Saints Row*, he noted, the story elements are conveyed primarily by cut scenes and by the missions you choose to go on, but also by the little choices you make. As a player, Jaros explains, "You are part of the storytelling process. You are an active participant in building the story. That's why it's so powerful."

Despite the lack of a sequential storyline, Jaros maintains that open world games do contain goals for the player to strive for. "No matter what, you need a goal," he emphasized. "Without a goal, there is no story." In *Saints Row*, these goals can be small things—getting rid of a particular enemy, for instance—or they can be major ambitions, like having your gang become the dominant criminal force in your city.

In *Saints Row*, characters can also have character arcs, as they do in movies and other linear dramas, but there are differences, too. "Characters need to grow and change," Jaros told me. "If nothing changes, the character is boring, right?" In a game like *Saints Row*, he added, "players decide what they feel is important and what they want to invest in, and that's what gives you the story." In contrast, in a third-person game like *Prince of Persia: Sands of Time*, the character arc is predetermined. "No matter what, you are on the journey of that character, the Prince of Persia, and that will take you screaming down his journey," he noted. Whereas in *Saints Row* the player and the character are one, "and it's not fair for me to have you feel sad about something you might feel totally justified by." In other words, in *Saints Row*, you can choose how you want to behave, what you want to be, and how you feel, and no value judgment is placed on those choices. Thus, the character arc in *Saints Row* is more of an exterior professional journey than an interior, emotional one. Jaros describes it as a "power fantasy," and described the character arc this way: "You go from being a nobody to becoming a street gang member to becoming the leader of a gang to becoming a pop culture icon to essentially declaring your own city state."

I asked Jaros if *Saints Row* has a traditional three-act structure (essentially, a beginning, middle, and end) and he replied affirmatively that it did, but on a smaller scale. "You aren't telling *a* story; you are telling lots of small stories. That's a total and fundamental shift. There's this myth that your game has to be about *a* thing, and that's not true," he asserted.

"I think the bigger question is do I think the three-act structure is the best way to tell a story in an open world game," he went on, "and I don't think it is." Naturally curious, I pressed him about what a better structural model might be. "This is where it gets tricky," he said. "For me, open worlds are about letting players get lost in the world and I think that telling smaller stories about the world is more interesting than telling a grand story about a character the player may or may not be involved in. It's about having a world full of stories and the player choosing what he wants to invest in rather than there being some grand story that I tell that you have to go on. It's not some arbitrary thing I'm telling you is important as a writer. People aren't picking up an open world game to go and hear my bull****. They are picking up an open world game so they can go and experience the world and be transported to this new place. Stories about the place are more interesting than me telling you what you should care about."

During the last remaining minutes we had to talk, we discussed the role of humor in open world games. According to Jaros, "How important humor is depends on the game you are making. I think humor is an important release for people, but sometimes you don't need a lot of humor. Sometimes you need a little. Sometimes you don't need any humor." When it comes to humor, he said: "I don't think there's a best practice for games." He noted that humor is subjective, and that different kinds of humor appeal to different people. Not everyone finds the same kind of thing funny. For example, he said that while he doesn't find toilet humor funny, many people do. In *Saints Row*, famous for its over-the-top humor, they make a point of including a wide variety of different kinds of humor. "There's a potpourri of different options," he told me. "That's the philosophy of Saint's Row, because our game is a crazy humor game, a wild crazy ride where anything goes. So we have to allow for all manner of humor" (see Figure 15.5).

Figure 15.5 The *Saints Row* games are known for their wacky, over-the-top humor. Image courtesy of Deep Silver Volition.

MASSIVELY MULTIPLAYER ONLINE ROLE-PLAYING GAMES (MMORPGS)

Massively multiplayer online games (MMOGs or MMOs), particularly massively multiplayer online role-playing games (MMORPGs), are among the most creatively demanding but financially lucrative forms of interactive entertainment ever to be devised. MMORPGs are mere youngsters compared to video games—the earliest ones, *Ultima Online* and *EverQuest*, were not launched until the late 1990s. Yet they've already drawn an intensely dedicated fan base in many parts of the world. In some regions, they are even more popular than traditional single-player video games. Though these games reside on the Internet, which is the only vehicle that can accommodate so many players simultaneously, they can be played on a variety of platforms: game consoles, personal computers, and even mobile devices.

MMORPGs are derived from MUDs, text-based adventure games in which players assume fictional personas, explore virtual worlds, and interact with each other. MUD stands for Multi-User Dungeon (or Multi-User Domain or Multi-User Dimension). The MUD, and its close cousin, the MOO (MUD, Object Oriented), can support the simultaneous play by a great number of participants. The first MUD (and *MUD* was indeed its name) was developed in Great Britain in 1978. It was a team effort of Richard Bartle and Roy Trubshaw, both students at the University of Essex. It is quite easy to detect the close family resemblance between the MUDs and MMORPGs. However, MUDs are text based, while MMORPGs immerse players in a world of richly animated graphics.

THE CHARACTERISTICS OF THE MMORPG

MMORPGs have several characteristics that set them apart from other games, even online games. For one thing, they are played simultaneously by tens of thousands of people, and the interactions between the players are a significant part of the experience. They are set in sprawling fictional landscapes that usually include multiple complex worlds, all of which may be populated. These game worlds are also persistent universes, meaning that the activities going on in them continue even after a player has logged off, just as in the real world things continue to happen even when we go to sleep.

MMORPGs observe many of the characteristics of the RPG, discussed previously in this chapter. Players create and control one or more avatars who are defined by a set of attributes, such as species, occupation, and special skill. These player-controlled characters strategize with each other, go on quests, and explore. Players work hard to advance their avatars' skills and powers. A great many MMORPGs revolve around so-called "sword and sorcery" medieval fantasies and feature bloody encounters with NPCs and player-controlled avatars.

Typically, MMORPGs are supported by subscriptions. To play them, people pay a regular monthly fee, much like a magazine subscription (although in some Asian countries, where MMORPGs are typically played in cafes, players may pay by the hour). In addition to the subscription, players usually have to purchase the initial software, often sold on a CD-ROM. Many games also come up with periodic expansion packs, and players are encouraged to buy them so they can have access to new features of the game. A MMORPG needs only to attract a few hundred thousand players to generate a considerable income, and over the course of several years, a successful MMORPG can take in more money than even a hit video game or movie.

THE MMORPG'S CLOSEST COUSIN: SOCIAL NETWORKING VIRTUAL WORLDS

Second Life and similar avatar-driven social networking sites are close cousins to MMORPGs. Residents of these virtual worlds can create their own avatars, explore vast landscapes, and socialize with each other, just as they do in MMORPGs. However, on closer inspection they have three important differences:

1. Social networking sites, unlike MMORPGs, are not games: participants do not go on quests, engage in combat, advance in skill level, or have any game-based goals to fulfill.

2. *Second Life* and other avatar-based virtual worlds do not contain any narrative elements. They are not stories in any way.

3. The focus of social networking sites is different from that of MMORPGs. As the term implies, the emphasis is heavily on socializing. Another important element, particularly in *Second Life*, is the commercial element. *Second Life* is a thriving marketplace, where residents buy, sell, or trade items with other residents. Although this sort of activity can also occur in MMORPGs, it plays a far greater role in *Second Life*.

NARRATIVE IN MMORPGS

Essentially, the production team for a MMORPG creates a framework for people to play in. They devise an intriguing backstory, various narrative elements to be discovered during play, and set up quests for players to undertake. They also create the virtual landscapes for the MMORPG and create the characters who will inhabit it: the NPCs and the types of avatars that players can build and control. But although MMORPGs contain a certain amount of story material created by the production team, they also contain narrative elements that the players themselves initiate, thus creating an emergent narrative.

A MMORPG typically contains a number of simultaneous storylines as well as an over-arching narrative. The over-arching storyline is set up in the backstory and gives context and excitement to the fictional world of the game. But within this framework are a number of mini-stories. In fact, each quest that a player goes on may be regarded as a story, with a starting point, a period of intense conflict and action, and a resolution—a traditional three-act structure. However, the over-arching storyline of the MMORPG is left open-ended.

EXPERT OBSERVATIONS: RESEMBLANCE TO SOAP OPERAS

The narrative elements in MMORPGs are in some respects quite similar to the type of storytelling found in soap operas, a point made by Nick Iuppa and Terry Borst in their book, *Story and Simulations for Serious Games*. As with a soap opera, the core story in a MMORPG is never resolved. This is quite different from the narratives found in movies, which have clear-cut endings, with all the pieces neatly tied up. Yet the audiences of soap operas and the players of MMORPGs find them intensely involving; the lack of closure of the central storyline does not diminish the pleasure of watching or participating in these stories, for there is always something new to discover and a new twist to the tale.

WHY SO POWERFULLY ADDICTIVE?

Much to the fascination of journalists and to the dismay of psychologists, parents, and spouses, MMORPGs are such a potent form of entertainment that some players have actually become addicted to them. These games are sometimes referred to as "heroinware" and the game *EverQuest* has been nicknamed "EverCrack." Gamers who cross the line from recreational play to something more serious exhibit all the classic signs of addiction. They lie about the time they spend playing; develop problems with work, school, or relationships; and are unable to stop playing, even when they try. In South Korea, there's even a documented case of a young man who dropped dead after playing a MMORPG for 50 hours straight.

Anyone with a professional interest in this arena has to wonder what it is that makes these games so compelling. They might also wonder if these factors can be incorporated into new games—not to make more MMORPG junkies, of course, but in order to attract new players to this arena.

Players cite these qualities that make MMORPGs so compelling:

- they provide an escape from the blandness of everyday life;

- via role-playing, players can become powerful, awe-inspiring figures;

- players have a great deal at stake in terms of the investments they've made in avatars and acquisitions and don't want to lose them, but because these games are persistent universes, this requires staying actively involved in the game;

- MMORPGs have a strong social component; people make close friends in these worlds, and want to stay connected to them;

- they are challenging and highly goal-oriented—every time a goal is achieved, there's a new one looming.

EXPERT OBSERVATIONS: THE COMMUNITY ASPECTS OF MMORPGS

Richard Bartle, co-designer of the world's first MUD, the predecessor to the MMORPG, does not consider MMORPGs to be games at all. Instead, he regards them as "places." In an article written for *Business Week Online* (December 13, 2001), he noted that MMORPGs, unlike games, offered a sense of community, which he believes makes them more like real life. This, he feels, is an important part of their appeal. He noted: "When you visit those places, you can play, sure, but you [also] can talk, you can explore, you can boss people around. They are environments, and they have real people in them." Many experts in the field agree with Bartle that the social aspect of MMORPGs, and the friendships formed while playing, are a major reason why people are drawn to them.

A PLAYER'S POINT OF VIEW

In order to gain a better understanding of how a fan experiences one of these games, and what in particular appeals to them, I spent an afternoon with 15-year-old Michael Loeser as he played the *Dark Age of Camelot*, a medieval fantasy game developed by Mythic Entertainment. Loeser, who had been playing the game for a month or so, said he liked it because it had good character control, was easy to use, and he could make his character look really cool. "I don't like games that are too difficult," he told me. "They are more annoying than fun." For him, he said, most of the satisfaction of this kind of game comes from "working up levels and getting cooler stuff and going into battle."

He said he particularly likes medieval games because of their magic and swordplay, and also because he thought it was an interesting time frame. He took me on a tour of his favorite realm in the game, the island of Albion, via his avatar, a poor but strapping warrior. I was struck by the lush exterior environments and the beautifully detailed interiors of the taverns and shops we visited. The island seemed immense. Loeser said it could take hours to cross on foot, though if you were in a hurry and had money, you could buy a ticket to ride a horse. Day also changes to night in this game, and Loeser told me weather could also change. Just as in England, it can be foggy and rainy here, making it difficult to spot your quarry (see Figure 15.6).

Figure 15.6   A misty landscape in Albion, one of the realms of the *Dark Age of Camelot*. Image courtesy of Mythic Entertainment.

Loeser enjoys playing in character, and demonstrated how he does this, begging a passerby, a wealthy looking nobleman, for some coins by way of a courtly typed message sprinkled with *thees* and *thous*. To my surprise, the passerby generously complied. And what would Loeser do with his newfound bounty? He promptly spent most of it to have all his clothes dyed red, along with much of his equipment. Clearly, this game was some kind of medieval fashion show. "If you have money, you may as well make your character look good," he told me. But he justified the expense by explaining "people are more eager to let you join their group if you look cool."

With that, Loeser activated a function that signaled he was looking for company, and in short order he hooked up with about a dozen other players and was off on a monster hunt. The fog was rolling in and dusk was falling, reducing visibility, but just enough light was left for the group to track a lumbering, furry looking creature, to surround it, and to do it in—the conclusion of a good day's work in Albion.

THE MMORPG-MAKERS' POINT OF VIEW

A player's point of view can be illuminating, but to understand how these games are put together, I talked with the duo that heads up production for *EverQuest*, developed and published by Sony Online Entertainment. *EverQuest*, like *The Dark Age of Camelot*, is a medieval fantasy game (see Figure 15.7). Until more recent ones came along, it was the most popular MMORPG in the Western hemisphere and is possibly the longest-running online game of all time.

Figure 15.7 *EverQuest*, a medieval fantasy game, belongs to the "sword and sorcery" genre of MMORPGs and is vast in scope. Image courtesy of Sony Online Entertainment.

My experts were the two people who headed up the game's day-to-day production work, and who probably know as much as anyone in the world about creating and producing MMORPGs: Rich Waters, Design Director, and Robert Pfister, Senior Producer. Waters and Pfister told me (answering my questions jointly) that one of the greatest challenges of producing a game like *EverQuest* is its vast scope. They compared what they did to running a small city, requiring the juggling of multiple and highly demanding responsibilities. At the time we talked, the game had 220 adventure zones, 16 city zones, and some 40,000 NPCs. "That's a lot to look after, each day, every day," they pointed out, an understatement if ever there was one. And, on top of that, they are continually writing new stories and developing new features.

Designing a new MMORPG, they told me, is a multiyear project requiring a staff of dozens of people. Among the first issues the team must address is defining the game's setting (Medieval times? Space? Post-apocalyptic?) and determining the basis of the game's conflict. Two elements that demand special attention, they said, are story and character. "Story is very important to a game," they asserted. In the context of a MMORPG, story is primarily considered to be the history, backstory, and lore of the fictional world, as well as the conflicts within it. Story, they explained, "can be introduced in a two-minute cut scene at the beginning of the game, or can be spread across the world in books, tales told, and in quest backgrounds … The richer you make your world, the more likely people are to come to visit and stay." They told me that players can, and do, spend years exploring *EverQuest*: "They find that every inch is covered with lore and story." But, they added, part of their job is also to create "very specific adventures for people to complete—fight this dragon, defeat this god, rescue that person."

As with video games, the characters in MMORPGs fall into two broad categories: the player characters and the NPCs. In *EverQuest*, the NPCs may be monsters you fight or human characters like shopkeepers or guild masters. The monsters fall into a category called a *MOB*, short for *Mobile Object*, which is an object in the game that moves, as opposed to an inanimate object like a door or chest that you must "attack" in order to open.

In developing an NPC that will have a role in a new quest, the design team works out what its function will be in the overall quest, what its backstory is, how players will interact with it, and what lines of dialogue it will speak. The artists will then do concept drawings of the new NPC, working with the designers to refine the look, and then add clothing and "attachments"—things like shields and hats. The final step is to animate the character, giving it actions like running, swimming, fighting, casting spells, or dying. That done, the character is imported into the game.

The design process for the avatars is somewhat different. In *EverQuest*, the basic character types are either drawn from standard mythology (archetypes like ogres, trolls, elves, and gnomes) or else from *EverQuest*'s own mythology. Waters and Pfister said that the critical thing, when designing a new class or race, is to take care that it does not create an overwhelming advantage to one particular group of characters. They consider how the character will work on its own, how it will play in a group, how it will play in a large raid, and what effect it will have on all the different types of NPCs.

Before any new features are added to the game, the designers must first consider all the different ways it might be used and how its presence might impact the gameplay. For example, Waters and Pfister told me they recently added horses to the game. In doing so, they had to address such questions as: Can people steal horses? Can horses be killed? What role will horses play with the most competitive players? With more casual ones?

Overall, they also cautioned against making a game too technically demanding, stressing instead that it must be enjoyable to play. This is, of course, the same point our 15-year-old informant stressed. Waters and Pfister asserted: "You can have the most detailed online world imaginable down to the cracks in the sidewalk, but if it isn't fun, no one will play."

BREAKING FRESH GROUND

Although a great many MMORPGs are sword and sorcery fantasies, Disney broke new ground by creating *Toontown Online*, a light-hearted game designed for a family audience. It was a totally radical concept at the time of its development, because of its use of humor and cartoon characters (see Figure 15.8). It was released in 2003 but discontinued after a successful 10-year run, in the fall of 2013, when it was replaced by other Disney Interactive projects.

Figure 15.8 A screenshot from *Toontown Online*, a fantasy world inhabited by Toons (cartoon characters). Image courtesy of © Disney.

Toontown was a colorful world inhabited by Toons, or cartoon characters. In the game, this cheerful place was being threatened by business-minded robotic creatures called Cogs with a single-minded agenda: to take over the Toons' buildings and convert them into drab office structures. As a player, your mission was to protect Toontown from the Cogs. To battle these robots, you launched "gags" at them. For example, you could pelt them with cream pies or drench them with your personal rain cloud.

This innovative, humorous approach to the MMORPG was dreamed up by Mike Goslin, who at the time was Vice President of Disney's Virtual Reality Studio. Goslin told me the idea came to him late one night in 1999, as he was working on an attraction for DisneyQuest, an urban interactive indoor theme park in Orlando. It was born out of a "what if" question: what if you took the skills and experience acquired from designing theme parks and applied them to a MMORPG? He told me it was like a light going on overhead, especially as he realized that a MMORPG was really "a place more than a game, and we know how to build places." Strikingly, though he was coming at it from a totally different set of experiences, Goslin's vision of the MMORPG as a "place" closely echoed that of Richard Bartle, quoted earlier in this chapter.

One of the innovations of the game was a trolley system to transport players around this world. The trolleys were devised to vastly speed up the time spent getting from one place to another in the game. Though time-consuming navigation is characteristic of most MMORPGs, Goslin's team realized it was not something young children were likely to have much patience with.

The Characters

Just as with MMORPGs for adults, this new game was to be populated both by NPCs and PCs. The NPCs would fall into two basic categories: Cogs (the game's antagonists) and other Toons (neutral characters). The creative team came up with 32 different types of Cogs, all based on the theme of big business. Four different variables would determine each Cog's persona: its name, physical appearance, dialogue, and mode of attack. For example, a Cog named Cold Caller would have a block of ice for a head, and his mode of attack might be to throw a telephone; when encountered in the street, he might say something like "Sorry to interrupt your dinner." The game would replenish any defeated Cogs; there would be no end to them.

The other group of NPCs, the non-player Toons, would mostly be shopkeepers, and about 800 of them would be dispersed around Toontown. They would be on hand to interact with player-controlled Toons and give them tasks to do. There would also be a special group of NPCs: several "star" Toons of the Disney universe, familiar characters like Mickey, Minnie, and Pluto. They would circulate through Toontown, and thrill players when they appeared.

As with adult MMORPGs, players would get to design their own avatars, molding them from a million possible combinations (see Figure 15.9). They could choose from six possible species—dog, cat, mouse, horse, rabbit, or duck—and pick different body types, color combinations, and clothing styles. They would then get to name their Toon. During the game, they

Figure 15.9 *Toontown Online* allows players to design their own avatars. Here, in the *Choose Your Clothing* feature, they can create their avatars' outfits. Image courtesy of © Disney.

would be viewing their Toon from a third-person point of view, which Goslin termed "the wing man view." It would be as if the camera were tethered right behind the Toon.

Reaching a Broad Demographic

During development, the team considered each demographic group they wanted to attract and built in elements that would appeal to each. For adults, for example, the primary attraction would be the game's sophisticated workplace humor and wordplay, such as the puns in the Toontown shop signs. Working in things for boys was not difficult, Goslin said, because, based on the history of how boys have responded to prior games, "we know what they like." But shaping the content to appeal to girls was harder, he noted, because "no one's done it before." The team felt girls would respond well to the emphasis on cooperative play and to the social aspects of the game, and would enjoy being able to customize the avatars. They also considered the tastes of girls in the visual design, with Toontown's bright colors and rounded shapes.

The design team also took steps to ensure that the game would not be plagued with *griefers* (players who deliberately make life miserable for other players). One way they handled this was by preventing unrestricted chat. Instead, they offered instead a "speed chat" system, giving players a selection of words and phrases to choose from. This short-circuited the ability of ill-mannered players to verbally harass others and also protected young users against predators and the invasion of privacy, an important consideration for families. The downside, of course, was that it could limit the social aspects of the game. However, with parental approval and a special code, kids could enjoy free chat privileges with people they knew from outside the game.

To further ensure a positive experience, the game encouraged good behavior by rewarding cooperation and team play. It offered no incentive to compete, and no opportunities for player versus player (PvP) battles. It thus circumvented the bloody player attacks prevalent in most MMORPGs. Even the battles between the players and the Cogs were non-gory affairs, emphasizing strategy and humor rather than physical force (see Figure 15.10). Not only would the Toons use gags for ammunition, but the Cogs would retaliate in kind. For example, they might spray a Toon with ink from a fountain pen, or fling half-Windsor neckties.

The Role of the Treadmill

One feature that can be found in classic MMORPGs like *EverQuest* and *World of Warcraft* is a device called a treadmill, and this device was built into *Toontown* as well. A treadmill is an internal structural system that keeps the player hooked, cycling repeatedly through the same types of beats in order to advance in the game.

In an old-line MMORPG, the treadmill might require players to kill monsters to earn money to buy swords to kill more monsters. But in *Toontown Online*, the treadmill worked like this: Toons played mini-games to earn jelly beans; Toons used the jelly beans to buy gags; Toons used the gags to fight the Cogs, at which point their inventory of gags was depleted; then, once again, the Toons must play mini-games to earn jelly beans. Players cannot advance in the game without using the gags, and the gags get better—more effective and more fun—as players work their way up. For instance, one line of progression begins with throwing cupcakes, advances

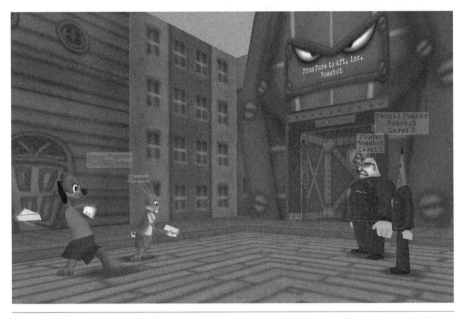

Figure 15.10 Screenshot of a Toontown battle: Toons on the left versus Cogs on the right. Image courtesy of © Disney.

to slices of pie, and then to entire wedding cakes. The best treadmills, according to Goslin, are integrated into the game in a natural way, as part of the overall game world.

STORY AND STRUCTURE

One of the toughest challenges Goslin found in developing *Toontown* was dealing with the story. In a shared world like a MMORPG, he said, "It is a unique challenge to do storytelling … you stretch the limits of storytelling in this kind of thing." As he pointed out, in a traditional story, you have one story structure featuring one hero and one major encounter. But in a MMORPG, each player is the hero of his or her own experience of the game. Furthermore, you need a reusable climax, something that can be played through by each person. This precludes having a fixed ending. And finally, you don't want the game to come to a conclusive and final end, because this would undercut its subscription basis.

NOTES FROM THE FIELD: THREE LEVELS OF STORY

Goslin sees stories in MMORPGs as operating on three levels—high, medium, and low. The high-level story, he feels, gives players a context and meaning to the overall state of affairs that they find in this world and for the core conflicts that exist there. In *Toontown*, this was the backstory of who the Cogs were and how they became unleashed on the Toons. The medium-level story, he feels, is a template everyone can share, perhaps a quest experience. He sees it as being a little like the season finale of a TV show, tying up some loose ends and shedding some new light on the high-level story. The low-level story, he suggests, is about the individual player's role in the story, that player's personal narrative within the game.

THE FUTURE OF MMORPGS

The long-term popularity of *Toontown Online* has demonstrated that MMORPGs can successfully be extended beyond the traditional "swords and sorcery" games and can appeal to a new demographic of gamers. Goslin believes the potential of MMORPGs is largely untapped. But he advises anyone venturing into this arena to be careful of making assumptions about the game's potential players. "If you think you know how they will use it, you will probably miss something," he asserts. He recommends thoroughly testing every aspect of the game before releasing it, and thinks the testing process should continue for weeks, even months. But he also believes this is not an area for the timid. Though it requires discipline, he said, it also requires passion. "It's not a mistake to aim high," he asserts. "If you aren't aiming high, you can't hit high."

Since the early days of *Toontown*, an extremely daring and ambitious new MMORPG project has been launched. Called *Defiance*, this sci-fi story is both a TV series and a MMORPG, with the same storyworld in both and with characters moving back and forth between both. Thus, not only is it an entirely new kind of transmedia endeavor, but the first time a MMORPG has been integrated into a TV show. It premiered early in 2013 on the Syfi channel. As of this writing, it is too soon to evaluate its success, but it is impressive to know that the producers spent five years and $150 million dollars preparing *Defiance* for its premiere. Echoing Goslin's advice, they are certainly aiming high.

Clearly, the process of developing a MMORPG is not suited to those with short attention spans, shallow pockets, or a lack of creative vision. The vast scale of MMORPGs, coupled with the fact that they must be able to support tens of thousands of simultaneous players, has substantial impact on story, structure, and character development. These games require that their creators be able to let go of familiar narrative techniques and regard storytelling in quite a new light.

THE RISE OF CASUAL GAMES

Casual games, as can be imaged from the term, are at the opposite end of the spectrum from MMORPs. In recent years, they have been one of the fastest growing sectors of the games market. Such games can be easily learned (though they are often challenging to master) and can be played in brief periods of time—they are little forms of recreation like coffee breaks or recess at school. They are also highly replayable; some would say addictive. They are played online, on game consoles, PCs, and all types of mobile devices. The development of the Wii helped increase their popularity and has pulled in a whole new demographic of gamers: senior citizens.

Casual games have their roots in the oldest types of video games, such as *Pong* and other arcade games, and include a wide variety of genres, such as abstract puzzle games, shooters, and racing games. Advergames, covered in Chapter 13, are often a form of casual gaming. New kinds of casual games, cognitive games, have been developed to help older individuals retain mental functions, serving as a form of exercise for the brain. Women are a substantial part of the player base, even outnumbering men, according to many studies. Players who are not hard-core gamers enjoy them because, unlike traditional video games, they are easy to play and can be satisfying without demanding a large investment of time.

Game developers have a different set of reasons for liking casual games: they are far less expensive to develop than a full-length video game, which now have average budgets of $28 million. Furthermore, the development cycle is considerably shorter. Developing a traditional video game can be a big gamble, because, while some are big hits, many others are big losers. Casual games, however, with their lower budgets and speedier development cycles, are substantially less risky.

Because casual games are so popular with players, and also so advantageous to developers, we can expect to see this sector of the market continue to grow. However, because casual games can only support a small amount of narrative, at best, they do not appear to be a promising arena for digital storytelling.

WHO PLAYS GAMES AND WHY?

While many people are under the impression that the majority of gamers are teenage boys, the truth is that the average age of gamers has been rising steadily. According to the latest figures of the Entertainment Software Association (ESA), the industry group dedicated to the video game business, the average age of gamers is now 30. Furthermore, ESA statistics show that male gamers only slightly outnumber female gamers, with 47 percent of all gamers being women. In fact, women over the age of 18 form a larger portion of the gaming population (30 percent) than boys 17 or younger (18 percent). In addition, thanks in part to the Wii and to casual games, a large number of seniors are also playing games.

Nevertheless, teens are, on the whole, avid gamers. A study conducted by the Pew Internet Project back in 2008 showed that the vast majority of teens, 97 percent, play video games. Though this study was done some years ago, there is no reason to doubt this figure has changed significantly.

While it is important to know who is playing games, an even more interesting question, especially to those of us who are interested in creating compelling interactive entertainment, is *why* people play games—what is it about games that makes them so appealing to those who play them?

For one thing, as we noted earlier in the book, games are experienced as fun. They satisfy a desire we all have to play, and that desire doesn't go away even after we've left our childhoods far behind. Games offer us a socially acceptable form of play at any age, and an enjoyable stimulus to the imagination. To maintain the sense of fun, a good game offers just the right amount of challenge—not too little, or it would be boring, and not too much, or it would be discouraging.

For another thing, games take you out of your ordinary life and give you a chance to do things you'd never be able to do in reality, and all without any actual risk to life or limb. You are given plenty to do in these game worlds and can pretty much decide how you want to interact with it. In other words, you control the shots—often literally.

EXPERT OBSERVATIONS: CLASSIC GAMER PERSONALITIES

William Fisher, the founder and president of Quicksilver Software, pointed out to me that not everyone plays games for the same reasons. Fisher, a seasoned games professional, who was in the business even before founding his company back in 1984, told me he has observed several kinds of "classic gamer personalities." People may play, he believes, for one of several reasons. It may be because they are:

- looking to escape;
- want to blow off steam;
- enjoy the intellectual challenge; or
- want to compete with other people.

"What hooks people initially is the visual and conceptual part of the game—what it looks like, and what it's about," he said. "What keeps them [hooked] is the progressive challenge of the game, the gradual increase in difficulty that keeps them scaling the mountain one step at a time." In other words, the challenges continue to escalate, keeping the player alert and involved.

Veteran game producer and designer Darlene Waddington, who worked on the classic game *Dragon's Lair*, offered up another reason people get hooked on games: the adrenaline rush. She believes players become caught up in the intense struggle to overcome a challenge. They're absorbed to the point of tunnel vision, and when they finally do succeed, they are rewarded with a gratifying sense of release. In other words, games can produce an emotion akin to catharsis.

GAMIFICATION

Video games have become so popular and so widely played that non-gaming entities have adapted certain techniques and mechanics from video games and are now employing them in something called gamification. Gamification is an especially popular new tool for promotion, and is also used in education. Gamification is explored in depth in Chapter 13.

WHAT CAN WE LEARN FROM GAMES?

Probably more than any other form of entertainment, video games are powerfully effective at actively involving users in a fictional experience. And despite the various criticisms leveled at them, games have clearly proven to be a compelling form of entertainment. Furthermore, games can teach us many useful lessons that can be applied to other forms of digital storytelling. For example:

- People are drawn to games as an enjoyable form of play, as an escape from the pressures of everyday life. Overcoming the challenges in a game offers players an empowering sense of achievement.

- Games are most effective when they give participants an opportunity to do things—to actively engage in an experience—and these tasks should be meaningful in the context of the game.

- To keep players involved, games use devices like a strong over-arching goal; a rewards system; challenges; and an escalation of suspense and tension.

- Games need to make sense and have an internal logic; this cannot be sacrificed to gameplay.

- Players are drawn to games for a variety of reasons, and it is important to understand one's target audience in order to create an experience that will please them.

These guidelines can be applied to virtually any type of interactive story experience just by removing the word "game" and substituting the appropriate interactive medium. Although some forms of interactive storytelling will lean more heavily to the gaming end of the spectrum and others toward the narrative end, the basic principles will still apply.

TIPS FOR NEWBIE GAME-MAKERS

People enjoy playing games so much that a certain number of these players will be inspired to make their own games, unaware of the pitfalls and challenges such an endeavor inevitably entails. If you are among this group of newbie game-makers, it might be helpful to you to review these tips.

1. Select your team carefully. Ideally, it will include at least one member who has had experience working on a game that has actually gone to market. It should also include individuals who will bring special skills to your team. Coding, graphics, and marketing are among the most valuable. Also consider the personalities of your potential teammates. It's best not to include individuals who are inherently negative or are excessively into socializing. Negative individuals will pull your team spirit down, while social butterflies will distract others from the work that needs to be accomplished.

2. Consider the scope of your game. It is unwise to be overly ambitious in terms of its size or in terms of breaking new ground. Making any kind of game is an extremely time-consuming task, and if you are new at this type of work, you will be surprised at

how labor-intensive it can be. It is best to have relatively modest ambitions for your first game than to aim for a magnificence you will almost certainly fail to achieve.

3. Set realistic milestones for the development of your game. Having certain dates by which certain key elements of your game must be completed will help you stay on course. Your milestones should be realistic in terms of being achievable. It can be helpful to pin your milestones to real life events, such as meetings of a local game developers' organization. That way, you will not only have a specific date to shoot for but also an opportunity to show off what your team has accomplished thus far.

ADDITIONAL RESOURCES

The Internet is full of excellent information about video games. Among them are:

- Gamespot (www.Gamespot.com).
- The International Game Developers Association (www.igda.org) and Gamasutra (www.gamasutra.com), which the IGDA hosts.
- Moby Games (http://www.mobygames.com/home).
- For books on video games, refer to the Bibliography.

CONCLUSION

Certainly, games have made a light year's worth of progress since the first games were introduced back in the 1970s. One need only compare *Pong* to the *BioShock* series to see how far they have come. What kinds of games might we be playing a few decades from now? And what role will games play in the overall universe of interactive entertainment, and entertainment in general? If only we could consult one of the wizards who populate so many role-playing games and learn the answers to these questions!

IDEA-GENERATING EXERCISES

1. To test your understanding of genre, take a game you are familiar with, name its genre, and then assign it an entirely different genre. What elements would need to be added or changed, and what could remain, to make the game fit the conventions of this new genre?

2. Analyze your own experiences in playing games. What about them makes them appealing to you? What makes you feel involved with a game, and what makes you want to spend time playing it? What emotions do you experience as you play?

3. Consider recent movies or TV shows that you have seen. What kinds of storylines, characters, or themes have they contained that you've never seen included in a game? Do you think it would be possible to include this kind of content in a game? How?

4. What experience from real life have you never seen tackled in a game but believe could be? How do you think this idea could be implemented?

5. Sketch out a premise for a MMORPG. What world or worlds would it be set in? What would the central conflict be? What kinds of characters would exist here? What would be of great value in this world, the equivalent of money in our own world? Once you have established these fundamentals of your MMORPG, try to construct a treadmill for it.

CHAPTER 16

The Internet

What are the unique characteristics of the Internet, and how can you make the most of them when creating narratives for this medium?

What is meant by "stickiness" when referring to content on the Internet?

In terms of story-based entertainment on the Internet, what do users find particularly attractive and what kinds of things risk being kisses of death?

How are Web-based technologies that were originally developed for non-fiction purposes now being used for digital storytelling?

THE EVOLUTION OF THE INTERNET

The Internet has been through some massive changes and several dramatic reversals of fortune since its origins in the late 1960s. As we saw in Chapter 2, it started out in relative obscurity, and with an entirely different name—ARPANET—and was developed to assist the military during the Cold War. But in a little over two decades, it underwent a name change and morphed into the more populist communications tool known as the Internet. By the mid-1990s, this once plebian communications tool was beginning to be perceived as a viable medium for entertainment, thanks to the development of the tools that made possible the World Wide Web. This was the time of the dot-com boom, and there was frenzied launching of new websites, many of them built for entertainment purposes. Everyone was hoping to "strike gold in cyberspace." Unfortunately, within a few short years, just after the new millennium arrived, it became evident that the great majority of these brash new websites were not generating the profits that were anticipated. The plug was pulled on many a site and we were suddenly looking at a dot-com bust.

In recent years, however, the Internet has not only rebounded but has become an even more robust medium for entertainment than almost anyone during the boom years could have predicted. In large part, this resurgence has been due to the growing numbers of households with broadband connectivity, which makes it possible to enjoy video on the Web, as well as other forms of entertainment that require high-speed access.

WORTH NOTING: THE DIFFERENCE BETWEEN THE INTERNET AND THE WEB

It should be noted that even though the terms "Internet" and "Web" are often used interchangeably, they are not the same thing. To be accurate, the Internet ("Net" for short) is a vast network of computer networks that are all linked together. It is made up of computer networks from the sectors of business, government, and academia, as well as personal computers. It allows any computer that's part of the Internet to communicate with any other computer. But despite the critical role played by the World Wide Web, the Internet itself remains an important way to communicate: email is sent through the Internet, not through the Web.

The World Wide Web (or Web, for short) is just a small portion of the Internet, but a critically important one, because it is the portion of the Internet that makes it possible to link Web pages with each other, and to search the entire Web for a particular topic or name. In a sense, the Web sits on top of the Internet and functions through the Internet. As one writer put it, paraphrasing somewhat, the Internet is like a restaurant, and the Web is the most popular dish on the menu (from About.com). For digital storytelling purposes, we are primarily but not exclusively interested in the Web.

The Internet is now home to a diverse array of narrative-based genres, a number of them unique to this medium. We have already touched on several of them in previous chapters, such as Web series/webisodes, faux blogs, and various types of games, such as MMOGs and casual games. We have also looked at another cyber experience made possible by the Web, the virtual world. In future chapters, we will be exploring alternate reality games (ARGs) and iCinema—other forms in which the Web often plays an important part. Furthermore, as we have seen, the Web is often used as a platform for narrative-rich projects used to teach, promote, and inform. And finally, as we have explored previously, there has been an explosion of user-generated material on social networking sites, some of which is narrative in nature.

In addition to all these relatively well-established types of content, the Internet is also home to such new forms of digital storytelling that they don't even have generic names yet. We will be looking at several of them in this chapter. Without question, the Internet plays an enormous role when it comes to digital media and storytelling.

INTERNET CONNECTIVITY ACROSS THE GLOBE

Without being connected to the Internet, it would not be possible to enjoy the enormous amount of digital storytelling this medium offers. And the number of individuals connected to the Internet, either at work or at home, grows larger every day. By June 30, 2012, the last quarter that figures were available, over seven billion people had access to the Internet.

The parts of the world with the greatest amount of connectivity, in terms of the percentage of the population, were North America (79 percent), Oceania/Australia (68 percent), and Europe (63 percent), according to Internet World Stats (www.internetworldstats.com/stats .htm). Africa was trailing far behind, with only 16 percent of the population in that part of the world connected to the Internet, but it was also experiencing astounding growth, an increase of 3606.7 percent in just two years.

In the United States, according to a 2013 Pew Study report, 70 percent of the population enjoys high-speed Internet access.

THE POPULARITY OF YOUTUBE VIDEOS

YouTube videos are not only one of the most popular forms of entertainment on the Web, but also one of the forms users are most eager to share. By 2013, people were watching six billion hours a month of YouTube videos, double the amount of the previous year. If that amount of video watching were dispersed around the world, it would work out to one hour a month for every person on Earth! (from Shelley Palmer's blog, May 2, 2013, http://www.shellypalmer.com/). A *New York Times* reporter calculated that it would take 72 hours to watch all the videos posted to YouTube in just one single minute (*New York Times*, February 13, 2013).

STRANGE BUT TRUE: SEX SELLS

Producers of emerging media entertainment have traditionally seen the value of adding racy content to their offerings. This has been true of photography, novels, movies, and DVDs. And the same is true for the Internet. It turns out that the most valuable URL in the history of the Web is Sex.com. That URL was sold by one company to another for a staggering $13 million dollars in 2010, without any concrete plans for how to monetize the URL—the URL alone was considered valuable enough to fetch that price.

YOUTUBE SUCCESS STORIES

It seems virtually impossible to predict the types of videos that will be enormously popular with viewers or that will be spread the most quickly through viral marketing. Two of the most successful videos of recent years could not be more different from each other. One is an earnest documentary called *Kony 2012*, about the Ugandan who runs the Lord's Resistance Army and forces youngsters to become child soldiers. The documentary was watched by 100 million people in six days, largely thanks to viral marketing. The other enormous hit was *Gangnam Style*, an upbeat music video by South Korean artist Psy. It was the first YouTube video to score one billion views. Why did a music video and a documentary both attain such popularity? We will try to answer this question during this chapter.

THE QUEST FOR "STICKINESS"

The Internet has many attributes which, when taken individually, may mirror other media, but when bundled together, make it a unique venue for enjoying entertainment. When a website contains a great many of these attributes, it is also likely to possess a quality known as *stickiness*, a term that was widely used in the years 2001 to 2003, and is still relevant and still being used today. Though stickiness is unwelcome when it comes to doorknobs or furniture, it is an extremely desirable attribute for a website. It connotes the ability to draw people to the site and entice them to linger for long periods of time. If you want to create an entertainment site that is sticky, and hence appealing to users, you will want to include as many sticky attributes as you can, providing, of course, that they make sense in terms of the project. Users are attracted to the Internet because it offers them experiences that are:

- *Community building*. One of the most unique aspects of the Web is that it allows individuals to communicate with each other and share their thoughts, concerns, and opinions. When they visit a website, particularly one that focuses on a fictional world they especially care about, they look for community-fostering options like comments boards and chat features.

- *Dynamic*. Well-maintained websites are refreshed on a regular basis, and users look forward to seeing new features on sites that they visit frequently. The adding of fresh content gives the website a vibrant, responsive quality. Websites that are not updated begin to seem stagnant and "canned," as if they had just been stuck up on the Internet and then abandoned.

- *Participatory*. Users want to interact with content; they look for ways of becoming involved with it. Participation in story-based entertainment on the Web can take many forms. It can mean chatting with a fictional character; suggesting new twists in a plot; creating and playing a character in an online story; snooping around in a character's computer files; or, in the case of a MMOG, creating an avatar and becoming an active character in a fictional game world.

- *Deep*. Users expect websites to offer them opportunities to dig down into the content. Even story-rich environments can offer a variety of ways to satisfy this expectation, from reading diaries "written" by the characters to viewing their "home movies" to visiting the online newspaper of their fictional hometown.

- *Edgy*. The Internet has something of the persona of a cheeky adolescent. Users enjoy irreverent humor, opinions that challenge conventional thinking, and content that they are unlikely to find in mainstream media like television and newspapers.

- *Personal*. The Web allows users to express themselves and be creative. Users enjoy customizing and personalizing content in various ways.

- *Easy to navigate and well-organized*. Users want to be able to quickly locate the content they are interested in and appreciate it when content is organized logically, or, as we discussed in Chapter 14, has a well-ordered *taxonomy*.

- *"Snackable."* Most users are looking for short entertainment breaks rather than extended ones, or, as *Wired* magazine puts it, *snack-o-tainment*. Content should be broken into consumable pieces that can be enjoyed within a few minutes of time.

YOUTUBE STICKINESS

What specifically makes a YouTube video sticky? Freddie Wong, one of the creators of the immensely successful YouTube series, *Video Game High School*, had some thoughts to share on a blog on RocketJump about the popularity of the Kony documentary (http://www.rocketjump.com/blog/the-secrets-of-YouTube-success-updated/2). Although he didn't feel it was particularly well-made, he did believe that the video offered users a terrific feeling when they shared it with family and friends. It made them feel worldly and committed to justice and as someone willing to act. "Kony was a drug in video form," Wong suggested. "And the method of administration was sharing it, spreading it further."

Kate Murphy in an article for the *New York Times* (February 13, 2013) offered some tips for making successful Internet videos:

- Have the right equipment. This needn't be elaborate—you can shoot on a smart phone. A lavalier microphone and some lights are also helpful.

- Be sure your performer is a good communicator. This person should be interesting and energetic, and give the impression that he's speaking to you as a friend.

- Offer content that is unique and cannot be found elsewhere.

In addition to these points, I would stress the importance of having a compelling story to tell. Even non-fiction works should have a story that people want to hear. Though the Kony documentary might not have been the most polished work of all time, it was about an evil strongman who committed barbaric acts of cruelty against vulnerable people, so the subject matter and the main character were unquestionably captivating, as was the overhanging question adding tension to the narrative: can this person be brought to justice? Thus it had many of the characteristics of a solid story.

TV AS A ROLE MODEL?

Because the Web supports audio and video, and because it is viewed on a monitor that looks much like a TV screen, inexperienced Web developers are sometimes lulled into the belief that creating stories for the Web is much like creating stories for TV. While many important similarities do exist, so do significant differences, and ignoring those differences can seriously undermine a project.

This was one of the most important lessons learned by writers and producers who worked on the Internet's earliest version of a Web series, *The Spot*, which began its run in 1995. The storylines revolved around a group of young singles living in a California beach house. Because of its focus on highly charged emotionally relationships, *The Spot* had much in common with television soap operas. However, unlike TV, each of their stories was told from a first-person point of view, largely through journals. And somewhat like the movie *Rashomon*, the characters often gave different versions of the same events.

Stewart St. John, a writer-producer with an extensive background in television, served as the Executive Producer and Head Writer of *The Spot* during its last year, from 1996 to 1997. But his work on *The Spot* quickly taught him to appreciate the differences between TV and the Internet.

EXPERT OBSERVATIONS: TV—A KISS OF DEATH

Looking back on his experience in working on *The Spot*, St. John said: "In the beginning, I brought my conventional TV background to it. I plotted it weeks and weeks in advance and expected the storyline to stay true to what I wrote, never straying. It was the kiss of death. The fans went berserk. They didn't feel emotionally connected. It was too much like television." Visitors to online fictional worlds want to be able to participate in the story, he stressed.

To allow for more user participation, St. John found ways to integrate input from the fans to shape the direction of the plot. Over time, he came to realize that it was particularly effective to build consequences—both positive and negative—into the choices the fans are offered in the narrative, believing this pulled them more deeply into the story. By loosening his control and becoming more flexible, he was able to provide an experience that was both narrative and interactive.

"You can't think in terms of the way you'd create for television," St. John asserted. "The Internet is its own world, and the language of that world is interactivity. This is the biggest mistake I've seen over the past few years; creators creating Internet sites using a television format. It won't work."

One way staff members on *The Spot* would involve fans in the story was to go into its chat room in character and chat with them. Some of these exchanges would be mentioned in the online journals "written" by fictitious characters, even weaving the users' names into the accounts. Not only did this give the fans a few minutes of glory but it also made the show seem all the more real. In fact, many fans of *The Spot* were under the impression that the characters were actual people, which put extra pressure on the writers to keep them consistent and believable.

SOME UNIQUE WEB GENRES

As noted earlier, a number of story-rich genres have been created specifically for the Web, and the Web also supports certain forms of narrative that blend several different media elements together, such as ARGs and transmedia storytelling. Let's take a look at some important Web-based narrative genres.

WEB SERIES, OR WEBISODE

Web series, which in the past were most often referred to as *webisodes*, are serialized stories that are broken into short installments, each just a few minutes long, and each of which often ends in a cliffhanger. The terms webisode and Web series can be used interchangeably. The genre evolved from *The Spot*, but while the storylines of *The Spot* were primarily conveyed by text and still images, today's webisodes use full motion video or animation. Most webisodes revolve around contemporary characters in modern settings and center on personal dramas. And, despite the lessons learned by Stewart St. John and others working on *The Spot*, many of today's webisodes are presented in a linear fashion, much like a TV show, with little or no opportunity for user participation.

WEB SERIES WITH HOLLYWOOD PARENTAGE

Some Web series, as we discussed in Chapter 10, are spin-offs of popular TV shows and are the product of Hollywood professionals. For example, *The Office: The Accountants* was the story of several regular characters from the hit TV show, *The Office*. Another now historic Web series was *Homicide: Life on the Streets*. It was based on the popular TV police drama, but contained original characters and incidents that were independent of the TV show. More recently, as noted in Chapter 10, Showtime created a Web series based on its hit TV show, *Dexter*, about a serial killer with a strong moral code. Some episodes of the Web series dealt with Dexter's backstory and others were about cases not featured on the TV series. Other Web series spun off from TV shows include those made for *Lost*, *Ugly Betty*, *Heroes*, *Scrubs*, *Grey's Anatomy*, *Pretty Little Liars*, and *The Vampire Diaries*.

In addition to direct spin-offs, professionals from TV and feature films have begun to get into original Web series in a big way. For example, *Prom Queen* was a major entry with impressive Hollywood connections. It was produced by the great Hollywood luminary, Michael Eisner, who once ran the Disney Studios. It debuted in 2007 and was shot on video. With 80 episodes, each just 90 seconds long, the steamy murder mystery revolved around a seminal high school event, prom night. On a completely different note, a comedy about gamers called *The Guild* was created and written by Hollywood actress Felicia Day, known for her performances in *Buffy the Vampire Slayer*. Day not only wrote the episodes of *The Guild*, but produced and starred in them as well. It was a big hit not only with gamers, but with people who enjoyed its offbeat humor, and ran for six seasons.

ORIGINAL WEB SERIES

In recent years, there has been a surge of interest in creating and producing original Web series. To my knowledge, no one is keeping a list of every produced series, but just to begin to put some sort of numbers on this phenomenon, in 2013 alone, almost 500 produced Web series were submitted to the Los Angeles Web Series Festival (nicknamed LA WEBFEST) by people hoping to have their work screened there (of this number, 262 were accepted). Applicants to this Web festival—the biggest and oldest one in the world—came from 15 different countries—some from as far away as Turkey and China. Approximately 4,000 people attended events there, and many of them were hoping to make, or were in the process of making, their own Web series. The LA WEBFEST has spurred interest in other parts of the United States and the world to hold similar events, starting in 2011 with France's Marseille Webfest, the brother to the LA WEBFEST. In 2013 alone, festivals have sprung up in Hong Kong (HK Webfest), Australia (Melbourne Webfest), England (London Urban Webfest), Belgium (Liege Webfest), and two in Italy (Rome and Campi Flegrei, near Naples). In addition, in the United States, there were Web festivals in Washington, DC and Atlanta, Georgia. Other parts of the world with plans to hold Web festivals include Polynesia, Singapore, Senegal, Russia, Canada, and, in the United States, Texas and New York.

The LA WEBFEST is under the helm of Michael Ajakwe, Jr., an Emmy-winning TV producer, NAACP Image Award-winning playwright, and veteran TV and screenwriter who has even written and produced his own Web series, *Who...*, on his web channel, www. Ajakwetv.com. He started the LA WEBFEST in 2010, and it has grown bigger with each subsequent year. In an interview during a brief break at the 2013 WEBFEST, I asked Ajakwe why he thought people were so interested in making Web series.

For one thing, he told me, making a Web series "is user friendly. Before, filmmaking was a rich man's game. And if you couldn't afford to make a film, a great voice might be lost." And, he added, "with a Web series, you can hear the voice of its creator. Web series offer more freedom. They are coming from the ground up, whereas other media come from the top down. Web series are almost like a pirate road. They let us hear stories you don't here anywhere else. They are more authentic, more honest."

Ajakwe hit on one of the major reasons people are attracted to Web series: they can offer their creators a powerful form of self-expression. In addition, people are drawn to them for professional reasons. They are a relatively inexpensive way to master filmmaking skills and demonstrate your talent; they offer an opportunity to get your foot in the door of the theater world and TV and film business.

Original Web series come in an enormous assortment of shapes, sizes, styles, and themes. *In Transition* is the story of three women getting out of prison and adjusting to life on the other side of the bars; *Betas* is about a group of young men who work in a digital startup company; *Video Game High School* is a comedy about a high school where prowess at playing video games is far more esteemed than prowess on the athletic field; *3X3* is a French transmedia Web series set in Paris about a young man with amnesia trying to find out who he is. There are even story-based Web series produced for pragmatic purposes, such as *In the Moment* (http://www.inthemoment.tv/#!home/mainPage), a sexy series designed to make young gay men more conscious of the risks of HIV and Aids.

A CLOSE LOOK AT A SUCCESSFUL WEB SERIES: *ENTER THE DOJO*

My own state of New Mexico is home to the successful Web comedy, *Enter the Dojo* (www.youtube.com/enterthedojoshow), a skillfully produced and extremely funny work written, produced, and directed by Matt Page, who also stars in the series. The series, a mockumentary, is set in a martial arts studio where students are instructed in a fictional and potentially deadly martial arts form, Ameri-Do-Te. Their over-the-top confident instructor is Master Ken, played by Page. The series, just starting its third season, has had approximately four million views on YouTube.

I sat down with Page at a local roadhouse and asked him why he decided to make *Enter the Dojo* and what he has learned from the process. Page noted that he had often been employed by various New Mexico entities to make promotional films for them and has made several short films on his own. But he told me he had become frustrated with the length of time it took to make and screen a short film—about two years—and that in the end only 500 people even saw it. But he had also worked on other people's Web series and had an opinion of what he'd do differently. He thought the Web series was an interesting format and a way to exert creative control of a project. He also believed making his own series could be a calling card for work in Hollywood.

Page selected his storyworld, which revolved around martial arts, in part because it was something he himself had practiced since he was 16. Master Ken is a hybrid and send-up of various instructors he has had over the years. He knew the world inside out, and believed he knew how to target a series to the martial arts community—something he was totally correct about, for the series is a big hit in that community. At some real-life dojos, the students watch the series as a group experience. Page told me that the show is "crazy popular" in the UK, and that as many as 10,000 fans turn up there at *Enter the Dojo* events. Fans like to participate in the story by sending in videos showing how they would perform "techniques" demonstrated on the series, like the "kill face" and the "hurricane." The series also has a presence on Facebook and Twitter.

But Page has encountered unexpected challenges. For one thing, three of the series stars, buoyed by their success on the series, have taken off to Hollywood and he can only infrequently get them back to New Mexico. Thus, scheduling has become a big problem. Also, because he is a trained filmmaker (he is a graduate of the Film School of Santa Fe University of Art and Design), it is difficult for him to quickly produce a story-based episode because he can't rush the process. "I still try to apply the craft I spent years learning," he told me (see Figure 16.1). He has discovered, though, that he can speedily turn out short episodes where he does monologues or where there is only one other actor. He can do three of these in a single weekend, and does them all in one take, so there is no editing to do. Editing, he noted, was incredibly time-consuming.

I asked Page what advice he would give to people wanting to make their own Web series. He offered the following:

- Take care to come up with a concept that is sustainable. You want to be able to roll out a multi-season series.
- Watch lots of shows on YouTube's different channels before you start, particularly in your subject area. Once you get going, you can send the creators personal invitations to watch your series. (That strategy helped Page get to 10,000 views quickly.)
- Don't shoot your series all at once. He told me "Make sure there's an audience for it, first. You don't know if anyone is going to give a s**t."

Figure 16.1   Matt Page, center, on the set of *Enter the Dojo*. Image courtesy of Matt Page.

- Don't make your series dependent on a large cast. Scheduling can become a major challenge, as it has in his case, with three of his actors now based in Hollywood.

- You have got to "feed the beast." In other words, you must keep producing and posting new material or people will unsubscribe.

- Interact with your fans. For instance, a disabled fan who was confined to a wheelchair and asked Page how he could still practice martial arts. Page responded as Master Ken, enthusiastically telling the fan what a great weapon a wheelchair could be and describing the ways it could be used.

- Modify your filmmaking technique to fit the medium. Page has had to learn to shoot his Web episodes more quickly than he would shoot a film.

- Create characters that can be quickly understood by your audience, especially when you first introduce them. You don't have the luxury of doing character arcs or detailed backstories in a Web series. Once the series is established, however, you can let your characters evolve and change to some degree.

Though Page believes doing a Web series can be "a terrible way to make money," he has found the experience of creating his series personally and professionally validating. On the professional side, it has generated new work for him as an actor and a director. And on the personal side, it has brought him recognition that his short films never have. "It feels good to know you have a dedicated fan base," he told me, "and that you are a positive part of people's lives."

NON-FICTION AND FICTIONAL BLOGS

The *blog*, short for Web log, is one of the most pervasive forms of communication on the Internet. A type of grassroots journalism, blogs are often highly personal and are written much like diaries, often with daily entries. Many blogs use not only text and stills but also video (and when a blog is video-based, it is known as *vlog*—short for video blog). As of July 2011, about 181 million blogs had been created around the world, according to NM Incite, a Nielsen McKinsey company.

Blogs, of course, are a form of storytelling. Originally, blogs were utilized to cover non-fiction subjects—everything from child-raising to politics to food—so first we'll look at non-fiction blogs and then turn to fictional or faux blogs—blogs that resemble their true-life cousins, but are actually make-believe stories.

NON-FICTION BLOGS

Individuals write non-fiction blogs for many reasons, and according to a survey reported by Right Mix Marketing, these reasons include the desire to write about areas of interest; to share expertise; to attract new clients; and to connect with like-minded people.

Michele C. Hollow, for example, writes a successful blog called *Pet News and Views* (www.petnewsandviews.com) and has been doing this blog since 2009. In an email interview, she told me: "The goal of my blog is to educate people about pet care, pet lifestyle topics, and to share information about people who are working on behalf of animals." She went on to say "I … highlight causes that are important to me, and more importantly, important to animal welfare." Hollow says it isn't difficult for her to find material to blog about because "I have a lot of contacts in the pet and wildlife world. People contact me on a daily basis with interesting stories to cover. If I posted daily, I still wouldn't be able to cover everything. So I pick and choose." She advises people who want to start a blog to "Pick a topic you deeply care about. You are going to be devoting a large part of your time covering this subject, so it must be something that excites you."

Jacqueline Herships, a first-time blogger, created and runs a blog called *The Little Old Lady Stays Put (or doesn't)* using Blogger, a free platform owned by Google. Herships is a journalist and publicist who started her blog in 2011 to explore the housing options available for older people and the housing issues seniors face, in part because she herself was growing older and was trying to find answers for herself. She told me in a phone interview that so far she has created about 177 posts using the phrase "little old lady" for her blog somewhat satirically. She admitted it has met with resistance from some of the people she wanted to interview who didn't want to be labeled that way, though others didn't seem to mind at all.

Over time the blog has evolved more into a lifestyle blog than a personal blog. Although Herships said she started to blog in part to find answers for herself, she has found that putting herself in the spotlight makes her uncomfortable, so now she is more likely to write about other people and their experiences. She said she hasn't found it challenging to find material for her blog, asserting she has "story radar," but she has encountered difficulties with the technical side of blogging, such as developing a comments section that will make it easy for people to post comments. On the other hand, she is pleased to have found blogging to be far more immediate than media she had used in the past, like newspapers and magazines. She confessed, though, that she misses the help that print publications provide, like proofreaders. She told me she is grateful that she is doing this blog because she is finding that it is a new way to engage with the world and with people. And as a result, she is slowly reaching her goal of solving her own issues as a senior citizen.

STRANGE BUT TRUE: NON-FICTION BLOGS THAT READ LIKE FICTION

For the most part, non-fiction blogs tackle serious issues or at least topics that are of personal concern for people, such as health. Partially for this reason, I believed for years that *Belle de Jour: Diary of a London Call Girl* was a fictional blog. It related the racy experiences of a London sex worker and seemed too lurid to be true. But on doing some additional research on the blog for this edition of the book, I discovered that the blog was in fact a real-life diary written by a real call girl, and one that happened to be highly educated—a Ph.D. scientist, in fact. It turns out she was using "Belle de Jour" as her pen name while finishing up her Ph.D. in forensic science, meanwhile covering her living expenses as a high-priced call girl. She has recently revealed her true identity because she was on the verge of being outed by a former boyfriend. Now married and living in the Scottish highlands, she has written two books based on her experiences and a TV series has been based on her blog. She continues to write under her real name about scientific topics and sexual politics.

FICTIONAL OR FAUX BLOGS

Non-fiction blogs have achieved massive popularity, so it was only a matter of time before the creative community recognized their potential for storytelling and started to develop faux or fictional blogs. Many of them look just like the real thing. We discussed one such faux blog in Chapter 10, *Nigelblog*, allegedly written by a character from the TV show *Crossing Jordan* in 2005–2006. Another pioneering blog, although one which looks far more like a Broadway musical than a blog, was *Dr. Horrible's Sing-Along Blog*. It was created by Josh Whedon, a highly successful TV writer who has worked on such shows as *Buffy the Vampire Slayer*. Done entirely in video and divided into three "posts" or acts, it is a strange blend of comedy and wistfulness, the story of a man who yearns to be a super villain. Produced in 2008, it was an enormous success, but had little apparent connection to blogging as it was known at the time or even today.

However, a number of faux blogs have been created that have no connection at all to Hollywood entertainment properties and for all intents and purposes seem real. *Ghost Town* was an early example of this. It was a blog "written" by a young Ukrainian woman named Elena who claims she likes to ride her motorcycle through the dead zone of Chernobyl decimated years after the disaster at the nuclear power plant. Her faux blog, illustrated with her own photographs, is a disturbing warning of the dangers of nuclear accidents. It is so convincingly done that it spread like wildfire around the Internet, with most people believing it was a true story.

A number of writers now believe that faux blogs can stand on their own as a form of fictional narrative. One fine example of fictional blogging is *Ben's Dive Blog*, written by experimental blogger Leo Thompson. His work looks like an authentic blog in every respect (see Figure 16.2), and the blog was presented as a work of undisclosed blog fiction, which means that Thompson did not tell readers the story was not true. Reflecting back on this, he told me in an email interview from Oman, where he now lives, that "I wanted my readers to believe it was genuine and make it more intense, though I also didn't want them to call the local police or ambulance service if my character went offline for a few days."

Figure 16.2 This page from *Ben's Dive Blog* looks like an authentic, non-fiction blog, but is actually a work of fiction. Image courtesy of Leo Thompson.

Ben's Dive Blog is a harrowing adventure story about cave diving, and involves two real and largely underwater cave systems in England: Wookey Hole and Swildon Hole. In the blog, two young men are trying to find an underwater passage that will link the two caves—a highly dangerous enterprise. To add drama to the story, a rival group of divers is trying to accomplish the same goal and will possibly try to sabotage the first group. The blog is told as a first-person account by one of the divers in the first group. The protagonist reports every day on their progress and setbacks—an approach that works perfectly in a blog format, and gives the story a gripping immediacy.

According to Thompson, he chose a blog format for his story because "there is something about their capacity to be personal, intimate and immediate that lent itself to a fictional project." In the course of writing it, he found that it evolved over time. He told me he had to adjust the tone, "which was too stiff and precise to fit the 'laying myself open rough feel' you often get with blogs. It also forced me to compress the daily episodes/posts and be more concise, which is something I have always struggled with as a writer." He would also deliberately make a few typos and comment on things going on in the news to give the blog an air of authenticity.

He made the story interactive by letting followers post comments, send email, follow on Twitter, and access a photo gallery using Flickr. He told me that "This enabled the protagonist to respond to comments left by real world followers who could cross the boundaries and play a part in this fictional universe." He found his biggest difficulty was the pressure to post every day, but on the whole found the experience a good one. "I learned that blogging is multidimensional in a way that 'old print' isn't," he said. For others interested in creating a fictional blog, he recommends considering form and function first. "Does the content and purpose of your story lend itself well to a blog?" he said to ask yourself. "If not then choose another medium. Push the envelope somewhere else." The blog is now archived at http://archive.org/web/, and can be found by searching for benlockhart.com and, once there, by clicking on the date August 27, 2010.

WEBCAM DRAMAS

A webcam drama (my term) is one of the most unique storytelling forms on the Web and would not work on any other medium. Essentially these stories are intimate online diaries in which the protagonists of the stories focus their webcams on themselves and relate what is currently taking place in their lives.

Rachel's Room, which debuted in 2001, introduced this highly innovative and organic approach to storytelling on the Web, and fully used everything the Internet had to offer at the time to serve the purposes of the narrative. It was developed as part of Sony's ambitious broadband initiative, *Sony Screenblast*, which catered to users with high bandwidth, and thus made heavy use of video, offering 50 video installments, each running between three and five minutes. It pushed the envelope of the Internet as a medium for fiction. Six long years later, the famous *LonelyGirl15* used an almost identical approach.

Rachel's Room is a story that could only exist on the Web—the very fact that it takes place on the Internet is an integral part of the concept. Here is the conceit: 16-year-old Rachel Reed is at a crisis point in her life. Her father has recently passed away and she is at war with her mother, who has a serious drinking problem. Like Holden Caulfield in *The Catcher in the Rye*, Rachel feels misunderstood by everyone around her. Thus, in an effort to break out of her isolation and get a handle on things, she makes a radical decision: she will open herself up to strangers in the outside world. So they can see who she really is, she will place webcams around her bedroom and let them roll (though she plans to edit out the "boring parts" before putting the videos up on the Web). Furthermore, she will keep an online journal and also go into a chat room every night to talk with members of her cyber support group (see Figure 16.3).

Arika Lisanne Mittman, who served as Producer and Head Writer of *Rachel's Room*, utilized both familiar and novel methods of telling Rachel's story and encouraging audience

Figure 16.3 *Rachel's Room* appeared to be the website of a real teenager, but it was actually a professionally written drama. Image courtesy of Sony Pictures Digital.

participation. Pieces of Rachel's story were revealed via the video episodes, her written journal, and the chat sessions, and all three were coordinated in terms of content. Viewers could express themselves via message boards, emails, chats, and in certain special ways, such as the "Dreams" section of the site. The chat sessions were an important part of the *Rachel's Room* experience. Mittman herself went into the chat room every weekday night, playing the part of Rachel. Sometimes these sessions contained serious discussions of teen-related issues, but sometimes they also advanced the story. In a clever blending of reality and fiction, she had Rachel meet a boy fan during one of these sessions, a charmer whom Rachel believes to be her soul mate. Against all common sense, she invites the boy (actually an actor playing a fan) to her room, unaware that he's made a bet with his friends that he could seduce her on camera. Naturally, the relationship ends badly, but it caused great anxiety among Rachel's real fans, many of whom were convinced that Rachel was a real girl and not a character in a fictional drama. Mittman says she developed this subplot in part as a cautionary tale for the site's visitors.

EXPERT OBSERVATIONS: DRAWING FROM TRADITIONAL MEDIA

By having Rachel share her most personal thoughts and her teenage angst, often breaking the fourth wall by addressing the viewers directly, the character touched a nerve among the site's fans. They closely identified with her and were intensely concerned with what happened to her. In creating such a compelling protagonist, *Rachel's Room* was actually borrowing a valuable technique from older forms of storytelling: good character development.

"It's wrong to think characters for the Web don't need much depth," Mittman asserted to me. She believes character development is as important for the Web as it is for any other medium. She strove to create a multidimensional, realistic teen, tapping into her own "inner teenager" to do so. She gave Rachel "a certain mopey cynicism" and had her do dumb things at times. In other words, she was flawed, which helped her seem real, and contributed to her appeal.

> Mittman also took pains to develop an overall good story for the series, "arcing it out" (constructing an arc for it) as would be done for a television drama. For the Web, she stressed, "you have to try that much harder to keep people coming back." To Mittman, that means not only constructing strong storylines with cliffhangers but also giving viewers a meaningful role in the story. "You have to keep them in mind," she told me, "and keep in mind why they are going to come back. You have to make them a part of it."

A number of other Web dramas have been presented as true-life video blogs made by someone using his or her own webcam. A series of such videos, purportedly made by a teenaged girl named Bree, caused a huge stir when they turned up on YouTube in 2006. The homemade looking videos, collectively known as *LonelyGirl15* (the fictional girl's user name), were an intimate portrait of a shy, awkward teenager and her friendship with a boy named Daniel. Bree corresponded with her fans by email (actually written by a woman involved with the production). Viewers in turn sent Bree videos they had made. The storylines of *LonelyGirl15* were shaped to some degree on viewers' feedback. Some of the videos contained hints that Bree was possibly being pulled into a sinister cult, and viewers grew increasingly alarmed by her situation. About four months after the first video appeared, however, it was revealed that Bree was actually an actress and that *LonelyGirl15* was a work of fiction, a discovery that brought the series even more attention (the making of *LonelyGirl15* is discussed in Chapter 25).

Though *LonelyGirl15* was by far the best known of these webcam dramas, it was not the first. Two such works, *Online Caroline* and *Planet Jemma*, were produced several years earlier in the UK, and *KateModern*, a sister series of *LonelyGirl15*, was launched in 2007, one year after *LonelyGirl15*. It was produced in the UK and made for Bebo, and used many elements from the *LonelyGirl15* plotline.

COMEDY SHORTS

Comedy shorts are immensely popular on the Web. Because they are amusing, and usually just a few minutes long, they work extremely well as a form of "snack-o-tainment." Many of these shorts tackle subject matter that would be considered in bad taste or too extreme for mainstream TV, further adding to their popularity. In some cases, a site will be an amalgamation of the work of various writers and producers. For example, *Icebox* specializes in animated shorts written by some of Hollywood's funniest writers. *Funny or Die*, founded by actor Will Ferrell, is another site with a great number of shorts, which are mostly shot in full motion video and seem to be primarily targeted to young males.

In many cases, a comedy will be a stand-alone work and not part of an amalgamated site. *Orlando's Joint* (http://blip.tv/orlandosjoint), for example, runs on Blib but is a stand-alone comedy. This animated series is set in the inner city and features a pot-smoking young man who runs a coffee shop.

INTERACTIVE MYSTERIES AND ADVENTURES

Although not at all as numerous compared to Web series and other forms of Internet narratives, interactive mysteries and adventures are a dynamic form of Web entertainment. Such narratives give viewers the opportunity to become a participant in a story and solve a crime or a mystery, sometimes for prize money. For example, *Save My Husband*, which will be discussed in Chapter 18, solicits the help of viewers in finding a man who has been kidnapped. In *Underground Bounty Hunter*, viewers "become" bounty hunters and try to track down a villain without getting wounded, captured, or killed. *Jamie Kane*, which was produced by the BBC, was a story about the mysterious death of a fictional British pop star and participants were asked to determine how he died.

The episodic mystery series *Stranger Adventures* sent viewers on a new adventure each week to help a character find a hidden treasure. Debuting in 2006, it was an anthology series, a form rare to the Web. A new story came online each week on a Sunday and ran until the following Saturday. It was a new kind of genre for the Internet and creating it was full of challenges for the development team. In devising this series, the producers chose to break new ground and take Internet entertainment in an entirely new direction. But in doing so, they took care to invest a great deal of creative energy early on to get the series off to a good start. They produced a demo episode and conducted five focus groups before moving ahead with the series.

The stories thrust viewers into a first-person drama that began when an individual they do not know (the "stranger" of the title) urgently requests their help in finding a treasure of some kind. Each story featured a different stranger with a different need for help, and finding the treasure required cracking a 10-digit code, which was done by uncovering clues embedded in the story. The first viewer to succeed received a thank you gift in the form of $25,000 in cash. Thus, *Stranger Adventures* combined some of the features of TV drama with some elements of video games, creating a unique narrative genre (see Figure 16.4).

Richie Solomon, the Supervising Producer of the series, described it as "a story that takes an ordinary person on an extraordinary adventure." The drama unfolded in real time through the emails and videos—usually several a day—sent to you by the stranger. If the stranger found herself in trouble and needed your help at 3:30 in the morning, for example, you would receive a communication from her at 3:30 in the morning. "Our format was something entirely new," Solomon said. "Our stories were extremely personal. The viewer needed to feel like the protagonist was talking directly to them. It was very intimate and confessional. It shattered the fourth wall." The pilot was so successful that it earned the show an Emmy nomination (the series went on to receive two more Emmy nominations).

Solomon, who was involved in hiring the writers for first season, told me how challenging many writers found this new form of writing to be. "Our writers had to relearn storytelling," he said. "Many of the writers we interviewed in the beginning of the season just couldn't get it … It's definitely a challenge to write a story that is told through video one moment and then through a text e-mail the next and then through a series of interactive animations, all the while keeping the adventure engaging and exciting from one day to the next. And the writer must provide ample material for the designers, animators, and puzzle master to work with, all the while keeping these separate elements organic to the storytelling."

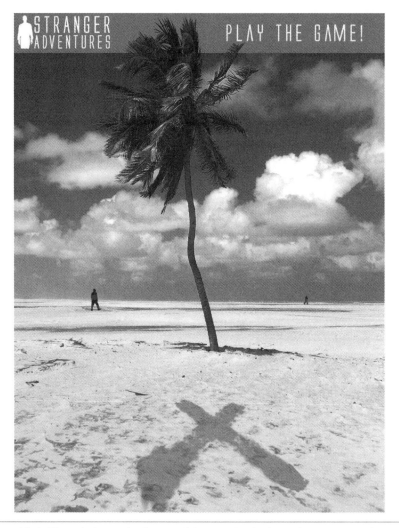

Figure 16.4 The anthology series *Stranger Adventures* involved users in a new interactive mystery each week. Image courtesy of Riddle Productions, Inc.

NOTES FROM THE FIELD: WHY SUSPENSE WORKS

Over time, Solomon told me, the creative staff found that the more suspenseful stories in the series received better viewer feedback. "You almost had to end every communication from the stranger with its own cliffhanger," he said. "That way the viewers were eagerly anticipating and actively checking for the next communication."

CONCLUSION

As we have seen, the Internet has successfully recovered from the dot-com bust at the turn of the millennium and has proven to be a robust vehicle for new kinds of entertainment experiences. In this chapter, we have seen some compelling examples of how stories developed for the Web can be told differently than stories developed for other media, especially TV. The most innovative of these new kinds of narratives are participatory and use a variety of Web-based technologies to advance the storyline. Many also break the fourth wall and blur reality and fiction in intriguing ways.

In addition to the genres discussed in this chapter, we have touched elsewhere in this book on other forms being used on the Web. They include: games of all kinds; virtual worlds; and music videos. And, as we saw in Chapter 3, Google Maps have been used as a storytelling device. It was utilized in a thriller called *21 Steps*.

In addition to forms already touched on, at least one soap opera has been developed for the Web, a work called *Crescent Heights*, which was produced for Tide. Another genre that might or might not gain traction is something called *lifecasting*. In lifecasting, a wearable camera is attached to a person, and the subject is videotaped live as he or she goes through the day. It's a little like an episode of Big Brother, but with only one participant. Lifecasting offers interactivity, because viewers can communicate with the subject with a chat window or cellphone.

Of course, we can have wonderful interactive stories that defy categorization. *Duck Has An Adventure* (http://e-merl.com/stuff/duckadv.html), for example, is an unpretentious interactive story about a duck. You, the user, can decide what the duck will do. He can go on a pirate adventure, acquire an education, or find romance. The story is told primarily in panels, like a comic strip, with occasional text and many quacks, and there are some surprises in the tale. It's a simple story told in a simple way, but highly interactive and charming.

As the Internet continues to mature, we can expect to see new kinds of narratives that will advance the art of digital storytelling on this medium. Some will succeed and some will fall by the wayside, but one thing we can count on: the Internet will continue to offer us new kinds of stories.

IDEA-GENERATING EXERCISES

1. Select a website that has story-rich content. What demographic do you think this content is designed to attract and why do you think this group would find it appealing? How, if at all, does it use the special attributes of the Web? What about it, if anything, do you think users might dislike? Can you suggest anything that might make it more enjoyable?

2. Sketch out an idea for an original fiction-based work for the Internet. How would you make it "sticky?" How could users become involved with the content?

3. Select a character you are extremely familiar with from a TV show or movie and write several entries for a faux blog in this person's voice. Alternatively, create a fictional character of your own and write a portion of this person's blog.

4. Many people enjoy dramas on the Internet that, like *Rachel's Room, LonelyGirl15*, and *Ben's Dive Blog*, are works of fiction but seem real. Other people, however, object to stories that blur fiction and reality in this way, feeling they are a form of lying and deception. What are your views of such stories, and why?

CHAPTER 17

Mobile Devices and Apps

How are portable devices like mobile phones and tablet computers being used for entertainment purposes?

What are some of the unique features of mobile devices that make them attractive as platforms for digital storytelling and other forms of entertainment?

What are some of the approaches app developers are using for digital storytelling?

THE METAMORPHOSIS OF THE TELEPHONE

Just a few short years ago, we used our telephones for just one purpose: to talk with other people. It was a convenient method of verbal communication. But thanks to the development of mobile phones, particularly smart phones, the possibilities for the once strictly utilitarian telephone have expanded exponentially. Smart phones are cell phones that can perform many of the functions of a computer, but in a far smaller package. Consider some of the things we can do with smart phones that we could never dream of doing with our old phones:

- send and receive text messages;
- connect to the Internet;
- take, send, and view digital photos;
- take, send, and watch videos (and even live-stream two-way videos);
- scan barcodes and QR codes;
- utilize apps;
- get updates on news, sports, and weather;
- use embedded GPS (Global Positioning System) technology and a compass;

- listen to music;
- watch comedy shows, cartoons, and dramas; and
- play games.

Clearly, the old rotary-dial telephone with its cumbersome cord has evolved into something far more sophisticated. The same goes for our computers, which once sat impressively on our desks and were often too heavy to lift. Over the years, though, thanks to technology, computers became lighter and more portable, and now many of us work exclusively on laptop computers. But in 2010—drum roll, please!—we were presented with the iPad, a portable computer that was just the size of a magazine but could do so much more than our old laptops! Since then, we have been flooded with new kinds of tablets. Many have cameras, microphones, accelerometers, and virtual keyboards, and most functions can be performed by swiping a touchscreen. Tablet computers can do virtually everything our older computers can do, even though they are not as useful for major computing tasks as our old desktops and laptops. Nevertheless, many analysts predict that tablets are killing off the older, larger forms of computers. In fact, laptop shipments declined recently for the first time since 2001 (from Shelley Palmer's blog, January 27, 2013).

The spread of cell phones across the globe has occurred with remarkable speed. The first cell phones were tested in 1979 in Chicago and Japan. By 2013, in less than 35 years, the International Telecommunications Union (ITU), a special agency of the UN, reported there were 6.8 billion active cell phone subscribers around the world, almost one subscriber for every person on Earth!

STRANGE BUT TRUE: CELL PHONES MORE POPULAR THAN TOOTHBRUSHES!

An infographic published by Digital Buzz (http://www.digitalbuzzblog.com/social-media-statistics-stats-2012-infographic/) noted that by early January 2012, although almost five billion people owned a cell phone, only 4.2 billion owned a toothbrush. Though this is a statistic that should make mobile developers happy, it is unlikely to please dentists!

It should be noted that the popularity of mobile devices and apps has spurred a new branch of the economy, the so-called app economy, and has been credited with creating 800,000 jobs worldwide since 2007 (as reported by the trade group TechNet).

THE PROGENITOR: A SNAKE

Given the short history of the mobile phone and the tablet computer, an impressive amount of entertainment, some of it highly innovative, has already been developed for this plat-form. Oddly enough, it was a serpent that started it all, the star of the mobile game, *Snake*. Nokia introduced *Snake*, a retooling of an old video game, in 1997 as a novelty on a new line of phones. Though it is rudimentary by today's standards, it is still being played. And, like the appearance of the serpent in the biblical Garden of Eden, its arrival on the wireless scene served as a major eye-opener, bringing about a dramatic change in perception. Before the arrival of *Snake*, we regarded our telephone as a utility device; thanks to *Snake*, we were able to see its potential for entertainment.

In the years since *Snake* first slithered across the screens of the world's cell phones, entertainment on mobile devices has evolved dramatically. Much of this entertainment comes to us in the form of apps. Downloading and utilizing apps is one of the popular functions of smart phones and tablets. An app (short for application) is a small dedicated program or piece of software that can be downloaded to a portable device like a phone or tablet to fulfill a particular function. Apps can be games, ebooks, or even a utilitarian program that turns your phone into a flashlight. The two most popular operating systems for apps are Apple's iOS (which used to stand for iPhone Operating System, but is now used for all Apple mobile devices) and Google's Android, a Linux-based operating system. Although there are other mobile operating systems, Apple and Google apps have been in a neck and neck race for popularity across the Globe. However, in the middle of 2013, Google became the winner when the Google Play store passed the one million mark, offering over one million apps for downloading, while Apple's iTunes trailed behind slightly at about 900,000 apps. ABI research estimated that by the end of 2013, consumers will have downloaded an astounding 70 billion apps, which works out to 10 apps for every person on Earth!

Owners of mobile devices appreciate receiving entertainment in this new way because it is immensely portable and because it offers content in bite-sized, easily consumed pieces. It's the perfect solution to those situations in life that are usually entertainment dead zones: riding elevators, waiting for buses, or sitting around in waiting rooms.

STRANGE BUT TRUE: APPS FOR APES

It turns out that humans are not the only species that enjoys playing with apps when things get a little boring—orangutans are highly enthusiastic about apps, too! *Apps for Apes* is a program in about 13 zoos worldwide designed to give these highly intelligent primates more stimulation. They are fond of a variety of different apps, such as playing the drums, finger painting, playing games, and watching videos, and are particularly excited about being able to interact with the tablets. They are given a choice of apps to use, and each orangutan seems to have his or her own preferences. As of yet, however, they can only interact with them through a small opening in the bars of their cages; they are regarded as too powerful to be allowed to hold the tablets themselves. The orangutans respond to tablets much like humans, with the young ones particularly excited about them. But a zoo in Miami (not part of this program but doing its own work with iPads) has discovered that its two oldest orangutans, unlike the young ones, respond much like seniors in the human species, and are not particularly interested in them.

Developers of entertainment content have also quickly gravitated to mobile devices, and for a number of reasons, including:

- they are an extremely common device, dwarfing the number of game consoles and computers in comparison, and thus offer a vast potential audience;

- mobile phone subscribers are highly diverse demographically, making it possible to reach new groups of users;

- the technology allows for fresh content to be offered on the fly;

- many apps are offered to consumers as a purchase, and even though the price is usually modest, it is often not free, unlike Web content;

- mobile devices are conducive to the use of social media, giving them a community-building aspect;

- producing content for mobile devices generally costs less than other forms of entertainment, such as TV shows and video games, and the development period is usually shorter as well.

STRANGE BUT TRUE: CELL PHONE DEPENDENCY

Along with all the positive aspects of mobile devices, there is at least one downside: people can become overly dependent on them. According to a study by TeleNav, Inc., more than half of Americans would rather do without caffeine, alcohol, or chocolate than part temporarily with their cell phones. Another third would give up sex; 20 percent would give up their toothbrushes, and 21 percent would do without shoes before they would do without their mobile phones. As a testament to their devotion to these devices, 66 percent of people surveyed reported sleeping with their cell phones next to them in bed.

GOOD FOR THE LITTLE ONES?

As many parents of babies and toddlers have discovered, their tots are enormous fans of tablet computers and can operate them almost instantly, without any instruction. Though their small hands still lack the dexterity to operate a mouse, a computer keyboard, or video game console, they can easily operate a touchscreen, and they are delighted when it responds. It's a form of instant gratification. But, parents wonder, is this a good thing or a bad thing for my child? Unfortunately, no one knows for sure. The touchscreen tablet is so new that very little scientific testing has been done on it. These little tots are, in a way, human guinea pigs.

What can be documented is the popularity of these digital devices with young users. Common Sense Media in San Francisco reported that by late 2013, 7 out of 10 children younger than 8 had used a mobile device, a figure that had doubled in only two years. Another study reported that over 80 percent of the top-selling apps in the educational category were for children and 72 percent of these were for preschoolers or elementary aged children (from the iLearn II study by the Joan Ganz Cooney Center at Sesame Workshop). Still another study reported that while 21 percent of 4–5-year-olds could operate a smart phone, only 14 percent of them could tie their shoes! (from *The Wall Street Journal*, January 19, 2011). And, in an unscientific but compelling viral video, we can watch a little one-year-old girl swipe and pinch a magazine, thinking it is an iPad, and finally declaring in frustration: "It not work!" A little later she is seen gleefully playing with an iPad.

With older children, cell phone ownership is almost universal. A Pew Report showed that 78 percent of youngsters aged between 12 and 17 have cell phones, and half of these phones are smart phones. It is extremely common for these older kids to use their phones, rather than computers, to access the Internet.

When it comes to touchscreen tablets and apps, parents worry about a variety of things, including:

- that the app or mobile device will be scrambling their tots' delicate little brains and impairing their ability to focus and develop social skills instead of being a tool for enrichment;
- that the apps are collecting personal information about their child;
- that their child will be taken advantage of and enticed into buying alluring-seeming add-ons to their apps;
- that the app will cause family friction, with the child wanting to play with it during dinner time or at other times when parents want a face-to-face relationship with the child; and
- that even though the parents might realize that a mobile device allows them to stay in contact with their child, which is a plus, their child can easily gain access to inappropriate materials.

As a content creator of mobile apps, we must be aware and respectful of these concerns. Although many of them are not within our powers to address, we can certainly accept the responsibility of developing quality content and not mindless fluff. To a large extent, it is a business decision rather than a creative one about whether or not we will develop content that will require additional purchases from the young user to move forward in the story or game. If we do decide to employ such a business model, however, the ethical approach is to offer such add-ons judiciously and only when they genuinely enhance the app.

Ongoing research still needs to be done to determine if using apps is a positive or negative thing for young minds. Such research is being done at PBS Kids, and according to PBS Kids Interactive Vice President Sara DeWitt, "We do a great deal of testing in the development process of our apps, and have also done some of the earliest studies in the kids mobile apps space to test our apps for educational impact." She said that a past study showed that children that played with one of their apps made significant learning gains, including a 31 percent increase in vocabulary skills. She also said: "We believe that mobile apps can be great learning tools for children—they can help provide learning moments on the go and can encourage children to look at the world around them" (as quoted in *Wired* magazine by writer Daniel Donahoo, July 27, 2012).

MOBILE'S SPECIAL CHALLENGES AND OPPORTUNITIES

Despite the enormous potential audience for mobile entertainment, and despite its many attractions for content creators, developing entertainment in this arena poses a unique set of significant challenges. For one thing, content creators must find ways to cope with tiny screen space, though this is less of an issue with full-sized tablet computers. In addition, it can be extremely difficult for the "little guys" who make games of mobile devices to market their products and to compete against the major players like Gameloft, Electronic Arts, and Rovio. And though on the plus side, mobile phones are something you always have with you and are always available, they also come with a host of new technologies to deal with, including:

- the *touchscreen*, which lets people employ fingers on the screen to touch and drag content, slide objects up and down or around the screen, and pinch to decrease or widen fingers to increase the content's size;

- a *QR code reader*, which is used to read a QR code, a type of bar code made up of black bars arranged into a square (see Figure 17.1);

- the *accelerometer*, which can compute roll and pitch;

- the *gyroscope*, which, when combined with the accelerometer, can compute how fast, how far, and in which direction an object has moved;

- a *compass*, which can be used to determine geographic direction;

- *face time* (Google Hangouts via Android or Skype on both) which is used to make video calls; and

- a *camera*, which can be used to take still photos or video, and even stream live video.

Though not all mobile devices come with all of these elements, most of them are common on smart phones, and developers need to be aware of what they can do and how they can possibly contribute to a story experience.

Bill Klein is someone who found some ways to address the challenges facing small mobile developers. Klein is now CEO of Rival Theory, a company that creates a new generation of smart NPCs, but he used to make mobile games when he headed Extreme AI, Inc. According to Klein, while you can't compete directly against the big companies, which have enormous resources, "you can compete in terms of novel ideas." Klein told me it is important not to look at mobile devices as "just a piece of hardware for playing video games, but as a device with special attributes, especially involving communications." He believes in order to compete, developers need to come up with new ways to incorporate these special attributes into the games they make.

http://reader.kaywa.com

cityofriddles.com   8675309

Figure 17.1 A QR code from *The Q Game*. Image courtesy of Extreme AI, Inc.

His company did just that when it developed and ran a multi-month game called *The Q Game: City of Riddles* (see Figure 17.2). "Q" is a nickname for Albuquerque, where the game was played, and the slogan for the game is "Do you Q?" Sponsored by local businesses, it was a community-based game that combined puzzle solving and a story with quest-like missions. Some of the clues contained images of unique landmarks in Albuquerque (see Figure 17.2). Klein and his team managed to develop a game that made good use of some of the unique qualities of mobile devices, yet by keeping it local and community-based, they did so in a way that was manageable by a small start-up and that did not directly compete with major game companies.

Figure 17.2 This old gas pump is a local landmark in Albuquerque and was one of the clues in *The Q Game*. Image courtesy of Extreme AI, Inc.

Players were dispatched to real-world locations to find clues, which in turn led them to other clues. For example, they were sent to an art museum to try to find a specific artwork. If they succeeded at locating it they would be startled to receive a call on their mobile while still standing in front of the artwork. The call would give them instructions for their next mission. Players were also asked to use their phones to photograph a QR code, which would then unlock a website offering an important clue.

Though set in the contemporary world, the narrative of *The Q Game* is based on Greek mythology. Klein describes the game this way: "The storyline is based on the return of the mythical Greek Titans to our world. In the game, the Titans are ordinary people, many of whom don't realize what they are. As the story progresses, one of the Titans enlists the aid of the players to reawaken the others and prepare them all for the coming conflict with Zeus." According to Klein, the clues are "not just interesting for their own sake but are relevant to the content of story or else lead you further into the game."

MOBILE DEVICES AND DIGITAL STORYTELLING

Just as *Snake* evolved into more sophisticated forms of games, character-based entertainment on mobile devices has also been evolving. In 2001, when cell phone graphics were still extremely primitive, a Finnish company, Riot-E, thought of a clever way to use text messages as a storytelling device. At the time, the movie *Bridget Jones' Diary*, the story of the world's most miserable unmarried woman, was a huge hit. Riot-E offered subscribers short daily SMS (SMS stands for Short Message Service) updates "written" by Bridget herself. For instance, one of her communications, referring to her dismal text-messaging habits, reads: "Text messages from Daniel: 0 (bad). Text messages sent and received regarding lack of text messages from Daniel: 492 (very, very bad)." Bridget also conducted polls, asking her wireless friends their opinion of the following: "Valentine's Day should be banned by law. Reply with Y/N." With *Bridget Jones' Diary*, Riot-E cleverly used SMS technology in a way that fit snugly with the persona of the fictional Bridget, and it was a big hit for its time.

Since 2001, when *Bridget Jones' Diary* was being played, several important new genres of storytelling have been introduced on mobile devices. They include:

- *Ebooks*, which are electronic books that are read on mobile devices. Ebooks vary a great deal in terms of the interactive features they offer. Some are very pure, with only text and sometimes illustrations, and only offer the user the ability to turn the page forward or backwards. Others offer video, animation, sound (often a voice narrating the story), pop-up elements, words that light up as the story is being narrated, and a connection to the Internet. Some even go beyond that, and send "readers" on a quest into real life, which can be to make an art project and to solve a mystery. They may have the reader call a telephone number, solve puzzles, read Facebook posts, or "look over" evidence, like letters or files. One particularly interactive ebook is *Little Red Riding Hood* from Nosy Crow, which offers multiple paths to Grandma's and eight possible endings.

- *Interactive adventures* using mobile devices are adventures set in real places but use mobile devices to guide players from one location to another while picking up clues. At least two such adventures have been made for Disney properties. The *Menahune Adventure Trail* is set at Disney's Aulani Resort Hotel in Hawaii. Players are given a specially designed mobile device, about the size of a cell phone, and sent on a scavenger-hunt-like quest involving the Menahune, or the magical little people of the islands who are somewhat like Ireland's leprechauns. As one goes on the adventure and finds a correct location, their mobile device can light torches and make rocks move and make drums play, and there's an Hawaiian auntie to call if one needs help. Another mobile adventure game, this one set at Disney's Epcot Theme Park, is *Disney Phineas and Ferb: Agent P's World Showcase Adventure*. As with the Hawaiian adventure, players use a special mobile device to follow clues in one of several different pavilions at Epcot.

- *Appisodes* are serialized stories, either animated or in video, that are made as apps, to be used on mobile devices. Unlike a webisode, an appisode often incorporates interactive features. Players can tap on characters on the screen to make them talk, find hidden objects, or collect items as part of a quest. Although some appisodes are simply linear stories, others contain a wealth of interactive features. As an example, a 13-part appisode series featuring Nurse Jeffrey, called *In House*, was made for the TV series *House*.

- *Character-based activities* are apps that heavily rely on characters to make them entertaining. For example, *Talking Friends* is a menagerie of interactive characters who will repeat anything you say, but in a funny voice. You can even poke them and feed them. One of them, Talking Angela, will even engage in a two-way conversation with you. These characters are so popular that they achieved a major landmark in 2013: one billion downloads.

- *Serialized movies* are being made for the iPad. They are much like appisodes but the episodes are longer. *Haunting Melissa* is an episodic horror movie that is being released at staggered intervals, and people who buy this app never know when they will receive another installment.

MOBILE GAMES

Snake pioneered the way for games on mobile devices, and they have become one of the most successful forms of apps. Mobile games contain varying degrees of narrative, much like games played on other digital platforms, and they offer built-in interactivity. Almost any type of game found on other platforms can be found on mobile devices: puzzle games, shooters, strategy games, racing games, war games, and even single-player versions of MMOGs.

The *Angry Birds* games alone have been downloaded by 1.7 billion people around the world and the birds have become a stunning phenomenon in their own right, spawning flush toys, playground equipment, t-shirts, and dozens of other spin-offs. Essentially, *Angry Birds* is a casual game with dozens of levels and sequels. The initial concept was extremely simple: some pigs have stolen eggs from a group of birds, and the birds wreck revenge by flinging themselves, via sling shots, at the pigs. Other than that, there is no story. Like all casual games, it is easy to learn to play but becomes increasingly difficult with each level and is increasingly addictive.

In contrast, *Alt-Minds*, a paranormal thriller, had an extremely rich narrative. It was an eight-week transmedia game based in Europe that relied heavily on mobile devices, but also used the Internet and involved geo-locative content. The story involved five brilliant young researchers who were kidnapped from Belgrade University and the mystery of why they disappeared. Players became investigators in the case and became heavily involved with helping to solve the mystery. It was played out in real time, but those who were not in Europe while the game was being played out, or who missed playing the live version, can still purchase the game (http://www.alt-minds.com/home.html?lang=en). The multi-lingual game was produced by Orange Transmedia and Lexis-Numerique.

CREATING CONTENT FOR MOBILE DEVICES

Because mobile devices and apps are quite new as storytelling platforms, the creative community is still learning which approaches work best and which lead to mediocre productions. I interviewed several experts on the topic to learn from their expertise.

One of my experts was Kate Wilson, the managing director of Nosy Crow, a UK publisher of ebooks and print books for children. Wilson told me in an email interview that most of their ideas for ebooks are generated internally, and "what sets these ideas apart is that the narratives have been imagined with interactivity embedded in them." And, she added, they are stories that "would work particularly well on screen." In contrast, she noted, "there are many stories that are simple, linear narratives, and/or stories told in rhyme which would be disrupted by having interactivity shoe-horned into them. There are many things that the printed page does best. Simply adding bells and whistles to a story that would be told better in a linear, non-interactive, text-and-illustration format isn't interesting to us."

In terms of ebooks, she told me that at Nosy Crow, they were often attracted to fairy tales "because they have such flexibility – they can be told in lots of different ways." She noted that they try to use interactivity appropriately. For example, in adapting Cinderella to an app, which opens "with Cinderella as a put-upon second-class citizen, we focus the interactivity of helping Cinderella with her chores. Later, when the story is about magical transformation, we focus the interactivity on that aspect of the story." She strongly believes in using interactivity appropriately, telling me that "I personally don't think there's much benefit in taking an existing picture book, adding a few sound effects and some animation loops, and thinking that you've made an interactive story. I think that the best apps are native to the devices, rather than translated from another medium."

I also interviewed Warren Buckleitner, the editor of *Children's Technology Review* and an acknowledged expert on children's digital media. I asked Buckleitner what he thought one should begin with when creating an app, and I was pleased, given my focus on storytelling, when he told me: "a good story is always the most important starting point. Good narrative is essential. If you don't start with good narrative, then you can't do anything whether it's in print or in digital. But people sometimes forget … they think they can just make an app and it will somehow magically help out." He also noted that you shouldn't talk down to children when making an app for them and, putting it beautifully, said the goal should be "to empower a young finger."

He advised a person setting out to make an app to study the market, especially the most successful works, and ask yourself if you can compete. He feels that adding special features can be dangerous, because serious money can be lost trying to compete with big companies like Disney or Rovio. Maybe, he suggested, you should not even try to add special features, and instead "let [children's] own software in their brain do the work." But if you are determined to use special features, he feels a good question to ask is "What can I turn the child's finger into that could never be done before?" For example, in the *War Horse* ebook, users could spin a soldier's helmet around and see it in 3D from all sides. In addition, geographic references are linked to real-time locations that are shown in Google Earth. "You might be surprised to see what was once a battlefield is now a shopping center," he told me. And in the *Voyage of Ulysses* app, users could actually take the tiller of Ulysses' sailboat and sail the boat themselves. These breakthrough ways of using the touch screen made these two works outstanding.

Buckleitner calls skillful ways of using interactivity "embedded reinforcement," meaning that "it has direct link to the narrative to help support your intended goal as a storyteller." And he pointed to a couple of things that he and others in the field believe can weaken an interactive project. One is an approach he terms a "page flipper"—an interactive book build around a navigation metaphor from the past, with the only interactivity being the ability to turn the pages. He notes, though, that some page flippers are actually quite good as ebooks, so one should not make a blanket rule against them. But, on the negative side, he told me that "sprinkles" can seriously undermine a project. Sprinkles, he said, were hot spots that trigger little animations that are scattered around the page that do not support the narrative in any way. He noted if you use hot spots, everything on the page that could come to life should have that capacity. For instance, if you have a kitchen scene with a toaster on the counter, children are naturally going to want to touch the toaster to see what it will do, and if it is lifeless, it will be disappointing. In sum, he said, imagination and authenticity are two important elements in creating apps, and that "the innovators will be richly rewarded because they can figure out how to use all this new potential ... That's why I say it is an art as much as it is a science."

I also talked with Grace Chen, a digital artist and user interface (UI) designer, to see what insights she could give me. She told me that when creating graphic images for an app, she was always guided by the context of the story. For instance, if the story was about the Wild West, she would use images relating to cowboys, while if it was an outer space-themed story, then images of stars or spaceships might be appropriate. Chen has been working on the *Yumby* series of games, which features a set of odd-looking little characters in different settings. In one game, *Yumby Smash*, they fling themselves at buildings infiltrated with monsters. The game has a steampunk theme, so the UI here uses steampunk-like imagery that is in keeping with the theme (see Figure 17.3). Chen said color, sound, and motion all come into play when designing the interface for an app, and she advises that text should be used very sparingly. She also noted that interface design for apps has a number of special challenges, such as the small screen size and the different aspect ratios between devices. Scaling the same app for different screen sizes, she said, is possible in most cases but made things more complicated. She told me most art can be re-used, but needs to be created with scalability in mind. In addition, she told me that designing works for children and for adults involves very different design issues. Sometimes, for instance, it is difficult to create an icon that both adults and children would recognize as the same thing, since their experiences of the object might be so different.

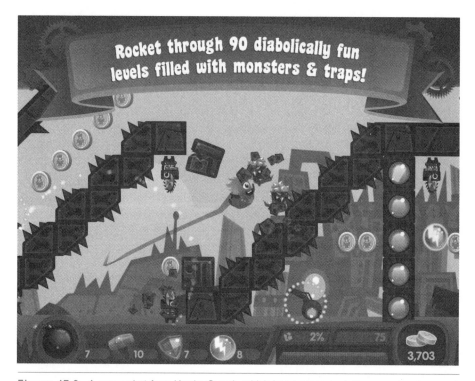

Figure 17.3 A screenshot from *Yumby Smash*, which has a steampunk theme and a steampunk UI. Image courtesy of PlayGearz, Inc. (www.Yumby.com).

Clearly, based on everything Wilson, Buckleitner, and Chen told me, story is central when creating an app, just as it is with other forms of digital storytelling, and the interactivity should spring from the narrative. But beyond that, there are dozens of issues to consider and a host of challenges to contend with. One question developers must ask and answer is whether they wish to focus their efforts on building native apps (ones that are made to run on a specific platform or device, and which must be installed in order to play) or whether to create a mobile Web app (which can access Web-based content directly through the Web browser on the device). In coming years, as more apps continue to be developed, we can expect that certain standard conventions will be developed for these mobile forms of entertainment. On one hand, that will make things easier for mobile content creators, but on the other hand, we may no longer see amazing innovations in the field.

PUTTING MOBILE DEVICES TO PRACTICAL USE

Businesses and educational entities have begun to see the potential of using mobile devices to teach and promote, and experimental projects using apps are underway, as well. Many of these projects are using entertainment techniques to accomplish their goals. As we have already seen in this chapter, there has been an explosion of apps developed for early childhood education.

In addition, projects have been developed for children with special needs, such as autism, and apps have been found to be an effective way of teaching them. And in a remote village in India, where homes have no running water and where even the local school lacks electricity, an experimental program has been instituted using tablet computers to teach educational basics, like colors and shapes, to the village children. They have responded with great enthusiasm and have mastered the new concepts, as you can see in this video tape of the project: http://www.youtube.com/watch?v=e4dnInmzm7o&feature=youtu.be. Adult literacy projects are underway, as well. In Spain, under the National Reading Plan, posters with QR codes have been placed in trains, and people with smart phones can use the QR codes to access the first chapters of several dozen books.

In another project aimed at adults, about 10 bulky wildlife guides in Florida have been merged into a single app called the *Ultimate Guide to Florida Nature*. Now, nature enthusiasts have a single small device to help them identify birds, mammals, reptiles, amphibians, fish, seashells, and plants, and, thanks to the audio this app contains, they can also listen to bird songs and identify birds through sound.

STRANGE BUT TRUE: SMART PHONES AS MUSICAL INSTRUMENTS

Students at the University of Michigan have been experimenting with ways to turn their smart phones into musical instruments, learning to design, build, and play them. Their professor, Georg Essl, said of the work he and his students are doing: "We're not tethered to the physics of traditional instruments. We can do interesting, weird, unusual things. This kind of technology is in its infancy, but it's a hot and growing area to use iPhones for artistic expression" (reported by Reuters, March 12, 2009). These new "instruments" utilize many of the unique attributes of the smart phone, including the touchscreen, the microphone, the GPS, the compass, and the accelerometer. One day, perhaps, we will have a new Beethoven who will be able to create a symphony for smartphones!

The US military, of course, always an early adopter of technology, is using smart phones and tablets to relay critical videos to troops on the ground. Meanwhile, commercial ventures with mobile devices abound. In 2013, mobile global advertising became a $8.9 billion business, a jump of 83 percent in a single year. Merchants are now employing something called *SoLoMo* to attract customers. The term is a mash-up of the words social, local, and mobile, and is a way of targeting consumers with information about retailers, often with special offers, based on their proximity to that place of business. Mobile promotion for business can be quite playful, of course. When the movie *Harry Potter and the Half-Blood Prince* came out, an app was developed that let players participate in the world of the film. They could even insert photos of themselves in a fictional newspaper, *The Daily Prophet*.

As to be expected, many mobile promotional ventures are more earnest, such as the World Wildlife Fund's *WWF Together*. This app tells the stories of eight threatened species of wildlife. Users can try out different activities such as "seeing" with tiger vision or "eating" bamboo like a panda. They can also play games and learn to make origami versions of the threatened animals, all in the hopes that the living animals will never be replaced by the paper ones.

A FEW CONSIDERATIONS

Mobile entertainment is evolving so quickly that it is difficult to nail down guidelines for how such projects should be developed. However, a few overall considerations can be extrapolated from the examples we have studied here and from comments made by professionals in the field. In general:

- Make the story central to your major creative decisions. Does it lend itself to interactivity? What sort of visual approach does it lend itself to? What would players gain by the story becoming interactive rather than being told in a linear fashion?

- If you want your content to stand out, be as original as possible, not derivative of works found on other media.

- Use the technology unique to mobile devices judiciously and as much as possible be innovative with it. Don't try to compete with the major mobile producers but aim to create your own individual approach to mobile content.

- When at all feasible, offer users a way to actively participate in the content.

- When at all feasible, promote social interaction among users.

- If a game, make it rewarding for the time invested, even if the player does not win.

- If a game, make it relatively simple to learn and fun for players who are not hard-core gamers.

- If story-based, the characters should have vivid personalities and their motivations should be clear.

- Use visuals that come through clearly on a small screen.

ADDITIONAL RESOURCES

To learn more about mobile entertainment and developments in the mobile industry, some helpful resources are:

- *GameSpot Mobile* (http://www.gamespot.com/mobile/index.html), which offers reviews of games and wireless devices as well as general articles on wireless entertainment.

- The Mobile Entertainment Forum (http://mobileentertainmentforum.org/), which is a global trade organization for the mobile industry.

- The LinkedIn group, MEF (Mobile Content), which offers free, expert information on mobile content: http://www.linkedin.com/groups/ Mobile-Content-61398?gid=61398&mostPopular=&trk=tyah&trkInfo= tas%3AMobile%20content%2Cidx%3A1-1-1.

- Fierce Mobile Content, (http://www.fiercemobileit.com/), which covers news, content, and apps (http://www.fiercemobileit.com/topics/mobile-content-and-services).

- Mobile Magazine (http://www.mobilemag.com/), which covers the mobile world.

- If you wish to enter a completed work in a mobile competition, consider the MoFilms competitions: http://www.mofilm.com/.

CONCLUSION

From the projects we have examined here, it is quite evident that mobile platforms can support a diverse array of entertainment experiences, including story-based narratives. Some of the projects featured in this chapter have made exciting use of the unique attributes of mobile devices and have found innovative ways to involve users. It will be interesting to see what new techniques developers will use in the future to integrate interactivity and narrative into mobile content, especially as increasingly sophisticated mobile devices become more widespread.

When thinking about what can or cannot be done with mobile devices, we must bear in mind that the very first wireless game, *Snake*, made its debut in 1997, a relatively short time ago. This medium is still in its early formative years. We are just beginning to understand its potential, and to comprehend how it may be used as a tool for digital storytelling. Without doubt, innovative digital storytellers will make new breakthroughs in this area and will discover ways to use it that we have not yet imagined.

IDEA-GENERATING EXERCISES

1. Consider the forms of mobile storytelling that you have experienced. What forms have you enjoyed most, and why?

2. Pick a children's fairy tale and try to devise a mobile app that could make the story interactive.

3. In terms of creating content for mobile devices, which factors do you think are most challenging, and why?

4. Pick a consumer product and devise a concept for mobile devices that could promote it.

CHAPTER 18

Alternate Reality Games (ARGs)

What makes alternate reality games different from other forms of gaming?

In the ARGs thus far produced, what techniques have proven to be most successful and why have some not done well?

What are some of the surprising elements that have found their way into ARGs?

How important is narrative in ARGs, and what kinds of stories do these works generally support?

SMUDGING THE BOUNDARY BETWEEN REAL LIFE AND FICTION

In three cities across the United States, dozens of people take part in stormy rallies opposing the emancipation of robots. The protests are real, although they pertain to issues set in the future, in the year 2142, not in 2001, when the rallies actually take place. At about the same time, a young girl sends a moving email to her friends, mourning the death of her grandmother, and she receives 340 sympathetic condolence messages in return. The young girl is a fictional character, but the people who write to her are real. And within that same few weeks, at some unidentified location, a musician tunes up his lute and prepares to play a piece of sixteenth-century music, hoping it will help him find clues to a murder mystery.

What exactly is going on here? As it happens, these people have not collectively lost their minds. Instead, they are all participating in a deeply immersive, narrative-rich game, a sci-fi murder mystery nicknamed *The Beast*. The game belongs to a relatively new but immensely successful genre of interactive entertainment called an alternate reality game, or ARG. *The Beast*, which ran in 2001, was the world's first ARG.

"THIS IS NOT A GAME"

We first touched on ARGs in Chapter 10, focusing particularly on how they figured into transmedia entertainment, and discussed them again in Chapters 12 and 13, when we examined how they can be used as vehicles for promotion and education. Now, however, let's look at ARGs specifically as a new form of digital storytelling.

ARGs, perhaps more than any other form of digital storytelling, tightly integrate story and game elements together. Typically, ARGS have a strong and complex narrative, but the story is broken into tiny fragments and embedded in a great variety of media assets and other forms of communication. In order to assemble the story and make sense of it, players have to solve a series of puzzles. These games often take players out into the real world in search of clues or to participate in story-related events.

ARGs are such intense experiences for both the players and the developers that they usually run for only a limited span of time, from just a few days to several months. They play out in real time, adding to the intensity of the experience, and unfold much like a serialized story, with new pieces of narrative being unlocked as players solve the puzzles.

ARGs have become so popular that at least several of them are usually running at the same time, and sometimes as many as two dozen or more. The current ones are generally mentioned in a website devoted to ARGs, *ARGNet.com*. The rapid rise of this new form of story-game has caught many people by surprise, for the phenomenon seems to have sprung up from nowhere. In point of fact, however, ARGs are closely related to live role-playing games, which have been around for decades. They also have some of the characteristics of earlier works of digital storytelling, such as *The Blair Witch Project* and *The Spot*, both of which presented fictional stories as true-life events. In addition, the antecedents of ARGs date back to even earlier forms of entertainment, such as mystery novels and scavenger hunts.

People who play ARGs call themselves ARGers, and they are often passionately devoted to the genre. They have coined a mantra for this type of entertainment: "This is not a game." It reflects the way ARGs spill out into the real world, and seem not to be fiction at all. In fact, ARGers use another term to describe works in this genre, "unfiction," which also happens to be the name of another website devoted to ARGs, *unfiction.com*. As a striking case of art imitating art, the characteristic blurring of gameplay and real life in ARGs was captured in 1997 in David Fincher's film, *The Game*, released four years before the first ARG was ever made.

The ARGs that have reached the public thus far have used an astounding variety of media and techniques to impart clues, puzzles, and bits of the story. The Internet has been employed in virtually every way imaginable, including faux websites and blogs, emails, webcams, podcasts, and instant messaging, with much use of audio, video, and animation. Mobile devices have also been pressed into service in a variety of ways, as we will see in Chapter 20, as have landline phones and even pay phones. Faxes, letters, and postcards have also played a role in ARGs, and so have full-length books. In addition, ARGs have partially played out in such "old media" forms of communication as newspapers, magazines, radio and TV commercials, TV shows, posters, and billboards. Clues have even been embedded in jars of honey and public library books. Clue-laden USB flash drives have been hidden in bathroom stalls and critical phone numbers have been written in the sky.

STRANGE BUT TRUE: CELL PHONE CAKES!

One of the most inventive elements of any ARG was a sequence of clues leading to the discovery of working cell phones baked into layer cakes. This clever device was developed for *Why So Serious?*, a game produced in conjunction with the Batman film, *The Dark Knight*. Players were sent on a wild chase to 22 widely disparate addresses and instructed to retrieve an unknown object that would be waiting for them under the name of Robin Banks (robbing banks—Joker humor!). The first 22 people to reach these addresses found them to be bakeries, and the retrieved article turned out to be a cake with a phone number written in the icing. When players called the number, a phone would ring from inside the cake! By digging through the cake, they would find the phone with a new number to call, which would instigate a new series of clues and tasks. The bakeries must have been mystified by these bizarre cakes they were commissioned to make!

Furthermore, virtually all ARGs include staged live events, with professional actors playing the parts of characters in the story. Three particularly dramatic scenes staged for ARGs were a fake fight that broke out at a video game conference; a SWAT team busting into a concert of a well-known band and halting the performance; and an extremely realistic break-in of an automobile showroom and the theft of a valuable car.

In addition to the ARGs which are centered around digital media, two ground-breaking ARGs have been built around prime time television series, as we saw in Chapter 10—the American TV drama, *Push, Nevada*, and the Swedish TV drama, *The Truth About Marika*.

ARGS: PROMOTIONAL VEHICLES OR ART FORM?

Because ARGs are often used as promotional vehicles, there has been some vigorous debate in transmedia and academic circles about whether they should be regarded primarily as a new type of advertising campaign or whether instead they could be considered an art form unto themselves.

While no definitive answer can be offered to this question, it is quite clear that ARGs are not inevitably employed for marketing purposes. Some ARGs are designed as a pure form of entertainment; some are created for educational purposes; still others are studded with factual information and almost serve as works of infotainment. The form is still in its infancy and still evolving. However, ARG producers who work outside of the promotional box continue to struggle with the question of how their work can be funded. The question of whether or not they are a pure art form is a far less pressing issue. As Jordan Weisman, a highly regarded ARG pioneer, put it at a conference at UCLA, "If we don't figure out how to charge for them, we don't have an art form." It should be noted that Weisman was the leader of the creative powerhouse team behind *The Beast*.

THE CREATION OF THE WORLD'S FIRST ARG

The Beast, described at the beginning of this chapter, was produced in 2001 by Microsoft to serve as a stealth marketing device to promote Steven Spielberg's movie, *AI*. The creative work fell to an enormously talented and visionary four-person team, headed up by Executive Producer Jordan Weisman, as noted above. In time, the players would affectionately dub this group "the Puppetmasters," a term that is now applied universally to all ARG creative teams.

Even though *The Beast* was designed to promote a major movie, it did so in a very surreptitious way. It was given no publicity but instead was spread by viral marketing. Furthermore, nothing in the game directly referred to the film. The project was not even given a formal name. According to one team member, it received its nickname, *The Beast*, because at one point its asset list totaled 666 items, the numeric sign of the Devil. *The Beast* name stuck, no doubt in part because its puzzles were so fiendishly difficult to solve and because its story elements were so complex and challenging to piece together.

STORY OR GAME?

The people who played *The Beast* were united by a common goal: to figure out who killed a fictional scientist named Evan Chan, and to learn why he was murdered. The mystery could only be solved by working through a series of complex puzzles. So, did that make *The Beast* a story or a game? With its well-structured story arcs, fully developed characters, and emotional punch, it had strong narrative elements. Yet, unlike other kinds of stories, it was broken into tiny fragments that had to be discovered and pieced together. And the use of puzzles gave it a strong, game-like quality. Unlike a game, however, it had no rules, no prizes, no victory conditions. When all was said and done, it was a new type of experience, both story and game, and not definitively one or the other.

The Beast was "told" in part via everyday methods of communications like telephone calls and emails. It penetrated the real world even further by staging live events, like the anti-robot rallies mentioned earlier. Websites, its major workhorse component, numbered in the hundreds. They looked completely realistic and bore no traceable link to the movie or to Microsoft. Both the copy and the graphic design of these sites were entirely in keeping with the various organizations or individuals who were purported to own them, and, like websites in the real world, they varied enormously in style. The copy for each was written in a manner appropriate for its owner, just as a character in a screenplay speaks in his or her own unique voice. For example, the *Belladerma* website "belonged" to a fictional enterprise that manufactured sexy artificial companions (see Figure 18.1). One of its products, a robot named Venus, is a suspect in the murder mystery.

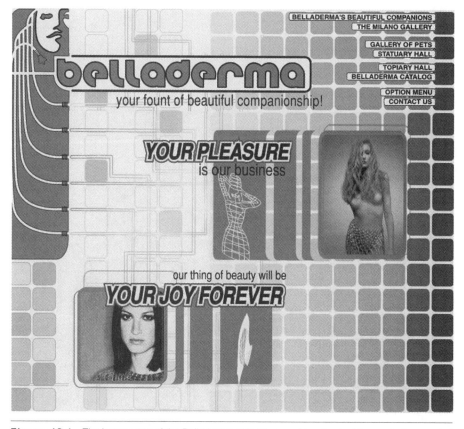

Figure 18.1   The home page of the *Belladerma* website, one of hundreds of faux websites created for *The Beast*. Image courtesy of Microsoft.

Only one aspect of these websites indicated that they were not as real as they seemed to be: they all pertained in one way or another to the future, to the year 2142. Though the players recognized that the mystery was a fiction, and that the story was set decades in the future, the realism of *The Beast* made it possible for them to temporarily suspend disbelief and to plunge fully into the drama.

According to Sean Stewart, the lead writer and co-designer of *The Beast*, the narrative contained five arcs, something like the acts in a play or the movements of a symphony. The plotlines started as far away as possible from the story in the film, but they gradually converged and pointed to the events portrayed in the movie. And although Stewart and others on the creative team controlled the basic beats of the story, they did give the players a hand in shaping certain aspects of the narrative and in giving them a say on how it would end. These openings in the story and the ability to impact the ending is the transmedia and ARG device that has become known as the *cheese hole*. The climax of *The Beast* revolved around whether or not the robots in this futurist world would be emancipated. The Puppetmasters put that decision up to the players, and let them vote on it. "The players genuinely affected the world," Stewart told me. "Their vote determined the fate of intelligent machines."

THE RABBIT HOLE

The first clue that tipped people off to the existence of the game was a strange piece of information included in a trailer for the movie. A woman named Jeanine Salla was given credit as the film's "sentient machine therapist"—in other words, a shrink who treated robots. A little online research by a curious observer of this credit would uncover the puzzling-looking Salla family website, made by Dr. Salla's granddaughter (see Figure 18.2). In turn, it linked to a

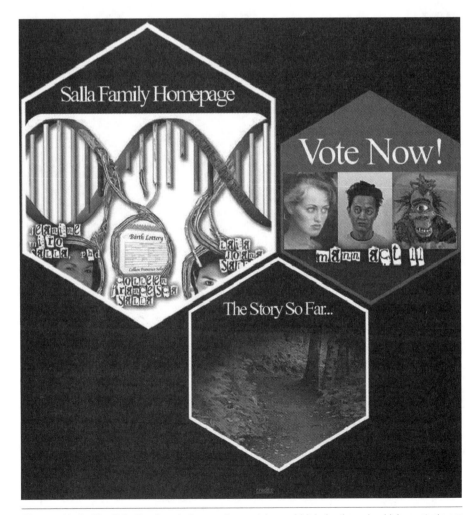

Figure 18.2 The Salla Family website was the portal, or rabbit hole, through which most players entered the futuristic world of *The Beast*. Image courtesy of Microsoft.

number of other odd websites, all set in the future, and the game was off and running. The Salla website was thus the path into the story, an entry point known in ARGs as *the rabbit hole*.

Soon after the game went live, several thousand hard-core players joined forces and worked together in a tightly knit online association, the Cloudmakers. They collaborated in finding and interpreting clues and solving the puzzles, and posted thousands of messages speculating with each other about the twists and turns of the story. This type of player collaboration and socialization has become a hallmark of ARG-playing.

THE PUZZLES

In order to follow the story of Evan Chan and the half-dozen or so other major characters, and to be able to solve the murder mystery, it was necessary to solve the puzzles. The Puppetmasters deliberately constructed them to promote collaborative puzzle solving, which was an enormous gamble, since nothing like this had been tried before. To get the players to work together, the Puppetmasters designed them in such a way that they required a greater sweep of knowledge than any single individual was likely to possess. Some, in order to be solvable, also required critical pieces of information found in geographically separate places. Others called for unusual devices or special technologies like a certain type of Japanese cell phone or sound editing software. Many required fairly uncommon skill sets like translating archaic languages or the ability to read and play sixteenth-century lute tablature.

However, not all the puzzles were meant to be tremendously difficult. Some, especially at the beginning of the game, were designed to appear baffling but to be fairly simple to figure out, to give players confidence in their puzzle-solving capability. For example, the game's chemistry puzzle looks extremely intimidating (see Figure 18.3), but can be worked out by pretty much anyone who thinks of downloading the periodic table of the chemical elements. The solution

Figure 18.3 The chemistry puzzle from *The Beast*. It appears much harder to solve than it actually is. Image courtesy of Microsoft.

to the puzzle spells out "coronersweborg," which is clearly the URL for a website—a coroner's office. Players who visited it could learn more about the murder victim, Evan Chan.

BUT CAN YOU TAKE OUT THE PUZZLES?

But what if you took away the puzzles, or had players who simply didn't want to spend time solving them … could *The Beast* just be enjoyed as a story? Stewart says many participants experienced *The Beast* in just that way. The Puppetmasters referred to them as *lurkers*, a term now widely used in discussions of ARGs. *The Beast*'s lurkers followed the events of the story and the puzzle solving by reading the discussions on the Cloudmakers site. This way, they could enjoy the vicarious pleasure of seeing puzzles solved without having to do the work themselves. They could receive emails, call the phone numbers of the fictional characters or institutions, and visit the websites that interested them. "Most people are lurkers," Stewart said. "They like to eavesdrop. You've got to make things fun for them, and not obligate them to play."

Nevertheless, Stewart believes both the story and the puzzles were critical parts of *The Beast*. The story was important, he said, because "if you don't have a cool story, you are dead. Narrative always works. It is a very well-tested medium." As for the puzzles, he said, they added the important element of interactivity and provided an impetus for the players to collaborate and form a community.

WHY SO COMPELLING?

Many players poured every free moment of their spare time into the game, and one has to ask what made it so compelling. Certainly, part of it was the desire to solve the puzzles and to uncover the secrets hidden in the story, and also to see the plotlines resolved. But Stewart points to two other possible reasons that are unique to the ARG: first, because *The Beast* entered the players' daily lives in the way it did, it pulled them right into the drama. The game gave them a heightened sense of reality, of their lives being less humdrum and more dramatic. Every aspect of their lives had the potential of being part of the unfolding murder mystery. When the phone rang, a player would never know whether it was his mom on the line, or one of the characters in the game.

Second, Stewart suggests that the game empowered the players in a highly intoxicating way. It gave them the sense that by working together, they could solve any challenge; that collectively they were incredibly smart, far smarter than they were as separate individuals.

A NEW FORM OF STORYTELLING?

Stewart's perspective of *The Beast* is that of a novelist, his primary occupation (he is the author of a number of highly regarded works of literary science fiction and fantasy). He regards *The Beast* as a prototype for a new form of fictional narrative, calling it "the storytelling of the twenty-first century." He labels this new genre a *distributed narrative*. This type of storytelling, he notes, places the onus on the audience to gather the pieces and make sense of them, somewhat like assembling a jigsaw puzzle.

Though working on the game required Stewart and the other Puppetmasters to be trailblazers, and had them bushwhacking through some totally unexplored territory, Stewart recognized that in some ways his writing role was not too unlike what other writers had done before him.

Essentially he saw himself as following the old-fashioned craft of serial writing, a form of fiction that Charles Dickens had practiced so successfully in the nineteenth century. But, of course, a few things made this particular writing job unique. The story was being told via methods of communication that had never before been used for telling stories, such as the Internet and phone calls, and it was a collaborative experience between the authors and "the audience."

NOTES FROM THE FIELD: "STAYING IN THE CAR"

At one point in his life, Stewart had been a game master of live role-playing games, and he recognized that an interactive game like *The Beast* had to be a two-way process. The creators could not just put something out there on the Internet and leave it at that. They had to be responsive to the players, and give them a certain amount of behind-the-scenes direction. As he put it: "Once you let them drive the car, you have to stay in the car."

Like almost all new developments in the arts, *The Beast* and other ARGs could only be possible because of technological advancements—in this case, digital media. As Stewart pointed out, the novel could not exist until someone invented the printing press. "Anything that allows you to lie will become an artistic medium," he asserted. "After all, what are stories, but artistically presented lies?" Of course, it takes time for a new art form to develop its own unique characteristics. For example, the first automobiles closely resembled the horse-drawn buggies they replaced because buggies were the logical model for the manufacturers to draw upon, and automobiles were even called "horseless carriages." Perhaps someday, Stewart speculated, *The Beast* will seem like a narrative version of the horseless carriage.

MAJESTIC WADES INTO THE WATERS

Just about the time *The Beast* was rolling to a close, another major ARG was launched, the highly anticipated *Majestic*, produced by heavy-hitter Electronic Arts (EA). Set in the contemporary world, the story revolved around an intense conspiracy-driven plot. Like *The Beast*, it was largely played on the Internet, and many of its narrative elements were embedded in realistic-looking websites. Its characters communicated with the participants by instant messaging and email, though they also sent faxes and made phone calls. Players could follow the story by downloading videos that had been "shot" by the characters and by listening to audio messages.

Pulling out all stops, EA hired a Hollywood feature film writer to write large parts of the story, and it got off to an ingenious start. Soon after players signed up for the game, they would receive a shocking fax saying that the game had to be suspended—a fire had destroyed *Majestic*'s development company, Anim-X studios. The fax was on the EA letterhead and signed by the EA customer service department; it looked completely authentic. Actually, of course, the document was just part of the game. It was an effective way to thrust the player into a tale involving youthful high-tech professionals—people probably much like themselves or their friends—who become unwittingly sucked into a conspiracy involving aliens, government mind control experiments, and New Age mysticism.

The game utilized technology in innovative ways, including a clever IM (instant messaging) system in which bots realistically conversed with the players. The story was well developed, and the game's assets were generally of high quality, with video and audio segments made by Hollywood professionals. Nevertheless, despite its ambitiousness and generous funding, estimated at some $10 million, *Majestic* fared poorly in the marketplace. The game was never able to achieve the critical mass it needed to sustain itself, and EA pulled the plug several months after its launch, long before the game's conclusion.

THE BEAST VERSUS *MAJESTIC*

Because *Majestic* made its debut several months after *The Beast*, in the summer of 2001, many people erroneously believed it was imitating the Microsoft game. In truth, however, the development teams of the two games just happened to be working along parallel tracks. The emergence of these games within such a close span of time was sheer coincidence. Certainly, however, they were both spurred by similar perceptions: that the Internet was robust enough to use for a new type of gaming and storytelling; that various communications technologies could be used in conjunction with the Internet to simulate real life; and that people might enjoy an experience that blurred the lines between games and reality.

However, significant differences existed between the two games. For one thing, *The Beast* took an under-the-radar approach to making itself known, depending on viral marketing, and hiding the fact it was a fiction. *Majestic*, on the other hand, mounted a multimillion-dollar marketing campaign to publicize itself, and in doing so, flagged the fact that it was a game. The publicity undermined *Majestic*'s ability to make the events of the story seem real and believable, and disenchanted hard-core ARGers, who enjoyed the illusion that "this is not a game." For another thing, *The Beast* was free, while *Majestic* was a subscription-based service. And *The Beast* was a continuous, unbroken playing experience, while *Majestic* was divided into episodes.

But perhaps more significant than any of these differences were their dissimilar approaches to content. *Majestic* was designed for solo play and did not lend itself to the collaboration so important to playing *The Beast*. Furthermore, players had virtually no way to have an impact on *Majestic*'s storyline or to affect the way the game proceeded. It was stubbornly unresponsive. The Puppetmasters of *The Beast*, on the other hand, stayed keenly in tune with their players. They tooled and retooled the game with them in mind, gave them ways to feel involved, and let them decide on the ending.

SERVING TWO MASTERS

Quite possibly, *Majestic* tried too hard to serve two masters, and was unable to please either one sufficiently well. According to Neil Young, the EA executive who created *Majestic*, the game hoped to attract both the newbie player and the experienced gamer. The company believed that by having an exciting story, by painting the game on a new kind of canvas, and by inventing a compelling concept—"the game that plays YOU"—they would draw people who did not normally play games. They also felt that by offering the game in monthly episodes, with about 30 minutes of playing time a day, they would appeal to older gamers. These gamers, it was felt, still yearned for interactive entertainment, but no longer had the time for demanding video games or MMOGs.

But in trying to serve two masters, *Majestic* ended up disappointing both. The newbies complained about having to download the tools needed to play the game, and had trouble following the clues and solving the puzzles. Meanwhile, the experienced gamers grumbled that the puzzles were not challenging enough.

PRODUCING AN ARG ON A SHOESTRING

Expensive and elaborate experiences like *The Beast* and *Majestic*, and works we will examine a little later in this chapter, may give the impression that ARGs require an enormous budget and the backing of a major media company or a Fortune 500 corporation. Such is not necessarily the case, however. Every year, a number of ARGs are launched by small teams operating with modest financing.

Furthermore, such ARGs can contain all the elements of a big budget work, though on a smaller scale. The scope of these less-well-funded ARGs is, as to be expected, partially dependent on the size of their budgets. Nonetheless, these more modest endeavors can be wonderfully innovative, and what they lack in expensively produced elements they often make up for with highly innovative assets. Companies that are interested in creating ARGs of their own, even well-funded ones, can learn a great deal by studying these smaller-scale undertakings, not only in terms of what works well but also in terms of mistakes to avoid.

ALIENS AND ARGS

One such highly inventive ARG, created on a minuscule budget, was *The Roswell Experience*. Though the work faced many challenges and was its creator's first foray into ARG development, it succeeded on many fronts, and valuable lessons were learned in the production of it. This ARG originated in the small town of Roswell, New Mexico, a place closely associated with UFOs and aliens. This unusual connection dates back to 1947 when an unidentified airborne object crash-landed near Roswell. Many people believe the object was a flying saucer and that it was carrying a crew of aliens. They further believe that at least one of these aliens was taken to a lab and autopsied by medical professionals. To this day, the town is decorated with numerous images of aliens, and despite the fact that Roswell is home to many normal and sedate organizations like the New Mexico Military Institute, the town gives off a somewhat wacky alien vibe (see Figure 18.4).

The Roswell Experience, a two-week ARG that took place in the summer of 2012, cleverly takes advantage of Roswell's unique history by incorporating aliens and UFOs into the narrative and game. It was created and produced by James Airhart with the assistance of a small team of helpers, and with a tiny budget of only $2000. At the time, Airhart was a Professor of Digital Media at New Mexico State University. As a life-long resident of Roswell, Airhart was well-acquainted with the town and surrounding area, and also well-versed in its history. This history included not only the speculation about aliens but also rich Native American lore and an association with one of the most famous celebrities of the Old West, Billy the Kid. Airhart recognized the potential of incorporating pieces of Roswell's history and also the area's striking natural outdoor attractions into an ARG.

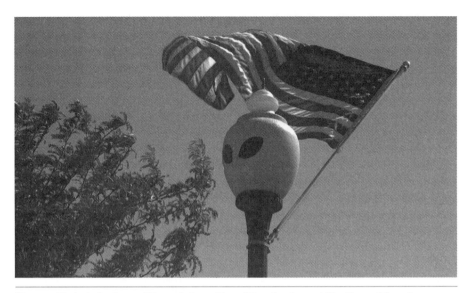

Figure 18.4 In the town of Roswell, the setting of the alien-themed *The Roswell Experience*, even the street lights look like aliens. Image courtesy of Robert Pratten.

His impetus for creating the ARG was his personal passion for transmedia. "I see ARGs as a whole new art form, and a new way of artists to express and represent their mediums," he explained to me with gusto one day over coffee. "That's why I'm so excited about doing them." And, he added, they can be good for education, creating as he put it, "a sense of wonder and magic." Thus, while being a highly engaging form of entertainment, they can also serve as vehicles for teaching. Airhart went on to say that one of his objectives in this ARG was to educate participants about Roswell, its surroundings and local history.

But to engage the participants, he intertwined the informational aspects of the work with an alien-themed sci-fi fantasy. The narrative centers around a powerful alien character named Vrillon, who threatens to destroy the earth unless an ancient amulet with links to his ancestors is returned to him. The story also spelled out that aliens would be landing on the summer solstice (one of several real astrological events that were woven into the game). It was up to the players to follow clues that would lead to the recovery of the amulet and also to follow clues to the landing place of the aliens by the time of the solstice. Everyone who was able to figure out the landing place and to arrive on time was rewarded by being present for the grand finale of the game—the arrival of Vrillon (an actor in an alien costume) and the handing over of the amulet (assuming it had been found), and thus the salvation of the Earth.

A LOCATION-BASED ARG

The type of work that Airhart created is essentially a location-based ARG—one that is rooted in a particular geographic place, and incorporates local elements into the narrative and gameplay. Location-based ARGs are generally easier to finance and manage than ARGs that are spread out over a vast area, like *The Art of the Heist*, which staged live events all over the

United States, or *Why So Serious*, the Batman ARG, which was fully international in scope, playing out in 75 countries.

The Roswell Experience kicked off with a dramatic incident well suited to the alien themes of the game: the discovery of a mysterious crop circle in a local farmer's field (see Figure 18.5). Airhart enlisted a friend to work out the coaxial of the enormous crop circle, which was

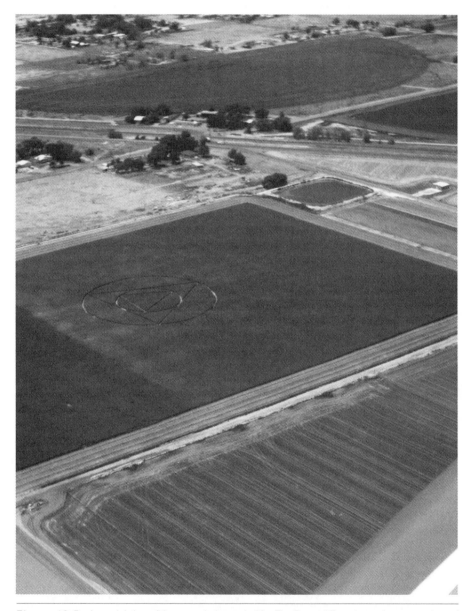

Figure 18.5 An aerial view of the crop circle created for *The Roswell Experience*. Image courtesy of James Airhart.

100 yards across, and to help make it. The discovery of the crop circle made local news, both in the paper and on TV. It was an auspicious start to *The Roswell Experience*.

To pull people into the ARG, Airhart planted a faux newspaper, *The Roswell Daily Planet*, around town. The paper contained bits of the narrative and some coded clues. He also put up posters in local businesses (with the cooperation of the merchants) with clues that would lead to the game's 29 different locations (see Figure 18.6). Once players arrived at one of the locations, they had to

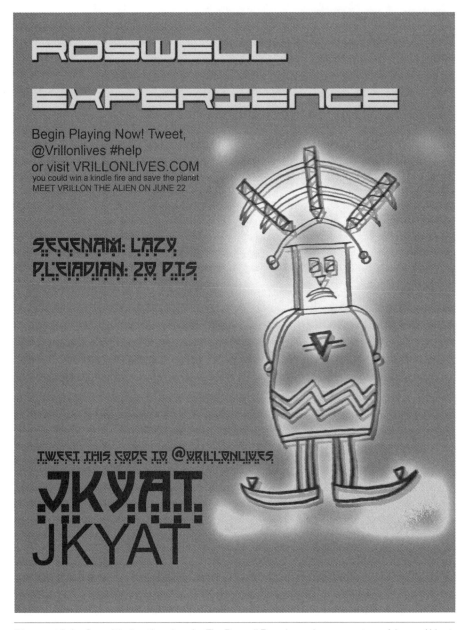

Figure 18.6 One of the location clues for *The Roswell Experience*. Image courtesy of James Airhart.

look around to find the next clue, which would be posted somewhere in the area. Once they found it, they would tweet or text the code to Vrillon, who would send them back a piece of the story.

The crop circle, the location posters, and *The Roswell Daily Planet* all functioned as rabbit holes to the game. As for cheese holes, the narrative spelled out that humans had acquired traits of two destructive ancient species, the Pleiadians and Reptoids, both threats to the planet, and that all humans were members of either one group or the other. Airhart felt that this narrative element would stimulate players to develop storylines or even create YouTube videos based on the groups they belonged to. To determine whether a player was a Pleiadian or a Reptoid, he created a mini-game which involved looking at one's palm to see if it contained certain lines in the shape of an M, and then tweeting the answer back to Vrillon. (For the record, I tweeted that I didn't see an M, and within a couple of minutes was rewarded by a reply from Vrillon himself: "You are a Pleiadian. Help your people save the planet from the Reptoid Army!") In addition to the Pleiadian and Reptoid element as a potential cheese hole, Airhart also believed players would dig deeper into the history of the area and share their findings with other players, and would create part of the storyworld together. Unfortunately, though, players failed to take advantage of these opportunities. The lack of robust and functioning cheese holes was one of the few weak aspects of *The Roswell Experience*.

However, Airhart's instincts to seed the town with materials about the game and to incorporate local history into it were right on target. After the game was over, the winner talked with Airhart about what had motivated her to play. She explained that she was new to Roswell and had found one of the faux newspapers, *The Roswell Daily Planet* (see Figure 18.7). She was intrigued by it and started following the clues, and kept playing because she enjoyed learning about the history of the area.

PRODUCING THE ARG'S COMPONENTS

Because the ARG was largely self-funded, aside from a small amount of advertising that Airhart managed to sell, he created most of the game's assets himself. Thanks to his training in graphic design, he told me, "I was able to quickly create the print material, which quickly became the center of the game." Along with the faux newspaper and posters, he also produced a book, *The Roswell Amulet*, which he "ghost wrote" for the powerful alien, Vrillon, so the fictional character could tell his story (see Figure 18.8). He also made use of his videography skills to produce several videos, which he posted on YouTube. In addition, a friend helped out by producing Native American themed artwork for the clues.

Other assets for the ARG included various communications from Vrillon, including a blog, tweets, and texts. They also included the clues that led to the locations and the codes that unlocked pieces of the narrative, and a virtual badge system. Airhart also created events that took place in real time. One night, for instance, he managed to insert an eerie warning, allegedly from Vrillon, into a radio music show, a bit like Orson Wells in 1938 with his seemingly authentic broadcast of an alien invasion, *The War of the Worlds*. In the Roswell version, the radio show is abruptly interrupted by a burst of static, and then the great alien Vrillon (voiced by Airhart, but with appropriate "other worldly" audio distortions) comes on the air to ominously announce that an alien space ship is making its way to Roswell. Airhart also orchestrated the game's live

The Roswell Daily Planet

THE VOICE OF VRILLON

Vol. 1111, Issue 1

DAILY NEWS

www.vrillonlives.com

JUNE 2012

$1.00

UNLOCK ROSWELL'S SECRET HISTORY

Oppenheimer: Rpetoid or Pliedian?

Did Billy the Kid hunt Chupacabra?

Was the father of modern Rock-etry influenced by the amulet?

You could be the one that finds the amulet and wins a Kindle Fire!!!

The Book, The Roswell Amulet, available on the Amazon Kindle Store.

Graves Farm and Garden in Roswell was the site of this crop circle June 4, 2012

The solar eclipse of 2012 has begun the Great Awakening . The Reptoid army will be rising up from the depths of the caverns and ground around Roswell on June 22. The Plieadians have marked the ground for there ships to arrive and fight the Reptoid army. Be on the look out in the skies above Roswell for the light of the Pliedian ships. They have made there presence known. If the amulet is not found before the summer solstice, then all hope may be lost. The amulet is out there around Roswell. Learn the location of the alien Vrillon's return in order to save the planet from annialation. Visit Cattlemans Steakhouse, Imagine That, Scrap-booking store, or Graves Farm and Garden for more information.

Where Will the Alien Spacecraft Land?

You have a chance to meet the alien Vrillon. The codes to his destination are located below. Tweet or text five codes to learn the location. Tweet or text all the codes to unlock the history of the amulet and earn points and badges. Play through Twitter and you will learn even more about Vrillon. If he thinks you are worthy, you could be the one who recieves the information that will lead you to the location of the hidden amulet.

The end of the world is near! We are facing a monster apocalypse if the amulet is not found. You could be the one who saves the world from annihilation!

The Codes Have Been Found!

The codes were recieved from the incoming Pleíadian ships. It is apparent the Pleiedians know of Vrillon's plan to destroy the world if the amulet is not found. The codes were delivered through the airwaves on the local station, JackFM, 106.5. Listen to the station for more clues to the amulets location. You could be the one Vrillon is looking for. You could be the one who saves the world.

TEXT AT LEAST FIVE OF THE 5 DIGIT CODES TO (575) 208-5005
OR TWEET AT LEAST FIVE, OF THE 5 DIGIT CODES @VRILLONLIVES

standard text and data rates may apply. Text stop at any time to stop receiving messages.

QGSJV ALGXV 6UDTU LNEBD KMWBB
FUAIV AER09 CIRJW ERTYG WQ27R
JKYAT MOPXE GJK83 BN34I KJFI3
XBM23 OIUS4 53FGH 5TFR1 90WER
19WIE UIFH2 AXB30 YP2H9 STW12
ZX06W QOP12 18W45 UWZTE

Figure 18.7 *The Roswell Daily Planet*, a faux newspaper that pulled many players into the ARG. Image courtesy of James Airhart.

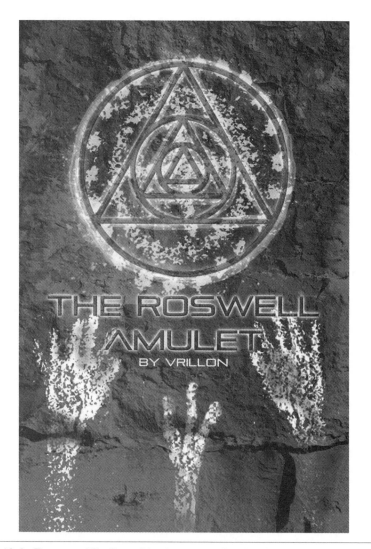

Figure 18.8 The cover of *The Roswell Amulet*, supposedly written by the fictional character, Vrillon. Image courtesy of James Airhart.

finale, previously described, with an actor costumed as an alien receiving the amulet on the space ship landing field.

Unfortunately, though, Airhart was unable to execute everything as planned because some financial backing he had anticipated fell through. That meant he had to cancel what probably would have been the game's highlight … a fly-over one night of a full scale flying saucer (which would have been pulled by a helicopter, invisible in the dark). But he was able to come up with an effective low budget substitute, using LED-lit balloons hovering overhead to represent the space ship. Fortunately, the bright lights of the balloons were convincing as the lights of an alien space ship.

Although Airhart was able to produce many of the assets himself, or with the help of a small group of colleagues, he found that once the ARG got underway, the task of managing it became almost overwhelming. "It was way too ambitious for one person to take on," he confessed to me. "I was guilty of thinking I could do everything myself. I was at the point of throwing in the towel at many points."

Fortunately, however, Airhart received a great deal of assistance from an experienced transmedia professional, Robert Pratten. Pratten, based in London, is CEO of Transmedia Storyteller Ltd. His company has developed a software program, *Conducttr*, which coordinates and manages all the assets of transmedia stories, including social media, and releases pieces of the story at appropriate times. His company also assists with the production of works of transmedia stories, such as the educational ARG, *Cosmic Voyage Enterprises*, discussed in Chapter 9. Pratten was onsite during the run of the game, and with his help, Airhart was able to use *Conducttr* to smoothly integrate and release all the disparate pieces of the game and the narrative. Pratten also assisted with the gaming aspects of *The Roswell Experience*, including the creation of clues, tweets, and text messages.

The onsite experience, according to Airhart, helped both of them learn a great deal about markets and audience and to tweak the game so it worked better. For example, they realized early on that they needed to change the primary method of communications that Airhart had set up for *The Roswell Experience*. Airhart notes that "We originally were only using Twitter as a way to play. But Roswellites do not use Twitter. So we switched to using text messaging. This worked much better."

Despite the sense of being overwhelmed at times by managing his ARG, Airhart regards it as a success. He was able to do everything that he had planned to do or to find reasonable alternatives, and the game and story came to a meaningful conclusion. He now looks back on the 2012 ARG as something of an experiment that he can build upon for a future iteration of *The Roswell Experience*.

LESSONS LEARNED

Airhart willingly shared with me many of the valuable lessons he learned from producing *The Roswell Experience*.

First of all, he stressed the importance of starting the preproduction phase of an ARG well in advance of the active start of the game. In his case, he feels he didn't start nearly soon enough, waiting until a month before the game began to nail down its locations and to obtain permissions for the placement of physical clues. "The preproduction process is vital!" he emphasized. "The most important part is to get all the people involved on board and in the know on event dates and places as soon as possible. An ARG is going to give you enough surprises with it being very well organized. During pre-production, you want to test and test, and try to discover all that might become an issue before it actually goes live." When asked what the ideal length of the preproduction period should be, he said it is partly dependent on the complexities of the work that is being created, but for a short ARG like his, of two weeks in length, he felt planning should start six months before the launch date.

An essential part of preproduction, Airhart stressed, is the development of the ARG's narrative. In hindsight, he regretted he didn't spend more effort working out his story. "You need a great story," he stated adamantly. "That's the most important element. If you don't have one, no one will want to be part of it. So it shouldn't just be thrown together. You should have the story and your main characters worked out in advance and solidified."

Airhart also stressed the importance of knowing who your target audience is. He recommended building your audience and your ARG community before starting the game. He noted that you need to understand what type of content your audience will enjoy, and what type they will not be interested in, and develop the story accordingly. For example, once his ARG went live, he realized that the residents of Roswell, being surrounded by "alien history" as they were, for the most part had no interest in becoming involved in an alien-themed experience. He came to realize that the ARG he developed would have been better suited for the town's annual UFO Festival, which draws a large crowd of out-of-towners, all of whom are presumably interested in aliens.

When it comes to your target audience, he also pointed out that you need to understand how they use technology. As noted earlier, he had to do a last-minute revision of his communications delivery methods when Twitter proved ineffectual. He also felt he made a miscalculation about the length of the game. Two weeks, he learned, was too long a period to keep his players involved, and he felt a four-day game would have been more popular. "You need to understand how long your audience will be willing to be involved in an ARG," he pointed out, "and set an appropriate running length for the active playing of it."

NOTES FROM THE FIELD: THE BEST MEDIUM TO USE

Newcomers to ARG design often wonder what platforms and forms of media they should utilize. Airhart feels there is no single answer. "I believe whatever an artist or ARG developer does best should be the most important part. You should branch out from what you do best. I am a videographer, so I should have focused more on developing videos for the project."

Airhart also recommended that ARGs be designed to be open-ended, which gives your audience a chance to contribute. In other words, you should create cheese holes that will entice your audience to add content to the narrative. He also noted the importance of planning live events for your audience to participate in. He told me: "An ARG should not just be a digital experience; it should have a social element as well. The live events are what will drive audiences to play. The players and audience are the culture and life of an ARG. Reward them with rich real world experience."

Finally, he also recommends having a budget and a business plan in place, and strongly advised against assuming that local businesses will support an ARG. He found it difficult to get local merchants to comprehend what ARGs are and how his ARG could potentially benefit their businesses. As a result, he did not get the anticipated financial support from local merchants, though many were willing to let him place location clues in their stores.

ADDITIONAL OBSERVATIONS

Robert Pratten, who assisted Airhart with *The Roswell Experience*, shared with me in an email interview some additional insights about what worked well with the project and what some of the trouble spots were.

He concurred with Airhart that the crop circle was a success and that starting with a dramatic element like that could make good sense. "The crop circle was great," he said, "because it gave the experience 'spectacle' and generated TV coverage." He also felt that the quick, easy-to-play games were very popular, such as the game where you looked for an M pattern in your palm. They worked well, he said, because "it was something everyone could do with little effort."

On the other hand, he felt that the location based posters were not as successful as they might have been. He felt that "although they looked great as storyworld artifacts … the messaging was not clear enough." The problem was, he told me, that they were often the first point of contact with the storyworld but had been designed as though for a player already familiar with *The Roswell Experience* and who wanted to go deeper. He felt that their purpose was not crystal clear and that impacted participation. He emphasized that with elements such as these, everything "needs to be in very plain English, easy to understand, and take no more than 3 seconds to read."

As Airhart came to realize, it's vital to have a good sense of one's audience and to do audience research as part of the preproduction work, something that Pratten feels is essential. For example, he told me, "we made a mistake by not doing that research ahead of time and went with Twitter because we wanted a social component to the experience. SMS worked perfectly for the game but it's one-to-one and not socially spreadable."

When I asked Pratten what he thought the role of video should be in an ARG, he replied that, since these works are intended to be participatory experiences, passive elements like video should be used sparingly, somewhat like cut scenes in games. He advocates that they should be used as rewards for achieving a certain level or progressing in the game. "It is the interactive storytelling that holds the secret to engagement and it's the videos that sit on top of that," he said. Even Airhart, though a videographer, concurs with Pratten's view of video. "Video has the most universal appeal," Airhart noted, "but it isn't vital to a great ARG."

Pratten also pointed me to some thoughtful observations about location-based storytelling that he wrote up in a blog post on his website (http://www.tstoryteller.com/location-based-storytelling).

For one thing, he advocates keeping game-based experiences as simple as possible. In other words, he feels, things should be low "in terms of intellectual demands, physical demands, time demands and technology demands." He notes that every time you increase one of those factors above the minimum, you reduce your potential audience.

Ironically, but sensibly, Pratten asserts in the same post that in location-based experiences, it is poor strategy to require players to visit specific locations. He says this is "likely to create a roadblock which could result in someone abandoning the experience." Instead, he advocates creating a story with "location aware" experiences, so people can access them online when and from wherever they wish. However, he goes on to say that while visiting a specific location should not be mandatory, players should be rewarded with an add-on value if they do visit the location.

In general, Pratten believes it is useful to understand what motivates people to play ARGs. He believes their appeal is connected to the satisfying of basic human needs: to be special; to be good at something; to be in control and direct events in some way; to be connected with other people (which, he notes, can include a connection with fictional characters); and to satisfy curiosity. But, he warns, projects should not rely too heavily on satisfying curiosity. "There's so much content available to be curious about it's not enough on its own."

One element that Pratten believes holds enormous power in an ARG is the staging of live events. As he beautifully put it, "Our lives should be measured not by how many breaths we take but how many experiences take our breath away. Live events have the power to do that—to really move people. They connect at an emotional level and bring people together in a shared experience—and that feeling can last a lifetime."

SOME OTHER NOTEWORTHY ARGs

As a genre, ARGs are still in their infancy, and almost every new ARG breaks fresh ground. In Chapter 10, for example, we saw how *Push, Nevada* was the first ARG to be built around a prime-time TV series. We also saw how *The Lost Experience* employed innovative elements like faux TV commercials and planting a "spokesman" from a fictitious organization on a TV talk show. In Chapter 12, we examined how ARGs could be used for educational purposes, with the example of the UK-produced *Routes*. In Chapter 17, we examined how mobile devices can be used as the fulcrum medium in an ARG, as was done with *The Q Game*.

Though space does not allow for a discussion of all the interesting ARGs that have been introduced since *The Beast*, let's look at a handful of noteworthy ones and examine what can be learned from them.

WHO IS BENJAMIN STOVE?

In Chapter 13, in our discussion of how ARGs are used in promotion, we briefly discussed the ARG, *Who is Benjamin Stove?* Let's take another look at this game, focusing particularly on its story and gameplay.

The rabbit hole in this case is a website that seeks information about a strange painting of crop circles and a man named Benjamin Stove who evidently has some connection to the mysterious artwork. To unravel this mystery, players must follow clues that lead them to certain books in various public libraries. If they succeed at this, they will find handwritten notes tucked inside the books that have supposedly been written by Benjamin Stove and contain valuable information relating to the story (see Figure 18.9). The concept of creating realistic "artifacts" in the form of handwritten notes and concealing them inside public library books are two of the highly innovative features of this ARG.

Figure 18.9 One of the artifacts from *Who is Benjamin Stove?*, a handwritten note that was tucked inside a library book in a public library in Seattle. Image courtesy of Dave Szulborksi and General Motors' Live Green, Go Yellow campaign.

I LOVE BEES

I Love Bees, an ARG that was developed to market the video game *Halo 2*, was created by the same team responsible for *The Beast*, though by this point they had formed their own company, 42 Entertainment. The game started off in an intriguing way, with influential ARGers

EXPERT OBSERVATIONS: THE PRESSURE TO BE INNOVATIVE

The late Dave Szulborski, who not only served on Benjamin Stove's creative team but on 11 other ARGs as well, and who was one of the world's most esteemed designers of ARGs, told me before his untimely passing that ARG designers are under constant pressure to find new ways "to move the narrative and interactivity into the real world, as well as incorporating new and exciting technologies into the structure of the ARG. It's important to remember, however," he added, "that no matter how clever or innovative the delivery mechanism may be, a well written and engaging story is still the single most important element of any successful ARG."

Thus, Szulborski reaffirmed what has been stressed throughout this book: that good solid storytelling is of critical importance in digital entertainment. Cutting-edge technology and clever approaches, while attractive assets, are no substitutes for strong narratives.

receiving jars of honey containing clues leading them to a website called *Ilovebees.com*. As clever as this was, however, the most innovative feature of this ARG was the use of payphones. Players would receive the GPS coordinates leading them to payphones all over the United States and would stand by the phones, waiting for them to ring. When they did, they would hear cryptic messages with important bits of the story. Sometimes the messages were delivered by a recorded voice and sometimes by a live actor representing a character in the story.

WHY SO SERIOUS?

Why So Serious?, mentioned briefly above in connection with the cell phone cakes, was developed to promote the Batman film *The Dark Knight* and serve as a bridge between that movie and the earlier Christopher Nolan Batman movie, *Batman Begins*. The game was "orchestrated" by the fictional character of the Joker from the Batman franchise and participants played as concerned citizens of Gotham City. As with many other high-profile ARGs, this one was seeded at the annual ComicCon convention in San Diego, California, though a handful of early clues had been planted beforehand. The ComicCon phase began with the discovery of "jokerized" one-dollar bills with the Joker's face inked on the bills, along with a URL for a website. Players who scrutinized the webpage found instructions to meet at a particular location the next morning at 10 a.m., and those who turned up were rewarded with a phone number written in the sky. At this point, the game moved into high gear.

One of the most inventive elements of this ARG, described earlier, was the sequence of clues that directed players to cakes with working cell phones baked inside the pastry, along with a charger and a joker card, all inside an "evidence bag." Once the phones had been retrieved, players were instructed to keep the phone with them, and charged, at all times, and it would ring periodically with additional clues for the game.

Why So Serious? is quite possibly the world's most successful ARG. The 18-month campaign, which began early in 2007, was played by over 10 million people in 75 countries. It was the subject of enormous media attention and created a massive amount of buzz for the film. As with many of the other ARGs described here, it was produced by 42 Entertainment, which, in this instance, was working with Warner Bros.

YEAR ZERO

Like *Why So Serious?*, *Year Zero* was devised to promote an entertainment property. Unlike most ARGs linked to entertainment properties, though, it was not created in connection with a film or a video game. Instead it was designed to promote a record album, which had never been done before. The album in question was *Year Zero* by the group Nine Inch Nails. The not-yet-released album gave its name to the ARG, which was produced by 42 Entertainment, with the close collaboration of Trent Reznor, of Nine Inch Nails.

Reznor saw the ARG as an engaging way to put the "end of the world" themed music on his new album into context. The rabbit holes included secret messages embedded on the group's t-shirts and USB flash drives discovered in bathroom stalls at the band's concert venues. The narrative is set in a dystopian future (the Year Zero), during an era dominated by a militant fundamentalist group that has managed to subdue the populace via a psychotropic drug they have injected into the water supply. Participants played as members of a resistance movement.

One of the most memorable sequences of live events of this ARG occurred when a group of the most successful players was directed to a pick-up location in Los Angeles, then herded into a bus with blacked-out windows, and dropped off at what seemed to be a deserted warehouse. There the group was subjected to an intense lecture by a resistance leader. After being pumped up with resistance zeal, they were led into another room, where they found themselves at a live performance of Nine Inch Nails. Suddenly, however, the excitement of being at the live performance was shattered when the concert was broken up by a menacing government SWAT team (actually actors posing as law enforcement agents). The players were able to race out of the venue and safely get back on the bus, though shaken and unsure of what had just happened. The game, which ran during 2007, reached a satisfying conclusion when a warning message was successfully sent by people in the future to people in the present time. The message alerted them to the dystopian future awaiting them in the Year Zero unless strong precautions were taken, and the people of the present were able to avert this grim fate.

TRACES OF HOPE

Traces of Hope, which ran in 2008, was the world's first ARG to be sponsored by a major charity, in this case, the British Red Cross. The narrative revolves around a teenager, Joseph, whose home is destroyed and his family scattered during a vicious civil war in northern Uganda. Joseph longs to be reunited with his mother, and can only do that with the players' help. The game was designed to raise awareness of the vulnerability of individuals during wartime. The British Red Cross estimates that the ARG reached 30 million people and significantly increased donations to its organization.

THE ART OF THE HEIST

The Art of the Heist was created to promote the Audi A3, and the ARG was a standout for its innovative use of staged events. It started off with the seeming break-in of an Audi showroom on Manhattan's upscale Park Avenue and the theft of a brand new A3. It was the players' "job" to track down the stolen car and to discover the role it played in a much larger criminal scheme involving an art heist. The game culminated at a live event in front of a New York hotel that revealed the identity of the story's master criminal. Thanks to this ARG, 1,000 of the new vehicles were sold and online purchase activity for Audi increased by 73 percent over previous marketing campaigns.

LAST CALL POKER

Like *I Love Bees*, *Last Call Poker* was created by 42 Entertainment and was also designed to promote a video game, in this case, the Western-themed *Gun*. Even the registration for *Last Call Poker* contained an odd twist, for instead of being asked your birth date, you were asked instead for the date of your death. True to its name, the game offered ample opportunities to play poker. You could play the game online, with long-dead characters from the old West. But, if that were not strange enough, you could join other players in the game's most unique feature, a live version of poker called *Tombstone Hold 'Em*. To play this version of poker participants needed to be at one of six cemeteries in the United States at an appointed time. Once there, they learned that the tombstones would be serving as "cards." Playing the game unlocked clues to the story, and ARGers flew in from distant locations to participate.

PERPLEX CITY

Perplex City is one of the rare big-time ARGs that was not designed as a promotional vehicle but instead functioned as an independent game. It was developed by the London-based company, Mind Candy, and created in part by two brothers who were avid players of *The Beast*. The storyline centers on the theft and attempted retrieval of a strange cube-shaped object that may have come from a foreign universe. ARGers were alerted to the game by a "lost and found" ad placed in English-language papers all over the world.

The most unique aspect of *Perplex City* was the role of collectible puzzle cards. About the size of standard postcards, they not only held clues to the game but were entertaining in their own right. The materials for the game also included a realistic-looking tourist brochure for the metropolis of the fictional Perplex City, complete with a map of its subway system. As an enticement to play, potential retrievers of the cube were offered a $200,000 reward.

SAVE MY HUSBAND

Initially, *Save My Husband* appeared to be a true-life crime story. It began with a distraught woman appearing in a video clip on a cable TV channel, pleading for the safe return of her kidnapped husband, and directing people to a website with more information. At first the website also looked authentic. It contained a grainy video of the kidnapping scene and additional video from the victim's wife. But soon disclaimers began to appear on the website, making it clear that this was a sponsored game, backed by a restaurant chain, a brand of automobile, and the cable TV channel.

The eight-day long game invited players to solve puzzles that would unlock clues to why the husband had been kidnapped and where he might be. Any players who correctly identified the kidnapper and the address where the victim was being held would receive a share of a $25,000 reward. As promising as the concept sounded, however, it was severely criticized both by experienced ARGers and by newbies, and for some of the same reasons leveled at *Majestic*.

First of all, the website's disclaimers and the heavy-handed promotion of the restaurant chain (where many of the game's videos were set, with the restaurant's logo featured prominently in the background) violated the "this is not a game" mantra of ARGers. Second of all, the developers thoroughly misjudged their audience. On one hand, they underestimated the sophistication of the experienced ARGers, who quickly figured out where the clues were "parked" and solved them long before they were even released. And the producers hadn't anticipated the confusion and anger of the newbies, who regarded the communal sharing of clues and information to be "cheating." In addition, many players found the story disjointed and the puzzles too easy, though it should also be noted that other players enjoyed the experience, despite the game's shortcomings.

EXPERT OBSERVATIONS: THE "OVALTINE MOMENT"

As we have seen here, ARGs are often used as promotional vehicles. The late designer Dave Szulborski advised that when ARGs are used for promotion, the creators should be careful to avoid what is known as the "Ovaltine Moment." The term comes from a scene in the movie *A Christmas Story* in which a boy named Ralphie eagerly uses a decoding ring to decipher an encrypted message only to discover it urges him to drink Ovaltine.

Szulborski had a strongly negative view of using such a blatant approach in an ARG: "It's not necessarily bad for an ARG to be obviously promotional," he told me. "What's critical, though, is that the corporate sponsorship of their message isn't part of the 'big reveal' or climax of the game. That's the Ovaltine Moment—when a player has devoted a lot of time and energy following a game and trying to figure out all its mysteries, only to have it all lead to a web page saying 'Drive Fords! They're great!'"

LESSONS FROM THE FIELD

Not all ARGs have been commercially successful or have reached their desired audiences, but the vast majority of them have been quite innovative, and some have been stunning achievements in breaking new narrative ground. As different as these various projects have been from each other, we can some learn important lessons both from the successful ARGs and the less successful ones:

- As always, you need to understand your audience, and provide them with an experience they will perceive as enjoyable, not as too difficult or too simple, or too confusing or overwhelming.

- In an ARG, story elements and gaming elements are both extremely important, and neither can be shortchanged without weakening the overall project. ARGs require a rich, engaging narrative that will captivate participants. They also require puzzles that will challenge participants, and ideally, some of these puzzles should require player collaboration in order to be solved.

- Members of the audience want to be able to participate in a meaningful way, and have some impact on the story or game.

- Live events, and events that take place in the real world, can insert an exciting jolt of electricity into an ARG, and should be built into an ARG whenever possible, but in ways that make sense in terms of the narrative and are not extraneous to it.

- The creative team cannot set the game in motion and then walk away from it; they need to "stay in the car" and be responsive to the players.

- The barriers to entry should be set as low as possible, so you don't discourage those who are less technologically sophisticated from participating.

- If possible, provide a way for people who are not hard-core gamers to enjoy the experience, but on the other hand, don't cater to the newbies to such an extent that serious gamers will be disenchanted.

- Construct the property in such a way that it will foster community-building and inter-player collaboration. ARGs are social experiences, and need to be designed as such.

ADDITIONAL RESOURCES

As noted earlier, two websites have been established that focus exclusively on ARGs. They are the ARG Network: www.argn.com, and Unfiction: www.unfiction.com.

Also, the players' website made for *The Beast* has been preserved. Called *Cloudmakers*, it contains links to its archived websites, a walkthrough, and a guide, which includes an excellent post-mortem. The materials on the site comprise a fascinating study of the game: www.cloudmakers.org.

A case study of *Why So Serious*, the Batman ARG, is available on YouTube http://www.youtube.com/watch?v=1pd74It-yVo, as is a video about the player experience for *I Love Bees*: http://www.youtube.com/watch?v=SNhurUnOWKQ&feature=player_embedded.

Pieces of the British Red Cross ARG, *Traces of Hope*, have been preserved at http://tracesofhope.com/register.php.

CONCLUSION

In essence, ARGs exemplify what digital storytelling is all about: they contain strong narratives; they offer robust interactivity and genuine agency; they are extremely engaging; and they make good use of the unique attributes of digital media.

Even though the first ARG debuted as recently as 2001, many outstanding works have already been produced for this genre, and as we have seen, the ARGs created so far have employed a wide variety of approaches. Still, Sean Stewart, lead writer for *The Beast* and other ARGs, suggests that ARGs are still in their "horseless carriage" days. If this is true, we have some exciting things to look forward to as this new form of narrative evolves.

IDEA-GENERATING EXERCISES

1. Have you personally played an ARG? If not, why have you not done so, and what do you think would make you more interested in entertaining yourself in this way? If you have, what about the experience did you enjoy most? What about it did you not enjoy? How do you think your own experiences and perceptions of ARGs could be used to make this form of narrative attractive to greater numbers of people?

2. Many ARGs include complex puzzles, and such puzzles often require the collaboration of many players in order to be solved. What specialized areas of knowledge do you have that might lend themselves to the development of puzzles? Can you suggest how a puzzle might be constructed based on one of your special areas of knowledge?

3. A variety of different media and communications tools have been employed in ARGs. Can you think of any media or tools that, to your knowledge, have not yet been used but might lend themselves to an ARG? If so, how do you think such media or tools could be employed?

4. Select a type of product that you feel could be promoted in an ARG. Sketch out an idea for an ARG that could be built around this product.

5. Imagine that you have been charged with creating a location-based ARG for your town or city. What is special about your area—in terms of its history, landmarks, or natural features—that you think would lend itself to an ARG? Come up with a narrative premise for your ARG that could incorporate these features.

CHAPTER 19

Interactive Television

How can TV, a linear platform, be turned into an interactive form of entertainment?

What are some of the terms people use to indicate different forms of interactive TV?

What are some of the interactive features that consumers are most drawn to when it comes to television?

What are some of the major creative hurdles that developers of interactive TV programming are faced with?

WINNING OVER THE COUCH POTATO

OK, Mr. or Ms. Couch Potato, which will it be?

- The chance to compete with other viewers and win prizes in a trivia competition based on the TV show you are watching?
- The chance to see highly personal and emotional "bonus" material from the point of view of one of the characters in a serialized drama?
- The chance to determine which Olympic competition to watch, and from which angle? Or …
- The chance to solve a mystery on your favorite crime show?

In truth, the most likely answer is "none of the above." Though all four of these interactive TV scenarios have been produced and broadcast, most viewers are not aware of them and would have trouble seeing them even if they wanted to. This is because interactive TV (iTV) is an area that has progressed in fits and starts, and has suffered significant setbacks over the years. It has yet to attain the critical mass necessary for genuine success.

Surprisingly, iTV has a very old history in terms of interactive media. The first public iTV trials date way back to the 1970s, when the Internet hadn't even been born. There was also an upsurge of iTV experimentation in the 1990s with Time Warner's Full Service Network and other cable companies, who were trying to deliver interactive apps through enhanced set-top boxes. Still later efforts at iTV only offered limited functionality, so most people ignored them. Unlike the Internet, which took off in a massive way, the progress of iTV has been unsteady and at times it has threatened to disappear altogether.

With the first forms of iTV, as with most early stage technologies, there were standards problems between competing systems backed by various companies. But the weak link in the system was the set-top box itself, especially in the United States, because the box did not contain the processing power or memory required to deliver visually exciting applications. In Europe, however, with a successful history of telephony-based teletext, government regulators mandated hardware upgrades, including the interactive "Red Button" system in the UK.

The development of iTV underwent a welcome and radical shift in the United States with the release of Apple's iOS-fueled iPad and iPhone, and later Google's Android platform. These platforms suddenly made the dream of "interactive TV" real, in large part because these devices could display HDTV-quality picture and stereo sound. They also allowed for third-party developers to create apps that would give both broadcasters and consumers a new world of media experiences. Some of these new apps were for experiences occurring entirely on the mobile device. But others could be linked to live or recorded television shows by means of sound technology, thus enabling a full second-screen experience. The United States, and the rest of the world, finally entered the era when consumers could, if they chose, do all sorts of things in conjunction with their favorite TV shows.

Unfortunately, despite the fact that millions of homes possess the capability of receiving some form of iTV, most viewers are under the impression that this form of entertainment is something for the far-off future, not something available in the here-and-now. In fact, when teaching Digital Storytelling classes, a number of my university students had never even heard of iTV. I would get comments like this: "I did not realize it exists. I thought it was a sci-fi kind of thing." Another student said: "I think the most interesting form of Digital Storytelling is the iTV. This is a part of storytelling that takes something very original and classic and makes it new and exciting."

The truth is, despite recent developments, iTV must overcome many problems if it is ever to become a mainstream form of entertainment. Professionals within the industry are even hard-pressed to agree on a uniform definition for it. Along with iTV, it was at one time also referred to as enhanced TV (eTV). Today the two most used terms are "second-screen TV" and "social TV," but some also use the term "app TV" or "multiscreen TV." In addition, in the UK we have "Red Button TV." What do all these terms mean and how are they different from each other?

Second-screen TV means watching a TV show on the main screen (your TV set) while also interacting, often through a special app, on your tablet or smart phone. Social TV is technology that supports communication and social interaction on your mobile devices while simultaneously watching a show on the main screen. Second-screen and social TV are often the same thing; the defining quality of social TV is the degree of interaction with other viewers. Multiscreen TV, as the term implies, means using more than one screen to enjoy TV, and app TV is simply using an app in conjunction with watching a TV show—the app enhances the TV program. As for BBC's Red Button TV in the UK, it is a service that allows viewers to see additional content by pushing the red button on their controller. As described by the BBC, Red Button is "an interactive TV service available via digital terrestrial television, satellite television and cable television." An estimated 20 million people a month press the red button there.

All of this is, to be honest, fairly confusing, especially because of the overlap of social and second-screen TV. I interviewed my colleague Nick DeMartino, a digital media strategy consultant, to help me get a clearer picture of the field. Unfortunately, although DeMartino did his best to clarify the terminology, it turns out that this is no easy job.

DeMartino noted that the original vision of iTV required set-top boxes, as noted above. But, he said, "this was single-screen interactivity, and it failed." Some companies were also trying to deliver interactivity by means of other devices, such as a game console, a cell phone, or the Internet, because back then we didn't have tablets and smart phones. When DeMartino was at the helm of AFI's cutting-edge Enhanced TV workshop, holding the position of Senior VP of Media and Technology for AFI, the lab experimented with a great number of variations of iTV. The lab was renamed the Digital Content Lab and unfortunately closed in 2010, which may (or may not) indicate the fading hopes for iTV.

Nonetheless, DeMartino said: "In the current incarnation, what we're essentially doing is reflecting the popularity of mobile devices—primarily the smartphones and tablets—which are small and light and powerful computers that consumers pretty much always have with them. Their presence in the room where the TV viewing is occurring … *that* is the breakthrough." In this new incarnation of iTV, we are watching TV and using our mobile phones at the same time. Before that, he noted, "this activity was happening asynchronously." But, he maintains, "The function of the second screen experience is still being explored and debated." He also notes that many second-screen apps are specialized for particular shows or broadcasters and the upside is that you receive a completely customized experience. But, he wonders, "Does everybody want to load a different app every time they change the channel?"

DeMartino suggests that there's a reason that the professional community is so interested in second-screen TV. "I think it's intriguing to a lot of people because, embedded within the idea is the notion that there is a deeper audience engagement opportunity that, for the first time, is supported by the infrastructure and the consumer behavior. You're encouraging people to use the device they're already using all the time for many other things, to connect it with the TV experience. This is the fundamental shift in the discussion of the interactivity." He notes that second-screen TV is only about two years old, emphasizing that "We're at the relatively beginning phases of a very different relationship between the audience and their content." He feels that we are just beginning to learn what can be done with it, telling me: "Second-screen is exciting people not because of what's done but what it's going to enable someone to do."

He feels that social TV, which is often just using Twitter to comment about the show you are watching, is "essentially social functionalities of these different second-screen apps." In other words, "just variations on the broad social media functions that we all take for granted."

One thing that surprised me was DeMartino's emphasis that second-screen was a *business* rather than an innovative way to present interactive content, telling me there are 138 different applications of second-screen, and counting. "It's a bunch of different functionalities and businesses that are all losing money, that are trying to find a market for this second-screen kind of experience." Since my emphasis is always on the storytelling side of digital media, I was disappointed with this characterization of second-screen TV, though I respected his insights.

Sensing my disappointment, he pointed me to some innovative storytelling work that is currently going on. For example, an app produced by HBO and Miso (a second-screen company) for the hit TV show, *Game of Thrones*, gives you a map of where the action is taking place and also offers the genealogy of the characters and other helpful features to assist the viewers in following the story. In addition, it gives fans a chance to add their own second-screen content: factoids, comments on the characters, and the like. Although this was not the kind of interactivity that I was hoping was going on with second-screen, at least it did enrich the story. Again, as if DeMartino could read my mind, he said: "It doesn't change the experience of watching a linear show, it enhances it. There really are not, to my knowledge, any real groundbreaking storytelling experiences that are second-screen." He notes that at present the media companies and the venture capitalists "are still struggling to find business models for all these things."

One of the experiences I enjoyed most, the *Psych* spin-off, *The Social Sector* (described in Chapter 9 and that DeMartino had pointed me to), was, according to DeMartino, not technically a form of second-screen TV because it didn't work simultaneously with the TV show, but outside of it, even though it had the same characters and milieu, used video, and was extremely interactive. Helpfully, he told me: "You want to be clear about what is the technology that's enabling experience and what is the experience. You can't conflate the two. The second-screen is a description of a technological infrastructure." He stressed that "It's nothing to do with the experience of the television." But, ending on a hopeful note, he added: "That doesn't mean the experiments aren't interesting."

EARLIER FORMS OF iTV

In addition to the new forms of iTV mentioned above, other types of video experiences that people in the industry have placed under the iTV umbrella are:

- Interactive programming furnished via a digital set-top box provided by a satellite or cable company, known as *single-screen interactivity*.
- The synchronization of content on TV and the Web, calling for a secondary device like an Internet-connected computer or cell phone, known as *dual screen* or *synchronous interactivity*.
- *Video on demand* (VOD), in which viewers can order movies or other video content from their TV sets or devices connected to the Internet.

- Devices like TiVO, which are known as personal video recorders or digital video recorders (PVRs or DVRs) and which offer features like pausing live TV and skipping commercials.

- Interactive program guides.

Beyond the issue of interactivity, the advent of digital technologies is rendering the very definition of television obsolete, DeMartino maintains. For instance, watching video on the Internet is sometimes called "Internet TV," and a few experts even predict that all forms of video entertainment will eventually be watched on the Internet. Indeed, virtually all TV is now "digital," whether it is broadcast or distributed via satellite, cable networks, or telephony networks. Suddenly new programming networks and content options are available "over the top"—meaning directly via the Internet, without going through the subscriptions-based providers like cable or satellite. Neflix is the most successful, having passed HBO by number of subscriptions in 2013. In addition, thanks to mobile devices, viewers no longer have to be tethered to a TV set or to a computer to enjoy video content. (People who abandon their TV sets are sometimes called "cord cutters.") While some of the video viewed on digital platforms is programming ported over from "regular" TV, an increasing percentage of it has been produced specifically for digital media.

Thus, we are not only looking at many ways of defining iTV, but also at a quickly changing landscape for video content in general. For our purposes, let's keep things simple and say that iTV is programming that allows viewers to interact in some meaningful way with the content of a television show or other forms of video, no matter what the platform (social TV and second-screen TV are discussed in Chapter 9).

MAJOR HURDLES

Even though our definition of iTV might be simple, little else about it is. This is especially true of single-screen interactivity in the United States. Deployment has been slow since no one uniform standard of iTV broadcasting using a set-top box has yet been adopted. Though several satellite and cable companies offer iTV service, they are not compatible with each other. Also, only a small number of homes are equipped with digital set-top boxes that are robust enough to receive iTV programming. Interface devices pose another obstacle. The most common type of interface device in the United States is the remote control, which is not as easy to use for iTV as the color-coded "fast keys" system found in the UK and Europe. In addition, no strong financial incentives exist among cable and satellite services, broadcasters, or advertisers to press for single-screen interactivity, leaving the creative end of the field under-supported and under-promoted to the public. DeMartino feels that single-screen interactivity is largely an outdated technology. He told me that "there's not much to be done with it. The sun has set on that as an innovation; it's fifteen years old."

NOTES FROM THE FIELD: THE CREATIVE CHALLENGERS OF iTV

As if the multitude of second-screen apps were not enough, developers face an incredibly difficult challenge when it comes to the creation of programming, and it is this: how do you design content for the interactive aspects of the program that enhances, and does not detract from, the linear content? This is the fundamental conundrum of all interactive TV content creators, and one for which no clear answers have yet been found. DeMartino, in quoting James Cameron, defined the ultimate dilemma. According to DeMartino, Cameron said, "'I don't believe that you come to my films in order to change the ending or to make your contribution. You come in order for me to tell you what the story is.'" If it is true that people are expecting a linear narrative from a master storyteller, then what is the role of interactivity?

It is not a surprising development that many television viewers have largely been left in the dark about what is happening with interactive TV. If Mr. or Ms. Couch Potato is ever going to become excited about it and eager to try it, significant creative breakthroughs will need to be made.

THE VIEW FROM THE FRONTIER

Some people working in the interactive television arena are more upbeat about its potential than DeMartino. One such person is Dale Herigstad, a leader in the multiscreen world and the Chief Interactive Officer of Possible Worldwide. He's been involved in interactive TV since Time Warner introduced the Full Service Network in Orlando, Florida, back in 1994. Herigstad, who is considered a visionary in the field, has probably brought interactivity to more American television shows than anyone in the business.

"This is the frontier," he told me during an interview some time ago, speaking with relish, not distress. "There are no books on this, no classes on this. We have to invent the rules and figure things out for ourselves. It's a learning experience for all of us." But he admits to certain impatience at how slowly the business side of things is moving: "My mind is exploding with stuff," he said in frustration, because the technology and the money aren't where they need to be yet.

One of Herigstad's best known projects is his groundbreaking work on the hit CBS crime series, *CSI* (*Crime Scene Investigation*), which was America's first interactive prime-time network drama. He and his company designed and produced single-screen iTV enhancements for every show in the first two seasons, a total of 48 episodes. In the linear version of the show, viewers watch a team of investigators as they visit crime scenes and uncover clues, using logic, experience, and scientific tools to solve their cases. Viewers fortunate enough to be able to see the interactive version of this show could probe more deeply into the cases, getting additional information, for example, on the science of fiber analysis or about the geographical relationships between the different locations in the mystery. One of the most unique aspects of the interactive version was the chance to solve the case alongside the fictional investigators, as if you were one of the team, with the chance of "becoming" a highly ranked investigator.

Herigstad termed *CSI* "the perfect show to work on" because it was so well suited for enhancements. Curiosity about the clues and the desire to figure out the mystery gave viewers a powerful incentive to utilize its interactive features. However, because his company did not have access to the set during filming, the enhancements had to be added after each show had already been shot. His company would get the work print of the show and watch it with an eye toward elements that would lend themselves to different types of enhancements and then his writer would work on the interactive content.

A "PERFECT WORLD" VISION

Although Herigstad called the *CSI* assignment "a dream job" and said he learned a great deal from it, he indicated that in a perfect world, he would have done some things differently. For example, he felt the enhanced version could have been richer if his team had had access to more assets, such as B-roll footage (scenes that focus on details or general shots rather than on the main characters), or even better, had been able to have a production crew on the set.

Had that been possible, he said, they could have shot special footage just for the enhancements. For instance, they could have added more of an emotional dimension to the story by creating flashbacks showing scenes from a character's past. They could also have shot footage that would have offered the viewer a choice of camera angles for important scenes.

EXPERT OBSERVATIONS: LESSONS LEARNED

For all the challenges developers of iTV programming face, Herigstad nevertheless remains enthusiastic about its possibilities, and shared with me some general lessons he has gleaned about developing interactive content for television. He said the work he has done so far has shown him that:

- Interactive enhancements should be choreographed to the program, and not forced upon it; the pacing is important.

- Ninety percent of what you are trying to figure out is the balance between the passive and the interactive elements.

- What constitutes a value-added experience is different for every show and what is successful for one will not necessarily be appropriate for another.

> - Because TV viewers are sitting back and can't see the TV very well, they need the visuals to be very clear and simple, and they don't want to read much text.
> - They like things to be easy and prefer to respond, not to initiate.
>
> Herigstad says he has a mantra about interactive television, and it is this: interactive TV is television, television, television. It's not the Web and it's not something else. And television, above all, has always been a simple experience.

PUSHING THE ENVELOPE

While AFI's wonderfully innovative Digital Content Lab was still in operation, it encouraged developers to think in terms of five possible ways to use interactivity with TV. These goals are as valid now as they were in 2010, when the lab closed. It suggested interactivity in television can be used:

- To add dimension to the show's characters (which can pertain to real people in non-fiction programs as well as characters in dramas and comedies).
- To allow viewers to delve more deeply into the subject matter.
- To serve as an educational springboard for young learners.
- To provide an opportunity for self-exploration.
- To explore sensitive social issues and offer a forum for community building.

Adding interactivity to a dramatic show has been one of the toughest nuts developers have tried to crack. AFI assigned a team to the drama *The L Word* to see what they could come up with. The Showtime cable series was an emotionally intense portrayal of a group of lesbian and bisexual women in Los Angeles (the "L" in the show's title stands both for love and lesbian). The team decided to do two things with the enhancements: to expand the narrative aspects of the show and to pull viewers into the story in a personal way. Thus, they gave viewers the opportunity to watch soliloquies of the characters, during which they revealed feelings that they hid from other characters in the show. In addition, the drama would pause at several key points and present viewers with multiple-choice questions about their own views of romance. At the end of each episode, the viewer would be rewarded by receiving a personal message from the character who most resembled her (as gauged by the answers she gave to the questions), offering additional comments on the theme of the show. While the soliloquies work well to add dimension to the story, some might question the validity of inserting the multiple-choice questions, seeing them more of a distraction than an enhancement.

Interactive TV is used for non-fiction programs as well, and many would say interactivity works better on non-fiction shows than on dramas or comedies. To some degree, the single-screen approach is still alive in the United States and the National Geographic has been using it for *Sunday Night Interactive*. The interactive options include trivia questions, polls, and previews.

Under the AFI Digital Content Lab, I had the opportunity to serve as a mentor for an educational show called *TV411*. A so-called "adult literacy" project, it was designed to help adults improve their reading and math skills. Our prototype actually made use of two platforms: interactive TV and cell phones. The interactive TV element worked as a tutorial for the subject matter addressed on the linear show, giving viewers extra help with the concepts covered in it. At the end, they could take an interactive quiz to test themselves, to see if they grasped the lesson. The cell phone enhancements were done as a game and tied to one of the concepts explored in the TV show. It was designed to be short and easy to play, in keeping with the limited literacy skills of the target audience.

Some years ago, while the Digital Content Lab was still in operation, Marcia Zellers told me that "We are in the early stages of this medium." She said content creators were still wrestling with the essential puzzle of interactive TV—how to enhance the content without being distracting. "It is a very tough thing to do," Zellers said. "I don't think we've found the golden nugget yet." Her words are still true today. However, a few general guidelines can be put forth:

- Broadcasters and advertisers don't want attention taken away from the commercials.

- Anything that makes it difficult to follow the story is distracting.

- Enhancements that are too fast or too difficult or that require too much thinking can be distracting.

- The typically chunky style of Web design is distracting on TV.

- The user interface must be clear, and must not be hard to figure out while looking at the TV screen.

EXPERT OBSERVATIONS: iTV'S TO DO LIST

In speaking of where further work needs to be done to advance iTV, Zellers told me: "I think we still need to keep hammering away at it … What is the right interface? What truly enhances the program? Technology is just bells and whistles. But how do the enhancements make television more compelling than if we didn't have this technology?"

WHEN iTV BECOMES "JUST TELEVISION"

At AFI's interactive TV events, one would often hear a wistful phrase: "Someday we'll just call it television." In this vision of the future, interactive TV will have become so widespread that it will just be a normal part of the entertainment landscape. Although still a long way off in the United States, the dream is already largely realized in the UK. This is thanks primarily to the BBC, though its interactivity is of limited robustness. However, over half the homes in the UK have access to two-way iTV services from the BBC. And these people don't just have access to interactive TV; they avail themselves of it. For example, during a recent Wimbledon tennis competition, 64 percent of those equipped with interactive TV technology took advantage of it to watch the tournament, switching at will between the action going on in five different courts.

A VARIETY OF APPROACHES

The BBC has taken a diversity of approaches toward interactive TV. With the *Antiques Roadshow*, for example, it employed an interactive overlay on top of the video that let viewers guess the value of the heirlooms being examined. This interactive gaming element helped the BBC solve a vexing problem: that of drawing younger viewers to a show that had primarily attracted an older demographic. The gaming overlay not only brought in a new audience, but did so without changing the show itself.

With the highly provocative series, *Diners*, the BBC used an approach similar to the Wimbledon telecast, but in this case the setting was a restaurant. And, as you would expect, the people in the room are eating and chatting. The twist here is that cameras are aimed at diners all over the room—real people, not actors—and the viewer can decide which table they'd like to "visit," and then eavesdrop on the conversation going on there. The multiple-camera approach used on *Diners* suggests some intriguing possibilities for a drama. One can imagine, for example, what Robert Altman could do with this.

The BBC has a large audience of older people and is using different approaches to bring such viewers into the interactive tent. For this demographic, the interactive features are designed to be uncomplicated but satisfying. Thus, the BBC designs shows for older viewers that give them an opportunity to vote on matters they care greatly about and, when feasible, these votes trigger an action. For example, in *Restoration*, a show about Britain's historic houses, they invited viewers to vote on which structure was the most deserving to receive a large grant for renovations. This type of interactivity has proven to be highly popular with the over-40 crowd.

The BBC's Red Button service proved to be enormously popular across all demographics during the 2012 London Olympics. Red Button offered multiple video streams of the events and each stream attracted at least 100,000 viewers. The tennis finals and the men's cycling proved to be the biggest hits. The BBC also offered a mobile app for the Olympics, and that, too, was extremely popular, with 1.9 million downloads. Phil Fearnley, General Manager of BBC Future Media, said: "Our aspiration was that just as the Coronation did for TV in 1953, the Olympics would do for digital in 2012. The demand and astonishing feedback we've seen from audiences accessing our Olympics content online, whenever they want, on the devices they choose, has exceeded our expectations and helped fulfill this aspiration."

APPLYING iTV TO DRAMA

The BBC has also experimented with iTV dramas. For example, it aired a hospital drama in which viewers could decide which of two patients' lives could be saved. And, in a trial in the north of England, it aired short daily segments of a month-long episodic drama called *Thunder Road* (see Figure 19.1). The drama was set in a real city, Hull, where the trial was taking place, and was presented as a blend of fiction and faux documentary. It revolved around a married couple that takes over a rundown pub, the Thunder Road, and has to make a success of it in 30 days or risk losing not only the pub, but also their livelihood and possibly their marriage. Each little episode ended on a cliffhanger.

Figure 19.1 The BBC's interactive episodic drama, *Thunder Road*, offered viewers a variety of ways to interact with the story. Image courtesy of the BBC.

Among the interactive possibilities was the chance to see, via VOD, additional "documentary footage" about the story. These video segments were monologues of each of the characters, shot with a hand-held camera to heighten the documentary effect, in which they revealed their thoughts and feelings about the unfolding events. Viewers could also participate in message boards and quizzes. The additional scenes did not change the story itself but gave viewers a greater understanding of the characters.

In a quite different iteration of interactive drama, the British series *Dubplate Drama*, which aired on Channel 4, gave viewers a choice over the storyline. Each episode ended on a cliffhanger and viewers were asked to vote on what they wanted to happen next. The plot development scoring the most votes became the storyline for the next episode. *Dubplate Drama* was about a group of aspiring musicians trying to secure a record label and featured highly popular British musicians. Rather than being a single-screen experience, it played on multiple channels and viewers made their choices known by voting online, on their mobile phones, or on their Sony PSPs. The show was targeted at a young audience and was successful enough to run for three seasons.

EXPERT OBSERVATIONS: NO "BOLT ONS"

Ashley Highfield, who was once in charge of BBC's interactive shows and is now CEO of Johnston Press, taking these local papers into the digital age, suggested to me in an email interview that one reason that the BBC has been able to produce so many breakthrough iTV projects is because of the broadcaster's approach to creating them. He said these projects are created from the very beginning to be interactive, instead of the interactivity being pasted onto already-produced linear shows. "Regardless of genre," he said, "All our interactive applications begin from the ground up at the time of the programme's commission. They are not considered 'bolt ons' to the linear programme." The BBC's approach encourages far greater freedom in designing the relationship between the linear and interactive content, and also means that the interactive elements can be produced at the same time as the linear ones, using the same actors, sets, and other assets. As discussed earlier in this chapter, this is the same approach that Dale Herigstad advocates and makes such good sense. Now that Highfield is no longer at the BBC, however, the interactivity there could be headed in another direction.

THE DUAL-SCREEN EXPERIENCE: A REAL-LIFE EXAMPLE

While the UK has an established infrastructure for single-screen interactivity, the same is not yet true in the United States, as we've noted. Until the use of the screens of mobile apps became feasible, most Americans experienced interactive TV through a dual-screen configuration. That meant watching the linear program on a TV set and interacting through a synchronized website or mobile device.

To get a sense of what such an iTV experience is like, allow me to describe a show I participated in, called *Boys' Toys*. It was a week-long series on the History Channel about gadgets and vehicles that particularly appeal to men—things like motorcycles, limos, private planes, and convertibles. The technology to make *Boys' Toys* operational was supplied by GoldPocket Interactive, which has been merged with Tandberg TV, a Norwegian company, which was then acquired by Ericsson Television, a Swedish company.

The main interactive enhancement of the series was a quiz game that viewers could play along with the show. Those with the highest scores for the week could win prizes in the sweepstakes. I logged onto the History Channel's website in order to register and to check starting times and subjects. Scanning the schedule, I decided to go for the one on private planes, which sounded like the most fun. To play, I'd need Macromedia's Shockwave plug-in, which I already had. The registration process was easy. I was asked to give my time zone, a password, a user name, and some contact information. Unfortunately, not seeing ahead, I typed in my real first name as a user name, never stopping to think how uncool a girlie name like Carolyn would look if I were lucky enough to make the leaderboard.

A few minutes before the show was to start, I logged on a little nervously and waited, not knowing quite what to expect. The action got going at 9 p.m., right on the dot, when the interactive interface popped up on my computer screen. It had an appropriately high-tech gadgety look, complete with gears, reflecting the theme of the series (see Figure 19.2). Soon I was engaged in the nonstop business of trying to accumulate points. I had no trouble watching the TV show while keeping up with what was happening on my computer, and the synchronization worked flawlessly; but the quiz kept me busy. Some of the questions were giveaways, earning you points just for participating in a poll ("if you could have your own private aircraft, which would you choose?"). But some questions required prior knowledge of aviation (a subject I knew pretty well, being a frequent flyer) and some were based on information already imparted on the show, and you had to stay alert. Slyly, some of the questions were based on commercials run by the sponsor, IBM, so you couldn't slip out for a bathroom break while they were running. The most stressful questions were those that had you wagering a percentage of your accumulated points, and being right or wrong here could drastically affect your total score.

Figure 19.2 The interface for *Boys' Toys*, as it looked on a computer screen. The interactivity was synchronized to the TV broadcast. Image courtesy of A&E Television Networks. Reprinted with permission. All rights reserved.

The first time the leaderboard popped up, I was thrilled to see my name on it, number 6! Though I hadn't intended to play for the whole show, I was hooked. But I certainly wished I'd picked a cooler user name, especially because my fellow high scorers had such macho ones—Gundoc, Scuba Steve, and White Boy. No time for reflection, though; the game was on again, and my adrenaline was pumping. Next time the leaderboard appeared, I had risen to number 5. But then came one of those wager questions, and I answered incorrectly. My score plummeted by 600 points and my ranking to 7. It was now the final stretch of the game and I vowed to regain those lost points. Sure enough, when the game ended, I had risen to number 4! I felt proud of upholding the honor of my gender, though if I were to do it again, I'd pick a name like ToughChik or SmartyPants, just to give the guys a poke. But overall, it was a completely enjoyable and engaging experience. The interactivity added a whole other dimension to TV viewing and kept me glued to the two screens. I had only one complaint with this interactive TV experience, as opposed to a more laid-back linear one: it was impossible to snack!

HOW SECOND-SCREEN TV IS BEING USED

Thus far, the most successful use of second-screen TV has been for game shows, sport shows, and live events. To some degree, it is also being utilized by advertisers. When used for dramatic series, the second-screen features are usually in the form of additional factual information about the show and the actors, but may also be used for polling or voting. According to Nielsen, 40–45 percent of viewers use their tablets or smart phones while watching TV, with 53 percent of teens doing this as well as 38 percent of people over 55. But the use of these mobile devices is not necessarily being done in conjunction with the TV show: in some cases, people are just checking their email.

Second-screen TV works particularly well for live events, because people tend to watch these shows as they are being aired rather than recording for later viewing. Having so many eyeballs fixed simultaneously on the TV screen, but hopefully ready for a richer experience, serves as an inducement to develop second-screen content. For example, during the 2012 Academy Awards, viewers could try to predict the winners of each category—the same kind of competition that takes place at many Oscar night parties, but this was a virtual party competition. Viewers could also answer trivia questions and rate the movies up for awards. Viggle, the second-screen app developer for the event, was planning to offer free movie tickets to viewers who scored enough points, though there was not enough time to implement this plan. The official iPad app of the awards show featured photos, videos, and interviews, so offered a significant amount of new content.

In another live event, the 2012 Super Bowl, Coca-Cola ran a clever and highly successful second-screen app, the *Coca Cola Polar Bear Party*. In this live app, two polar bears, "fans" of the rival teams, sit on a couch made of ice and react in real time to the events of the game. One wears a red scarf and the other a blue scarf. When the team favored by the bear with the blue scarf is winning, he's jubilant, while the bear with the red scarf looks upset and begins to pace nervously, and they continue to react realistically throughout the game. At times other Nordic characters would wander across the screen, like a penguin or a small polar bear. As this animated feature was running, people could send in pictures of their Super Bowl parties with the bears in the background. The 2012 and 2013 Super Bowls were also major tweeting events, with a total of 13.7 million tweets during the 2012 game and 24.1 million tweets during the 2013 game.

Game shows seem to be a natural arena for second-screen TV, since viewers enjoy trying to compete against the onscreen players. The British game show, *The Million Pound Drop*, offered viewers at home a unique way to participate. They played the same game as the onscreen contestants, but had to put a wad of money on the answer they believed was the correct choice. But if they were incorrect, the money would fall through a trap door! In addition, the on-air host would make comments about how the players at home were doing compared to the players in the TV studio. This added an extra edge of competition to the game.

Second-screen TV has been developed for dramatic shows, as well. We mentioned above the approach taken with the hit HBO series, *Game of Thrones*. In addition, users of the Miso iOS app could create second-screen content themselves and submit it to the show. Another drama with a second-screen app is the VH1 show, *Hit the Floor*, about the dancers who perform for a professional basketball team. The app extends the fictional lives of the characters through social media and fictional websites. You can read their email exchanges and also listen to their voicemail while the show is airing. And the USA Network sitcom, *Modern Family*, a mockumentary about a blended contemporary family, uses the second screen to let fans access trivia and participate in polling, voting, and games. You can also answer questions about your biggest lie (Was it epic? Or not?).

STRANGE BUT TRUE: SECOND-SCREEN MOVIES

Although it is generally annoying when someone in the audience of a movie theater lights up their cell phone and checks their messages during a film, a couple of apps have been specifically produced to be used in conjunction with the movie on the screen. Two of these films, both called *App the Movie*, have used this technique. The one coming out of AFI is a romantic comedy while the other, a Dutch film, is a heart-pounding thriller. The intent of both apps is to add another layer of entertainment and "realism" to the fictional story.

SOCIAL TV

Most second-screen apps have a social media component, but some apps augment the TV show almost exclusively through social media and use it in somewhat unexpected ways. For example, *Dirty Work*, a Web series that is part of Rides.TV, uses social media to add to the story rather than to connect viewers with each other. *Dirty Work* (http://rides .tv/dirty-work/) is the story of a trio of 20-somethings whose grisly job it is to clean up crime scenes and other biologically contaminated environments. People who sign up for the second-screen enhancements receive text messages, emails, and phone calls during the show from the fictional characters, and also additional videos. This is one of the few instances of the second-screen components actually enhancing the story content rather than adding a little layer of inconsequential material over the story.

Pretty Little Liars, a teen drama, employs a more conventional, but highly successful approach to social TV. The show follows four teenage girls who are being terrorized by an unknown person. It was ranked Tuesday's "most social" program in 2012. ABC has been extremely active in stimulating social media activity for the show. It has a popular Facebook page (with 10 million fans) and special Facebook tabs which unlock special content. It also uses hashtags to stimulate tweets that are posted during the show as well as Twitter-based scavenger hunts, endeavors that have reaped rich rewards: *Pretty Little Liars* was mentioned 1.4 million times on Twitter in 2012. ABC also developed an eight-part Web series, *Pretty Dirty Secrets*, to run between seasons. The show's social media approach works perfectly for its target demographic, women between 18 and 49.

USING THE WEB TO DIMENSIONALIZE A TV DRAMA

Using gaming techniques to draw viewers into a linear program, as *Boys' Toys* did so compellingly, has become a fairly standard strategy in interactive TV, with voting, polling, and informational overlays being other popular strategies. But in some cases, as with *Dirty Work*, storytelling techniques have been used to add interactivity and to enrich the linear program. Another example of this approach is *Cisco's Journal*, an interactive enhancement of the PBS series, *American Family*, produced by El Norte Productions. Though it was made before second-screen TV became a widespread development, it uses a number of techniques that can also be used for second-screen dramatic endeavors. *Cisco's Journal* was enhanced with a website, and a new installment of the website was launched with each new episode of the show. Although it lacked synchronous interactivity, the show and the website were designed to be enjoyed alongside each other.

The series revolves around a multigenerational Latino family in East Los Angeles. One of the members of this large family is Cisco, a talented teenager who is an aspiring filmmaker and artist. Each week that the series was on the air, Cisco would post his artwork online on his blog. It is this intensely personal artwork that comprises *Cisco's Journal* and enhances the linear TV show. Thus, Cisco used his blog to reach out to the world much like Rachel did in *Rachel's Room*, described in Chapter 16.

I was fortunate enough to interview Barbara Martinez-Jitner about *Cisco's Journal*. She was the show's supervising producer, writer, and director (sharing writing and directing tasks with producer Gregory Nava). She told me: "I wanted to see what you could do with this [augmenting the series with a dedicated website] as a narrative experience." She said she wanted to explore "how to transport people emotionally." She felt *Cisco's Journal* could be a powerful tool, especially with younger viewers, and might help draw them to the show.

The journal developed for the website is more akin to an artist's sketchpad than a journal. The use of visuals, sounds, and interactivity proved to be a surprisingly effective way to add an extra dimension to the story of the Gonzalez family and to get underneath the skin of the characters, particularly Cisco. The journal functioned as "an emotional extension" of Cisco and of the TV series.

Cisco is a young man who is wrestling with his identity as a member of his family, as a Latino, and as an American, and all of this is reflected in the pages of the journal. It is a densely layered portrait of a complex character. In the course of doing the journal, he matures. He comes to appreciate himself more, discovers his powers as an artist, and gains a deeper appreciation of his culture. In other words, he moves through a classic character arc.

Cisco's growth as a character is portrayed viscerally, through his artwork. Each new entry is thematically tied to a specific episode in the series and is presented as a diptych, an artwork made up of two parts. It is reminiscent of an altarpiece made up of two tablets, though in this case, the two parts are two pages of an open journal, with the spiral spine down the center. Sometimes the diptych would illustrate emotional conflict (with each side representing an opposing feeling) and sometimes it would show complementary versions of the same subject, as in the tribute Cisco made for his recently deceased mother (see Figure 19.3). In this diptych, her memorial candles are on one side (and they light up when you roll your cursor over them); on the other side is her beloved sewing machine (which clatters when you run your cursor over it). Another entry about his mother features an image of her pearl necklace. It is coiled in such a way that it spells out her name, Berta. But if you roll your cursor over it, the pearls will drop to the floor one by one, like teardrops.

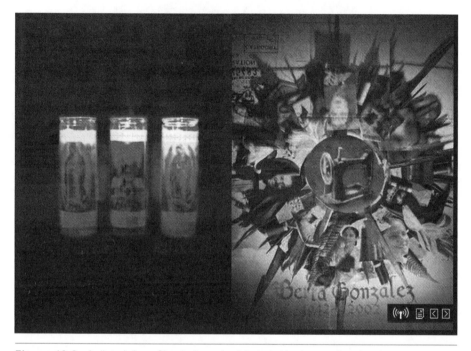

Figure 19.3 A diptych from *Cisco's Journal,* a tribute to his deceased mother. Image courtesy of Twentieth Century Fox Film Corporation, PBS, and KCET.

A mixture of artistic styles was used to convey Cisco's inner life, often referencing Latino artistic styles and folkloric traditions. One work features dancing Day of the Dead figures; another is an old-fashioned linoleum cut; still another models popular mural art. Most contain an interactive element that lets the viewer participate in the story in some way. I particularly enjoyed the episode about spray painting that let you test your skill with a can of spray paint. It turned out to be harder than it looked! (See Figure 19.4.)

The producers now maintain they were not consciously trying to push the envelope, although that is exactly what they achieved. At the time they were just asking themselves who Cisco was as a character, how he would react to a particular situation, and what materials he would have on hand. But by staying focused on these questions, they were able to create a completely new way to enhance a television program, one that portrays a sophisticated character arc and resonates on a deep emotional level, all with a minimum use of words.

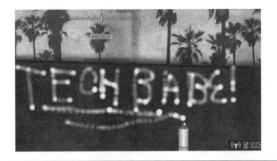

Figure 19.4 In this episode of *Cisco's Journal*, viewers can become a spray paint artist. Image courtesy of Twentieth Century Fox Film Corporation, PBS, and KCET.

ADDITIONAL RESOURCES

To stay abreast of interactive TV developments, go to:

- iTVT, a publication devoted to iTV: http://www.itvt.com/.
- The Interactive Television Alliance (ITA): http://www.itvalliance.org/.
- The Second Screen Society: http://www.2ndscreensociety.com/.

CONCLUSION

It would be nice to think that interactive TV, like the fictional Cisco, could move through a character arc and could metamorphose from an unsure adolescence into a more mature and dependable entity, capable of supporting strong artistic visions. Certainly, we can find some hopeful indications that this day is coming. We can also find a number of creative individuals who believe in its potential and are pushing forward on the development front. If and when the creative, technological, and financial hurdles are eventually surmounted, it is possible that interactive TV may finally become, in the words of the folks at AFI, "just television."

IDEA-GENERATING EXERCISES

1. If possible, watch and interact with a second-screen enhancement. Analyze the experience, noting whether the interactivity detracted from the linear program or whether it made you feel more involved with it. What aspects of the interactivity, if any, did you think worked particularly well? What aspects did you think were less than successful? What changes would you suggest making?

2. Record a non-fiction TV show, such as a cooking show, a news analysis show, or a children's show, so you can study it. Once you are extremely familiar with it, work out some ways to add interactive enhancements to it.

3. Record a TV show with a strong narrative line, such as documentary, drama, or comedy. Once you have studied it closely, work out some ways to add interactive enhancements to it, first deciding what the goal of these enhancements should be.

4. Sketch out an idea of an original interactive TV show, either a single program or a series, in which the interactivity is integrated into the concept. What would the objective of these interactive elements be and how would they work with the linear content?

CHAPTER 20

Smart Toys and Life-Like Robots

What could smart toys and life-like robots possibly have in common with other types of digital entertainment?

When you are dealing with life-like physical characters, what special challenges do you face?

How is it possible for robots, no matter how life-like, to arouse powerful emotions in humans?

VENTURING INTO THE METAPHYSICAL

The area of smart toys and life-like robots is an immensely intriguing sector of digital entertainment. It not only involves storytelling skills but also bends one's mind in ways one might never believe possible. I have worked on several smart toy projects myself and can personally attest to the fact that they are uniquely challenging. The work done in this arena alternates between fascinating and frustrating, but is never humdrum.

Not surprisingly, one finds oneself dealing with a host of creative and technical issues. But in addition, because these objects blur the lines between what is alive and what is mechanical, you must also grapple with perplexing questions touching on psychology, human development, ethics, and even metaphysics. At one point or another, if you work in this area long enough, you will find yourself asking such questions as: "What is intelligence?" or "What is the dividing line between a living creature and a human-made creation?" You might also find yourself pondering this one: "Is it immoral to create a life-like object that can elicit deep emotions from a human?" Or this one: "Is it irresponsible to create objects that blur reality and make-believe to the point where it is difficult to tell them apart?"

WORTH NOTING: EXPLORING THE HUMAN–NON-HUMAN CONNECTION

MIT professor Sherry Turkle has spent years investigating the relationships between virtual pets and smart dolls and their human owners. In an article for UNESCO's magazine, *Courier* (September 2000), she said "when we are asked to care for an object, when this cared-for object thrives and offers us its attention and concern, we experience it as intelligent, but more important, we feel a connection to it. The old AI debates were about the technical abilities of machines. The new ones will be about the emotional vulnerabilities of people."

It is unlikely that any other sector of interactive entertainment raises as many profound questions that go to the heart of our identity as humans and as creators.

SMART TOYS AND LIFE-LIKE ROBOTS: WHAT DO THEY HAVE IN COMMON?

This chapter focuses on the types of smart toys and robots that either have some of the attributes of fictional characters or that can be incorporated into interactive stories. These creations actually span work that is going on in a number of different fields, but we are combining them into a single chapter because of the characteristics they have in common. They are:

- life-like;
- interactive;
- physical, as opposed to virtual;
- operated by computer technology; and
- endowed with enough personality to enable them to become part of a storytelling experience.

In addition, working with any of these creations involves answering a similar set of questions. How do you use physical, life-like creations in a narrative framework? How do you advance the plot of such a story? How do you involve the user in it? How do you give personality to an artificial character? How do you communicate with a physical, life-like artificial character?

Smart toys and robots, are, of course, usually designed for quite different uses—one for play, the other for pragmatic purposes, although the dividing line is not a rigid one. Smart toys are an enormous sector of the toy market. They include any kind of plaything with a built-in microprocessing chip. The chips operate like tiny computers; they are programmable and hold the instructions and memory of the toy, controlling what they do. Smart toys can include educational playthings that are the equivalent of electronic flash cards. They can also be musical games, touch-sensitive picture books, or child-friendly computers designed for the toddler set (so-called "lapware"). For our purposes, though, we are going to focus on three-dimensional toys that represent living things—humans or animals or fantasy creatures—or playsets that tell a story.

Like smart toys, robots are an enormous category. A robot is generally defined as a device that operates either by remote control or on its own, and relates in some way to its surroundings. Some robots are designed to be playthings for children or adults and are actually a type of smart toy, and others are built to be part of entertainment or educational experiences. Some robots are also used in the medical field. For example, Keepon is a bright yellow dancing creature that looks like two tennis balls, and is employed to help children with autism. Many robots are specifically built for highly pragmatic functions. In fact, the word "robot" is a variation of the Czech word, *robota*, which means slave-like labor or drudgery.

Robots can be programmed to work in factories and in outer space. Specialized robots perform hazardous duties like defusing bombs and miniature robots perform various functions inside the human body. Many of these "employed" robots do not resemble in any way what we commonly think of as a robot—an anthropomorphic mechanical creature with arms and legs, capable of movement and sometimes of speech. However, two members of the robot family, androids and animatronic characters, can look, move, and make sounds like living beings and respond to humans in a life-like way. These robots have particular relevance to digital storytelling.

A LONG HISTORY

Although computerized versions of living beings are a relatively new phenomenon, people throughout history have been beguiled by the idea of a nonliving creature coming to life. Myths, legends, and works of literature and popular entertainment are filled with such tales. One of the best-known Greek myths, that of Pygmalion and Galatea, is about a sculptor whose carving of a beautiful woman comes to life. The story inspired the musical comedy, *My Fair Lady*, as well as the work of interactive fiction, *Galatea*, described in Chapter 4.

In medieval times, Jews told a story about the Golem, a mystically created monster made out of clay who was called upon to protect the Jewish community from attackers. Children have their beloved story of Pinocchio, of course, about the puppet who longs to be a real boy. Science fiction writer Brian Aldiss wrote a short story, *Supertoys Last All Summer*, based on a similar theme, about a robotic boy who longs to become human. Steven Spielberg turned the story into the movie *AI*. If you saw it, you might remember that the little robotic boy in the film has a smart toy of his own, a wise and endearing teddy bear. *AI* was, in turn, the springboard for the ARG, *The Beast*, described in Chapter 17, which is all about robots intermingling with humans.

But robotic characters do not merely exist in works of the imagination. Almost as long as we have told tales about such beings, we have also tried to construct them. Over 2,000 years ago, for example, a brilliant Greek engineer named Hero of Alexandria was famous for inventing a number of astounding *automata*—self-operating mechanical figures that could move, and, in some cases, make life-like sounds. Among his works were singing birds; a satyr pouring wine; and a scene depicting Hercules shooting an arrow into a dragon, which hisses. The demanding craft of constructing automata was taken up by Arabians and then revived in Europe in the Middle Ages, leading to wondrous clocks that featured parades of mechanical characters when the hours were struck. One craftsman even invented a duck that could supposedly eat, digest food, and eliminate the waste. Many of the most illustrious scientists of the day worked on automata, leading to some important breakthroughs in science and engineering. The tradition continued into the nineteenth century, with no less an inventor than Thomas Edison applying his genius to the construction of life-like animated figures. Edison successfully created a talking doll, patented in 1878, which caused a sensation. It used a miniaturized version of another of his inventions, the phonograph record.

TODAY'S SMART TOYS

Beginning in 1985, the first true smart toys entered the world, led by Teddy Ruxpin, a singing, storytelling teddy bear. Each new generation of smart toys has been increasingly sophisticated. Many of the smart toys available now have various types of sensors that enable them to "perceive" things like sound, touch, or changes in position or light. Sensors can also enable them to "recognize" objects—pretend food, an article of clothing, or a playpiece like a sword or magic wand. They may also have sensors that enable them to recognize and interact with fellow toys. A number of smart toys also "talk"; some even have voice recognition and can carry on a simple conversation. They may also have individualized emotional responses and in turn may be designed to elicit emotions from their owners. Smart toys may develop intellectually and physically over time like a real puppy or human child. Some even have built-in calendars and can wish their owners happy birthday or Merry Christmas on the appropriate days. It is no wonder that a toy that possesses many of these traits is called smart.

Smart toys utilize some of the most advanced technology of any of the interactive platforms. Thus, breakthroughs in smart toys can potentially lead to breakthroughs in other areas, just as the work done on automata in the Middle Ages led to advances in science and engineering. Furthermore, designers of smart playsets deal with many of the same spatial, structural, and architectural issues as designers of video games and interactive cinema, potentially leading to a cross-fertilization of works in these areas.

The latest toys do things that were pretty much unthinkable back when children only had wooden blocks and electric trains to play with. For instance, a new model of Barbie is now embedded with a digital camera. By plugging her USB cord into the computer, you can download the images and put together slide shows. The latest Furby (a fantasy stuffed animal originally introduced in 1998), the Furby Boom, can learn language over time and can sing songs with other Furbys. By pulling its tale, it will fall asleep and snore softly. And this new Furby also interacts with the iPad. Via a special app, you can give your Furby showers, though you must change the temperature of the water, depending on how hot or cold your Furby likes it.

You can also feed it smoothies (and each Furby has its own preferences in terms of the combinations of fruits it prefers), and even help it hatch an egg, which is a baby Furbling.

Many smart toys now connect to the Internet or to game consoles. By purchasing a plastic toy or stuffed animal doll and using the secret code that comes with it, or placing it on a special *reader pad*, or putting it near a smart phone, where it is read by NFC (Near Field Communication), the user is transported to a game or a virtual world where their toy or animal comes to life. *Webkinz*, introduced in 2005, operates this way with fluffy stuffed animals, while *Skylanders*, launched in 2011, operates this way with little plastic figurines.

In 2013, Disney entered this field with an enormously ambitious game called *Disney Infinity*. The game's plastic figures are all models of characters from popular Disney and Pixar films, including Sully and Mike from *Monster University*, Lightning McQueen from *Cars*, and Jack Sparrow from *Pirates of the Caribbean*. Each starter pack comes with three toys and a reader pad, and new characters will be introduced on an ongoing basis. Users can choose either to play mission-based games in the world of the character or enjoy free-form play in a virtual world where any of these characters can interact with any other. In other words, in free-form play, you might have Jack Sparrow fighting a duel with Lightning McQueen, or set up a horseback race with Jack Sparrow racing against Woody from *Toy Story*. You'll be able to choose your own backgrounds and props. *Disney Infinity* plays on major game consoles, including the Microsoft Xbox, Sony PlayStation3, and Nintendo Wii U.

THE CHALLENGES OF CREATING A SMART TOY

To illustrate some of the challenges one is faced with in designing a new smart toy, let's look at a project I was called in to work on, an interactive dollhouse populated by a family of four tiny dolls. I was part of the development team assembled by a subcontractor to the large toy company that would be manufacturing it. At the time we were brought in, the toy manufacturer had already done considerable groundwork in terms of the architecture of the house and had also determined that its residents would be a mother, father, and two girls. It had also been determined that by moving the dolls to different sensors, users would elicit different responses. Our job would be to work out what happened when a child actually played with the dollhouse—the nature of the interactivity and how the dollhouse could "tell" stories. Among the questions we had to ask ourselves (and which we eventually managed to answer, after much brainstorming and hair tugging) were:

- What kinds of stories could you tell in a little physical world, especially when you did not know when a particular character would be present or what room they would be in?

- How could we control the action or flow of a story in this environment? What would trigger the advancement of the storyline? What kind of structure could work here?

- What genres of stories could work in an environment like this? Was the dollhouse best suited to realistic narratives, to fantasy, or to mystery? What about humor?

- What kinds of controls could we give the child over the experience? Could we let the child determine the time of day, what the weather was, or the season? If so, how would these choices determine the narrative experiences?

- How much personality could we give to the residents of the house and how would they relate to each other? Would they break the fourth wall and address us directly, or would they be oblivious of our presence?

THE PROCESS OF DEVELOPING A SMART TOY

Smart toys reflect the increasingly computerized world around us. Electronics have become so cheap and pervasive that even toys for infants light up and sparkle. Microchips are coming down in price and size, while increasing in power, so they can be inserted into more things and given more to do. Despite the opportunities presented by technological advances, however, it is not easy for a new toy to become successful. Thousands of new toys are introduced each year, and they have to compete for limited shelf space and also capture the fancy of the consumer. Before a toy ever reaches the stores, it has to be invented, developed, manufactured, and marketed, and each step is filled with challenges.

THE TOY INVENTOR'S PERSPECTIVE

How does someone go about creating a smart toy that has a chance of becoming a winner? Let's hear what Judy Shackelford, a prominent toy inventor, has to say about the process. Shackelford's creations include the landmark doll, Amazing Amy, plus many other groundbreaking toys. Before launching her own company, J. Shackelford and Associates, she had a 10-year stint at Mattel toys, rising to the position of Executive Vice President of Marketing and Product Development Worldwide.

The main challenge in inventing a new toy, Shackelford told me, is to find the point of differentiation—to come up with something that hasn't been done before; something that makes it unlike other toys. This point of differentiation can be a look, a mechanism, or any number of other things. "People like me figure out new applications for interactive toys, often by incorporating technology used in computers or other electronics," she explained. "I invent something when there was nothing there before. I conceptualize it and then I hire the appropriate people to work on it on a for-hire basis to help get it born. In a sense, I'm the producer of the toy."

Shackelford describes the process as being highly collaborative, calling for an assortment of experts in various fields, from people who specialize in doll hair design to sculptors to various kinds of technicians. She said an array of factors must be considered when inventing a toy. One of the most important is its play pattern—what you want to happen between the child and the toy. You also need to consider how it will appeal to the prospective purchaser (usually a parent or grandparent) and what its competition will be. In designing a toy, Shackelford cautioned, you have to avoid the temptation to throw everything into it that the toy could possibly do. "That would make it far too expensive," she pointed out. "You can't make a toy the dumping ground for every new technology." Altogether, she said, it takes "an unbelievably complex blend of things to successfully bring a toy to market."

One of Shackelford's most recent inventions was a doll called Baby Bright Eyes, which was manufactured by Playmates Toys. In this case, her starting point was a new technology, a miniature motor developed by a company called Nano-Muscle. She realized that this tiny motor could be used to give a doll extremely realistic eye movements. Out of this idea Baby Bright Eyes was born, a doll who is about 18 months old, with large expressive eyes and a sweet face (see Figure 20.1). Her eyes, Shackelford said, convey the doll's feelings and give her the semblance of artificial intelligence. Though Baby Bright Eyes has the limited vocabulary of an 18-month-old child, what she does say and do is synchronized with her eye movements.

Figure 20.1   Baby Bright Eyes utilizes nanotechnology for realistic eye movement. Image courtesy of Playmates Toys.

Like the Amazing Amy doll, she contains special sensors that enable her to "recognize" objects. She knows when you put a bottle in her mouth or a teddy bear in her hand … and she'll look at these objects when you give them to her. She conveys shyness by partially closing her eyes and shows surprise by opening her eyes wide. The toy illustrates that technology and design can be used to give personality to a doll.

NOTES FROM THE FIELD: TOO SPOOKY?

New technologies, such as the miniature motor used in Baby Bright Eyes, are giving dolls the ever-increasing ability to model living creatures. I asked Shackelford if dolls could possibly become too realistic, even to the point of being scary, as some people allege? Shackelford insists this is not the case. "I think the kinds of interactive properties we design in dolls are gentle and natural. They're not scary," she asserted. "An adult may look at a life-like doll and say: 'Oh, that's spooky.' but it's not spooky to kids. It's just real." Referring to the graphic violence in many video games, she added: "Now, that's what I think is spooky!"

A TOY MANUFACTURER'S PERSPECTIVE

An inventor like Shackelford must try to anticipate what toy manufacturers will find attractive. And what, in general, do they look for? To find out, I talked with Lori Farbanish, Vice President of Girls' Marketing for Playmates Toys, a leader in interactive dolls. According to Farbanish, for a smart doll to succeed, it must possess an illusive quality she termed "magical"—the quality to excite the child and capture her imagination. This is one of the biggest challenges of toy design, she told me, trying to "bring magic to a toy in a totally different way."

Playmates gives great consideration to how a child will most likely play with the toy and what type of play pattern it fits into, and looks for ways for the smart features to enhance the anticipated play experience. Doll babies like Baby Bright Eyes typically elicit nurturing play, with the little girl taking care of the doll much as a mother does a baby. Nurturing activities include amusing the baby with a plaything, giving it a bottle, and putting it to bed. A child can do all of these things with Baby Bright Eyes and receive a response back from the toy, both with her eye movements and her baby-like vocabulary.

A second type of play Farbanish mentioned was *fiddle play*. It's the kind of activity that keeps little fingers busy, doing things like pulling open little drawers or rolling tiny supermarket carts or opening and closing doors. Opportunities for fiddle play are built into many interactive playsets. In working out how a smart toy will be played with, Playmates makes sure it offers not only interactive features but also opportunities for traditional imaginative play, things like combing the doll's hair, dressing it up, or inventing little scenarios for it.

In a third type of play, the child relates to the doll as a friend or companion. Sometimes this companion doll is regarded as an aspirational figure—someone the child looks up to and hopes to be like. This is the type of relationship Playmates Toys wanted to build into their Belle doll when they adapted the character from Disney's movie, *The Beauty and the Beast*. The challenge here was to find a way for the doll to come to life and tell you about her romance with the Beast, but to do so without it being a passive experience, with the doll telling the story and the child just sitting there listening. The solution that Playmates Toys came up with was to give the child an opportunity to participate in Belle's story via "costume changes" and an array of talking props (see Figure 20.2).

Figure 20.2 Little girls share in Belle's adventure by exploring the enchanted castle with her and attending the ball. The costume change is to the right, and the props in the foreground. MA courtesy of Playmates Toys. Belle © Disney Enterprises, Inc. Used by permission from Disney.

The adventure story the child shares with Belle is broken into two parts, roughly following the plot of the movie. Part one is devoted to the exploration of the castle and meeting some of its inhabitants. Part two, which is triggered when the child removes Belle's workaday pinafore and changes her into her beautiful party gown, takes place at the ball and climaxes when Belle dances with the Beast. The story is conveyed primarily through sound—by dialogue, music, and lively sound effects. As Farbanish puts it, "your imagination is the set."

In addition to the change in costume, the story is advanced by inserting the different props into Belle's hand. Some of the props even speak in their character voices from the movie. Among them are Mrs. Potts, the chatty, motherly teapot, and Lumiere, the candelabra, who speaks with a French accent. In many of these little scenes, the characters acknowledge the child's presence as Belle's friend, as if she were standing there right beside Belle. These encounters help personalize the story for the child.

Thus, Belle is a companion doll who is also aspirational. She includes the child in an exciting adventure, and the doll's smart features make the experience interactive and advance the story. Most important of all, the child has a meaningful role: she helps Belle explore the castle; gets her ready for the ball; and prepares her for her encounter with the Beast.

THE TOY DEVELOPER'S PERSPECTIVE

Toy manufacturers like Playmates often collaborate closely with outside development companies when they are bringing out a new toy, and much of the actual work of creating a toy's personality and "intelligence" may be done by these specialists. One such company is Pangea Corp., which developed Belle, among many other smart toys. Two of the company's principals, John Schulte and John C. Besmehn, who use the titles "Big Dog" and "Little Dog," respectively, talked to me about their company's role in bringing dolls to life, and jointly shared their observations of smart toys in general.

Schulte and Besmehn believe today's children are far more excited about playthings that offer a multisensory experience than they are about static toys, and will no longer settle for "inert chunks of plastic." But they also feel that if a toy is too smart, it becomes too limiting. Children, they say, become disenchanted when a doll is overly bossy, narrowly restricting their experience by demanding that they "do this; do this; do this." They believe that the best smart toys serve as a stimulus, kindling the child's own sense of imaginative play, and that's the approach they take with the dolls they develop. There's a lot to be said, John Schulte told me, about technology "being used cleverly to open doors to parts of a girl's imagination she would otherwise ignore with a 'dumb' doll. That's why we try to imagine open-ended play patterns; we conjure up creative situations and scenarios that will evoke emotional responses, but allow for the girl herself to travel pathways of logic or illogic in a more open manner. We create the frame and provide the canvas. It's up to the girl to paint the picture as she sees it and feels it."

In working with a manufacturer on a new toy, Pangea comes aboard the project at an early concept stage and stays involved until the chips are burned. The development process starts by fleshing out each character and its world, looking for ways to harness the technology so that it will bring the character to life—by how it speaks or moves or reacts to a playpiece.

Biographies are written for each character, sometimes done as autobiographies, as if written by the characters themselves. If they are developing a multi-toy line, they also consider the other characters in the line, looking for balance and variety. Everything, they say, always leads back to the essence of the toy: what is the play pattern and what will the child's experience of it be? These are the concepts upon which the toy is built.

Once they've gotten the basics nailed down, they begin to map out the interactivity, working out the variables and laying down the protocols for the most likely and least likely choices the child will make. All of this is written out in a document that goes by various names in the toy business: a logic flow chart, a logic script, a matrix, or a flow chart. Once the interactivity is worked out, a branching if/then script is written for the experience, much as it would be for any other interactive narrative.

One of the biggest challenges, they say, is writing the dialogue, because storage is at such a premium on the chips, and it competes for room with programming code, sound effects, and music. The chips for Belle, for example, could contain a maximum of eight minutes of sound. To get the most mileage possible from the available storage, they make use of *concatenation*, a technique of efficiently reusing words and phrases. Common words, phrases, and sound effects are stored in a "sound data bank" and pulled out whenever needed. For example, it may store words for all the common colors, and if an NPC talks at one point about her friend's blue eyes and at another point about her new blue dress, the same word ,"blue," would be used both times.

Once the script is complete, they do a table reading and time it all out before giving it to the actors to record. For a toy like Belle, which was based on a hit movie, the stars of the film do the voices. For example, Angela Lansbury, who played Mrs. Potts in the film, does the voice of Mrs. Potts for the toy. However, they said, it can be a major adjustment for actors to work within the time constraints of a toy script, which may give them just 3.2 seconds per line to express their character's personality.

Interestingly, Schulte and Besmehn consider the development process for a smart doll to be very much like a video game, requiring many of the same considerations in terms of characters, interactivity, and script writing. The goal is to make the play experience as nonrestrictive as possible, letting the child feel in control, while inconspicuously channeling her toward an end goal.

Of course, smart toys need not resemble human beings, as we have seen with the Furby Boom. One group of hot toys that has been immensely popular is the collection of hamster-like creatures produced by Zhu Zhu Pets. Unlike living hamsters, these stuffed animals don't make messes and don't smell and don't hide in places that are out of reach, all of which have been strong selling points to the parents. Children love these cute stuffed beings because they can make 40 different sounds, race through tunnels, slide down chutes, and even act unpredictably. Sometimes they get stuck and need their human's help, just like real hamsters.

In recent years, holiday catalogues offering expensive merchandise have been featuring smart toys that resemble everything from adorable baby dinosaurs, each with its own personality, to insect-like creatures with unquenchable curiosity. These new smart toys all have their own set of characteristics and all of them are capable of some form of interaction with their human playmates.

TOY ROBOTS: NOT JUST FOR KIDS

As we noted earlier, robots are devices that operate either by remote control or on their own and respond in some way to their environment. Robots can closely resemble living creatures like humans, dogs, and other animals. In fact, dolls like Belle and Baby Bright Eyes are really robots, though they do not look like the stereotypical robots with the jerky movements and hard metal bodies that we are familiar with from the movies. A smart toy named Robosapien, however, very much does resemble these movie robots.

With his black and white body made of manufactured material, enormous arms, bowed legs, and glowing red eyes, one could never mistake Robosapien for a human. Yet he can actually "walk" on those two bowed legs, moving one leg in front of the other, just like a human, though an extremely ungainly one. Furthermore, he can execute 67 commands that are much like a verb set from a video game, including throw, kick, and pick up. Others, however, such as belch, are of a more earthy nature and are meant to give him "attitude." Surprisingly, Robosapien robots can be purchased for under $100 and are marketed as children's toys.

Not all robotic toys are meant to be children's playthings, however. In 1999, Sony introduced a sophisticated robotic "companion" dog named Aibo to the public. With a price tag of over $2,000, it was definitely not a kid's toy. These smart dogs can see (via a camera), hear, walk, obey commands, do tricks, and express canine-appropriate emotions. They love being petted and are responsive to their masters; their personalities are shaped by how they are treated. Some adult enthusiasts have acquired whole packs of them and swear that each dog has its own personality. A number of owners get together regularly with other owners for the equivalent of "play dates." Students at some universities have even programmed teams of Aibos to take part in soccer matches. Impressively, the dogs can play the game autonomously, on their own, without the use of remote controls. It is hardly surprising, then, that Aibo owners were dismayed when Sony announced in 2006 that they were discontinuing production of Aibos in a cost-cutting move.

A more serious type of robot, much closer to the robots found in works of science fiction, is Robonaut 2, created by NASA to be an assistant on space voyages. R2, as he is known, looks vaguely human, with a thick torso, shoulders, arms, head (in a helmet), and extremely dexterous fingers. However, at this point, he only exists from the torso up. He sits on a wheeled platform, though his developers say in the future he will have legs. His hands are particularly important, because they can perform more movements than the gloved hands of a human astronaut and thus can perform more tasks. R2 has already visited the Space Station and worked with the crew there.

R2 is not the only intelligent robot around. Simon is a humanoid robot that is being created by students at Georgia Tech. Simon's purpose is to demonstrate how robots can take part in social interactions with human beings and work alongside them. Simon can understand spoken sentences and reply, and makes gestures (nods, shrugs, and the like) that are quite human. And then there's DeeChee, a three-foot baby-like robot developed by researchers in England who is programmed to learn language just like a baby human does. DeeChee acquires a vocabulary of shapes and colors by interacting with human volunteers, who are instructed to talk with it like adults talk to babies.

STRANGE BUT TRUE: ROBOTIC FISH

Robofish are a school of bright yellow fish, about five feet long, designed by researchers of the Shoal Consortium to check for pollution in harbors and other bodies of water. The fish propel themselves realistically by their tails rather than by propellers, thus reducing the chance of getting snagged in seaweed. They can see underwater, communicate with each other, and analyze the data they collect. Though they offer great potential to scientists and environmentalists, they are unlikely to become popular at fish fries!

ANIMATRONIC CHARACTERS: STARS OF THE STAGE AND SCREEN

Animatronic characters are a particular type of robot that is made to look believably life-like. They are primarily found in motion pictures and theme parks and are also turning up frequently in museum installations. These specialized robots can resemble historic and contemporary figures, birds, bugs, sea creatures, and animals. Animatronic characters can move, talk, and sing, but the movements and sounds they make are preprogrammed or prerecorded. Essentially, they are mechanized puppets. The term Audio-Animatronic is a Walt Disney Engineering trademark and dates back to 1961.

Some of the first animatronic characters played important roles in movies (these include the giant squid in *20,000 Leagues Under the Sea* and the human-eating shark in *Jaws*). In Chapter 22, we describe a number of animatronic characters who play parts in theme parks, shows, and museum displays, including a giant grasshopper, a fierce pirate, and a soldier from the American Revolutionary War.

ANDROIDS: TOO MUCH LIKE US?

An android is a type of robot that is meant to look and act as much like a human being as possible, ideally to the point of passing as human. The world "android" comes from the Greek, meaning "resembling man." Unlike mechanized robots, androids are capable of responding to visual and vocal stimuli. Some androids are capable of voice recognition and can converse in a fairly believable way.

Androids are often used for training purposes in the military and in medical schools. For example, life-sized androids serve in the US Army, where they simulate wounded patients and are used by medics in training to prepare them for field conditions. With realistic faces and the height and weight of adult men and women, they look extremely convincing. But what makes them even more compelling is the fact that their chests rise and fall with healthy or raspy wheezy sounds. In addition, they possess an artificial pulse; their eyes tear; and they bleed and expel mucus. And when the wounded soldiers are not given the proper medical treatment, they can die.

Far away from the battlefield, a pretty blond android named Noelle is being used for medical school training. Like the android soldiers, she has a pulse and can breathe and bleed; she can also urinate. But what makes Noelle particularly interesting is that she is pregnant. She goes through labor and, if all goes well, she will give birth, even to twins. But, just as in real life, serious complications can develop and the medical students have to handle the crises well in order to keep Noelle and the baby or babies alive. Unlike real life, however, the complications are orchestrated by an instructor who controls Noelle via a laptop and in a sense serves as a dungeon master.

While the creation of the field of robotics used to be the domain of engineers and technology-minded scientists, a newer type of roboticist has become active in this arena. These scientists are particularly interested in robot–human interaction, and in creating robots that communicate in a life-like way, with nods, gestures, and eye contact, such as Simon, introduced above. Such androids, they believe, can eventually perform important services in taking care of the elderly, the disabled, and other dependent individuals.

STRANGE BUT TRUE: THE "UNCANNY VALLEY SYNDROME"

Roboticists are striving to make their creations seem as human as possible, but they have discovered that too much realism can have an unwanted negative effect. Known as "the uncanny valley syndrome," a term coined by Japanese roboticist Masahiro Mori, it seems that when a robot resembles a human too closely, people will find it too eerie and reject it. Thus, roboticists walk a thin line between making their androids convincingly human, but not *too* human.

One of the most realistic androids ever designed is a Japanese creation called Repliee Q1, developed by Professor Hiroshi Ishiguro of Osaka University. The slender, dark-haired, extremely feminine android caused a sensation when she appeared at the 2005 World Expo and even appeared on CNN and other TV news outlets. Called Q1 for short, she can converse in a believable fashion and gestures much like a real person. To contribute to her realism, she is programmed with 42 points of articulation in her upper body; she "breathes" with the aid of an air compressor; and her skin is made of soft, pliant silicone. And if Q1 receives too much annoying attention from a male admirer, she will react just like a real woman might, swatting him away with her hand.

At present Q1 is an experimental model, and despite her celebrity, she has not become involved in any works of digital storytelling. But it is interesting to speculate how androids like Q1, Noelle, and the wounded soldiers might be used in the future, playing life-like roles in productions that blend reality and fantasy in entirely new ways. Certainly, compelling scenarios could be built around their capabilities.

RESOURCES

To learn more about smart toys and robots, the following resources may be helpful:

- *Children's Technology Review*, http://www.childrenssoftware.com/, both a print and electronic magazine and also a website, carries articles and reviews of smart toys, with a focus on their educational value.

- Timetoplaymag (http://www.timetoplaymag.com) has news and reviews of all types of toys.

- Animatronics.org is a clearinghouse of information about animatronics and other types of robots.

- *Robotics Trends*, an online publication about robots: http://www.roboticstrends.com/.

CONCLUSION

As we've seen with the Belle doll from *Beauty and the Beast*, smart toys can be given personalities and support interactive narratives. And as we've seen with Noelle, the pregnant android, robots can be the center of life-like dramas. In addition, theme parks and museums are finding innovative ways to employ animatronic characters. Even though the work being done in robotics does not often intersect with the work going on in smart toys, both fields can contribute concepts and technology to new kinds of digital storytelling experiences.

The challenges of creating compelling interactive narratives with physical, life-like characters can be daunting, as this chapter has illustrated. Yet Lori Farbanish of Playmates Toys has a valuable piece of advice for creating smart toys that can be applied in general to all of these characters. "Sometimes," she says, "we think too much like adults. Sometimes you just have to dump all the pieces on the floor and play."

IDEA-GENERATING EXERCISES

1. Select an existing smart toy—one that has narrative features or a developed personality—and spend some time playing with it. Analyze what is compelling about the toy and where it may fall short. Do you think it could be improved, and if so, how? Can you see a way to use it as a model for another toy? How like or unlike do you think this toy is to other forms of interactive entertainment, such as a video game or VR installation?

2. Describe an android or an animatronic character that you have seen at a theme park, museum, or elsewhere. What about the character made it life-like? What about it did not seem "real"?

3. Sketch out an idea for an interactive talking character. How would it be part of an overall narrative experience? How would it communicate its personality? Would it require props, and if so, what kind?

CHAPTER 21

Interactive Cinema

Movie stories traditionally follow a linear path, and movie-going has always been a passive experience, so how do you open up a movie to a nonlinear narrative and give the audience a dynamic way to interact with it?

What is "group-based interactivity" and how does it fit into an interactive movie experience?

How is it similar to or different from multi-user interactivity found in such areas as MMOGs and iTV?

What narrative models are being used for small-screen interactive movies?

HOLD THE POPCORN!

Consider these three movie scenarios:

- An astroscientist, on a return trip from Mars, is struck by a mysterious and life-threatening illness after her space ship collides with some debris in outer space.

- An emotional family drama, a true story, reveals what it is like to grow up poor and black in the segregated American south.

- Cloned twins confront the drug-addicted scientist who created them.

All three stories have an intriguing premise and would seem to promise good movie entertainment. But if you planned on watching any of them while munching popcorn and reclining in a theater seat or on your couch at home, you'd have a problem. That's because all three are interactive movies. In other words, they are works of interactive cinema, or iCinema, and in order to enjoy them, you would need to be an active participant. This is no place for popcorn. You'd be too busy using your hands to eat it.

Most interactive movies fall into one of two quite different categories. One type is designed for a large theater screen and usually intended to be a group experience (although in some cases these large-screen works are meant for a solo participant). The other type is for a small screen and is usually viewed at home. It is a much more intimate experience, meant to be enjoyed by a single individual. Of the three movie scenarios described above, the first, the outer space story, was designed for a group experience in a theater; the second and third are small-screen films. Although the kinds of interactivity and the overall experience offered by the two types of iCinema are quite dissimilar, they do share some important characteristics:

- they are story driven;
- they have dimensional characters;
- even if and when they have some game-like features, narrative plays an essential role;
- choices made by the users profoundly affect how the story is experienced.

A BIRD'S EYE VIEW OF THE FIELD

Because interactive cinema is a direct descendent of the movies, one of the contemporary world's most beloved forms of entertainment, and because movies are so heavily narrative driven, one might expect that interactive cinema would be ground zero for digital storytelling. Unfortunately, such is not the case. Relatively little work is currently being done either for large-screen or small-screen interactive cinema.

Large-screen interactive movies can primarily be found in museums and other cultural institutions. The field has been dominated by one innovative company based in Toronto. As for small-screen interactive movies, most that have been produced to date have been made under the umbrella of universities or government-funded film institutes, where interactive storytellers can get the necessary support to work in this field. One exception to this is the interactive documentary, a narrative form that several print publications have been experimenting with (and several were discussed in Chapter 14). With the exception of interactive documentaries, the public has not been particularly receptive to small-screen iCinema, making it extremely difficult for such movies to succeed commercially. So far, only a small niche market exists for them, primarily among people in academic circles and those with a strong interest in cutting-edge storytelling. But even though this is hardly a booming field, the work being done in iCinema continues to break fresh ground in terms of devising new ways to combine story and interactivity, and gives us a number of useful examples of digital storytelling.

LARGE-SCREEN INTERACTIVE CINEMA

The film that is regarded as the world's first large-screen interactive movie was shown at the Montreal World's Fair in 1967. The film, produced in Czechoslovakia, was called *Kinoautomat* and was written by Radúz Činčera. It was the story of a man who felt a guilty responsibility about his apartment building burning down, and was told via flashbacks. The film contained nine choice points. The audience could vote on what they wanted to happen next by pressing a red or green button on their seats. What the audience didn't realize, however, was that no matter what they chose, the next scene would always be the same. Thus, it was not true interactivity. Nevertheless, it was a big hit at the World's Fair.

It was not until 1992 that the first true large-screen interactive movies were released to the public. These films were produced by a company called Interfilm, and were offered to the public between 1992 and 1995. They were released under a four-picture deal with Sony, with such titles as *Mr. Payback* and *I'm Your Man*. However, these movies offered extremely limited interactivity, especially for anyone used to the fast pace of video games, and they did little to impact the plotline. Very much like the Czech film at the World's Fair, people made their choices known via a button system embedded in the armrests of the theater seats (three buttons rather than two, thus offering them three possible choices). Otherwise, the audience had no role in the film. The branching storyline structure they used was thus quite similar to the old *Choose Your Own Adventure* books and offered about the same amount of meaningful agency … none, really. Furthermore, the storylines, acting, and production values were quite weak. Not surprisingly, they were commercially unsuccessful, and their failure to generate any enthusiasm from the public pretty much killed off interest in this area for many years.

In 1997, however, a Canadian company called Immersion Studios opened its doors and demonstrated considerable interest in this type of interactivity, particularly for projects that combined entertainment and education. In other words, they were works of edutainment. Many of them tackled scientific themes such as human biology, pollution, and nuclear energy. Based in Toronto, the company produced large-screen interactive films for a prestigious roster of international clients, including the Smithsonian Institution in the United States; La Cité in Paris; and the Science Museum in the UK. Although Immersion Studios ceased operations in 2006, the work produced there gives us an excellent view of the potential of large-screen cinema.

At Immersion Studios, they termed the work they did "immersive cinema," and immersion is the operative word here. Audiences were enveloped by surround sound and images projected on a large screen, and the films combined dramatic storylines with fast-paced gaming elements. These movies used both live action and 3D animation, sometimes in the same production. The interactivity offered to audiences was far richer and more dynamic than the old Interfilm model, and more purposeful, too.

With an Immersion Studios film, audience members were made to feel they had an essential role to play in the unfolding drama. In one case, for example, they played time travelers and their decisions helped determine what species would survive into the present day. In another case, they took on the role of marine biologists and tried to prevent the depletion of the population of sea lions.

Furthermore, the interactivity was far more versatile and extensive. Each single-person or two-person team was seated beside a touchscreen computer console, through which they indicated their choices. In addition, the computer gave them a way to dig deeply into the subject matter, somewhat like exploring a website. During the game-like segments, it served as a virtual control panel to direct the action. Thus, the Immersive Studio approach combined an audience-shared large-screen theatrical experience with a more personal small-screen experience and control system (see Figure 21.1).

Figure 21.1 At this large-screen work of iCinema, *Vital Space*, members of the audience sit in front of touchscreen consoles and help direct the action through the small screens. Image courtesy of Immersion Studios.

GROUP-BASED INTERACTIVITY

While participating in an Immersion Studios film, audience members were called upon to interact with each other, sometimes by competing and sometimes by collaborating. Some exchanges were done electronically, but at other times, people communicated the old-fashioned way—by talking with each other. At least one of the Immersion Studio projects was also networked, linking students at several different institutions. This type of shared communication, *group-based interactivity*, also known as *multi-user interactivity*, was the hallmark of an Immersion Studios experience.

WORTH NOTING: TYPES OF GROUP-BASED INTERACTIVITY

The group-based interactivity that is built into productions made by Immersion Studios bears an interesting similarity to the types of interactivity found in second-screen TV, in MMOGs, and in a few multiplayer motion-based games found at theme parks. All three are enjoyed simultaneously by multiple users/viewers, and the actions of the users help impact the outcome. It remains to be seen if these three areas will cross-pollinate each other in ways that will lead to advances in multi-user digital storytelling.

INVOLVING THE AUDIENCE

Stacey Spiegel, the CEO of Immersion Studios, believed his company's approach to iCinema was highly effective for teaching, and for three important reasons. First of all, he pointed out, the immersiveness of the stories facilitated the suspension of disbelief. In traditional media, he noted, "You are outside the window looking in. But here, the window disappears and you feel you are a part of what's happening." Second of all, the members of the audience were put in the position of having to make decisions, and their decisions had consequences. This caused them to be extremely alert and mindful of the material they were dealing with. And third, the collaborative social element—being an active participant in a group drama—reinforced learning. This type of audience involvement thus combined peer-to-peer and active learning, both described in Chapter 12. Spiegel noted that the company's philosophy of engaging the audience is reflected in the old proverb that goes: "Tell me and I'll forget; show me and I may remember; involve me and I'll understand."

Competitive gameplay was often built into these productions, because, Spiegel reported, their audiences responded so positively to it. Still, he stressed, narrative remained a vital element, giving their films a context and framework and contributing to their emotional power.

A SAMPLE LARGE-SCREEN EXPERIENCE

To see how an Immersion Studios movie worked, let's take a closer look at one of its films, *Vital Space*. The educational goal here was to give the audience an inside look at the major human body systems. The story, briefly sketched out at the opening of this chapter, is set in outer space. As the film opens, two space scientists, a married couple, have just completed a successful mission to Mars. Commander Susan Grant is examining a vial of Martian soil while her husband, Dr. John Osborne, is busy in another part of the space ship. Suddenly, the ship is struck by space debris, causing the soil sample to spill and contaminate the chamber where she is working. Thinking quickly, Commander Grant seals herself off in the lab to prevent further contamination, but she is already experiencing symptoms of a serious health problem.

At this point, just a few minutes into the movie, the audience is about to become intimately involved in the story, and their actions will determine Commander Grant's fate. Her husband informs us that since she has quarantined herself, making it impossible for him to examine her, the only way to diagnose and treat her illness is by using an experimental, remote-controlled medical system called VIVISYS, never utilized before under field conditions. And he'll need the help of those of us in "ground control" (the audience) to guide and direct VIVISYS, which we'll do via our touchscreen consoles. From this point on, we are faced with a series of decisions, such as selecting which type of microrobot should begin the diagnostic process (see Figure 21.2).

Figure 21.2   Screen capture of the microrobots in *Vital Space*. Image courtesy of Immersion Studios.

In a race against time, members of the audience try to determine the cause of Commander Grant's illness by investigating the various systems of her body. But her condition worsens, and in a dramatic twist, VIVISYS picks up a second heartbeat—shades of the movie *Alien!*—and is at the point of destroying it. But at the last moment, Commander Grant, writhing in pain, orders the procedure halted. It is a good thing she does, because it turns out that the second heartbeat belongs to her unborn child—unbeknownst to the couple, they have a baby on the way. As the investigation into her illness proceeds, the audience may or may not find the true cause of her problem: a lethal parasitic infection. If the audience does find it, the film turns more game-like, somewhat like a first-person shooter, with audience members trying to shoot down the intruders. Thus, the life or death drama of the plot helps keep the audience engaged in the film, and the combination of the large theater screen and the small console screens gives them the means to become deeply immersed in this unique journey through the human body.

SPECIAL CHALLENGES OF LARGE-SCREEN INTERACTIVE CINEMA

According to Brian Katz, who was the VP of Corporate Development at Immersion Studios, most of the films made by the company were for cultural institutions, who liked them because they help attract visitors. Although such large-screen installations required a great deal of special hardware and servicing, which could be expensive, they furthered the educational goals of these institutions. Also, because these films were suitable for all ages, they offered visitors a positive family experience. However, not all audience members were comfortable with this type of media-rich interactivity, Katz said. While young people were used to multitasking and had no problems with the large-screen/small-screen configuration, he reported that some older people become confused and wondered "where should I look?" Often the kids fell into the role of coaching their parents, he said.

Katz also noted some of the special creative challenges posed by large-screen interactive cinema, including:

- Devising a scenario that is gripping right from the start and that thrusts the audience members into the action.
- Avoiding a presentation that is overly complicated and could turn people off.
- Creating gameplay that is exciting and complements the narrative.
- Devising interactivity that calls for meaningful choices and not just guesswork.

EXPERT OBSERVATIONS: TYING THE LARGE AND SMALL SCREENS TOGETHER

One special challenge with the type of iCinema produced by Immersive Studios was tying together the content of the large and small screens. To illustrate how the action on the two screens could be made into a cohesive whole, Spiegel

> described a scene from a film they'd made on the space program. On the large
> screen, astronauts are seen outside the space station working on a robotic arm
> system. But when they try to return to the space station, they find the door is
> locked! While the astronauts hover helplessly in space, their oxygen running
> low, members of the audience feverishly work at their consoles, trying to find a
> way to unlock the door. Thus the action on the large and small screens is closely
> and dramatically integrated.

OTHER VENUES FOR LARGE-SCREEN iCINEMA

Unfortunately, Immersion Studios is no longer able to lead the way with large-screen iCinema and group-based interactivity, but large-screen iCinema has managed to find some new homes. As we will see in the next chapter, it is being used in immersive training simulations for military and law enforcement personnel. In addition, selected large-screen immersive iCinema experiences are offered at theme parks, as with Disney's set of works produced for the *Living Landscapes* pre-show for the *Soarin'* ride, described in Chapter 15.

SMALL-SCREEN INTERACTIVE CINEMA

Examples of small-screen interactive movies are somewhat easier to find than their larger relatives, but they are by no means abundant, even though most people have the hardware necessary to play them. These movies are made for the Internet, DVD-ROM and DVD-Video, and mobile devices, and thus they can be played on a variety of familiar platforms. The awareness of iCinema is greater in Europe than in the United States, but there are indications that even in the United States interest in them may slowly be growing. Some of these productions are now being shown at international festivals, and they are also being sold at brick-and-mortar bookstores and at online sites like Amazon.com, all signs that a market for them may gradually be developing.

These productions are somewhat like the films one can find in art house movie theaters. Unlike blockbuster commercial movies, they are not fantasies about comic book heroes or gory action-adventure pictures. Instead, they are apt to have an intellectual underpinning and focus more on human relationships and sophisticated psychological or philosophical themes. Unlike linear films, they lend themselves well to telling a story from multiple points of view, and often offer viewers a wealth of visual material to investigate. Filmmakers working in this area have developed several different models of interactive narrative, including:

- the hyperstory;
- the database narrative;
- interactive documentaries;

- the user as fulcrum; and
- the spatial narrative.

THE HYPERSTORY

Hyperstory is a term used by filmmaker Margi Szperling to describe the works of iCinema she produces. A hyperstory, like hypertext, links different elements together, but instead of linking a word to another piece of text, a visual element is linked to another visual element, offering a different view of the same scene or story. Szperling believes her hyperstory approach to filmmaking offers a deeper and more complex view of the world than the typical Hollywood linear movie.

Before becoming interested in interactive media, Szperling had been an architect, and told me the disciplines have much in common, since both deal with structure, the movement through space, and design issues. In describing her hyperstory approach to me, Szperling said: "We can tell different kinds of stories in this medium, from multiple perspectives. These are databases that respond to people's choices." Among her influences, she said, were the novels of James Joyce, the movie *Rashomon*, and the theories of the Russian experimental documentary filmmaker, Dziga Vertov (1896–1954). Vertov expounded an idea of "film truth," holding that fragments of film, when organized, could reveal a truth not perceptible to the naked eye.

Szperling's first film, *Uncompressed*, was, at its core, a science fiction drama about a drug-addicted scientist and the set of twins he has cloned in his lab. However, with its six intersecting storylines, the film is far more layered than a typical sci-fi film. The stories of the scientist and the twins form two of the narrative paths. Other narrative paths follow a man with a life-threatening illness; a telepathic grandmother and granddaughter; a woman who has passed away; and the man who still loves her. Unlike the typical Hollywood movie, *Uncompressed* does not have a central protagonist. Instead, each character or set of characters serves as the protagonist of their individual storylines.

Though the characters all seem to live in disparate worlds, their stories are all interconnected. The drama culminates with a violent confrontation in which a gun is fired and someone is shot, but unless you work your way through all six paths, you cannot have a clear understanding of what has happened. To some degree, therefore, the film uses a *Rashomon* model, in which a single event is seen through the eyes of different characters.

When playing *Uncompressed*, the first thing one comes to is a screen divided into six frames. Each frame contains an image of the characters, singly or in pairs (see Figure 21.3). By running your cursor over any of the frames, the character or characters inside will reveal a brief bit about themselves. By clicking on one of the frames, you will go to their storyline. The characters' paths cross at various points in the film. If you wish, you can follow each of the six stories from start to finish, in a linear fashion, but you can also switch to another character's perspective at various junctions. In addition, you can choose specific scenes to watch by going to the chapter index.

Figure 21.3 The six characters and pairs of characters featured in *Uncompressed*. Image courtesy of Margi Szperling and substanz.

According to Szperling, *Uncompressed* allows the viewer to "see between the panes of glass." Her hope in making this work, she told me, "was to create a series of subtle questions meant to discredit and validate themselves within the storyline. I realize this is a conundrum," she admitted, but added that "most provocative artwork contains opposites. Every storyline shows how different the same reality can appear; it shows perspectives as they intersect with each other. This is where the strength of the piece lies. With this vast an amount of interactive content, much is learned by traveling in between the layers." All told, the work has six storylines, and the user can jump at will between them and experience the six variations of the story (see Figure 21.4).

Uncompressed runs for 36 minutes, though it takes hours to play in all its variations. Despite the low budget and the various challenges encountered while making it, the film has notably high production values. This, coupled with its innovative design and intricately crafted story, has earned it nominations in about 50 international competitions and awards in several of them. Szperling believes her narrative model, the hyperstory, has great potential, and looks at *Uncompressed* as a prototype of what is possible. She believes this form can give us "a way to understand who we are and to understand the complexities of the world around us."

Figure 21.4 The chapter index of *Uncompressed*, one of several ways in which viewers can change perspectives. Image courtesy of Margi Szperling and substanz.

DATABASE NARRATIVES

The Labyrinth Project at the University of Southern California specializes in what it calls "database narratives." These are works of iCinema made up of tiny pieces of data that users can assemble in various ways to form their own versions of the narrative. The Labyrinth Project is under the direction of cultural theorist Marsha Kinder, who serves as executive producer of the works made under its auspices. These interactive narratives explore, as Kinder terms it, "the border between documentary and fiction."

The website for the Labyrinth Project explains: "Although a database narrative may have no clear-cut beginning, no narrative closure, no three-act structure, and no coherent chain of causality, it still presents a narrative field full of story elements that are capable of arousing a user's curiosity and desire."

Documentaries, compiled as they are from a great mass of material, are particularly well suited to the database narrative approach. In linear documentaries, the production team decides which version of the truth to present. It selects which materials to show the viewer and which to exclude and it arranges the order in which the scenes will be shown. But in a nonlinear documentary, the selection process is turned over to the viewers, and ultimately, they can form their own version of the truth.

Unlike traditional linear documentaries, database narratives "frequently have a subversive edge," the Labyrinth Project website asserts. "For, in calling attention to the database infrastructure of all narratives, they reveal a fuller range of alternatives. In this way, they expose the arbitrariness of so-called master narratives, which are frequently designed to appear natural or inevitable."

The Labyrinth Project has undertaken a variety of disparate projects, many of them based on the works of artists and writers. For example, *The Dawn at My Back*, a DVD-ROM, is a memoir created by an African-American woman about her life and family. It relates what it was like to grow up poor and black in Texas and uses a quilt metaphor to present the different pieces of her story. Like a handmade quilt, the memoir is composed of many small fragments. The task of stitching them together, however, is given to the viewer. The pieces of the quilt are an assortment of old photos, contemporary videos, interviews, voices, and animations. The quilt that forms the backdrop of this work is an heirloom from the filmmaker's own family, giving her story an even deeper emotional resonance.

Bleeding Through: Layers of Los Angeles is another film made under the umbrella of the Labyrinth Project. As the title suggests, it takes a layered approach to narrative. It also boldly intertwines historic fact and invented fiction. Set in downtown Los Angeles and spanning over 60 years, from 1920 to 1986, it tells the story of a fictitious woman named Molly (based on a real person) who may—or may not—have murdered one of her husbands. Users are invited to piece together their own version of Molly's alleged crime, which they can do by sifting through a great amount of historical material. The narrative thus uses the archeological dig structural model described in Chapter 7.

The work is the creation of Norman Klein, a novelist, historian, and cultural critic. He not only wears all three hats in this interactive narrative but also appears in a window on the screen, adding his own commentary. The work, presented on a DVD-ROM, was an international coproduction of the ZKM Center for Art and Media in Germany and the Labyrinth Project at USC's Annenberg Center.

Although Molly is an invented character, her story is shaped by the history of her time and place. It is set in downtown Los Angeles during a period when that part of the city was undergoing profound cultural change. *Bleeding Through* uses vintage film clips, maps, reconstructed scenes of actual events, historic photos, and contemporary interviews to tell Molly's story (see Figure 21.5). Klein notes: "We're a civilization of layers. We no longer think in montage and collage; we multitask in layers more and more" (as reported in the *San Francisco Chronicle*, in a story by Glen Hellfand, September 18, 2003).

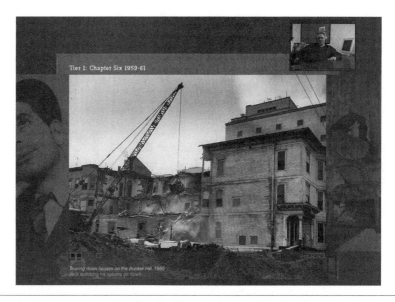

Figure 21.5 A screenshot from *Bleeding Through: Layers of Los Angeles*. Image courtesy of the Labyrinth Project of USC's Annenberg Center for Communication and the ZKM Center for Art and Media.

Like other database narratives produced by the Labyrinth Project, *Bleeding Through* is highly cinematic and visually arresting. One particularly striking feature is the way old and new photos of Los Angeles, taken from exactly the same angle, are layered on top of each other. By sliding between them, users can see the images literally bleed through each other and watch landmarks appear and disappear. It is a visual metaphor for the way the present overtakes the past, but by peeling back the present, the past can be revealed.

OTHER DOCUMENTARY FORMS

The database narrative approach is an extremely interesting way to present documentary material, but as we saw in Chapter 14, there are many other ways, as well. In *Snow Fall: The Avalanche at Tunnel Creek* and in *The Jockey*, the *New York Times* created two works in which we had a gripping interplay between larger pieces of video, audio, and text, and one through which we could assemble our own personalized narrative.

A somewhat different approach, both simpler and more complex, is employed in *Clouds over Cuba*, an interactive documentary about the Cuban Missile Crisis produced in 2012 by the John F. Kennedy Presidential Library and Museum. The documentary, made to commemorate the fiftieth anniversary of the Cuban missile crisis, was designed to be played on the Web, on the iPad, and on other mobile devices. It thus uses a common feature of Web pages, the menu, and breaks the material into seven chapters. But it also covers a wealth of documentary materials (including letters, government papers, and still photos) which you can scrutinize while watching the video footage or can save in your "dossier" to examine later. The documentary can also be viewed using a "real time calendar" of the events, watching them in chronological order. One of the most unique features of the documentary is a totally fictional and haunting "what if" segment, a video supposedly shot in 2012 discussing the disaster that "occurred" 50 years earlier, when diplomacy failed and bombs were dropped on Cuba, the United States, and the Soviet Union. Clouds over Cuba can be viewed at http://cloudsovercuba.com/.

Manuela's Children is an interactive documentary that uses a multiple person point of view. The film, created by artist Eva Koch, was funded by the Danish Film Institute. It is a highly personal saga of five Spanish children torn apart by personal and national tragedy. Soon after the children's father dies, their mother, the Manuela of the title, becomes too ill to care for them. When the Spanish Civil War breaks out, the children are separated and scattered to various places. One dies in infancy and another ends up in Scandinavia—the woman who is destined to become the mother of filmmaker Koch. Years later, Koch travels back to Spain to reconstruct her family's history on film and reunite as many of her kin as she can.

However, instead of taking the familiar documentary approach, which would force her to take a restrictive linear path, she chose to use the interactive features of the DVD, which offered her a more fluid, open framework. She gives the siblings' accounts as individual but parallel chronological journeys, using a variation of the *Rashomon* model described in Chapter 7. Each account contributes a different layer to the narrative. Viewers can choose to follow one sibling's story at a time, or, more provocatively, can switch back and forth between them, allowing them to view this family drama from alternate viewpoints. This approach reflected the reality of the situation: each member of the family had a unique and personal view of their family's history. To try to present their memories as a single united version of the truth would have done their stories a disservice.

In *Bear71*, an interactive documentary produced by the National Film Board of Canada, our central character is a female grizzly bear. The 20-minute film was released at Sundance in 2012, and recreates the habitat and challenges faced by wildlife when its environment is encroached by modern technology. We meet the bear right after she is trapped and watch her being tagged with a radio collar, thus becoming Bear71. The radio collar allows us to follow her story from there on an interactive grid of her rangeland in Banff National Park, and it eventually comes to a sad end. We can click at will on other tagged wildlife as well, see videos of ones that have been caught on hidden cameras and learn more about them. The bear herself is given an anthropomorphic treatment by the script which is read by an actress, which unfortunately clashes with the realism of the piece, but the documentary is effective nonetheless.

USER AS FULCRUM

In the *user as fulcrum* model of iCinema, the viewer is actually inserted into the story, and the decisions that he or she makes drive the narrative forward. Unlike a role-playing game, however, users do not take on a fictional identity. Instead, they step into the story as the person they are in real life.

To date, the best example of this approach to iCinema is a work called *Façade*. Although sometimes described as a video game, *Façade* is a domestic drama. It contains just three characters: a married couple, Trip and Grace (both NPCs), and you, an old friend of theirs.

You experience the drama from the first-person POV, and it begins when you accept Trip's invitation to come over to their apartment for an evening of socializing. However, after a few pleasantries, the façade of their happy marriage slips off and the true strains become too obvious to miss, a shade like an interactive version of Edward Albee's play, *Who's Afraid of Virginia Woolf*. Things become even more awkward when one of the characters begins to flirt with you. The way you handle the situation and how you interact with the two (which is done by typing in your end of the conversation) shapes the way the evening unfolds. The characters of Grace and Trip have been given a robust amount of AI and the twists and turns of the drama are not pre-scripted; they are rendered on the fly.

One of the most noteworthy aspects of *Façade*, aside from its impressive use of AI, is the intent behind it—to produce a believable interactive drama with psychologically complex characters and emotional intensity. The work, created by Andrew Stern and Michael Mateas, was five years in the making. According to the *Façade* website, the pair did not want the work to be like a typical fantasy video game, "about manipulating magical objects, fighting monsters, and rescuing princesses." Instead, they wanted to make something about real human relationships. "Rather than focusing on the traditional gamer market, we are interested in interactive experiences that appeal to the adult, non-computer geek, movie-and-theater-going public."

THE SPATIAL NARRATIVE

A *spatial narrative* is an interactive drama in which the story elements are embedded in a three-dimensional space, and the user discovers narrative fragments while exploring the fictional environment. One excellent example of this approach to iCinema is a work called *A Space of Time*, created by Dr. Diego Bonilla several years ago. The story is about a homeless man who lives in an abandoned school building. As you navigate around the building, you get glimpses not only of his past and present life there, but also of other individuals who spent time in the school. *A Space of Time* is composed of over 700 QuickTime videos, making the possible permutations of this story enormous.

Another extremely interesting spatial narrative is a work by Julia Heyward called *Miracles in Reverse*. A story about the trauma of child sexual abuse, it is at once deeply personal and profoundly surrealistic. In order to put the pieces of the story together, one must first select one of three possible ways to enter it … from the point of view of a mom, an alien, or Jesus Christ. Once one of these characters is selected, the user is free to explore the protagonist's home, garden, tool shed, and neighborhood, uncovering pieces of her disturbing story along the way.

OTHER FICTION-BASED SMALL-SCREEN FORMS OF iCINEMA

Digital storytellers have found a multitude of other ways to harness technology to create works of iCinema. Among them are:

Multiplot Stories on a Grid

In *Crossed Lines*, Dr. Sarah Atkinson of the University of Brighton created a multiplot film using nine characters and connecting them all via conversations on the telephone.

The characters are arranged on the screen in three rows of three characters each, in other words, on a grid. You, the user, can make any character telephone any other character. The work contains no central plot but is made up of numerous subplots. She uses a real telephone keypad as the interface device, a clever and totally appropriate device considering the subject matter. For example, by pressing keys number 4 and number 8, you can have character number 4 call character number 8 and then speak with each other (see Figure 21.6). The characters are presented somewhat as if a webcam is directed on them at all times. We can see what each is doing when not talking on the phone. The grid presentation is somewhat similar to *Uncompressed*, though unlike *Uncompressed*, there is no central plot. The work can be viewed both on a large screen and on a small screen.

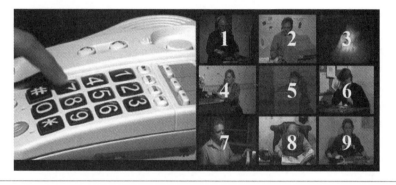

Figure 21.6 In *Crossed Lines*, we can connect characters by having them talk with each other on the telephone. Image courtesy of Dr. Sarah Atkinson.

Employing DVD Technology

Both *Scourges of the World* and *Late Fragment* are interactive movies released on DVD, and have taken advantage of the DVD's generous storage capacity and menu system to produce multilayered stories, but do so in quite different ways. *Scourges of the World* is a dungeons and dragons animated adventure with multiple branches. Viewers are asked to make decisions at critical parts of the story (using the menu system and the DVD remote), and their choices determine what version of the narrative they see and how the version ends. This branching tree structure is, of course, not exactly a novel one. It's the same concept that was used in the old *Choose Your Own Adventure* books, mentioned several times in this book, and has been the underlying structure for many interactive screen-based narratives. According to the producers, the Canadian company DKP Effects, it contains 996 possible variations and four possible endings, thus offering a fairly generous amount of agency for a branching tree structure.

Late Fragment (http://www.latefragment.com/), on the other hand, uses an approach its creators term 360-degree storytelling. It is a story focusing on just three contemporary characters, and by clicking on the remote when a particular character is on the screen, you are offered a piece of that character's backstory or point of view, and can uncover secrets about that character. The three characters have quite different lifestyles and issues, but they are united by all belonging to a type of therapy group called Restorative Justice. The work contains 137 scenes that viewers can piece together in a variety of ways. It was produced by the CFC Media Lab in co-production with the National Film Board of Canada.

Stories with User-Generated Characters

Beckinfield and *Aurelia: Edge of Darkness* are both works made for the Internet which are in part populated by characters that members of the audience have invented and actually portray in videos. The users upload their videos to a website powered by the Theatrics collaborative storytelling platform. The two works are both multi-episode stories, and thus are a bit more like a television series than a movie. *Beckinfield* (http://www.theatrics.com/beckinfield/), produced by Theatrics, is a science fiction story about the mysterious goings-on in a fictional town. Its creators refer to it as "a never-ending soap opera" and as "mass participation TV." The site has 4,000 registered users, and 10 percent of them, or about 400 people, regularly upload content to the ongoing story. Users receive a weekly newsletter and a story bible to help them contribute to the narrative, which is plotted, but not scripted.

Aurelia: Edge of Darkness (http://enteraurelia.com/) is described by its producers as a "steampunk fantasy Web drama." It utilizes the toolset offered by Theatrics (the producers of *Beckinfield*), which now offers a self-service version of its software. The story revolves around a city built by the survivors of an ecological cataclysm. Unfortunately, the city is running out of power and its inhabitants may perish if a solution is not found. As with *Beckinfield*, participants create a character, videotape themselves reciting a monologue, and submit it to the company. Their characters may then be integrated into the story by writer Lisa Walker England. The 16-week series was launched in the summer of 2013.

iCinema Works Driven by Social Media

In some cases, the events or the outcome of an iCinema story are controlled by users on social media sites. *Inside* was such a work, and furthermore, it played out in real time. It is a thriller about a 24-year-old woman who is being held captive in an unknown place by an unknown person for an unknown reason. However, the room where she is kept contains a laptop computer, and with this computer she reaches out to friends and to others on social media sites (Facebook, YouTube, and Twitter) who have heard of her terrifying plight. These connections help her decipher clues in her room that will lead to her release and solve the mystery of her captivity. The video episodes ran one to four minutes long and new ones were posted every few days, with posts on social media sites in between. The work was a branded property sponsored by Toshiba and Intel: her laptop is a Toshiba, powered by an Intel chip.

iCinema Works Controlled by the Movements of Audience Members

Professor Martin Rieser of De Montfort University in the UK has been creating narrative installations in which the distance of the audience member to the screen or projection affects what the audience member sees and hears. For instance, in *Understanding Echo*, a flickering image of a woman is projected in a shallow pool in the middle of the room. She is a reference to the mythological figure of the nymph, associated with lakes and wells. She is speaking, and as a member of the audience draws nearer to her, her comments become more intimate. Conversely, the further away the audience member, the more impersonal her comments.

In *Secret Garden*, Rieser explores the *Garden of Eden* story in the Bible through words, dance, and song. The scenes from the story are displayed on 11 iPads arranged in a circle, and audience members wear headphones to experience 3D animated images and spatialized acapella singing. Each iPad contains one scene from the story, and as an audience member approaches a particular iPad, that scene is triggered. Thus, audience members can assemble the story in any order, depending on the order in which they approach the iPads. In a way, this work is a bit like *Uncompressed*, because members of the audience can create their version of the story from a number of offered scenes, but the big difference is that *The Secret Garden* is played out on multiple screens in a physical space.

Rieser also led *The Third Woman* project (2008–2011) under the European emobilArt initiative. This project was, in part, an interactive mobile film. It was set in contemporary Vienna, revisiting the territory of post-war film *The Third Man* and re-imagining it for the twenty-first century. The public participated by using their mobile phones to trigger QR codes for film-noir fragments and text messages, which moved them through a scenario. The film itself was structured into three parallel dramas where the same scene was available in three different emotional moods. The work toured internationally—in Austria, Greece, Britain, China, and the United States—and was reworked substantially for each succeeding venue. Other aspects of this project were discussed in Chapter 17.

WORTH NOTING: iCINEMA AND ACADEMIA

As we have noted throughout this chapter, much of the work done in iCinema has been under the helm of academic institutions. To a large degree, colleges, universities, and film schools are the major force pushing this field forward. The Labyrinth Project (http://thelabyrinthproject.com/), with its innovative program on database narrative, is under the wing of the famed School of Cinematic Arts at the University of Southern California. And the iCinema Centre for Interactive Cinema Research at the University of New South Wales is another program to keep an eye on, even though a great deal of this program's emphasis is on virtual reality and other forms of immersive experiences. Nevertheless, its website (http://www.icinema.unsw.edu.au/) contains much of interest.

CONCLUSION

As we have seen in this chapter, the field of iCinema may be small, but the work that is being produced here is dynamic and innovative. It encompasses both large-screen theatrical experiences and intimate small-screen interactivity, sometimes within the same work, and the practitioners of iCinema employ highly diverse approaches for the works they create.

Each new venture in iCinema pushes the envelope of digital storytelling a little bit further. It is a field that cries out for more study and more experimentation. Advances, however, have been slowed by the dearth of successful business models. Even more daunting, however, has been the lack thus far of a receptive audience for this type of storytelling. Some critics have argued that iCinema has not caught on because it is simply not a viable form of entertainment, and that cinematic storytelling and interactivity cannot be melded together in a satisfactory way.

However, it must be remembered that in the early days of linear cinema, it too met with a negative reception. Audiences reacted to the first movies they saw with bewilderment and hardly knew what to make of them. With time and increased familiarity, however, they came to accept and understand the grammar of this new medium—techniques like the montage, the dissolve, and the flashback. In fact, if we look at the history of each new art form, we will usually find that the public reacts with skepticism and an initial lack of enthusiasm. Not so long ago, when music videos were first aired on TV, they too had a chilly reception, especially from adults who had grown up watching the more sedately paced movies of the mid-twentieth century. Many found music videos to be a dizzying barrage of unconnected images and could find nothing to enjoy about them. Although some people will never like them, they have become an immensely popular and influential part of contemporary culture.

As for interactive cinema, it is critically important that it, too, develop a support base of users. Otherwise, its creators are laboring in a vacuum. Josephine Anstey, who created the VR work *A Thing Growing* (described in Chapter 22), stated this dilemma eloquently when she said: "We need practitioners and experimentalists, but we also need an increasingly sophisticated audience and the feedback between the two. No interactive fiction can be made without constant testing and feedback from users" (*Computer Graphics World*, February, 2001).

Hopefully, as more people are exposed to iCinema, they will begin to develop an understanding and appreciation of a new cinematic language and a new storytelling art form, and this promising arena will receive the support it needs to move forward.

IDEA-GENERATING EXERCISES

1. What do you think might eventually help iCinema reach a greater audience?

2. Pick a subject that you think might work well as a fiction-based interactive movie. Do you think this topic would be better suited to a large-screen experience or a small-screen experience, and why? Which approach to iCinema described in this chapter do you think would be most appropriate for your premise, or do you feel that you would need to work out an original approach of your own?

3. Pick a subject that you think lends itself well to a documentary work for iCinema. How would you take advantage of the interactivity that digital media provides?

4. Sketch out an idea for an interactive movie that involves a large-screen and small-screen configuration, as with the Immersive Studios model, and work out one sample idea that offers multi-user interactivity. What would be happening on the large screen, and what would participants be doing on the small screen?

CHAPTER 22

Immersive Environments

What is meant by an "immersive environment?"

What are some of the special methods used to create the illusion of being "inside" a digitally created virtual world?

What are some of the greatest challenges of creating a story-based experience for immersive environments?

What unique opportunities do these virtual worlds present to storytellers?

SCIENCE FICTION TERRITORY

In real life, it is highly unlikely you'd get to go on a dangerous military reconnaissance mission behind enemy lines without risk of injury or death. And unless you had supernatural powers, you couldn't expect to hear the voices of the departed when you visited a graveyard. And you'd certainly have to have a pretty powerful imagination to see yourself going on a guided tour of the ocean by a friendly dolphin. But thanks to various forms of virtual reality (VR) and other digitally created immersive environments, you can experience all of these things, and in a way that is convincingly life-like.

When we move into the world of immersive environments, we are entering serious science fiction territory—but science fiction that has become entertainment fact. A dramatic vision of this type of experience, as portrayed by the media, was introduced to us in the pilot episode of *Star Trek: The Next Generation* TV series, with a device called the holodeck. In this make-believe vision of VR, the crew of the starship Enterprise and its successor, Voyager, could entertain themselves in their off hours by visiting the holodeck and becoming actors in computer-generated dramas. These experiences were much like novels that had come to life, complete with props, sets, life-like characters, virtual food, tactile sensations, and scenarios capable of eliciting intense emotions. The holodeck was such a compelling vision of the possibilities of marrying narrative to digital technology that Janet Murray even named her book on the future of storytelling after it, calling it *Hamlet on the Holodeck*.

To date, of course, nothing as convincing and detailed as the alternate reality of the *Star Trek* holodeck has been achieved here on Planet Earth. However, computer scientists and imaginative twenty-first-century storytellers, progressing in small increments, are moving ever closer. Before we investigate what they've accomplished, and discuss the implications their work has for new types of narratives, let's first take a moment to pin down what we are talking about.

DEFINING IMMERSIVE ENVIRONMENTS

Immersive environments can be roughly defined by what they are intended to do. The goal of a digitally created, or digitally enhanced, immersive environment is to give users an intense and seemingly real experience they could not otherwise have. They put the participants right "inside" a digitally created world, hence the term *environment*. In other words, the participant is not just looking at something on a screen or monitor but is instead surrounded by the work and, in many cases, is interacting with it.

A number of these experiences fall into a category of works called *Location Based Entertainment* (LBE), which are entertainment experiences that take place outside the home. LBE includes various kinds of theme park attractions as well as multiplayer competitions like racing simulations and outer space combats. It also includes attractions set in museums and other cultural institutions, visitors' centers, and Las Vegas hotels.

Immersive environments encompass a very broad and diverse group of digital works, with at least eight different subgenres, and we will be examining each of them in this chapter. They include:

- virtual reality (VR);
- mixed reality;
- augmented reality (AR);
- large-screen immersive experiences for audiences (also known as ridefilms and 4D dark rides);
- large-screen immersive experiences for single participants;
- immersive multiplayer motion-based games;
- interactive theme park rides; and
- fulldome productions.

Immersive environments use a large palette of techniques to create their fantasy worlds. Some, like virtual reality, require the user to wear heavy-duty hardware. Others utilize large curved screens. Still others employ animatronic characters. Often, immersive environments are *multi-sensory*, meaning they stimulate the senses in a number of ways. While traditional screen-based works like movies and television only employ the senses of seeing and hearing, immersive environments also may employ touch and smell, making them uniquely powerful. Techniques for doing this may include variations in room temperature; special effects like snow and fog; various forms of tactile sensations such as vibrations and sprays of water; the movement of a seat or floor; and artificially produced smells.

Like other forms of digital storytelling, immersive environments contain narrative elements, like plots, characters, and dramatic situations. However, telling stories with this type of technology can be challenging. While many works of immersive environments are designed for pure entertainment, they are used for other purposes as well. These include teaching and training; psychotherapy; promotion; and the enhancement of information, particularly in cultural institutions.

VIRTUAL REALITY: WELCOME TO THE OUTER EDGES OF CYBERSPACE

A true VR environment is an extreme form of cyberspace, a 3D artificial world generated by computers, and a world that seems believably real. Within such a space, one is able to move around and view the virtual structures and objects from any angle. But a VR world requires special hardware to be perceived. In one of its most common forms, visitors are outfitted with a helmet-like device with goggles and ear phones called a *head-mounted display* (HMD) and special gloves, which gives them the ability to perceive and manipulate the computer-generated representations. Another important type of VR is called the *CAVE*, where the users are surrounded by rear-view projection screens and wear stereoscopic glasses to see 3D images.

It should be noted, however, that we are talking about immersive VR experiences here, and that VR is not necessarily a space that one enters. Some VR creations are designed just for observation purposes. They may be quite small, just of tabletop size. Such VR creations are chiefly constructed for scientific, engineering, or architectural purposes, not for entertainment.

While most individuals have had at least one experience inside an immersive environment, usually as an attraction at a theme park, true VR installations are much harder to come by. Except for a small handful of theme parks, most VR is confined to the research divisions of academic, military, or industrial organizations. But to make matters a bit more complicated, the term "virtual reality" is often applied indiscriminately to immersive experiences that have some, but not all, of the components of true VR.

A CLOSE-UP LOOK AT A WORK OF VR

Let's examine a true work of VR in more detail. Our example will be *DarkCon*, an intensely gripping military simulation discussed briefly in Chapter 6. The name, *DarkCon*, comes from "dark reconnaissance mission." It was created as part of the US Army's endeavor to utilize interactive digital media to create safe but effective training methods. *DarkCon* was produced for the Army by the USC Institute for Creative Technologies (ICT), which is a research arm of the University of Southern California.

To experience *DarkCon*, each soldier/trainee, one by one, dons a HMD and earphones and steps onto a large bare platform. Via the 3D images seen through the HMD and the sounds heard through the earphones, the soldier is plunged into a frighteningly realistic surveillance mission. As the soldier turns or moves in one direction or another, specific images and sounds are activated. In a sense, the soldier acts as a computer cursor. By moving to position A, one type of response from the program will be triggered; moving to position B will trigger another.

The soldier's assignment is to observe members of a rogue paramilitary troop suspected of stockpiling illegal weapons, moving as close to them as possible, but to avoid attracting their attention; otherwise the consequences could be fatal. The mission begins in a dark culvert near a bridge and an abandoned mill (see Figure 22.1). Although there is no dialogue, sound effects—such as dripping water, a barking dog, or the scurrying of a rat—play an important role. The participant will even hear the sound of his own footsteps as he moves through the virtual landscape, and they'll match the terrain he or she is moving over—the squishing of mud, the crunch of gravel, the rustling of dry leaves. The footsteps are also synced up to the soldier's movements. If he or she starts to run, the footsteps will quicken.

Figure 22.1 The *DarkCon* VR simulation begins inside a dark culvert. Image courtesy of USC's Institute for Creative Technologies.

The realism of the simulation is further enhanced by both a *scent necklace* and a *rumble floor*. The rumble floor is built into the platform the trainee moves across during the mission, and vibrates when cued by certain events, such as an explosion or a truck passing over the bridge. The "scent necklace," worn around the neck, gives off specific smells at key points during the simulation, and is geared to enhance the frightening moments as well as the moments of relief. For instance, while moving through the dark and dangerous culvert, the trainee might smell a mustiness that hints of decay or rats, but at better moments, such as emerging unharmed from the culvert, the necklace might emit the fragrance of fresh pine.

Writer Larry Tuch, a professional screenwriter with a Hollywood television background and a long-term involvement with ICT, was given the task of writing the initial demo script for *DarkCon*. In describing his role to me, he said he was called upon to create a context for the surveillance mission and a structural spine for the experience. He also had to find ways of ramping up the tension and the soldier's sense of jeopardy. He scripted in a number of objects, events, and visual clues for the soldier to discover during the mission. One of them was a child's broken doll, which was possibly abandoned by a family of fleeing refugees. Another was a blood-spattered wall, possibly evidence of a slaughter.

From his television experience, Tuch was used to developing stories with three acts, and used this model for *DarkCon*. The first act set up the mission and the second act introduced a series of complications, much like a typical Hollywood script. However, the third act was left open-ended, without a fixed resolution; the ending would be shaped by the decisions the soldier/trainee made along the way. Thus, although *DarkCon* might not contain as complex a story as a Hollywood movie, it does contain many important narrative elements: a protagonist, opponents, a goal, obstacles, a structural spine, and an increasing degree of jeopardy. And it is these narrative elements, plus the unique aspects of VR, that make it so gripping and effective as a simulation.

USING VR FOR ARTISTIC EXPRESSION AND STORYTELLING

Outside of the military, the most adventurous storytelling in VR work often takes place within academic institutions. In this setting, professors and students are keen to push the boundaries of this medium and have more latitude to experiment than they would in the outside world, where commercial considerations are often constricting. At Iowa State University, for example, faculty and students have worked together within the university's Virtual Reality Applications Center to produce some extremely innovative work.

One of their projects, *Ashes to Ashes*, is particularly dramatic. It is an emotional memorial to the victims and survivors of the New York City terrorist attacks on 9/11. It was built for a six-sided CAVE called the C6, which offers 360-degree immersion. In a C6, the ceiling, walls, and floor are all stereoscopic screens, and it has a 3D sound system as well. An extremely ambitious undertaking, *Ashes to Ashes* combines abstract dance, music, and narrative accounts of the survivors and witnesses, all in a technical environment which does not normally support any of these things (see Figure 22.2).

Figure 22.2 In *Ashes to Ashes*, VR is used to recreate the events of 9/11. Here, users listen to the final comments of survivors while surrounded by the rubble of the World Trade Towers. Image courtesy of the Virtual Reality Applications Center of Iowa State University.

To help shape the work and give it a narrative cohesion, the VRAC team brought in writer Larry Tuch from Los Angeles. Tuch had had a positive experience working on the *DarkCon* VR project for the Army, and understood many of the challenges of story creation in a VR environment. Nevertheless, Tuch told me he found the project a tough nut to crack. He felt it "would not jell unless it had structure and meaning for the participant." And he wrestled with how to integrate all its disparate elements. "You have to decide what experience you want to offer people," he said, "and how you'll use these elements you have—the cube, the surround sound, the dancers, and so on—to give them that experience." He was also well aware of the risk of basing an experimental artistic work on such a well-known, profoundly emotional tragedy. If handled in the wrong way, he could inadvertently trivialize it. Yet, handled in the right way, the work had the potential to be truly cathartic.

Another tough challenge was the C6 itself, which to him seemed like an unnatural space for a narrative experience. "Who'd want to tell a story in a box?" he wondered. Designing for the cube meant taking everything into account, including the floor, which, like all the other walls, was a projection surface for digital images. But he didn't want the C6's shape to impose on the experience. "Literalness is the enemy," he said. "You aren't just doing it for four or six walls." In other words, you have to try to make those walls disappear, to push the experience beyond the physical boundaries. So he worked on devising ways to help participants forget they were in a cube.

Fortunately, he had one major asset going for him: access to audiotapes of survivors giving eyewitness accounts of the event. From these, he shaped a through-line using the harrowing account of a fireman named Billy, with other survivors' stories branching out from it. This yielded the framework that enabled participants to relive the drama of that fateful day.

A VIRTUAL FOREST

A work called *Summerbranch*, developed in the UK by an artists' group called Igloo, uses VR and other digital techniques to recreate a piece of England's New Forest. The New Forest isn't actually new—it was created by William the Conqueror as a hunting ground in 1079, and thus contains some very old stands of trees. In the *Summerbranch* installation, users can explore the woodland by daylight or by moonlight. If they explore carefully, they will encounter some dancers dressed in camouflage who blend into the vegetation and who have an important role to play in the theme of this installation. In a large part because of the dancers, the work explores stillness and movement in nature. Though this is an extremely slender storyline, if it can be called a story at all, one of the artists, Bruno Martelli, explained that the installation raises the question "what is truth, what is artifice in our attempt to reproduce nature?" This peaceful work is at the opposite end of the spectrum from *DarkCon*, and exemplifies the two extremes of VR environments and storytelling.

DISCOVERING THE DRAMATIC POTENTIAL OF VR

In some cases, digital storytellers are going beyond classic techniques and experimenting with new ways to tell stories in VR environments. Such is the case with *Conversations*, a work produced by iCinema Centre for Interactive Cinema Research at the University of New South Wales in Australia.

Conversations is a dramatic reenactment of a famous prison escape that took place in Australia in the mid-1960s. During the escape, a prison guard was shot and killed. Later, one of the prison escapees, Ronald Ryan, was convicted of his murder and executed. However, the case remains highly disputed. *Conversations* uses a VR installation to let participants make their own determination of the truth.

Part one of *Conversations* recreates the prison escape and shooting, thrusting users into the center of the chaotic events. Users, wearing HMDs and earphones, can view the action from all angles, but because so much is going on at once, it is impossible to take in everything. Part two is set in a virtual investigation room, where users can interrogate key people (played by actors) involved in the case.

Unlike traditional dramas, users have a proactive role in the narrative: to decide how to observe the crime scene, to determine which people to interrogate, and to decide what questions to ask. And ultimately, the users must decide for themselves what really happens. Consider how different this is from watching a film, where the screenwriter has selected what the audience will see and has scripted one particular version of a drama.

THE IMPORTANCE OF FINDING A "GRAMMAR" FOR VR

Jacquelyn Ford Morie, the producer of the *DarkCon* military simulation, is one of the leading pioneers in terms of using VR as a dramatic medium. She is also a fine artist, which very much informs her approach to VR. In recent years, she has been working on a project called *Memory Stairs*, which, like *A Thing Growing*, sharply focuses on the emotions of the participant.

The physical centerpiece of *Memory Stairs* is a spiral staircase (see Figure 22.3). Each stair that the participant steps on will trigger a memory experience, nine recollections in all, from prebirth to old age. The stairway thus serves as a linear pathway, and the participant ascends it as if going on a chronological journey through key life experiences. Participants will wear HMDs and other devices to be able to see, hear, and smell the virtual memories, and use a joystick to maneuver through the 3D images.

Figure 22.3 A concept rendering of the spiral stairway of *Memory Stairs*. Spectators can watch the screens on the sides to view images that the participant is seeing. Computer concept rendering by Jared Leshin. Image courtesy of Jacquelyn Ford Morie.

In part, Morie is creating the project to explore how personal memories can be translated into universal ones, and how emotions can be integrated into a VR experience. (Her work in creating an emotional score for *DarkCon* was previously discussed in Chapter 6.) But another important goal for her in *Memory Stairs* is to explore the possible "grammar"—artistic principles or rules—that can be employed in VR. She feels VR still relies heavily on older concepts borrowed from earlier forms of entertainment, in part because the practitioners in this field have placed more emphasis on developing hardware and software than on exploring content. As a result, it is short on artistic ideas that are specifically geared for VR's unique attributes. Every new medium requires its own artistic vocabulary, but that takes time to develop, and audiences often have trouble at first in interpreting what they are experiencing. For instance, when the jump cut was first introduced in the early development of cinema, people didn't understand what it meant.

"But what is the equivalent of a 'jump cut' in VR?" she wonders. "Can you do a break in time and make it work? And is there a way for the participant to control time?" These are some of the questions Morie would like to see addressed in VR works. She feels that answers to these and other questions will come from the artists who are working in VR, not from the technologists. "I think the artists push more than the technologists," she asserted.

VR IN ENTERTAINMENT

To an extremely limited degree, VR can also be found in commercial entertainment venues. Probably the most impressive example of this is the DisneyQuest indoor theme park. Within this five-story structure in Orlando, DisneyQuest offers a diverse array of VR amusements utilizing HMDs, CAVE environments, and simulators. For example, visitors can take a ride on Aladdin's magic carpet, go on a jungle riverboat ride, or have a swashbuckling laser sword fight with super villains from the world of comic strips. They can also become virtual pirates of the Caribbean and sail their own pirate ship, or even design a roller coaster at a touchscreen kiosk, and then, via a simulator, take a ride in it. But few commercial venues other than DisneyQuest are currently offering guests the opportunity to sample VR.

PRAGMATIC USES OF VR TECHNOLOGY

Although VR has not yet become a major medium for entertainment, and perhaps never will, it has an important role to play in other areas. They include:

1. *Teaching and training*: as we have seen, VR is being used by the military as a training tool. It is also being used in the classroom to teach difficult subjects. For instance, a VR program on chemistry lets students play a game where they catch protons and electrons and make atoms.

2. *Product promotion*: several industries are turning to VR for promotional purposes. Some have even utilized portable, suitcase-sized VR units for cutting-edge promotions. One model even comes with a head-mounted device that has its own built-in scent dispenser. Buick commissioned such a unit so it could take potential customers on a virtual test drive. The "drivers" were treated to the scent of fresh-cut grass as they tooled along the virtual road.

3. *Science*: at the Los Alamos National Laboratory in New Mexico, scientists use the CAVE VR system to investigate details of the effects of foam being crushed under a gravitational load and to investigate details of astronomic simulations. With VR, they can examine details that would otherwise be missed, and to see the objects of their investigations in 3D.

4. *Medicine*: as we saw in Chapter 12, a VR simulation called *Snow World* is used to help burn victims deal with the intense pain caused by the treatments they must receive.

5. *Psychotherapy*: VR is being used by therapists to help patients overcome a variety of phobias, including the fear of spiders, the fear of driving, and the fear of flying. It is also being used to treat soldiers suffering from Post-Traumatic Stress Disorder. The patients are enveloped in a virtual experience that resembles the real life event that caused them so much stress. Done in sessions with a skilled therapist, and in a controlled environment, the patients gradually become desensitized to the situations that cause them anxiety. This type of therapy is called "prolonged exposure therapy" or "immersion therapy."

For example, *Virtual Iraq* is designed to treat the "ground pounders" of the war—soldiers who served or who are still serving in the heart of the action. The simulation incorporates a modified version of the video game *Full Spectrum Warrior* and can be modified in innumerable ways by either the therapist or the patient. The soldier, for example, can be a driver of a Humvee, a rider in it, or sitting in a turret behind a machine gun. The speed of the vehicle can be slowed down or sped up; the time of day can be changed; the action and behaviors of the people on the street can be changed and so can the smells. This degree of modification creates a scene that almost exactly replicates a traumatic experience the soldier suffered while on duty. The sights, sounds, and smells are added gradually, to give the soldier time to become accustomed to them, and ultimately, the scenario loses its power to induce stress. With this type of VR therapy, he or she will no longer have a panicked reaction to a once-frightening cue in real life like the sound of a car backfiring. Essentially, it works because patients revisit the stories of their traumas until they cease to hold power over them.

These various applications of VR are used to deal with real-world situations, some of them quite serious. But it is quite possible that forward progress in one of these arenas could spur new advances in using VR for entertainment purposes.

WORTH NOTING: THE CHALLENGES OF CREATING NARRATIVES IN VR

As we have seen from the various VR projects we've examined, developing narrative-based projects for VR can be difficult due to a number of factors, including:

- Creators must deal with an entirely new paradigm. In traditional media, such as movies, television, and theater, viewers watch something that takes place in front of them. This is true even with video games and content made for mobile devices. But in VR, the participant is *inside* the entertainment content and is surrounded by it. We do not yet have a body of experience to guide us in creating content for such a medium.

- Storytelling tends to take a back seat to technology in this field, and most developments are spurred by scientific interests, not by entertainment objectives.

- Creators in the field have a lack of models to draw upon—few successful projects are available to serve as examples.

- The field still lacks a developed aesthetic grammar of its own, and has not yet found commonly recognized ways of dealing with creative issues.

All of these factors call for developers in this arena to stretch themselves to the limits creatively, and to be willing to break new artistic ground.

MIXED REALITY

In *mixed reality* immersive environments, digital technology is used in conjunction with physical props or in real-life physical settings to create a variety of unique experiences. These works have one thing in common: digitally created elements and real physical objects (including people) are intermixed and contained within the same space and may interact with each other.

MIXED REALITY IN A MILITARY SCENARIO

In *Flat World*, an experimental military installation being developed by ICT, participants wear lightweight stereoscopic glasses to make the virtual elements seem real. The title *Flat World* refers to the idea that part of the environment is made up of theatrical-style flats, which are the painted walls of the scenery, and does not refer to the antiquated idea that the world is flat. The scenario is set in a compound in the Middle East that is being bombarded by enemy fire. When you are inside this environment, you can duck into a building and watch the virtual warfare out the window. You can see and hear a helicopter passing by overhead and land in the distance. Suddenly you might hear pounding at the door and open it to a virtual soldier who warns you to leave immediately, saying it is too dangerous to remain where you are! If you look up as you hurry out of the building, you will see a young boy on a roof of the building across the way—also a virtual character—preparing to hurl a rock at you. Though the digital characters are not realistic enough to be entirely believable, *Flat World* demonstrates the potential of mixing the real and the virtual in the same setting.

CULTURAL INSTITUTIONS: A NEW HOME FOR MIXED REALITY

In recent years, museum designers and curators have begun to appreciate how augmenting their exhibits with mixed reality environments can make their exhibits more interesting and exciting to the general public, and they are borrowing techniques more commonly found at theme parks to do this. For example, at the Abraham Lincoln Presidential Library and Museum, visitors encounter the "ghosts" of Lincoln and some of his contemporaries. At the American Museum of Natural History in New York, visitors "feel" the impact of a meteorite slamming into the earth. At the Pirate Soul Museum in Key West, Florida, visitors encounter a menacing animatronic Blackbeard. At the visitors' complex at Mount Vernon, where President George Washington lived, visitors to the exhibit portraying the disastrously cold winter of the Revolutionary War feel a sharp drop in temperature. Inside a wooden hut, they will see a sickly looking soldier lying under a blanket. The chest of this animatronic character rises and falls, and he coughs and moans plaintively. And at the Getty Museum in LA, at an exhibit called *Please Be Seated*, visitors could sit in a replica of a chair once belonging to Marie Antoinette and be virtually transported into her bedroom at the Petit Trianon.

EXPERT OBSERVATION: MUSEUMS AND STORYTELLING

Jeff Rosen, Director of Project Development for BRC Imagination Arts, the multinational firm that developed the innovative exhibits for both the Civil War Museum and the Lincoln Library, made a strong statement about the importance of good storytelling on the firm's website. He asserted: "As a result of shorter attention spans, the 21st Century will need even better storytellers in cultural attractions. We must capture the public's imagination in less time and hold it for longer. We must be worthy of the … [subject matter] … entrusted to our care."

GHOSTS IN THE GRAVEYARD; DOLPHINS IN THE OCEAN; COYOTES IN THE DESERT

Sometimes mixed reality uses sound to bring a place to life. Such works are sometimes called *locative storytelling* or *narrative archeology*. Unlike the artificially constructed settings of the museum exhibits just described, a project called *The Voices of Oakland* is a mixed reality work set square in the middle of a real life environment—an old cemetery in Atlanta, Georgia. Visitors to the cemetery, wearing headphones and carrying a tracking device and laptop, select gravestones that catch their interest and listen to the voices of the dead beneath their feet. They can also opt to hear audio segments about the history, art, and architecture of the graveyard that surrounds them. The work was devised by students at the Georgia Institute of Technology.

A similar type of sound walk was designed for the campus of the Institute of American Indian Arts (IAIA) in Santa Fe. Called *No Places with Names*, it utilized an iPhone app and a GPS device which picked up your position as you walked along a special trail. The app and the GPS were the digital components, while the "reality" was the trail and the landscape surrounding it. As you were walking, your position would trigger the sounds of virtual humans and animals, as well as the sound of the changing weather.

The landscape in this area is now mostly dry desert, but it might once have been fertile. As you passed a relatively flat area, you could hear the sound of tools rhythmically chopping at the earth—the sound of people hoeing and preparing the soil for planting—perhaps pre-Columbian Native Americans. A little later, off in the distance, came the sound of coyotes howling, and then harshly blowing wind and rolls of thunder, followed by the splatter of rain drops on the dusty soil. But your skin and clothes remained perfectly dry—all of these sounds were part of the project; none existed in reality. The coyotes, the wind, and the rain are sounds one hears frequently enough in Santa Fe so they could have been real, but the sound of hoeing done by unseen people was quite stirring, making me picture what this land and its now vanished inhabitants might once have been like, and for me was the most evocative sound.

DRU, quite another type of mixed reality work, is set in a very different environment than the desert or a graveyard—in this case, the Caribbean ocean. DRU stands for Dolphin Robotic Unit, and as the name suggests, DRU is a life-like robotic dolphin, a free-swimming Audio-Animatronics puppet. It is the exact size and weight of a real dolphin and its swimming motions are precisely like a living dolphin as well.

DRU was introduced to the world at an aquarium at a Walt Disney resort in Florida, and after initial testing, he was taken out of the tank and given a chance to swim in the real ocean. He became the star of a prototype "swimming with the dolphins" attraction for snorkelers at Disney's private island, Castaway Cay (see Figure 22.4).

Figure 22.4   DRU, an Audio-Animatronics Dolphin conceived and tested by Walt Disney Imagineers, on an ocean swim with a Disney cast member. Image courtesy of © Disney.

As with many immersive environments, a story was created to enhance this new attraction. Roger Holzberg, Senior Show Producer of Walt Disney Imagineering, described the story to me as a mix of scientific fact and Disney fantasy. The idea was that a pod of intelligent dolphins lived just off the island's coast. By successfully summoning one of them (DRU, of course, who was actually controlled by an operator disguised as a fellow guest), the friendly animal would give the snorklers a personal tour of the ocean from a dolphin's perspective, communicating with the snorklers by nodding or shaking its head or opening its mouth and splashing water, all in a friendly manner.

Even though the people who participated in this attraction were told in advance that DRU was not a living creature, Holzberg says "every single human being who swam with the Audio-Animatronics dolphin believed it was real." He told me that at one point they were considering adding a shark to the act, but knowing how convincing DRU had been, they were afraid that the sudden appearance of a shark, up close and personal, might be a bit more than the guests could handle.

Holzberg feels that attractions like DRU and other immersive theme park experiences are very much in keeping with an idea called *dimensional storytelling*, a concept articulated by that master storyteller himself, Walt Disney. Disney, he said, saw dimensional storytelling as a way for kids and parents to become involved with the stories he created, and it was this idea that lead to the creation of the original Disneyland Park. Holzberg believes that everything done by Walt Disney Imagineering (the division of the Walt Disney Company that designs and builds the theme parks and attractions) is a story of some kind, "Though it isn't always traditional storytelling," he said, "it *is* storytelling. Writing, filmmaking, and interactive design are what the storytelling of today is all about," and, he added, "this type of immersive storytelling takes a story from make-believe to real."

AUGMENTED REALITY

Augmented reality (AR) is a technology that synchronizes digital data, including text, images, video, and sound, with the real world. AR is usually experienced through mobile devices like smart phones and tablet computers. Although scientists have been experimenting with VR for many years, dating back to the early 1990s, it is only recently that the public has been able to enjoy this form of immersive environments. AR offers a diverse variety of experiences and is used for a variety of endeavors, including:

- *Books*: *Who's Afraid of Bugs?* is an AR enabled pop-up book created by AR specialist Helen Papagiannis. Thanks to AR technology, it lets the reader meet bugs in a highly personal way. For example, when you focus your mobile device on a tarantula, the furry looking spider will grow in size and become three-dimensional and actually crawl over your hand.

- *Architecture*: in Rotterdam, people who passed by the massive horse-shoe-shaped Market Hall building (an indoor food market) while it was undergoing construction could point their smartphones at the site and see what it would look like once it was completed, not just the exterior, but the interior as well.

STRANGE BUT TRUE: AN INTELLIGENT STAMP

The UK's Royal Mail service issued the world's first "intelligent stamp" in 2010 in conjunction with a special stamp issue called the Great British Railway. By focusing your smartphone on the stamp, you are treated to a video of an actor reciting the poem *Night Mail* by W.H. Auden. According to a BBC article on the stamp, it is the first time a national postal service has employed AR technology on a stamp.

- *Sports*: the 2013 America's Cup Race, one of the major races in sailing, used AR technology to help spectators unfamiliar with sailing to understand what was going on. The spectators sat in comfortable bean bag chairs watching large screens right on the edge of San Francisco Bay as the race was going on just yards from where they were sitting. The screens showed close-ups of the boats in the competition, supplemented, thanks to AR, with critical information, such as the distance between the boats and the speeds at which they were traveling.

- *Science education*: at the Kennedy Space Center Visitor Complex, you can have a virtual seat in the cockpit of the Space Shuttle Atlantis, and thanks to AR, you can investigate the entire flight deck.

- *Product promotion*: toy companies like Lego are now using AR to make their toys come to life while in a toy store. Children can hold up the box containing the Star Wars Death Star Lego set in front of a kiosk screen and not only see what the set would look like when put together, but could also see miniature guards shooting at each other with light sabers. In addition, the child could see an image of himself or herself holding the box.

- *Gaming*: *Ingress*, a location-based game, is one of the first games to use AR technology as a key component. To play the game, you must go out into the real world, to places like Times Square in New York City, and use your smartphone to control and capture portals. An earlier AR game, *Lantern Worthy*, simultaneously promoted the *Green Lantern* movie and the drinking of milk. Players were challenged with three tasks—involving strength, focus, and agility—which they could see and do through their webcam.

LARGE-SCREEN IMMERSIVENESS FOR AUDIENCES—THE *4-D DARK RIDE*

Immersive environments sometimes make use of theatrical-sized movie screens to envelop participants in a dramatic experience. These experiences are variously known by two different terms: the *ridefilm* and the *4-D Dark Ride*, and are becoming popular attractions in theme parks, vistors' centers, and cultural venues like zoos and historic sites. The "4-D" in the term *4-D Dark Ride* refers to the fact that these rides involve other senses beyond vision and sound, including touch, smell, and temperature changes, and in doing so, strive to bring the audience into the fourth dimension. These experiences are set in specially designed theaters and they usually include seats that move in synch with the story's action (*motion base chairs*). In this type of attraction, one stays seated and cannot move around as one can in other forms of immersive environments. In some regards, these projects are easier to design than VR experiences, because they draw upon cinematic narrative tools that the creative community is already quite familiar with, though imagination comes heavily into play when designing the 4-D elements.

Large-screen experiences lend themselves well to taking participants on a fictional journey, much like a movie. Even though they typically offer little or no opportunity for interaction, unlike the large-screen works of iCinema, discussed in the last chapter, they can offer an intensely involving, even enthralling, experience. This is due both to good storytelling and to how these films are shown. The screens are not only tall but have a wraparound 180-degree curve, thus totally encompassing each person's peripheral vision. They also use state-of-the art surround sound systems and technology to stimulate the other senses. Audience members view these films from a first-person perspective, as if they were right in the heart of the action.

A BUGGY 4-D DARK RIDE

A 4-D Dark Ride called *It's Tough to be a Bug* is a popular attraction at Disney's California Adventure theme park. It features a 3D film, an animatronic grasshopper, and a cast of amusing characters to give audiences an inside view on what it's like to be a bug. To enhance the "buggy" experience even further, giant spiders drop on top of you from the ceiling; you "feel" bugs crawling on you (via vibrations in your seats); you are misted with "acid" by termites; and you get squirted by a smelly stick bug. The shocker in this ridefilm occurs when you are swarmed by angry wasps and "stung" in the back (also via the motion base chair). At this point, the screams of audience members almost drown out the soundtrack.

Ridefilms cannot only be found in IMAX theatres and at theme parks, but are even finding their way into cultural institutions. For instance, at historic Mount Vernon, when visitors watch a film called *Revolutionary War Immersive Experience*, snowflakes fall down on them from the sky, fog rolls in, and through their chairs—which are actually rumble seats—they can feel the thudding of cannons going off. And, in a very different kind of 4-D Dark Ride, this one designed for the toddler set, audience members can join the beloved Dora the Explorer and her friend Diego at various cultural institutions like the Central Park Zoo in New York for *Dora and Diego's 4-D Adventure*. The adventure is set in a tropical rainforest, and thanks to the "magic" of 4-D technology, the audience members, wearing 3D glasses, can almost touch Dora and Diego as they swing from vines right towards them. They join the characters as they ride over water in a helicopter and feel the water splashing in their faces, and they can even smell the bananas that a character snatches from a tree.

SINGLE-PARTICIPANT LARGE-SCREEN IMMERSIVENESS

In some cases, large-screen immersive environments are designed for a solo participant. Most frequently, they are used for cutting-edge training simulations. They often employ sophisticated AI, synthetic characters, voice recognition systems, and multi-sensory stimuli.

Mission Rehearsal, a military training project, is a good example of a single-participant large-screen simulation. Like many of the military simulations already discussed, it was produced by ICT, and writer Larry Tuch, who scripted many of the other simulations, wrote this one as well. *Mission Rehearsal* is set in a war zone and requires the trainee, a young officer, to handle a volatile situation—a child has been run over and severely injured by a military vehicle, attracting a hostile crowd.

The trainee stands in a physical space surrounded by the life-like virtual characters on the screen (see Figure 22.5). To diffuse the rapidly escalating crisis, the trainee must obtain essential information from the synthetic characters on the screen, particularly from the central onscreen figure, the platoon sergeant. (This character has been built with a high degree of AI, and can understand spoken language and respond convincingly.) Once the trainee has a grasp of the situation, he or she must give the appropriate orders to peacefully resolve it. Otherwise, things get even more dangerously out of hand.

Figure 22.5 *Mission Rehearsal* makes use of a large curved screen, surround sound, and virtual characters. Image courtesy of USC's Institute for Creative Technologies.

As with the other military simulations he worked on, Tuch said the events unfolded at a relentless pace, with unexpected twists and turns. Unlike a TV set, it cannot be turned off. "You're inside the story," Tuch explained, "and there's no pausing or doing it on your own time. It doesn't wait for you." This type of pressure, intertwined with the unfolding drama, calls for quick decisions and prepares the trainees for situations that they may well encounter during actual military operations.

Very similar techniques are being used to train law officers in how to handle particularly volatile situations, such as when hostages are involved. One company, VirTra Systems, employs a five-screen system that completely surrounds the trainees, creating a full 360-degree perimeter. The characters on the screen are rendered with photorealistic precision, making the drama extremely compelling. The trainees have to be aware of what's going on all around them, and the situations they are faced with call for both good judgment and good marksmanship. They hold a prop gun, and if they discharge it at one of the virtual characters, it can actually "kill" the person struck. But it is also possible to hit the wrong target and set off an explosive device. Furthermore, the trainees themselves can be "shot." In some of these simulations, they are wired to a special device, and if they are "hit" by a bullet, they will receive an electric jolt.

However, not all large-screen, single-participant environments are designed for training. Some are meant for leisure-time enjoyment. For instance, the School of Computing at the University of Utah has designed a system that incorporates a treadmill and three large screens for a 180-degree view, and as individuals walk or run on the treadmill, they feel as if they are hiking or running in various exotic spots. They call this method of employing a treadmill in a large-screen environment a *locomotion interface*.

IMMERSIVE MULTIPLAYER MOTION-SENSING GAMES

In Chapter 15, on video games, we briefly described a new type of game called (for lack of a better term) an immersive multiplayer motion-sensing game. A set of these games was developed for Disney's Epcot Theme Park in Florida, for the *Living Landscapes* pre-show for the *Soarin'* ride. These games were created to help entertain the guests while they were waiting in a long line for the *Soarin'* ride, a major attraction at the park, and the games were developed under the helm of Disney Imagineer Dean Orion. Orion is a writer/producer and creative director of traditional and interactive media, which gives him a valuable viewpoint for narrative-based interactive works. While I was in Los Angles a few months ago, I was lucky enough to snag an interview with him about the process of developing these games—a type of gaming that had never been done before.

He told me that essentially he had started with a blank canvas, only knowing that he had to come up with something to amuse the people in this line, something that would fit into a 150-foot hallway, 15 feet in depth, crowded with 250 people. As if that were not challenge enough, he said, "you can't use buttons and you can't use levers!"

Initially, he and his team managed to come up with four screen-based motion-sensitive games that they believed could work in this space. Using motion-sensitive technology for multiplayer gaming was revolutionary at the time, and in the beginning, Orion confessed, he didn't even know it would work. But he did his research and found a company that had created projects with the kind of technology he had in mind, a camera-based infrared technology similar to the Kinect, though it would be several years before the Kinect would come out. Orion's team then managed to produce four working games using this technology. However, when they tested them with real guests, they discovered problems. "One of the biggest things I learned working at Disney on location-based projects is that there's a lot of emergent behavior with experiences," Orion told me. "You design something thinking people will behave the way you designed it. Then you put it in, install it, and you see them behaving in ways you never expected."

When they first tested these games, he said, "The very first thing we observed was that people would be in line, and they'd be with their family or their friends or whatever, and they're not all necessarily facing the screen. They're all in different jumbles." Thus, they would miss the introduction to the game and wouldn't understand how to play it. To solve this problem, Orion had his team come up with a little song, and when the music started to play, people would turn and look at the screen. Now that they had their attention, they were able to do a short intro with instructions on how to play, and then, Orion said "dramatically people were able to enjoy the game, much much better than before."

Orion and his team faced another problem with one of the games, *Air Race*, where the audience could direct the flight of a bird by leaning to the right or the left as a team, dodging rocks and trees. Each team would have its own colored bird and the five teams would all race against each other. But, Orion told me, "What happened was that we noticed that people would get tired. Some people can't lean for two minutes, left and right, left and right. On a particular team,

I'd say we started with 50 people, then after 30 seconds we were down to 35 or 30 because people dropped out. But the system would still be looking for those other 15 or 20 people, so it wouldn't steer the bird correctly because it would just see [the ones who dropped away] as not leaning. That meant the people still wanting to play would end up losing." Orion thought that was unfair. So he had his programmers add a little program called "adaptive sensitivity." Every five seconds the program would look around and say "okay, how many people are playing? 50? Okay, we'll have 50 steer the bird." Five seconds later it would say "okay, how many now? 45? Okay, 45 steer the bird." So in a sense it would "take readings" every few seconds and would allow the people still playing to correctly steer the bird. Orion added: "That was one of those things [that we gathered from continual observation] that we were able to adjust, and make it an enjoyable experience for as many people who wanted to play at any given moment." He also told me working on location-based projects requires a focused period of testing in the field and readjustments based on what you learn. "Everything you build for a location, every interactive experience, needs to have on-site field testing and revision time built into the schedule," he emphasized.

After the first four games had been installed, the team learned they still had a sizeable sum left in the budget, and they realized that they must use it or the budget for the following year would be reduced. That was the impetus to come up with a fifth game, *Balloon Odyssey*, and it turned out to be the game in this set that Orion is most proud of. It was a narrative-based game powered by kinetic energy—the clapping, jumping, or waving movements done by the audience. The idea they came up with "was to do a side-scrolling game that had a balloon that could go up and down based on the amount of kinetic energy produced by the players in front of the screen," Orion told me. And, to add drama to this game, they invented a scenario based loosely on Homer's *Odyssey*.

The action starts at a beautiful palace full of jewels. But a bandit balloon comes along and, using a vacuum cleaner, sucks a mass of jewels out of the palace (see Figure 22.6).

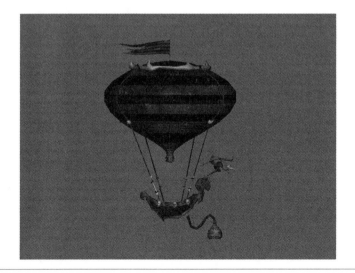

Figure 22.6 Concept art for the bandit balloon, complete with vacuum cleaner, from *Balloon Odyssey*. Image courtesy of © Disney Enterprises, Inc.

You, the audience, give chase in your own balloon and try to wrest the stolen jewels from the bandit balloon. In a sense the jewels are a stand in for Helen of Troy, from Homer's other great work, the *Iliad*. Orion describes the chase as an exciting journey. "You can go up into the sky, into the stratosphere. Or you can descend into the underworld, which kind of looks hellish, or you can stay in the earth plane. And in each one of those planes there are all these mythological monsters; there are trolls who throw rocks at you and dragons that fly and breathe fire at you, and spiders that try to attack you in the underworld." And then, he adds, "at the third act break, the bandit balloon makes another appearance and starts to chase you. And then eventually you get away from him as the whole experience comes to a close, the balloon settles back down at home, just like Odysseus coming home to Ithaca. And you get a little final score at the end."

INTERACTIVE THEME PARK RIDES

Most theme park rides, though they can be extremely exciting, are passive experiences—the riders cannot interact in any way with the objects or characters they see around them. Today's theme park designers, however, recognize that the new generation of park visitors enjoys interactive experiences, and thus have begun to create new kinds of attractions. One such ride is The *Buzz Lightyear AstroBlaster*, built around one of the primary characters of the *Toy Story* films, the toy space ranger, Buzz Lightyear. This ride has a clear storyline: you, the rider, play an ally of Buzz, and you are sent off on an intergalactic mission to fight the evil emperor Zurg.

In this highly interactive ride, you can manipulate your Star Cruiser spacecraft, tilting it and spinning it around in any direction, and can shoot your hand-held laser cannon at various types of outerspace villains. You play against others who are taking the ride at the same time and you can compare your score to theirs at the end of the space voyage. At one point in this adventure, a picture is snapped of you engaged in battle, and when you dismount from your Star Cruiser, you can view your photo at kiosks lining the wall, and even email it to admiring friends and family members back home.

Toy Story Mania is another interactive ride based on the *Toy Story* franchise, and riders can enjoy it both at Disney's Hollywood Studios in Florida and at Disney's California Adventure. The conceit revolves around a new birthday present Andy has just received, the Toy Story Midway Games Play Set. It's a box full of carnival attractions, and once it is set up, Mr. Potato Head invites all the toys to play. Park guests play as honorary toys and ride from carnival attraction to carnival attraction in special trams, from which they can throw virtual eggs, pies, darts, and other objects. The 3D characters in the ride duck realistically in response, making it not only thoroughly interactive, but in addition, scores are tallied for all the riders, making it thoroughly game-like, too.

FULLDOME PRODUCTIONS

One of the newest forms of immersive environments are works called *fulldome*. In these works, images are projected onto the entire surface of a planetarium dome or a similarly shaped theater. To get a sense of what watching a fulldome work is like, picture yourself sitting inside a huge upside-down bowl, surrounded on all sides by moving images.

The fulldome area is one of the fastest growing of all forms of immersive entertainment and edutainment, now numbering hundreds of theaters since its beginnings in 1999. Like other forms of immersive environments, fulldome has the power to transport you to a place you could probably never visit in real life, and to give you an experience you could not otherwise have. Many fulldome productions are set in outer space or in the ocean, perhaps because these themes lend themselves well to narratives about all-enveloping environments. One of the more adventurous of these scientifically themed works is a trip inside a black hole and to the other side of infinity, a visualized representation of Einstein's equations. Another is a dazzling, kaleidoscopic investigation of the mathematic patterns known as fractals. Some people working in the dome arena are now using vDome software, which can be used to produce interactive dome experiences, such as moving an avatar around the space and creating a painting based on the movement of the audience.

ADDITIONAL RESOURCES

For information on fulldome experiences, go to the Fulldome Database at http://www.fddb.org/.

For information on DomeFest, go to **http://www.domefestival.com/.**

In addition, teams of people around the world are actively experimenting with fulldome works that are purely narrative or artistic in nature. For example, the well-known artist and muralist, Gronk, created a stunning semi-abstract piece called *Gronk's BrainFlame*, which is about the power of imagination and the birth of artistic ideas. And a team at the University of New Mexico has been working on a fulldome adaptation of Gerald McDermott's Caldecott Medal winning children's book, *Arrow to the Sun*. This myth-like story is about a Native American boy from a Southwestern pueblo who discovers his father is the sun god.

AN ARTIST'S TAKE ON CREATING FOR FULLDOME

To try to understand what it is like to create artistic and narrative works for fulldome, I met with Hue Walker, a poet and fine artist and one of the pioneering practitioners of this field, or a "domer," as these digital artists call themselves. Walker not only creates original works for fulldome but also served as producer of *BrainFlame* and the adaptation of *Arrow to the Sun*. Until recently, Walker taught fulldome classes at the University of New Mexico (UNM). We met inside UNM's small-scale, portable fulldome, a perfect place for such a conversation.

Walker's own fulldome works are highly personal and rich with poetic imagery. For example, in *Wings of Memory*, Walker explored the power of memory and why one life moment flows forward throughout one's lifetime and even beyond while other memories disappear. The piece combines old family photos and moving images, including a dancer dressed in white and beating wings. The wings, she said, represent "the memories moving along with us" (see Figure 22.7). The piece won a Domie award for Best Art Piece at the 2004 Domefest, an annual festival of fulldome works.

Figure 22.7 An image from Hue Walker's *Wings of Memory*, a fulldome work. Note that the image is a 180° fish-eye projection to conform to the shape of the dome. Image courtesy of Hue Walker.

Walker told me one of the greatest challenges of creating fulldome pieces was dealing with the shape of the dome. In today's world, we are totally familiar with setting our work inside a frame—the rectangle of a canvas or a movie screen, for example—but we are not at all used to setting a work inside a domed space. "It's closer to the images we see in our mind when we hear a story around a campfire, more like how we dream," she said. "There's no frame around these images."

In creating for a domed space, familiar film techniques like close-ups and cuts either do not work at all or are confusing to the audience. Domers have to learn to work with a 180-degree by 360-degree viewpoint and have to create for a fish-eye shape. Just as with VR installations, it calls for the creation of a new visual vocabulary.

Walker does not believe that there is one particular genre of storytelling or another that is more or less suited to fulldome. The important thing, she stresses, is that your storytelling should relate to the space and make good use of it. "If you are attracted to it because this is where the story belongs, then it will happen," she asserted.

EXPERT OBSERVATIONS: THE EMOTIONAL POWER OF FULLDOME

Walker stressed that there are positive trade-offs to the challenges the domed shape presents. Foremost of these is the power of the dome to elicit intense emotions in the audience—emotions like joy, fear, mistrust, and enthrallment. She explained that triggering these emotions is connected to the sense of body weight, body position, and velocity and can be induced by how images and sounds are used within the dome. For instance, you can elicit a feeling of mistrust or fear by having an image sneak up behind the audience. And having an image plunge downwards can produce a dropping sensation, which sometimes can feel like doom or death, while a soaring image can produce a sense of weightlessness, which is interpreted emotionally as joy.

Another domer, visual artist Ethan Bach, who until recently was the Digital Dome Director for the Institute of American Indian Arts (IAIA), believes that fulldome offers great artistic and narrative possibilities. He told *InPark News*: "I believe digital domes are a great way to share many expressions of art, culture, and storytelling. The immersive high resolution images paired with surround sound has a strong influence on the audience that is very different than traditional flat screen."

COMING DOWN THE PIKE

Developments in immersive environments keep sprouting up at such a breathtaking pace that it can be difficult to keep up with them. One of the latest developments in this arena is a high-tech form of spectacles called *Google Glass*. Essentially, Google Glass is a wearable form of augmented reality. Despite the name, it contains no glass; it most closely resembles the top part of a frame of eyeglasses, with a small touchscreen above the right eye. Google Glass is essentially a tiny, powerful computer. As of this writing, it is still in beta testing, but David Pogue, the *New York Times* technology columnist, had the opportunity to wear one and asserted it was even lighter than a pair of sunglasses. Google Glass is allegedly capable of voice, face, and mood recognition; contains a camera and a speaker; an accelerometer; a gyroscope; a compass; and, fortunately, a battery. It is being tested out by a select few people in the gaming community, so the potential for storytelling is still unknown. However, like forms of AR that we are already familiar with, it has the potential for making experiences richer by adding real-time information.

Experiments with various forms of VR goggles are also taking place. The *Oculus Rift* is a headset that immerses the wearer in a VR world and *Avegant goggles* deliver VR directly to your retina. One thing that developers of VR goggles must contend with is something called "simulation sickness." It is similar to sea sickness, but caused by a different set of circumstances.

With simulation sickness, your body is still but you are receiving different visual cues in your inner ear. Despite simulation sickness, however, it is possible to imagine how these goggles can be used for storytelling, extrapolating from models found in other forms of VR. It seems as if the fictional holodeck from *Star Trek* is getting ever closer to reality!

CONCLUSION

More than any other set of technologies, immersive environments and VR give us the ability to create deeply dimensional narratives and simulations that put the user in the center of the action. These works can visualize abstract concepts and can seemingly make fantasies come to life in real physical spaces. Not only do they possess all the components of other engaging forms of digital entertainment—sound and moving images; interactivity; and computer-generated intelligent characters—they offer storytellers additional tools to use, as well. These include 3D images, props and sets, animatronic characters, new types of spaces, and multi-sensory stimuli.

Yet, despite all the creative opportunities they offer, there are serious hurdles standing in the way of some of these forms becoming widely utilized by the creative community or enjoyed by the public. These include issues like the complexity and costs of the technologies involved, the fact that some of these forms can only be enjoyed by one individual at a time, and, in some cases, the lack of financial support for artistic productions. However, as the examples in this chapter illustrate, immersive environments can offer unparelled storytelling opportunities to individuals who have the vision and pioneering spirit to work in this arena.

IDEA-GENERATING EXERCISES

1. Describe an immersive environment that you have personally visited. What about the experience made it seem believable to you? What about it did not feel like "real life"? If you could improve anything about this particular immersive environment, without having to consider cost or technical impediments, what would it be?

2. What kind of narrative experience could you imagine creating for an immersive environment? Which of these eight forms described in this chapter would you use? Sketch out this experience, describing some of the visuals, sounds, and other elements it might contain. Describe how it would start and how it would end.

3. Can you think of any component or element that might be used for an immersive environment, but to your knowledge, has not thus far been used? How would you use this element? What kind of experience could it help create?

4. On a piece of paper, list the eight forms of immersive environments described in this chapter. Then take a current news story, a scientific idea, a short story, or even a movie or TV show you saw recently, and try to adapt it to each of these forms. Why do you think your idea adapts itself relatively easily to some of these genres and not to others?

CHAPTER 23

Electronic Kiosks

How can something as utilitarian as an electronic kiosk be transformed into an attractive medium for storytelling?

What are some of the features that make kiosks especially desirable for use in public places?

Why do museums and other cultural institutions often incorporate kiosks into their exhibits, and why do companies frequently use kiosks as part of their displays at trade shows?

What are the most important considerations to keep in mind when developing a narrative-based kiosk project?

A HUMBLE BEGINNING

The electronic kiosk, sometimes also called the multimedia kiosk or the interactive kiosk, is perhaps the most modest and unassuming of all interactive platforms. Essentially, kiosks are simply booths or other small structures that offer the user an easy-to-operate computerized service, often via a touchscreen. Kiosks are so universal and so much a part of our everyday landscape that we barely give them a second thought, though we are constantly using them to obtain cash, buy gas, or find books in the library. Yet these plain-Jane devices are capable of supporting some surprisingly creative projects, and can be transported into excellent vehicles for entertainment, information, or promotion. In a way, they are a bit like an electronic version of Cinderella—the scorned stepchild who metamorphoses into a beautiful young woman when her fairy godmother dresses her up for the ball. Today, there are an estimated 131,000 kiosks in operation.

The electronic kiosk had a humble beginning, devised for an entirely pragmatic purpose: to reduce the number of tellers in banks. The first electronic kiosk was the handy Automated Teller Machine (ATM), introduced by Chemical Bank in 1969. Since then, however, kiosks have been used for a vast array of purposes. They are particularly well suited for use in public places, either indoors or outdoors. Their popularity continues to grow as the cost of hardware and computer technology drops and the speed of computers increases, making kiosks ever more affordable and useful. Sophisticated technological advances have also increased the kinds of tasks the kiosk can perform. Furthermore, members of the public have become so accustomed to using ATM machines that it is not much of a leap for them to use a kiosk for many other kinds of tasks.

WORTH NOTING: WHAT KIOSKS CAN DO

Kiosks are immensely versatile in how they operate and what they can do. They are inherently interactive and can:

- be used for any type of content enjoyed on any other computerized system, including games;
- accommodate both single users and small groups;
- read credit cards;
- scan codes;
- print out receipts and other documents;
- be equipped with teleconferencing capability;
- be connected to the Internet;
- be operated by touchscreens, keyboards, track balls, videogame controllers, and push buttons;
- be networked together so users can communicate with each other and share interactive experiences with people in distant places;
- record audio, still photographs, and video.

THE KIOSK'S VERSATILITY

Kiosks are particularly useful in spaces with high pedestrian traffic, such as shopping malls, airports, trade shows, lobbies of large buildings, and theme parks. Because they are typically rugged and designed for ease of use, they require no staffing and little maintenance. They have the excellent advantage of being operational 24 hours a day, seven days a week. Furthermore, they are quite portable, and thus are highly suitable for traveling exhibits and trade shows. In terms of cost, they are cheap to run and relatively inexpensive to build.

Though a great many of the services provided by kiosks are strictly utilitarian, the jobs they do so efficiently can be harnessed equally well for entertainment, infotainment, or promotion. If you can create a virtual tour of a retail store, for example, can you not just as easily create a virtual tour of the solar system, or of a historic battleground, or a theme park? And if you can ask a kiosk to print out a receipt for an ATM transaction, can you not also ask it to print out a prize for playing a game, a list of fun facts, or information about a new product?

THE KIOSK AS A MEDIUM FOR STORYTELLING

As versatile as kiosks can be, they do have limitations when it comes to offering pure storytelling experiences. These limitations have nothing to do with technology. From a technological point of view, kiosks are fully capable of supporting rich interactive narratives. It is more a matter of how kiosks are perceived and how they are used. Typically, they are regarded as a "workhorse" medium, designed to fulfill specific pragmatic functions. Furthermore, they are almost always intended to serve a high volume of users, each spending just a few minutes interacting with the content. These short sessions of usage are antithetical to content that contains complex storylines or characters.

Storytelling does play an important role, however, when it comes to making the utilitarian functions of the kiosk inviting and enjoyable to the user. We will be discussing strategies for applying narrative techniques to kiosk programs later in this chapter.

DEVELOPING CONTENT FOR THE KIOSK

As one might expect, the process of developing content for the kiosk is somewhat different from developing content for other interactive platforms. The differences are guided by two important factors. First, as we have already noted, kiosks are usually placed in public spaces. Second, they are typically used by individuals from an extremely wide demographic pool. Users will be of different ages, educational backgrounds, and socioeconomic groups, and they will have different attitudes about computer technology as well. With these factors in mind, here are some key guidelines for developing content for this medium:

1. The kiosk should capture the attention of passersby with an enticing onscreen visual. In the kiosk world, this visual is known as the *attract mode* or the *attract routine*. This little visual tease should loop continuously until a user engages with the kiosk and triggers the opening screen. The attract mode should be friendly and welcoming.

2. The program should be easy to start. It should not require any training, the need for a manual, or detailed written instructions.

3. The interface and navigation should be as intuitive as possible. Prompts and other kinds of help should be built in to assist users who are having trouble. Whenever possible, audio prompts should be used instead of written instructions. If you must use text, keep it to a bare minimum, and use a large, legible font.

4. Input devices should be easy to use. Most kiosk designers prefer touchscreens, track balls, or video game controllers to keyboards. Not all users are comfortable with typing. Also, keyboards are prone to break.

5. The user interface should be as easy to operate as possible. Buttons should be large and decision trees should be streamlined.

6. The content should be extremely engaging, and presented in as visual and interactive a manner as possible.

7. The script or text should be written with a general audience in mind, suitable for users of different educational backgrounds. The vocabulary and grammar should be simple, though expressive. Difficult concepts should be explained in an engaging way. On the other hand, the material should not be over-simplified in such a way that it sounds patronizing.

8. The user's role should be clear and immediately apparent, so people will be able to use the kiosk immediately, and without confusion.

9. The program should be designed to be a brief experience from start to finish, just a few minutes in length. Keep in mind that many users stop at kiosks on impulse, on their way to do something else. Also, others may be waiting to use the kiosk.

10. As with all interactive content, it is wise to test your program on a representative group of users before making it available to the public.

AN INTERACTIVE MICKEY

To get an idea of how the humble kiosk can be transformed into a medium for a richly inventive and entertaining experience, let's take a look at a project developed for the four Walt Disney World Resort theme parks near Orlando, Florida. Called *Discover the Stories Behind the Magic*, these 42 kiosks were built as part of the *100 Years of Magic* celebration to celebrate the centennial of Walt Disney's birth. According to Roger Holzberg of Walt Disney Imagineering, who was creative lead for the celebration project (and was previously introduced in Chapter 22), the goal of the kiosks was to give park guests an appreciation of the breadth of Walt Disney's imagination. And, for people who knew nothing about Disney history, and thought Walt Disney "was just a brand name like Sara Lee," they wanted to demonstrate that a real person existed behind the familiar name, Holzberg said. To do this in a way that would be enjoyable both for adult guests and for young visitors they decided to present the content in the form of a game.

Each of the Florida theme parks (Disney's Hollywood Studios, Epcot, Magic Kingdom, and Disney's Animal Kingdom) had its own style of kiosk and its own game, though all four games employed the same fundamental approach, interface, and style. The housing for the four kiosks had a distinctive feature in common as well: the main body of all four models resembled Mickey Mouse. And they all operated in the same way, too. Visitors spun Mickey's ears and pushed his nose to interact with the content (see Figure 23.1).

One special feature of this kiosk project was its multi-user design. It was envisioned as an experience that parents could enjoy with their children. Thus, the interface was designed in such a way that two to four people could play the game in tandem. A stair step was even built into the kiosk to make it easier for small children to play.

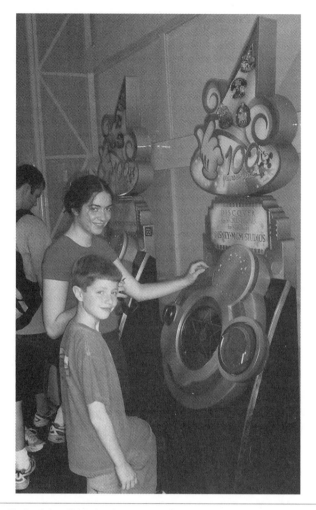

Figure 23.1   Each of the 43 kiosks designed for Disney's *Discover the Stories Behind the Magic* resembles Mickey Mouse. Visitors spin the ears and push the nose to interact with the content. Image courtesy of Roger Holzberg.

INTERACTIVITY ON A TINY SCALE

This kiosk project included another innovative element: tiny interactive collectable pins. Called the *Magic Moment Pins*, they came in five different styles (see Figure 23.2). The pins were embedded with tiny lights that lit up and became animated when the guest interacted with the kiosk, as well with other attractions and entertainment in all four theme parks. Holzberg, one of the inventors of the pins and one of the three people who contributed to the patent, calls the concept *merchant-tainment*. In other words, they are physical items that you can purchase and that will contribute to the entertainment experience.

Although guests didn't need to wear a pin to enjoy the kiosks, Holzberg said, it added "an additional interactive overlay." The pin would start to flash as the guest approached the kiosk,

Figure 23.2   The five different interactive Magic Moment pins.

and if the wearer did well in the game, he said, "it would go crazy." The design of the little pins was echoed in the design of the kiosks themselves. The *headers* (the marquees) of the kiosk structures were giant versions of the pins, done in the same five patterns. Like the pins, they lit up in response to the guest's interactions.

THE GAMES FOR THE MICKEY KIOSKS

All four games used the same attract mode. Pixie dust floated across the screen and set the interface aglow. Text appeared, inviting the guest to "spin the ear" (see Figure 23.3). In addition, Mickey's nose flashed, as did the lights in the kiosk's header. When a guest pressed Mickey's nose or spun his ear, the attract mode dissolved into the primary interface screen of the game.

The interface was a stylized map of the theme park the player was in. To move through the map and select a particular land, the player spun Mickey's ear. The movement through the park was synchronized with the direction in which the ear was spun. Instead of a cursor, an area would be lit up to indicate it was "hot." A hot item would be selected by pressing Mickey's nose.

To play a kiosk game, guests answered multiple-choice questions about various attractions in the particular theme park they were visiting (for a sample script, see Figure 23.4). The games were designed in such a way that children might know some of the answers while their parents might know others. To avoid unhappiness, guests could not lose the game; they could only win, or win bigger. Each time they answered a question, they'd learn a little bit about the attraction and how its inspiration had been drawn from Walt Disney himself. When a question was answered correctly, the guest would be rewarded by seeing a 3D animated model of that attraction materialize on the screen. By answering all the questions correctly, the entire theme park would be assembled on the screen and Mickey himself would congratulate the guest. Thus, guests would be using Disney's imagination to build a theme park; they would literally be experiencing the connection between Disney's imagination and the parks he inspired.

CATCHING THE EYE

The Mickey Mouse kiosks are not only fun to use, but also do a good job of catching the eye of passersby and enticing them to give the kiosks a whirl. Kiosk designers on other projects

Figure 23.3   The attract screen for *Discover the Stories Behind the Magic* kiosk game. Image courtesy of © Disney.

```
100 Years of Magic
Magic Kingdom - Cinderella Castle


The signature animation of the Sorcerer's Hat plays.  The hat lifts up, magic
spills out and the camera pushes into the hat.

Beauty shot image of Cinderella Castle.

                    NARRATOR
          Cinderella Castle at the Magic Kingdom in Walt
          Disney World is taller than Sleeping Beauty Castle
          at Disneyland in California.  Can you guess how
          much?

Cinderella Castle "slides over" and makes way for Sleeping Beauty Castle as
it slides into frame and stops next to its east coast sister.  To start out,
the two side-by-side castles are the same size.

                    NARRATOR (cont'd)
          Is it 10 feet taller?

In the side-by-side comparison, Cinderella Castle grows 10 feet (accompanied
by slide whistle sound effect).

                    NARRATOR (cont'd)
          32 and 1/2 feet taller?

Cinderella Castle grows 32 and 1/2 feet taller.

                    NARRATOR (cont'd)
          Or 112 feet taller?

Cinderella Castle grows 112 feet taller!

TEXT APPEARS:  TURN EAR AND PRESS BUTTON TO MAKE A SELECTION.

                    NARRATOR (cont'd)
          Turn Mickey's ear to select your answer and press
          his nose when you're ready.

As guest turns ear, each answer choice highlights in sequence.  If guest
leaves a choice highlighted for more than a second, the NOSE BUTTON flashes.

WHEN GUEST MAKES A SELECTION, his or her magic pin activates.
```

(Continued)

```
Montage of concept sketches of Sleeping Beauty Castle.

                    NARRATOR (cont'd)
            When Walt Disney was designing Disneyland, he
            dreamed of having a beautiful fairy tale castle at
            the heart of his Magic Kingdom.

Footage of the first-ever children running through.

                    NARRATOR (cont'd)
            And when his dream came true, Sleeping Beauty
            Castle, at 77 feet tall, was just the right size for
            his 50-acre park.

Footage of Walt pointing to a map of central Florida.

                    NARRATOR (cont'd)
            But when Walt started dreaming about Walt Disney
            World, he had nearly 30,000 acres to build on!
            That's twice the size of Manhattan Island!

Special effect of Cinderella Castle popping into the New York City skyline.

                    NARRATOR (cont'd)
            And even though there was enough land to build a
            skyscraper-sized castle...

Overlay of Sleeping Beauty Castle against Cinderella Castle.

                    NARRATOR (cont'd)
            ...Cinderella Castle measured in at 'only' 112 feet
            taller than its little sister in California.

Footage of fireworks exploding over Sleeping Beauty Castle.

                    NARRATOR
            After all, it's not the size of the castle that
            counts...

Tinker Bell flies in and changes the scene with her magic wand to fireworks
exploding above Cinderella Castle..

                    NARRATOR (cont'd)
            ...it's the size of the magic in the Kingdom!

IF GUEST HAD SELECTED "112 FEET TALLER," TEXT APPEARS:   "YOU'RE RIGHT!"

                    MICKEY MOUSE
            You're right!  Great job!

IF GUEST HAD SELECTED ANOTHER ANSWER:

                    MICKEY MOUSE (cont'd)
Gosh, I didn't know that!
```

Figure 23.4 A script for *Magic Kingdom: Cinderella Castle*, one of the *Discover The Stories Behind the Magic* kiosk games. The script was written by Kevin P. Rafferty, Senior Concept Writer and Director, Walt Disney Imagineering. Script courtesy of © Disney.

have used a similar approach, creating housing that not only attracts attention but also reflects the theme or message that the kiosk is meant to send out.

For example, the University of North Carolina, which is located near the coast, developed a kiosk program called *Surf the Seaweb* that would give students and visitors easy access to information about the school. The kiosk designed for this project resembles a full-size surfboard, in keeping with both its seashore location and with the metaphor of surfing for information.

A chain of movie theaters in Canada has installed "character kiosks" in its movie house lobbies to serve as ticket sellers and ticket takers. Each reflects the theme of the movie house where it is located. One of the most colorful, set in an Egyptian themed theater, is an exotic jackal figure. Standing on two legs and the height of a tall man, it looks as if it had sprung right out of an Egyptian pyramid.

And, as a final example, a firm in North Carolina created a teepee-like structure to promote the work of Native American artists. It is constructed along traditional lines, supported in the center by tent poles and decorated with authentic Native American symbols. Yet it is a fully functional kiosk, fitted out with three computer units and monitors.

USING KIOSKS AS PART OF A LARGER EXPERIENCE

Kiosks are often used as adjuncts to cultural exhibits, trade shows, and other types of installations. In such cases, the kiosk's program is usually coordinated with other parts of the exhibition so that it is thematically in keeping with them, both visually and in terms of style and subject matter. This integrated approach is similar to the philosophy of designing a transmedia production, discussed in Chapter 10.

Since different users will come to the kiosk with different degrees of interest in the subject matter it presents and different degrees of knowledge about it, a well-designed kiosk program will offer visitors as much choice as possible about what they can see or do. Some of the choices may be geared for those who just have a passing curiosity about the subject, while other choices might be suitable for those who want to delve deeper.

Ideally, the kiosk will offer users an opportunity to experience some element of the exhibit in greater depth, or in a way that would not otherwise be possible. And even when kiosks are expected to fulfill some type of pragmatic goal, they will be more effective if the contents are entertaining.

THE KIOSK AS A VIRTUAL EYE

Kiosks can give users an opportunity to see things that are impossible to view under any other circumstance. For instance, in its exhibit of antique Greek vases, the Getty Museum in Los Angeles designed a kiosk that let visitors examine a precious vase from any angle they chose, as if they were holding the vase in their own hands, and even as if examining it through a magnifying glass. In reality, of course, a museum visitor would never be allowed to touch such a vase, so the kiosk offered them a special experience.

In a similar fashion, the Galleria dell'Accademia in Florence, Italy, installed a kiosk in conjunction with its display of the world famous statue of Michelangelo's David. The kiosk allowed museum visitors to view parts of the giant statue at close range, including parts of the statue that are normally hidden from view.

MIXING IN THE ENTERTAINMENT

To better understand the process of designing a kiosk project that has a purposeful goal, yet is also highly entertaining, let's take a look at an air pollution project on which I served as a consultant. The client was a government environmental protection agency in the state of California. Here are some of the questions we needed to address right at the start of the project, and how we answered them.

1. What is the goal of the project? We established that the goal was to increase the kiosk visitor's awareness of air pollution, especially pollution produced by motor vehicles.

2. Who would our target audience be? We determined that the program would be directed at adult drivers. However, because the kiosks would be placed in various public spaces, we realized we could have no direct control over who might be visiting them, so we had to make the program meaningful to others as well.

3. What was the project's objective? We established three objectives. First, to raise awareness that the air pollution problem in California was not "solved," and that motor vehicles were a large part of the problem. Second, to educate visitors about the harmful effects of air pollution. And third, to inform users of simple steps they could take, as drivers, to reduce air pollution.

4. What format would we use to get our message across? Since this would be reaching an extremely broad demographic, we wanted to make the program as entertaining and engaging as possible. Thus, we decided to design a game around the core message. We wanted the game to be fun, yet relatively quick to play.

5. What would the thrust of the game be, and how would it be structured? We built the game around the idea of an imaginary road trip, appropriate for a target audience of drivers. The player would travel along a fictional highway and could stop at various roadside attractions along the way, advertised by humorous looking billboards. Each attraction would be a module devoted to one aspect of air pollution and would contain a brief, light introduction and a trivia game relating to the topic.

6. How would we reward the players for playing the game? In addition to verbal rewards for answering the trivia questions correctly, we decided to make use of the kiosk's ability to print. Players would receive a souvenir bumper sticker for each of the attractions they visited (thus reinforcing what they learned in the module) and also get one random "air pollution resolution"—an easy-to-apply idea for reducing motor vehicle emissions.

Based on these initial decisions, we could then go ahead and do the other development tasks that needed to be done. These included working out a concept for the attract mode, deciding on the theme of each module, and determining the game's overall visual style. Finally, we'd turn to the time-consuming job of filling in the details: putting together a list of the facts we wanted to impart; writing the trivia questions; and producing the artwork.

PLUMBING THE CREATIVE POSSIBILITIES OF THE KIOSK

One of the most attractive attributes of the kiosk is its versatility and the ease with which it lends itself to various add-ons. In a way, the kiosk is like a bland food, such as a chicken breast, that can be dressed up in an endless variety of sauces and served in many delectable ways. Just as chefs make good use of the adaptability of the chicken, we can put our inventive powers to work to plumb the possibilities of the kiosk.

For example, INTOUCH Kiosk has produced a great number of kiosk projects, and two of them, just as a sample, were completely different from each other. One was produced for Mattel, as a way to celebrate Barbie's 50th anniversary. It encouraged users to share their own personal Barbie stories, which they could record just by using the kiosk. The second, called T-Rex Café, was a suite of games and activities all built around our favorite prehistoric reptile. You could create your own dino, make a volcano erupt by answering trivia questions correctly, and play a fossil-matching game. The kiosks were part of a dinosaur attraction in downtown Orlando, Florida, and in Kansas City.

TIME-TRAVEL VIA KIOSK

A project called *An Imagined Place* is an excellent example of how the basic kiosk can be enriched by using sophisticated technologies. *An Imagined Place* was developed by designer Greg Roach, introduced earlier. He describes *An Imagined Place* as "a way to be a tourist in time," and to virtually travel to some of the greatest archeological sites in the world. The project has been developed with the encouragement of Microsoft, Cambridge University, and UNESCO. Although still in its conceptual stage, with its ultimate destiny still unknown, enough groundwork has been done on it to illustrate how a specially outfitted kiosk can transport users to a lost civilization and allow them to have a unique interactive journey.

Roach named the prototype for his project *Virtual Luxor* because he conceived of his idea while visiting the temples of ancient Egypt. The portal into this lost world of ancient Egypt would be through a specially outfitted kiosk (see Figure 23.5). Once visitors entered the kiosk booth, an Internet connection and videoconferencing would be used to transport them back in time to the temple complex at Luxor. There they would see their own image inside the ancient tomb complex (via the teleconferencing technology) and be able to interact with virtual characters from ancient Egypt.

The technology for producing a project like *Virtual Luxor* would seem to be extremely expensive and perhaps difficult to execute, but Roach asserts that this is no longer the case. He points out that thanks to advances in graphics, bandwidth, and computing power, a project like this can almost be done with an "off the shelf" approach.

ASSISTING IN LIFE AND DEATH

With the technology that has become available since 1969, when the first ATMs were introduced, kiosks are being called upon to handle tasks that were unimaginable back then. For

An Imagined Place

Video conferencing camera

LCD display/ touch screen

Trackball

Shared CPU unit

Blue screen surface

Figure 23.5 The specially outfitted kiosk booth for *Virtual Luxor*. Image courtesy of Hyperbole Studios.

example, a cosmetics company has developed kiosks that can not only show informational videos about its product line but also dispense sample fragrances. Called the *In-Store Interactive Fragrance Assistant*, the kiosk lets customers sniff a whiff of a selected scent. It then quickly dissipates the perfume, leaving the air fragrance-free for another choice.

Kiosks can now even "eat" no longer wanted electronics, and will pay you for them, as well. Developed by ecoATM, the kiosks will accept cell phones, laptop computers, video games, and a host of other electronic devices. The kiosks are even programmed to identify the user, making sure the device you offer was not stolen.

Kiosks are also assisting those who have passed away, and the ones who grieve for them, projecting images of the deceased from beyond the grave. Mourners or people who plan well ahead can now commission a tombstone—a so-called *vidstone*—to commemorate the life of the deceased individual. The tombstone kiosk contains a video record of the departed's life. The vidstones utilize solar-powered technology and weatherproof LCD panels. A smaller version, called the *VIDpet memorial*, is now available for cherished animal companions.

THE KIOSK AS AVATAR

Certainly one of the most unique examples of kiosk technology is the robotic kiosk project known as *PEBBLES*. PEBBLES stands for Providing Education By Bringing Learning Environments to Students, and these kiosks are designed to connect hospitalized children with their schools. The system makes use of two matching life-sized robotic kiosks and videoconferencing technology, with a monitor embedded in the robot's "face" (see Figure 23.6).

Figure 23.6   PEBBLES, the robotic kiosk, serves as an avatar for hospitalized children. Image courtesy of the PEBBLES project.

One unit is deployed to the patient's school and acts as the child's avatar, while the second unit stays beside the patient's bed and serves as a window into the classroom. Using video game controls to manipulate the avatar at school, the child can direct it to move around the classroom, zoom into the blackboard for a better look at what the teacher is writing, turn its robotic head to see what the students in the back of the room are doing, or even raise its hand to ask a question. The units also contain printers and scanners so the patient and teacher can exchange documents—homework, tests, handouts, and so on. The monitor in the classroom unit shows a live video feed of the patient in the hospital, creating a real sense that the child is actually present. Furthermore, the school-based robotic kiosk is not just restricted to a single classroom. It can move from room to room, hang out with friends at the cafeteria, and even participate in school performances.

The PEBBLES units have full-time jobs connecting sick children to their classrooms, but imagine the possibilities if similar robotic kiosks were available for other types of activities. For example, they might be employed to take part in role-playing games, or be put to work exploring a dangerous terrain, or be used to visit places the person operating it cannot visit in person. In terms of storytelling, these robotic kiosks could become leading characters in the digital dramas of the future.

OTHER RESOURCES

News and feature articles about kiosks can be viewed at the *Self Service World* website, http://www.selfserviceworld.com/. The publication, which was begun in 1999 and which was formally known as *Kiosk* magazine, carries information on all aspects of interactive kiosks.

In addition, the Summit Research Association (http://www.summit-res.com/index.html) researches and sells highly specialized reports on kiosks, on topics ranging from market segments, design and development issues, to statistics about the kiosk business.

CONCLUSION

Although the basic kiosk is quite simple—just a computer and screen placed within some kind of rugged housing—we have seen how it can be dressed up in a great variety of ways. Because of its versatility, the kiosk can readily be combined with other technologies to give users unique kinds of experiences. As the projects described in this chapter have illustrated, the humble kiosk can be transformed into a dynamic medium for entertainment, education, information, and social interaction.

The kiosk is an exceptionally democratic tool, well suited for use in public places and for all types of users. It offers interactive experiences to any and all, usually free of charge. And even those who might normally consider themselves technophobic are apt to find kiosks user-friendly and not at all intimidating.

Furthermore, kiosks adapt readily to new technologies. Almost certainly, innovative designers and content creators will be putting them to work in ways we cannot yet imagine as new technologies come down the pike.

IDEA-GENERATING EXERCISES

1. List the various things you have been able to do via electronic kiosks, including utilitarian tasks as well as other kinds of experiences. What was the most inventive use of a kiosk that you've personally encountered? Are there certain things you think could be done via a kiosk, but have not yet seen offered?

2. Pick a topic that one might find as the subject of a museum exhibition, historic site, or other type of cultural or recreational institution. Sketch out an idea related to this topic that could be explored via an electronic kiosk. How would this kiosk program broaden the visitor's understanding of the exhibit? What kinds of things would it allow the user to do?

3. Imagine that you are in charge of a large public facility such as a hospital, train station, or theater lobby—a place where people often have time on their hands. What type of entertainment experience could you provide via a kiosk that would be appropriate to your facility? If money were no object, what kind of design would you choose for the physical housing of this kiosk, and for the interface devices?

PART 5

Career
Considerations

Working as a Digital Storyteller

How do you find work as a digital storyteller?

If you've got a great idea for a video game or other work of interactive entertainment, how do you sell it?

How do you build a career in such a quickly changing field as digital storytelling?

A NEW OCCUPATION

The pioneering individuals that we've met along the way in this book are all practitioners of a new type of creative endeavor, a craft that did not even exist a few decades ago. They are digital storytellers. The work they do spans an assortment of technologies, and the projects they create are a contrast in opposites—everything from talking baby dolls to gritty video games. Some of these creations appear on the tiny screens of wireless devices, while others play out on huge movie screens. The venues where these works are enjoyed run a gamut of possibilities, too. They may be seen in one's living room, in a theme park, in a schoolroom, in an office—even in the ocean, as with the robotic dolphin, DRU. Yet, despite the great differences among them, the works they create have significant points in common. All of them:

- utilize digital technologies;
- tell a story;
- are perceived as being entertaining;
- engage the users in an interactive experience.

Even though being a digital storyteller is a relatively new occupation, it is a type of work that is increasingly in demand. True, you won't find jobs for "digital storytellers" listed in the want ads. That's because the jobs in this arena go by a great variety of titles and call for various kinds of skill sets. As we've seen throughout this book, the people that we would consider to be digital storytellers carry many official titles, including designer, graphic artist, information architect, producer, project manager, writer, and director. The most visionary of the digital storytellers may work across a number of different platforms and media.

The great news about this new profession is that it can pay quite well. According to the annual salary review published in the 2013 issue of *Game Developer* magazine, on average, programmers earn $92,151; producers earn $84,127; and designers earn $75,065. As to be expected, the top executives and the legal professionals earn the most of all, an average of $103,934. Unfortunately, no salary statistics are being gathered for other sectors of digital entertainment, but one might expect the salary ranges in the most established arenas to be more or less consistent with the games industry.

Another interesting point about digital media: these companies are scattered all over the world, meaning you don't need to live in New York City or Silicon Valley to be employed. The game developer's map (http://www.gamedevmap.com/) shows how widely dispersed game development companies are throughout the world, with at least a few on every continent except for Antarctica.

This chapter will explore ways of finding work and developing a career in the field of digital storytelling.

THE LIFE OF A DIGITAL STORYTELLER

If you were to round up 10 people who could be described as digital storytellers and ask them how they got started, the chances are that they would give you 10 entirely different answers. Many, especially the younger ones, will probably have had some kind of college training in the area, but almost certainly, their career paths will not have been straight ones. Most will have come to their present job by following a dream, by hard work, and by a willingness to take chances.

Kevin Rafferty's career is a perfect illustration of this. Rafferty is a Senior Concept Writer and Director for Walt Disney Imagineering, the group at Disney that creates attractions for the theme parks. It's work that Rafferty and other Imagineers refer to as the "dimensional entertainment" side of the storytelling fence, as we saw in Chapter 22. As you may recall, Rafferty was the writer of the kiosk script in Chapter 23 for the *Discover the Stories Behind the Magic* project. Rafferty's job calls for a mixture of tasks besides writing. He also creates ideas for theme park attractions and helps to take them from concept all the way to completion. In addition, he writes original music; casts and directs voice and camera talent; and directs show programming and figure animation … and that's just a partial list of his responsibilities.

Not surprisingly, Rafferty's dream job at Disney didn't start out on this level. His career path actually started with a humble dishwashing job at Disneyland while he was still in college, where he was an art major. After college, he worked for a while as an advertising copywriter. When he heard that Disney was hiring people to work on the new Epcot theme park, he applied for a job as a writer, figuring he knew a little something about theme parks from his old dishwashing job. He succeeded in getting hired, but not as a writer. Instead, he found himself dusting show models and cutting mats for artwork. But still, he had his foot in the door at Epcot, and made the most of the opportunity. Working on his own time after hours he created and developed some original ideas and ran them by a friendly vice president, and "after paying a lot of dues and trying to prove my creative worth," he told me, "I was finally and officially accepted into the creative division."

Thus, a path that began with dishwashing led to an exciting array of assignments at various Disney theme parks. Looking back on his experience, Rafferty quips in classic Disney fashion, "I guess it's true what they say: 'When you DISH upon a star, your dreams come true.'"

Rafferty's career path is typical of many others who have found their way into digital storytelling. A straight, clear-cut route is quite rare. It's not like deciding you want to go into dentistry and knowing that step number one is applying to dental school. In Rafferty's case, his career aspirations evolved over time, and once he knew what he wanted to do—to become a creative part of Walt Disney Imagineering—he focused his efforts and sacrificed his free time to get where he wanted to be.

NOTES FROM THE FIELD: SOME KEYS TO SUCCESS

Although new media involves cutting-edge technology, two industry pros who were queried on advice for establishing a career in this field mentioned some tried and true old-fashioned values (*GIGnews*, March 2002). In fact, the answers they gave would have worked as well for a Stone-Age hatchet maker. For example, Stevie Case said the three keys to success were drive, dedication, and the desire to learn, while John Romero named passion, hard work, and an optimistic outlook. And both also stressed the importance of being a finisher— to complete any project you commit yourself to doing.

One thing most people who work in the field will agree upon is the importance of good storytelling. Mark Harris, a software architect who was also the creator of the transmedia film, *The Lost Children*, was asked in an interview for *Filmmaker Magazine* (April 4, 2013) what he believed were the most important tools for an interactive storytelling. Harris answered: "Empathy, character, story. I believe that an 'interactive storyteller' should focus on the same skills utilized by every other storyteller. Technologies come and go. But I don't think they fundamentally change human behavior."

SELLING AN ORIGINAL IDEA

What if, unlike Rafferty, your dream is not to work within a particular company or hold a particular job, but instead to sell your own original ideas for a game or other type of interactive entertainment? No question, this is an appealing goal, one shared by many hopeful individuals. Sad to say, however, it is not particularly realistic, for several reasons.

For one thing, ideas are plentiful, to the point that most companies are flooded with their own internal ideas generated by employees of the company, and thus they are not looking for ideas from the outside. For another thing, as they say in Hollywood, ideas are cheap; execution is everything. Execution is where the real challenge lies, and execution takes experience, talent, time, and often an investment of money. To convince a company that your concept has merit, you'll need more than an idea. You'll want to have something to show them—a concept document, a design document, or, even better, a working prototype. And you'll also need to consider the pitching strategy for your project. Who is the target audience for this product, and why would they like it? What competing projects already exist, and how is yours different and better? And how would your project be a good fit with other offerings in the company's line?

But even if you've done all the necessary groundwork, the companies you are planning to approach are unlikely to give you a warm reception if you are an unknown quantity to them. Developing a game or other work of interactive entertainment is a risky proposition that can cost millions of dollars. If a company is interested at all in hearing pitches from outside vendors, they will be far more likely to be receptive to a known developer with a proven track record than they would be to a stranger.

WORTH NOTING: HELPING HANDS

Despite these discouraging words, if you are convinced that you have a stellar idea and want to have a go at trying to sell it, you can obtain some excellent guidance from a document prepared by the International Game Developers Association (IGDA), the premiere organization of game developers. Called the *Game Submission Guide* (http://www.igda.org/sites/default/files/IGDA_Game_Submission_Guide_0.pdf), it offers information about the pitching process and includes a checklist of what you will need to include for a professional-looking submission. Although written with video games in mind, the information pertains equally well to other forms of interactive entertainment. Although it was written a number of years ago, its points are as relevant as ever.

In addition, the IGDA site has a great deal of other helpful information for newbies in the field. If you are seriously interested in getting a job in digital media, especially video games, and want to know how to get into the field, visit the section of the IGDA website called *Breaking In*: http://www.igda.org/breakingin. The site includes an excellent section on major career paths;

interviews with professionals in games describing how they broke in; and a list of resources. Another good source of information on the site is an excellent column written by game industry veteran Tom Sloper called *The Games Game* (http://www.igda.org/games-game).

Outside of the IGDA site, game designer Ernest Adams has a Web page devoted to breaking into the game business: *The Wanna-Be Page*: http://www .designersnotebook.com/Wanna-be/wanna-be.htm.

As to be expected, your chances of selling a game or other interactive project are far better if you are a development company that has a track record of producing games rather than someone new to the field. But even so, it is a difficult path. At the Game Developer's Conference in Europe in 2012, Pete Smith, Sony's director of product development, offered a number of practical tips about pitching to Sony (as reported by Jessica Conditt in Joystig on August 18, 2012). They work well in terms of pitching to any major publisher.

- Be able to pitch your idea quickly, in about 30 seconds.
- Practice your pitch before the meeting.
- Select the best person from your team to deliver the pitch. It might not be the CEO.
- Keep your visuals simple and bold.
- Tailor your pitch to the specific publisher you are meeting with and make sure it is an appropriate work for this company.
- Sell your company and your team. Even if your project isn't what the publisher is looking for, your team might be.
- Leave time for the publisher to ask questions.
- Don't be boring, late, or hung over!

Although the report did not mention it, it is also important to leave some documentation describing your IP with the publisher. A concise concept document, described in Chapter 11, works perfectly for this.

WORTH NOTING: ANOTHER ROUTE

Pitching a project to a publisher is not the only way to finance a project and get it made. Many teams have raised money for projects through Kickstarter and other crowdsourcing sites, and it can be a highly successful way to obtain the funding you and your team need. For example, the little game console OUYA, smaller than a soft drink can and with an intended sales price of $99, raised $8 million on Kickstarter (as reported on Mashable, January 3, 2013).

THINKING OUTSIDE THE BOX

Some digital storytellers grab the reins and create their own media outlets, rather than trying to sell an idea to another party. This is the entrepreneurial approach, and it can be a very successful way to go. For example, Freddie Wong and his team not only produced the Web series *Video Game High School*, as of this writing starting its third season, but actually built a website to host it, Rocket Jump (http://www.rocketjump.com/). In the storyworld of *Video Game High School*, gamers and their games have become the rock stars of their high school, leaving jocks in the dust. The series has been an enormous success, with its first series being seen by 50 million viewers, and raising over $800,000 on Kickstarter for its second season, shattering the Kickstarter record for a film campaign (from *The Wrap*, February 13, 2013). Though the series is also available on YouTube, Wong told *The Wrap* (August 22, 2012) that having their own website gives his team more financial opportunities. "We need our own place to exhibit our own content," he said, "and we need to be able to control that user experience, and have a way to guide viewers through content." In terms of content, they can add behind-the-scenes material, a better commenting system, and potentially, transmedia experiences. And, in terms of financial opportunities, they can recruit sponsors, sell merchandise, and do a great deal of product placement. Thus, being entrepreneurial can offer substantial benefits, though of course it can also be a risky approach to content creation. A successful project needs to be highly original and well-targeted for a specific audience. In Wong's case, his story is a refreshing take on high school and is targeted primarily to gamers.

Two additional routes to fund one's projects or to receive funding for yet unmade projects are through YouTube partnerships and through grants. By becoming a YouTube partner (https://support.google.com/youtube/answer/72851?hl=en), ads may be implanted on eligible videos you have made and you share the proceeds with YouTube. Grants and funding for unmade projects often come from nonprofit organizations like Games for Health (http://www.healthgamesresearch.org/).

THE DIFFERENT EMPLOYMENT PATHS

If you are interested in finding full-time employment in interactive media, you will be happy to know that a surprisingly wide variety of businesses employ staff members who specialize in this field. The most obvious are the game publishers and game developers. The publishers have deeper pockets than the developers, and may either develop projects in-house or farm them out to developers, who do the actual creative work, which the publishers then package and market. These publishers and developers do not necessarily restrict themselves to video games. They may also make games for mobile devices and for the Web, including MMOGs.

In addition to game publishers and developers, another group of entities focuses on interactive media: the design firms that deal with interactive media. Some of them specialize in Web design work, while others pursue cutting-edge projects in immersive reality. Some work in a wide sweep of interactive media, a mix of platforms and approaches including kiosks, wireless devices, the Web, and transmedia storytelling.

One entire industry that is becoming increasingly involved in interactive media is the Hollywood entertainment business, as we've seen throughout this book. Not only are movie studios making games based on their films, but they are also promoting their films on the Internet and on mobile devices, sometimes using highly creative approaches. Television networks also promote their shows via new media. Public broadcasters are particularly aggressive in using interactive media to maximize the content of their programming, developing projects for the Web, DVDs, and iTV. Thus, traditional entertainment studios and broadcasters are definitely worth investigating for employment opportunities.

In considering possible employers, do not by any means overlook major corporations. Most of today's large companies have internal divisions that produce content for the Web and other interactive media, work that is often done under the umbrella of the promotion or marketing departments. Other entities that do work in interactive media are toy companies, ad agencies, and PR companies, as well as companies that specialize in interactive training programs. Another group of organizations to consider are cultural institutions—museums, historic sites, aquariums, and so on—all of which may use interactive displays to make their exhibits come to life. And theme park companies employ individuals like Kevin Rafferty to create attractions that take advantage of the latest interactive technologies. In addition, government agencies sometimes produce interactive programming for educational, informational, or training purposes.

COMMON ENTRY POINTS

Although, as we've seen from Kevin Rafferty's story, the path to a great job in digital media is not necessarily a straight one, a couple of traditional routes do exist. One is by becoming a beta tester, which is particularly attractive to people who want to work in games. Beta testers are hired to look for bugs in games before they are released to the public, and this type of work is often a stepping-stone to a higher level job within the same company. One of my students, Trevor Weisberg, who became a beta tester, had this to say to those wishing to follow the same path: "One thing I strongly advise—do NOT become a tester to play games. Become a tester to TEST games. I know with all these never-before-released titles it's enticing to play for fun, but when I was given a job I had to drop the game immediately to get it done." In other words, the job sounds like a wonderful opportunity to play games all day, but that isn't what testing is all about. He also warned that the job can entail long hours: "Be prepared to work 60 hour weeks. When I was at XXXXX, I was at work 12 hours a day, 6 days a week." He reports that his present job has far more manageable hours, and on the whole, he is happy with working as a beta tester.

Another proven route is via student internships. Internships offer first-hand exposure to a professional new media workplace. Not only are they educational, but such experiences are also good to have on a résumé. And, best of all, they can lead to full-time employment.

Aside from scoring an internship or a job as a beta tester, the pathway into digital storytelling is much like that for any other kind of work. You need to research the field to determine which segment of the industry would offer you the most potential, given your particular talents, interests, and skill set. It is also quite helpful to network and to attend industry events, which we will be discussing in more detail later in the chapter. And before setting out on a job search, you'll want to give serious consideration to creating a portfolio of sample work, which is discussed in detail in Chapter 25. Once you have some experience under your belt, you can visit job boards to see if there might be a good fit for you. An extremely large list of jobs, primarily in games, can be found at *Mary-Margaret Network*, http://www.mary-margaret.com/. The site also contains articles with good advice for job seekers.

WORKING AS A FREELANCER

What if you would prefer to be your own boss rather than to be a full-time employee of an organization—is this an option in new media? The answer is a tentative yes. It depends on your experience, on your specialty, and the tenor of the times. Back in the 1990s, it was quite customary to be hired to work on a specific project and then move on once the project had been completed. People who worked on a project to project basis, instead of being employed full time by one company, are known as *contract workers*, and that is the path that I personally prefer because of the creative opportunities it offers. Currently, however, most companies work entirely with full-time staffers. One of the few professional areas that still offers opportunities to freelancers is in writing, my own specialty. The more credits you have and the more people you know in the industry, the more likely you are to find freelance writing work.

The work one does as a freelance writer varies tremendously from project to project. Some of the assignments you snag are not much different from doing piece goods work in a factory. You may be expected to churn out hundreds of lines of dialogue, sometimes with little variation between the lines, and the work can be quite tedious. On the other hand, some writing jobs are highly creative. You may have a chance to collaborate on the overall design and content of a project and to develop original characters; you may also be able to help develop what the interactivity will be and how it will work. Each type of interactive medium poses its own challenges. Writing a script for a kiosk will be quite different from writing one for a smart toy, and both will be different again from writing an ARG or a serious game or a virtual world.

One of the most stimulating things about being a freelance writer is being able to take on projects that are quite different from each other; your work is always creatively challenging. However, being a freelancer also means dealing with issues that one does not have to worry about as a full-time employee. For example, you might have to chase after a client to get paid, or find yourself mired in an unpleasant situation called *project creep*, in which a project grows much bigger than it was originally understood to be. Project creep can cause you to spend many more weeks than you had planned on an assignment, but without receiving additional compensation. It should also be noted that one faces a host of uncertainties when working for a start-up company. Start-ups lack the experience of a long-established company and their expectations may be off-kilter and payments might also be slow in coming. However, start-ups can offer creative opportunities not found at long established companies, so they can be exciting to work for, despite the risks.

Fortunately, freelance writers do not have to go it entirely alone anymore. The IGDA has a SIG (special interest group) for writers. The Writers Guild of America, west, offers staff support, a games committee, and two special contracts for interactive writing. The first contract, called the Interactive Program Contract, or IPC, covers writing for most types of interactive media, including video games and mobile entertainment, while the second, called the Made for Internet Contract, specifically covers original writing done for the Internet. Both contracts are available directly from the Guild's organizing department. Qualified new media writers can even obtain membership in the Guild, which once just included writers of motion pictures and television.

LEGAL CONSIDERATIONS

At some point or other, if you are working in new media, you are bound to run into legal situations. For example, you are quite likely to be faced with issues involving intellectual property (IP). Intellectual properties are unique works of human intelligence—images, writings, music, pieces of animation, even game engines or an invention for a toy—that are given certain legal protections, which include copyrights, patents, and trademarks. Intellectual properties can be extremely valuable, and they are fiercely guarded in interactive media with a zeal bordering on paranoia. You may become involved with IP questions when it comes to protecting your own creations; you may also run into IP issues when you want to use the creative work of others in a project.

IP issues can be highly complex, but one thing about them is quite simple: you don't want someone stealing your intellectual property and you don't want to be accused of stealing intellectual property that belongs to someone else. The first situation can result in your losing a significant amount of income; the second can result in a lawsuit. To prevent either situation from occurring, you need to familiarize yourself with the basics of intellectual property law. One place to start is with the website of entertainment and new media attorney and IP specialist Michael Leventhal (http://www.mcsquaredlaw.com/). The site contains a number of articles relating to IP.

Another legal matter you will need to be familiar with is a document called a Non-Disclosure Agreement, or NDA, often used in high-tech circles. You will no doubt become aware of NDAs if you are submitting a project to a company in the hopes of selling it or if a company is interested in hiring you for a project, but first needs to share with you what has been done with the project to date. Both situations raise the risk of valuable information being seen by strangers who might possibly use it without authorization. To avert such a risk, it is customary for one party to request the other to sign an NDA. When someone signs such a document, he or she promises to keep the information they are receiving confidential (see Figure 24.1).

If you are working as a freelancer or are running your own development or design company, you will also need some legal protections in the form of a contract. You will definitely want a contract if you are entering into a new employment relationship; that is, if you or your firm is being hired to do some work for another entity. A contract should specify what your responsibilities will be and what you will be paid at each juncture, often tying payments to the completion of various milestones (points in the project, like a character bible, when particular parts of the project and payments are due). It should spell out what happens if the work expands beyond what has been assigned,

NON-DISCLOSURE AGREEMENT

This non-disclosure agreement ("Agreement") is entered into as of _____ ("Effective Date") by and between _____, located at _____ ("Artist"), and _____, located at _____ ("Recipient"). Artist and Recipient are engaged in discussions in contemplation of or in furtherance of a business relationship. In order to induce Artist to disclose its confidential information during such discussions, Recipient agrees to accept such information under the restrictions set forth in this Agreement.

1.   Disclosure of Confidential Information. Artist may disclose, either orally or in writing, certain information which Recipient knows or has reason to know is considered confidential by Artist relating to the [NAME] Project ("Artist Confidential Information"). Artist Confidential Information shall include, but not be limited to, creative ideas, story-lines, characters, trade secrets, know-how, inventions, techniques, processes, algorithms, software programs, schematics, software source documents, contracts, customer lists, financial information, sales and marketing plans and business plans.

2.   Confidentiality. Recipient agrees to maintain in confidence Artist Confidential Information. Recipient will use Artist Confidential Information solely to evaluate the commercial potential of a business relationship with Artist. Recipient will not disclose the Artist Confidential Information to any person except its employees or Artist's to whom it is necessary to disclose the Artist Confidential Information for such purposes. Recipient agrees that Artist Confidential Information will be disclosed or made available only to those of its employees or Artist's who have agreed in writing to receive it under terms at least as restrictive as those specified in this Agreement. Recipient will take reasonable measures to maintain the confidentiality of Artist Confidential Information, but not less than the measures it uses for its confidential information of similar type. Recipient will immediately give notice to Artist of any unauthorized use or disclosure of the Artist Confidential Information. Recipient agrees to assist Artist in remedying such unauthorized use or disclosure of the Artist Confidential Information. This obligation will not apply to the extent that Recipient can demonstrate that: (a) the Artist Confidential Information at the time of disclosure is part of the public domain; (b) the Artist Confidential Information became part of the public domain, by publication or otherwise, except by breach of the provisions of this Agreement; (c) the Artist Confidential Information can be established by written evidence to have been in the possession of Recipient at the time of disclosure; (d) the Artist Confidential Information is received from a third party without similar restrictions and without breach of this Agreement; or (e) the Artist Confidential Information is required to be disclosed by a government agency to further the objectives of this Agreement, or by a proper court of competent jurisdiction; provided, however, that Recipient will use its best efforts to minimize the disclosure of such information and will consult with and assist Artist in obtaining a protective order prior to such disclosure.

3.   Materials. All materials including, without limitation, documents, drawings, models, apparatus, sketches, designs and lists furnished to Recipient by Artist and any tangible materials embodying Artist Confidential Information created by Recipient shall remain the property of Artist. Recipient shall return to Artist or destroy such materials and all copies thereof upon the termination of this Agreement or upon the written request of Artist.

4.   No License. This Agreement does not grant Recipient any license to use Artist Confidential Information except as provided in Article 2.

5.   Term.

(a)   This Agreement shall terminate three (3) years after the Effective Date unless terminated earlier by either party. Artist may extend the term of the Agreement by written notice to Recipient. Either party may terminate this Agreement, with or without cause, by giving notice of termination to the other party. The Agreement shall terminate immediately upon receipt of such notice.

(b)   Upon termination of this Agreement, Recipient shall cease to use Artist Confidential Information and shall comply with Paragraph 3 within twenty (20) days of the date

(Continued)

of termination. Upon the request of Artist, an officer of Recipient shall certify that Recipient has complied with its obligations in this Section.

        (c)   Notwithstanding the termination of this Agreement, Recipient's obligations in Paragraph 2 shall survive such termination.

    6.   <u>General Provisions</u>.

        (a)   This Agreement shall be governed by and construed in accordance with the laws of the United States and of the State of California as applied to transactions entered into and to be performed wholly within California between California residents. In the event of any action, suit, or proceeding arising from or based upon this agreement brought by either party hereto against the other, the prevailing party shall be entitled to recover from the other its reasonable attorneys' fees in connection therewith in addition to the costs of such action, suit, or proceeding.

        (b)   Any notice provided for or permitted under this Agreement will be treated as having been given when (a) delivered personally, (b) sent by confirmed telefacsimile or telecopy, (c) sent by commercial overnight courier with written verification of receipt, or (d) mailed postage prepaid by certified or registered mail, return receipt requested, to the party to be notified, at the address set forth above, or at such other place of which the other party has been notified in accordance with the provisions of this Section. Such notice will be treated as having been received upon the earlier of actual receipt or five (5) days after posting.

        (c)   Recipient agrees that the breach of the provisions of this Agreement by Recipient will cause Artist irreparable damage for which recovery of money damages would be inadequate. Artist will, therefore, be entitled to obtain timely injunctive relief to protect Artist's rights under this Agreement in addition to any and all remedies available at law.

        (d)   This Agreement constitutes the entire agreement between the parties relating to this subject matter and supersedes all prior or simultaneous representations, discussions, negotiations, and agreements, whether written or oral. This Agreement may be amended or supplemented only by a writing that is signed by duly authorized representatives of both parties. Recipient may not assign its rights under this Agreement. No term or provision hereof will be considered waived by either party, and no breach excused by either party, unless such waiver or consent is in writing signed on behalf of the party against whom the waiver is asserted. No consent by either party to, or waiver of, a breach by either party, whether express or implied, will constitute a consent to, waiver of, or excuse of any other, different, or subsequent breach by either party. If any part of this Agreement is found invalid or unenforceable, that part will be amended to achieve as nearly as possible the same economic effect as the original provision and the remainder of this Agreement will remain in full force.

        (e)   This Agreement may be executed in counterparts and all counterparts so executed by all parties hereto and affixed to this Agreement shall constitute a valid and binding agreement, even though the all of the parties have not signed the same counterpart.

    IN WITNESS WHEREOF, the parties have executed this Agreement as of the Effective Date.

RECIPIENT   ARTIST

_____   _____
Typed Name   Typed Name

_____   _____
Title   Title

Figure 24.1   A model NDA document. Document courtesy of Michael Leventhal.

thus avoiding the problem of project creep, discussed earlier. The contract may also include language about the kind of credit you will receive and where the credit will appear, and may note who will hold the copyright to the completed work. If you are inexperienced in negotiating contracts, you would be well advised to seek the help of an attorney. Even if you think you are savvy in such matters, it is always a good idea to have a lawyer look things over before signing.

But even before you reach the contract stage, you need to take some steps to protect yourself against an unscrupulous or inept employer. (Working for a well-intentioned but inexperienced client can be as perilous as working for one who deliberately intends to take advantage of you.) Before going too far in any discussion with a new client, try to learn as much about the company as you can, either by doing some research or by asking the prospective employer a series of focused questions. Asking the right questions about the company and the project will help you determine whether this is something you'll want to pursue—or if it is something you should run from.

EDUCATING YOURSELF

In any case, concerns about contracts and protecting your intellectual property are matters to be dealt with once a career is established. Let's take a few steps back and discuss how one prepares for a career in new media. It usually begins, as you might expect, with the right education. In terms of a formal education, you have a choice of two different paths. Path number one is to get a good foundation in the liberal arts, and then pick up specialized training, if needed, after graduation. Path number two is a more focused route: to enroll in an undergraduate program in computer science or in digital/media arts. Digital/media arts programs are becoming increasingly common at institutions of higher learning all over the world, both as undergraduate programs and as master degree programs. Specialized programs can give you a good background on theory and invaluable hands-on experience in creating interactive projects; they sometimes offer internship programs and can serve as fairly smooth stepping-stones to a good job. The Entertainment Software Alliance provides a list of schools that offer video game courses and degrees: http://www.theesa.com/games-improving-what-matters/schools.asp.

EXPERT OBSERVATION: BUT WHAT IF YOU ARE A LUDDITE?

Not everyone feels that it is good to focus on new media as an undergraduate. For example, designer Greg Roach, introduced in Chapter 4, strongly believes that no matter what position you are angling for in interactive media, you should first have a liberal arts education. He says "A grounding in the classical humanities is critical. Programmer, 3D artist, designer, whatever ... I'd much rather hire a traditional painter who's a Luddite [a person who rejects technology] but who understands color theory—and then train her in Maya—than hire a hot-shot 3D modeler whose aesthetic has been shaped exclusively by console games."

One excellent way to get hands-on experience working on a game is by participating in a Global Game Jam. Participants in these events form small teams and develop a game within a very short time frame—usually in just a single weekend. To level the playing field, all participants are given the same theme to work on. Some of these games are later polished and released commercially. In 2013, for example, 319 teams in 63 countries created original games based on the theme of the sound of a heartbeat.

If you are already out of college or if going to college is not an option for you, you might consider a certificate program in new media arts. Such programs are offered by many community colleges and by university extensions, and many can be taken online. Or you might select just a few courses that prepare you in the direction you wish to go in—classes in Flash animation, for example, or Web design. How much technical know-how you need varies from position to position. It is always helpful to have a general understanding of digital technology and a grasp of basic software programs, but if you want to be a digital storyteller, it is even more important to understand the fundamentals of storytelling, drama, and literature. You would be well advised to take a course that teaches narrative structure, or one in world mythology, and you should definitely take at least one course in dramatic writing.

Not all of your education has to take place in a classroom. If you don't already, spend some time playing games, trying out different genres and different platforms. Include first-person shooters, MMOGs, ARGs, mobile and casual games on your "to play" list so you can see how the experiences differ. Even if you aren't interested in working in games, they can teach you a great deal about design and interactivity. If a particular area of gaming is unfamiliar to you, find someone who plays this kind of game—a relative, a local student, a family friend—and ask them to give you a tour of one or two. Most people are happy to oblige, but you can always make it more attractive by treating your guide to a pizza.

Finally, you can get an excellent free education online by visiting websites devoted to various aspects of interactive media. You can also sign up to receive electronic and print trade publications. Each segment of the new media arena has several websites devoted to it and usually several electronic publications. Many have been mentioned in this book, and a diligent online search will turn up others.

INDUSTRY EVENTS

Another excellent way to educate yourself is by attending conferences, trade shows, and other industry events. Most of these gatherings are divided into two quite different parts, a conference and an exposition. By strolling around the expo floor, you get a chance to see demonstrations of the latest hardware and software in the field, often given by some of the creators of these very products. And by attending the conference sessions, you will hear talks by industry leaders and learn about the latest developments in the field. Although these trade events can be expensive, many of them offer student discounts and many also have volunteer programs. By working as a volunteer, you can take in as much of the event as you want during your off hours.

Virtually every sector of the interactive arena holds at least one annual event. Two major international conferences are MIPTV featuring Milia, which is held in Cannes, France, and the Tokyo Game Show in Japan. In the United States, the Game Developers Conference (GDC) is well worth attending. It offers excellent presentations on every facet of game design and production, including mobile games, MMOGs, and serious games, and many of the topics are of particular interest to digital storytellers. The Austin Game Conference is another high quality event.

If you are interested in computer graphics, you will definitely want to attend the annual SIGGRAPH conference. It is also one of the few shows where significant attention is paid to VR. The training field has its special gatherings, too, with *Training Magazine*'s annual conference and expo being just one example. The events mentioned here are just a small sampling of trade shows, conferences, and conventions that involve interactive media; new ones are started every year, and a few older ones sometimes fall by the wayside. The best way to find out about the industry events in your particular area of interest is by subscribing to electronic and print publications that specialize in the field.

THE PEOPLE CONNECTION

Industry events, excellent as they are, only take place at infrequent intervals. To stay more closely involved, and to connect with others who work in new media, you would be well advised to join one of the many professional organizations in this field. Networking with others in the field is one of the best ways to find work and stay on top of developments in the industry, as virtually any career counselor will tell you. It is even more important in a fast moving field like interactive media. Merely joining and attending an occasional meeting, however, brings limited benefits; you'll reap far greater rewards if you join a SIG (special interest group) or a committee within the organization and become an active, contributing member. By participating on a deeper level, you are more likely to form valuable connections that can lead to jobs. Two such organizations are the Academy of Interactive Arts and Sciences (AIAS) and the International Game Developers Association (IGDA).

A number of guilds and other organizations within the Hollywood system now welcome members who specialize in interactive media. Among these mainstream organizations are the Writers Guild, noted earlier, the Producers Guild, and the Academy of Television Arts and Sciences, generally known as the TV Academy. These organizations all have active committees or peer groups made up of new media members and put on special events focusing on interactive entertainment.

Unfortunately, many of the organizations mentioned here only hold meetings in certain geographical regions, and if you live outside these regions, it is difficult to become actively involved. However, you might also look into the possibility of forming a local branch, which can be a great way to meet other members in a less congested setting.

SOME POINTERS FOR A CAREER IN NEW MEDIA

Here are some helpful ideas for establishing and maintaining a career as a digital storyteller:

- Anticipate change. This field does not stay still, so you need to continually educate yourself on digital technologies and new forms of digital entertainment.

- Don't restrict your vision only to this field. Indulge your interests in the world beyond. Not only will this be of value to you in your professional work but it will also help keep you balanced.

- Educate yourself on narrative techniques. All good storytelling relies on certain basic principles.

- Stay tuned to traditional popular culture—to television, film, and music. To a large extent, new media and traditional media intersect and influence each other.

- If you are angling for a first job or a better job, consider building your own showcase. Not only will it give you a way to display your talents, but you will also learn something in the process. For more on showcases, see the next chapter.

- Remember that digital media can be a feast-or-famine type of industry and it is wise to be prepared for busts in certain media, in terms of having both a savings account and a good mental attitude. I have already weathered the bust in the CD-ROM market and the dot-com bust and will not be surprised if there's another bust ahead.

- As one of our experts said in Chapter 20, referring to smart toys, sometimes you have to dump all the pieces on the floor and play with them. Playing games and participating in interactive experiences is the single best way to keep your edges sharp.

CHAPTER 25

Creating Your Own Showcase

Is it a good investment of your time to create an original piece of work or a portfolio of samples to show off your talents?

If you do decide to create your own showcase, what should it include, and what is the best way to highlight your strengths?

What sorts of things do not belong in a showcase and can make a negative impression?

SHOWCASING YOUR WORK: IS IT WORTHWHILE?

It is reasonable to wonder, given how much effort it takes to create an original piece of work, if it is ever worth the investment of your time and energy to put together your own showcase. I would answer this question with a resounding yes, based on my own observations of the interactive entertainment industry, and also based on the interviews I've done for this book. A little later in this chapter, we will examine some actual situations in which people have successfully showcased their work. Creating your own showcase can benefit you if one of these scenarios fits your personal situation:

1. You have not yet had any professional experience in interactive media, but are interested in working in the field.

2. You are already working in digital entertainment, but are considering moving into a different area within it or would like to move to a higher level.

3. You are working as an employee in the field, but want to work as a freelancer.

4. You are working as a freelancer, and want to attract new clients.

Having an original piece of work to show, or a portfolio of work, is of particular importance if you have not yet had any experience in the field. How else will you be able to demonstrate to a prospective employer what you are capable of doing? A well thought out "calling card" of original work illustrates what your special talents are, where your creative leanings lie, and also reveals something about who you are as a person. A showcase of original work also bears a powerful subtext: you are serious enough about working in this field to spend your own time putting together a demonstration of your work. It carries the message that you are energetic, enterprising, and committed.

Producing a showcase project is a strategy used by small companies as well as by individuals. For example, Free Range Graphics undertook *The Meatrix* (described in Chapter 13) as a *pro bono* project in part to stimulate new business, a gamble that paid off handsomely for it.

However, the advice to build a promotional calling card must be given with a serious note of caution. If you do undertake such a significant self-assigned task, you need to go about it in a way that will set off your abilities in the most positive light possible and avoid doing things that can undermine your prospects.

CONSIDERATIONS IN CREATING A PROFESSIONAL SHOWCASE

For some people, putting together a showcase is a relatively easy task, because they can use samples of student projects or volunteer work that they did, or even of professional assignments. But if you don't have any such samples, or the samples you have are not well suited to your current goal, you are faced with the daunting job of creating something original from scratch. You will have a number of things to consider before you actually begin. Among the questions that will almost certainly cross your mind are:

PORTFOLIO OR SINGLE-PIECE APPROACH?

A portfolio approach includes several brief examples of work, while a single-piece approach focuses on one well-developed project. Each tactic has its own pros and cons. With the portfolio approach, you can effectively demonstrate your ability to work in a range of styles and on different types of subject matter. However, the portfolio approach also means that you will have to undertake several different projects and build them out to the point that they are solid enough to serve as good samples.

By showcasing a single piece, on the other hand, you can present a more fleshed out and complete project than you'd have in a portfolio, where the samples tend to be short and fairly superficial. But having just one piece of work to showcase can be a little risky, because the work you are exhibiting might not be what the prospective employer or client is looking for, and you will have nothing else to illustrate what you are capable of.

So where does this leave you? It's best to make the call based on your own individual situation. If you already have a couple of samples you can use, and have some ideas about another one or two you could put together, then you are probably already well down the path toward the portfolio approach. On the other hand, if you feel confident you've got a great concept to showcase, and that it would work well as a demo piece, then that's probably the best way for you to proceed. There's no right or wrong answer here.

DISTRIBUTION METHOD?

You will need to determine what method you will use to make your showcase available to the people you want to see it. The three most obvious choices are the Internet, CD-ROMs, and DVDs. Virtually any prospective employer or client should be able to view your work on any one of these platforms, so ease of viewing is not a factor here. Your work itself, and your own leanings, are really your best guides. It makes sense to distribute your showcase on the medium in which you are most interested in working. But if you want to work in an area that falls outside of the three already mentioned avenues of distribution—if you are interested in VR, say, or in alternate reality games—then pick the medium that you feel would display your material to the best advantage. One final consideration for a multi-project portfolio: it is advisable to package your showcase on a single platform rather than having a jumble of different works that cannot easily be viewed together. If you have both Web and CD-ROM samples, you might want to put your Web pages on the CD-ROM with the other examples, or vice versa. As another possibility, you could embed links to your Web pages in your CD-ROM.

SUBJECT MATTER AND APPROACH?

One of the most important questions you will be faced with is what the content of your showcase will be. The honest answer is that no one can tell you what to do here. The best choices are the ones that most closely reflect your own personal interests, talents, and expertise. By picking a subject you really care about, you have the best chance of producing something that will be strong and will stand out from the crowd. The way you decide to construct your showcase should also reflect your personal taste and style—within limits, of course. Coarse humor and disparaging portrayals of any particular ethnic group are never appropriate. Also, you do yourself no favors by employing a sloppy, unprofessional looking style.

But what if you have tried your best to think of some topics for your showcase and still come up blank? Then you might consider volunteering your services for a nonprofit institution in your community. Possible choices include your church, synagogue, or mosque; the local chamber of commerce or a community service group; or a school sports team or Brownie troop. Another alternative is to create a promotional piece for a business belonging to a friend or relative.

Although on the surface such projects seem to be creatively limiting, you may be inspired to create something quite clever. For instance, you could design an amusing advergame for your brother-in-law's landscaping business, or an interactive adventure tale about Brownies for your niece's troop. Volunteer projects for nonprofit organizations or for businesses have some solid advantages. They give you hands-on practical experience, and also give you a professional sample to include in your showcase, even if the work was done without monetary compensation.

GAPS IN NECESSARY SKILLS?

Lacking all the skills necessary to put together one's own showcase is a common problem, because few people are equipped with the full range of talents necessary for building an effective sample piece. The problem can be solved in two ways: by teaching yourself what you don't already know, or by teaming up with someone who is strong where you are weak. Teaching yourself a new skill like Flash animation may seem like an intimidating project, but as we will see from the

Odd Todd case study later in this chapter, it is manageable. Software is becoming ever easier to use, and books are available that teach animation programs, image manipulation, Web page design, and media authoring. You might also take a community college course to fill in a particular gap.

But if you prefer to team up with a colleague instead, keep in mind you need not even be in the same community. Many collaborations take place in cyberspace, and sometimes occur between people who have never met in person. Perhaps your strengths are in art, writing, and conceptualizing, while the other person excels at the more technical side of things. If you work together, you can create a project that is more effective than either of you could do alone, and also demonstrates your special abilities. This can be a win-win solution for both parties. Of course, you will want to be sure that each person's contribution is made clear in the credits, and that no one is claiming solo authorship for the entire project.

ODD TODD: A CASE STUDY

While it is important for a personal showcase to look professional, this does not necessarily mean it needs to follow a conservative, play-by-the-rules approach. If you take a look at the website *Odd Todd* (www.oddtodd.com), you will find an immensely quirky piece of work that breaks almost all the rules and yet has become a wildly successful endeavor. This is not to say that everyone should build a project as idiosyncratic as this one is, but it does effectively illustrate the power of being fresh and original, and of having something meaningful to say. Essentially a one-person operation and done on a tiny budget, *Odd Todd* thrust its creator, Todd Rosenberg, into the spotlight and changed his life. He's been featured on *Good Morning America, Nightline, ABC World News*, and *National Geographic*.

The site is named for a fictitious character, Odd Todd, and is loosely based on the experiences of the site's creator, Todd Rosenberg, who lost his job with a dot-com company during a radical downsizing. In a series of Flash-animated episodes, we watch Todd as he futilely searches for a new job and gives in to such distractions as fudge-striped cookies, long naps, and fantasies about large-breasted women. The artwork in the cartoons is rough and child-like, and the only human speaking character is Todd, who chronicles his hero's struggles in a voice-over narration (see Figure 25.1). The voice he uses is distinctive, marked by a puzzled kind of irony and bewilderment at his predicament, and further made unique by his urban drawl and a

Figure 25.1   Odd Todd is the fictional protagonist of the *Odd Todd* website, an endeavor that has turned its creator's life around. Image courtesy of Todd Rosenberg.

particular way of stretching out the end vowels in such words as money (mon-aaay) and cookie (cook-aaay). And though the site is extremely funny, it does have a serious side, touching on the painful issues of being unemployed and serving as a kind of cyberspace support system for laid off white-collar workers.

Beginning with just a single animated episode, the site has mushroomed into a full array of features. It includes dozens of cartoons and games, all relating to Odd Todd and his life and obsessions. It also includes a variety of specials such as a feature called "What's Happening," a diary-like log of Todd's life, Daily Good News, Coolio Funlinks, and Mov-ay Reviews.

THE HOWS AND WHYS OF *ODD TODD*

Why has a site featuring roughly drawn cartoons about an unshaven, unemployed guy in a blue bathrobe become such a hit? How did Todd Rosenberg set about making this site and how does he keep it going? And as a showcase, what has it done for his career? The real Todd shed some light on these questions during a phone interview and several follow-up emails.

First of all, let's address one burning question right away. No, the real Todd does not sound like the voice he uses on the website. That is a made-up voice, and many of the situations depicted in the cartoons are invented as well. But the core conceit—that an unemployed dot-comer built the site—is totally true. The authenticity of the character's predicament, the real Todd believes, is an important reason why *Odd Todd* has become so immensely popular. People identify with it, Rosenberg explained. "They see it and say to themselves: 'It's so me!' or 'Someone else is doing exactly what I'm doing!'"

A DO-IT-YOURSELF APPROACH

Although Rosenberg had learned basic HTML at a prior job and had taught himself to draw (by using *Mad Magazine* as a model), he lacked training in almost every other skill he would need in order to build and maintain his new site. When asked what he'd studied in college, the University of Hartford, he confessed: "I never studied in college. I wasn't much of a student." He admitted to filling up his notebooks with cartoons instead of lecture notes. He had no training in screenwriting—he owned books on the subject, he said, but had never read them—and had never acquired experience in acting, either, because he had stage fright.

One of the first things he needed to learn, in order to bring *Odd Todd* to life, was Flash animation. He taught himself how with the help of a book called *Flash 5 Cartooning*. His "studio" was his apartment in New York, and he did everything from there. To lay down the soundtrack for the cartoons, he used the microphone that came with his computer and did all the voice work himself, including the strange chirps and other sound effects for the site's non-human characters. As a result, he managed to keep his start-up costs low, estimating that during his first year he spent under $1,000.

Rosenberg began the site after he was laid off from AtomFilms.com. Thinking he'd only be out of work for a few months, he decided to spend some of it doing something he'd always enjoyed—cartooning—and create something that might possibly help him become employed again. The result was the first episode of *Odd Todd*. The debut episode was a humorous take on what it is like to be newly laid off, with too much time and too little money.

KEEPING THINGS GOING

Though Rosenberg's cartoons have an unpolished, homemade appearance, he can actually draw much better than the work on his website would suggest. In doing the animation for his first cartoon, he made a quick series of drawings, intending to use them as placeholders. But after he refined them, he discovered he much preferred the look of the rough first set, and discarded the more polished ones. Even now, with multiple episodes behind him, he still makes five or six versions of each cartoon before he has one that he feels is right. Making the website look quickly dashed out and candid is totally in keeping with the fictional Odd Todd character, though accomplishing the right look actually takes a great deal of work.

In the beginning, however, Rosenberg's abilities in many areas truly were less than polished. His Odd Todd character would look different from picture to picture; he had trouble making him consistent. In addition, he didn't know how to synch the sound and the picture properly, or how to make a button to let users replay an episode or game. He kept going back to his books and asking more knowledgeable friends for help before he mastered what he felt he needed to know.

Now that the site has been up and running for a number of years, it still requires regular maintenance and new content. He continues to update it with new cartoons, games, and other features.

A CYBER SUPPORT SYSTEM

Rosenberg has managed to keep his expenses low in part by developing an informal exchange system. For instance, his site is hosted for free by Peak Webhosting, which saves him a great deal of money. In return, he promotes Peak Webhosting on his site, which has brought them business. He has also received significant volunteer assistance from one of his fans, Stacey Kamen, a website designer. Rosenberg reciprocates by prominently promoting her design skills and her website business on his site (Kamen and her work will be discussed in more detail later in this chapter).

Another fan, Geoffrey Noles, volunteers his services to the site by programming the *Odd Todd* games, such as the enormously amusing and popular *Cook-ay Slots*, a wacky slot machine game. Noles, too, receives credit on *Odd Todd*, as well as a link to his site. Rosenberg has never met either of these two important contributors face to face. They communicate by various electronic means, including, in the case of Noles and Rosenberg, by webcam.

Since its launch late in 2001, *Odd Todd* has been visited by millions of unique users and has attracted major media attention. Dozens of articles have been written about the site, and Rosenberg has been featured on a great number of TV and radio shows. Loyal fans have contributed thousands of dollars to *Odd Todd*'s online tip jar, one dollar at a time, and they also support the site by buying a great variety of *Odd Todd* merchandise, from t-shirts to coffee mugs. The site has also spawned a book, *The Odd Todd Handbook: Hard Times, Soft Couch*, which, like the site, was created by Rosenberg.

Over time, however, the lives of the fictitious Todd and the real Todd have diverged. While an episode might show a dejected Todd sending out résumés and trying to find work, in actuality Rosenberg is no longer dejected or looking for full-time employment. Instead, he makes enough money from the site and related merchandise, plus freelance work, to keep going. The success of the site, he said, and the creative satisfaction it has brought him, has caused him to lose interest in returning to the 9-to-5 corporate world. Ironically, he's actually making a living by being unemployed.

SOME OTHER APPROACHES TO SHOWCASING

The Internet, especially with the rapid spread of broadband, has proven to be an extremely effective platform for getting one's work seen. Some people, like Rosenberg, have created an entire website to promote their work, while others post their creations on sites like YouTube and MySpace. Still others, like Rosenberg's cyber support team, show off their work by collaborating with others.

A TWO-PRONGED APPROACH

Stacey Kamen, a Web and graphic designer with a specialty in business imaging (giving businesses a particular image via websites, brochures, and other materials), has taken two routes to making her work known. She contributes design work to the *Odd Todd* site and has built a site of her own (www.StaceyKamen.com), which is totally different from Rosenberg's.

Interestingly, when she first approached Rosenberg and volunteered her services, she wasn't thinking about how helping him out might boost her own career. She first learned of Rosenberg's website when she was working at a dot-com company and it became clear that she was about to lose her job. A friend sent her a link to *Odd Todd*, and she visited it every day. "It made me laugh, and it took away that alone feeling," she told me. "It had a big draw, apart from the humor. You felt you were in good company."

Still, she told me, the site was driving her nuts because the home page was so disorganized and the navigation was so clumsy. She contacted Rosenberg and offered to help, but he wasn't interested, maintaining that the unprofessional look was part of the *Odd Todd* mystique. She persisted anyway, and even sent him a plan of what she had in mind. Finally, the day before Rosenberg was due to make an appearance on CNN, he agreed to let her redesign the home page. She had just one day to do it, but managed to tidy things up and add a smoothly functioning, jaunty new navigation bar on the left-hand side of the screen.

That was the beginning of their successful collaboration. Kamen continues to help him out with special tasks, like adding falling snowflakes to the site for Christmas, and giving it an appropriate seasonal look for other holidays. In return for her help, Rosenberg makes a point of promoting Kamen throughout his site as "The Official Web Designer of *OddTodd.com*!" As a result, Kamen reports, 90 percent of the inquiries she gets from prospective clients have come to her from the *Odd Todd* site. She's also getting more of her dream clients—companies and individuals from the arts and entertainment world, including musicians.

Looking back on how she first hooked up with Rosenberg and started working with him, Kamen said: "I was coming out of a corporate situation, always working with the same color palette. I was looking for more creative opportunities. It turned out to be the best business move I ever made."

Kamen's own website for her freelance design business, which she launched soon after she was laid off from her dot-com job, is entirely different from the casual bachelor style of *Odd Todd*. It is crisp, polished, and elegant, laid out in a highly organized way (see Figure 25.2). Its design earned it a Golden Web Award from the International Association of Webmasters and Designers.

"My website says a lot about me," Kamen said. "For instance, I love nature and earth tones, and I'm organized." She says the site also reflects her skills and style at a glance, without making the visitor sift through mountains of text. She wanted her site to show her creative side and eclectic nature. "A site like everyone else's—standard layout, standard buttons, standard navigation—wouldn't be 'me,'" she asserted. "I created my site with the idea of doing something different, not only its visual structure, but in navigation as well." The samples of her work that are included on the site reveal the diversity of her design approaches. "If you are going to be successful in the design business," she said, "you need to be flexible, and be able to shift gears easily."

Figure 25.2 The elegant style Kamen uses for her website utilizes a totally different approach than the *Odd Todd* website. Image courtesy of Stacey Kamen.

LONELY NO MORE

LonelyGirl15 is another self-made venture that, like *Odd Todd*, was produced on a shoestring budget and yet thrust its creators into the limelight. Unlike *Odd Todd*, however, this faux video blog, discussed in Chapter 15, was released at first as individual videos on YouTube (the series now has its own website). The project is the joint effort of Miles Beckett, a young doctor who dropped out of his residency program to do something more creative, and Ramesh Flinders, an aspiring screenwriter.

The two met at a karaoke bar birthday party and discovered they shared a vision of producing a new kind of entertainment specifically geared for the Internet, one that would use the kind of video blogging found on sites like YouTube to tell a fictional story and that would seem so real that it would pull viewers into the lives of the characters. Together they created *LonelyGirl15*, shooting it in Flinders' bedroom with a cheap webcam, inexpensive props, and unpaid actors. They planned their strategy carefully, giving the episodes a rough-hewn look like other YouTube amateur videos and even having the main character, Bree, refer to recent videos posted on YouTube to make her seem all the more authentic.

STAKING OUT NEW TERRITORY

LonelyGirl15 has been a huge hit, and not even the discovery that Bree was not a real girl has managed to derail it. As of this writing 328 episodes have been released and Beckett and Flinders are now represented by a major Hollywood talent agency. Interestingly, although they have had meetings with top TV producers, they steadfastly refuse to turn *LonelyGirl15* into just another TV series, preferring instead to stake out uncharted creative territory. As Beckett told a writer from *Wired Magazine* (December, 2006): "The Web isn't just a support system for hit TV shows. It's a new medium. It requires new storytelling techniques. The way the networks look at the Internet now is like the early days of TV, when announcers would just read radio scripts on camera."

AN ALMIGHTY HIT

Mr. Deity, which made its debut in 2006, is another Web-based video series made on a tiny budget that has given its creator enormous visibility. The *Mr. Deity* of this comedy series is God himself and he is portrayed as a visionary who is not especially good with the details. The videos are far too quirky to ever find a home on television but are a great fit for the Web, which loves edgy humor. Though they do not actually mock religion, they do pose some thorny theological questions in a humorous way. For example, why does God allow terrible things to happen to innocent people, and why do so many prayers seem to go unanswered? The series creator, Brian Keith Dalton, it should be noted, is not only an independent filmmaker, but was at one time training to be a missionary and asserts that he has great respect for religious people.

Like *LonelyGirl15*, the first episodes of *Mr. Deity* were released as individual videos on YouTube. They feature a revolving cast of four characters, including God, Jesus, Lucifer, and God's right-hand assistant, the highly efficient Larry. Dalton himself does almost everything: he writes, directs, edits, produces, and stars in the videos and even wrote the theme music. A one-person crew handles both the camera and sound. *Mr. Deity* has not only been a major hit on YouTube but has also attracted the attention of Sony Pictures Entertainment, which now features two new episodes a month of *Mr. Deity* on its website, *Crackle*.

Mr. Deity is yet another example of how high originality is more important than a high budget when it comes to creating a showcase for your talent.

GETTING YOUR WORK SEEN

One excellent way to bring attention to your work is to enter it in contests and competitions. A number of new ones have gotten started in recent years, and we can expect to see more of them all the time. It's a good idea to keep your eyes open for them, because winning one can bring your work tremendous exposure.

POINTERS FOR MAKING YOUR OWN SHOWCASE

If you are planning to create and build your own professional showcase, the following suggestions are helpful to keep in mind:

1. Don't imitate others; be an original. Let your showcase reflect what you really care about. This is the same advice offered by professionals in every creative field to anyone endeavoring to make something to show off their talents, be it a painting or a movie script or a novel or an interactive game.

2. Define your ultimate objectives and mold your showcase accordingly. The material it contains should demonstrate your abilities in the type of work you want to do and be appropriate to the general arena where you hope to find employment.

3. Don't confuse the making of a showcase with the making of a vanity piece. This isn't the place to display cute pet pictures or to brag about your snowboarding trophies. It is, however, appropriate to include your professional credits and contact information.

4. Be sure your showcase actually works. Try to get a friend to beta test it for you. If the piece is for the Web, look at it on different browsers and on both Macs and PCs.

5. If you are lacking in a particular skill, don't let that be a roadblock. Either teach yourself that skill or team up with more skilled colleagues.

6. Humor can be an asset in a showcase, but inappropriate humor can backfire. If you think your piece is comic, run it by other people to see if they agree. Ideally, seek the opinions of people who are about the same age and at the same professional level as your target audience.

7. If your work includes text, keep it concise and easy to read. Try whenever possible to find a way to do something visually rather than by printed words.

8. Make sure that the interactive elements you include are well integrated into the overall concept, have a legitimate function, and demonstrate that you understand how to use interactivity effectively.

9. If you are taking a portfolio approach instead of showcasing a single piece, select pieces that contain different types of subject matter and display different styles and approaches.

10. Get feedback from others, and be open to what they say. Receiving feedback can be uncomfortable, but it is the only way you will find out how others see your work. Don't become so attached to any one feature that you are unable to discard it, even if it detracts from other aspects of your showcase. As a story editor once said to me: "Sometimes you have to kill your babies."

The process of creating an effective showcase will take time, but be patient. You will probably experience some frustrations and hit some walls. Such setbacks indicate you are stretching yourself, which is a positive thing. If you persist, you will end up knowing more than you did when you began the project, and are likely to create something of which you can be proud.

Conclusion

As this book has demonstrated, digital storytelling is a vast and quickly changing field, one full of unique challenges and opportunities. Nevertheless, many of the old principles of storytelling, dating back to preliterate times, still apply. In this book, I have tried to tie the old and the new together to make the path into this field less intimidating.

I hope you have enjoyed this journey through this world of digital stories, and feel inspired to create your own works of digital storytelling. Producing a new work in this arena, while inevitably challenging, can also be enormous fun, and I hope the fun part of the experience shines through in the case studies and examples.

There's one thing that I would like to leave you with: to wring the best possible results out of an innovative product, the project's producers have first taken pains to understand the platform it would play on. They studied what the platform could offer and what its limitations were. As new platforms come along that are not covered in this book, you can apply these principles to your own work, to explore the possibilities of a new platform as a vehicle for storytelling.

Please visit the book's companion website for updates and resources at www.focalpress.com/cw/miller. And I also welcome questions and comments, which can be addressed to me at Carolyn@CarolynMiller.com.

And here's to storytelling, old and new!

Glossary

3G: See *third generation*.

4-D dark ride: An immersive experience that takes place in a space with theatrical seating and a large curved screen. In these experiences, the seats may move to give the audience members the sensation of traveling. (Such a seat is called a *motion base chair*). In addition, these rides involve other senses beyond vision and sound, including touch, smell, and temperature change. These sensations are used to bring the audience into the fourth dimension. Such experiences may also be called *ridefilms*.

accelerometer: A device embedded in smart phones and tablets that can compute roll and pitch. It can track the way in which the smart phone or tablet is being moved. For instance, the accelerometer can track a virtual marble a user is rolling around the screen and make the marble appear to be moving realistically, using the rules of physics.

active learning: See *experiential learning*.

Advanced TV Enhancement Forum (ATVEF): Set of standards that allows Web-based content to be broadcast on TV.

advergaming: An entertainment that incorporates advertising into a game. Such games appear on the Web and on wireless devices. They are generally short, designed as a quick burst of fun.

agency: The user's ability to control aspects of an interactive narrative. Essentially, agency gives the user the ability to make choices and to experience the results of those choices. Agency also allows the user to navigate through the story space, create an avatar, change points of view, and enjoy many other kinds of interactive experiences.

agon: Greek for a contest for a prize at a public game; a contest or conflict. The words "antagonist" and "protagonist" are both formed around this root. The protagonist is the one who goes after the prize and the antagonist is the one who tries to prevent this; their struggle is the core of dramatic narrative.

AI: See *artificial intelligence*.

algorithm: A logical system that determines the triggering of events. In a game, an algorithm may determine such things as what the player needs to do before gaining access to "X" or what steps must be taken in order to trigger "Y." An algorithm is a little like a recipe, but instead of the ingredients being foods, they are events or actions.

alternate reality game (ARG): An interactive game that blurs real life with fiction, and that combines a rich narrative with puzzle-solving. ARGs usually involve multiple media and incorporate types of communications not normally associated with games, such as telephone calls, ads in newspapers, and faxes.

analog: One of two ways of transmitting and storing information, including entertainment content, electronically; the other being digital. Analog information is continuous and unbroken. Film, video, LPs, and audiotape are all analog storage media.

ancillary market: The secondary use of an entertainment property. Typical ancillary markets for movies and TV shows are videos, DVDs, music CDs, and video games. Wireless games are also becoming part of the ancillary market.

android: A type of robot that is meant to look and act as much like a human being as possible, ideally to the point of passing as human. The word comes from the Greek, meaning "resembling man." Unlike mechanized robots, androids are capable of responding to visual and vocal stimuli, and some are capable of voice recognition and can converse in a fairly believable way.

Android: the Google operating system for mobile devices. It is a Linux-based operating system. It is used primarily for mobile devices like tablet computers and mobile phones.

animatronic character: A replica of a living creature that is computer-operated but moves in a life-like way and may also speak.

antagonist: In a drama, the adversary of the story's central character. Their opposition gives heat to the drama and provides the story with exciting conflict. The word is formed around the Greek root, *agon*, meaning contest or prize. See *agon*.

app: See *application*.

application or app: A small downloadable program designed for a particular purpose. "App" is an abbreviation of the term. Apps include ebooks and games as well as programs designed for pragmatic purposes.

arcade game: A game designed to be played on an arcade machine, generally having a great deal of fast action and designed for a short playing time, or a video game that is made in the style of an arcade game.

arcade machine: A coin-operated video game designed for play in public spaces.

ARG: See *alternate reality game*.

artificial intelligence (AI): Computer intelligence that simulates human intelligence. A digital character with artificial intelligence seems to understand what the player is doing or saying, and acts appropriately in response.

assessment tool: A method of analyzing a learner's performance in an interactive project designed to teach or train.

attract mode: A visual tease on a kiosk screen that loops continuously until a user engages with the kiosk and triggers the program. It is also known as an attract routine.

ATVEF: See *Advanced TV Enhancement Forum*.

augmented reality: A type of immersive environment in which digital technology is used in conjunction with physical props or in a real-life physical setting to create a unique experience. In such works, digitally created elements and physical objects (including people) are contained within the same space and may interact with each other.

automata: Self-operating mechanical figures that can move, and, in some cases, make life-like sounds. Automata have been made since ancient times and are the forerunners of smart toys.

avatar: A graphic representation of the character controlled by the player. Players often have the opportunity to construct their own avatar from a selection of choices.

backstory: Background material relating to a drama that explains events that happened or relationships that were established before the current narrative begins.

bandwidth: The capacity of a communications channel to receive data; usually measured in bits or bytes per second. The higher the bandwidth connection, the better able the user is to receive streaming video and to enjoy a high-quality Internet experience. High bandwidth connections are also called broadband and are available via DSL lines and cable and satellite services. Dial-up modems are only able to support low bandwidth; such connections are quite slow and do not support streaming video well. See also *broadband*.

beta tester: A person who looks for bugs in a software program or game before it is released to the public. This type of job is often a stepping-stone to a higher level position in the software industry.

bible: A document that describes all the significant elements of a work that is in development. The term comes from television production and is used in the development of interactive content. The bible includes all the settings or worlds and what happens in them, as well as all the major characters. It may also give the backstories of these characters. Some bibles, called character bibles, only describe the characters.

binary choice: Having only two possible options for each decision or action offered to the user.

blog: A Web log. An online diary or journal that is accessible to anyone on the Web, or a site that expresses a personal opinion.

Bluetooth: A protocol that enables high-speed wireless connections to the Internet.

Boolean logic: Logic that uses only two variables, such as 0 and 1, or true and false. A string of such variables can determine a fairly complex sequence of events. Boolean logic can be regarded as a series of conditions that determine when a "gate" is opened—when something previously unavailable becomes available, or something previously undoable becomes doable. Boolean logic is also used to do searches on the Web.

BOOM (Binocular Omni Orientation Monitor): A type of VR device that works like a HMD but is mounted on a rotating arm rather than on one's head. See also *head-mounted display*.

boss battle: a fight between a boss monster and the player. See *boss monster*.

boss monster: In a video game, the most formidable opponent that the player encounters in a level or segment of the game. The boss monster will usually make an appearance toward the end of the segment, and must be defeated in order for the player to make further progress in the game.

bot: Short for robot; an artificial character. On the Internet, bots are programs that can access websites and gather information that is used by search engines.

branching structure: A classic structure in interactive works. It is a little like a pathway over which the user travels. Every so often, the user comes to a fork and will be presented with several different choices. Upon selecting one, the user will then travel a bit further until reaching another fork, with several more choices, and so on.

branded content: Programming that is funded by an advertiser and integrates promotional elements with the entertainment content. Unlike traditional advertising sponsorship, where the advertising is done through commercials, the entire program can be thought of as a "soft" commercial.

branding: A way of establishing a distinctive identity for a product or service; an image that makes it stand out from the crowd. By successful branding, the product is distinguished from its competitors and is made to seem alluring in a unique way.

broadband: A transmission medium capable of supporting a wide range of frequencies. Broadband can transmit more data and at a higher speed than narrowband, and can support streaming audio and video. The term is often used to mean high-speed Internet access. See also *bandwidth*.

canon: the official version of a narrative, consistent on all the different media on which the story is carried. *Canon* is a term often used in discussions of transmedia storytelling.

casual game: A game that can be easily learned and can be played in a brief period of time, but is highly replayable. Such games are played online and on game consoles, PCs, cell phones, and other portable devices. They include a wide variety of genres, such as abstract puzzle games, shooters, racing games, and advergames.

CAVE (CAVE Automatic Virtual Environment): An extremely immersive type of VR environment in which the user is surrounded by rear-view projection screens and the 3D images are seen through stereoscopic glasses.

CD-i (Compact Disc-interactive): A multimedia system developed jointly by Philips and Sony and introduced in 1991. It was the first interactive technology geared for a mass audience. CD-i discs were played on special units designed for the purpose, and connected to a TV set or color monitor.

CD-ROM (Compact Disc-Read Only Memory): A storage medium for digital data—text, audio, video, and animation—which can be read by a personal computer. The CD-ROM was introduced to the public in 1985 and could store a massive amount of digital data compared to the other storage media of the time.

CGI: See *common gateway interface; computer generated image*.

character arc: The transformation that a character, usually the protagonist, undergoes during the course of a story; the way a character evolves and changes. For example, a character might start off as cowardly but grow into a hero by the end of the narrative. The character arc is a staple element of linear drama, but can also be found in works of digital storytelling.

chatterbot: An artificial character, or bot, with whom users can chat.

cheese hole: Spaces in transmedia stories which are designed to encourage members of the audience to contribute content.

cinematic: A cut scene. See *cut scene*.

Cloud computing: A method of using, managing, and processing data on remote servers rather than on personal computers.

common gateway interface (CGI): A Web term for a set of rules that govern how a Web server communicates with another piece of software.

computer generated image (CGI): An image produced by a computer rather than being hand-drawn, often used as shorthand for computer animation.

concatenation: The efficient reuse of words and phrases to maximize space on a chip.

console game: A game played on a game console. See also *game console*.

contract worker: An employee of a digital media company who works on a project to project basis instead of being employed full time by one company. They are also called *freelance* employees.

convergence: A blending together of two or more entities into one seamless whole. In terms of interactive media, it may be used to mean the integration of telecommunications and broadcasting or the integration of the PC and the TV.

critical story path: The linear narrative line through an interactive work. This path contains all the sequences a user must experience, and all the information that must be acquired, for the user to achieve the full story experience and reach a meaningful ending point.

cross-media production: The merging of a single entertainment property over multiple platforms or venues. See also *transmedia entertainment*.

cut scene: A linear story segment in an interactive work; also called a cinematic. Cut scenes are used to establish the story or to serve as a transition between events; they are also shown at the culmination of a mission or at the end of a game.

cyberspace: A term used to refer to the nonphysical world created by computer communications. It was coined in 1984 by William Gibson in his sci-fi novel, *Neuromancer*.

database narrative: A type of interactive movie whose structure allows for both the selection and the combining of narrative elements from a number of categories drawn from a deep database.

design document: The written blueprint of an interactive work used as a guide during the development process and containing every detail of the project. It is a living document, begun during preproduction but never truly completed until the project itself is finished.

developer: A company that does the development work for a new software product, such as a game or smart toy.

diagesis: A term used, particularly in academic circles, to mean a *storyworld*.

dialogue tree: A form of interactive dialogue in which the player character or user is presented with several lines of dialogue to choose from. Each line will trigger a different response from the NPC being addressed and in some cases may even take the user or player character down different narrative paths.

digital: One of two ways of transmitting and storing information, including entertainment content, electronically, the other being analog. Digital information is made up of distinct, separate bits: the zeroes and ones that feed our computers. DVDs, CD-ROMs, CDs, and digital video are all digital storage media. Digital information can be stored easily, accessed quickly, and can be transferred among a great variety of devices.

digital video recorder (DVR): One of several terms for devices that enable viewers to select and record television programs; the best-known device is the TiVo. Other generic terms for this type of device are *personal digital recorder* and *personal video recorder*. These devices offer viewers more control than VCRs and include features like pausing live TV and the ability to skip commercials.

disruptive media: An innovation in media that creates a new market, thereby disrupting an existing market.

drill and kill game: Educational games that drill children in particular skills.

dual-screen iTV: A form of iTV in which a television show and a website are synchronized, and thus employ both a TV screen and a computer or mobile device screen. This form of iTV is available to anyone with a computer or mobile device, online access, and a TV set; it does not require any special equipment. It is also known as *synchronous interactivity*. See also *single-screen iTV*.

dungeon master: The person who, during the playing of an RPG or a real-time simulation, helps shape the action, serves as the game's referee, and manipulates the game's nonplayer characters. Dungeon masters were first introduced in LARPs and are a feature of MMOGs and other interactive experiences, including training simulations. See also *LARP* and *MMOG*.

DVD: An electronics platform that plays digitized programs, particularly movies and compilations of TV shows, on special discs, also called DVDs. The initials DVD once stood for "Digital Video Disc," but now the initials do not stand for any particular words; the initials themselves are the name of the technology.

DVR: See *digital video recorder*.

early adopter: A person who is one of the first to use a new technology or device.

ebook: See *electronic book*.

edutainment: An interactive program for children that combines entertainment and education; one of the most successful categories of children's software.

e-learning: Online education and training. College courses, university extension courses, and adult education courses are all offered as e-learning opportunities.

electronic book: A book that can read on a mobile device. Electronic books, also called ebooks, offer varying degrees of interactivity and media features. Some are quite limited, only letting the user "turn" the pages, while others offer video, animation, sound (often a voice narrating the story), pop-up elements, and a connection to the Internet.

electronic kiosk: A booth or other small structure that offers the user an easy-to-operate computerized experience, often via a touchscreen. Although usually used for pragmatic services like banking (ATM machines), they are also used for entertainment and informational purposes.

electronic literature: A form of literature that is not printed but instead makes use of the special capabilities of computer technology; also known as hyperliterature. See *hyperliterature*.

email: Short for electronic mail, mail that is sent over the Internet.

emergent behavior: A computer-controlled character acting in ways that go beyond the things it has been specifically programmed to do; unpredictable behavior. When an NPC exhibits emergent behavior, it seems to have an inner life and almost be capable of human thought.

emergent story: A story that is not fixed or embedded within a game or interactive work, but that takes shape as the user plays the game or interactive work.

emoticon: Symbols used in text messages to express emotions.

engine: The computer programming that operates a game or other piece of software.

experiential learning: Learning by doing, acting, and experiencing, as opposed to passive forms of learning, such as listening to lectures or reading books. Also known as *active learning*.

exposition: Information that is essential for the understanding of a story and must be incorporated into it for the story to make sense. It includes the background and relationships of the characters; their aspirations; and important events that took place in their past that relate to the story.

F2P: See *free-to-play*.

fan fiction (fanfic): A type of narrative that is based on a printed or produced story or drama, but is written by fans instead of by the original author.

fanfic See *fan fiction*.

first-person point of view: The perspective we have while participating in an interactive work in which we see the action as if we were in the middle of it and viewing it through our own eyes. We see the world around us, but we don't see ourselves, except for perhaps a hand or a foot. It is the "I" experience. See also *third-person point of view*.

first-person shooter (FPS): A shooting game in which the player is given a first-person point of view of the action. The players control and play the protagonist, but they cannot see themselves, though they may be able to see a weapon they are holding. See also *first-person point of view*.

Flash animation: An animated film created with Adobe Flash animation software. It supports interactivity and is a common form of animation on the Internet.

flowchart: A visual expression of the through line of an interactive project. Flowcharts illustrate important aspects of the content and a project's interactive structure.

FMV: See *full motion video*.

fourth wall: The invisible boundary that, in the theater, separates the audience from the characters on the stage, and in any dramatic work divides reality (the audience side) from fiction (the characters' side). Works of digital storytelling often break the fourth wall by bringing the participant into the fictional world or by the fictional world invading the real world.

FPS: See *first-person shooter*.

fractal structure: A structural model in which the essence of the story does not advance or change, but instead grows in scope as the player interacts with it. The term is based on the mathematic concept of the fractal, a pattern that repeats itself endlessly in smaller and larger forms.

free-to-play (F2P): A game that is free to play, or free to download. It can be virtually any genre. Players, however, may be invited to make small payments for in-game items or to enhance the gameplay experience. In some cases, a F2P version of a game is designed as a way to promote the pay-to-play version of the game.

full motion video (FMV): Live action video seen on a computer.

fulldome: A type of immersive environment in which images are projected onto the entire inner surface of a planetarium dome or a similarly shaped theater. For audience members, it is somewhat like sitting inside a huge upside-down bowl, surrounded on all sides by moving images.

functionality: How an interactive program works, particularly its interactive elements and its interface.

game console: A device made for playing video games. Some consoles plug into a TV set and use the TV as a monitor; others are self-contained hand-held devices. Most can support multiplayer games and the majority of the current generation of consoles can connect to the Internet and can play DVDs.

gameplay: The elements that make a game fun; also, the way players play a game—how they control it and how the game responds. It consists of the specific challenges that are presented to the player and the actions the player can take in order to overcome them; it also includes victory and loss conditions and the rules of the game. In addition, it provides instantaneous feedback to the players' input and choices.

gamification: The application of gaming techniques such as rewards and scores to projects that are not games and not designed for entertainment. Gamification has become a highly popular method for businesses and organizations to promote their messages to the public.

genre: A category of programming that contains certain characteristic elements. Major types of entertainment properties, like movies and video games, are broken into genres to distinguish them from each other.

gesampkunstwerk: A German word meaning a synthesis of various art forms, like an opera, which can incorporate music, dancing, set design, and performance. *Gesampkunstwerk* thus indicates that a work is a form of convergence, where various art forms have been melded together.

global positioning system (GPS): A satellite-based navigation system that allows individuals with receivers to pinpoint their geographic location.

GPS: See *global positioning system*.

grammar, artistic: The artistic principles or rules that can be employed in a creative field; a visual vocabulary. Every artistic medium requires its own specialized grammar; this is necessary for the artists who work in the field as well as the audiences who experience it. For example, jump cuts, dissolves, and montages are all part of the grammar of the cinema.

griefer: A player in a MMOG who enjoys killing off new players and otherwise making life miserable for them.

gyroscope: A device embedded in smart phones and tablets which, when combined with the *accelerometer*, can compute how fast, how far, and in which direction an object has moved. See also *accelerometer*.

head-mounted display (HMD): A device worn on the head in a virtual reality simulation that enables the user to see the digital images.

hero's journey, the: Myths, and stories based on this type of myth, about the coming of age experience. Joseph Campbell analyzed this type of myth in his seminal work, *The Hero with a Thousand Faces*. Its core elements and recurring characters have been incorporated into many popular movies, and it has also served as a model for innumerable works of digital storytelling, particularly video games.

hidden story structure: A structural form that contains two layers of narrative. The top layer contains clues to a story that took place in the past. The user explores this top layer to uncover the second layer, the hidden story, and to assemble the pieces of the hidden story into a coherent and linear whole.

high bandwidth: See *bandwidth*.

HMD: See *head-mounted display*.

hot spot: An image or area on the screen that the user can click on to produce a reaction, such as a little piece of animation, a bit of audio, or a short video clip.

HTML (Hypertext Markup Language): The software language used to create Web pages and hyperlinks.

HTTP (Hypertext Transfer Protocol): Protocol used to transfer files, including text, sound, video, and graphics, on the Web.

hub-and-spoke structure: A modular structure for video games in which the player starts from a central location (the hub), and all the modules radiate out from there (the spokes). This structure is extremely clear and simple to navigate, making it especially suitable for children's projects. See also *module*.

hyperlink: A word or image that is linked to another word or image. See also *hypertext*.

hyperliterature: A catch-all phrase for a number of forms of computer-based literature, including hypertext, digital poetry, nonlinear literature, electronic literature, and cyberliterature. Since it is computer-based, it is able to make use of elements that are not possible in printed literature, such as interactivity, animations, sound effects, and hypertext (the ability to link various pieces of text together.) See *hypertext*.

hyperstory: A form of iCinema in which one visual element is linked to another visual element, offering a different view of the same scene or story. It is similar to hypertext, but uses visuals instead of text. See *hypertext*.

hypertext: A technique used in digital works that enables the linking of words or phrases to other related "assets," such as photographs, sounds, video, or other text. The user makes the connection to the linked asset by clicking on the hyperlinked word or phrase, which usually stands out by being underlined or by being in a different color. See also *hyperlink*.

hypertext markup language: See *HTML*.

hypertext transfer protocol: See *HTTP*.

iCinema: An interactive movie. Such works fall into two broad categories. One type is designed for a large theater screen and is usually intended to be a group experience; the other type is for a small screen and meant to be enjoyed by a solo viewer.

if/then construct: A fundamental way of expressing choice and consequence in an interactive work. In an if/then scenario, if the user does A, then B will happen. Or, to put it slightly differently, choosing or doing A will link you to B.

IF: See *interactive fiction*.

IM or IMing (Instant Message or Instant Messaging): See *instant messaging*.

immersive environment: An artificially created environment or installation that seems real. Virtual reality is a type of immersive environment. See also *virtual reality*.

incunabula: the very first works produced for a new medium. The term comes from the Latin word for cradle or swaddling clothes, and thus means something still in its infancy. The term was first applied to the earliest printed books, those made before 1501, but now the term is used more broadly to apply to the early forms of any new medium, including works made for various types of digital technology.

independent game: a game that has been made without the financial support of a publisher and that usually has been produced on an extremely small budget and by an extremely small team or a single individual. This independence gives the developers full artistic control of their games, and these games can be far more experimental and artistic than games that have been made with a publisher's support. They are usually referred to as *indie games*.

indie game: See *independent game*.

infotainment: A presentation that combines information and entertainment.

instant messaging (IM or IMing): A method of exchanging messages with another person while you are both online, much like a conversation. Although IMing began as a text-only medium, some service providers offer graphic and audio options as well.

intellectual property (IP): A unique work of human intelligence—such as a photograph, a script, a song, a piece of animation, or a game engine—that is given legal protection such as a copyright, patent, or trademark. Intellectual properties can be extremely valuable and are closely guarded.

interactive fiction (IF): A work of interactive narrative, usually text based, into which users input their commands via their computer keyboard. Works of IF are available on the Internet and as CD-ROMs and sometimes contain graphics and video. Works of IF resemble text-based adventure games (MUDs), but are engaged in by a solo user, not multiple players. They also lack a win/lose outcome. See also *MUD*.

interactive television (iTV): A form of television that gives the viewer some control over the content or way of interacting with it.

interactive voice response (IVR): Communications that take place on the telephone that facilitate the acquisition of information. The user is asked a series of questions by a recorded voice and responds by pressing the telephone's number keys or by speaking. Based on the caller's input, the system retrieves information from a database. IVR systems are commonly used by banks to provide account information to customers. They are also being called into play for games.

interface: The elements of an interactive work that enable the users to communicate with the material, to make choices and navigate through it. Among the many visual devices used in interface design are menus, navigation bars, icons, buttons, and cursors.

Internet 2: A faster, more robust form of the Internet. It is used by government and academic organizations; it is not accessible to the general public.

iOS: An abbreviation used to stand for iPhone Operating System, but now is used to indicate the operating system for all Apple mobile devices.

IP: See *intellectual property*.

iTV: See *interactive television*.

IVR: See *interactive voice response*.

kiosk: See *electronic kiosk*.

landline telephones: Telephones that are connected to wires and cables, as opposed to wireless phones.

lapwear: Software products made for youngsters between nine months and two years of age. The term springs from the fact that children often sit on a parent's lap while playing with such products.

LARP: See *live action role-playing game*.

laser disc: A storage and playback format, also called a video disc, introduced in the late 1970s and used for watching movies and for educational and training purposes, as well as for arcade games. They have largely been replaced by DVDs, though a small number of devoted fans still use them.

latency: The time it takes for a program to react.

LBE: See *location-based entertainment*.

leaderboard: A list of the top scorers in a game.

level: A structural device in a game or other interactive work; it is a section of the work, akin to a chapter or an act. Each level has its own physical environment, characters, and challenges. Games may also be "leveled" in terms of degree of difficulty, with levels running from easy to difficult. Characters, too, can attain an increase in level in terms of their powers or skills; they are "leveled up."

licensed character: See *licensed property*.

licensed property: A piece of intellectual property, often a movie, a novel, or other work of entertainment, or even a fictional character, that is covered by a licensing agreement, allowing another entity to use it. Licensed properties and characters are generally highly recognizable and popular, and their use can add value to a new work. The Harry Potter novels are licensed properties and Lara Croft is a licensed character.

lifecasting: A form of Web-based entertainment in which a wearable camera is attached to a person and the subject is videotaped live as he or she goes through the day. It's a little like an episode of *Big Brother*, but with only one participant. Lifecasting offers interactivity, because viewers can communicate with the subject via a chat window or cell phone. A lifecasting subject need not be human; they are sometimes animals or birds.

linearity: A state in which events are fixed in a set, unchangeable sequence, and one event follows another in a logical, fixed, and progressive sequence. Films and novels are linear, while interactive works are nonlinear.

live action role-playing game (LARP): Games that are played by participants in the real world as opposed to role-playing games played on computers or online. The earliest LARPs were war game simulations. Such games were the predecessors of the highly popular Dungeons and Dragons LARPs, which evolved into today's MMORPGs. See also *MMORPGs*.

location-based entertainment (LBE): Entertainment that takes place away from the home. Venues can include museums, theme parks, and retail malls. In many cases, LBE experiences involve immersive environments. See also *immersive environment*.

location-based gaming: A type of game that is set and played out in real-world locations, usually in urban settings.

locative journalism: An information-based work that takes place in a specific location and uses audio and GPS units to tell the story of a physical place. LoJo is a nickname used for this form. Audio-based storytelling set in a real physical space can also be called *narrative archeology* or *locative storytelling*, and is a form of mixed reality.

locative storytelling: One of several terms used to label a form of narrative set in a specific location that uses audio and GPS units to tell the story of the place in which it is set. It may also be called *narrative archeology* or *locative journalism*. It is a type of mixed reality.

locomotion interface: A type of immersive environment that employs a treadmill in a large-screen environment. As the participant walks or runs on the treadmill, the images on the screen change.

log line: A clear and vivid description of the premise of an entertainment property, usually no more than one sentence long. When used for an interactive project, it describes the concept in a way that indicates the nature of the interactivity, what the challenges might be, and what will hook the users. The term got its name from the concise descriptions of movies given in television logs and other entertainment guides.

low bandwidth: See *bandwidth*.

ludology: One of two major and opposing ways of studying games, the other being narratology. Ludologists assert that even though games have elements of narrative like characters and plot, this is incidental to the things that make them a distinct creative form, such as gameplay. Thus, they assert, games should be studied as unique constructs. The term ludology comes from the Latin word *ludus*, for game. See also *narratology*.

Machinima: A form of filmmaking that borrows scenery and characters from video games but creates original stories with them. The term combines the words "machine" and "cinema." Works of Machinima are often humorous, possibly because the characters, borrowed as they are from video games, are not capable of deep expression.

malleable linear path: A narrative through-line for a video game or other interactive work; similar to a *critical story path*. The malleable linear path includes the major actions the user must take or events the user must experience in order for the narrative to make sense and to reach a conclusion, but these actions or events do not need to occur in a specific order. See also *critical story path*.

massively multiplayer online game (MMOG): An online game that is played simultaneously by tens of thousands of people and is typically set in a sprawling fictional landscape. MMOGs are persistent universes, meaning that the stories continue even after a player has logged off.

massively multiplayer online role-playing game (MMORPG): An online role-playing game played simultaneously by thousands of participants, and one of the most popular forms of MMOGs. MMORPGs contain many of the elements of video game RPGs, in which the player controls one or more avatars and goes on quests. These avatars are defined by a set of attributes, such as species, occupation, skill, and special talents.

massively multiplayer online war game leveraging the Internet (MMPWGLI): A type of multiplayer game played online that deals with complex problems. These games are often message based, as opposed to games that use cinematic visuals.

matrix: A table-like chart with rows and columns that is used to help assign and track the variables in an interactive project.

merchant-tainment: Physical items that can be purchased and that can contribute to an entertainment experience.

message-based game: A game which usually does not possess highly cinematic visuals and in which player exchanges are conveyed via test.

metatag: Information used by search engines, important for constructing indexes.

milestone: A project marker that specifies when the different elements of a project must be completed.

mission: An assignment given to a player in a video game. Some video games are organized by missions rather than by levels, and the player must complete the missions one by one. See also *level*.

MMOG: See *massively multiplayer online game*.

MMORPG: See *massively multiplayer online role-playing game*.

MMOWGLI: See *massively multiplayer online war game leveraging the Internet*.

MMS: See *multimedia service*.

MOB (mobile object): An object in a game that moves.

MOBA: See *multiplayer online battle arena*.

mobisode: A serialized story or multi-episode entertainment series made for mobile devices, similar to a webisode.

module: A method of organizing or structuring an interactive work, often used in educational and training projects. Each module customarily focuses on one element in the curriculum or one learning objective.

MOO (MUD, Object Oriented): A text-based adventure game that is a close cousin to the MUD. See also *MUD*.

motion base chair: A theater-style seat used in ridefilms that moves in synchronization with the story's action. See also *ridefilm*.

motion capture: An animation technique for producing life-like movements and facial expressions in characters. This technique calls for attaching sensors to an individual (who might be an actor, dancer, or athlete) and digitally tracking this individual's movements and expressions. These movements and expressions are then "transferred" to an animated character.

MUD: A text-based adventure game in which multiple players assume fictional personas, explore fantasy environments, and interact with each other. MUD stands for Multi-User Dungeon (or Multi-User Domain or Multi-User Dimension). Aside from being text based, MUDs are much like today's MMOGs.

multimedia service (MMS): A feature offered on wireless phones that enables users to send and receive more data than with SMS. It can support a variety of media, including photographs, long text messages, audio, and video, and different media can be combined in the same message. See also *short messaging service*.

multi-modal: The use of various methods of communication, such as spoken dialogue, text, animation, sound effects, and video, within the same work.

multi-platforming: The development of an entertainment property for many different platforms, both traditional (theatrical motion pictures and television) and new (video games, the Internet, and so on).

multiplayer online battle arena (MOBA): A sub-genre of the real-time strategy game in which two teams of players compete against each other. Each player controls a single character. Ideally, teams are made up of characters with different and complementary strengths.

multi-sensory: A technique used in simulations, virtual reality, and other forms of immersive environments in which multiple senses are stimulated. While most forms of media only involve hearing and seeing, a multi-sensory approach might also include tactile sensations, smells, motion, and so on.

multitask: To simultaneously perform several things at once, such as being online while also talking on the phone, listening to the radio, or watching TV.

narrative archeology: A form of storytelling set in a specific location that uses audio and GPS to tell the story of the place in which it is set. It is a type of mixed reality.

narratology: One of two major and opposing ways of studying games, the other being ludology. Narratologists assert that games are a form of storytelling and they can be studied as narratives. See *ludology*.

natural language interface: A life-like method of communication between a user and an artificial character, in which the artificial character can "understand" the words the user types or says, and is able to respond appropriately.

navigation: In interactive media, the method by which users move through a work. Navigational tools include menus, navigation bars, icons, buttons, cursors, rollovers, maps, and directional symbols.

NDA: See *nondisclosure agreement*.

near field communication (NFC): Near field communications are a set of standards that allow smart phones and other devices to communicate with each other when they are brought close together.

networked gaming environment: The linking of computers together into a network that allows many users to participate in an interactive experience. Such networks may be used for educational and training purposes as well as for gaming.

newbie: A new player or new user.

news game: An informational game built around a subject currently in the news.

NFC: See *near field communication*.

node: A design term sometimes used to indicate the largest organizational unit of a game (similar to a level or world) and sometimes used to indicate a point where a user can make a choice.

nondisclosure agreement (NDA): A document used when potentially valuable information is about to be shared with another party. The party that is to receive the information, in signing the NDA, agrees to keep the information confidential.

nonlinearity: Not having a fixed sequence of events; not progressing in a preset, progressive manner. Nonlinearity is a characteristic of interactive works. Though the work may have a central storyline, players or users can weave a varied path through the material, interacting with it in a highly fluid manner.

nonplayer character (NPC): A character controlled by the computer, not by the player.

NPC: See *nonplayer character*.

open world game: A nonlinear game in which players can freely choose where to go, what to do, and when to do it, and even fully customize the character they play. They are typically set in vast environments which the player can explore freely, and they offer players a rich variety of activities to enjoy, from shopping to fighting to operating a variety of vehicles and aircraft. They do, however, contain narrative elements.

otame game: A game genre born in Japan and typically designed for female players. These games generally feature a romantic plot and the usual objective is to end up with the desired boyfriend. Their visual style resembles manga (Japanese comic books).

parallel world: A quasi-linear structure that contains several layers of story, each set in its own virtual world, and the user can jump between them. Often each world is a persistent universe, meaning that events continue to unfurl there even when the user is not present.

PC game: A game that is played on a computer.

PDA: See *personal digital assistant*.

PDR: See *personal digital recorder*.

peer-to-peer learning: An educational environment that facilitates collaborative learning. Online peer-to-peer learning environments may include such features as instant messaging, message boards, and chat rooms.

persistent universe: A virtual environment that continues to exist and evolve after the user has logged off or gone away; a common feature of MMOGs.

personal digital assistant (PDA): A wireless device that serves as an electronic Rolodex, calendar, and organizer. PDAs can download material from the Internet and from PCs.

personal digital recorder (PDR): Same as a personal video recorder and digital video recorder. See *personal video recorder*.

personal video recorder (PVR): One of several terms for devices that enable viewers to select and record television programs; the best-known of such devices is the TiVo. Two other generic terms for this type of device are *personal digital recorder* and *digital video recorder*. These devices offer viewers more control than VCRs and include features like pausing live TV and the ability to skip commercials.

phablet: A convergent device that combines many of the features of a smartphone and a tablet and is in between them in size.

pixel: Short for Picture Element. A pixel is a single tiny unit of a digital graphic image. Graphic images are made up of thousands of pixels in rows and columns, and they are so small that they are usually not visible to the naked eye. The smaller the pixels, the higher the quality of the graphic.

platform: A hardware/software system for running a program or a game.

platform game: A genre of game that is very fast paced and calls for players to make their characters jump, run, or climb through a challenging terrain, often while dodging falling objects or avoiding pitfalls. Such games require quick reflexes and manual dexterity.

player character: A character controlled by the player.

player versus player (PvP): A competitive encounter between two players in a video game, as opposed to a competitive encounter between a player and an NPC. PvP combats can be quite violent and can result in the virtual death of one of the players.

podcast: A form of broadcasting distributed over the Internet and designed for playback on portable digital devices, though the audio or video material can also be enjoyed directly from the Internet. The term podcast combines the words "broadcast" and "iPod." The iPod (a portable MP3 player made by Apple) is one of the devices used to listen and watch such broadcasts, though Apple did not invent the term.

point of view (POV): In interactive media, the way the user views the visual content. The two principal views are first person and third person. See *first-person point of view* and *third-person point of view*.

POV: See *point of view; first-person point of view*; and *third-person point of view*.

procedural animation: An animation technique for endowing characters with life-like behavior and a wide range of actions. In procedural animation, characters are created in real time, rather than being pre rendered. To make such a character, the animator provides a set of rules and initial conditions—in other words, a procedure.

product placement: An advertising technique in which advertisers pay a fee to a movie or television production company to have their product prominently displayed in a scene in a movie or television show. This practice is now becoming widespread in video games.

project creep: A situation in which a project expands beyond its original concept and swallows up unexpected staff time, often without additional financial compensation. Also called scope creep.

proprietary: The state of being owned or controlled by an individual or organization. In interactive entertainment, certain software is sometimes called proprietary, meaning that it is the exclusive property of that developer.

protagonist: The central figure of the drama, whose mission, goal, or objective provides the story with its forward momentum. The word is formed around the Greek root, *agon*, meaning contest or prize. See *agon*.

protocol: A set of instructions or rules for exchanging information between computer systems or networks.

prototype: A working model of a small part of an overall project.

publisher: A company that funds the development of a game or other software product and packages and markets it. A publisher may also develop projects in-house.

PvP: See *player versus player*.

PVR: See *personal video recorder*.

QR code: A code made up of black bars arranged into a square that can be "read" by a smart phone or other device and is often used to link to Web pages.

Rashomon structure: A structural form that contains several versions of the same story and users can experience each version from the POV of the different characters. The model resembles the Japanese movie, *Rashomon*, about a crime viewed by four people, each of whom saw it differently.

reader pad: A specialized device in which to set a smart toy or other object, and that can transport the toy or object into an online world or a game and make it "come to life." For example, reader pads are used for Webkinz stuffed animals and Skylanders plastic figurines.

Really Simple Syndication (RSS): RSS, which stands for both Really Syndication and Rich Site Summary, is a family of formats for distributing content to websites; it is a form of syndication.

real-time 3D graphic (RT3D): Three-dimensional animation that is rendered in real time instead of being prerendered. In a game environment, the images respond to the players' actions.

real-time strategy game (RTS): A genre of game that emphasizes the use of strategy and logic. In these games, the players manage resources, military units, or communities. In a real-time strategy game, the play is continuous, as opposed to a turn-based strategy game, where players take turns.

Red Button TV: An interactive service in the UK that allows viewers to see additional TV content by pushing the red button on their controller. It is available via digital terrestrial television, satellite television, and cable television.

repeatability: A quality, also known as *replayability*, possessed by some video games and other interactive works that lends itself to more than one play, because each play offers a new experience, a new version of the narrative, or new challenges. Educational games that contain several layers of difficulty also possess this quality.

replayability: See *repeatability*.

repurposing: Taking content or programming models from older media and porting them over to a new medium, often with little or no change. For instance, the first movies were filmed stage plays, and the first CD-ROMs were encyclopedias, and the first types of content available on Video iPods were reruns of TV shows.

rhizome structural model: A structural form that takes its name from the field of botany, where it is used to describe an interconnecting root system. In interactive stories using this structure, each piece can be connected to every other piece. Thus, it is much like a maze.

Rich Site Summary (RSS): See *Really Simple Syndication*.

ridefilm: An entertainment experience that takes place in a specially equipped theater. The audience may sit in special seats (motion base chairs) that move in sync with the action taking place on the screen. This gives them the illusion that they are traveling, though they are not actually going anywhere. See also *motion base chair*.

robot: A device that operates either by remote control or on its own, and relates in some way to its surroundings. Some are designed to be playthings for children or adults; others are built to be part of entertainment or educational experiences. Many, however, are specifically built for highly pragmatic functions. The word "robot" is a variation of the Czech word, *robota*, which means slave-like labor or drudgery.

role-playing game (RPG): A genre of game in which the player controls one or more characters, or avatars, and vicariously goes on adventures. These games evolved from the pre-computer version of *Dungeons and Dragons*. See also *avatar*.

RPG: See *role-playing game*.

RSS: See *Really Simple Syndication*.

RT3D: See *real-time 3D graphic*.

RTS: See *real-time strategy game*.

rumble floor: A device used to enhance the realism of an immersive environment. The rumble floor is built into the platform that participants move across, and vibrates when cued by certain virtual events, such as an explosion or an earthquake.

sandbox game: A game set in a large environment that can be explored freely and that allows players to decide what they want to do throughout the game. The term is often used interchangeably with an open-world game. While these two genres of gaming have much in common, sandbox games are regarded as a "toy box" that contains tools that players can use to modify the game world and gameplay. Instead of containing set story elements like an open-world game, players can construct a narrative while playing: an emergent story.

sandbox structure: A structural model that offers the user a great deal of freedom. Unlike a game, this type of structure does not set specific goals for the user to achieve and has no victory conditions. And unlike narrative-based works, it has no plot. However, such models do provide users with objects to manipulate and things to do, and they do have spatial boundaries.

scent necklace: A device used to enhance the realism of an immersive environment. It is worn around the neck of the participant and gives off specific aromas at key points during the simulation, in keeping with the virtual landscape or action of the piece.

schematic: An easy-to-understand diagram that illustrates how something works.

second-screen TV: The use of a device like a smart phone or tablet computer in conjunction with a broadcast TV show, which is done to augment the content of the TV show. It can be used to gain access to additional information about the show, to post or read comments about the show, and to play games in conjunction with the show.

sequential linearity: An interactive structure that channels the user down a linear path and is quite restrictive in terms of the freedom of movement it offers to the user.

serious game: A game designed to teach a difficult subject, either to advanced students or to learners outside of academic settings. Because serious games are meant to be entertaining as well as teaching vehicles, they make intensive use of digital storytelling techniques.

short messaging service (SMS): A feature offered on wireless phones that enables users to send and receive short text messages up to 160 characters in length.

SIG: See *special interest group*.

silo: media organizations like TV production companies, ad agencies, and newspaper publishers that are used to operating independently and being non-collaborative. In transmedia storytelling, "navigating silos" is often a major challenge.

simulation: A realistic and dramatic scenario in which users make choices that determine how things turn out. Simulations are featured in many types of interactive environments, including virtual reality and CD-ROM programs, and are used for entertainment and educational and training purposes.

single-screen interactivity: A form of iTV in which interactive programming is furnished via a digital set-top box provided by a satellite or cable company and is viewed on one's television set. It thus requires just one screen, as opposed to dual-screen iTV. See also *dual-screen iTV*.

skeuomorph: A design approach that is sometimes employed in user interface where an icon is made to resemble its real-life equivalent. For example, an icon that indicates you can watch a video might look like a TV set.

smart phone: a cell phone that can perform many of the functions of a computer, but in a far smaller package.

smart toy: Any type of plaything with a built-in microprocessing chip. Such toys can include educational games and life-like dolls, animals, or fantasy creatures that seem intelligent and can interact with the child playing with it. They can also include playsets that tell a story as the child interacts with it.

SME: See *subject matter expert*.

SMS: See *short messaging service*.

social marketing: A specialized form of promotion that is designed to change the way people behave—to motivate them to break harmful habits like smoking or overeating, and to encourage them to take up positive behaviors, like wearing seat belts or exercising.

social networking site: A website that contains content that is largely created by the users themselves and that facilitates communications between users. Such sites are virtual communities, and they may be populated by virtual inhabitants in the form of user-controlled avatars. See also *avatar*.

social object: A term used to indicate a shared interest in a subject, often online, which can be the focus of an online social network.

social TV: Technology that supports communication and social interaction on mobile devices while simultaneously watching a show on a TV screen.

SoLoMo: A mash-up of the words social, local, and mobile. SoLoMo is a way of targeting individuals carrying mobile phone with information about nearby retailers. The individuals may be offered special discounts, based on their proximity to that place of business.

spatial narrative: An interactive drama in which the story elements are embedded in a three-dimensional space, and the user discovers narrative fragments while exploring the fictional environment.

special interest group (SIG): A group of individuals with similar interests formed within a larger organization.

state engine approach: An interactive mechanism that allows for a greater range of responses to stimuli than a simple if/then construct, which allows for only one possible outcome for every choice. See also *if/then construct*.

stereoscope: A device that enables people to see images in 3D. Stereoscopic devices are used in VR installations.

stickiness: The ability to draw people to a particular website and entice them to linger for long periods of time; also the ability to draw visitors back repeatedly.

storyboard: A series of drawings that illustrate the flow of action, the interactivity, and important pieces of the content of an interactive project, displayed sequentially, much like a comic book. Essentially, a storyboard is an illustrated flowchart. See also *flowchart*.

storyline: The way a narrative unfolds and is told, beat-by-beat. In traditional linear narratives, the storyline is all-important and very clear; it is "the bones" of a story. In interactive media, however, storylines tend to be less defined and apparent, because such works are nonlinear. In video games that contain a narrative, the storyline takes second place to gameplay, although the storyline serves to give context to the game.

storyworld: the universe of the story. A storyworld can be either fiction or non-fiction, but should always contain everything the story revolves around. This includes the plot, the characters, and the setting. The term is used in all forms of digital storytelling as well as in traditional media, but it is a particularly important term in transmedia storytelling.

streaming: Receiving video or audio in real time, without a delay, as it downloads from the Internet. Video received this way is called streaming video; audio received this way is called streaming audio.

string of pearls structure: A structural model for the linear story path in a video game or other interactive work. Each of the "pearls" is a world, and players are able to move freely inside each of them. But in order to progress in the story, the player must first successfully perform certain tasks in each pearl.

subject matter expert (SME): An individual with special expertise who is consulted for a new media project, especially one designed for teaching or training. These specialists may offer advice about the target learners, the content of the project, or the teaching objectives.

synchronous interactivity: A form of interactive television in which the content of a television program and the content of a website are synchronized and designed for viewer interactivity;

also known as *dual-screen iTV*. The type of interactivity calls for a secondary device like an Internet-connected computer or cell phone, as well as a television set.

synthetic character: A highly intelligent computer-controlled character. Such characters are capable of "understanding" the words typed or spoken by the user, and are able to respond appropriately. Unlike a chatterbot, characters with this capacity are fully animated and highly life-like. See also *chatterbot*.

taxonomy: In biology, the discipline of classifying and organizing plants and animals. In interactive media, a systematic organizing of content. As in biology, it is a hierarchical system, starting with the largest category at the top, and then dividing the content into smaller and smaller categories, organized logically by commonalities. The word comes from the Greek and is composed of two parts: *taxis*, meaning order or arrangement, and *nomia*, meaning method or law.

TCP/IP: See *Transmission Control Protocol/Internet Protocol*.

third generation (3G): A stage of development in wireless technology that enables wireless telephones to have high-speed access to the Internet.

third screen: A term that includes many forms of screen-based new media entertainment, including video games and content developed for the Internet and cell phones. While once there were only two types of entertainment screens—TV screens and movie screens—the third screen is a powerful newcomer to the entertainment world.

third-person point of view: The perspective we have in an interactive work in which we watch our character from a distance, much as we watch the protagonist in a movie. We can see the character in action and can also see their facial expressions. Cut scenes show characters from the third-person POV, and when we control an avatar, we are observing it from this POV as well. See also *first-person point of view*.

three-act structure: The classic structure of theatrical dramas and screenplays. This structural form was first articulated by Aristotle, who noted that effective dramas always contained a beginning (Act 1); a middle (Act 2); and an end (Act 3).

ticking clock: A dramatic device used to keep the audience glued to the story. It is found in both linear and nonlinear narrative works. With a ticking clock, the protagonist is given a specific and limited period of time to accomplish a goal. Otherwise there will be serious and perhaps even deadly consequences.

TiVo: The brand name for a device that allows TV viewers to select and record TV programs and play them back whenever they wish. Viewers also have the option of fast forwarding through the commercials. The generic terms for such devices are personal video recorder (PVR), personal digital recorder (PDR), and digital video recorder (DVR).

touchscreen: The screen of a smart phone or tablet that responds to touch. Virtual objects on the screen react accordingly. Objects can be moved, shrunk in size, expanded, or activated by touch.

tragic flaw: A negative character trait possessed by the protagonist of a drama. Though this character may be noble in many ways, he or she also has a fatal weakness such as jealousy, self-doubt, or ambition, and this trait leads to the character's undoing.

transmedia entertainment: Entertainment properties that combine at least two media, one of which is interactive, to tell a single story. Possible linear components include movies, TV shows, and novels, while possible new media components include websites, video games, and mobile devices. In addition, these projects may also utilize everyday communication tools like faxes, voicemail, and instant messaging. This approach to entertainment goes by many different names, including *multi-platforming*, *cross-media production*, *networked entertainment*, and *integrated media*. Gaming projects that use the transmedia approach may be called *alternate reality games*. See also *alternate reality game.*

Transmission Control Protocol/Internet Protocol (TCP/IP): A protocol developed for ARPANET, the forerunner of the Internet, by Vint Cerf and Bob Kahn. It is the basic communication language of the Internet, and allowed the Internet to grow into the immense international mass-communication system that it has become.

treadmill: An internal structural system of a MMOG that keeps the user involved playing it, cycling repeatedly through the same types of beats in order to advance in the game.

Turing test: a rigorous set of standards to judge artificial intelligence (AI) in a computer program, set in 1950 by Alan Turing. In what is now known as the "Turing Test," both a human and a computer are asked a series of questions. If the computer's answers cannot be distinguished from the human's, the computer is regarded as having AI. See also *artificial intelligence.*

UI: See *user interface.*

uncanny valley syndrome: A term coined by Japanese roboticist Masahiro Mori to describe the uncomfortable reaction people have to robots that seem too life-like and human.

URL (Uniform Resource Locator): A website address.

user interface: The way users of digital media make their wishes known to the program and control what they see and do and where they go. The many visual devices used in interface design and navigation include menus, navigation bars, icons, buttons, cursors, rollovers, maps, and directional symbols. Sound effects also play a role in user interface. Hardware devices for user interface include video game controllers, touch screens, and VR wands.

user-generated content: Content that is created by the users themselves. Such content includes everything from the avatars and objects found in virtual worlds to homemade videos and animations. It also includes Machinima, fan fiction, and the personal profiles and other content found on social networking sites.

verb set: The actions that can be performed in an interactive work. The verb set of a game consists of all the things that players can make their characters do. The most common verbs are walk, run, turn, jump, pick up, and shoot.

video blog (vlog): A blog that contains video. See *blog*.

video on demand (VOD): A system that lets viewers select video content to watch from the Internet or from digital cable or satellite systems.

viral marketing: A marketing strategy that encourages people to pass along a piece of information; originally used in Web marketing but now also used for wireless devices.

virtual channel: A designated channel where VOD videos are "parked." See also *video on demand*.

virtual reality (VR): A 3D artificial world generated by computers that seems believably real. Within such a space, one is able to move around and view the virtual structures and objects from any angle. A VR world requires special hardware to be perceived.

virtual world: An online environment where users control their own avatars and interact with each other. These worlds may have richly detailed landscapes to explore, buildings that can be entered, and vehicles that can be operated, much like a massively multiplayer online game (MMOG). However, these virtual worlds are not really games, even though they may have some game-like attributes. Instead, they serve as virtual community centers, where people can get together and socialize, and, if they wish, conduct business. See also *MMOG*.

vlog: See *video blog*.

VOD: See *video on demand*.

VR: See *virtual reality*.

walled garden: An area of restricted access, generally relating to Internet content.

WAP: See *wireless application protocol*.

webcam: A stationary digital video camera that captures images and broadcasts them on the Web. Webcams often run continually and the footage is broadcast without being edited.

webinar: An educational or training session that takes place in a classroom and that combines Web-based and live instruction, with a live instructor acting as facilitator.

webisode: A story-based serial on the Web that is told in short installments using stills, text, animation, or video.

Wi-Fi: A protocol that enables a mobile device to have a high-speed connection to the Internet and to connect with other devices, like game consoles and DVRs.

wireless application protocol (WAP): A set of instructions that enables mobile devices to connect with the Internet and perform other functions.

wireless telephony: Communications systems that enable the transmission of sound, text, and images without the use of wires, unlike landline telephony.

world structure: A structural device used in interactive narratives. In such structures, the narrative is divided into different geographical spaces—the rooms of a house, different parts of a town, or different planets.

Additional Readings

The following books offer additional information on various aspects of classic narrative, digital storytelling, design, and career issues:

- Adams, Ernest, *Break into the Game Industry: How to Get a Job Making Video Games* (Emeryville, CA, McGraw-Hill Osborne Media, 2003). A good guide to careers in the game industry.

- Adams, Ernest, *Fundamentals of Game Design*, Second Edition (Indianapolis, IN, New Riders, 2009). An excellent, clear, and extremely thorough guide to game design.

- Aristotle, *The Poetics* (New York, Hill & Wang, 1961). The classic treatise on dramatic writing.

- Bernardo, Nuno, *The Producer's Guide to Transmedia: How to Develop, Fund, Produce and Distribute Compelling Stories Across Multiple Platforms* (Lisbon, Sao Paulo, Dublin, and London, Beactive Books, 2011). A solid work about producing works of transmedia storytelling, written by one of the creative forces behind some major transmedia narratives.

- Bogost, Ian, *Persuasive Games, The Expressive Power of Videogames* (Cambridge, MA, MIT Press, 2010). A book focusing on serious games by one of the leaders in the field.

- Campbell, Joseph, *The Hero with a Thousand Faces*, Second Edition (Princeton, NJ, Princeton University Press, 1972). A classic study of mythology and particularly of the hero's journey, a universal myth that many dramatic works, including digital stories, are modeled on.

- Crawford, Chris, *Chris Crawford on Game Design* (Indianapolis, IN, New Riders, 2003). A somewhat idiosyncratic but lively look at game design by a well-known game guru.

- Frazel, Madge, *Digital Storytelling Guide for Educators* (Washington, DC, International Society for Technology in Education, 2010). This book defines digital storytelling in the way that it is used in schools: as a tool for personal expression or as a way to build narrative around a curriculum topic (such as history). A useful guide for teachers who want to employ this form of digital storytelling in the classroom.

- Fullerton, Tracy, *Game Design Workshop*, Second Edition: *A Playcentric Approach to Creating Innovative Games* (Burlington, MA, Morgan Kaufmann, 2008). A solid and user-friendly work on game design written by a well-respected designer and professor.

- Garrand, Timothy Paul, *Writing for Multimedia and the Web*, Third Edition (Burlington, MA, Focal Press, 2006). A good general book about writing for interactive media, with a particular focus on the Internet.

- Gee, James Paul, *What Video Games Have to Teach Us About Learning and Literacy*, Second Edition (Houndmills, Palgrave Macmillan, 2007). A book that promotes the positive aspect of video games and how games can facilitate learning.

- Giovagnoli, Max, *Transmedia Storytelling: Imagery, Shapes and Techniques* (Lulu.com, 2011). A thorough approach to transmedia storytelling by a practitoner in the field.

- Herz, J. C., *Joystick Nation: How Videogames Ate Our Quarters, Won Our Hearts, and Rewired Our Minds* (New York, Little Brown-Warner Books, 1997). Though an older book, this is a provocative and interesting work on the cultural impact of video games.

- Iuppa, Nicholas V., *Designing Interactive Digital Media* (Burlington, MA, Focal Press, 1998). A very thorough and practical book that primarily addresses design issues.

- Iuppa, Nicholas and Borst, Terry, *End-to-End Game Development: Creating Independent Serious Games and Simulations from Start to Finish* (Burlington, MA, Focal Press, 2009). An in-depth examination of the role of narrative in serious games and simulations, based in part on case studies of projects the two have worked on.

- Jenkins, Henry, *Convergence Culture: Where Old and New Media Collide* (New York, NYU Press, 2008). A well-regarded book about transmedia storytelling.

- Mankovitch, Lev, *The Language of New Media* (Cambridge, MA, MIT Press, 2002). A heavily theoretical and scholarly look at where new media fits into the general media landscape, written by a well-respected academician.

- McGonigal, Jane, *Reality Is Broken: Why Games Make Us Better and How They Can Change the World* (London, Penguin Books, 2011). A meditation about the power of games to do good by a game designer who brings real-world experience to her topic.

- Meadows, Mark Stephen, *Pause and Effect: The Art of Interactive Narrative* (Indianapolis, IN, New Riders, 2002). A beautifully illustrated and thoughtful examination of interactive narrative with an emphasis on design.

- Montfort, Nick, *Twisty Little Passages: An Approach to Interactive Fiction* (Cambridge, MA, MIT Press, 2005). A good book for anyone interested in electronic literature and how narratives can be interactive.

- Murray, Janet, *Hamlet on the Holodeck: The Future of Narrative in Cyberspace* (Cambridge, MA, MIT Press, 1998). A highly regarded and thoughtful book about the potential of digital storytelling. One of the first books written on the subject, the book is still extremely valuable for its ideas, even though some of the references are dated.

- Pearce, Celia, *Communities of Play: Emergent Cultures in Multiplayer Games and Virtual Worlds* (Cambridge, MA, MIT Press, 2011). An examination of massively multiplayer online games and, more specifically, of the players themselves and their impact on the games they play.

- Pearce, Celia, *The Interactive Book: A Guide to the Interactive Revolution* (Indianapolis, IN, Macmillan Technical Publishing, 1997). A collection of essays exploring the social, cultural, and psychological impact of interactive media.

- Phillips, Andrea, *A Creator's Guide to Transmedia Storytelling* (New York, McGraw-Hill, 2012). A thorough book on transmedia storytelling by a practitioner in the field.

- Reddish, Janice, *Letting Go of the Words*, Second Edition: *Writing Web Content that Works* (Burlington, MA, Morgan Kaufmann, 2012). A solid book about Web design and writing, focusing on non-fiction and commercial website work.

- Rollings, Andrew and Ernest, Adams, *Andrew Rollings and Ernest Adams on Game Design* (Indianapolis, IN, New Riders, 2003). A solid book on game design.

- Rose, Frank, *The Art of Immersion: How the Digital Generation Is Remaking Hollywood, Madison Avenue, and the Way We Tell Stories* (New York, WW Norton, 2012). A journalist's investigation of digital storytelling containing an examination of some ground breaking works, written in an entertaining fashion.

- Schell, Jesse, *The Art of Game Design: A Book of Lenses* (Burlington, MA, Morgan Kaufmann, 2008). A book on game design and game theory, by a seasoned practitioner in the field. A very helpful book for those who want to learn more about game design.

- Squire, Kurt, *Video Games and Learning: Teaching and Participatory Culture in the Digital Age* (New York, Teachers College Press, 2011). A look at how games can be used in education, and also an examination of what makes games fun.

- Thomas, Sue, *Technobiophilia: Nature and Cyberspace* (London, Bloomsbury Academic, 2013). An exploration of the connection between the natural world and cyberspace.

- Vogler, Chris and Montez, Michele, *The Writers Journey: Mythic Structure for Writers*, Third Edition (Studio City, CA, Michael Wiese Productions, 2007). An examination of Joseph Campbell's theory of *The Hero with a Thousand Faces*, a mythic structure which is the basis of many games; this book is geared toward writers.

- Wardrip-Fruin, Noah and Harrigan, Pat, *Second Person: Role-Playing and Story in Games and Playable Media* (Cambridge, MA, MIT Press, 2010). A collection of readings, focusing primarily on role-playing games.

- Wardrip-Fruin, Noah and Harrigan, Pat, *The New Media Reader* (Cambridge, MA, MIT Press, 2003). A remarkable and exhaustive archive of writings about new media, particularly about the early days of the field.
- Wardrip-Fruin, Noah and Harrigan, Pat, *Third Person: Authoring and Exploring Vast Narratives* (Cambridge, MA, MIT Press, 2009). A collection of readings, primarily delving into virtual worlds and multiplayer games.

Project Index

Subject Index

Note: page numbers in italic type refer to Figures.

W

X

Y

Z